QUITY

A® Program Curriculum
16 • LEVEL II • VOLUME 4

CFA Institute | WILEY

Please visit our website at
www.WileyGlobalFinance.com.

FSC
www.fsc.org

MIX

Paper from
responsible source

FSC® C00592

CONTENTS

How to Use the CFA Program Curriculum   vi
    Curriculum Development Process   vi
    Organization of the Curriculum   vii
    Features of the Curriculum   viii
    Designing Your Personal Study Program   ix
    Feedback   xi

Equity Valuation 4 case 20%.

Study Session 10   **Equity Valuation: Valuation Concepts**   3

Reading 29   **Equity Valuation: Applications and Processes**   5
    Introduction   5
    Value Definitions and Valuation Applications   6
        What Is Value?   6
        Applications of Equity Valuation   9
    The Valuation Process   11
        Understanding the Business   12
        Forecasting Company Performance   21
        Selecting the Appropriate Valuation Model   22
        Converting Forecasts to a Valuation   29
        Applying the Valuation Conclusion: The Analyst's Role and
            Responsibilities   30
    Communicating Valuation Results   32
        Contents of a Research Report   32
        Format of a Research Report   34
        Research Reporting Responsibilities   35
    Summary   37
    Practice Problems   40
    Solutions   44

Reading 30 1/2   **Return Concepts**   47
    Introduction   48
    Return Concepts   48
        Holding Period Return   48
        Realized and Expected (Holding Period) Return   49
        Required Return   49
        Expected Return Estimates from Intrinsic Value Estimates   51
        Discount Rate   53
        Internal Rate of Return   53
    The Equity Risk Premium   54
        Historical Estimates   55
        Forward-Looking Estimates   64
    The Required Return on Equity   67
        The Capital Asset Pricing Model   67

	Multifactor Models	75
	Build-Up Method Estimates of the Required Return on Equity	81
	The Required Return on Equity: International Issues	85
	The Weighted Average Cost of Capital	86
	Discount Rate Selection in Relation to Cash Flows	88
	Summary	89
	Practice Problems	92
	Solutions	97
Study Session 11	**Equity Valuation: Industry and Company Analysis in a Global Context**	**101**
Reading 31	**The Five Competitive Forces that Shape Strategy**	**103**
	The Idea in Brief	104
	The Idea in Practice	104
	Introduction	105
	Forces that Shape Competition	107
	Factors, Not Forces	115
	Changes in Industry Structure	117
	Implications for Strategy	118
	Competition and Value	122
	Practice Problems	125
	Solutions	127
Reading 32	**Your Strategy Needs a Strategy**	**129**
	Finding the Right Strategic Style	130
	Classical	131
	Adaptive	132
	Shaping	133
	Visionary	134
	Avoiding the Traps	135
	Misplaced Confidence	135
	Unexamined Habits	135
	Culture Mismatches	136
	Operating in Many Modes	136
Reading 33	**Industry and Company Analysis**	**139**
	Introduction	140
	Financial Modeling: An Overview	140
	Income Statement Modeling: Revenue	140
	Income Statement Modeling: Operating Costs	146
	Income Statement Modeling: Non-operating Costs	158
	Income Statement Modeling: Other Items	164
	Balance Sheet and Cash Flow Statement Modeling	164
	Scenario Analysis and Sensitivity Analysis	167
	The Impact of Competitive Factors on Prices and Costs	168
	Inflation and Deflation	177
	Sales Projections with Inflation and Deflation	177
	Cost Projections with Inflation and Deflation	182

◙ indicates an optional segment

Contents

Technological Developments | **185**
Long-Term Forecasting | **195**
  Case Study: Estimating Normalized Revenue | **196**
Building a Model | **202**
  Industry Overview | **202**
  Company Overview | **203**
  Construction of Pro Forma Income Statement | **204**
  Construction of Pro Forma Cash Flow Statement and Balance Sheet | **209**
  Valuation Inputs | **214**
Conclusions and Summary | **215**
Practice Problems | **217**
Solutions | **224**

Reading 34 1/2

Discounted Dividend Valuation | **229**
Introduction | **230**
Present Value Models | **231**
  Valuation Based on the Present Value of Future Cash Flows | **231**
  Streams of Expected Cash Flows | **233**
The Dividend Discount Model | **239**
  The Expression for a Single Holding Period | **239**
  The Expression for Multiple Holding Periods | **240**
The Gordon Growth Model | **242**
  The Gordon Growth Model Equation | **242**
  The Links Among Dividend Growth, Earnings Growth, and Value
    Appreciation in the Gordon Growth Model | **249**
  Share Repurchases | **250**
  The Implied Dividend Growth Rate | **251**
  The Present Value of Growth Opportunities | **252**
  Gordon Growth Model and the Price-to-Earnings Ratio | **254**
  Estimating a Required Return Using the Gordon Growth Model | **256**
  The Gordon Growth Model: Concluding Remarks | **257**
Multistage Dividend Discount Models | **257**
  Two-Stage Dividend Discount Model | **258**
  Valuing a Non-Dividend-Paying Company | **261**
  The H-Model | **262**
  Three-Stage Dividend Discount Models | **264**
  Spreadsheet (General) Modeling | **269**
  Estimating a Required Return Using Any DDM | **271**
  Multistage DDM: Concluding Remarks | **272**
The Financial Determinants of Growth Rates | **273**
  Sustainable Growth Rate | **273**
  Dividend Growth Rate, Retention Rate, and ROE Analysis | **275**
  Financial Models and Dividends | **278**
Summary | **279**
Practice Problems | **283**
Solutions | **291**

◙ indicates an optional segment

Study Session 12   **Equity Investments: Valuation Models**   299

Reading 35   **Free Cash Flow Valuation**   301
                              Introduction to Free Cash Flows   302
I case   FCFF and FCFE Valuation Approaches   303
                                  Defining Free Cash Flow   303
                                  Present Value of Free Cash Flow   304
                                  Single-Stage (Constant-Growth) FCFF and FCFE Models   305
                              Forecasting Free Cash Flow   307
                                  Computing FCFF from Net Income   307
                                  Computing FCFF from the Statement of Cash Flows   311
                                  Noncash Charges   313
                                  Computing FCFE from FCFF   319
                                  Finding FCFF and FCFE from EBIT or EBITDA   324
                                  FCFF and FCFE on a Uses-of-Free-Cash-Flow Basis   326
                                  Forecasting FCFF and FCFE   327
                                  Other Issues in Free Cash Flow Analysis   332
                              Free Cash Flow Model Variations   337
                                  An International Application of the Single-Stage Model   337
                                  Sensitivity Analysis of FCFF and FCFE Valuations   339
                                  Two-Stage Free Cash Flow Models   340
                                  Three-Stage Growth Models   347
                              Nonoperating Assets and Firm Value   349
                              Summary   350
                              Practice Problems   353
                              Solutions   366

Reading 36   **Market-Based Valuation: Price and Enterprise Value Multiples** 379
1/2   Introduction   380
                              Price and Enterprise Value Multiples in Valuation   381
                                  The Method of Comparables   381
                                  The Method Based on Forecasted Fundamentals   383
                              Price Multiples   384
                                  Price to Earnings   384
                                  Price to Book Value   416
                                  Price to Sales   427
                                  Price to Cash Flow   433
                                  Price to Dividends and Dividend Yield   439
                              Enterprise Value Multiples   442
                                  Enterprise Value to EBITDA   442
                                  Other Enterprise Value Multiples   448
                                  Enterprise Value to Sales   449
                                  Price and Enterprise Value Multiples in a Comparable Analysis:
                                      Some Illustrative Data   449
                              International Considerations When Using Multiples   451
                              Momentum Valuation Indicators   453
                              Valuation Indicators: Issues in Practice   459
                                  Averaging Multiples: The Harmonic Mean   459
                                  Using Multiple Valuation Indicators   461

◙ indicates an optional segment

Contents

Summary	**465**
Practice Problems	**470**
Solutions	**479**

Reading 37 | case

Residual Income Valuation — **487**

Introduction — **488**
Residual Income — **488**
  The Use of Residual Income in Equity Valuation — **490**
  Commercial Implementations — **492**
The Residual Income Model — **493**
  The General Residual Income Model — **496**
  Fundamental Determinants of Residual Income — **500**
  Single-Stage Residual Income Valuation — **502**
  Multistage Residual Income Valuation — **503**
Residual Income Valuation in Relation to Other Approaches — **507**
  Strengths and Weaknesses of the Residual Income Model — **510**
  Broad Guidelines for Using a Residual Income Model — **510**
Accounting and International Considerations — **511**
  Violations of the Clean Surplus Relationship — **512**
  Balance Sheet Adjustments for Fair Value — **520**
  Intangible Assets — **521**
  Nonrecurring Items — **524**
  Other Aggressive Accounting Practices — **524**
  International Considerations — **525**
Summary — **525**
Practice Problems — **529**
Solutions — **536**

Reading 38
1/2

Private Company Valuation — **547**
Introduction — **548**
The Scope of Private Company Valuation — **548**
  Private and Public Company Valuation: Similarities and Contrasts — **549**
  Reasons for Performing Valuations — **550**
Definitions (Standards) of Value — **552**
Private Company Valuation Approaches — **554**
  Earnings Normalization and Cash Flow Estimation Issues — **555**
  Income Approach Methods of Private Company Valuation — **561**
  Market Approach Methods of Private Company Valuation — **571**
  Asset-Based Approach to Private Company Valuation — **578**
  Valuation Discounts and Premiums — **580**
  Business Valuation Standards and Practices — **587**
Summary — **588**
Practice Problems — **591**
Solutions — **598**

Glossary — **G-1**
Index — **I-1**

◙ indicates an optional segment

How to Use the CFA Program Curriculum

Congratulations on reaching Level II of the Chartered Financial Analyst (CFA®) Program. This exciting and rewarding program of study reflects your desire to become a serious investment professional. You are embarking on a program noted for its high ethical standards and the breadth of knowledge, skills, and abilities it develops. Your commitment to the CFA Program should be educationally and professionally rewarding.

The credential you seek is respected around the world as a mark of accomplishment and dedication. Each level of the program represents a distinct achievement in professional development. Successful completion of the program is rewarded with membership in a prestigious global community of investment professionals. CFA charterholders are dedicated to life-long learning and maintaining currency with the ever-changing dynamics of a challenging profession. The CFA Program represents the first step toward a career-long commitment to professional education.

The CFA examination measures your mastery of the core skills required to succeed as an investment professional. These core skills are the basis for the Candidate Body of Knowledge (CBOK™). The CBOK consists of four components:

- A broad outline that lists the major topic areas covered in the CFA Program (www.cfainstitute.org/cbok);
- Topic area weights that indicate the relative exam weightings of the top-level topic areas (www.cfainstitute.org/level_II);
- Learning outcome statements (LOS) that advise candidates about the specific knowledge, skills, and abilities they should acquire from readings covering a topic area (LOS are provided in candidate study sessions and at the beginning of each reading); and
- The CFA Program curriculum, which contains the readings and end-of-reading questions, that candidates receive upon exam registration.

Therefore, the key to your success on the CFA examinations is studying and understanding the CBOK. The following sections provide background on the CBOK, the organization of the curriculum, and tips for developing an effective study program.

CURRICULUM DEVELOPMENT PROCESS

The CFA Program is grounded in the practice of the investment profession. Beginning with the Global Body of Investment Knowledge (GBIK), CFA Institute performs a continuous practice analysis with investment professionals around the world to determine the knowledge, skills, and abilities (competencies) that are relevant to the profession. Regional expert panels and targeted surveys are conducted annually to verify and reinforce the continuous feedback from the GBIK collaborative website. The practice analysis process ultimately defines the CBOK. The CBOK reflects the competencies that are generally accepted and applied by investment professionals. These competencies are used in practice in a generalist context and are expected to be demonstrated by a recently qualified CFA charterholder.

The Education Advisory Committee, consisting of practicing charterholders, in conjunction with CFA Institute staff, designs the CFA Program curriculum in order to deliver the CBOK to candidates. The examinations, also written by charterholders, are designed to allow you to demonstrate your mastery of the CBOK as set forth in the CFA Program curriculum. As you structure your personal study program, you should emphasize mastery of the CBOK and the practical application of that knowledge. For more information on the practice analysis, CBOK, and development of the CFA Program curriculum, please visit www.cfainstitute.org.

ORGANIZATION OF THE CURRICULUM

The Level II CFA Program curriculum is organized into 10 topic areas. Each topic area begins with a brief statement of the material and the depth of knowledge expected.

Each topic area is then divided into one or more study sessions. These study sessions—18 sessions in the Level II curriculum—should form the basic structure of your reading and preparation.

Each study session includes a statement of its structure and objective and is further divided into specific reading assignments. An outline illustrating the organization of these 18 study sessions can be found at the front of each volume of the curriculum.

The readings and end-of-reading questions are the basis for all examination questions and are selected or developed specifically to teach the knowledge, skills, and abilities reflected in the CBOK. These readings are drawn from content commissioned by CFA Institute, textbook chapters, professional journal articles, research analyst reports, and cases. All readings include problems and solutions to help you understand and master the topic areas.

Reading-specific Learning Outcome Statements (LOS) are listed at the beginning of each reading. These LOS indicate what you should be able to accomplish after studying the reading. The LOS, the reading, and the end-of-reading questions are dependent on each other, with the reading and questions providing context for understanding the scope of the LOS.

You should use the LOS to guide and focus your study because each examination question is based on the assigned readings and one or more LOS. The readings provide context for the LOS and enable you to apply a principle or concept in a variety of scenarios. The candidate is responsible for the entirety of the required material in a study session, which includes the assigned readings as well as the end-of-reading questions and problems.

We encourage you to review the information about the LOS on our website (www.cfainstitute.org/programs/cfaprogram/courseofstudy/Pages/study_sessions.aspx), including the descriptions of LOS "command words" (www.cfainstitute.org/programs/Documents/cfa_and_cipm_los_command_words.pdf).

FEATURES OF THE CURRICULUM

OPTIONAL
SEGMENT

Required vs. Optional Segments   You should read all of an assigned reading. In some cases, though, we have reprinted an entire chapter or article and marked certain parts of the reading as "optional." The CFA examination is based only on the required segments, and the optional segments are included only when it is determined that they might help you to better understand the required segments (by seeing the required material in its full context). When an optional segment begins, you will see an icon and a dashed vertical bar in the outside margin that will continue until the optional segment ends, accompanied by another icon. *Unless the material is specifically marked as optional, you should assume it is required.* You should rely on the required segments and the reading-specific LOS in preparing for the examination.

End-of-Reading Problems/Solutions   *All problems in the readings as well as their solutions (which are provided directly following the problems) are part of the curriculum and are required material for the exam.* When appropriate, we have included problems within and after the readings to demonstrate practical application and reinforce your understanding of the concepts presented. The problems are designed to help you learn these concepts and may serve as a basis for exam questions. Many of these questions are adapted from past CFA examinations.

Glossary and Index   For your convenience, we have printed a comprehensive glossary in each volume. Throughout the curriculum, a **bolded** word in a reading denotes a term defined in the glossary. The curriculum eBook is searchable, but we also publish an index that can be found on the CFA Institute website with the Level II study sessions.

Source Material   The authorship, publisher, and copyright owners are given for each reading for your reference. We recommend that you use the CFA Institute curriculum rather than the original source materials because the curriculum may include only selected pages from outside readings, updated sections within the readings, and problems and solutions tailored to the CFA Program.

LOS Self-Check   We have inserted checkboxes next to each LOS that you can use to track your progress in mastering the concepts in each reading.

DESIGNING YOUR PERSONAL STUDY PROGRAM

Create a Schedule   An orderly, systematic approach to exam preparation is critical. You should dedicate a consistent block of time every week to reading and studying. Complete all reading assignments and the associated problems and solutions in each study session. Review the LOS both before and after you study each reading to ensure that you have mastered the applicable content and can demonstrate the knowledge, skill, or ability described by the LOS and the assigned reading. Use the LOS self-check to track your progress and highlight areas of weakness for later review.

As you prepare for your exam, we will e-mail you important exam updates, testing policies, and study tips. Be sure to read these carefully. Curriculum errata are periodically updated and posted on the study session page at www.cfainstitute.org. You can also sign up for an RSS feed to alert you to the latest errata update.

Successful candidates report an average of more than 300 hours preparing for each exam. Your preparation time will vary based on your prior education and experience. For each level of the curriculum, there are 18 study sessions. So, a good plan is to devote 15–20 hours per week for 18 weeks to studying the material. Use the final four to six weeks before the exam to review what you have learned and practice with topic and mock exams. This recommendation, however, may underestimate the hours needed for appropriate examination preparation depending on your individual circumstances, relevant experience, and academic background. You will undoubtedly adjust your study time to conform to your own strengths and weaknesses and to your educational and professional background.

END OPTIONAL SEGMENT

You will probably spend more time on some study sessions than on others, but on average you should plan on devoting 15–20 hours per study session. You should allow ample time for both in-depth study of all topic areas and additional concentration on those topic areas for which you feel the least prepared.

An interactive study planner is available in the candidate resources area of our website to help you plan your study time. The interactive study planner recommends completion dates for each topic of the curriculum. Dates are determined based on study time available, exam topic weights, and curriculum weights. As you progress through the curriculum, the interactive study planner dynamically adjusts your study plan when you are running off schedule to help you stay on track for completion prior to the examination.

CFA Institute Topic Exams   The CFA Institute topic exams are intended to assess your mastery of individual topic areas as you progress through your studies. After each test, you will receive immediate feedback noting the correct responses and indicating the relevant assigned reading so you can identify areas of weakness for further study. For more information on the topic tests, please visit www.cfainstitute.org.

CFA Institute Mock Exams   The three-hour mock exams simulate the morning and afternoon sessions of the actual CFA examination, and are intended to be taken after you complete your study of the full curriculum so you can test your understanding of the curriculum and your readiness for the exam. You will receive feedback at the end of the mock exam, noting the correct responses and indicating the relevant assigned readings so you can assess areas of weakness for further study during your review period. We recommend that you take mock exams during the final stages of your preparation for the actual CFA examination. For more information on the mock examinations, please visit www.cfainstitute.org.

Preparatory Providers   After you enroll in the CFA Program, you may receive numerous solicitations for preparatory courses and review materials. When considering a prep course, make sure the provider is in compliance with the CFA Institute Prep Provider Guidelines Program (www.cfainstitute.org/utility/examprep/Pages/index.aspx). Just remember, there are no shortcuts to success on the CFA examinations; reading and studying the CFA curriculum is the key to success on the examination. The CFA examinations reference only the CFA Institute assigned curriculum—no preparatory course or review course materials are consulted or referenced.

SUMMARY

Every question on the CFA examination is based on the content contained in the required readings and on one or more LOS. Frequently, an examination question is based on a specific example highlighted within a reading or on a specific end-of-reading question and/or problem and its solution. To make effective use of the CFA Program curriculum, please remember these key points:

1   All pages of the curriculum are required reading for the examination except for occasional sections marked as optional. You may read optional pages as background, but you will not be tested on them.

2   All questions, problems, and their solutions—found at the end of readings—are part of the curriculum and are required study material for the examination.

3   You should make appropriate use of the topic and mock examinations and other resources available at www.cfainstitute.org.

4   Use the interactive study planner to create a schedule and commit sufficient study time to cover the 18 study sessions, review the materials, and take topic and mock examinations.

5   Some of the concepts in the study sessions may be superseded by updated rulings and/or pronouncements issued after a reading was published. Candidates are expected to be familiar with the overall analytical framework contained in the assigned readings. Candidates are not responsible for changes that occur after the material was written.

FEEDBACK

At CFA Institute, we are committed to delivering a comprehensive and rigorous curriculum for the development of competent, ethically grounded investment professionals. We rely on candidate and member feedback as we work to incorporate content, design, and packaging improvements. You can be assured that we will continue to listen to your suggestions. Please send any comments or feedback to info@cfainstitute.org. Ongoing improvements in the curriculum will help you prepare for success on the upcoming examinations and for a lifetime of learning as a serious investment professional.

Equity Valuation

STUDY SESSIONS

Study Session 10   Valuation Concepts

Study Session 11   Industry and Company Analysis in a Global Context

Study Session 12   Valuation Models

TOPIC LEVEL LEARNING OUTCOME

The candidate should be able to analyze and evaluate equity securities using appropriate valuation concepts and techniques. The candidate should also be able to estimate risk and expected return of equities in global contexts.

10

Equity Valuation

Valuation Concepts

This study session lays a foundation for the study of equity valuation. The first reading provides an overview of major themes and important models in equity valuation. The session ends with a presentation of topics relating to returns and discount rates, which are essential to equity valuation.

READING ASSIGNMENTS

Reading 29   Equity Valuation: Applications and Processes
by Jerald E. Pinto, PhD, CFA, Elaine Henry, PhD, CFA,
Thomas R. Robinson, PhD, CFA, and John D. Stowe, PhD,
CFA

Reading 30   Return Concepts
by Jerald E. Pinto, PhD, CFA, Elaine Henry, PhD, CFA,
Thomas R. Robinson, PhD, CFA, and John D. Stowe, PhD,
CFA

READING

29

Equity Valuation: Applications and Processes

by Jerald E. Pinto, PhD, CFA, Elaine Henry, PhD, CFA, Thomas R. Robinson, PhD, CFA, and John D. Stowe, PhD, CFA

Jerald E. Pinto, PhD, CFA, is at CFA Institute (USA). Elaine Henry, PhD, CFA, is at Fordham University (USA). Thomas R. Robinson, PhD, CFA, is at CFA Institute (USA). John D. Stowe, PhD, CFA, is at Ohio University (USA).

LEARNING OUTCOMES

Mastery	The candidate should be able to:
☐	a. define valuation and intrinsic value and explain sources of perceived mispricing;
☐	b. explain the going concern assumption and contrast a going concern value to a liquidation value;
☐	c. describe definitions of value and justify which definition of value is most relevant to public company valuation;
☐	d. describe applications of equity valuation;
☐	e. describe questions that should be addressed in conducting an industry and competitive analysis;
☐	f. contrast absolute and relative valuation models and describe examples of each type of model;
☐	g. describe sum-of-the-parts valuation and conglomerate discounts;
☐	h. explain broad criteria for choosing an appropriate approach for valuing a given company.

INTRODUCTION

1

Every day, thousands of participants in the investment profession—investors, portfolio managers, regulators, researchers—face a common and often perplexing question: What is the value of a particular asset? The answers to this question usually influence success or failure in achieving investment objectives. For one group of those

The data and examples for this reading were updated in 2014 by Professor Stephen Wilcox, CFA.

Equity Asset Valuation, Second Edition, by Jerald E. Pinto, CFA, Elaine Henry, CFA, Thomas R. Robinson, CFA, and John D. Stowe, CFA. Copyright © 2009 by CFA Institute.

participants—equity analysts—the question and its potential answers are particularly critical, because determining the value of an ownership stake is at the heart of their professional activities and decisions. **Valuation** is the estimation of an asset's value based on variables perceived to be related to future investment returns, on comparisons with similar assets, or, when relevant, on estimates of immediate liquidation proceeds. Skill in valuation is a very important element of success in investing.

In this introductory reading, we address some basic questions: What is value? Who uses equity valuations? What is the importance of industry knowledge? How can the analyst effectively communicate his analysis? This reading answers these and other questions and lays a foundation for the remaining valuation readings.

The balance of this reading is organized as follows: Section 2 defines value and describes the various uses of equity valuation. Section 3 examines the steps in the valuation process, including a discussion of the analyst's role and responsibilities. Section 4 discusses how valuation results are communicated and provides some guidance on the content and format of an effective research report. The final section summarizes the reading, and practice problems conclude.

2 VALUE DEFINITIONS AND VALUATION APPLICATIONS

Before summarizing the various applications of equity valuation tools, it is helpful to define what is meant by "value" and to understand that the meaning can vary in different contexts. The context of a valuation, including its objective, generally determines the appropriate definition of value and thus affects the analyst's selection of a valuation approach.

2.1 What Is Value?

Several perspectives on value serve as the foundation for the variety of valuation models available to the equity analyst. Intrinsic value is the necessary starting point, but other concepts of value—going-concern value, liquidation value, and fair value—are also important.

2.1.1 Intrinsic Value

A critical assumption in equity valuation, as applied to publicly traded securities, is that the market *price* of a security can differ from its intrinsic *value*. The **intrinsic value** of any asset is the value of the asset given a hypothetically complete understanding of the asset's investment characteristics. For any particular investor, an estimate of intrinsic value reflects his or her view of the "true" or "real" value of an asset. If one assumed that the market price of an equity security perfectly reflected its intrinsic value, "valuation" would simply require looking at the market price. Roughly, it is just such an assumption that underpins traditional efficient market theory, which suggests that an asset's market price is the best available estimate of its intrinsic value.

An important theoretical counter to the notion that market price and intrinsic value are identical can be found in the Grossman–Stiglitz paradox. If market prices, which are essentially freely obtainable, perfectly reflect a security's intrinsic value, then a rational investor would not incur the costs of obtaining and analyzing information to obtain a second estimate of the security's value. If no investor obtains and analyzes information about a security, however, then how can the market price reflect the security's intrinsic value? The **rational efficient markets formulation** (Grossman and Stiglitz, 1980) recognizes that investors will not rationally incur the expenses of gathering information unless they expect to be rewarded by higher gross returns compared with the free alternative of accepting the market price. Furthermore, modern theorists recognize that when intrinsic value is difficult to determine, as is the case for common stock, and when trading costs exist, even further room exists for price to diverge from value (Lee, Myers, and Swaminathan, 1999).

Thus, analysts often view market prices both with respect and with skepticism. They seek to identify mispricing. At the same time, they often rely on price eventually converging to intrinsic value. They also recognize distinctions among the levels of **market efficiency** in different markets or tiers of markets (for example, stocks heavily followed by analysts and stocks neglected by analysts). Overall, equity valuation, when applied to market-traded securities, admits the possibility of mispricing. Throughout these readings, then, we distinguish between the market price, P, and the intrinsic value ("value" for short), V.

For an active investment manager, valuation is an inherent part of the attempt to produce investment returns that exceed the returns commensurate with the investment's risk; that is, positive excess risk-adjusted returns. An excess risk-adjusted return is also called an **abnormal return** or **alpha**. (Return concepts will be more fully discussed in a later reading.) The active investment manager hopes to capture a positive alpha as a result of his or her efforts to estimate intrinsic value. Any departure of market price from the manager's estimate of intrinsic value is a perceived **mispricing** (a difference between the estimated intrinsic value and the market price of an asset).

These ideas can be illuminated through the following expression that identifies two possible sources of perceived mispricing:[1]

$$V_E - P = (V - P) + (V_E - V)$$

where

V_E = estimated value
P = market price
V = intrinsic value

This expression states that the difference between a valuation estimate and the prevailing market price is, by definition, equal to the sum of two components. The first component is the true mispricing, that is, the difference between the true but unobservable intrinsic value V and the observed market price P (this difference contributes to the abnormal return). The second component is the difference between the valuation estimate and the true but unobservable intrinsic value, that is, the error in the estimate of the intrinsic value.

To obtain a useful estimate of intrinsic value, an analyst must combine accurate forecasts with an appropriate valuation model. The quality of the analyst's forecasts, in particular the expectational inputs used in valuation models, is a key element in determining investment success. For active security selection to be consistently successful, the manager's expectations must differ from consensus expectations and be, on average, correct as well.

Uncertainty is constantly present in equity valuation. Confidence in one's expectations is always realistically partial. In applying any valuation approach, analysts can never be sure that they have accounted for all the sources of risk reflected in an asset's price. Because competing equity risk models will always exist, there is no obvious final resolution to this dilemma. Even if an analyst makes adequate risk adjustments, develops accurate forecasts, and employs appropriate valuation models, success is not assured. Temporal market conditions may prevent the investor from capturing the benefits of any perceived mispricing. Convergence of the market price to perceived intrinsic value may not happen within the investor's investment horizon, if at all.

---

1 Derived as $V_E - P = V_E - P + V - V = (V - P) + (V_E - V)$.

So, besides evidence of mispricing, some active investors look for the presence of a particular market or corporate event (**catalyst**) that will cause the marketplace to re-evaluate a company's prospects.

2.1.2 *Going-Concern Value and Liquidation Value*

A company generally has one value if it is to be immediately dissolved and another value if it will continue in operation. In estimating value, a **going-concern assumption** is the assumption that the company will continue its business activities into the foreseeable future. In other words, the company will continue to produce and sell its goods and services, use its assets in a value-maximizing way for a relevant economic time frame, and access its optimal sources of financing. The **going-concern value** of a company is its value under a going-concern assumption. Models of going-concern value are the focus of these readings.

Nevertheless, a going-concern assumption may not be appropriate for a company in financial distress. An alternative to a company's going-concern value is its value if it were dissolved and its assets sold individually, known as its **liquidation value**. For many companies, the value added by assets working together and by human capital applied to managing those assets makes estimated going-concern value greater than liquidation value (although a persistently unprofitable business may be worth more "dead" than "alive"). Beyond the value added by assets working together or by applying managerial skill to those assets, the value of a company's assets would likely differ depending on the time frame available for liquidating them. For example, the value of nonperishable inventory that had to be immediately liquidated would typically be lower than the value of inventory that could be sold during a longer period of time, i.e., in an "orderly" fashion. Thus, concepts such as **orderly liquidation value** are sometimes distinguished.

2.1.3 *Fair Market Value and Investment Value*

For an analyst valuing public equities, intrinsic value is typically the relevant concept of value. In other contexts, however, other definitions of value are relevant. For example, a buy–sell agreement among the owners of a private business—specifying how and when the owners (e.g., shareholders or partners) can sell their ownership interest and at what price—might be primarily concerned with equitable treatment of both sellers and buyers. In that context, the relevant definition of value would likely be fair market value. **Fair market value** is the price at which an asset (or liability) would change hands between a willing buyer and a willing seller when the former is not under any compulsion to buy and the latter is not under any compulsion to sell. Furthermore, the concept of fair market value generally includes an assumption that both buyer and seller are informed of all material aspects of the underlying investment. Fair market value has often been used in valuation related to assessing taxes. In a financial reporting context—for example, in valuing an asset for the purpose of impairment testing—financial reporting standards reference **fair value**, a related (but not identical) concept.[2]

Assuming the marketplace has confidence that the company's management is acting in the owners' best interests, market prices should tend, in the long run, to reflect fair market value. In some situations, however, an asset is worth more to a particular buyer (e.g., because of potential operating synergies). The concept of value to a specific buyer taking account of potential synergies and based on the investor's requirements and expectations is called **investment value**.

---

2 Accounting standards provide specific definitions of fair value. Fair value is the amount for which an asset could be exchanged, a liability settled, or an equity instrument granted could be exchanged between knowledgeable, willing parties in an arm's length transaction.

2.1.4 Definitions of Value: Summary

Analysts valuing an asset need to be aware of the definition or definitions of value relevant to the assignment. For the valuation of public equities, an intrinsic value definition of values is generally relevant. Intrinsic value, estimated under a going-concern assumption, is the focus of these equity valuation readings.

2.2 Applications of Equity Valuation

Investment analysts work in a wide variety of organizations and positions; as a result, they apply the tools of equity valuation to address a range of practical problems. In particular, analysts use valuation concepts and models to accomplish the following:

- *Selecting stocks.* Stock selection is the primary use of the tools presented in these readings. Equity analysts continually address the same question for every common stock that is either a current or prospective portfolio holding, or for every stock that he or she is responsible for covering: Is this security fairly priced, overpriced, or underpriced relative to its current estimated intrinsic value and relative to the prices of comparable securities?

- *Inferring (extracting) market expectations.* Market prices reflect the expectations of investors about the future performance of companies. Analysts may ask: What expectations about a company's future performance are consistent with the current market price for that company's stock? What assumptions about the company's fundamentals would justify the current price? (**Fundamentals** are characteristics of a company related to profitability, financial strength, or risk.) These questions may be relevant to the analyst for several reasons:
  - The analyst can evaluate the reasonableness of the expectations implied by the market price by comparing the market's implied expectations to his own expectations.
  - The market's expectations for a fundamental characteristic of one company may be useful as a benchmark or comparison value of the same characteristic for another company.

  To extract or reverse-engineer a market expectation, the analyst selects a valuation model that relates value to expectations about fundamentals and is appropriate given the characteristics of the stock. Next, the analyst estimates values for all fundamentals in the model except the fundamental of interest. The analyst then solves for that value of the fundamental of interest that results in a model value equal to the current market price.

- *Evaluating corporate events.* Investment bankers, corporate analysts, and investment analysts use valuation tools to assess the impact of such corporate events as mergers, acquisitions, divestitures, spin-offs, and going private transactions. (A **merger** is the general term for the combination of two companies. An **acquisition** is also a combination of two companies, with one of the companies identified as the acquirer, the other the acquired. In a **divestiture**, a company sells some major component of its business. In a **spin-off**, the company separates one of its component businesses and transfers the ownership of the separated business to its shareholders. A **leveraged buyout** is an acquisition involving significant leverage [i.e., debt], which is often collateralized by the assets of the company being acquired.) Each of these events affects a company's future cash flows and thus the value of its equity. Furthermore, in mergers and acquisitions, the acquiring company's own common stock is often used as currency for the purchase; investors then want to know whether the stock is fairly valued.

- *Rendering fairness opinions.* The parties to a merger may be required to seek a fairness opinion on the terms of the merger from a third party, such as an investment bank. Valuation is central to such opinions.

- *Evaluating business strategies and models.* Companies concerned with maximizing shareholder value evaluate the effect of alternative strategies on share value.

- *Communicating with analysts and shareholders.* Valuation concepts facilitate communication and discussion among company management, shareholders, and analysts on a range of corporate issues affecting company value.

- *Appraising private businesses.* Valuation of the equity of private businesses is important for transactional purposes (e.g., acquisitions of such companies or buy–sell agreements for the transfer of equity interests among owners when one of them dies or retires) and tax reporting purposes (e.g., for the taxation of estates) among others. The absence of a market price imparts distinctive characteristics to such valuations, although the fundamental models are shared with public equity valuation. An analyst encounters these characteristics when evaluating initial public offerings, for example. An **initial public offering** (IPO) is the initial issuance of common stock registered for public trading by a company whose shares were not formerly publicly traded, either because it was formerly privately owned or government-owned, or because it is a newly formed entity.

- *Share-based payment (compensation).* Share-based payments (e.g., restricted stock grants) are sometimes part of executive compensation. Estimation of their value frequently depends on using equity valuation tools.

EXAMPLE 1

Inferring Market Expectations

On 21 September 2000, Intel Corporation (NASDAQ-GS: INTC)[3] issued a press release containing information about its expected revenue growth for the third quarter of 2000. The announced growth fell short of the company's own prior prediction by 2 to 4 percentage points and short of analysts' projections by 3 to 7 percentage points. In response to the announcement, Intel's stock price fell nearly 30 percent during the following five days—from $61.50 just prior to the press release to only $43.31 five days later.

To assess whether the information in Intel's announcement was sufficient to explain such a large loss of value, Cornell (2001) estimated the value of a company's equity as the present value of expected future cash flows from operations minus the expenditures needed to maintain the company's growth. (We will discuss such *free cash flow models* in detail in a later reading.)

Using a conservatively low discount rate, Cornell estimated that Intel's price before the announcement, $61.50, was consistent with a forecasted growth rate of 20 percent a year for the subsequent 10 years and then 6 percent per year thereafter. Intel's price after the announcement, $43.31, was consistent with a decline of the 10-year growth rate to well under 15 percent per year. In the final year of the forecast horizon (2009), projected revenues with the lower growth rate would be $50 billion below the projected revenues based on the

---

3 In these readings, the shares of real companies are identified by an abbreviation for the stock exchange or electronic marketplace where the shares of the company are traded, followed by a ticker symbol or formal acronym for the shares. For example, NASDAQ-GS stands for "NASDAQ Global Select Market," and INTC is the ticker symbol for Intel Corporation on the NASDAQ-GS. (Many stocks are traded on a number of exchanges worldwide, and some stocks may have more than one formal acronym; we usually state just one marketplace and one ticker symbol.)

pre-announcement price. Because the press release did not obviously point to any changes in Intel's fundamental long-run business conditions (Intel attributed the quarterly revenue growth shortfall to a cyclical slowing of demand in Europe), Cornell's detailed analysis left him skeptical that the stock market's reaction could be explained in terms of fundamentals.

Assuming Cornell's methodology was sound, one interpretation is that investors' reaction to the press release was irrational. An alternative interpretation is that Intel's stock was overvalued prior to the press release, and the press release was "a kind of catalyst that caused movement toward a more rational price, even though the release itself did not contain sufficient long-run valuation information to justify that movement" (Cornell 2001, p. 134). How could one evaluate these two possible interpretations?

Solution:

To evaluate whether the market reaction to Intel's announcement was an irrational reaction or a rational reduction of a previously overvalued price, one could compare the expected 20 percent growth implicit in the pre-announcement stock price to some benchmark—for example, the company's actual recent revenue growth, the industry's recent growth, and/or forecasts for the growth of the industry or the economy. Finding the growth rate implied in the company's stock price is an example of using a valuation model and a company's actual stock price to infer market expectations.

Note: Cornell (2001) observed that the 20 percent revenue growth rate implied by the pre-announcement stock price was much higher than Intel's average growth rate during the previous five years, which occurred when the company was much smaller. He concluded that Intel's stock was overvalued prior to the press release.

This example illustrates the role of expectations in equity valuation and a typical situation in which a given set of facts may be given various interpretations. This example also illustrates that differences between market price and intrinsic value can occur suddenly, offering opportunities for astute investment managers to generate alpha.

THE VALUATION PROCESS

3

In general, the valuation process involves the following five steps:

1 *Understanding the business.* Industry and competitive analysis, together with an analysis of financial statements and other company disclosures, provides a basis for forecasting company performance.

2 *Forecasting company performance.* Forecasts of sales, earnings, dividends, and financial position (pro forma analysis) provide the inputs for most valuation models.

3 *Selecting the appropriate valuation model.* Depending on the characteristics of the company and the context of valuation, some valuation models may be more appropriate than others.

4 *Converting forecasts to a valuation.* Beyond mechanically obtaining the "output" of valuation models, estimating value involves judgment.

5 *Applying the valuation conclusions.* Depending on the purpose, an analyst may use the valuation conclusions to make an investment recommendation about a particular stock, provide an opinion about the price of a transaction, or evaluate the economic merits of a potential strategic investment.

Most of these steps are addressed in detail in the succeeding valuation readings; here, we provide an overview of each.

3.1 Understanding the Business

To forecast a company's financial performance as a basis for determining the value of an investment in the company or its securities, it is helpful to understand the economic and industry contexts in which the company operates, the company's strategy, and the company's previous financial performance. Industry and competitive analysis, together with an analysis of the company's financial reports, provides a basis for forecasting performance.

3.1.1 Industry and Competitive Analysis

Because similar economic and technological factors typically affect all companies in an industry, industry knowledge helps analysts understand the basic characteristics of the markets served by a company and the economics of the company. An airline industry analyst will know that labor costs and jet fuel costs are the two largest expenses of airlines, and that in many markets airlines have difficulty passing through higher fuel prices by raising ticket prices. Using this knowledge, the analyst may inquire about the degree to which different airlines hedge the commodity price risk inherent in jet fuel costs. With such information in hand, the analyst is better able to evaluate risk and forecast future cash flows. In addition, the analyst would run sensitivity analyses to determine how different levels of fuel prices would affect valuation.

Various frameworks exist for industry and competitive analysis. The primary usefulness of such frameworks is that they can help ensure that an analysis gives appropriate attention to the most important economic drivers of a business. In other words, the objective is *not* to prepare some formal framework representing industry structure or corporate strategy, but rather to use a framework to organize thoughts about an industry and to better understand a company's prospects for success in competition with other companies in that industry. Further, although frameworks can provide a template, obviously the informational content added by an analyst makes the framework relevant to valuation. Ultimately, an industry and competitive analysis should highlight which aspects of a company's business present the greatest challenges and opportunities and should thus be the subject of further investigation, and/or more extensive **sensitivity analysis** (an analysis to determine how changes in an assumed input would affect the outcome of an analysis). Frameworks may be useful as analysts focus on questions relevant to understanding a business.

■ *How attractive are the industries in which the company operates, in terms of offering prospects for sustained profitability?*

Inherent industry profitability is one important factor in determining a company's profitability. Analysts should try to understand **industry structure**—the industry's underlying economic and technical characteristics—and the trends affecting that structure. Basic economic factors—supply and demand—provide a fundamental framework for understanding an industry.

Porter's (1985, 1998, 2008) five forces characterizing industry structure are summarized below with an explanation of how that force could positively affect inherent industry profitability. For each force, the opposite situation would negatively affect inherent industry profitability.

  i. *Intra-industry rivalry.* Lower rivalry among industry participants—for example, in a faster growing industry with relatively few competitors and/or good brand identification—enhances inherent industry profitability.

  ii. *New entrants.* Relatively high costs to enter an industry (or other entry barriers, such as government policies) result in fewer new participants and less competition, thus enhancing inherent industry profitability.

  iii. *Substitutes.* When few potential substitutes exist and/or the cost to switch to a substitute is high, industry participants are less constrained in raising prices, thus enhancing inherent industry profitability.

  iv. *Supplier power.* When many suppliers of the inputs needed by industry participants exist, suppliers have limited power to raise prices and thus would not represent inherent downward pressure on industry profitability.

  v. *Buyer power.* When many customers for an industry's product exist, customers have limited power to negotiate lower prices and thus would not represent inherent downward pressure on industry profitability.

Analysts must also stay current on facts and news concerning all the industries in which the company operates, including recent developments (e.g., management, technological, or financial). Particularly important to valuation are any factors likely to affect the industry's longer term profitability and growth prospects such as demographic trends.

■ *What is the company's relative competitive position within its industry, and what is its competitive strategy?*

The level and trend of the company's market share indicate its relative competitive position within an industry. In general, a company's value is higher to the extent that it can create and sustain an advantage relative to its competition. Porter identifies three generic corporate strategies for achieving above-average performance:

  i. Cost leadership: being the lowest cost producer while offering products comparable to those of other companies, so that products can be priced at or near the industry average;

  ii. Differentiation: offering unique products or services along some dimensions that are widely valued by buyers so that the company can command premium prices; and

  iii. Focus: seeking a competitive advantage within a target segment or segments of the industry, based on either cost leadership (cost focus) or differentiation (differentiation focus).

The term "business model" refers generally to how a company makes money: which customers it targets, what products or services it will sell to those customers, and how it delivers those products or services (including how it finances its activities). The term is broadly used and sometimes encompasses aspects of the generic strategies described above. For example, an airline with a generic cost leadership strategy might have a business model characterized as a low-cost carrier. Low-cost carriers offer a single class of service and use a single type of aircraft to minimize training costs and maintenance charges.

■ *How well has the company executed its strategy and what are its prospects for future execution?*

Competitive success requires both appropriate strategic choices and competent execution. Analyzing the company's financial reports provides a basis for evaluating a company's performance against its strategic objectives and for developing expectations about a company's likely future performance. A historical analysis means more than just reviewing, say, the 10-year historical record in the most recent annual report. It very often means looking at the annual reports from 10 years prior, 5 years prior, and the most recent two years. Why? Because looking at annual reports from prior years often provides useful insights into how management has historically foreseen challenges and has adapted to changes in business conditions through time. (In general, the investor relations sections of most publicly traded companies' websites provide electronic copies of their annual reports from at least the most recent years.)

In examining financial and operational strategic execution, two caveats merit mention. First, the importance of qualitative, that is, non-numeric factors, must be considered. Such non-numeric factors include, for example, the company's ownership structure, its intellectual and physical property, the terms of its intangible assets such as licenses and franchise agreements, and the potential consequences of legal disputes or other contingent liabilities. Second, it is important to avoid simply extrapolating past operating results when forecasting future performance. In general, economic and technological forces can often contribute to the phenomenon of "regression toward the mean." Specifically, successful companies tend to draw more competitors into their industries and find that their ability to generate above average profits comes under pressure. Conversely, poorly performing companies are often restructured in such a manner as to improve their long-term profitability. Thus, in many cases, analysts making long-term horizon growth forecasts for a company's earnings and profits (e.g., forecasts beyond the next 10 years) plausibly assume company convergence toward the forecasted average growth rate for the underlying economy.

3.1.2 *Analysis of Financial Reports*

The aspects of a financial report that are most relevant for evaluating a company's success in implementing strategic choices vary across companies and industries. For established companies, financial ratio analysis is useful. Individual drivers of profitability for merchandising and manufacturing companies can be evaluated against the company's stated strategic objectives. For example, a manufacturing company aiming to create a sustainable competitive advantage by building strong brand recognition could be expected to have substantial expenditures for advertising but relatively higher prices for its goods. Compared with a company aiming to compete on cost, the branded company would be expected to have higher gross margins but also higher selling expenses as a percent of sales.

EXAMPLE 2

Competitive Analysis

Based on 2012 revenues, the six largest providers of oilfield services are:

- Schlumberger Ltd. (NYSE: SLB)
  - Revenues: $42.1 billion
  - Net income: $5.5 billion
- Halliburton (NYSE: HAL)
  - Revenues: $28.5 billion
  - Net income: $2.6 billion
- Baker Hughes Inc. (NYSE: BHI)

- Revenue: $21.4 billion
- Net income: $1.3 billion
- National Oilwell Varco Inc. (NYSE: NOV)
  - Revenues: $20.0 billion
  - Net income: $2.5 billion
- Weatherford International Ltd. (NYSE: WFT)
  - Revenues: $15.2 billion
  - Net loss: −$778 million
- Cameron (NYSE: CAM)
  - Revenues: $8.5 billion
  - Net income: $751 million

These companies provide tools and services—often of a very technical nature—to expedite the drilling activities of oil and gas producers and drilling companies.

1 Discuss the economic factors that may affect demand for the services provided by oilfield services companies, and explain a logical framework for analyzing and forecasting revenue for these companies.

2 Explain how comparing the level and trend in profit margin (net income/sales) and revenue per employee for the above companies may help in evaluating whether one of these companies is the cost leader in the peer group.

Solution to 1:

Because the products and services of these companies relate to oil and gas exploration and production, the levels of exploration and production activities by oil and gas producers are probably the major factors that determine the demand for their services. In turn, the prices of natural gas and crude oil are important in determining the level of exploration and production activities. Therefore, among other economic factors, an analyst should research those relating to supply and demand for natural gas and crude oil.

- Supply factors in natural gas, such as natural gas inventory levels.
- Demand factors in natural gas, including household and commercial use of natural gas and the amount of new power generation equipment being fired by natural gas.
- Supply factors in crude oil, including capacity constraints and production levels in OPEC and other oil producing countries, as well as new discoveries of off-shore, and land-based oil reserves.
- Demand factors in crude oil, such as household and commercial use of oil and the amount of new power generation equipment using oil products as its primary fuel.
- For both crude oil and natural gas, projected economic growth rates could be examined as a demand factor and depletion rates as a supply side factor.

Solution to 2:

Profit margin reflects cost structure; in interpreting profit margin, however, analysts should evaluate any differences in companies' abilities to affect profit margin through power over price. A successfully executed cost leadership strategy will lower costs and raise profit margins. All else equal, we would also expect a cost leader to have relatively high sales per employee, reflecting efficient use of human resources.

Note: Energy analysts should be familiar with sources for researching supply and demand information, such as the International Energy Agency (IEA), the European Petroleum Industry Association (EUROPIA), the Energy Information Administration (EIA), the American Gas Association (AGA), and the American Petroleum Institute (API).

With newer companies, or companies involved in creating new products or markets, nonfinancial measures may be critical to obtaining an accurate picture of corporate prospects. For example, a biotechnology company's clinical trial results or an internet company's unique visitors per day may provide information helpful for evaluating future revenue.

3.1.3 *Sources of Information*

An important perspective on industry and competition is sometimes provided by companies themselves in regulator-mandated disclosures, regulatory filings, company press releases, investor relations materials, and contacts with analysts. Analysts can compare the information provided directly by companies to their own independent research.

Regulatory requirements concerning disclosures and filings vary internationally. In some markets, such as Canada and the United States, some mandatory filings require management to provide industry and competitive information and access to those filings is freely available on the internet (e.g., www.sedar.com for Canadian filings and at www.sec.gov for US filings). To take the case of the United States, in annual filings with the Securities and Exchange Commission made on Form 10-K for US companies and Form 20-F for non-US companies, companies provide industry and competitive information in the business description section and in the management discussion and analysis (MD&A). Interim filings (e.g., the quarterly SEC Form 10-Q for US companies and Form 6-K for non-US companies) provide interim financial statements but typically less detailed coverage of industry and competition.

So far as analyst–management contacts are concerned, analysts must be aware when regulations (e.g., Regulation FD in the United States) prohibit companies from disclosing material nonpublic information to analysts without also disseminating that information to the public.[4] General management insights based on public information, however, can still be useful to analysts, and many analysts consider in-person meetings with a company's management to be essential to understanding a company.

The CFA Institute Code of Ethics and Standards of Professional Conduct prohibit use of material inside information, and Regulation FD (and similar regulations in other countries) is designed to prohibit companies from selectively offering such information. These ethical and legal requirements assist analysts by clarifying their main role and purpose.

Company-provided sources of information in addition to regulatory filings include press releases and investor relations materials. The press releases of most relevance to analysts are the press releases that companies issue to announce their periodic earnings. Companies typically issue these earnings press releases several weeks after the end of an accounting period and several weeks before they file their interim financial statements. Earnings press releases summarize the company's performance for the period, usually include explanations for the performance, and usually include financial

---

4 There may be special filings, for example Form 8-K in the United States, associated with public disclosure of material corporate events.

statements (often abbreviated versions). Following their earnings press releases, many companies host conference calls in which they further elaborate on their reported performance and typically allocate some time to answer questions posed by analysts. On their corporate websites, many companies post audio downloads and transcripts of conference calls and of presentations made in analyst conferences. The audio files and transcripts of conference calls and conference presentations provide access not only to the company's reports but also to analysts' questions and the company's answers to those questions.

Apart from company-provided sources of information, analysts also obtain information from third party sources such as industry organizations, regulatory agencies, and commercial providers of market intelligence.

3.1.4 *Considerations in Using Accounting Information*

In evaluating a company's historical performance and developing forecasts of future performance, analysts typically rely heavily on companies' accounting information and financial disclosures. Companies' reported results vary in their persistence, i.e., sustainability. In addition, the information that companies disclose can vary substantially with respect to the *accuracy* of reported accounting results as reflections of economic performance and the detail in which results are disclosed.

The term **quality of earnings analysis** broadly includes the scrutiny of *all* financial statements, including the balance sheet, to evaluate both the sustainability of the companies' performance and how accurately the reported information reflects economic reality. Equity analysts will generally develop better insights into a company and improve forecast accuracy by developing an ability to assess a company's quality of earnings. With regard to sustainability of performance, an analyst aims to identify aspects of reported performance that are less likely to recur. For example, earnings with significant components of nonrecurring events such as positive litigation settlements, nonpermanent tax reductions, or gains on sales of nonoperating assets are considered to be of lower quality than earnings derived mainly from the company's core business operations.

In addition to identifying nonrecurring events, an analyst aims to identify reporting decisions that may result in a level of reported earnings that are unlikely to continue. A good starting point for this type of quality of earnings analysis is a comparison of a company's net income with its operating cash flow. As a simple hypothetical example, consider a company that generates revenues and net income but no operating cash flow because it makes all sales on account and never collects its receivables. One systematic way to make the comparison is to decompose net income into a cash component (combining operating and investing cash flows) and an accrual component (defined as net income minus the cash component). Capital markets research shows that the cash component is more persistent than the accrual component of earnings, with the result that a company with a relatively higher amount of current accruals will have a relatively lower ROA in the future (Sloan 1996). Here, greater persistency means that, compared to accruals in the current period, the cash component in the current period is more predictive of future net income. A relatively higher proportion of accruals can be interpreted as lower earnings quality.

A quality of earnings analysis for a particular company requires careful scrutiny of accounting statements, footnotes, and other relevant disclosures. Sources for studying quality of earnings analysis and accounting risk factors include Mulford and Comiskey (2005) and Schilit and Perler (2010), as well as American Institute of Certified Public Accountants *Consideration of Fraud in a Financial Statement Audit* (28 February 2002) and International Federation of Accountants, International Standards on Auditing 240, *The Auditor's Responsibility to Consider Fraud and Error in an Audit of Financial Statements* (2008). Examples of a few of the many available indicators of possible problems with a company's quality of earnings are provided in Exhibit 1.

Exhibit 1	Selected Quality of Earnings Indicators	
Category	**Observation**	**Potential Interpretation**
Revenues and gains	Recognizing revenue early, for example: ▪ bill-and-hold sales, and ▪ recording sales of equipment or software prior to installation and acceptance by customer.	Acceleration in the recognition of revenue boosts reported income, masking a decline in operating performance.
	Classification of nonoperating income or gains as part of operations.	Income or gains may be nonrecurring and may not relate to true operating performance, possibly masking declines in operating performance.
Expenses and losses	Recognizing too much or too little reserves in the current year, such as: ▪ restructuring reserves; ▪ loan-loss or bad-debt reserves; and ▪ valuation allowances against deferred tax assets.	May boost current income at the expense of future income, or alternatively may decrease current year's earnings to boost future years' performance.
	Deferral of expenses by capitalizing expenditures as an asset, for example: ▪ customer acquisition costs, and ▪ product development costs.	May boost current income at the expense of future income. May mask problems with underlying business performance.
	Use of aggressive estimates and assumptions, such as: ▪ asset impairments; ▪ long depreciable lives; ▪ long periods of amortization; ▪ high assumed discount rate for pension liabilities; ▪ low assumed rate of compensation growth for pension liabilities; and ▪ high expected return on assets for pension.	Aggressive estimates may indicate actions taken to boost current reported income. Changes in assumptions may indicate an attempt to mask problems with underlying performance in the current period.
Balance sheet issues (may also affect earnings)	Use of **off-balance sheet financing** (financing that does not appear on the balance sheet), such as leasing assets or securitizing receivables.	Assets and/or liabilities may not be properly reflected on the balance sheet.
Operating cash flow	Characterization of an increase in a bank overdraft as operating cash flow.	Operating cash flow may be artificially inflated.

The following example illustrates the importance of accounting practices in influencing reported financial results and the need for analysts to exercise judgment when using those results in any valuation model.

EXAMPLE 3

Quality of Earnings Warning Signs: Aggressive Estimates

In the section of his 2007 letter to the shareholders of Berkshire Hathaway titled "Fanciful Figures—How Public Companies Juice Earnings," Warren Buffett referred to the investment return assumption (the anticipated return on a defined-benefit pension plan's current and future assets):

> "Decades of option-accounting nonsense have now been put to rest, but other accounting choices remain—important among these [is] the investment-return assumption a company uses in calculating pension expense. It will come as no surprise that many companies continue to choose an assumption that allows them to report less-than-solid 'earnings.' For the 363 companies in the S&P that have pension plans, this assumption in 2006 averaged 8%."

(www.berkshirehathaway.com/letters/2007ltr.pdf. See pp.18–19.)

In his explanation, Buffett assumes a 5 percent return on cash and bonds, which averaged 28 percent of US pension fund assets. Therefore, this implies that the remaining 72 percent of pension fund assets—predominately invested in equities—must earn a return of 9.2 percent, after all fees, to achieve the 8 percent overall return on the pension fund assets. To illustrate one perspective on an average pension fund achieving that 9.2 percent return, he estimates that the Dow Jones Industrial Index would need to close at about 2,000,000 on 31 December 2099 (compared to a level under 13,000 at the time of his writing) for this century's returns on that US stock index to match just the 5.3 percent average annual compound return achieved in the 20th century.

1 How do aggressively optimistic estimates for returns on pension assets affect pension expense?

2 Where can information about a company's assumed returns on its pension assets be found?

Solution to 1:

The amount of "expected return on plan assets" associated with the return assumption is a deduction in calculating pension expense. An aggressively optimistic estimate for the rate of return that pension assets will earn means a larger-than-warranted deduction in calculating pension expense, and subtraction will lead to understating pension expense and overstating net income. In fact, pension expense could become pension income depending on the numbers involved.

Solution to 2:

Information about a company's assumed return on its pension assets can be found in the footnotes to the company's financial statements.

The next example of poor earnings quality, in which management made choices going beyond making an aggressive estimate, is reminiscent of a humorous vignette from Benjamin Graham in which the chairman of a company outlines plans for return to profitability, as follows: "Contrary to expectations, no changes will be made in the company's manufacturing or selling policies. Instead, the bookkeeping system is to be entirely revamped. By adopting and further improving a number of modern accounting and financial devices, the corporation's earning power will be amazingly transformed."[5]

EXAMPLE 4

Quality of Earnings Warning Signs: An Extreme Case

Livent, Inc. was a publicly traded theatrical production company that staged a number of smash hits such as Tony-award winning productions of *Showboat* and *Fosse*. Livent capitalized preproduction costs including expenses for pre-opening advertising, publicity and promotion, set construction, props, costumes, and salaries and fees paid to the cast, crew, and musicians during rehearsals. The company then amortized these capitalized costs over the expected life of the theatrical production based on anticipated revenues.[6]

1   State the effect of Livent's accounting for preproduction costs on its reported earnings per share.

2   State the effect of Livent's accounting for preproduction costs on its balance sheet.

3   If an analyst calculated EBITDA/interest expense and debt/EBITDA based on Livent's accounting for preproduction costs without adjustment, how might the analyst be misled in assessing Livent's financial strength? (Recall that EBITDA is defined as earnings before interest, taxes, depreciation, and amortization. Ratios such as EBITDA/interest expense and debt/EBITDA indicate one aspect of a company's financial strength, debt-paying ability.)

Solution to 1:

Livent's accounting for preproduction costs immediately increased reported earnings per share because it deferred expenses.

Solution to 2:

Instead of immediately expensing costs, Livent reported the amounts on its balance sheet as an asset. The warning signal—the deferral of expenses—can indicate aggressive accounting; preproduction costs should have been expensed immediately because of the tremendous uncertainty about revenues from theatrical productions. There was no assurance that there would be revenues against which expenses could be matched.

Solution to 3:

Livent did not deduct preproduction costs from earnings as expenses. If the amortization of capitalized preproduction costs were then added back to earnings, the EBITDA/interest and debt/EBITDA ratios would not reflect in any way the cash outflows associated with items such as paying pre-opening salaries; but cash outflows reduce funds available to meet debt obligations. The analyst who mechanically added back amortization of preproduction costs to calculate EBITDA would be misled into overestimating Livent's financial strength. Based on a closer look at the company's accounting, the analyst would properly not add back amortization of preproduction expenses in computing EBITDA. If

---

5 Graham 1936.
6 The discussion in this example is indebted to Moody's (2000).

preproduction expenses are not added back, a very different picture of Livent's financial health would emerge. In 1996, Livent's reported debt/EBITDA ratio was 1.7, but the ratio without adding back amortization for preproduction costs was 5.5. In 1997, debt/EBITDA was 3.7 based on positive EBITDA of $58.3 million, but EBITDA without the add-back was *negative* $52.6 million.

Note: In November 1998, Livent declared bankruptcy and is now defunct. The criminal trial, in Canada, concluded in 2009 with the conviction of Livent's co-founders on charges of fraud and forgery.

In general, growth in an asset account (such as deferred costs in the Livent example) at a much faster rate than the growth rate of sales may indicate aggressive accounting. Analysts recognize a variety of risk factors that may signal possible future negative surprises. A working selection of these risk factors would include the following (AICPA 2002):

- Poor quality of accounting disclosures, such as segment information, acquisitions, accounting policies and assumptions, and a lack of discussion of negative factors.
- Existence of related-party transactions.
- Existence of excessive officer, employee, or director loans.
- High management or director turnover.
- Excessive pressure on company personnel to make revenue or earnings targets, particularly when combined with a dominant, aggressive management team or individual.
- Material nonaudit services performed by audit firm.
- Reported (through regulatory filings) disputes with and/or changes in auditors.
- Management and/or directors' compensation tied to profitability or stock price (through ownership or compensation plans). Although such arrangements are usually desirable, they can be a risk factor for aggressive financial reporting.
- Economic, industry, or company-specific pressures on profitability, such as loss of market share or declining margins.
- Management pressure to meet debt covenants or earnings expectations.
- A history of securities law violations, reporting violations, or persistent late filings.

3.2 Forecasting Company Performance

The second step in the valuation process—forecasting company performance—can be viewed from two perspectives: the economic environment in which the company operates and the company's own operating and financial characteristics.

Companies do business within larger contexts of particular industries, national economies, and world trade. Viewing a company within those larger contexts, a top-down forecasting approach moves from international and national macroeconomic forecasts to industry forecasts and then to individual company and asset forecasts.[7]

---

7 A related but distinct concept is **top-down investing** versus **bottom-up investing** as one broad description of types of active investment styles. For example, a top-down investor uses macroeconomic forecasts to identify sectors of the economy representing potentially attractive investment opportunities. In contrast, an investor following a bottom-up investing approach might decide that a security is undervalued based on some valuation indicator, for example, without making an explicit judgment on the overall economy or the relative value of different sectors.

For example, a revenue forecast for a major home appliance manufacturer could start with industry unit sales forecasts that are in turn based on GDP forecasts. Forecasted company unit sales would equal forecasted industry unit sales multiplied by the appliance manufacturer's forecasted market share. A revenue projection would be based on forecasted company unit sales and sales prices.

Alternatively, a bottom-up forecasting approach aggregates forecasts at a micro level to larger scale forecasts, under specific assumptions. For example, a clothing retailer may have several stores in operation with two new stores about to open. Using information based on the sales per square meter of the existing stores (perhaps during their initial period of operation), the analyst could forecast sales per square meter of the new stores that, added to forecasts of a similar type for existing stores, would give a sales forecast for the company as a whole. In making such a bottom-up sales forecast, the analyst would be making assumptions about selling prices and merchandise costs. Forecasts for individual retailers could be aggregated into forecasts for the group, continuing in a bottom-up fashion.

In general, analysts integrate insights from industry and competitive analysis with financial statement analysis to formulate specific forecasts of such items as a company's sales, earnings, and cash flow. Analysts generally consider qualitative as well as quantitative factors in financial forecasting and valuation. For example, an analyst might modify his or her forecasts and valuation judgments based on qualitative factors, such as the analyst's opinion about the business acumen and integrity of management, and/or the transparency and quality of a company's accounting practices. Such qualitative factors are necessarily subjective.

3.3 Selecting the Appropriate Valuation Model

This section discusses the third step in the valuation process—selecting the appropriate model for the valuation task at hand. Detailed descriptions of the valuation models are presented in later readings. Absolute valuation models and relative valuation models are the two broad types of valuation models that incorporate a going-concern assumption. Here, we describe absolute and relative valuation models in general terms and discuss a number of issues in model selection. In practice, an analyst may use a variety of models to estimate the value of a company or its common stock.

3.3.1 *Absolute Valuation Models*

An **absolute valuation model** is a model that specifies an asset's intrinsic value. Such models are used to produce an estimate of value that can be compared with the asset's market price. The most important type of absolute equity valuation models are present value models. In finance theory, present value models are considered the fundamental approach to equity valuation. The logic of such models is that the value of an asset to an investor must be related to the returns that investor expects to receive from holding that asset. Generally speaking, those returns can be referred to as the asset's cash flows, and present value models are also referred to as discounted cash flow models.

A **present value model** or **discounted cash flow model** applied to equity valuation derives the value of common stock as the present or discounted value of its expected future cash flows.[8] For common stock, one familiar type of cash flow is dividends, which are discretionary distributions to shareholders authorized by a corporation's board of directors. Dividends represent cash flows at the shareholder level in the sense that they are paid directly to shareholders. Present value models based on dividends are called **dividend discount models**. Rather than defining cash flows as dividends, analysts frequently define cash flows at the company level. Common shareholders in

---

8 In private business appraisal, such models are known as income models of valuation.

principle have an equity ownership claim on the balance of the cash flows generated by a company after payments have been made to claimants senior to common equity, such as bondholders and preferred stockholders (and the government as well, which takes taxes), whether such flows are distributed in the form of dividends.

The two main company-level definitions of cash flow in current use are free cash flow and residual income. Free cash flow is based on cash flow from operations but takes into account the reinvestment in fixed assets and working capital necessary for a going concern. The **free cash flow to equity model** defines cash flow net of payments to providers of debt, whereas the **free cash flow to the firm model** defines cash flows before those payments. We will define free cash flow and each model with more precision in later readings. A **residual income model** is based on accrual accounting earnings in excess of the opportunity cost of generating those earnings.

Because the present value approach is the familiar technique for valuing bonds,[9] it is helpful to contrast the application of present value models to equity valuation with present value models as applied to bond valuation. The application of present value models to common stock typically involves greater uncertainty than is the case with bonds; that uncertainty centers on two critical inputs for present value models—the cash flows and the discount rate(s). Bond valuation discounts a stream of cash payments specified in a legal contract (the **bond indenture**). In contrast, in equity valuation an analyst must define the specific cash flow stream to be valued—dividends or free cash flow—and then forecast the amounts of those cash flows. Unlike bond valuation, no cash flow stream is contractually owed to common stockholders. Clearly, a company's total cash flows, and therefore the cash flows potentially available to common stockholders, will be affected by business, financial, technological, and other factors and are subject to greater variation than the contractual cash flow of a bond. Furthermore, the forecasts for common stock cash flows extend indefinitely into the future because common stock has no maturity date. In addition to the greater uncertainty involved in forecasting cash flows for equity valuation, significant uncertainty exists in estimating an appropriate rate at which to discount those cash flows. In contrast with bond valuation, in which a discount rate can usually be based on market interest rates and bond ratings, equity valuation typically involves a more subjective and uncertain assessment of the appropriate discount rate.[10] Finally, in addition to the uncertainty associated with cash flows and discount rates, the equity analyst may need to address other issues, such as the value of corporate control or the value of unused assets.

The present value approach applied to stock valuation, therefore, presents a high order of complexity. Present value models are ambitious in what they attempt—an estimate of intrinsic value—and offer many challenges in application. Graham and Dodd (1934) suggested that the analyst consider stating a range of intrinsic values, and that suggestion remains a valid one. To that end, **sensitivity analysis** is an essential tool in applying discounted cash flow valuation. We discuss sensitivity analysis in more detail below.

Another type of absolute valuation is **asset-based valuation** that values a company on the basis of the market value of the assets or resources it controls. For appropriate companies, asset-based valuation can provide an independent estimate of value, and an analyst typically finds alternative, independent estimates of value to be useful. The following example describes instances in which this approach to absolute valuation could be appropriate.

---

9 The word "bond" throughout this section is used in the general sense and refers to all debt securities and loans.

10 For some bond market instruments such as mortgage-backed securities and structured notes the estimation of cash flows and an appropriate discount rate can pose challenges comparable to equity investment.

EXAMPLE 5

Asset-Based Valuation

Analysts often apply asset-based valuation to natural resource companies. For example, a crude oil producer such as Petrobras (NYSE: PBR) might be valued on the basis of the market value of its current proven reserves in barrels of oil, minus a discount for estimated extraction costs. A forest industry company such as Weyerhaeuser (NYSE: WY) might be valued on the basis of the board meters (or board feet) of timber it controls. Today, however, fewer companies than in the past are involved only in natural resources extraction or production. For example, Occidental Petroleum (NYSE: OXY) features petroleum in its name but also has substantial chemical manufacturing operations. For such cases, the total company might be valued as the sum of its divisions, with the natural resource division valued on the basis of its proven resources.

3.3.2 Relative Valuation Models

Relative valuation models constitute the second broad type of going-concern valuation models. A **relative valuation model** estimates an asset's value relative to that of another asset. The idea underlying relative valuation is that similar assets should sell at similar prices, and relative valuation is typically implemented using price multiples (ratios of stock price to a fundamental such as cash flow per share) or enterprise multiples (ratios of the total value of common stock and debt net of cash and short-term investments to certain of a company's operating assets to a fundamental such as operating earnings).

Perhaps the most familiar price multiple is the price-to-earnings ratio (P/E), which is the ratio of a stock's market price to the company's earnings per share. A stock selling at a P/E that is low relative to the P/E of another closely comparable stock (in terms of anticipated earnings growth rates and risk, for example) is *relatively undervalued* (a good buy) relative to the comparison stock. For brevity, an analyst might state simply *undervalued*, but the analyst must realize that if the comparison stock is overvalued (in an absolute sense, in relation to intrinsic value), so might be the stock being called undervalued. Therefore, it is useful to maintain the distinction between *undervalued* and *relatively undervalued*. Investing to exploit perceived mispricing in either case (absolute or relative mispricing) relies on a basis of differential expectations, that is, investor expectations that differ from and are more accurate than those reflected in market prices, as discussed earlier.

The more conservative investing strategies based on relative valuation involve overweighting (underweighting) relatively undervalued (overvalued) assets, with reference to benchmark weights. The more aggressive strategies allow short selling of perceived overvalued assets. Such aggressive approaches are known as relative value investing (or relative spread investing, if using implied discount factors). A classic example is **pairs trading** that utilizes pairs of closely related stocks (e.g., two automotive stocks), buying the relatively undervalued stock and selling short the relatively overvalued stock. Regardless of which direction the overall stock market goes, the investor will be better off to the extent that the relatively undervalued stock ultimately rises more (falls less) than the relatively overvalued stock.

Frequently, relative valuation involves a group of comparison assets, such as an industry group, rather than a single comparison asset. The application of relative valuation to equity is often called the method of comparables (or just comparables) and is the subject of a later reading.

> **EXAMPLE 6**
>
> ## Relative Valuation Models
>
> While researching Smithson Genomics, Inc., a (fictitious) healthcare information services company, you encounter a difference of opinions. One analyst's report claims that Smithson is at least 15 percent *overvalued*, based on a comparison of its P/E with the median P/E of peer companies in the healthcare information services industry and taking account of company and peer group fundamentals. A second analyst asserts that Smithson is *undervalued* by 10 percent, based on a comparison of Smithson's P/E with the median P/E of the Russell 3000 Index, a broad-based US equity index. Both analyses appear to be carefully executed and reported. Can both analysts be right?
>
> ### Solution:
>
> Yes. The assertions of both analysts concern *relative* valuations, and their benchmarks for comparisons differ. The first analyst compared Smithson to its peers in the healthcare information services industry and considers the company to be *relatively overvalued* compared to that group. The second analyst compared Smithson to the overall market as represented by the Russell 3000 and considers the company to be *relatively undervalued* compared to that group. If the entire healthcare information services industry is undervalued in relation to the Russell 3000, both analysts can be right because they are making relative valuations.
>
> The investment implications of each analyst's valuation generally would depend on additional considerations including whether the market price of the Russell 3000 fairly represents that index's intrinsic value and whether the market liquidity of an otherwise attractive investment would accommodate the intended position size. The analyst in many cases may want to supplement relative valuation with estimates of intrinsic value.

The method of comparables is characterized by a wide range of possible implementation choices; a later reading discusses various alternative price and enterprise multiples. Practitioners will often examine a number of price and enterprise multiples for the complementary information they can provide. In summary, the method of comparables does not specify intrinsic value without making the further assumption that the comparison asset is fairly valued. The method of comparables has the advantages of being simple, related to market prices, and grounded in a sound economic principle (that similar assets should sell at similar prices). Price and enterprise multiples are widely recognized by investors, so analysts can communicate the results of an absolute valuation in terms of a price or enterprise multiple.

3.3.3 *Valuation of the Total Entity and Its Components*

A variation to valuing a company as a single entity is to estimate its value as the sum of the estimated values of its various businesses considered as independent, going-concern entities. A valuation that sums the estimated values of each of the company's businesses as if each business were an independent going concern is known as a **sum-of-the-parts valuation**. (The value derived using a sum-of-the-parts valuation is sometimes called the **breakup value** or **private market value**.)

Sum-of-the-parts analysis is most useful when valuing a company with segments in different industries that have different valuation characteristics. Sum-of-the-parts analysis is also frequently used to evaluate the value that might be unlocked in a restructuring through a spin-off, split-off, tracking stock, or equity (IPO) carve-out.

Example 7 shows a case in which a sum-of-the-parts valuation could be used to gain insight into a company's future prospects. In practice, a detailed breakdown of each business segment's contribution to earnings, cash flow, and value would be needed.

EXAMPLE 7

Sum-of-the-Parts Valuation

Donaldson Company, Inc. (NYSE: DCI) is one of the largest and most successful filtration manufacturers in the world. Consistent with FASB guidance related to segment reporting, the company has identified two reportable segments: Engine Products and Industrial Products. Segment selection was based on the internal organizational structure, management of operations, and performance evaluation by management and the Company's Board of Directors. 2012 10-K data (in thousands of US dollars) for the segments appear in the table below.

The Engine Products segment sells to original equipment manufacturers (OEMs) in the construction, mining, agriculture, aerospace, defense, and truck markets and to independent distributors, OEM dealer networks, private label accounts, and large equipment fleets. Products include air filtration systems, exhaust and emission systems, liquid filtration systems including hydraulics, fuel, and lube, and replacement filters.

The Industrial Products segment sells to various industrial end-users, OEMs of gas-fired turbines, and OEMs and end-users requiring clean air. Products include dust, fume, and mist collectors, compressed air purification systems, air filtration systems for gas turbines, membrane-based products, and specialized air and gas filtration systems for applications including computer hard disk drives and other electronic equipment.

	Engine Products	Industrial Products	Total Company*
2012			
Net sales	$1,570,140	$923,108	$2,493,248
Earnings before income taxes	227,941	149,249	370,780
Total assets	845,176	520,739	1,730,082
Capital expenditures**	46,816	24,083	78,139
2011			
Net sales	$1,440,495	$853,534	$2,294,029
Earnings before income taxes	211,255	123,871	312,263
Total assets	888,080	519,730	1,726,093
Capital expenditures	36,423	19,442	60,633
2010			
Net sales	$1,126,007	$751,057	$1,877,064
Earnings before income taxes	155,833	91,084	230,176

	Engine Products	Industrial Products	Total Company*
Total assets	702,300	477,154	1,499,506
Capital expenditures	24,355	15,250	43,149

*Total company results differ from the sum of the two divisions by allocated corporate and unallocated amounts.
**Capital expenditures are reported net of acquired businesses.

1 Why might an analyst use a sum-of-the-parts approach to value Donaldson's?

2 How might an analyst use the provided information in an analysis and valuation?

Solution to 1:

The Engine Products segment is already significantly larger than the Industrial Products segment and is growing at a much faster rate. Annual sales growth over 2010–2012 was 18.1 percent versus 10.9 percent, and annual capital expenditure growth was 38.6 percent versus 25.7 percent, both in favor of Engine Products. On the other hand, profit margins appear to be higher for Industrial Products. In 2012, the EBIT-to-sales ratio was 16.2 percent versus 14.5 percent, and the EBIT-to-assets ratio was 28.6 percent versus 27.0 percent, both in favor of Industrial Products.

An investor presentation by Donaldson's management in May 2013 indicated that they expected Industrial Products to become 48 percent of the company's product portfolio by 2021. However, the recent results noted above show that the Engine Products segment has become a larger and larger part of Donaldson's total business and lower margins are associated with this growth. Whether or not the company will ultimately be successful in changing their product mix is fundamental to an analyst forming an opinion on Donaldson's share price.

Solution to 2:

An analyst might use the above information to develop separate valuations for each of the segments, based on forecasts for each segment's sales and profitability. The value of the company in total would be the sum of the value of each of the segments, adjusted for corporate items such as taxes, overhead expenses, and assets/liabilities not directly attributable to the separate operating systems.

The concept of a conglomerate discount often arises in connection with situations warranting a sum-of-the parts valuation. **Conglomerate discount** refers to the concept that the market applies a discount to the stock of a company operating in multiple, unrelated businesses compared to the stock of companies with narrower focuses. Alternative explanations for the conglomerate discount include 1) inefficiency of internal capital markets (i.e., companies' allocation of investment capital among divisions does not maximize overall shareholder value), 2) endogenous factors (i.e., poorly performing companies tend to expand by making acquisitions in unrelated businesses), and 3) research measurement errors (i.e., conglomerate discounts do not actually exist, and evidence suggesting that they do is a result of flawed measurement).[11] Examples in which conglomerate discounts appear most observable occur when companies divest parts of the company that have limited synergies with their core businesses.

Note that a break-up value in excess of a company's unadjusted going-concern value may prompt strategic actions such as a divestiture or spin-off.

3.3.4 *Issues in Model Selection and Interpretation*

How does one select a valuation model? The broad criteria for model selection are that the valuation model be:

- consistent with the characteristics of the company being valued;
- appropriate given the availability and quality of data; and
- consistent with the purpose of valuation, including the analyst's perspective.

Note that using more than one model can yield incremental insights.

Selection of a model consistent with the characteristics of the company being valued is facilitated by having a good understanding of the business, which is the first step in the valuation process. Part of understanding a company is understanding the nature of its assets and how it uses those assets to create value. For example, a bank is composed largely of marketable or potentially marketable assets and securities, and thus for a bank, a relative valuation based on assets (as recognized in accounting) has more relevance than a similar exercise for a service company with few marketable assets.

In selecting a model, data availability and quality can be limiting factors. For example, a dividend discount model is the simplest discounted cash flow model; but if a company has never paid dividends and no other information exists to assess a company's future dividend policy, an analyst may have more confidence applying an apparently more complex present value model. Similar considerations also apply in selecting a specific relative valuation approach. For example, meaningful comparisons using P/Es may be hard to make for a company with highly volatile or persistently negative earnings.

Model selection can also be influenced by the purpose of the valuation or the perspective of the analyst. For example, an investor seeking a controlling equity position in a company may elect to value the company based on forecasted free cash flows rather than forecasted dividends because such flows might potentially be redirected by such an acquirer without affecting the value of the acquisition (this valuation approach will be discussed in detail in another reading). When an analyst reads valuations and research reports prepared by others, the analyst should consider how the writer's perspective (and potential biases) may have affected the choice of a particular valuation approach and/or valuation inputs. Later readings, discussing present value models and price multiples, offer specific guidance on model selection.

As a final note to this introduction of model selection, it is important to recognize that professionals frequently use multiple valuation models or factors in common stock selection. According to the *Merrill Lynch Institutional Factor Survey (2006)*, respondent institutional investors report using an average of approximately nine valuation factors in selecting stocks.[12] There are a variety of ways in which multiple factors can be used in stock selection. One prominent way, stock screens, will be discussed in a later reading. As another example, analysts can rank each security in a given investment universe by relative attractiveness according to a particular valuation factor. The

---

11 See, for example, Lamont and Polk (2002) and Burch and Nanda (2003).
12 In the report, the term *factors* covers valuation models as well as variables such as return on equity.

rankings for individual securities could be combined into a single composite ranking by assigning weights to the individual factors. Analysts may use a quantitative model to assign those weights.

3.4 Converting Forecasts to a Valuation

Converting forecasts to valuation involves more than inputting the forecast amounts to a model to obtain an estimate of the value of a company or its securities. Two important aspects of converting forecasts to valuation are sensitivity analysis and situational adjustments.

Sensitivity analysis is an analysis to determine how changes in an assumed input would affect the outcome. Some sensitivity analyses are common to most valuations. For example, a sensitivity analysis can be used to assess how a change in assumptions about a company's future growth—for example, decomposed by sales growth forecasts and margin forecasts—and/or a change in discount rates would affect the estimated value. Other sensitivity analyses depend on the context. For example, assume an analyst is aware that a competitor to the target company plans to introduce a competing product. Given uncertainty about the target company's competitive response—will the company lower prices to retain market share, offer discounts to its distributors, increase advertising, or change a product feature—the analyst could create a baseline forecast and then analyze how different competitive responses would affect the forecasted financials and in turn the estimated valuation.

Situational adjustments may be required to incorporate the valuation impact of specific issues. Three such issues that could affect value estimates are control premiums, lack of marketability discounts, and illiquidity discounts. A controlling ownership position in a company (e.g., more than 50 percent of outstanding shares, although a far smaller percentage often affords an investor the ability to significantly influence a company) carries with it control of the board of directors and the valuable options of redeploying the company's assets or changing the company's capital structure. The value of a stock investment that would give an investor a controlling position will generally reflect a **control premium**; that is, it will be higher than a valuation produced by a generic quantitative valuation expression that did not explicitly model such a premium. A second issue generally not explicitly modeled is that investors require an extra return to compensate for lack of a public market or lack of marketability. The value of non-publicly traded stocks generally reflects a **lack of marketability discount**. Among publicly traded (i.e., marketable) stocks, the prices of shares with less depth to their markets (less liquidity) often reflect an **illiquidity discount**. An illiquidity discount would also apply if an investor wishes to sell an amount of stock that is large relative to that stock's trading volume (assuming it is not large enough to constitute a controlling ownership). The price that could be realized for that block of shares would generally be lower than the market price for a smaller amount of stock, a so-called **blockage factor**.[13]

---

13 Note, however, that the US fair value accounting standard (SFAS No. 157) does not permit a blockage factor adjustment for actively traded shares. The value of a position is the product of the quoted price times the quantity held.

3.5 Applying the Valuation Conclusion: The Analyst's Role and Responsibilities

As noted earlier, the purposes of valuation and the intended consumer of the valuation vary:

- Analysts associated with investment firms' brokerage operations are perhaps the most visible group of analysts offering valuation judgments—their research reports are widely distributed to current and prospective retail and institutional brokerage clients. Analysts who work at brokerage firms are known as **sell-side analysts** (because brokerage firms sell investments and services to institutions such as investment management firms).[14]

- In investment management firms, trusts and bank trust departments, and similar institutions, an analyst may report valuation judgments to a portfolio manager or to an investment committee as input to an investment decision. Such analysts are widely known as **buy-side analysts**. The analyst's valuation expertise is important not only in investment disciplines involving security selection based on detailed company analysis, but also in highly quantitative investment disciplines; quantitative analysts work in developing, testing, and updating security selection methodologies.[15]

- Analysts at corporations may perform some valuation tasks similar to those of analysts at money management firms (e.g., when the corporation manages in-house a sponsored pension plan). Both corporate analysts and investment bank analysts may also identify and value companies that could become acquisition targets.

- Analysts at independent vendors of financial information usually offer valuation information and opinions in publicly distributed research reports, although some focus solely on organizing and analyzing corporate information.

In conducting their valuation activities, investment analysts play a critical role in collecting, organizing, analyzing, and communicating corporate information, and in some contexts, recommending appropriate investment actions based on sound analysis. When they do those tasks well, analysts help their clients, the capital markets, and the suppliers of capital:

- Analysts help their clients achieve their investment objectives by enabling those clients to make better buy and sell decisions.

- Analysts contribute to the efficient functioning of capital markets by providing analysis that leads to informed buy and sell decisions, and thus to asset prices that better reflect underlying values. When asset prices accurately reflect underlying values, capital flows more easily to its highest-value uses.

- Analysts benefit the suppliers of capital, including shareholders, when they are effective monitors of management's performance. This monitoring can serve to keep managers' actions more closely aligned with shareholders' best interests.[16]

---

14 **Brokerage** is the business of acting as agents for buyers or sellers, usually in return for commissions.
15 Ranking stocks by some measure(s) of relative attractiveness (subject to a risk control discipline), as we will discuss in more detail later, forms one key part of quantitative equity investment disciplines.
16 See Jensen and Meckling (1976) for a classic analysis of the costs of stockholder–manager conflicts.

EXAMPLE 8

What Are Analysts Expected to Do?

When analysts at brokerage firms recommend a stock to the public that later performs very poorly, or when they fail to uncover negative corporate activities, they can sometimes come under public scrutiny. Industry leaders may then be asked to respond to such criticism and to comment on expectations about the role and responsibilities of analysts. One such instance occurred in the United States as a consequence of the late 2001 collapse of Enron Corporation, an energy, utility, trading, and telecommunication company. In testimony before the US Senate (excerpted below), the President and CEO of AIMR (predecessor organization of CFA Institute) offered a summary of the working conditions and responsibilities of brokerage analysts. In the following passage, **due diligence** refers to investigation and analysis in support of a recommendation; the failure to exercise due diligence may sometimes result in liability according to various securities laws. "Wall Street analysts" refers to analysts working in the US brokerage industry (sell-side analysts).

> What are Wall Street analysts expected to do? These analysts are assigned companies and industries to follow, are expected to research fully these companies and the industries in which they operate, and to forecast their future prospects. Based on this analysis, and using appropriate valuation models, they must then determine an appropriate fair price for the company's securities. After comparing this fair price to the current market price, the analyst is able to make a recommendation. If the analyst's "fair price" is significantly above the current market price, it would be expected that the stock be rated a "buy" or "market outperform."
>
> How do Wall Street analysts get their information? Through hard work and due diligence. They must study and try to comprehend the information in numerous public disclosure documents, such as the annual report to shareholders and regulatory filings . . . and gather the necessary quantitative and qualitative inputs to their valuation models.
>
> This due diligence isn't simply reading and analyzing annual reports. It also involves talking to company management, other company employees, competitors, and others, to get answers to questions that arise from their review of public documents. Talking to management must go beyond participation in regular conference calls. Not all questions can be voiced in those calls because of time constraints, for example, and because analysts, like journalists, rightly might not wish to "show their cards," and reveal the insights they have gotten through their hard work, by asking a particularly probing question in the presence of their competitors.
>
> Wall Street analysts are also expected to understand the dynamics of the industry and general economic conditions before finalizing a research report and making a recommendation. Therefore, in order for their firm to justify their continued employment, Wall Street

analysts must issue research reports on their assigned companies and must make recommendations based on their reports to clients who purchase their firm's research.[17]

From the beginnings of the movement to organize financial analysis as a profession rather than as a commercial trade, one guiding principle has been that the analyst must hold himself accountable to both standards of competence and standards of conduct. Competence in investment analysis requires a high degree of training, experience, and discipline.[18] Additionally, the investment professional is in a position of trust, requiring ethical conduct toward the public, clients, prospects, employers, employees, and fellow analysts. For CFA Institute members, this position of trust is reflected in the Code of Ethics and Standards of Professional Conduct, as well as in the Professional Conduct Statement that they submit annually. The Code and Standards, which guide the analyst to independent, well-researched, and well-documented analysis, are described in the following sections.

4   COMMUNICATING VALUATION RESULTS

Writing is an important part of an analyst's job. Whether a research report is for review by an investment committee or a portfolio manager in an investment management firm, or for distribution to the retail or institutional clients of a brokerage firm, research reports share several common elements. In this section we discuss the content of an effective research report, one adaptable format for writing such a report, and the analyst's responsibilities in preparing a research report. In many cases, institutional norms will guide the format and content of the written report.

4.1 Contents of a Research Report

A primary determinant of a research report's contents is what the intended readers seek to gain from reading the report. From a sell-side analyst's report, an intended reader would be interested in the investment recommendation. In evaluating how much attention and weight to give to a recommendation, the reader will look for persuasive supporting arguments. A key element supporting any recommendation is the intrinsic value of the security.

Given the importance of the estimated intrinsic value of the security, most research reports provide the reader with information about the key assumptions and expectations underlying that estimated intrinsic value. The information typically includes an update on the company's financial and operating results, a description of relevant aspects of the current macroeconomic and industry context, and an analysis and forecast for the industry and company. Because some readers of research reports are interested in background information, some reports contain detailed historical descriptive statistics about the industry and company.

A report can include specific forecasts, key valuation inputs (e.g., the estimated cost of capital), a description of the valuation model, and a discussion of qualitative factors and other considerations that affect valuation. Superior research reports also

---

17 Thomas A. Bowman, CFA. Testimony to the Committee on Governmental Affairs (excerpted) US Senate, 27 February 2002.

18 Competence in this sense is reflected in the examination and work experience requirements that are prerequisites for obtaining the CFA designation.

objectively address the uncertainty associated with investing in the security, and/ or the valuation inputs involving the greatest amount of uncertainty. By converting forecasts into estimated intrinsic value, a comparison between intrinsic value and market price provides the basis for an investment recommendation. When a research report states a target price for a stock (based on its intrinsic value) in its investment recommendation, the report should clarify the basis for computing the target, a time frame for reaching the target, and information on the uncertainty of reaching the target. An investment recommendation may be accompanied by an explanation of the underlying rationale, i.e., investment thesis, which summarizes why a particular investment offer would provide a way to profit from the analyst's outlook.

Although a well-written report cannot compensate for a poor analysis, a poorly written report can detract from the credibility of an excellent analysis. Writing an effective research report is a challenging task. In summary, an effective research report:

- contains timely information;
- is written in clear, incisive language;
- is objective and well researched, with key assumptions clearly identified; .
- distinguishes clearly between facts and opinions;
- contains analysis, forecasts, valuation, and a recommendation that are internally consistent;
- presents sufficient information to allow a reader to critique the valuation;
- states the key risk factors involved in an investment in the company; and
- discloses any potential conflicts of interests faced by the analyst.

Although these general characteristics are all desirable attributes of a useful and respected report, in some situations the requirements are more specific. For example, regulations governing disclosures of conflicts and potential conflicts of interest vary across countries, so an analyst must remain up-to-date on relevant disclosure requirements. As another example, in some situations, investment recommendations are affected by policies of the firm employing an analyst; for example, a policy might require that a security's price must be X percent below its estimated intrinsic value to be considered a "buy." Even in the absence of such a policy, an analyst needs to maintain a conceptual distinction between a "good company" and a "good investment" because returns on a common stock investment always depend on the price paid for the stock, whether the business prospects of the issuing company are good, bad, or indifferent.

EXAMPLE 9

Research Reports

The following two passages are closely based on the valuation discussions of actual companies in two actual short research notes. The dates and company names used in the passages, however, are fictional.

A At a recent multiple of 6.5, our earnings per share multiple for 2012, the shares were at a discount to our projection of 14 percent growth for the period ... MXI has two operating segments ... In valuing the segments separately, employing relative acquisition multiples and peer mean values, we found fair value to be above recent market value. In addition, the shares trade at a discount to book value (0.76). Based on the value indicated by these two valuation metrics, we view the shares as worth holding. However, in light of a weaker economy over the near term, dampening demand for MXI's services, our enthusiasm is tempered. [*Elsewhere in the report, MXI is evaluated as being in the firm's top category of investment attractiveness.*]

B　　Although TXI outperformed the overall stock market by 20 percent since the start of the year, it definitely looks undervalued as shown by its low multiples ... [*the values of the P/E and another multiple are stated*]. According to our dividend discount model valuation, we get to a valuation of €3.08 implying an upside potential of 36.8 percent based on current prices. The market outperform recommendation is reiterated. [*In a parenthetical expression, the current dividend, assumed dividend growth rates, and their time horizons are given. The analyst also briefly explains and calculates the discount rate. Elsewhere in the report the current price of TXI is given as €2.25.*]

Although some of the concepts mentioned in the two passages may not yet be familiar, you can begin to assess the two reporting efforts.

Passage A communicates the analysis awkwardly. The meaning of "the shares were at a discount to our projection of 14 percent growth for the period" is not completely clear. Presumably the analyst is projecting the earnings growth rate for 2012 and stating that the P/E is low in relation to that expected growth rate. The analyst next discusses valuing MXI as the sum of its divisions. In describing the method as "employing relative acquisition multiples and peer mean values," the analyst does not convey a clear picture of what was done. It is probable that companies similar to each of MXI's divisions were identified; then the mean or average value of some unidentified multiple for those comparison companies was calculated and used as the basis for valuing MXI. The writer is vague, however, on the extent of MXI's undervaluation. The analyst states that MXI's price is below its book value (an accounting measure of shareholders' investment) but draws no comparison with the average price-to-book value ratio for stocks similar to MXI, for example. (The price-to-book ratio is discussed in a later reading.) Finally, the verbal summation is feeble and hedged. Although filled with technical verbiage, Passage A does not communicate a coherent valuation of MXI.

In the second sentence of Passage B, by contrast, the analyst gives an explicit valuation of TXI and the information needed to critique it. The reader can also see that €3.08, which is elsewhere stated in the research note as the target price for TXI, implies the stated price appreciation potential for TXI [(€3.08/€2.25) − 1, approximately 37 percent]. In the first sentence in Passage B, the analyst gives information that might support the conclusion that TXI is undervalued, although the statement lacks strength because the analyst does not explain why the P/E is "low." The verbal summary is clear. Using less space than the analyst in Passage A, the analyst in Passage B has done a better job of communicating the results of his valuation.

4.2 Format of a Research Report

Equity research reports may be logically presented in several ways. The firm in which the analyst works sometimes specifies a fixed format for consistency and quality control purposes. Without claiming superiority to other ways to organize a report, we offer Exhibit 2 as an adaptable format by which the analyst can communicate research and valuation findings in detail. (Shorter research reports and research notes obviously may employ a more compact format.)

Exhibit 2	A Format for Research Reports		
Section	**Purpose**	**Content**	**Comments**
Table of Contents	■ Show report's organization	■ Consistent with narrative in sequence and language	This is typically used in very long research reports only.
Summary and Investment Conclusion	■ Communicate the large picture ■ Communicate major specific conclusions of the analysis ■ Recommend an investment course of action	■ Capsule description of the company ■ Major recent developments ■ Earnings projections ■ Other major conclusions ■ Valuation summary ■ Investment action	An executive summary; may be called simply "Summary."
Business Summary	■ Present the company in more detail ■ Communicate a detailed understanding of the company's economics and current situation ■ Provide and explain specific forecasts[a]	■ Company description to the divisional level ■ Industry analysis ■ Competitive analysis ■ Historical performance ■ Financial forecasts	Reflects the first and second steps of the valuation process. Financial forecasts should be explained adequately and reflect quality of earnings analysis.
Risks	■ Alert readers to the risk factors in investing in the security	■ Possible negative industry developments ■ Possible negative regulatory and legal developments ■ Possible negative company developments ■ Risks in the forecasts ■ Other risks	Readers should have enough information to determine how the analyst is defining and assessing the risks specific to investing in the security.
Valuation	■ Communicate a clear and careful valuation	■ Description of model(s) used ■ Recapitulation of inputs ■ Statement of conclusions	Readers should have enough information to critique the analysis.
Historical and Pro Forma Tables	■ Organize and present data to support the analysis in the Business Summary		This is generally a separate section in longer research reports only. Many reports fold all or some of this information into the Business Summary section.

[a] Actual outcomes can and generally will differ from forecasts. A discussion of key random factors and an examination of the sensitivity of outcomes to the outcomes of those factors are useful.

4.3 Research Reporting Responsibilities

All analysts have an obligation to provide substantive and meaningful content in a clear and comprehensive report format. Analysts who are CFA Institute members, however, have an additional and overriding responsibility to adhere to the Code of Ethics and the Standards of Professional Conduct in all activities pertaining to their research reports. The CFA Institute Code of Ethics states:

Members of CFA Institute must . . . use reasonable care and exercise independent professional judgment when conducting investment analysis, making investment recommendations, taking investment actions, and engaging in other professional activities.

Going beyond this general statement of responsibility, some specific Standards of Professional Conduct particularly relevant to an analyst writing a research report are shown in Exhibit 3.

Exhibit 3	Selected CFA Institute Standards of Professional Conduct Pertaining to Research Reports*
Standard of Professional Conduct	**Responsibility**
I(B)	Members and Candidates must use reasonable care and judgment to achieve and maintain independence and objectivity in their professional activities. Members and Candidates must not offer, solicit, or accept any gift, benefit, compensation, or consideration that reasonably could be expected to compromise their own or another's independence and objectivity.
I(C)	Members and Candidates must not knowingly make any misrepresentations relating to investment analysis, recommendations, actions, or other professional activities.
V(A)1	Members and Candidates must exercise diligence, independence, and thoroughness in analyzing investments, making investment recommendations, and taking investment actions.
V(A)2	Members and Candidates must have a reasonable and adequate basis, supported by appropriate research and investigation, for any investment analysis, recommendation, or action.
V(B)1	Members and Candidates must disclose to clients and prospective clients the basic format and general principles of the investment processes used to analyze investments, select securities, and construct portfolios and must promptly disclose any changes that might materially affect those processes.
V(B)2	Members and Candidates must use reasonable judgment in identifying which factors are important to their investment analyses, recommendations, or actions and include those factors in communications with clients and prospective clients.
V(B)3	Members and Candidates must distinguish between fact and opinion in the presentation of investment analysis and recommendations.
V(C)	Members and Candidates must develop and maintain appropriate records to support their investment analysis, recommendations, actions, and other investment-related communications with clients and prospective clients.

*See the most recent edition of the CFA Institute *Standards of Practice Handbook* (www.cfainstitute.org).

SUMMARY

In this reading, we have discussed the scope of equity valuation, outlined the valuation process, introduced valuation concepts and models, discussed the analyst's role and responsibilities in conducting valuation, and described the elements of an effective research report in which analysts communicate their valuation analysis.

- Valuation is the estimation of an asset's value based on variables perceived to be related to future investment returns, or based on comparisons with closely similar assets.

- The intrinsic value of an asset is its value given a hypothetically complete understanding of the asset's investment characteristics.

- The assumption that the market price of a security can diverge from its intrinsic value—as suggested by the rational efficient markets formulation of efficient market theory—underpins active investing.

- Intrinsic value incorporates the going-concern assumption, that is, the assumption that a company will continue operating for the foreseeable future. In contrast, liquidation value is the company's value if it were dissolved and its assets sold individually.

- Fair value is the price at which an asset (or liability) would change hands if neither buyer nor seller were under compulsion to buy/sell and both were informed about material underlying facts.

- In addition to stock selection by active traders, valuation is also used for:
  - inferring (extracting) market expectations;
  - evaluating corporate events;
  - issuing fairness opinions;
  - evaluating business strategies and models; and
  - appraising private businesses.

- The valuation process has five steps:
  1 Understanding the business.
  2 Forecasting company performance.
  3 Selecting the appropriate valuation model.
  4 Converting forecasts to a valuation.
  5 Applying the analytical results in the form of recommendations and conclusions.

- Understanding the business includes evaluating industry prospects, competitive position, and corporate strategies, all of which contribute to making more accurate forecasts. Understanding the business also involves analysis of financial reports, including evaluating the quality of a company's earnings.

- In forecasting company performance, a top-down forecasting approach moves from macroeconomic forecasts to industry forecasts and then to individual company and asset forecasts. A bottom-up forecasting approach aggregates individual company forecasts to industry forecasts, which in turn may be aggregated to macroeconomic forecasts.

- Selecting the appropriate valuation approach means choosing an approach that is:
  - consistent with the characteristics of the company being valued;
  - appropriate given the availability and quality of the data; and

- consistent with the analyst's valuation purpose and perspective.
- ▪ Two broad categories of valuation models are absolute valuation models and relative valuation models.
  - Absolute valuation models specify an asset's intrinsic value, supplying a point estimate of value that can be compared with market price. Present value models of common stock (also called discounted cash flow models) are the most important type of absolute valuation model.
  - Relative valuation models specify an asset's value relative to the value of another asset. As applied to equity valuation, relative valuation is also known as the method of comparables, which involves comparison of a stock's price multiple to a benchmark price multiple. The benchmark price multiple can be based on a similar stock or on the average price multiple of some group of stocks.
- ▪ Two important aspects of converting forecasts to valuation are sensitivity analysis and situational adjustments.
  - Sensitivity analysis is an analysis to determine how changes in an assumed input would affect the outcome of an analysis.
  - Situational adjustments include control premiums (premiums for a controlling interest in the company), discounts for lack of marketability (discounts reflecting the lack of a public market for the company's shares), and illiquidity discounts (discounts reflecting the lack of a liquid market for the company's shares).
- ▪ Applying valuation conclusions depends on the purpose of the valuation.
- ▪ In performing valuations, analysts must hold themselves accountable to both standards of competence and standards of conduct.
- ▪ An effective research report:
  - contains timely information;
  - is written in clear, incisive language;
  - is objective and well researched, with key assumptions clearly identified;
  - distinguishes clearly between facts and opinions;
  - contains analysis, forecasts, valuation, and a recommendation that are internally consistent;
  - presents sufficient information that the reader can critique the valuation;
  - states the risk factors for an investment in the company; and
  - discloses any potential conflicts of interests faced by the analyst.
- ▪ Analysts have an obligation to provide substantive and meaningful content. CFA Institute members have an additional overriding responsibility to adhere to the CFA Institute Code of Ethics and relevant specific Standards of Professional Conduct.

REFERENCES

Burch, Timothy R., and Vikram Nanda. 2003. "Divisional Diversity and the Conglomerate Discount: Evidence from Spinoffs." *Journal of Financial Economics*, vol. 70, no. 1:69–98.

Cornell, Bradford. 2001. "Is the Response of Analysts to Information Consistent with Fundamental Valuation? The Case of Intel." *Financial Management*, vol. 30, no. 1:113–136.

Graham, Benjamin, and David L. Dodd. 1934. *Security Analysis.* McGraw-Hill Professional Publishing.

Grossman, Sanford, and Joseph Stiglitz. 1980. "On the Impossibility of Informationally Efficient Markets." *American Economic Review*, vol. 70, no. 3:393–408.

Jensen, Michael C., and William H. Meckling. 1976. "Theory of the Firm: Managerial Behavior, Agency Costs and Ownership Structure." *Journal of Financial Economics*, vol. 3, no. 4:305–360.

Lamont, Owen A., and Christopher Polk. 2002. "Does Diversification Destroy Value? Evidence from the Industry Shocks." *Journal of Financial Economics*, vol. 63, no. 1:51–77.

Lee, Charles M.C., James Myers, and Bhaskaran Swaminathan. 1999. "What is the Intrinsic Value of the Dow?" *Journal of Finance*, vol. 54, no. 5:1693–1741.

Merrill Lynch & Co. *2006 Institutional Factor Survey.* Quantitative Strategy: Global Securities Research & Economics Group.

Moody's. 2000. *Putting EBITDA in Perspective.* Moody's Investors Service Global Credit Research.

Mulford, Charles W., and Eugene F. Comiskey. 2005. *Creative Cash Flow Reporting: Uncovering Sustainable Financial Performance.* Hoboken, NJ: John Wiley & Sons.

Porter, Michael E. 1985. *The Competitive Advantage: Creating and Sustaining Superior Performance.* New York: Free Press. (Republished with new introduction in 1998.)

Porter, Michael E. 2008. "The Five Competitive Forces that Shape Strategy." *Harvard Business Review*, vol. 86, no. 1:78–93.

Schilit, Howard, and Jeremy Perler. 2010. *Financial Shenanigans: How to Detect Accounting Gimmicks & Fraud in Financial Reports*, 3rd edition. New York: McGraw-Hill.

Sloan, Richard G. 1996. "Do Stock Prices Fully Reflect Information in Accruals and Cash Flows About Future Earnings?" *Accounting Review*, vol. 71, no. 3:289–315.

PRACTICE PROBLEMS

1 Critique the statement: "No equity investor needs to understand valuation models because real-time market prices for equities are easy to obtain online."

2 The reading defined intrinsic value as "the value of an asset given a hypothetically complete understanding of the asset's investment characteristics." Discuss why "hypothetically" is included in the definition and the practical implication(s).

3 **A** Explain why liquidation value is generally not relevant to estimating intrinsic value for profitable companies.

  B Explain whether making a going-concern assumption would affect the value placed on a company's inventory.

4 Explain how the procedure for using a valuation model to infer market expectations about a company's future growth differs from using the same model to obtain an independent estimate of value.

5 Example 1, based on a study of Intel Corporation that used a present value model (Cornell 2001), examined what future revenue growth rates were consistent with Intel's stock price of $61.50 just prior to its earnings announcement, and $43.31 only five days later. The example states, "Using a conservatively low discount rate, Cornell estimated that Intel's price before the announcement, $61.50, was consistent with a forecasted growth rate of 20 percent a year for the subsequent 10 years and then 6 percent per year thereafter." Discuss the implications of using a higher discount rate than Cornell did.

6 Discuss how understanding a company's business (the first step in equity valuation) might be useful in performing a sensitivity analysis related to a valuation of the company.

7 In a research note on the ordinary shares of the Milan Fashion Group (MFG) dated early July 2007 when a recent price was €7.73 and projected annual dividends were €0.05, an analyst stated a target price of €9.20. The research note did not discuss how the target price was obtained or how it should be interpreted. Assume the target price represents the expected price of MFG. What further specific pieces of information would you need to form an opinion on whether MFG was fairly valued, overvalued, or undervalued?

8 You are researching XMI Corporation (XMI). XMI has shown steady earnings per share growth (18 percent a year during the last seven years) and trades at a very high multiple to earnings (its P/E is currently 40 percent above the average P/E for a group of the most comparable stocks). XMI has generally grown through acquisition, by using XMI stock to purchase other companies whose stock traded at lower P/Es. In investigating the financial disclosures of these acquired companies and talking to industry contacts, you conclude that XMI has been forcing the companies it acquires to accelerate the payment of expenses before the acquisition deals are closed. As one example, XMI asks acquired companies to immediately pay all pending accounts payable, whether or not they are due. Subsequent to the acquisition, XMI reinstitutes normal expense payment patterns.

A What are the effects of XMI's pre-acquisition expensing policies?

B The statement is made that XMI's "P/E is currently 40 percent above the average P/E for a group of the most comparable stocks." What type of valuation model is implicit in that statement?

The following information relates to Questions 9–16

Guardian Capital is a rapidly growing US investment firm. The Guardian Capital research team is responsible for identifying undervalued and overvalued publicly traded equities that have a market capitalization greater than $500 million.

Due to the rapid growth of assets under management, Guardian Capital recently hired a new analyst, Jack Richardson, to support the research process. At the new analyst orientation meeting, the director of research made the following statements about equity valuation at Guardian:

Statement 1 "Analysts at Guardian Capital seek to identify mispricing, relying on price eventually converging to intrinsic value. However, convergence of the market price to an analyst's estimate of intrinsic value may not happen within the portfolio manager's investment time horizon. So, besides evidence of mispricing, analysts should look for the presence of a particular market or corporate event,— that is, a catalyst— that will cause the marketplace to re-evaluate the subject firm's prospects."

Statement 2 "An active investment manager attempts to capture positive alpha. But mispricing of assets is not directly observable. It is therefore important that you understand the possible sources of perceived mispricing."

Statement 3 "For its distressed securities fund, Guardian Capital screens its investable universe of securities for companies in financial distress."

Statement 4 "For its core equity fund, Guardian Capital selects financially sound companies that are expected to generate significant positive free cash flow from core business operations within a multiyear forecast horizon."

Statement 5 "Guardian Capital's research process requires analysts to evaluate the reasonableness of the expectations implied by the market price by comparing the market's implied expectations to his or her own expectations."

After the orientation meeting, the director of research asks Richardson to evaluate three companies that are retailers of men's clothing: Diamond Co., Renaissance Clothing, and Deluxe Men's Wear.

Richardson starts his analysis by evaluating the characteristics of the men's retail clothing industry. He finds few barriers to new retail entrants, high intra-industry rivalry among retailers, low product substitution costs for customers and a large number of wholesale clothing suppliers.

While conducting his analysis, Richardson discovers that Renaissance Clothing included three non-recurring items in their most recent earnings release: a positive litigation settlement, a one-time tax credit, and the gain on the sale of a non-operating asset.

To estimate each firm's intrinsic value, Richardson applies appropriate discount rates to each firm's estimated free cash flows over a ten-year time horizon and to the estimated value of the firm at the end of the ten-year horizon.

Michelle Lee, a junior technology analyst at Guardian, asks the director of research for advice as to which valuation model to use for VEGA, a fast growing semiconductor company that is rapidly gaining market share.

The director of research states that "the valuation model selected must be consistent with the characteristics of the company being valued."

Lee tells the director of research that VEGA is not expected to be profitable for several more years. According to management guidance, when the company turns profitable, it will invest in new product development; as a result, it does not expect to initiate a dividend for an extended period of time. Lee also notes that she expects that certain larger competitors will become interested in acquiring VEGA because of its excellent growth prospects. The director of research advises Lee to consider that in her valuation.

9 Based on Statement 2, which of the following sources of perceived mispricing do active investment managers attempt to identify? The difference between:

   A intrinsic value and market price.

   B estimated intrinsic value and market price.

   C intrinsic value and estimated intrinsic value.

10 With respect to Statements 3 and 4, which of the following measures of value would the distressed securities fund's analyst consider that a core equity fund analyst might ignore?

   A Fair value

   B Liquidation value

   C Fair market value

11 With respect to Statement 4, which measure of value is *most* relevant for the analyst of the fund described?

   A Liquidation value

   B Investment value

   C Going-concern value

12 According to Statement 5, analysts are expected to use valuation concepts and models to:

   A value private businesses.

   B render fairness opinions.

   C extract market expectations.

13 Based on Richardson's industry analysis, which of the following characteristics of men's retail clothing retailing would *positively* affect its profitability? That industry's:

   A entry costs.

   B substitution costs.

   C number of suppliers.

14 Which of the following statements about the reported earnings of Renaissance Clothing is *most accurate*? Relative to sustainable earnings, reported earnings are likely:

   A unbiased.

   B upward biased.

   C downward biased.

15 Which valuation model is Richardson applying in his analysis of the retailers?

  A Relative value

  B Absolute value

  C Sum-of-the-parts

16 Which valuation model would the director of research *most likely* recommend Lee use to estimate the value of VEGA?

  A Free cash flow

  B Dividend discount

  C P/E relative valuation

SOLUTIONS

1   The statement is flawed in at least two ways. First, active investors believe that stock prices do not always accurately reflect all relevant information on the security; for such investors, knowledge of equity valuation models is important for identifying investment opportunities because they represent a way to translate the investor's forecasts into value estimates for comparison with market prices. Thus, the "all" in "all investors" is misleading. Second, not all equities are publicly traded and have market prices, and the most recent market price can be stale for the many public equities that trade only infrequently.

2   No matter how diligent the analyst, some uncertainty always exists concerning 1) the accuracy of the analyst's forecasts and 2) whether an intrinsic value estimate accounts for all sources of risk reflected in market price. Thus, knowledge of a stock's investment characteristics is always incomplete. The practical consequences are that an investor can only estimate intrinsic value and active security selection carries the risk of making mistakes in estimating value.

3   A   Liquidation value is typically not relevant to estimating intrinsic value for profitable companies because, in general, value would be destroyed by selling such a company's assets individually. Stated another way, the value added by being a going concern is a relevant investment characteristic that an intrinsic value estimate would recognize.

    B   A going-concern assumption generally increases the value placed on a company's inventory relative to not making that assumption. Usually, inventory that can be sold in the company's regular distribution channels would realize higher amounts than inventory that must be sold immediately because a company is being liquidated.

4   The key difference is that for inferring investor expectations the market price is used as the model input for value whereas for obtaining an independent estimate of value, value is left as the unknown in the model. In the latter case, value is estimated based on the analyst's estimates for the variables that determine value.

5   Consider the present value of a single cash flow. If one increased the discount rate, one would also need to increase the cash flow if a constant present value were to be maintained. By a similar argument, if Cornell had used a higher discount rate, he would have needed to project a higher level of assumed future cash flows than he did for their present value to have been consistent with the given pre-announcement price of $61.50. Thus, the implied growth rate consistent with a price of $61.50 would have been higher than the 20 percent growth rate estimated by Cornell.

6   An understanding of the company's business facilitates a focus on the key business aspects that affect value, and from a practical perspective, highlights the critical inputs to a forecast that should be tested using sensitivity analysis.

7   You need to know 1) the time horizon for the price target and 2) the required rate of return on MFG. The price target of €9.20 represents a potential 20 percent return from investing in the stock if the time horizon is one year, calculated as (€9.20 + €0.05)/€7.73 − 1.0 = 0.197; without a time frame, however, you cannot evaluate the attractiveness of that return. Given that the time frame for the return is established, you need to have an estimate of the required rate of return over the same time horizon.

If the expected return of 19.7 percent exceeds the security's required return for the same horizon—in other words, if the share's expected alpha is positive—then MFG would appear to be undervalued.

8 A Accelerating the payment of expenses reduces the acquired companies' last reported pre-acquisition cash flow. Accelerating expense recognition reduces the acquired companies' last reported pre-acquisition earnings. XMI's cash flow and earnings growth rates following the acquisitions would be expected to be biased upwards because of the depressed levels for the acquirees.

B That is an example of a relative valuation model (or the method of comparables), which compares a company's market multiple to the multiples of similar companies.

9 A is correct. The difference between the true (real) but unobservable intrinsic value and the observed market price contributes to the abnormal return or alpha which is the concern of active investment managers.

10 B is correct. The measure of value the distressed securities fund's analyst would consider that the core equity fund analyst might ignore is liquidation value. The liquidation value of a company is its value if it were dissolved and its assets sold individually.

11 C is correct. For its core equity fund, Guardian Capital screens its investable universe of securities for well-capitalized companies that are expected to generate significant future free cash flow from core business operations. The concern with future free cash flows implies that going-concern value is relevant.

12 C is correct. Market prices reflect the expectations of investors about the future performance of companies. The analyst can evaluate the reasonableness of the expectations implied by the market price by comparing the market's implied expectations to his own expectations. This process assumes a valuation model, as discussed in the text.

13 C is correct. The men's retail clothing industry is characterized by a large number of wholesale clothing suppliers. When many suppliers of the products needed by industry participants exist, competition among suppliers should limit their ability to raise input prices. Thus the large number of suppliers is a factor that should positively affect industry profitability.

14 B is correct. The effects of favorable nonrecurring events in reported earnings would tend to bias reported earnings upward relative to sustainable earnings because non-recurring items are by definition not expected to repeat. Renaissance Clothing included three non-recurring items in their most recent earnings release that all led to higher earnings for the current period: a positive litigation settlement, a one-time tax credit, and the gain on the sale of a non-operating asset.

15 B is correct. An absolute valuation model is a model that specifies an asset's intrinsic value. The most important type of absolute equity valuation models are present value models (also referred to as discounted cash flow models) and the model described by Richardson is of that type.

16 A is correct. The broad criteria for model selection are that a valuation model be consistent with the characteristics of the company being valued, appropriate given the availability and quality of the data and consistent with the purpose of the valuation. VEGA currently has negative earnings, making the use of P/E relative valuation difficult if not impossible. As VEGA does not pay a dividend and is not expected to for the foreseeable future; this would make the application of a dividend discount model problematic. However, the lack of a dividend would not be an obstacle to free cash flow valuation. Furthermore, the director of research has advised that the possibility that competitors may seek to acquire VEGA be taken in to account in valuing VEGA. The reading states that free cash flow valuation can be appropriate in such circumstances. Thus, the director of research would be most likely to recommend free cash flow valuation.

READING
30

Return Concepts

by Jerald E. Pinto, PhD, CFA, Elaine Henry, PhD, CFA,
Thomas R. Robinson, PhD, CFA, and John D. Stowe, PhD, CFA

Jerald E. Pinto, PhD, CFA, is at CFA Institute (USA). Elaine Henry, PhD, CFA, is at Fordham University (USA). Thomas R. Robinson, PhD, CFA, is at CFA Institute (USA). John D. Stowe, PhD, CFA, is at Ohio University (USA).

LEARNING OUTCOMES

Mastery	The candidate should be able to:
☐	**a.** distinguish among realized holding period return, expected holding period return, required return, return from convergence of price to intrinsic value, discount rate, and internal rate of return;
☐	**b.** calculate and interpret an equity risk premium using historical and forward-looking estimation approaches;
☐	**c.** estimate the required return on an equity investment using the capital asset pricing model, the Fama–French model, the Pastor–Stambaugh model, macroeconomic multifactor models, and the build-up method (e.g., bond yield plus risk premium);
☐	**d.** explain beta estimation for public companies, thinly traded public companies, and nonpublic companies;
☐	**e.** describe strengths and weaknesses of methods used to estimate the required return on an equity investment;
☐	**f.** explain international considerations in required return estimation;
☐	**g.** explain and calculate the weighted average cost of capital for a company;
☐	**h.** evaluate the appropriateness of using a particular rate of return as a discount rate, given a description of the cash flow to be discounted and other relevant facts.

The data and examples for this reading were updated in 2014 by Professor Stephen Wilcox, CFA.

Equity Asset Valuation, Second Edition, by Jerald E. Pinto, CFA, Elaine Henry, CFA, Thomas R. Robinson, CFA, and John D. Stowe, CFA. Copyright © 2009 by CFA Institute.

1

INTRODUCTION

The return on an investment is a fundamental element in evaluating an investment:

- Investors evaluate an investment in terms of the return they expect to earn on it compared to a level of return viewed as fair given everything they know about the investment, including its risk.

- Analysts need to specify the appropriate rate or rates with which to discount expected future cash flows when using present value models of stock value.

This reading presents and illustrates key return measures relevant to valuation and is organized as follows. Section 2 provides an overview of return concepts. Section 3 presents the chief approaches to estimating the equity risk premium, a key input in determining the required rate of return on equity in several important models. With a means to estimate the equity risk premium in hand, Section 4 discusses and illustrates the major models for estimating the required return on equity. Section 5 presents the weighted average cost of capital, a discount rate used when finding the present value of cash flows to all providers of capital. Section 6 presents certain facts concerning discount rate selection. A summary and practice problems conclude the reading.

RETURN CONCEPTS

A sound investment decision depends critically on the correct use and evaluation of rate of return measures. The following sections explain the major return concepts most relevant to valuation.[1]

2.1 Holding Period Return

The holding period rate of return (for short, the **holding period return**)[2] is the return earned from investing in an asset over a specified time period. The specified time period is the holding period under examination, whether it is one day, two weeks, four years, or any other length of time. To use a hypothetical return figure of 0.8 percent for a one-day holding period, we would say that "the one-day holding period return is 0.8 percent" (or equivalently, "the one-day return is 0.8 percent" or "the return is 0.8 percent over one day"). Such returns can be separated into investment income and price appreciation components. If the asset is a share purchased now (at $t = 0$, with t denoting time) and sold at $t = H$, the holding period is $t = 0$ to $t = H$ and the holding period return is

$$r = \frac{D_H + P_H}{P_0} - 1$$

$$= \frac{D_H}{P_0} + \frac{P_H - P_0}{P_0} \tag{1}$$

$$= \text{Dividend yield} + \text{Price appreciation return}$$

where D_t and P_t are per-share dividends and share price at time t. Equation 1 shows that the holding period return is the sum of two components: dividend yield (D_H/P_0) and price appreciation return ($[P_H - P_0]/P_0$), also known as the capital gains yield.

---

1 This is by no means an exhaustive list of return concepts. In particular, other areas of finance such as performance evaluation make use of return concepts not covered here (e.g., time-weighted rate of return).
2 References to *return* in this reading refer to *rate of return*, not a money amount of return.

Equation 1 assumes, for simplicity, that any dividend is received at the end of the holding period. More generally, the holding period return would be calculated based on reinvesting any dividend received between $t = 0$ and $t = H$ in additional shares on the date the dividend was received at the price then available. Holding period returns are sometimes annualized—e.g., the return for a specific holding period may be converted to an annualized return, usually based on compounding at the holding period rate. For example, $(1.008)^{365} - 1 = 17.3271$ or $1,732.71$ percent, is one way to annualize a one-day 0.80 percent return. As the example shows, however, annualizing holding period returns, when the holding period is a fraction of a year, is unrealistic when the reinvestment rate is not an actual, available reinvestment rate.

2.2 Realized and Expected (Holding Period) Return

In the expression for the holding period return, the selling price, P_H, and in general, the dividend, D_H, are not known as of $t = 0$. For a holding period in the past, the selling price and the dividend are known, and the return is called a realized holding period return, or more simply, a realized return. For example, with a beginning price of €50.00, an ending or selling price of €52.00 six months later, and a dividend equal to €1.00 (all amounts referring to the past), the realized return is €1.00/€50.00 + (€52.00 − €50.00)/€50.00 = 0.02 + 0.04 = 0.06 or 6 percent over 6 months. In forward-looking contexts, holding-period returns are random variables because future selling prices and dividends may both take on a range of values. Nevertheless, an investor can form an expectation concerning the dividend and selling price and thereby have an **expected holding-period return**, or simply expected return, for the stock that consists of the expected dividend yield and the expected price appreciation return.

Although professional investors often formulate expected returns based on explicit valuation models, a return expectation does not have to be based on a model or on specific valuation knowledge. Any investor can have a personal viewpoint on the future returns on an asset. In fact, because investors formulate expectations in varying ways and on the basis of different information, different investors generally have different expected returns for an asset. The comparison point for interpreting the investment implication of the expected return for an asset is its required return, the subject of the next section.

2.3 Required Return

A **required rate of return** (for short, required return) is the minimum level of expected return that an investor requires in order to invest in the asset over a specified time period, given the asset's riskiness. It represents the opportunity cost for investing in the asset—the highest level of expected return available elsewhere from investments of similar risk. As the opportunity cost for investing in the asset, the required return represents a threshold value for being fairly compensated for the risk of the asset. If the investor's expected return exceeds the required return, the asset will appear to be undervalued because it is expected to return more-than-fair compensation for the asset's risk. By contrast, if the expected return on the asset falls short of the required rate of return, the asset will appear to be overvalued.

The valuation examples presented in these readings will illustrate the use of required return estimates grounded in market data (such as observed asset returns) and explicit models for required return. We will refer to any such estimate of the required return used in an example as *the* required return on the asset for the sake of simplicity, although other estimates are usually defensible. For example, using the capital asset pricing model (discussed in more detail later), the required return for an asset is equal to the risk-free rate of return plus a premium (or discount) related to the asset's sensitivity to market returns. That sensitivity can be estimated based on returns for an observed market portfolio and the asset. That is one example of a required return estimate grounded in a formal model based on marketplace variables (rather than a single investor's return requirements). Market variables should contain information about investors' asset risk perceptions and their level of risk aversion, both of which are important in determining fair compensation for risk.

The concept of risk-free rate mentioned in the previous paragraphs is important in valuation. "Risk-free rate" in financial theory is the rate of return on an asset that produces the same, known rate of return in all future economic states. In investment practice, "risk-free rate" typically refers to a rate of return on an investment with assured (or nearly assured) payments. This risk-free rate then serves as a reference rate for practical purposes such as valuing other investments. In a given market, the yield on a sovereign debt instrument (e.g., Treasury bills or Treasury bonds in the United States and German Treasury bills [Schätze] in the eurozone) is typically used by practitioners to represent the risk-free rate.

In this reading, we use the notation r for the required rate of return on the asset being discussed. The required rate of return on common stock and debt are also known as the **cost of equity** and **cost of debt**, respectively, taking the perspective of the issuer. To raise new capital, the issuer would have to price the security to offer a level of expected return that is competitive with the expected returns being offered by similarly risky securities. The required return on a security is therefore the issuer's marginal cost for raising additional capital of the same type.

The difference between the expected return and the required rate of return on an asset is the asset's expected alpha (or *ex ante* alpha) or expected abnormal return:

Expected alpha = Expected return − Required return   **(2a)**

When an asset is efficiently priced (its price equals its intrinsic value), expected return should equal required return and the expected alpha is zero. In investment decision-making and valuation, the focus is on expected alpha. However, to evaluate the actual results of an investment discipline, the analyst would examine realized alpha. Realized alpha (or *ex post* alpha) over a given holding period is

Realized alpha = Actual holding-period return

          − Contemporaneous required return   **(2b)**

Estimates of required returns are essential for using present value models of value. Present value models require the analyst to establish appropriate discount rates for determining the present values of expected future cash flows.

Expected return and *required rate of return* are sometimes used interchangeably in conversation and writing.[3] As discussed, that is not necessarily correct. When current price equals perceived value, expected return should be the same as the required rate of return. However, when price is below (above) the perceived value, expected return will exceed (be less than) the required return as long as the investor expects price to converge to value over his or her time horizon.

Given an investor's expected holding-period return, we defined expected alpha in relation to a required return estimate. In the next section, we show the conversion of a value estimate into an estimate of expected-holding period return.

---

3 Some financial models—such as the standard capital asset pricing model discussed later—assume that investors have the same expectations about the parameters of assets' return distributions and derive the level of required return for risky assets that clears the market for those assets. In the context of such a model with homogenous expectations, the required return is also *the* expected return for the asset. In discussions of such models, therefore, *expected return* and *required return* are used interchangeably.

2.4 Expected Return Estimates from Intrinsic Value Estimates

When an asset is mispriced, one of several outcomes is possible. Take the case of an asset that an investor believes is 25 percent undervalued in the marketplace. Over the investment time horizon, the mispricing may:

- increase (the asset may become more undervalued);
- stay the same (the asset may remain 25 percent undervalued);
- be partially corrected (e.g., the asset may become undervalued by 15 percent);
- be corrected (price changes to exactly reflect value); or
- reverse, or be overcorrected (the asset may become overvalued).

Generally, convergence of price to value is the equilibrium and anticipated outcome when the investor's value estimate is more accurate than the market's, as reflected in the market price. In that case, the investor's expected rate of return has two components: the required return (earned on the asset's current market price) and a return from convergence of price to value.

We can illustrate how expected return may be estimated when an investor's value estimate, V_0, is different from the market price. Suppose the investor expects price to fully converge to value over τ years. $(V_0 - P_0)/P_0$ is an estimate of the return from convergence over the period of that length, essentially the expected alpha for the asset stated on a per-period basis. With r_τ being the required return on a periodic (not annualized) basis and $E(R_\tau)$ the expected holding-period return on the same basis, then:

$$E(R_\tau) \approx r_\tau + \frac{V_0 - P_0}{P_0}$$

Although only an approximation, the expression does illustrate that an expected return can be viewed as the sum of two returns: the required return and a return from convergence of price to intrinsic value.[4]

To illustrate, in August of 2013, one estimate of the required return for Toyota Motors (TYO: 7203 and NYSE: TM) shares was 6.3 percent. At a time when Toyota's American Depository Receipt (ADR) market price was \$127.97, a research report estimated the company's intrinsic value at \$176.30 per share. Thus, in the report author's view, Toyota was undervalued by $V_0 - P_0 =$ \$176.30 − \$127.97 = \$48.33, or 37.77 percent as a fraction of the market price (\$48.33/\$127.97). If price were expected to converge to value in exactly one year, an investor would earn 37.77% + 6.3% = 44.07%. The expected alpha of Toyota is about 37.8 percent per annum. But if the investor expected the undervaluation to disappear by the end of nine months, then the investor might anticipate achieving a return of approximately 42.5 percent over the 9-month period. The required return on a nine-month basis ($\tau = 9/12 = 0.75$) is $(1.063)^{0.75} - 1 = 0.0469$ or 4.69 percent, so the total expected return is

$$
\begin{aligned}
E(R_\tau) &\approx r_\tau + \frac{V_0 - P_0}{P_0} \\
&= 4.69\% + 37.77\% \\
&= 42.46 \text{ percent}
\end{aligned}
$$

---

4 The expression assumes that the required rate of return and intrinsic value are static over the holding period and that convergence happens smoothly over the holding period (or all at once at its end). We conduct the analysis on a periodic (holding period) basis because one cannot assume reinvestment at a rate incorporating a return from convergence is feasible. For example, a 12.4 percent return from convergence earned over a month would be over 300 percent annualized, which is not meaningful as a performance expectation.

In this case, expected alpha is 37.77 percent on a nine-month basis which, when added to the required return of 4.69 percent on a nine-month basis, gives an estimate of the nine-month holding period return of approximately 42.5 percent. Another possibility is that price converges to value in two years. The expected two-year expected holding period return would be 13.00% + 37.77% = 50.77%, in which the required return component is calculated as $(1.063)^2 - 1 = 0.1300$. This expected return based on two-year convergence could be compared to the expected return based on one-year convergence of 44.07 percent by annualizing it: $(1.5077)^{1/2} - 1 = 0.2279$ or 22.79 percent per year.

Active investors essentially "second-guess" the market price. The risks of that activity include the risks that 1) their value estimates are not more accurate than the market price, and that, 2) even if they are more accurate, the value discrepancy may not narrow over the investors' time horizon. Clearly, the convergence component of expected return can be quite risky.

EXAMPLE 1

An Analyst Case Study (1): The Required Return on Microsoft Shares

Thomas Weeramantry and Françoise Delacour are co-managers of a US-based diversified global equity portfolio. They are researching Microsoft Corporation (NASDAQ-GS: MSFT),[5] the largest US-headquartered technology sector company. Weeramantry gathered a number of research reports on MSFT and began his analysis of the company in May 2013, when the current price for MSFT was $33.31. In one research report, the analyst offered the following facts, opinions, and estimates concerning MSFT:

▪ The most recent quarterly dividend was $0.23 per share. Over the coming year, two more quarterly dividends of $0.23 are expected, followed by two quarterly dividends of $0.25 per share.

▪ MSFT's required return on equity is 7.0 percent.

▪ A one-year target price for MSFT is $37.50.

An analyst's target price is the price at which the analyst believes the security should sell at a stated future point in time. Based only on the information given, answer the following questions concerning MSFT. For both questions, ignore returns from reinvesting the quarterly dividends.

1   What is the analyst's one-year expected return?

2   What is a target price that is *most* consistent with MSFT being fairly valued?

Solution to 1:

Over one year, the analyst expects MSFT to pay $0.23 + $0.23 + $0.25 + $0.25 = $0.96 in dividends. Using the target price of $37.50 and dividends of $0.96, the analyst's expected return is ($0.96/$33.31) + ($37.50 − $33.31)/$33.31 = 0.029 + 0.126 = 0.155 or 15.5 percent.

Solution to 2:

If MSFT is fairly valued, it should return its cost of equity (required return), which is 7.0 percent. Under that assumption, Target price = Current price × (1 + Required return) − Dividend = $33.31(1.07) − $0.96 = $34.68; the dividend

---

5 NASDAQ-GS: The Global Select Market tier of NASDAQ.

is subtracted to isolate the return from price appreciation. Another solution approach involves subtracting the dividend yield from the required return to isolate the anticipated price appreciation return: 7.0% − 2.9% = 4.1%. Thus, (1.041)($33.31) = $34.68.

2.5 Discount Rate

Discount rate is a general term for any rate used in finding the present value of a future cash flow. A discount rate reflects the compensation required by investors for delaying consumption—generally assumed to equal the risk-free rate—and their required compensation for the risk of the cash flow. Generally, the discount rate used to determine intrinsic value depends on the characteristics of the investment rather than on the characteristics of the purchaser. That is, *for the purposes of estimating intrinsic value*, a required return based on marketplace variables is used rather than a personal required return influenced by such factors as whether the investor is diversified in his or her personal portfolio. On the other hand, some investors will make judgmental adjustments to such required return estimates, knowing the limitations of the finance models used to estimate such returns.

In principle, because of varying expected future inflation rates and the possibly varying risk of expected future cash flows, a distinct discount rate could be applicable to each distinct expected future cash flow. In practice, a single required return is generally used to discount all expected future cash flows.[6]

Sometimes an internal rate of return is used as a required return estimate, as discussed in the next section.

2.6 Internal Rate of Return

The **internal rate of return** (IRR) on an investment is the discount rate that equates the present value of the asset's expected future cash flows to the asset's price—i.e., the amount of money needed today to purchase a right to those cash flows.

In a model that views the intrinsic value of a common equity share as the present value of expected future cash flows, if price is equal to current intrinsic value—the condition of market informational efficiency—then, generally, a discount rate can be found, usually by iteration, which equates that present value to the market price. An IRR computed under the assumption of market efficiency has been used to estimate the required return on equity. An example is the historical practice of many US state regulators of estimating the cost of equity for regulated utilities using the model illustrated in Equation 3b below.[7] (The issue of cost of equity arises because regulators set prices sufficient for utilities to earn their cost of capital.)[8]

To illustrate, the simplest version of a present value model results from defining cash flows as dividends and assuming a stable dividend growth rate for the indefinite future. The stable growth rate assumption reduces the sum of results in a very simple expression for intrinsic value:[9]

$$\text{Intrinsic value} = \frac{\text{Year-ahead dividend}}{\text{Required return} - \text{Expected dividend growth rate}} \qquad \textbf{(3a)}$$

---

6 When analysts sort expected future cash flows into multiple groups and each group has a different assumed growth rate, analysts sometimes apply different required returns to the different groups in discounting expected cash flows.

7 See Cornell (1999), p. 103, or Brealey, Myers, and Allen (2006) for an introduction to this use.

8 To avoid circularity, analysts must avoid using such an estimate as the discount rate in the same or closely similar present value model solved for intrinsic value.

9 This will be discussed in more detail in the reading on discounted dividend valuation.

If the asset is correctly valued now (Market price = Intrinsic value), given consensus estimates of the year-ahead dividend and future dividend growth rate (which are estimates of the dividend expectations built into the price), we can solve for a required return—an IRR implied by the market price:

$$\text{Required return estimate} = \frac{\text{Year-ahead dividend}}{\text{Market price}}$$
$$+ \text{Expected dividend growth rate} \qquad \textbf{(3b)}$$

The use of such an IRR as a required return estimate assumes not only market efficiency, but also the correctness of the particular present value model (in the above example, the stable growth rate assumption is critical) and the estimated inputs to the selected model. In Equation 3b and similar cases, although the asset's risk is incorporated indirectly into the required return estimate via the market price, the adjustment for risk is not explicit as it is in many competing models that will be presented.

Finally, obtaining an IRR from a present value model should not be confused with the somewhat similar-looking exercise that involves inferring what the market price implies about future growth rates of cash flows, given an independent estimate of required return: that exercise has the purpose of assessing the reasonableness of the market price.

3   THE EQUITY RISK PREMIUM

The equity risk premium is the incremental return (*premium*) that investors require for holding equities rather than a risk-free asset. Thus, it is the difference between the required return on equities and a specified expected risk-free rate of return. The equity risk premium, like the required return, depends strictly on expectations for the future because the investor's returns depend only on the investment's future cash flows. Possibly confusingly, *equity risk premium* is also commonly used to refer to the realized excess return of stocks over a risk-free asset over a given past time period. The realized excess return could be very different from the premium that, based on available information, was contemporaneously being expected by investors.[10]

Using the equity risk premium, the required return on the broad equity market or an average-systematic-risk equity security is

$$\text{Required return on equity} = \text{Current expected risk-free return} +$$
$$\text{Equity risk premium}$$

where, for consistency, the definition of risk-free asset (e.g., government bills or government bonds) used in estimating the equity risk premium should correspond to the one used in specifying the current expected risk-free return.

The importance of the equity risk premium in valuation is that, in perhaps a majority of cases in practice, analysts estimate the required return on a common equity issue as either

$$\text{Required return on share } i = \text{Current expected risk-free return}$$
$$+ \beta_i (\text{Equity risk premium}) \qquad \textbf{(4)}$$

---

10 Arnott and Bernstein (2002) underscore and discuss this topic at length.

or

$$\text{Required return on share } i = \text{Current expected risk-free return}$$
$$+ \text{ Equity risk premium}$$
$$\pm \left(\frac{\text{Other risk premia}}{\text{discounts appropriate for } i} \right)$$

(5)

- Equation 4 adjusts the equity risk premium for the share's particular level of systematic risk as measured by beta (β_i)—an average systematic risk security has a beta of 1, whereas beta values above and below 1 indicate greater-than-average and smaller-than-average systematic risk. Equation 4 will be explained in Section 4.1 as the capital asset pricing model (CAPM).

- Equation 5 does not make a beta adjustment to the equity risk premium but adds premia/discounts required to develop an overall equity risk adjustment. Equation 5 will be explained in Section 4.3 as the build-up method for estimating the required return. It is primarily used in the valuation of private businesses.

Typically, analysts estimate the equity risk premium for the national equity market of the issues being analyzed (but if a global CAPM is being used, a world equity premium is estimated that takes into account the totality of equity markets).

Even for the longest established developed markets, the magnitude of the equity risk premium is difficult to estimate and can be a reason for differing investment conclusions among analysts. Therefore, we will introduce the topic of estimation in some detail. Whatever estimates analysts decide to use, when an equity risk premium estimate enters into a valuation, analysts should be sensitive to how their value conclusions could be affected by estimation error.

Two broad approaches are available for estimating the equity risk premium. One is based on historical average differences between equity market return and government debt returns, and the other is based on current expectational data. These are presented in the following sections.

3.1 Historical Estimates

A historical equity risk premium estimate is usually calculated as the mean value of the differences between broad-based equity-market-index returns and government debt returns over some selected sample period. When reliable long-term records of equity returns are available, historical estimates have been a familiar and popular choice of estimation. If investors do not make systematic errors in forming expectations, then, over the long term, average returns should be an unbiased estimate of what investors expected. The fact that historical estimates are based on data also gives them an objective quality.

In using a historical estimate to represent the equity risk premium going forward, the analyst is assuming that returns are stationary—that is, the parameters that describe the return-generating process are constant over the past and into the future.

The analyst's major decisions in developing a historical equity risk premium estimate include the selection of:

- the equity index to represent equity market returns;
- the time period for computing the estimate;
- the type of mean calculated; and
- the proxy for the risk-free return.

Analysts try to select an equity index that accurately represents the average returns earned by equity investors in the market being examined. Broad-based, market-value weighted indices are typically selected.

Specifying the length of the sample period typically involves trade-offs. Dividing a data period of a given length into smaller subperiods does not increase precision in estimating the mean—only extending the length of the data set can increase precision.[11] Thus, a common choice is to use the longest reliable returns series available. However, the assumption of stationarity is usually more difficult to maintain as the series starting point is extended to the distant past. The specifics of the type of nonstationarity are also important. For a number of equity markets, research has brought forth abundant evidence of nonconstant underlying return volatility. Nonstationarity—in which the equity risk premium has fluctuated in the short term, but around a central value—is a less serious impediment to using a long data series than the case in which the risk premium has shifted to a permanently different level.[12] Empirically, the expected equity risk premium is countercyclical in the United States—that is, the expected premium is high during bad times but low during good times.[13] This property leads to some interesting challenges: For example, when a series of strong market returns has increased enthusiasm for equities and raised historical-mean equity risk premium estimates, the forward-looking equity risk premium may have actually declined.

Practitioners taking a historical approach to equity premium estimation often focus on the type of mean calculated and the proxy for the risk-free return. There are two choices for computing the mean and two broad choices for the proxy for the risk-free return.

The mean return of a historical set of annual return differences between equities and government debt securities can be calculated using a geometric mean or an arithmetic mean:

- A geometric mean equity risk premium estimate equal to the compound annual excess return of equities over the risk-free return, or

- An arithmetic mean equity risk premium estimate equal to the sum of the annual return differences divided by the number of observations in the sample.

The risk-free rate can also be represented in two ways:

- as a long-term government bond return, or

- as a short-term government debt instrument (Treasury bill) return.

Dimson, Marsh, and Staunton (2008) presented authoritative evidence on realized excess returns of stocks over government debt ("historical equity risk premia") using survivorship-bias free return datasets for 17 developed markets for the 108 years extending from 1900 through 2007.[14] In their 2013 update, they provided the risk premiums for 20 markets.[15] Exhibit 1 excerpts their findings, showing results for the four combinations of mean computation and risk-free return representation (two mean return choices × two risk-free return choices). In the table, *standard error* and *standard deviation* are those of the annual excess return series.

---

11 See Merton (1980). This result contrasts with the estimation of variance and covariance in which higher frequency of estimation for a given time span does increase the precision in estimating variance and covariance.
12 See Cornell (1999).
13 Fama and French (1989) and Ferson and Harvey (1991).
14 In a given year, the excess return of stocks over government debt is calculated as [(1 + Equity market return)/(1 + Risk-free rate of return)] − 1 ≈ Equity market return − Risk-free rate of return, where a specified government debt instrument return represents the risk-free rate of return.
15 *Credit Suisse Global Investment Returns Sourcebook*, 2013. Credit Suisse/London Business School.

Exhibit 1   Historical Equity Risk Premia: Twenty Major Markets, 1900–2012

Panel A: Historical Equity Risk Premia Relative to Bonds, 1900–2012

Country	Geometric Mean	Arithmetic Mean	Standard Error	Standard Deviation
Australia	5.6%	7.5%	1.9%	19.9%
Austria	2.8	22.1	14.7	154.8
Belgium	2.3	4.3	2.0	21.0
Canada	3.4	5.0	1.7	18.3
Denmark	1.8	3.3	1.6	17.5
Finland	5.3	8.9	2.8	30.1
France	3.0	5.3	2.1	22.8
Germany	5.2	8.6	2.7	28.4
Ireland	2.6	4.6	1.9	19.8
Italy	3.4	6.8	2.8	29.5
Japan	4.8	8.9	3.1	32.7
Netherlands	3.3	5.6	2.1	22.2
New Zealand	3.7	5.3	1.7	18.1
Norway	2.2	5.2	2.6	27.8
South Africa	5.4	7.1	1.8	19.5
Spain	2.1	4.1	1.9	20.7
Sweden	2.9	5.1	2.0	20.8
Switzerland	2.0	3.5	1.7	17.6
United Kingdom	3.7	5.0	1.6	17.1
United States	4.2	6.2	1.9	20.5
World-ex US	3.0	4.1	1.4	14.7
World	3.2	4.4	1.4	15.3

Panel B: Historical Equity Risk Premia Relative to Bills, 1900–2012

Country	Geometric Mean	Arithmetic Mean	Standard Error	Standard Deviation
Australia	6.6%	8.1%	1.7%	17.6%
Austria	5.6	10.5	3.6	37.7
Belgium	2.7	5.2	2.3	24.0
Canada	4.1	5.5	1.6	17.1
Denmark	2.8	4.6	1.9	20.5
Finland	5.8	9.3	2.8	30.0
France	5.9	8.6	2.3	24.4
Germany	5.9	9.8	3.0	31.7
Ireland	3.2	5.4	2.0	21.3
Italy	5.6	9.5	3.0	31.8
Japan	5.7	8.9	2.6	27.6
Netherlands	4.2	6.4	2.1	22.7
New Zealand	4.2	5.8	1.7	18.3
Norway	2.9	5.8	1.7	18.3
South Africa	6.3	8.3	2.1	21.9
Spain	3.1	5.3	2.0	21.7
Sweden	3.6	5.7	1.9	20.6

(continued)

Exhibit 1	(Continued)			

Panel B: Historical Equity Risk Premia Relative to Bills, 1900–2012

Country	Geometric Mean	Arithmetic Mean	Standard Error	Standard Deviation
Switzerland	3.4	5.1	1.8	18.8
United Kingdom	4.3	6.0	1.9	19.8
United States	5.3	7.2	1.8	19.6
World-ex US	3.5	5.1	1.8	18.6
World	4.1	5.5	1.6	17.0

Note: "World" represents a market-capitalization-weighted (in early decades, GDP-weighted) average of country results in USD terms. Statistics for Austria exclude 1921–22, and statistics for Germany exclude 1922–23.
Source: Damodaran (2013), Table 6.

The excerpt from Exhibit 1 presented below presents a comparison of historical equity risk premium estimates for the United States and Japan. This comparison highlights some of the issues that can arise in using historical estimates. As background to the discussion, note that as a mathematical fact, the geometric mean is always less than (or equal to) the arithmetic mean; furthermore, the yield curve is typically upward sloping (long-term bond yields are typically higher than short-term yields).

Exhibit 1	Historical Equity Risk Premia: 1900–2012 (excerpted)			
	United States		**Japan**	
	Geometric Mean	Arithmetic Mean	Geometric Mean	Arithmetic Mean
Premium relative to bills	5.3%	7.2%	5.7%	8.9%
Premium relative to bonds	4.2	6.2	4.8	8.9

For the United States, estimates of the equity risk premium relative to long-term government bonds runs from 4.2 percent (geometric mean relative to bonds) to 7.2 percent (arithmetic mean relative to bills). The United States illustrates the typical case in which realized values relative to bills, for any definition of mean, are higher than those relative to bonds.

The premium estimates for Japan are notably higher than for the United States. Because the promised yield on long-term bonds is usually higher than that on short-term bills, the equal arithmetic mean premium relative to bonds compared to bills in the case of Japan is atypical. The analyst would need to investigate the reasons for it and believe they applied to the future before using the estimate as a forecast for the future. In all markets, the geometric mean premium relative to long-term bonds gives the smallest risk premium estimate. Note the following:

- For each market, the variation in year-to-year results is very large as shown by the standard deviations. As a result, the sample mean estimates the true mean with potentially substantial error. To explain, the standard deviation of the sample mean in estimating the underlying mean (the standard error) is given by sample standard deviation ÷ square root of the number of observations: For example, 20.5 percent ÷ $\sqrt{113}$ ≈ 1.9 percent for the United States relative to bonds.[16] So a two standard deviation interval for the underlying mean (an interval within which the underlying mean is expected to lie with a 0.95 probability) is a wide 2.4 percent to 10.0 percent (i.e., 6.2% arithmetic mean ± 3.8% standard deviation) even with 113 years of data. This problem of sampling error becomes more acute, the shorter the series on which the mean estimate is based.

■ The variation in the historical equity risk premium estimates across countries is substantial. Referring to Panel A of Exhibit 1, the histogram in Exhibit 2, focusing on the geometric mean, shows that 75 percent of values fall in one-percentage-point intervals from 2 percent to 5 percent. The modal interval is 2–3 percent with the 3–4 percent interval as a close second. As Exhibit 1, Panel A shows, the mean ("World") value is 3.2 percent. However, approximately 25 percent of values fall in the two extreme intervals.

Exhibit 2	Distribution of Geometric Mean Realized Premium Relative to Bonds

Interval for Realized Premium x (in percent):

No. of Markets		$1 \leq x < 2$	$2 \leq x < 3$	$3 \leq x < 4$	$4 \leq x < 5$	$5 \leq x < 6$
	8					
	7		Switzerland			
	6		Spain	France		
	5		Norway	Netherlands		
	4		Belgium	Canda		Germany
	3		Ireland	Italy		Finland
	2		Austria	New Zealand	Japan	South Africa
	1	Denmark	Sweden	United Kingdom	United States	Australia

The next two sections discuss choices related to the calculation of a historical equity risk premium estimate.

3.1.1 Arithmetic Mean or Geometric Mean

A decision with an important impact on the risk premium estimate is the choice between an arithmetic mean and a geometric mean: the geometric mean is smaller by an amount equal to about one half the variance of returns, so it is always smaller than the arithmetic mean given any variability in returns (the geometric mean is equal to the arithmetic mean when the returns for all periods are equal).

In actual professional practice, both means have been used in equity risk premium estimation.

The arithmetic mean return as the average one-period return best represents the mean return in a single period. There are two traditional arguments in favor of using the arithmetic mean in equity risk premium estimation, one relating to the type of model in which the estimates are used and the second relating to a statistical property. The major finance models for estimating required return—in particular the CAPM

---

16 The statement can be made by appealing to the central limit theorem which states, informally, that the sample mean is approximately normally distributed for large samples. The calculation shown assumes that returns are serially uncorrelated and provides a lower limit for the standard error of the mean. In the case where returns are serially correlated, the standard error is larger.

and multifactor models—are single-period models; so the arithmetic mean, with its focus on single-period returns, appears to be a model-consistent choice. A statistical argument has also been made for the arithmetic mean: With serially uncorrelated returns and a *known* underlying arithmetic mean, the unbiased estimate of the expected terminal value of an investment is found by compounding forward at the arithmetic mean. For example, if the arithmetic mean is 8 percent, an unbiased estimate of the expected terminal value of a €1 million investment in 5 years is €1$(1.08)^5$ = €1.47 million. In practice, however, the underlying mean is not known. It has been established that compounding forward using the *sample* arithmetic mean, whether or not returns are serially uncorrelated, overestimates the expected terminal value of wealth.[17] In the example, if 8 percent is merely the sample arithmetic mean (used as an estimate of the unknown underlying mean), we would expect terminal wealth to be less than €1.47 million. Practically, only the first traditional argument still has force.

The geometric mean return of a sample represents the compound rate of growth that equates the beginning value to the ending value of one unit of money initially invested in an asset. Present value models involve the discounting over multiple time periods. Discounting is just the reverse side of compounding in terms of finding amounts of equivalent worth at different points in time; because the geometric mean is a compound growth rate, it appears to be a logical choice for estimating a required return in a multiperiod context, even when using a single-period required return model. In contrast to the sample arithmetic mean, using the sample geometric mean does not introduce bias in the calculated expected terminal value of an investment.[18] Equity risk premium estimates based on the geometric mean have tended to be closer to supply-side and demand-side estimates from economic theory than arithmetic mean estimates.[19] For the above reasons, the geometric mean is increasingly preferred for use in historical estimates of the equity risk premium.

3.1.2 Long-Term Government Bonds or Short-Term Government Bills

The choices for the risk-free rate are a short-term government debt rate, such as a 30-day T-bill rate, or a long-term government bond yield to maturity (YTM). Government bonds are preferred to even the highest rated corporate bonds as they typically have less (near zero) default and equity market risk.

A bond-based equity risk premium estimate in almost all cases is smaller than a bill-based estimate (see Exhibit 1). But a normal upward-sloping yield curve tends to offset the effect of the risk-free rate choice on a required return estimate, because the current expected risk-free rate based on a bond will be larger than the expectation based on a bill. However, with an inverted yield curve, the short-term yields exceed long-term yields and the required return estimate based on using a risk-free rate based on a bill can be much higher.

Industry practice has tended to favor use of a long-term government bond rate in premium estimates despite the fact that such estimates are often used in one-period models such as the CAPM. A risk premium based on a bill rate may produce a better estimate of the required rate of return for discounting a one-year-ahead cash flow, but a premium relative to bonds should produce a more plausible required return/discount rate in a multiperiod context of valuation.[20]

---

17 See Hughson, Stutzer, and Yung (2006) for a proof. Even when returns are not serially uncorrelated, using the arithmetic mean (even a known value) tends to overestimate the expected value of terminal wealth. Returns that revert to the mean are one example of serial correlation of practical concern.
18 See Hughson, Stutzer, and Yung (2006).
19 The relatively large size of the historical US equity premium relative to that predicted by demand-side theory is known as the "equity premium puzzle" (Mehra and Prescott 1985). Cornell (1999) provides an accessible summary of the research.
20 The argument is also made by Arzac (2005).

To illustrate a reason for the preference, take the case of bill-relative and bond-relative premia estimates of 5.5 percent and 4.5 percent, respectively, for a given market. Assume the yield curve is inverted: The current bill rate is 9 percent and the bond rate is 6 percent, respectively. The required return on average-risk equity based on bills is 14.5 percent (9% + 5.5%) compared with 10.5 percent based on bonds (6% + 4.5%). That 14.5 percent rate may be appropriate for discounting a one-year-ahead cash flow in a current high interest and inflation environment. The inverted yield curve, however, predicts a downward path for short-rates and inflation. Most of the cash flows lie in the future and the premium for expected average inflation rates built into the long-bond rate is more plausible. A practical principle is that for the purpose of valuation, the analyst should try to match the duration of the risk-free-rate measure to the duration of the asset being valued.[21] If the analyst has adopted a short-term risk-free rate definition, nevertheless, a practical approach to dealing with the situation just presented would be to use an expected average short-term bill rate rather than the current 9 percent rate. Advocates of using short-term rates point out that long-term government bonds are subject to risks, such as interest rate risk, that complicate their interpretation.

In practice, many analysts use the current YTM on a long-term government bond as an approximation for the expected return on it. The analyst needs to be clear that he or she is using a current yield observation, reflecting current inflation expectations. The yield on a recently issued ("on the run") bond mitigates distortions related to liquidity and discounts/premiums relative to face value. The available maturities of liquid government bonds change over time and differ among national markets. If a 20-year maturity is available and trades in a liquid market, however, its yield is a reasonable choice as an estimate of the risk-free rate for equity valuation.[22] In many international markets, only bonds of shorter maturity are available or have a liquid market. A 10-year government bond yield is another common choice.

Valuation requires definite estimates of required returns. The data in Exhibit 1 provide one practical starting point for an estimate of equity risk premium for the markets given. As discussed, one mainstream choice among alternative estimates of the historical equity risk premium is the geometric mean historical equity risk premium relative to government bonds.

3.1.3 *Adjusted Historical Estimates*

A historical risk premium estimate may be adjusted in several ways to neutralize the effect of biases that may be present in the underlying equity market return series. One type of adjustment is made to offset the effect of biases in the data series being used to estimate the equity risk premium. A second type of adjustment is made to take account of an independent estimate of the equity risk premium. In both cases the adjustment could be upward or downward.

One issue is **survivorship bias** in equity market data series. The bias arises when poorly performing or defunct companies are removed from membership in an index, so that only relative winners remain. Survivorship bias tends to inflate historical estimates of the equity risk premium. For many developed markets, equity returns series are now available that are free or nearly free of survivorship bias. When using a series that has such bias, however, the historical risk premium estimate should be adjusted downward. Guidance for such adjustment based on research is sometimes available.[23]

---

21 Duration is a measure of the price sensitivity of an asset (or liability) to interest-rate changes.
22 The Ibbotson US long-term government bond yield is based on a portfolio of 20-year average maturity T-bonds. We use that series in the suggested historical estimate of the US equity risk premium.
23 Copeland, Koller, and Murrin (2000) recommend a downward adjustment of 1.5 percent to 2.0 percent for survivorship bias in the S&P 500 Index, using arithmetic mean estimates. See also Dimson, Marsh, and Staunton (2002), which explains survivorship bias in greater detail.

A conceptually related issue with historical estimates can arise when a market has experienced a string of unexpectedly positive or negative events and the surprises do not balance out over the period of sampled data. For example, a string of positive inflation and productivity surprises may result in a series of high returns that increase the historical mean estimate of the equity risk premium. In such cases, a forward-looking model estimate may suggest a much lower value of the equity risk premium. To mitigate that concern, the analyst may adjust the historical estimate downward based on an independent forward-looking estimate (or upward, in the case of a string of negative surprises). Many experts believe that the historical record for various major world markets has benefited from a majority of favorable circumstances that cannot be expected to be duplicated in the future; their recommended adjustments to historical mean estimates is downward. Dimson, Marsh, and Staunton (2002) have argued that historical returns have been advantaged by re-pricings as increasing scope for diversification has led to a lower level of market risk. In the case of the United States, Ibbotson and Chen (2001) recommended a 1.25 percentage point downward adjustment to the Morningstar (Ibbotson) historical mean US equity risk premium estimate based on a lower estimate from a supply-side analysis of the equity risk premium.

Example 2 illustrates difficulties in historical data that could lead to a preference for an adjusted historical or forward-looking estimate.

EXAMPLE 2

The Indian Equity Risk Premium: Historical Estimates of the Equity Risk Premium in a Developing Market[24]

Historical estimates of the equity risk premium in developing markets are often attended by a range of concerns. The case of India can serve as an example. A number of equity indexes are available and each has possible limitations. Although not as broad-based as the alternatives, the S&P BSE Sensex Index (Sensex), a market-capitalization weighted index of the shares of 30 leading companies, has the longest available record: Compiled since 1986, returns go back to 1979. Note the following facts concerning this index and other issues relevant to estimating the equity risk premium:

- The backfilled returns from 1979 to 1985 are based on the initial 30 issues selected in 1986, which were among the largest market-cap as of 1986.

- The Sensex is a price index; a total return version of the index incorporating dividends is available from 1997 forward.

- Interest rates in India were suppressed by regulation prior to 1991 and were much more volatile thereafter. The benchmark interest rate reported by the Reserve Bank of India has averaged 6.57 percent from 2000 until 2013, reaching an all-time high of 14.50 percent in August of 2000 and a record low of 4.25 percent in April of 2009. In August 2013, the rate was 7.25 percent. The post-regulation period appears to be associated with higher stock market volatility.

- In 2000, the exchange used this index to open its derivatives market via the trading of Sensex futures contracts. The development of Sensex options followed in 2001.

---

24 Jayanth R. Varma and Samir K. Barua, "A First Cut Estimate of the Equity Risk Premium in India," Indian Institute of Management Ahmedabad, Working Paper No. 2006-06-04, June 2006, is the source for most of the institutional background used in this example.

- Valuation levels have changed significantly in the last two decades. The price-to-earnings ratio for the Sensex was 45.5 in 1994 and reached a low of 13.0 in 1998. In August 2013, the price-to-earnings ratio was 17.3.
- Objective estimates of the extent of any bias can be developed.

Based only on the information given, address the following.

1 What factors could bias an unadjusted historical risk premium estimate upward?

2 What factors could bias an unadjusted historical risk premium estimate downward?

3 State and explain two indications that the historical time series is nonstationary.

4 Recommend and justify a preference for a historical or an adjusted historical equity risk premium estimate.

Solution to 1:

The backfilling of returns from 1979 to 1985 based on companies selected in 1986 could upward bias the estimate because of survivorship bias. The companies that were selected in 1986 are likely to have been among the most successful of the companies on the exchange as of 1979. Another but less clear factor is the suppression of interest rates prior to 1991. An artificially low risk-free rate would bias the equity risk premium estimate upward unless the required return on equity was smaller by an equal amount. Finally, derivative contracts on the Sensex have been available only since the early 2000s. The ability to hedge market risk may result in future equity risk premiums being lower.

Solution to 2:

The failure to incorporate the return from dividends biases the equity risk premium estimate downward. Risk premiums are also generally believed to be inversely related to valuation ratios. The price-to-earnings ratio is currently well below its 1994 level, suggesting that the historical premium estimate may be biased downward.

Solution to 3:

The different levels of interest rates before and after the lifting of regulation in 1991 is one indication that the equity risk premium pre- and post-1991 could be different and that the overall series is nonstationary. A second is the higher level of stock market volatility pre- and postregulation.

Solution to 4:

Given that objective estimates of the extent of biases can be developed, an adjusted historical estimate would be preferred because such an estimate is more likely to be unbiased and accurate.

In Example 2, one criticism that could be raised concerning any historical estimate is the shortness of the period in the data set—the post-1991 reform period—that is definitely relevant to the present. Sampling error in any mean estimate—even one based on clean data—would be a major concern for this data set; recall that the earlier discussion of a two standard deviation interval for the US equity risk premium was based on 113 years of data. The analyst might address specific concerns through an adjusted historical estimate. The analyst may also decide to investigate one or more forward-looking estimates. Forward-looking estimates are the subject of the next section. A later section on international issues will have more information on equity risk premium estimation for emerging markets such as India.

3.2 Forward-Looking Estimates

Because the equity risk premium is based only on expectations for economic and financial variables from the present going forward, it is logical to estimate the premium directly based on current information and expectations concerning such variables. Such estimates are often called forward-looking or *ex ante* estimates. In principle, such estimates may agree with, be higher, or be lower than historical equity risk premium estimates.[25] *Ex ante* estimates are likely to be less subject to an issue such as nonstationarity or data biases than historical estimates. However, such estimates are often subject to other potential errors related to financial and economic models and potential behavioral biases in forecasting.

3.2.1 *Gordon Growth Model Estimates*

Probably the most frequently encountered forward-looking estimate of the equity risk premium is based on a very simple form of a present value model called the constant growth dividend discount model or Gordon growth model, already shown as Equation 3a. For mature developed equity markets such as Eurozone, the United Kingdom, and North American markets, the assumptions of this model are often met, at least approximately. Broad-based equity indices are nearly always associated with a dividend yield, and year-ahead dividend payment may be fairly predictable. The expected dividend growth rate may be inferred based on published analyst or economic expectations, such as consensus analyst expectations of the earnings growth rate for an equity market index (which may be based on forecasts for the constituent companies or a top-down forecast). Specifically, the Gordon growth model (GGM) equity risk premium estimate is:[26]

> GGM equity risk premium estimate
>
> = Dividend yield on the index based on year-ahead aggregate forecasted
>
>   dividends and aggregate market value   **(6)**
>
>   + Consensus long-term earnings growth rate
>
>   − Current long-term government bond yield

We can illustrate with the case of the United States. As of July 2013, the dividend yield on the S&P 500 as defined in Equation 6 was approximately 2.1 percent based on a price level of the S&P 500 of 1,685.73. The consensus analyst view was that earnings on the S&P 500 would grow from a trailing amount of $91.53 to $109.09 over the next year, a 19.1 percent growth rate. However, reported earnings have grown at approximately a 7 percent rate over the last four decades.[27] We will use the 7 percent long-term average growth rate as the long-term earnings growth forecast. Dividend

---

25 Fama and French (2001) found that prior to 1950, the historical and Gordon growth model estimates for the US equity risk premium agree, but from 1950–99, the Gordon growth model estimate averages less than half the historical estimate. They attribute the difference to the effect of positive earnings surprises relative to expectations on realized returns.

26 Recent examples of the application of this model (to US markets) are Jagannathan, McGrattan, and Scherbina (2000) and Fama and French (2001). The GGM estimate has also been used in institutional research for international markets (Stux 1994). Most analysts forecast the earnings growth rate rather than the dividend growth rate, which is technically specified in theory, so we use the earnings growth rate in the expression. Given a constant dividend payout ratio, a reasonable approximation for broad equity indexes, the two growth rates should be equal.

27 www.standardandpoors.com.

growth should track earnings growth over the long term. The 20-year US government bond yield was 3.0 percent. Therefore, according to Equation 6, the Gordon growth model estimate of the US equity risk premium was 2.1% + 7.0% − 3.0% or 6.1%. Like historical estimates, Gordon growth model estimates generally change through time. For example, the risk premium estimate of 6.1 percent just given compares with a GGM estimate of 2.4 percent (computed as 1.2% + 7% − 5.8%) made in the first edition of this reading, as of the end of 2001. In the second edition of this reading, the GGM estimate was 3.9 percent (computed as 1.9% + 7.0% − 5%), as of the end of 2009.

Equation 6 is based on an assumption of earnings growth at a stable rate. An assumption of multiple earnings growth stages is more appropriate for very rapidly growing economies. Taking an equity index in such an economy, the analyst may forecast a fast growth stage for the aggregate of companies included in the index, followed by a transition stage in which growth rates decline and a mature growth stage characterized by growth at a moderate, sustainable rate. The discount rate r that equates the sum of the present values of the expected cash flows of the three stages to the current market price of the equity index defines an IRR. Letting PVFastGrowthStage(r) stand for the present value of the cash flows of the fast earnings growth stage with the present value shown as a function of the discount rate r, and using a self-explanatory notation for the present values of the other phases, the equation for IRR is as follows:

$$\text{Equity index price} = \text{PVFastGrowthStage}(r) + \text{PVTransition}(r)$$
$$+ \text{PVMatureGrowthStage}(r)$$

The IRR is computable using a spreadsheet's IRR function. Using the IRR as an estimate of the required return on equities (as described in Section 2.6), subtracting a government bond yield gives an equity risk premium estimate.

A consequence of the model underlying Equation 6, making assumptions of a constant dividend payout ratio and efficient markets, is that earnings, dividends, and prices are expected to grow at dividend growth rate, so that the P/E ratio is constant. The analyst may believe, however, that the P/E ratio will expand or contract. Some analysts make an adjustment to the estimate in Equation 6 to reflect P/E multiple expansion or contraction. From a given starting market level associated with a given level of earnings and a given P/E ratio, the return from capital appreciation cannot be greater than the earnings growth rate unless the P/E multiple expands. P/E multiple expansion can result from an increase in the earnings growth rate and/or a decrease in risk.

3.2.2 Macroeconomic Model Estimates

Using relationships between macroeconomic variables and the financial variables that figure in equity valuation models, analysts can develop equity risk premium estimates. Such models may be more reliable when public equities represent a relatively large share of the economy, as in many developed markets. Many such analyses focus on the supply-side variables that fuel gross domestic product (GDP) growth (and are thus known as supply-side estimates). The Gordon growth model estimate, when based on a top-down economic analysis rather than using consensus analyst estimates, can be viewed as a supply-side estimate.[28]

To illustrate a supply-side analysis, the total return to equity can be analyzed into four components as explained by Ibbotson and Chen:[29]

- expected inflation: EINFL;

---

[28] Demand-side models estimate the equity risk premium based on estimates of investors' average risk aversion and the correlation of asset returns with changes in consumption. Such models are rarely encountered in professional practice, however.

[29] This is based on Ibbotson and Chen's (2003) method 3, the earnings method.

- expected growth rate in real earnings per share: EGREPS;
- expected growth rate in the P/E ratio (the ratio of share price to earnings per share): EGPE; and
- expected income component (including return from reinvestment of income): EINC.

The growth in P/E arises as a factor from a decomposition of the capital appreciation portion of returns.[30] So,

$$\text{Equity risk premium} = \left\{\left[(1 + \text{EINFL})(1 + \text{EGREPS})(1 + \text{EGPE}) - 1.0\right]\right. + \left.\text{EINC}\right\} - \text{Expected risk-free return}$$ (7)

In the following we illustrate this type of analysis using data for US equity markets as represented by the S&P 500.

- *Expected inflation.* A market forecast is available from the US treasury and US treasury inflation protected securities (TIPS) yield curve:

$$\text{Implicit inflation forecast} \approx \frac{1 + \text{YTM of 20-year maturity T-bonds}}{1 + \text{YTM of 20-year maturity TIPS}} - 1$$

$$= \frac{1.03}{1.0098} - 1$$

$$= 0.020 \text{ or } 2.0 \text{ percent.}$$

We will use an estimate of 2.0 percent per year, consistent with the TIPS analysis and other long-term forecasts. So, 1 + EINFL = 1.02.

- *Expected growth in real earnings per share.* This quantity should approximately track the real GDP growth rate. An adjustment upward or downward to the real GDP growth rate can be made for any expected differential growth between the companies represented in the equity index being used to represent the stock market and the overall economy.

  According to economic theory, the real GDP growth rate should equal the sum of labor productivity growth and the labor supply growth rate (which can be estimated as the sum of the population growth rate and the increase in the labor force participation rate). A forecasted 2 percent per year US labor productivity growth rate and 1 percent per year labor supply growth rate produces a 3 percent overall real GDP growth rate estimate of 3 percent. So, 1 + EGREPS = 1.03.

- *Expected growth in the P/E ratio.* The baseline value for this factor is zero, reflecting an efficient markets view. When the analyst views a current P/E level as reflecting overvaluation or undervaluation, however, a negative or positive value, respectively, can be used, reflecting the analyst's investment time horizon. So, without presenting a case for misevaluation, 1 + EGPE = 1.

- *Expected income component.* Historically, for US markets the long-term value has been close to 4.5 percent (including reinvestment return of 20 bps).[31] However, the current S&P 500 dividend yield is below the long-term average. A forward looking estimate based on the forward expected dividend yield of 2.1 percent and 10 bps reinvestment return is 2.2 percent. So, EINC = 0.022.

---

30 That is, $(P_t/P_{t-1}) - 1.0 = [(P_t/E_t)/(P_{t-1}/E_{t-1})](E_t/E_{t-1}) - 1.0 = (1 + \text{EGPE})(1 + \text{EGREPS}) - 1.0$.
31 See Ibbotson and Chen (2003), p. 90.

Using the Ibbotson–Chen format and a risk-free rate of 3 percent, an estimate of the US equity risk premium estimate is

$$\left\{\left[(1.02)(1.03)(1) - 1.0\right] + 0.022\right\} - 0.03 = 0.0726 - 0.03 = 4.26\%$$

The supply side estimate of 4.26 percent is very close to the historical geometric mean estimate of 4.2 percent (see Exhibit 1).[32]

3.2.3 Survey Estimates

One way to gauge expectations is to ask people what they expect. Survey estimates of the equity risk premium involve asking a sample of people—frequently, experts—about their expectations for it, or for capital market expectations from which the premium can be inferred.

For example, Fernandez, Aguirreamalloa, and L. Corres (2011) compared equity risk premium estimates for analysts, companies, and academics in the United States. The average estimate of analysts was lowest at 5.0 percent, followed by companies at 5.5 percent, and academics at 5.6 percent.

The monograph *Rethinking the Equity Risk Premium* (Hammond, Leibowitz, and Siegel, 2011) included the opinion of many financial experts regarding the future US equity risk premium. The range of equity risk premium estimates was 2.5 percent to 6.0 percent, with a mean forecast of about 3.25 percent.

THE REQUIRED RETURN ON EQUITY

4

With means to estimate the equity risk premium in hand, the analyst can estimate the required return on the equity of a particular issuer. The choices include the following:

- the CAPM;
- a multifactor model such as the Fama–French or related models; and
- a build-up method, such as the bond yield plus risk premium method.

4.1 The Capital Asset Pricing Model

The CAPM is an equation for required return that should hold in **equilibrium** (the condition in which supply equals demand) if the model's assumptions are met; among the key assumptions are that investors are risk averse and that they make investment decisions based on the mean return and variance of returns of their total portfolio. The chief insight of the model is that investors evaluate the risk of an asset in terms of the asset's contribution to the systematic risk of their total portfolio (systematic risk is risk that cannot be shed by portfolio diversification). Because the CAPM provides an economically grounded and relatively objective procedure for required return estimation, it has been widely used in valuation.

---

32 Strictly speaking, standard errors apply only to the arithmetic mean; but as an approximate guide to "closeness," they have also been applied to the geometric mean. See Dimson, Marsh, and Staunton (2002), p. 168.

The expression for the CAPM that is used in practice was given earlier as Equation 4:[33]

Required return on share i = Current expected risk-free return +
$$\beta_1(\text{Equity risk premium})$$

For example, if the current expected risk-free return is 3 percent, the asset's beta is 1.20, and the equity risk premium is 4.5 percent, then the asset's required return is

Required return on share i = 0.030 + 1.20(0.045) = 0.084 or 8.4 percent

The asset's beta measures its market or systematic risk, which in theory is the sensitivity of its returns to the returns on the "market portfolio" of risky assets. Concretely, beta equals the covariance of returns with the returns on the market portfolio divided by the market portfolio's variance of returns. In typical practice for equity valuation, the market portfolio is represented by a broad value-weighted equity market index. The asset's beta is estimated by a least squares regression of the asset's returns on the index's returns and is available also from many vendors. In effect, in Equation 4 the analyst is adjusting the equity risk premium up or down for the asset's level of systematic risk by multiplying it by the asset's beta, adding that asset-specific risk premium to the current expected risk-free return to obtain a required return estimate.

In the typical case in which the equity risk premium is based on a national equity market index and estimated beta is based on sensitivity to that index, the assumption is being made implicitly that equity prices are largely determined by *local* investors. When equities markets are *segmented* in that sense (i.e., local market prices are largely determined by local investors rather than by investors worldwide), two issues with the same risk characteristics can have different required returns if they trade in different markets.

The opposite assumption is that all investors worldwide participate equally in setting prices (perfectly integrated markets). That assumption results in the international CAPM (or world CAPM) in which the risk premium is relative to a world market portfolio. Taking an equity view of the market portfolio, the world equity risk premium can be estimated historically based on the MSCI World index (returns available from 1970), for example, or indirectly as the (US equity risk premium estimate)/(beta of US stocks relative to MSCI World) = 4.5%/0.81 = 5.6%. Computing beta relative to MSCI World and using a national risk-free interest rate, the analyst can obtain international CAPM estimates of required return. In practice, the international CAPM is not commonly relied on for required return on equity estimation.[34]

---

33 Formally, the CAPM is $E(R_i) = R_F + \beta_i[E(R_M) - R_F]$ where $E(R_i)$ is asset i's expected return in equilibrium given its beta, equal to its required return, R_F is the risk-free rate of return, and $E(R_M)$ is the expected return on the market portfolio. In theory, the market portfolio is defined to include all risky assets held according to their market value weights. In typical practice when applying the CAPM to value equities, a broad equity index is used to represent the market portfolio and an estimate of the equity risk premium is used for $E(R_M) - R_F$.

34 Other methods appear to give more plausible estimates in practice. See Morningstar (2007), pp. 177–179, 184. One variation on the international CAPM, called the Singer–Terhaar method, that does find use in professional practice, particularly for asset classes, is discussed in Calverley, Meder, Singer, and Staub (2007); this approach involves taking a weighted average of domestic and international CAPM estimates.

4.1.1 *Beta Estimation for a Public Company*

The simplest estimate of beta results from an ordinary least squares regression of the return on the stock on the return on the market. The result is often called an unadjusted or "raw" historical beta. The actual values of beta estimates are influenced by several choices:

- *The choice of the index used to represent the market portfolio.* For a number of markets there are traditional choices. For US equities, the S&P 500 and NYSE Composite have been traditional choices.

- *The length of data period and the frequency of observations.* The most common choice is five years of monthly data, yielding 60 observations

> (a number of vendors including Morningstar and Compustat make that choice). Value Line uses five years of weekly observations. The Bloomberg default is two years of weekly observations, which can be changed at the user's option. One study of US stocks found support for five years of monthly data over alternatives.[35] An argument can be made that the Bloomberg default can be especially appropriate in fast growing markets.

The beta value in a future period has been found to be on average closer to the mean value of 1.0, the beta of an average-systematic-risk security, than to the value of the raw beta. Because valuation is forward looking, it is logical to adjust the raw beta so it more accurately predicts a future beta. The most commonly used adjustment was introduced by Blume (1971):

$$\text{Adjusted beta} = (2/3)(\text{Unadjusted beta}) + (1/3)(1.0) \qquad \textbf{(8)}$$

For example, if the beta from a regression of an asset's returns on the market return is 1.30, adjusted beta is (2/3)(1.30) + (1/3)(1.0) = 1.20. Vendors of financial information often report raw and adjusted beta estimates together. Although most vendors use the Blume adjustment, some do not. For example, Morningstar (Ibbotson) adjusts raw beta toward the peer mean value (rather than toward the overall mean value of 1.0). The analyst of course needs to understand the basis behind the presentation of any data that he or she uses.

The following examples apply the CAPM to estimate the required return on equity.

EXAMPLE 3

An Analyst Case Study (2): The Required Return on Larsen & Toubro Shares

While Weeramantry has been researching Microsoft, his colleague Delacour has been investigating the required return on Larsen & Toubro Ltd. shares (BSE: 500510, NSE: LT).[36] Larsen & Toubro Ltd. is the largest India-based engineering and construction company. Calling up the beta function for LT on her Bloomberg terminal on 31 July 2013, Delacour sees the screen shown in Exhibit 3.

---

35 Bartholdy and Peare (2003).
36 BSE: Bombay Stock Exchange; NSE: National Stock Exchange. The Bloomberg reference for the company is LT IN whereas the Reuters reference is LART.BO.

Exhibit 3   A Bloomberg Screen for Beta Larsen & Toubro Ltd.

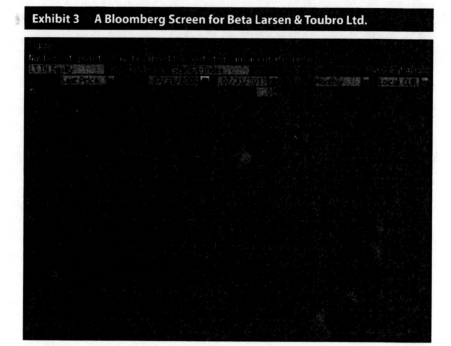

Delacour notes that Bloomberg has chosen the Sensex as the equity index for estimating beta. Delacour changes the Bloomberg default for time period/ frequency to the specification shown in the exhibit for consistency with her other estimation work; in doing so, she notes approvingly that the beta estimate is approximately the same at both horizons.

Raw beta, 1.537, is the slope of the regression line running through the scatterplot of 60 points denoting the return on LT (y-axis) for different returns on the Sensex (x-axis); a bar graph of the distribution of returns in local currency terms is superimposed over the x-axis.

Noting from R^2 that beta explains more than 73 percent of variation in LT returns—an exceptionally good fit—Delacour also decides to use the CAPM to estimate LT stock's required return.[37] Delacour has decided to use her own adjusted historical estimate of 4.0 percent for the Indian equity risk premium and the 10-year Indian government bond yield of 8.7 percent as the risk-free rate.[38] Delacour notes that a 8.7 percent yield is shown on the Bloomberg cost of capital screen for LT (as the "bond rate") and that the same screen shows an estimate of the Indian equity risk premium ("country premium") of 3.3 percent—close to her own estimate of 4.0 percent.

Based only on the information given, address the following:

1 Demonstrate the calculation of adjusted beta using the Blume method.

---

[37] The Bloomberg screen interprets R^2 as "correlation." More precisely, in a univariate regression as here, it is equivalent to the squared correlation between the dependent (stock return) and independent (market return) variables. It is interpreted as the fraction of the variation in the dependent variable explained by the independent variable.

[38] Varma and Barua (2006) estimated a historical geometric mean equity risk premium of 8.75 percent for Indian equities using their own database. This was adjusted downward by 1.7 percentage points based on a supply-side analysis. Some estimates of the Indian equity risk premium, e.g., country risk rating estimates, are much higher.

2 Estimate the required return on LT using the CAPM with an adjusted beta.

3 Explain one fact from the Bloomberg screen as evidence that beta has been estimated with accuracy.

Solution to 1:

The calculation for adjusted beta is (2/3)(1.537) + (1/3)(1.0) = 1.358.

Solution to 2:

r = 8.7% + 1.358(4%) = 14.1 percent.

Solution to 3:

The standard error of beta at 0.121 is relatively small in relation to the magnitude of the raw estimate, 1.537.

EXAMPLE 4

Calculating the Required Return on Equity Using the CAPM (1)

Exxon Mobil Corporation, BP p.l.c., and Total S.A. are three "super major" integrated oil and gas companies headquartered, respectively, in the United States, the United Kingdom, and France. An analyst estimates that the equity risk premium in the United States, the United Kingdom, and the Eurozone are, respectively, 4.5 percent, 4.1 percent, and 4.0 percent. Other information is summarized in Exhibit 4.

Exhibit 4   Exxon Mobil, BP, and Total

Company	Beta	Estimated Equity Risk Premium	Risk-Free Rate
Exxon Mobil Corp (NYSE: XOM)	0.77	4.5%	3.20%
BP p.l.c. (LSE SETS: BP, NYSE: BP)	1.99	4.1	3.56
Total S.A. (Euronext: FR0000120271, NYSE: TOT)	1.53	4.0	2.46

Sources: Financial Times, Yahoo.

Using the capital asset pricing model, calculate the required return on equity for

1 Exxon Mobil.

2 BP p.l.c.

3 Total.

Solution to 1:

The required return on Exxon Mobil according to the CAPM is 3.20% + 0.77(4.50%) = 6.67 percent.

Solution to 2:

The required return on BP according to the CAPM is 3.56% + 1.99(4.10%) = 11.72 percent.

Solution to 3:

The required return on Total stock according to the CAPM is 2.46% + 1.53(4.0) = 8.58 percent.

EXAMPLE 5

Calculating the Required Return on Equity Using the CAPM (2): Non-Traded Asset Case

Jill Adams is an analyst at a hedge fund that has been offered an equity stake in a privately held US property and liability insurer. Adams identifies Alleghany Corporation (NYSE: Y) as a publicly traded comparable company, and intends to use information about Alleghany in evaluating the offer. One sell-side analyst that Adams contacts puts Alleghany's required return on equity at 10.0 percent. Researching the required return herself, Adams determines that Alleghany has the historical betas shown in Exhibit 5 as of late August 2007:

Exhibit 5 Alleghany Corporation: Historical Betas	
5-Year Beta	**10-Year Beta**
0.56	0.40

Source: Reuters.

The estimated US equity risk premium (relative to bonds) is 4.20 percent. The YTM for:

- 91-day US Treasury bills is 0.03 percent.
- 2-year US government bonds is 3 percent.

Adams follows the most common industry practices concerning time period for estimating beta and adjustments to beta.

1 Estimate Alleghany Corporation's adjusted beta and required return based on the CAPM.

2 Is the sell-side analyst's estimate of 10 percent for Alleghany's cost of equity *most* consistent with Alleghany shares having above-average or below-average systematic risk?

Solution to 1:

Adjusted beta = (2/3)(0.56) + (1/3) = 0.707 or 0.71. Using a five-year horizon for calculating beta is the most common practice. Consistent with the definition of the equity risk premium, a long-bond yield is used in the CAPM: 3.00% + 0.71(4.20%) = 5.982% or 6.0 percent, approximately.

Solution to 2:

The analyst's estimate implies above-average systematic risk. A beta of 1 by definition represents the beta of the market and so shares of average systematic risk. A beta of 1 implies a required return of 3.00% + 1.0(4.20%) = 7.2% or 7.2 percent.

When a share issue trades infrequently, the most recent transaction price may be stale and not reflect underlying changes in value. If beta is estimated based on, for example, a monthly data series in which missing values are filled with the most recent transaction price, the estimated beta will be too small and the required return on equity will be underestimated. There are several econometric techniques that can be used to estimate the beta of infrequently traded securities.[39] A practical alternative is to base the beta estimate on the beta of a comparable security.

4.1.2 *Beta Estimation for Thinly Traded Stocks and Nonpublic Companies*

Analysts do not have access to a series of market price observations for nonpublic companies with which to calculate a regression estimate of beta. However, using an industry classification system such as the MSCI/Standard & Poor's Global Industry Classification Standard (GICS) or the FTSE Industry Classification Benchmark (ICB) to identify publicly traded peer companies, the analyst can estimate indirectly the beta of the nonpublic company on the basis of the public peer's beta.

The procedure must take into account the effect on beta of differences in financial leverage between the nonpublic company and the benchmark. First, the benchmark beta is unlevered to estimate the beta of the benchmark's assets—reflecting just the systematic risk arising from the economics of the industry. Then, the asset beta is re-levered to reflect the financial leverage of the nonpublic company.

Let β_E be the equity beta before removing the effects of leverage, if any. This is the benchmark beta. If the debt of the benchmark is high quality (so an assumption that the debt's beta is zero should be approximately true), analysts can use the following expression for unleveraging the beta:[40]

$$\beta_U \approx \left[\frac{1}{1 + (D/E)}\right]\beta_E \tag{9a}$$

Then, if the subject company has debt and equity levels D′ and E′, respectively, and assuming the subject company's debt is high grade, the subject company's equity beta, β'_E, is estimated as follows:

$$\beta'_E \approx \left[1 + (D'/E')\right]\beta_U \tag{9b}$$

Expressions 9a and 9b hold under the assumption that the level of debt adjusts to the target capital structure weight as total firm value changes, consistent with the definition for the weighted average cost of capital that will be presented later.[41] Exhibit 6 summarizes the steps.

---

39 See Elton, Gruber, Brown, and Goetzmann (2006) for a summary of the methods of Scholes and Williams (1977) and Dimson (1979).

40 Equation 9a comes from the expression $\beta_U \approx [1 + (D/E)]^{-1}[\beta_E + (D/E)\beta_D]$, making the assumption that $\beta_D = 0$. The expression in this footnote can be used when the debt's beta is known to be definitely non-zero.

41 See Miles and Ezzell (1985). Another expression (the one usually presented by textbooks) is appropriate under the typically less plausible assumption that the level of debt is constant from period to period: Still assuming the beta of debt is zero, the correct expression to unlever is then $\beta_U = [1 + (1 - t)(D/E)]^{-1} \beta_E$ and re-leveraging is done using $\beta_E = [1 + (1 - t)(D'/E')]\beta_U$ as shown by Hamada (1972). See Arzac (2005) for a more detailed presentation.

Exhibit 6	Estimating a Beta for a Non-Traded Company

Step 1
Select the benchmark (comparable)
⬇
Step 2
Estimate benchmark's beta
⬇
Step 3
Unlever the benchmark's beta
⬇
Step 4
Lever the beta to reflect the
subject company's financial leverage

To illustrate, suppose that a benchmark company is identified (Step 1) that is 40 percent funded by debt. By contrast, the weight of debt in the subject company's capital structure is only 20 percent. The benchmark's beta is estimated at 1.2 (Step 2). The 40 percent weight of debt in the benchmark implies that the weight of equity is 100% – 40% = 60 percent. Unlevering the benchmark beta (Step 3):

$$\beta_U \approx \left[\frac{1}{1+(D/E)}\right]\beta_E = \left[\frac{1}{1+(40/60)}\right]1.2 = 0.6 \times 1.2 = 0.72$$

Next, the unlevered beta of 0.72 is re-levered according to the financial leverage of the subject company, which uses 20 percent debt and 80 percent equity:

$$\beta'_E \approx \left[1+(D'/E')\right]\beta_U = \left[1+(20/80)\right]0.72 = 1.25 \times 0.72 = 0.90$$

Sometimes, instead of using an individual company as a benchmark, the required return will be benchmarked on a median or average industry beta. A process of unlevering and re-levering can be applied to such a beta based on the median or average industry capital structure.

EXAMPLE 6

Calculating the Required Return on Equity Using the CAPM (3)

Adams turns to determining a beta for use in evaluating the offer of an equity stake in a private insurer and rounds her beta estimate of Alleghany, the public comparable, to 0.70. As of the valuation date, Alleghany Corporation has no debt in its capital structure. The private insurer is 20 percent funded by debt.

If a beta of 0.70 is assumed for the comparable, what is the estimated beta of the private insurer?

Solution:

Because Alleghany does not use debt, its beta does not have to be unlevered. For the private insurer, if debt is 20 percent of capital then equity is 80 percent of capital and D'/E' = 20/80 = 0.25. Therefore, the estimate of the private insurer's equity beta is (1.25)(0.70) = 0.875 or 0.88.

The CAPM is a simple, widely accepted, theory-based method of estimating the cost of equity. Beta, its measure of risk, is readily obtainable for a wide range of securities from a variety of sources and can be estimated easily when not available from a vendor. In portfolios, the idiosyncratic risk of individual securities tends to offset against each other leaving largely beta (market) risk. For individual securities, idiosyncratic risk can overwhelm market risk and, in that case, beta may be a poor predictor of future average return. Thus the analyst needs to have multiple tools available.

4.2 Multifactor Models

A substantial amount of evidence has accumulated that the CAPM beta describes risk incompletely. In practice, coefficients of determination (R-squared) for individual stocks' beta regressions may range from 2 percent to 40 percent, with many under 10 percent. For many markets, evidence suggests that multiple factors drive returns. At the cost of greater complexity and expense, the analyst can consider a model for required return based on multiple factors. Greater complexity does not ensure greater explanatory power, however, and any selected multifactor model should be examined for the value it is adding.

Whereas the CAPM adds a single risk premium to the risk-free rate, arbitrage pricing theory (APT) models add a set of risk premia. APT models are based on a multifactor representation of the drivers of return. Formally, APT models express the required return on an asset as follows:

$$r = R_F + (\text{Risk premium})_1 + (\text{Risk premium})_2 + \dots$$
$$+ (\text{Risk premium})_K \tag{10}$$

where $(\text{Risk premium})_i = (\text{Factor sensitivity})_i \times (\text{Factor risk premium})_i$. **Factor sensitivity** or **factor beta** is the asset's sensitivity to a particular factor (holding all other factors constant). In general, the **factor risk premium** for factor i is the expected return in excess of the risk-free rate accruing to an asset with unit sensitivity to factor i and zero sensitivity to all other factors.[42]

One of the best known models based on multiple factors expands upon the CAPM with two additional factors. That model, the Fama–French model, is discussed next.

4.2.1 The Fama–French Model

By the end of the 1980s, empirical evidence had accumulated that, at least over certain long time periods, in the US and several other equity markets, investment strategies biased toward small-market capitalization securities and/or value might generate higher returns over the long-run than the CAPM predicts.[43]

In 1993, researchers Eugene Fama and Kenneth French addressed these perceived weaknesses of the CAPM in a model with three factors, known as the Fama–French model (FFM). The FFM is among the most widely known non-proprietary multifactor models. The factors are:

- RMRF, standing for $R_M - R_F$, the return on a market value-weighted equity index in excess of the one-month T-bill rate—this is one way the equity risk premium can be represented and is the factor shared with the CAPM.

---

[42] In the case of the Fama–French model, however, the premiums of two factors are not stated as quantities in excess of the risk-free rate.

[43] For example, Fama and French (1993) and Strong and Xu (1997) documented size and book-to-market premiums for the United States and the United Kingdom, respectively. Capaul, Rowley, and Sharpe (1993) and Chen and Zhang (1998) documented a value premium in developed markets internationally.

- SMB (small minus big), a size (market capitalization) factor. SMB is the average return on three small-cap portfolios minus the average return on three large-cap portfolios. Thus SMB represents a small-cap return premium.

- HML (high minus low), the average return on two high book-to-market portfolios minus the average return on two low book-to-market portfolios.[44] With high book-to-market (equivalently, low price-to-book) shares representing a value bias and low book-to-market representing a growth bias, in general, HML represents a value return premium.

Each of the factors can be viewed as the mean return to a zero–net investment, long–short portfolio. SMB represents the mean return to shorting large-cap shares and investing the proceeds in small-cap shares; HML is the mean return from shorting low book-to-market (high P/B) shares and investing the proceeds in high book-to-market shares. The FFM estimate of the required return is:

$$r_i = R_F + \beta_i^{mkt}RMRF + \beta_i^{size}SMB + \beta_i^{value}HML \qquad\qquad (11)$$

Historical data on the factors are publicly available for at least 24 countries.[45] The historical approach is frequently used in estimating the risk premia of this model. The definitions of RMRF, SMB, and HML have a specificity that lends itself to such estimation. Nevertheless, the range of estimation approaches discussed earlier could also be applied to estimating the FFM factors. Note the definition of RMRF in terms of a short-term rate; available historical series are in terms of a premium over a short-term government debt rate. In using Equation 11, we would take a current short-term risk-free rate. Note as well that because other factors besides the market factor are included in Equation 11, the beta on the market in Equation 11 is generally not exactly the same value as the CAPM beta for a given stock.

We can illustrate the FFM using the case of the US equity market. Assume the short-term interest rate is 0.03 percent. Historical market, size, and value premiums based on Fama–French data from 1926 to 2012 are 5.9 percent, 2.6 percent, and 4.1 percent, respectively. However, over the last quarter century (1986 to 2012) the realized SMB premium has averaged 0.3 percent and the realized HML premium has averaged 2.7 percent while the average RMRF has remained at 5.9 percent. Thus, based on risk premiums for the last 25 years, one estimate of the FFM expected return for the US market as of year-end 2012 is:

$$r_i = 0.0003 + \beta_i^{mkt}0.059 + \beta_i^{size}0.003 + \beta_i^{value}0.027$$

Consider the case of a small-cap issue with value characteristics and above-average market risk—assume the FFM market beta is 1.20. If the issue's market capitalization is small, we expect it to have a positive size beta; for example, $\beta_i^{size} = 0.5$. If the shares sell cheaply in relation to book equity (i.e., they have a high book-to-market ratio), the value beta is also expected to be positive; for example, $\beta_i^{value} = 0.8$. For both the size and value betas, zero is the neutral value, in contrast with the market beta, where the neutral value is 1. Thus, according to the FFM, the shares' required return is close to 10 percent:

$$r_i = 0.0003 + 1.20(0.059) + 0.5(0.003) + 0.8(0.027) = 0.0942$$

---

44 See http://mba.tuck.dartmouth.edu/pages/faculty/ken.french/ for more information on the Fama–French model and factor data information.

45 The countries include Australia, Austria, Belgium, Canada, Denmark, Finland, France, Germany, Hong Kong, Ireland, Italy, Japan, Malaysia, Netherlands, New Zealand, Norway, Singapore, Spain, Sweden, Switzerland, the United Kingdom, and the United States. See http://mba.tuck.dartmouth.edu/pages/faculty/ken.french/ for more information on the Fama–French model and factor data information.

The FFM market beta of 1.2 could be above or below the CAPM beta, but for this comparison, suppose it is 1.20. The CAPM estimate would be 0.0003 + 1.20(0.059) = 0.0711 or less by about 9.42 − 7.11, or 2.31 percentage points. In this case, positive size and value exposures help account for the different estimates in the two models.

Returning to the specification of the FFM to discuss its interpretation, note that the FFM factors are of two types:

- an equity market factor, which is identified with systematic risk as in the CAPM; and
- two factors related to company characteristics and valuation, size (SMB) and value (HML).

The FFM views the size and value factors as representing ("proxying for") a set of underlying risk factors. For example, small market-cap companies may be subject to risk factors such as less ready access to private and public credit markets and competitive disadvantages. High book-to-market may represent shares with depressed prices because of exposure to financial distress. The FFM views the return premiums to small size and value as compensation for bearing types of systematic risk. Many practitioners and researchers believe, however, that those return premiums arise from market inefficiencies rather than compensation for systematic risk.[46]

EXAMPLE 7

An Analyst Case Study (3): The Required Return on Microsoft Shares

Weeramantry's next task in researching Microsoft shares is to estimate a required return on equity (which is also a required return on total capital because Microsoft has no long-term debt). Weeramantry uses an equally weighted average of the CAPM and FFM estimates unless one method appears to be superior as judged by more than a five point difference in adjusted R^2; in that case, only the estimate with superior explanatory power is used. Exhibit 7 shows the cost of equity information for Microsoft Corporation. All the beta estimates in Exhibit 7 are significant at the 5 percent level.

Exhibit 7	CAPM and FFM Required Return Estimates, Microsoft Corporation	
	Model A	**Model B**
1) Current risk- free rate	0.03%	0.03%
2) Beta	0.93	0.96
3) Market (equity) risk premium	5.9%	5.9%
Premium for stock: (2) × (3) =	5.49%	5.66%
4) Size beta	—	−0.17
5) Size Premium (SMB)	—	2.6%
Premium for stock: (4) × (5) =	—	−0.44%
6) Value beta	—	−0.15
7) Value Premium	—	4.1%
Premium for stock: (6) × (7) =	—	−0.62%

(continued)

---

[46] Lakonishok, Shleifer, and Vishny (1994) and La Porta, Lakonishok, Shleifer, and Vishny (1997).

	Model A	Model B
Exhibit 7 (Continued)		
R^2	0.54	0.55
Adjusted R^2	0.53	0.52

Sources: http://mba.tuck.dartmouth.edu/pages/faculty/ken.french/data_library.html for size and value historical premia data (1926–2012) and Morningstar Ibbotson, The Cost of Capital Resources (March 2013 report for Microsoft) for CAPM and FFM betas and R^2.

Weeramantry's and Delacour's fund holds positions for 4 years on average. Weeramantry and his colleague Delacour are apprised that their firm's economic unit expects that the marketplace will favor growth-oriented equities over the coming year. Reviewing all the information, Delacour makes the following statements:

■ "Microsoft's cost of equity benefits from the company's above average market capitalization."

■ "If our economic unit's analysis is correct, growth-oriented portfolios are expected to outperform value-oriented portfolios over the next year. As a consequence, we should favor the CAPM required return estimate over the Fama–French estimate."

Using only the above information, address the following.

1 Estimate Microsoft's cost of equity using the:

   A   CAPM.

   B   Fama–French model.

2 Judge whether Delacour's first statement, concerning Microsoft's cost of equity, is accurate.

3 Judge whether Delacour's second statement, concerning the expected relative performance of growth-oriented portfolios and the use of the CAPM and FFM required return estimates, is correct.

Solution to 1:

A   The required return according to the CAPM is 0.03% + 0.93(5.9%) = 0.03% + 5.49% = 5.52%

B   The required return according to the FFM is 0.03% + 0.96(5.9%) + (−0.17)(2.6%) + (−0.15)(4.1%) = 0.03% + 5.66% + (−0.44%) + (−0.62%) = 4.63 percent.

Solution to 2:

The statement is accurate. The SMB premium is positive and Microsoft has negative exposure to it, resulting in the required return estimate being lower by 440 bps.

Solution to 3:

The statement is incorrect. It suggests that computing a required return using a positive value premium is questionable when the investor short-term forecast is for growth to outperform value. Required return estimates should reflect the expected or long-run compensation for risk. The positive value of the value premium in the FFM reflects expected compensation for bearing risk over the long run, consistent with the company's cash flows extending out to the indefinite future. The economic unit's prediction for a short-term time horizon does not invalidate the use of a positive value premium for the Fama–French model.

The regression fit statistics for both the CAPM and FFM in Example 7 were high. There is more to learn about the relative merits of the CAPM and FFM in practice, but the FFM appears to have the potential for being a practical addition to the analyst's toolkit. One study contrasting the CAPM and FFM for US markets found that whereas differences in the CAPM beta explained on average 3 percent of the cross-sectional differences in returns of the stocks over the next year, the FFM betas explained on average 5 percent of the differences.[47] Neither performance appears to be impressive, but keep in mind that equity returns are subject to a very high degree of randomness over short horizons.

4.2.2 Extensions to the Fama–French Model

The thought process behind the FFM of extending the CAPM to capture observed patterns in equity returns that differences in the CAPM beta appear not to explain has been extended by other researchers. One well-established relationship is that investors demand a return premium for assets that are relatively illiquid—assets that cannot be quickly sold in quantity without high explicit or implicit transaction costs. Pastor and Stambaugh (2003) extended the FFM to encompass compensation for the degree of liquidity of an equity investment.

This model has been applied to public security investment as well as certain private security investments.[48] The Pastor–Stambaugh model (PSM) adds to the FFM a fourth factor, LIQ, representing the excess returns to a portfolio that invests the proceeds from shorting high-liquidity stocks in a portfolio of low-liquidity stocks:

$$r_i = R_F + \beta_i^{mkt} RMRF + \beta_i^{size} SMB + \beta_i^{value} HML + \beta_i^{liq} LIQ \qquad (12)$$

An estimate of the liquidity premium for US equity markets is 4.5 percent.[49] An estimate of the PSM model for US markets is:

$$r_i = 0.003 + \beta_i^{mkt} 0.059 + \beta_i^{size} 0.003 + \beta_i^{value} 0.027 + \beta_i^{liq} 0.045$$

An average-liquidity equity should have a liquidity beta of 0, with no impact on required return. But below-average liquidity (positive liquidity beta) and above-average liquidity (negative liquidity beta) will tend to increase and decrease required return, respectively.

EXAMPLE 8

The Required Return for a Common Stock Investment

A common stock has the following characteristics:

Market beta	1.50
Size beta	0.15
Value beta	−0.52
Liquidity beta	0.20

Based only on the information given, infer the style characteristics of the above common stock issue.

---

47 Bartholdy and Peare (2003).
48 See Metrick (2007).
49 Metrick (2007), pp. 77–78, applied the PSM to venture capital fund investment.

Solution:

The issue appears to be small-cap and have a growth orientation. The positive size beta indicates sensitivity to small-cap returns as would characterize small-cap stocks. (A positive liquidity beta, as shown, would also be typical for small-cap stocks because they usually trade in less liquid markets than do large-cap stocks.) The negative value beta indicates a growth orientation.

The concept of liquidity may be distinguished from marketability. With reference to equities, liquidity relates to the ease and potential price impact of the sale of an equity interest into the market. Liquidity is a function of several factors including the size of the interest and the depth and breadth of the market and its ability to absorb a block (i.e., a large position) without an adverse price impact. In the strictest sense, marketability relates to the right to sell an asset.

Barring securities law or other contractual restrictions, all equity interests are potentially marketable, i.e., they can be potentially marketed for sale in the sense of the existence of a market into which the security can be sold. However, in private business valuation, the two terms are often used interchangeably.[50] The typical treatment in that context is to take a discount for lack of marketability (liquidity) from the value estimate, where justified,[51] rather than incorporate the effect in the discount rate, as in the PSM.

4.2.3 *Macroeconomic and Statistical Multifactor Models*

The FFM and PSM are examples of one type of a range of models for required return that are based on multiple fundamental factors (factors that are attributes of the stocks or companies themselves, e.g., the price-to-earnings ratio for a share or the company's financial leverage); the group includes several proprietary models as well. Models for required return have also been based on macroeconomic and statistical factors.

- In macroeconomic factor models the factors are economic variables that affect the expected future cash flows of companies and/or the discount rate that is appropriate to determining their present values.

- In statistical factor models, statistical methods are applied to historical returns to determine portfolios of securities (serving as factors) that explain those returns in various senses.

A specific example of macroeconomic factor models is the five-factor BIRR model, presented in Burmeister, Roll, and Ross (1994), with factor definitions as follows:

1 Confidence risk: the unanticipated change in the return difference between risky corporate bonds and government bonds, both with maturities of 20 years. To explain the factor's name, when their confidence is high, investors are willing to accept a smaller reward for bearing the added risk of corporate bonds.

2 Time horizon risk: the unanticipated change in the return difference between 20-year government bonds and 30-day Treasury bills. This factor reflects investors' willingness to invest for the long term.

3 Inflation risk: the unexpected change in the inflation rate. Nearly all stocks have negative exposure to this factor, as their returns decline with positive surprises in inflation.

---

50 Hitchner (2006), p. 390.
51 See Hitchner (2006), pp. 390–391.

4 Business cycle risk: the unexpected change in the level of real business activity. A positive surprise or unanticipated change indicates that the expected growth rate of the economy, measured in constant dollars, has increased.

5 Market timing risk: The portion of the total return of an equity market proxy (e.g., the S&P 500 for the United States) that remains unexplained by the first four risk factors. Almost all stocks have positive sensitivity to this factor.

The fifth factor acknowledges the uncertainty surrounding the correct set of underlying variables for asset pricing; this factor captures influences on the returns to the market proxy not explained by the first four factors. For example, using such a model, the required return for a security could have the form

r_i = T-bill rate + (Sensitivity to confidence risk × 2.59%) − (Sensitivity to time horizon risk × 0.66%) − (Sensitivity to inflation risk × 4.32%) + (Sensitivity to business-cycle risk × 1.49%) + (Sensitivity to market-timing risk × 3.61%)

where the risk premia estimates are developed using econometric techniques referenced in Burmeister, et al. (1994). Similar to models based on fundamental factors, models based on macroeconomic and statistical factors have various proprietary implementations.

4.3 Build-Up Method Estimates of the Required Return on Equity

Widely used by valuators of closely held businesses, the build-up method estimates the required return on an equity investment as the sum of the risk-free rate and a set of risk premia:

r_i = Risk-free rate + Equity risk premium ± One or more premia (discounts)

The build-up method parallels the risk premium approach embodied in multifactor models with the difference that specific beta adjustments are not applied to factor risk premiums.

4.3.1 Build-Up Approaches for Private Business Valuation

The need for estimates of the required return on the equity of a private business arises when present value models—known in such contexts as income models—are used in the process of valuing business interests. Because the valuation of such interests takes place not only for completely private investment purposes but where courts and tax authorities may play a role—e.g., in the valuation of a business included in an estate or the valuation of an equity interest for a legal dispute—the valuator may need to research which methods such authorities have found to be acceptable.

Standard approaches to estimating the required return on equity for publicly traded companies, such as the CAPM and the FFM, are adaptable for estimating the required rate of return for non-publicly traded companies. However, valuators often use an approach to valuation that relies on building up the required rate of return as a set of premia added to the risk-free rate. The premia include the equity risk premium and one or more additional premia, often based on factors such as size and perceived company-specific risk, depending on the facts of the exercise and the valuator's analysis of them. An expression for the build-up approach was presented in Equation 5. A traditional specific implementation is as follows:[52]

$$r_i = \text{Risk-free rate} + \text{Equity risk premium} + \text{Size premium}_i +$$
$$\text{Specific-company premium}_i$$

Exhibit 8 explains the logic for a typical case. The equity risk premium is often estimated with reference to equity indices of publicly traded companies. The market's largest market-capitalization companies typically constitute a large fraction of such indices' value. With a beta of 1.0 implicitly multiplying the equity risk premium, the sum of the risk-free rate and equity risk premium is effectively the required return on an average-systematic-risk large-cap public equity issue. In the great majority of cases, private business valuation concerns companies much smaller in size than public large-cap issues. Valuators often add a premium related to the excess returns of small stocks over large stocks reflecting an incremental return for small size. (The premium is typically after adjustment for the differences in the betas of small- and large-cap stocks to isolate the effect of size—a beta-adjusted size premium.) The level of the size premium is typically assumed to be inversely related to the size of the company being valued. When the size premium estimate is appropriately based on the lowest market-cap decile—frequently the case because many private businesses are small relative to publicly traded companies—the result corresponds to the return on an average-systematic-risk micro-cap public equity issue. An analysis of risk factors that are incremental to those captured by the previously included premia may lead the valuator to add a specific company premium. This risk premium sometimes includes a premium for unsystematic risk of the subject company under the premise that such risk related to a privately-held company may be less easily diversified away.

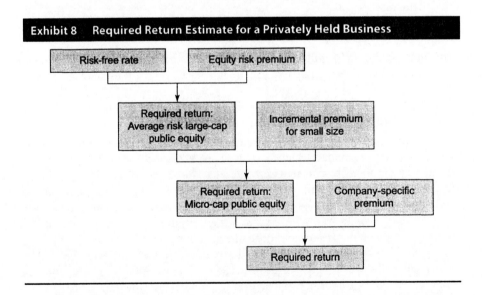

Exhibit 8   Required Return Estimate for a Privately Held Business

Two additional issues related to required return estimation for private companies include 1) consideration of the relative values of controlling versus minority interests in share value and 2) the effect on share value of the lack of ready marketability for a small equity interest in a private company. Lack of marketability is the inability to

---

[52] See Hitchner (2006), p. 173.

immediately sell shares due to lack of access to public equity markets because the shares are not registered for public trading. (Marketability may also be restricted by contractual or other reasons.)

With respect to the potential adjustment for the relative control associated with an equity interest in a private company, any adjustments related to the type of interest (controlling or minority) are traditionally not made in the required return but, if appropriate, directly to the preliminary value estimate. The issues involved in such adjustments are complex with some diversity of viewpoints among practitioners. Given these considerations, a detailed discussion is outside the scope of this reading.[53] Similarly, adjustments for lack of marketability are traditionally taken as an adjustment to the estimated value for an equity interest after any adjustment for the degree of control of the equity interest.

To illustrate, suppose an analyst is valuing a private integrated document management solutions company. The risk-free rate is 3.00 percent, the analyst's estimate of the equity risk premium is 4.20 percent, and based on assets and revenues the company appears to correspond to the top half of the 10th decile of US public companies, which is decile 10a in Exhibit 9 with market capitalizations of equity ranging from over $129 million to about $207 million.

Exhibit 9	Estimates of US Beta Adjusted Size Premia	
Market Cap Decile	**Market Cap of Largest Company (in thousands)**	**Size Premium**
6	$1,620,860	1.75%
7	1,090,515	1.77
8	682,750	2.51
9	422,811	2.80
10	206,795	6.10
	Breakdown of the 10th Decile	
10a	206,795	4.34%
10b	128,672	9.81

Source: SBBI Valuation Yearbook (2012), p. 86–90.

Thus, ignoring any appropriate specific-company premium, an estimate of the required return on equity is 3.00% + 4.20% + 4.34% = 11.54%. A caution is that the size premium for the smallest decile (and especially the 10b component) may reflect not only the premium for healthy small-cap companies, but former large-cap companies that are in financial distress. If that is the case, the historical estimate may not be applicable without a downward adjustment for estimating the required return for a small but financially healthy private company.

A so-called modified CAPM formulation would seek to capture departures from average systematic risk. For example, if the analyst estimated that the company would have a beta of 1.2 if publicly traded, based on its publicly traded peer group, the required return estimate would be

Risk-free rate + Beta × Equity risk premium + Size premium

---

[53] For more information on adjustments for relative control, see Hitchner (2006), ch. 8, and Bruner (2004), ch.15.

or 3.00% + 1.2 × 4.20% + 4.34% = 12.38%. This result could be reconciled to a simple build-up estimate by including a differential return of (1.2 − 1.0)(4.20%) = 0.84% in the specific-company premium.

4.3.2 Bond Yield Plus Risk Premium

For companies with publicly traded debt, the **bond yield plus risk premium method** provides a quick estimate of the cost of equity.[54] The estimate is

$$\text{BYPRP cost of equity} = \text{YTM on the company's long-term debt} \\ + \text{Risk premium}$$

(13)

The YTM on the company's long-term debt includes:

- a real interest rate and a premium for expected inflation, which are also factors embodied in a government bond yield; and

- a default risk premium.

The default risk premium captures factors such as profitability, the sensitivity of profitability to the business cycle, and leverage (operating and financial) that also affect the returns to equity. The risk premium in Equation 13 is the premium that compensates for the additional risk of the equity issue compared with the debt issue (recognizing that debt has a prior claim on the cash flows of the company). In US markets, the typical risk premium added is 3–4 percent, based on experience.

EXAMPLE 9

The Cost of Equity of IBM from Two Perspectives

You are valuing the stock of International Business Machines Corporation (NYSE: IBM) as of early August 2013, and you have gathered the following information:

30-year T-bond YTM:	3.70%
IBM 4s of 2042 YTM:	4.43%

The IBM bonds, you note, are investment grade (rated AA− by Standard & Poor's, Aa3 by Moody's Investors Service, and A+ by Fitch). The beta on IBM stock is 0.73. In prior valuations you have used a risk premium of 3 percent in the bond yield plus risk premium approach. However, the estimated beta of IBM has decreased over the past five years. As a matter of judgment, you have decided as a consequence to use a risk premium of 2.75 percent in the bond yield plus risk premium approach.

1   Calculate the cost of equity using the CAPM. Assume that the equity risk premium is 4.20 percent.

2   Calculate the cost of equity using the bond yield plus risk premium approach, with a risk premium of 2.75 percent.

3   Suppose you found that IBM stock, which closed at $195.04 on 31 July 2013, was slightly undervalued based on a DCF valuation using the CAPM cost of equity from Question 1. Does the alternative estimate of the cost of equity from Question 2 support the conclusion based on Question 1?

---

[54] Although simple, the method has been used in serious contexts. For example, the Board of Regents of the University of California in a retirement plan asset/liability study (July 2000) used the 20-year T-bond rate plus 3.3 percent as the single estimate of the equity risk premium.

Solution to 1:

3.70% + 0.73(4.20%) = 6.77%.

Solution to 2:

Add 2.75 percent to the IBM bond YTM: 4.43% + 2.75% = 7.18%. Note that the difference between the IBM bond YTM and T-bond YTM is 0.73 percent, or 73 basis points. This amount plus 2.75 percent is the total estimated risk premium versus Treasury debt, 0.73% + 2.75% = 3.48%.

Solution to 3:

Not necessarily; *undervalued* means that the value of a security is greater than market price. All else equal, the lower the discount rate, the higher the estimate of value. The inverse relationship between discount rate and value, holding all else constant, is a basic relationship in valuation. If IBM appears to be undervalued using the CAPM cost of equity estimate of 6.77 percent, that does not necessarily mean it will also appear to be undervalued using a 7.18 percent cost of equity based on the bond yield plus risk premium method.

The bond yield plus risk premium method can be viewed as a build-up method applying to companies with publicly traded debt. The estimate provided can be a useful check when the explanatory power of more rigorous models is low. Given that a company's shares have positive systematic risk, the yield on its long-term debt is revealing as a check on cost of equity estimate. For example, Sprint's 6.875 debentures (rated BB– by Standard & Poor's, B1 by Moody's, and B+ by Fitch) mature in 2028 and were priced to yield 7.60 percent as of early August 2013, so required return estimates for its stock (NYSE: S) not greater than 7.60 percent would be suspect.

4.4 The Required Return on Equity: International Issues

Among the issues that concern analysts estimating the required return of equities in a global context are:

- exchange rates, and
- data and model issues in emerging markets.

An investor is ultimately concerned with returns and volatility stated in terms of his or her own currency. Historical returns are often available or can be constructed in local currency and home currency terms. Equity risk premium estimates in home currency terms can be higher or lower than estimates in local currency terms because exchange rate gains and losses from the equity component are generally not exactly offset by gains and losses from the government security component of the equity risk premium. For example, Dimson, Marsh, and Staunton (2011) report that the real geometric mean Swiss premium over 1900 to 2010 was approximately 3.3 percent in Swiss franc terms but for a US investor it was approximately 4.2 percent due to the franc appreciating in value relative to the dollar. The US dollar estimate more accurately reflects a US investor's historical experience. A sound approach for any investor is to focus on the local currency record, incorporating any exchange rate forecasts.

The difficulty of required return and risk premium estimation in emerging markets has been previously mentioned. Of the numerous approaches that have been proposed to supplement or replace traditional historical and forward looking methods, we can mention two.

▪ The country spread model for the equity risk premium. For an emerging equity market, this states that:

Equity risk premium estimate = Equity risk premium for a developed market + Country premium

The country premium represents a premium associated with the expected greater risk of the emerging market compared to the benchmark developed market. Typically, analysts hope that a sovereign bond yield spread is adequate for approximating this premium. Thus, the country premium is often estimated as the yield on emerging market bonds (denominated in the currency of the developed market) minus the yield on developed market government bonds.

To illustrate, the yield premium on Indian companies' dollar bonds over US Treasuries decreased to 3.19 percent in March 2013. Taking this premium as the country premium for India and using an estimate of 4.20 percent for the US equity risk premium, the Indian equity risk premium equals 4.20% + 3.19% = 7.39%.

▪ The country risk rating model[55] provides a regression-based estimate of the equity risk premium based on the empirical relationship between developed equity market returns and Institutional Investor's semi-annual risk ratings for those markets. The estimated regression equation is then used with the risk ratings for less developed markets to predict the required return for those markets. This model has been recommended by Morningstar (Ibbotson).

5 THE WEIGHTED AVERAGE COST OF CAPITAL

The overall required rate of return of a company's suppliers of capital is usually referred to as the company's cost of capital. The cost of capital is most commonly estimated using the company's after-tax weighted average cost of capital, or weighted average cost of capital (WACC) for short: a weighted average of required rates of return for the component sources of capital.

The cost of capital is relevant to equity valuation when an analyst takes an indirect, total firm value approach using a present value model. Using the cost of capital to discount expected future cash flows available to debt and equity, the total value of these claims is estimated. The balance of this value after subtracting off the market value of debt is the estimate of the value of equity.

In many jurisdictions, corporations may deduct net interest expense from income in calculating taxes owed, but they cannot deduct payments to shareholders, such as dividends. The following discussion reflects that base case.

If the suppliers of capital are creditors and common stockholders, the expression for WACC is

$$\text{WACC} = \frac{\text{MVD}}{\text{MVD} + \text{MVCE}} r_d (1 - \text{Tax rate}) + \frac{\text{MVCE}}{\text{MVD} + \text{MVCE}} r \qquad \textbf{(14)}$$

55 Erb, Claude, Campbell R. Harvey, and Tadas Viskanta, "Country Credit Risk and Global Portfolio Selection," *Journal of Portfolio Management*, Winter 1995: 74–83.

where MVD and MVCE are the current market values of debt and (common) equity, not their book or accounting values. Dividing MVD or MVCE by the total market value of the firm, which is MVD + MVCE, gives the proportions of the company's total capital from debt or equity, respectively. These weights will sum to 1.0. The expression for WACC multiplies the weights of debt and equity in the company's financing by, respectively, the after-tax required rates of return for the company's debt and equity under current market conditions. "After-tax," it is important to note, refers to just corporate taxes in this discussion. Multiplying the before-tax required return on debt (r_d) by 1 minus the marginal corporate tax rate (1 – Tax rate) adjusts the pretax rate r_d downward to reflect the tax deductibility of corporate interest payments that is being assumed. Because distributions to equity are assumed not to be deductible by the corporations, a corporation's before and after-tax costs of equity are the same; no adjustment to r involving the corporate tax rate is appropriate. Generally speaking, it is appropriate to use a company's marginal tax rate rather than its current effective tax rate (reported taxes divided by pretax income) because the effective tax rate can reflect nonrecurring items. A cost of capital based on the marginal tax rate usually better reflects a company's future costs in raising funds.

Because the company's capital structure (the proportions of debt and equity financing) can change over time, WACC may also change over time. In addition, the company's current capital structure may also differ substantially from what it will be in future years. For these reasons, analysts often use *target* weights instead of the current market-value weights when calculating WACC. These target weights incorporate both the analyst's and investors' expectations about the target capital structure that the company will tend to use over time. Target weights provide a good approximation of the WACC for cases in which the current weights misrepresent the company's normal capital structure.[56]

The before-tax required return on debt is typically estimated using the expected YTM of the company's debt based on current market values. Analysts can choose from any of the methods presented in this reading for estimating the required return on equity, r. No tax adjustment is appropriate for the cost of equity assuming payments to shareholders such as dividends are not tax deductible by companies.

EXAMPLE 10

The Weighted Average Cost of Capital for IBM

Taking an indirect, total firm value approach to valuing equity, suppose you have the inputs for estimating the cost of capital shown in Exhibit 10. Based only on the information given, estimate IBM's WACC.

Exhibit 10 Cost of Capital Data: IBM	
Panel A: Capital Structure	**Value**
Long-term debt as a percent of total capital, at market value	36%
Tax rate	25%

(continued)

---

56 See a modern corporate finance textbook, such as Brealey, Myers, and Allen (2013), for a review of capital structure theory.

Exhibit 10 (Continued)	
Panel B: Component Costs of Capital	**Value**
Cost of equity: CAPM estimate	7.1%
YTM of IBM long bond	4.4%

Source: Estimates based on data collected from Morningstar and Value Line.

Solution:

Long-term debt as a percent of total capital stated at market value is the weight to be applied to IBM's after-tax cost of debt in the WACC calculation. Therefore, IBM's WACC is approximately 5.73 percent, calculated as follows:

$$WACC = 0.36(4.4\%)(1 - 0.25) + 0.64(7.1\%)$$
$$= 1.188\% + 4.544\% = 5.732 \text{ percent}$$

6   DISCOUNT RATE SELECTION IN RELATION TO CASH FLOWS

When used as discount rates in valuation, required returns need to be defined appropriately relative to the cash flows to be discounted.

A cash flow after more senior claims (e.g., promised payments on debt and taxes) have been fulfilled is a cash flow to equity. When a cash flow to equity is discounted, the required return on equity is an appropriate discount rate. When a cash flow is available to meet the claims of all of a company's capital providers—usually called a cash flow to the firm—the firm's cost of capital is the appropriate discount rate.

Cash flows may be stated in nominal or real terms. When cash flows are stated in real terms, amounts reflect offsets made for actual or anticipated changes in the purchasing power of money. Nominal discount rates must be used with nominal cash flows and real discount rates must be used with real cash flows. In valuing equity, we will use only nominal cash flows and therefore we will make use of nominal discount rates. Because the tax rates applying to corporate earnings are generally stated in nominal money terms—such and such tax rates applying at stated levels of nominal pretax earnings—using nominal quantities is an exact approach because it reflects taxes accurately.

Equation 14 presents an after-tax weighted average cost of capital using the after-tax cost of debt. In later readings, we will present cash flow to the firm definitions for which it is appropriate to use that definition of the cost of capital as the discount rate (i.e., rather than a pretax cost of capital reflecting a pretax cost of debt). The exploration of the topic is outside the scope of this reading because the definitions of cash flows have not been introduced and explained.[57]

---

57 Technically, in discounting a cash flow to the company, the definitions of the cash flow and cost of capital should be coordinated so the value of the tax saving associated with the deductibility of interest expense is not counted twice (i.e., in the cash flow and the discount rate).

In short, in later readings we will be able to illustrate present value models of stock value using only two discount rates: the nominal required return on equity when the cash flows are those available to common shareholders, and the nominal after-tax weighted average cost of capital when the cash flows are those available to all the company's capital providers.

SUMMARY

In this reading we introduced several important return concepts. Required returns are important because they are used as discount rates in determining the present value of expected future cash flows. When an investor's intrinsic value estimate for an asset differs from its market price, the investor generally expects to earn the required return plus a return from the convergence of price to value. When an asset's intrinsic value equals price, however, the investor only expects to earn the required return.

For two important approaches to estimating a company's required return, the CAPM and the build-up model, the analyst needs an estimate of the equity risk premium. This reading examined realized equity risk premia for a group of major world equity markets and also explained forward-looking estimation methods. For determining the required return on equity, the analyst may choose from the CAPM and various multifactor models such as the Fama–French model and its extensions, examining regression fit statistics to assess the reliability of these methods. For private companies, the analyst can adapt public equity valuation models for required return using public company comparables, or use a build-up model, which starts with the risk-free rate and the estimated equity risk premium and adds additional appropriate risk premia.

When the analyst approaches the valuation of equity indirectly, by first valuing the total firm as the present value of expected future cash flows to all sources of capital, the appropriate discount rate is a weighted average cost of capital based on all sources of capital. Discount rates must be on a nominal (real) basis if cash flows are on a nominal (real) basis.

Among the reading's major points are the following:

- The return from investing in an asset over a specified time period is called the *holding period return*. *Realized return* refers to a return achieved in the past, and *expected return* refers to an anticipated return over a future time period. A *required return* is the minimum level of expected return that an investor requires to invest in the asset over a specified time period, given the asset's riskiness. The (*market*) *required return*, a required rate of return on an asset that is inferred using market prices or returns, is typically used as the *discount rate* in finding the present values of expected future cash flows. If an asset is perceived (is not perceived) as fairly priced in the marketplace, the required return should (should not) equal the investor's expected return. When an asset is believed to be mispriced, investors should earn a *return from convergence of price to intrinsic value*.

- An estimate of the equity risk premium—the incremental return that investors require for holding equities rather than a risk-free asset—is used in the CAPM and in the build-up approach to required return estimation.

- Approaches to equity risk premium estimation include historical, adjusted historical, and forward-looking approaches.

- In historical estimation, the analyst must decide whether to use a short-term or a long-term government bond rate to represent the risk-free rate and whether to calculate a geometric or arithmetic mean for the equity risk premium estimate. Forward-looking estimates include Gordon growth model estimates, supply-side models, and survey estimates. Adjusted historical estimates can involve an adjustment for biases in data series and an adjustment to incorporate an independent estimate of the equity risk premium.

▪ The CAPM is a widely used model for required return estimation that uses beta relative to a market portfolio proxy to adjust for risk. The Fama–French model (FFM) is a three factor model that incorporates the market factor, a size factor, and a value factor. The Pastor-Stambaugh extension to the FFM adds a liquidity factor. The bond yield plus risk premium approach finds a required return estimate as the sum of the YTM of the subject company's debt plus a subjective risk premium (often 3 percent to 4 percent).

▪ When a stock is thinly traded or not publicly traded, its beta may be estimated on the basis of a peer company's beta. The procedure involves unlevering the peer company's beta and then re-levering it to reflect the subject company's use of financial leverage. The procedure adjusts for the effect of differences of financial leverage between the peer and subject company.

▪ Emerging markets pose special challenges to required return estimation. The country spread model estimates the equity risk premium as the equity risk premium for a developed market plus a country premium. The country risk rating model approach uses risk ratings for developed markets to infer risk ratings and equity risk premiums for emerging markets.

▪ The weighted average cost of capital is used when valuing the total firm and is generally understood as the nominal after-tax weighted average cost of capital, which is used in discounting nominal cash flows to the firm in later readings. The nominal required return on equity is used in discounting cash flows to equity.

REFERENCES

Arnott, Robert D., and Peter L. Bernstein. 2002. "What Risk Premium Is 'Normal'?" *Financial Analysts Journal*, vol. 58, no. 2:64–85.

Arzac, Enrique R. 2005. *Valuation for Mergers, Buyouts, and Restructuring*. Hoboken, NJ: John Wiley & Sons.

Bartholdy, Jan, and Paula Peare. 2003. "Unbiased Estimation of Expected Return Using CAPM." *International Review of Financial Analysis*, vol. 12, no. 1:69–81.

Blume, Marshall. 1971. "On the Assessment of Risk." *Journal of Finance*, vol. 26, no. 1:1–10.

Brealey, Richard A., Stewart C. Myers, and Franklin Allen. 2006. *Principles of Corporate Finance*. New York: McGraw-Hill/Irwin.

Brealey, Richard A., Stewart C. Myers, and Franklin Allen. 2013. *Principles of Corporate Finance*, 11th edition. New York: McGraw-Hill/Irwin.

Bruner, Robert K. 2004. *Applied Mergers and Acquisitions*. Hoboken, NJ: John Wiley & Sons.

Burmeister, Edwin, Richard Roll, and Stephen A. Ross. 1994. "A Practitioner's Guide to Arbitrage Pricing Theory." *A Practitioner's Guide to Factor Models*. Charlottesville, VA: The Research Foundation of the Institute of Chartered Financial Analysts.

Calverley, John, Alan Meder, Brian Singer, and Renato Staub. 2007. "Capital Market Expectations." *Managing Investment Portfolios: A Dynamic Process*, 3rd edition. John Maginn, Donald Tuttle, Jerald Pinto, and Dennis McLeavey, eds. Hoboken, NJ: John Wiley & Sons.

Capaul, Carlo, Ian Rowley, and William F. Sharpe. 1993. "International Value and Growth Stock Returns." *Financial Analysts Journal*, vol. 49, no. 1:27–36.

Chen, Nai-fu, and Feng Zhang. 1998. "Risk and Return of Value Stocks." *Journal of Business*, vol. 71, no. 4: 501–535.

Copeland, Tom, Tim Koller, and Jack Murrin. 2000. Valuation: *Measuring and Managing the Value of Companies*, 3rd edition. Hoboken, NJ: John Wiley & Sons.

Cornell, Bradford. 1999. *The Equity Risk Premium*. Hoboken, NJ: John Wiley & Sons.

Dimson, Elroy. 1979. "Risk Measurement When Shares Are Subject to Infrequent Trading." *Journal of Financial Economics*, vol. 7, no. 2:197–226.

Dimson, Elroy, Paul Marsh, and Mike Staunton. 2002. *Triumphs of the Optimists: 101 Years of Global Investment Returns*. Princeton, NJ: Princeton University Press.

Dimson, Elroy, Paul Marsh, and Mike Staunton. 2008. *Global Investment Returns Yearbook 2008.* ABN-AMRO, Royal Bank of Scotland, and London Business School.

Dimson, Elroy, Paul Marsh, and Mike Staunton. 2011. "Equity Premiums Around the World." In *Rethinking the Equity Risk Premium*, 2011. P. Brett Hammond, Jr., Martin L. Leibowitz, and Laurence B. Siegel, eds. Charlottesville, VA: Research Foundation of CFA Institute.

Damodaran, Aswath. 2013. "Equity Risk Premiums (ERP): Determinants, Estimation and Implications—The 2013 Edition." Available at SSRN: http://ssrn.com/abstract=2238064.

Elton, Edwin J., Martin J. Gruber, Stephen J. Brown, and William N. Goetzmann. 2006. *Modern Portfolio Theory and Investment Analysis*, 7th edition. New York: John Wiley & Sons.

Fama, Eugene F., and Kenneth R. French. 1989. "Business Conditions and Expected Returns on Stocks and Bonds." *Journal of Financial Economics*, vol. 25, no. 1:23–50.

Fama, Eugene F., and Kenneth R. French. 1993. "Common Risk Factors in the Returns on Stocks and Bonds." *Journal of Financial Economics*, vol. 33, no. 1:3–56.

Fama, Eugene F., and Kenneth R. French. 2001. "Disappearing Dividends: Changing Firm Characteristics of Lower Propensity to Pay?" *Journal of Financial Economics*, vol. 60, no. 1:3–43.

Fernandez, P., J. Aguirreamalloa, and L. Corres. 2011. "Equity Premiums Used in 2011 for the USA by Analysts, Companies and Professors: A Survey." Working paper available at http://papers.ssrn.com/sol3/papers/cfm?abstract_id=1805852&rec=1&srcabs=1822182.

Ferson, Wayne E., and Campbell R. Harvey. 1991. "The Variation of Economic Risk Premiums." *Journal of Political Economy*, vol. 99, no. 2:385–415.

Hamada, Robert. 1972. "The Effect of the Firm's Capital Structure on the Systematic Risk of Common Stocks." *Journal of Finance*, vol. 27, no. 2:435–452.

Hammond, P. Brett, Martin L. Leibowitz, and Laurence B. Siegel. 2011. *Rethinking the Equity Risk Premium*. Charlottesville, VA: Research Foundation of CFA Institute.

Hitchner, James R. 2006. *Financial Valuation: Applications and Models*, 2nd edition. Hoboken, NJ: John Wiley & Sons.

Hughson, Eric, Michael Stutzer, and Chris Yung. 2006. "The Misuse of Expected Returns." *Financial Analysts Journal*, vol. 62, no. 6:88–96.

Ibbotson, Roger, and Peng Chen. 2003. "Long-Run Stock Returns: Participating in the Real Economy." *Financial Analysts Journal*, vol. 58, no. 1:88–98.

Jagannathan, Ravi, Ellen McGrattan, and Anna Scherbina. 2000. "The Declining U.S. Equity Premium." *Quarterly Review.* Federal Reserve Bank of Minnesota, vol. 24, no. 4:3–19.

La Porta, Rafael, Josef Lakonishok, Andrei Shleifer, and Robert Vishny. 1997. "Good News for Value Stocks: Further Evidence on Market Efficiency." *Journal of Finance*, vol. 52, no. 2:859–874.

Lakonishok, J., A. Shleifer, and R.W. Vishny. 1994. "Contrarian Investment, Extrapolation and Risk." *Journal of Finance*, vol. 49, no. 5:1541–1578.

Mehra, Rajnish, and Edward C. Prescott. 1985. "The Equity Premium: A Puzzle." *Journal of Monetary Economics*, vol. 15, no. 2:145–161.

Merton, Robert C. 1980. "On Estimating the Expected Return on the Market: An Exploratory Investigation." *Journal of Financial Economics*, vol. 8, no. 4:323–361.

Metrick, Andrew. 2007. *Venture Capital and the Finance of Innovation.* Hoboken, NJ: John Wiley & Sons, Inc.

Miles, James A., and John R. Ezzell. 1985. "Reformulating Tax Shield Valuation: A Note." *Journal of Finance*, vol. 40, no. 5:1484–1492.

Morningstar. 2007. "Stocks, Bonds, Bills, and Inflation." *2007 Valuation Edition Yearbook*. Chicago: Morningstar, Inc.

Pastor, Lubos, and Robert F. Stambaugh. 2003. "Liquidity Risk and Expected Stock Returns." *Journal of Political Economy*, vol. 111, no. 3:642–685.

Scholes, Myron, and Joseph T. Williams. 1977. "Estimating Betas from Nonsynchronous Data." *Journal of Financial Economics*, vol. 5, no. 3:309–327.

Strong, Norman, and Zinzhong G. Xu. 1997. "Explaining the Cross-Section of UK Expected Stock Returns." *British Accounting Review*, vol. 29, no. 1:1–23.

Stux, Ivan E. 1994. "Earnings Growth: The Driver of Equity Value." Morgan Stanley *Global Equity and Derivatives Markets*.

Varma, Jayanth R., and Samir K. Barua. 2006. "A First Cut Estimate of the Equity Risk Premium in India." Indian Institute of Management Ahmedabad. Working Paper No. 2006-06-04.

PRACTICE PROBLEMS

1 A Canada-based investor buys shares of Toronto-Dominion Bank (Toronto: TD.TO) for C$72.08 on 15 October 2007 with the intent of holding them for a year. The dividend rate was C$2.11 per year. The investor actually sells the shares on 5 November 2007 for C$69.52. The investor notes the following additional facts:

   ● No dividends were paid between 15 October and 5 November.

   ● The required return on TD.TO equity was 8.7 percent on an annual basis and 0.161 percent on a weekly basis.

   A State the lengths of the expected and actual holding-periods.

   B Given that TD.TO was fairly priced, calculate the price appreciation return (capital gains yield) anticipated by the investor given his initial expectations and initial expected holding period.

   C Calculate the investor's realized return.

   D Calculate the realized alpha.

2 The estimated betas for AOL Time Warner (NYSE: AOL), J.P. Morgan Chase & Company (NYSE: JPM), and The Boeing Company (NYSE: BA) are 2.50, 1.50, and 0.80, respectively. The risk-free rate of return is 4.35 percent and the equity risk premium is 8.04 percent. Calculate the required rates of return for these three stocks using the CAPM.

3 The estimated factor sensitivities of TerraNova Energy to Fama–French factors and the risk premia associated with those factors are given in the table below:

	Factor Sensitivity	Risk Premium (%)
Market factor	1.20	4.5
Size factor	−0.50	2.7
Value factor	−0.15	4.3

   A Based on the Fama–French model, calculate the required return for TerraNova Energy using these estimates. Assume that the Treasury bill rate is 4.7 percent.

   B Describe the expected style characteristics of TerraNova based on its factor sensitivities.

4 Newmont Mining (NYSE: NEM) has an estimated beta of −0.2. The risk-free rate of return is 4.5 percent, and the equity risk premium is estimated to be 7.5 percent. Using the CAPM, calculate the required rate of return for investors in NEM.

5 An analyst wants to account for financial distress and market-capitalization as well as market risk in his cost of equity estimate for a particular traded company. Which of the following models is *most appropriate* for achieving that objective?

   A The capital asset pricing model (CAPM).

   B The Fama–French model.

   C A macroeconomic factor model.

6   The following facts describe Larsen & Toubro Ltd's component costs of capital and capital structure. Based on the information given, calculate Larsen & Toubro's WACC.

Component Costs of Capital	(%)
Cost of equity based on the CAPM:	15.6
Pretax cost of debt:	8.28
Tax rate:	30
Target weight in capital structure:	Equity 80, Debt 20

The following information relates to Questions 7–12

An equity index is established in 2001 for a country that has relatively recently established a market economy. The index vendor constructed returns for the five years prior to 2001 based on the initial group of companies constituting the index in 2001. Over 2004 to 2006 a series of military confrontations concerning a disputed border disrupted the economy and financial markets. The dispute is conclusively arbitrated at the end of 2006. In total, ten years of equity market return history is available as of the beginning of 2007. The geometric mean return relative to 10-year government bond returns over 10 years is 2 percent per year. The forward dividend yield on the index is 1 percent. Stock returns over 2004 to 2006 reflect the setbacks but economists predict the country will be on a path of a 4 percent real GDP growth rate by 2009. Earnings in the public corporate sector are expected to grow at a 5 percent per year real growth rate. Consistent with that, the market P/E ratio is expected to grow at 1 percent per year. Although inflation is currently high at 6 percent per year, the long-term forecast is for an inflation rate of 4 percent per year. Although the yield curve has usually been upward sloping, currently the government yield curve is inverted; at the short-end, yields are 9 percent and at 10-year maturities, yields are 7 percent.

7   The inclusion of index returns prior to 2001 would be expected to:

    A   bias the historical equity risk premium estimate upwards.

    B   bias the historical equity risk premium estimate downwards.

    C   have no effect on the historical equity risk premium estimate.

8   The events of 2004 to 2006 would be expected to:

    A   bias the historical equity risk premium estimate upwards.

    B   bias the historical equity risk premium estimate downwards.

    C   have no effect on the historical equity risk premium estimate.

9   In the current interest rate environment, using a required return estimate based on the short-term government bond rate and a historical equity risk premium defined in terms of a short-term government bond rate would be expected to:

    A   bias long-term required return on equity estimates upwards.

    B   bias long-term required return on equity estimates downwards.

    C   have no effect on long-term required return on equity estimates.

10   A supply side estimate of the equity risk premium as presented by The Ibbotson–Chen earnings model is *closest* to:

    A   3.2 percent.

    B   4.0 percent.

    C 4.3 percent.

11 Common stock issues in the above market with average systematic risk are *most likely* to have required rates of return:

    A between 2 percent and 7 percent.

    B between 7 and 9 percent.

    C 9 percent or greater.

12 Which of the following statements is *most accurate*? If two equity issues have the same market risk but the first issue has higher leverage, greater liquidity, and a higher required return, the higher required return *is most likely* the result of the first issue's:

    A greater liquidity.

    B higher leverage.

    C higher leverage and greater liquidity.

Questions 13 through 19 relate to Horizon Asset Management

Judy Chen is the primary portfolio manager of the global equities portfolio at Horizon Asset Management. Lars Johansson, a recently hired equity analyst, has been assigned to Chen to assist her with the portfolio.

    Chen recently sold shares of Novo-Gemini, Inc. from the portfolio. Chen tasks Johansson with assessing the return performance of Novo-Gemini, with specific trade information provided in Exhibit 1.

Exhibit 1   Novo-Gemini, Inc. Trade Details

    1 Novo-Gemini shares were purchased for $20.75 per share.

    2 At the time of purchase, research by Chen suggested that Novo-Gemini shares were expected to sell for $29.00 per share at the end of a 3-year holding period.

    3 At the time of purchase, the required return for Novo-Gemini based upon the capital asset pricing model (CAPM) was estimated to be 12.6% on an annual basis.

    4 Exactly 3 years after the purchase date, the shares were sold for $30.05 per share.

    5 No dividends were paid by Novo-Gemini over the 3-year holding period.

Chen explains to Johansson that, at the time of purchase, the CAPM used to estimate a required return for Novo-Gemini incorporated an unadjusted historical equity risk premium estimate for the US equity market. Chen notes that the US equities market has experienced a meaningful string of favorable inflation and productivity surprises in the past. She asks Johansson whether the historical equity risk premium should have been adjusted before estimating the required return for Novo-Gemini.

    For another perspective on the reward to bearing risk, Chen asks Johansson to calculate a forward looking equity risk premium for the US equity market using data on the S&P 500 index in Exhibit 2.

Exhibit 2	S&P 500 Index Data
Dividend yield, based on year-ahead aggregate forecasted dividends	1.2%
Consensus long-term earnings growth rate	4%
20-year US government bond yield	3%

Chen is now considering adding shares of Bezak, Inc. to the portfolio. Chen asks Johansson to calculate Bezak's weighted average cost of capital using the CAPM with the information provided in Exhibit 3.

Exhibit 3	Bezak, Inc.
Pretax cost of debt	4.9%
Long-term debt as a percent of total capital, at market value	25%
Marginal tax rate	30%
Bezak, Inc. beta	2.00
Estimated equity risk premium	5.5%
Risk-free rate	3.0%

Lastly, Chen asks Johansson to evaluate Twin Industries, a privately owned US company that may initiate a public stock offering. Johansson decides to adapt CAPM to estimate the required return on equity for Twin Industries. Using the MSCI / Standard & Poor's Global Industry Classification Standard (GICS), Johansson identifies a publicly traded peer company with an estimated beta of 1.09 that is much larger but otherwise similar to Twin Industries. Twin Industries is funded 49% by debt while the publicly traded peer company is funded 60% by debt.

13 Based upon Exhibit 1, the expected three-year holding period return for Novo-Gemini Inc. at the time of purchase was *closest* to:

A 39.76%.

B 42.76%.

C 44.82%.

14 Based upon Exhibit 1, the realized three-year holding period return for Novo-Gemini Inc. was *closest* to:

A 39.76%.

B 42.76%.

C 44.82%.

15 Based on the historical record of surprises in inflation and productivity, the historical equity risk premium for the US equity market, if it is used as an estimate of the forward-looking equity risk premium, should *most likely* be:

A left unchanged.

B adjusted upward.

C adjusted downward.

16 Based on Exhibit 2, the forward-looking estimate for the US equity risk premium is *closest* to:

A 2.2%.

B 5.8%.

C   8.2%.

17 Based on Exhibit 3, and assuming interest on debt is tax-deductible, the weighted average cost of capital (WACC) for Bezak, Inc. is *closest* to:

A   10.87%.

B   11.36%.

C   13.61%.

18 The estimate of beta for Twin Industries is *closest* to:

A   0.44.

B   0.85.

C   0.89.

19 A potential weakness of Johansson's approach to estimating the required return on equity for Twin Industries is that the return estimate:

A   does not include a size premium.

B   may overstate potential returns over the long-term.

C   does not consider systematic risk arising from the economics of the industry.

SOLUTIONS

1 A The expected holding was one year. The actual holding period was from 15 October 2007 to 5 November 2007, which is three weeks.

    B Given fair pricing, the expected return equals the required return, 8.7 percent. The expected price appreciation return over the initial anticipated one-year holding period must be equal to the required return minus the dividend yield, 2.11/72.08 = 0.0293 or 2.93 percent. Thus expected price appreciation return was 8.7% – 2.93% = 5.77 percent.

    C The realized return was ($69.52 – $72.08)/$72.08 = –0.03552 or negative 3.55 percent over three weeks. There was no dividend yield return over the actual holding period.

    D The required return over a three-week holding period was $(1.00161)^3 - 1 =$ 0.484 percent. Using the answer to C, the realized alpha was –3.552 – 0.484 = –4.036 percent or –4.04 percent.

2 For AOL Time Warner, the required return is

$$r = R_F + \beta\big[E(R_M) - R_F\big] = 4.35\% + 2.50(8.04\%) = 4.35\% + 20.10\%$$
$$= 24.45\%$$

For J.P. Morgan Chase, the required return is

$$r = R_F + \beta\big[E(R_M) - R_F\big] = 4.35\% + 1.50(8.04\%) = 4.35\% + 12.06\%$$
$$= 16.41\%$$

For Boeing, the required return is

$$r = R_F + \beta\big[E(R_M) - R_F\big] = 4.35\% + 0.80(8.04\%) = 4.35\% + 6.43\%$$
$$= 10.78\%$$

3 A The Fama–French model gives the required return as

      r = T-bill rate

        + (Sensitivity to equity market factor × Equity risk premium)

        + (Sensitivity to size factor × Size risk premium)

        + (Sensitivity to value factor × Value risk premium)

    For TerraNova Energy, the required return is

$$r = 4.7\% + (1.20 \times 4.5\%) + (-0.50 \times 2.7\%) + (-0.15 \times 4.3\%)$$
$$= 4.7\% + 5.4\% - 1.35\% - 0.645\%$$
$$= 8.1\%$$

    B TerraNova Energy appears to be a large-cap, growth-oriented, high market risk stock as indicated by its negative size beta, negative value beta, and market beta above 1.0.

4 The required return is given by

$$r = 0.045 + (-0.2)(0.075) = 4.5\% - 1.5\% = 3.0\%$$

This example indicates that Newmont Mining has a required return of 3 percent. When beta is negative, an asset has a CAPM required rate of return that is below the risk-free rate. Cases of equities with negative betas are relatively rare.

5 B is correct. The Fama–French model incorporates market, size, and value risk factors. One possible interpretation of the value risk factor is that it relates to financial distress.

6 Larsen & Toubro Ltd's WACC is 13.64 percent calculated as follows:

	Equity	Debt	WACC
Weight	0.80	0.20	
After-Tax Cost	15.6%	(1 – 0.30)8.28%	
Weight × Cost	12.48%	+ 1.16%	= 13.64%

7 A is correct. The backfilling of index returns using companies that have survived to the index construction date is expected to introduce a positive survivorship bias into returns.

8 B is correct. The events of 2004 to 2006 depressed share returns but 1) are not a persistent feature of the stock market environment, 2) were not offset by other positive events within the historical record, and 3) have led to relatively low valuation levels, which are expected to rebound.

9 A is correct. The required return reflects the magnitude of the historical equity risk premium, which is generally higher when based on a short-term interest rate (as a result of the normal upward sloping yield curve), and the current value of the rate being used to represent the risk-free rate. The short-term rate is currently higher than the long-term rate, which will also increase the required return estimate. The short-term interest rate, however, overstates the long-term expected inflation rate. Using the short-term interest rate, estimates of the long-term required return on equity will be biased upwards.

10 C is correct. According to this model, the equity risk premium is

$$\text{Equity risk premium} = \left\{\left[(1 + \text{EINFL})(1 + \text{EGREPS})(1 + \text{EGPE}) - 1.0\right] + \text{EINC}\right\}$$
$$- \text{Expected risk-free return}$$

Here:

> EINFL = 4 percent per year (long-term forecast of inflation)
>
> EGREPS = 5 percent per year (growth in real earnings)
>
> EGPE = 1 percent per year (growth in market P/E ratio)
>
> EINC = 1 percent per year (dividend yield or the income portion)
>
> Risk-free return = 7 percent per year (for 10-year maturities)

By substitution, we get:

$$\left\{\left[(1.04)(1.05)(1.01) - 1.0\right] + 0.01\right\} - 0.07 = 0.113 - 0.07$$
$$= 0.043 \text{ or } 4.3 \text{ percent.}$$

11 C is correct. Based on a long-term government bond yield of 7 percent, a beta of 1, and any of the risk premium estimates that can be calculated from the givens (e.g., a 2 percent historical risk premium estimate or 4.3 percent supply side equity risk premium estimate), the required rate of return would be at least 9 percent. Based on using a short-term rate of 9 percent, C is the correct choice.

12 B is correct. All else equal, the first issue's greater liquidity would tend to make its required return lower than the second issue's. However, the required return on equity increases as leverage increases. The first issue's higher required return must result from its higher leverage, more than offsetting the effect of its greater liquidity, given that both issues have the same market risk.

13 A is correct. This is the expected 3-year holding period return, calculated as:

$$\text{3-year expected return} = (V_0 - P_0) / P_0 = (\$29.00 - \$20.75) / \$20.75$$
$$= 39.76\%.$$

14 C is correct. The realized holding period return (note that no dividends were paid during the 3-year holding period) is 44.82%. Specifically, the realized 3-year holding period is calculated as calculated as:

$$\text{3-year realized return} = (P_H - P_0) / (P_0) = (30.05 - 20.75) / 20.75 = 44.82\%.$$

15 C is correct. A string of favorable inflation and productivity surprises may result in a series of high returns that increase the historical mean estimate of the equity risk premium. To mitigate that concern, the analyst may adjust the historical estimate downward based on an independent forward-looking estimate.

16 A is correct. Given the data presented, the equity risk premium can be estimated as:

Equity risk premium = dividend yield on the index based on year-ahead aggregate forecasted dividends and aggregate market value + consensus long-term earnings growth rate – current long-term government bond yield. The equity risk premium = 1.2% + 4.0% – 3.0% = 2.2%.

17 B is correct. The weighted average cost of capital is taking the sum product of each component of capital multiplied by the component's after-tax cost.

First, estimate the cost of equity using the CAPM:

Cost of equity = Risk-free rate + [Equity Risk Premium × Beta]

Cost of equity = 3.0% + [5.5% × 2.00] = 14%

Now, calculate Bezak's WACC:

	Equity	Debt	WACC
Weight	0.75	0.25	
After Tax Cost	14%	(1 – 0.30) × 4.9%	
Weight × After Tax Cost	10.5% +	0.8575%	=11.36%

18 B is correct. The steps to estimating a beta for a non-traded company are:

Step 1   Select the comparable benchmark

Step 2   Estimate benchmark's beta

Step 3   Un-lever the benchmark's beta

Step 4   Lever the beta to reflect the subject company's financial leverage

The beta of the benchmark peer company data is given as 1.09. Next, this beta needs to be unlevered, calculated as:

$$\beta_u = \left[\frac{1}{1 + \left(\dfrac{D}{E} \right)} \right] \beta_l$$

$$\beta_u = \left[\cfrac{1}{1 + \left(\cfrac{0.60}{0.40}\right)} \right](1.09)$$

β_u = 0.436, or 0.44

Then, the unlevered beta needs to be levered up to reflect the financial leverage of Twin Industries, calculated as:

$$\beta'_E \approx \left[1 + \left(\frac{D'}{E'}\right) \right]\beta_u$$

$$\beta'_E \approx \left[1 + \left(\frac{0.49}{0.51}\right) \right](0.436)$$

β_u = 0.8549, or 0.85

19 A is correct. Johansson intends to estimate a required return on equity using a modified CAPM approach. Twin Industries is stated to be smaller than the chosen proxy benchmark being used and there is no size premium adjustment in the CAPM framework; the framework adjusts the beta for leverage differences but this does not adjust for firm size differences. The build-up method may be more appropriate as it includes the equity risk premium and one or more additional premia, often based on factors such as size and perceived company-specific risk.

11

Equity Valuation

Industry and Company Analysis in a Global Context

This study session provides insights on issues that affect security valuation internationally. Analyzing industries in a global context and evaluating competitive forces that will affect returns provide a foundation for security valuation decisions. Discounted dividend models are examined in detail.

READING ASSIGNMENTS

Reading 31   The Five Competitive Forces That Shape Strategy
                      by Michael E. Porter

Reading 32   Your Strategy Needs a Strategy
                      by Martin Reeves, Claire Love, and Philipp Tillmanns

Reading 33   Industry and Company Analysis
                      by Matthew L. Coffina, CFA, Anthony M. Fiore, CFA, and
                      Antonius J. van Ooijen, CFA

Reading 34   Discounted Dividend Valuation
                      by Jerald E. Pinto, PhD, CFA, Elaine Henry, PhD, CFA,
                      Thomas R. Robinson, PhD, CFA, and
                      John D. Stowe, PhD, CFA

The Five Competitive Forces that Shape Strategy

by Michael E. Porter

Michael E. Porter (USA).

LEARNING OUTCOMES

Mastery	The candidate should be able to:
☐	**a.** distinguish among the five competitive forces and explain how they drive industry profitability in the medium and long run;
☐	**b.** describe why industry growth rate, technology and innovation, government, and complementary products and services are fleeting factors rather than forces shaping industry structure;
☐	**c.** identify changes in industry structure and forecast their effects on the industry's profit potential;
☐	**d.** explain how positioning a company, exploiting industry change, and shaping industry structure may be used to achieve a competitive advantage.

Editor's Note: In 1979, *Harvard Business Review* published "How Competitive Forces Shape Strategy" by a young economist and associate professor, Michael E. Porter. It was his first HBR article, and it started a revolution in the strategy field. In subsequent decades, Porter has brought his signature economic rigor to the study of competitive strategy for corporations, regions, nations, and, more recently, health care and philanthropy. "Porter's five forces" have shaped a generation of academic research and business practice. With prodding and assistance from Harvard Business School Professor Jan Rivkin and longtime colleague Joan Magretta, Porter here reaffirms, updates, and extends the classic work. He also addresses common misunderstandings, provides practical guidance for users of the framework, and offers a deeper view of implications for strategy today.

Awareness of the five forces can help a company understand the structure of its industry and stake out a position that is more profitable and less vulnerable to attack.

The Idea in Brief

You know that to sustain long-term profitability you must respond strategically to competition. And you naturally keep tabs on your **established rivals**. But as you scan the competitive arena, are you also looking *beyond* your direct competitors? As Porter explains in this update of his revolutionary 1979 HBR article, four additional competitive forces can hurt your prospective profits:

- Savvy **customers** can force down prices by playing you and your rivals against one another.
- Powerful **suppliers** may constrain your profits if they charge higher prices.
- Aspiring **entrants**, armed with new capacity and hungry for market share, can ratchet up the investment required for you to stay in the game.
- **Substitute offerings** can lure customers away.

Consider commercial aviation: It's one of the least profitable industries because all five forces are strong. **Established rivals** compete intensely on price. **Customers** are fickle, searching for the best deal regardless of carrier. **Suppliers**—plane and engine manufacturers, along with unionized labor forces—bargain away the lion's share of airlines' profits. **New players** enter the industry in a constant stream. And **substitutes** are readily available—such as train or car travel.

By analyzing all five competitive forces, you gain a complete picture of what's influencing profitability in your industry. You identify game-changing trends early, so you can swiftly exploit them. And you spot ways to work around constraints on profitability—or even reshape the forces in your favor.

The Idea in Practice

By understanding how the five competitive forces influence profitability in your industry, you can develop a strategy for enhancing your company's long-term profits. Porter suggests the following:

Position Your Company Where the Forces Are Weakest

- Example:

  In the heavy-truck industry, many buyers operate large fleets and are highly motivated to drive down truck prices. Trucks are built to regulated standards and offer similar features, so price competition is stiff; unions exercise considerable supplier power; and buyers can use substitutes such as cargo delivery by rail.

  To create and sustain long-term profitability within this industry, heavy-truck maker Paccar chose to focus on one customer group where competitive forces are weakest: individual drivers who own their trucks and contract directly with suppliers. These operators have limited clout as buyers and are less price sensitive because of their emotional ties to and economic dependence on their own trucks.

For these customers, Paccar has developed such features as luxurious sleeper cabins, plush leather seats, and sleek exterior styling. Buyers can select from thousands of options to put their personal signature on these built-to-order trucks.

Customers pay Paccar a 10% premium, and the company has been profitable for 68 straight years and earned a long-run return on equity above 20%.

Exploit Changes in the Forces

- Example:

  With the advent of the Internet and digital distribution of music, unauthorized downloading created an illegal but potent substitute for record companies' services. The record companies tried to develop technical platforms for digital distribution themselves, but major labels didn't want to sell their music through a platform owned by a rival.

  Into this vacuum stepped Apple, with its iTunes music store supporting its iPod music player. The birth of this powerful new gatekeeper has whittled down the number of major labels from six in 1997 to four today.

Reshape the Forces in Your Favor

Use tactics designed specifically to reduce the share of profits leaking to other players. For example:

- To neutralize **supplier power**, standardize specifications for parts so your company can switch more easily among vendors.
- To counter **customer power**, expand your services so it's harder for customers to leave you for a rival.
- To temper price wars initiated by **established rivals**, invest more heavily in products that differ significantly from competitors' offerings.
- To scare off **new entrants**, elevate the fixed costs of competing; for instance, by escalating your R&D expenditures.
- To limit the threat of **substitutes**, offer better value through wider product accessibility. Soft-drink producers did this by introducing vending machines and convenience store channels, which dramatically improved the availability of soft drinks relative to other beverages.

INTRODUCTION

1

In essence, the job of the strategist is to understand and cope with competition. Often, however, managers define competition too narrowly, as if it occurred only among today's direct competitors. Yet competition for profits goes beyond established industry rivals to include four other competitive forces as well: customers, suppliers, potential entrants, and substitute products. The extended rivalry that results from all five forces defines an industry's structure and shapes the nature of competitive interaction within an industry.

As different from one another as industries might appear on the surface, the underlying drivers of profitability are the same. The global auto industry, for instance, appears to have nothing in common with the worldwide market for art masterpieces or the heavily regulated health-care delivery industry in Europe. But to understand industry competition and profitability in each of those three cases, one must analyze the industry's underlying structure in terms of the five forces. (See Exhibit 1, "The Five Forces that Shape Industry Competition.")

If the forces are intense, as they are in such industries as airlines, textiles, and hotels, almost no company earns attractive returns on investment. If the forces are benign, as they are in industries such as software, soft drinks, and toiletries, many companies are profitable. Industry structure drives competition and profitability, not whether an industry produces a product or service, is emerging or mature, high tech or low tech, regulated or unregulated. While a myriad of factors can affect industry profitability in the short run—including the weather and the business cycle—industry structure, manifested in the competitive forces, sets industry profitability in the medium and long run. (See Exhibit 2, "Differences in Industry Profitability.")

Exhibit 1   The Five Forces That Shape Industry Competition

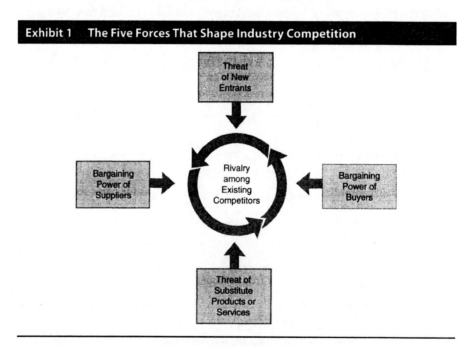

Exhibit 2   Differences in Industry Profitability

The average return on invested capital varies markedly from industry to industry. Between 1992 and 2006, for example, average return on invested capital in US industries ranged as low as zero or even negative to more than 50%. At the high end are industries like soft drinks and prepackaged software, which have been almost six times more profitable than the airline industry over the period.

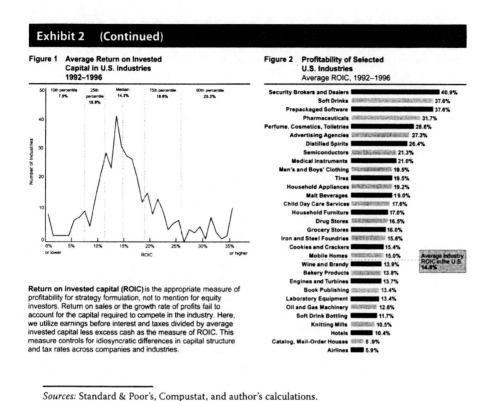

Exhibit 2 (Continued)

Figure 1 Average Return on Invested Capital in U.S. Industries 1992–1996

Figure 2 Profitability of Selected U.S. Industries
Average ROIC, 1992–1996

Industry	ROIC
Security Brokers and Dealers	40.9%
Soft Drinks	37.6%
Prepackaged Software	37.6%
Pharmaceuticals	31.7%
Perfume, Cosmetics, Toiletries	28.6%
Advertising Agencies	27.3%
Distilled Spirits	26.4%
Semiconductors	21.3%
Medical Instruments	21.0%
Men's and Boys' Clothing	19.5%
Tires	19.5%
Household Appliances	19.2%
Malt Beverages	19.0%
Child Day Care Services	17.6%
Household Furniture	17.0%
Drug Stores	16.5%
Grocery Stores	16.0%
Iron and Steel Foundries	15.6%
Cookies and Crackers	15.4%
Mobile Homes	15.0%
Wine and Brandy	13.9%
Bakery Products	13.8%
Engines and Turbines	13.7%
Book Publishing	13.4%
Laboratory Equipment	13.4%
Oil and Gas Machinery	12.6%
Soft Drink Bottling	11.7%
Knitting Mills	10.5%
Hotels	10.4%
Catalog, Mail-Order Houses	5.9%
Airlines	5.9%

Average industry ROIC in the U.S. 14.9%

Return on invested capital (ROIC) is the appropriate measure of profitability for strategy formulation, not to mention for equity investors. Return on sales or the growth rate of profits fail to account for the capital required to compete in the industry. Here, we utilize earnings before interest and taxes divided by average invested capital less excess cash as the measure of ROIC. This measure controls for idiosyncratic differences in capital structure and tax rates across companies and industries.

Sources: Standard & Poor's, Compustat, and author's calculations.

Understanding the competitive forces, and their underlying causes, reveals the roots of an industry's current profitability while providing a framework for anticipating and influencing competition (and profitability) over time. A healthy industry structure should be as much a competitive concern to strategists as their company's own position. Understanding industry structure is also essential to effective strategic positioning. As we will see, defending against the competitive forces and shaping them in a company's favor are crucial to strategy.

FORCES THAT SHAPE COMPETITION

2

The configuration of the five forces differs by industry. In the market for commercial aircraft, fierce rivalry between dominant producers Airbus and Boeing and the bargaining power of the airlines that place huge orders for aircraft are strong, while the threat of entry, the threat of substitutes, and the power of suppliers are more benign. In the movie theater industry, the proliferation of substitute forms of entertainment and the power of the movie producers and distributors who supply movies, the critical input, are important.

The strongest competitive force or forces determine the profitability of an industry and become the most important to strategy formulation. The most salient force, however, is not always obvious.

For example, even though rivalry is often fierce in commodity industries, it may not be the factor limiting profitability. Low returns in the photographic film industry, for instance, are the result of a superior substitute product—as Kodak and Fuji, the world's leading producers of photographic film, learned with the advent of digital photography. In such a situation, coping with the substitute product becomes the number one strategic priority.

Industry structure grows out of a set of economic and technical characteristics that determine the strength of each competitive force. We will examine these drivers in the pages that follow, taking the perspective of an incumbent, or a company already present in the industry. The analysis can be readily extended to understand the challenges facing a potential entrant.

Threat of Entry   New entrants to an industry bring new capacity and a desire to gain market share that puts pressure on prices, costs, and the rate of investment necessary to compete. Particularly when new entrants are diversifying from other markets, they can leverage existing capabilities and cash flows to shake up competition, as Pepsi did when it entered the bottled water industry, Microsoft did when it began to offer internet browsers, and Apple did when it entered the music distribution business.

The threat of entry, therefore, puts a cap on the profit potential of an industry. When the threat is high, incumbents must hold down their prices or boost investment to deter new competitors. In specialty coffee retailing, for example, relatively low entry barriers mean that Starbucks must invest aggressively in modernizing stores and menus.

The threat of entry in an industry depends on the height of entry barriers that are present and on the reaction entrants can expect from incumbents. If entry barriers are low and newcomers expect little retaliation from the entrenched competitors, the threat of entry is high and industry profitability is moderated. It is the *threat* of entry, not whether entry actually occurs, that holds down profitability.

Barriers to entry.   Entry barriers are advantages that incumbents have relative to new entrants. There are seven major sources:

1 *Supply-side economies of scale.* These economies arise when firms that produce at larger volumes enjoy lower costs per unit because they can spread fixed costs over more units, employ more efficient technology, or command better terms from suppliers. Supply-side scale economies deter entry by forcing the aspiring entrant either to come into the industry on a large scale, which requires dislodging entrenched competitors, or to accept a cost disadvantage.

   Scale economies can be found in virtually every activity in the value chain; which ones are most important varies by industry.[1] In microprocessors, incumbents such as Intel are protected by scale economies in research, chip fabrication, and consumer marketing. For lawn care companies like Scotts Miracle-Gro, the most important scale economies are found in the supply chain and media advertising. In small-package delivery, economies of scale arise in national logistical systems and information technology.

2 *Demand-side benefits of scale.* These benefits, also known as network effects, arise in industries where a buyer's willingness to pay for a company's product increases with the number of other buyers who also patronize the company. Buyers may trust larger companies more for a crucial product: Recall the old adage that no one ever got fired for buying from IBM (when it was the dominant computer maker). Buyers may also value being in a "network" with a larger number of fellow customers. For instance, online auction participants are attracted to eBay because it offers the most potential trading partners. Demand-side benefits of scale discourage entry by limiting the willingness of customers to buy from a newcomer and by reducing the price the newcomer can command until it builds up a large base of customers.

---

1 For a discussion of the value chain framework, see Michael E. Porter, *Competitive Advantage: Creating and Sustaining Superior Performance* (The Free Press, 1998).

3   *Customer switching costs.* Switching costs are fixed costs that buyers face when they change suppliers. Such costs may arise because a buyer who switches vendors must, for example, alter product specifications, retrain employees to use a new product, or modify processes or information systems. The larger the switching costs, the harder it will be for an entrant to gain customers. Enterprise resource planning (ERP) software is an example of a product with very high switching costs. Once a company has installed SAP's ERP system, for example, the costs of moving to a new vendor are astronomical because of embedded data, the fact that internal processes have been adapted to SAP, major retraining needs, and the mission-critical nature of the applications.

4   *Capital requirements.* The need to invest large financial resources in order to compete can deter new entrants. Capital may be necessary not only for fixed facilities but also to extend customer credit, build inventories, and fund start-up losses. The barrier is particularly great if the capital is required for unrecoverable and therefore harder-to-finance expenditures, such as up-front advertising or research and development. While major corporations have the financial resources to invade almost any industry, the huge capital requirements in certain fields limit the pool of likely entrants. Conversely, in such fields as tax preparation services or short-haul trucking, capital requirements are minimal and potential entrants plentiful.

It is important not to overstate the degree to which capital requirements alone deter entry. If industry returns are attractive and are expected to remain so, and if capital markets are efficient, investors will provide entrants with the funds they need. For aspiring air carriers, for instance, financing is available to purchase expensive aircraft because of their high resale value, one reason why there have been numerous new airlines in almost every region.

5   *Incumbency advantages independent of size.* No matter what their size, incumbents may have cost or quality advantages not available to potential rivals. These advantages can stem from such sources as proprietary technology, preferential access to the best raw material sources, preemption of the most favorable geographic locations, established brand identities, or cumulative experience that has allowed incumbents to learn how to produce more efficiently. Entrants try to bypass such advantages. Upstart discounters such as Target and Wal-Mart, for example, have located stores in free-standing sites rather than regional shopping centers where established department stores were well entrenched.

6   *Unequal access to distribution channels.* The new entrant must, of course, secure distribution of its product or service. A new food item, for example, must displace others from the supermarket shelf via price breaks, promotions, intense selling efforts, or some other means. The more limited the wholesale or retail channels are and the more that existing competitors have tied them up, the tougher entry into an industry will be. Sometimes access to distribution is so high a barrier that new entrants must bypass distribution channels altogether or create their own. Thus, upstart low-cost airlines have avoided distribution through travel agents (who tend to favor established higher-fare carriers) and have encouraged passengers to book their own flights on the internet.

7   *Restrictive government policy.* Government policy can hinder or aid new entry directly, as well as amplify (or nullify) the other entry barriers. Government directly limits or even forecloses entry into industries through, for instance, licensing requirements and restrictions on foreign investment. Regulated industries like liquor retailing, taxi services, and airlines are visible examples. Government policy can heighten other entry barriers through such means as expansive patenting rules that protect proprietary technology from imitation

or environmental or safety regulations that raise scale economies facing new-comers. Of course, government policies may also make entry easier—directly through subsidies, for instance, or indirectly by funding basic research and making it available to all firms, new and old, reducing scale economies.

Entry barriers should be assessed relative to the capabilities of potential entrants, which may be start-ups, foreign firms, or companies in related industries. And, as some of our examples illustrate, the strategist must be mindful of the creative ways newcomers might find to circumvent apparent barriers.

Expected retaliation. How potential entrants believe incumbents may react will also influence their decision to enter or stay out of an industry. If reaction is vigorous and protracted enough, the profit potential of participating in the industry can fall below the cost of capital. Incumbents often use public statements and responses to one entrant to send a message to other prospective entrants about their commitment to defending market share.

Newcomers are likely to fear expected retaliation if:

- Incumbents have previously responded vigorously to new entrants.

- Incumbents possess substantial resources to fight back, including excess cash and unused borrowing power, available productive capacity, or clout with distribution channels and customers.

- Incumbents seem likely to cut prices because they are committed to retaining market share at all costs or because the industry has high fixed costs, which create a strong motivation to drop prices to fill excess capacity.

- Industry growth is slow so newcomers can gain volume only by taking it from incumbents.

BOX 1 INDUSTRY ANALYSIS IN PRACTICE

Good industry analysis looks rigorously at the structural underpinnings of profitability. A first step is to understand the appropriate time horizon. One of the essential tasks in industry analysis is to distinguish temporary or cyclical changes from structural changes. A good guideline for the appropriate time horizon is the full business cycle for the particular industry. For most industries, a three-to-five-year horizon is appropriate, although in some industries with long lead times, such as mining, the appropriate horizon might be a decade or more. It is average profitability over this period, not profitability in any particular year, that should be the focus of analysis.

The point of industry analysis is not to declare the industry attractive or unattractive but to understand the underpinnings of competition and the root causes of profitability. As much as possible, analysts should look at industry structure quantitatively, rather than be satisfied with lists of qualitative factors. Many elements of the five forces can be quantified: the percentage of the buyer's total cost accounted for by the industry's product (to understand buyer price sensitivity); the percentage of industry sales required to fill a plant or operate a logistical network of efficient scale (to help assess barriers to entry); the buyer's switching cost (determining the inducement an entrant or rival must offer customers).

The strength of the competitive forces affects prices, costs, and the investment required to compete; thus the forces are directly tied to the income statements and balance sheets of industry participants. Industry structure defines the gap between revenues and costs. For example, intense rivalry drives down prices or elevates the costs of marketing, R&D, or customer service, reducing margins. How much? Strong suppliers drive up input costs. How much? Buyer power lowers prices or elevates the costs of meeting buyers' demands, such as the requirement to hold more inventory or provide financing. How much? Low barriers to entry or close substitutes limit the level of sustainable prices. How much? It is these economic relationships that sharpen the strategist's understanding of industry competition.

Finally, good industry analysis does not just list pluses and minuses but sees an industry in overall, systemic terms. Which forces are underpinning (or constraining) today's profitability? How might shifts in one competitive force trigger reactions in others? Answering such questions is often the source of true strategic insights.

An analysis of barriers to entry and expected retaliation is obviously crucial for any company contemplating entry into a new industry. The challenge is to find ways to surmount the entry barriers without nullifying, through heavy investment, the profitability of participating in the industry.

The Power of Suppliers   Powerful suppliers capture more of the value for themselves by charging higher prices, limiting quality or services, or shifting costs to industry participants. Powerful suppliers, including suppliers of labor, can squeeze profitability out of an industry that is unable to pass on cost increases in its own prices. Microsoft, for instance, has contributed to the erosion of profitability among personal computer makers by raising prices on operating systems. PC makers, competing fiercely for customers who can easily switch among them, have limited freedom to raise their prices accordingly.

Companies depend on a wide range of different supplier groups for inputs. A supplier group is powerful if:

- It is more concentrated than the industry it sells to. Microsoft's near monopoly in operating systems, coupled with the fragmentation of PC assemblers, exemplifies this situation.

- The supplier group does not depend heavily on the industry for its revenues. Suppliers serving many industries will not hesitate to extract maximum profits from each one. If a particular industry accounts for a large portion of a supplier group's volume or profit, however, suppliers will want to protect the industry through reasonable pricing and assist in activities such as R&D and lobbying.

- Industry participants face switching costs in changing suppliers. For example, shifting suppliers is difficult if companies have invested heavily in specialized ancillary equipment or in learning how to operate a supplier's equipment (as with Bloomberg terminals used by financial professionals). Or firms may have located their production lines adjacent to a supplier's manufacturing facilities (as in the case of some beverage companies and container manufacturers). When switching costs are high, industry participants find it hard to play suppliers off against one another. (Note that suppliers may have switching costs as well. This limits their power.)

- Suppliers offer products that are differentiated. Pharmaceutical companies that offer patented drugs with distinctive medical benefits have more power over hospitals, health maintenance organizations, and other drug buyers, for example, than drug companies offering me-too or generic products.

- There is no substitute for what the supplier group provides. Pilots' unions, for example, exercise considerable supplier power over airlines partly because there is no good alternative to a well-trained pilot in the cockpit.

- The supplier group can credibly threaten to integrate forward into the industry. In that case, if industry participants make too much money relative to suppliers, they will induce suppliers to enter the market.

The Power of Buyers   Powerful customers—the flip side of powerful suppliers—can capture more value by forcing down prices, demanding better quality or more service (thereby driving up costs), and generally playing industry participants off against one another, all at the expense of industry profitability. Buyers are powerful if they have negotiating leverage relative to industry participants, especially if they are price sensitive, using their clout primarily to pressure price reductions.

As with suppliers, there may be distinct groups of customers who differ in bargaining power. A customer group has negotiating leverage if:

- There are few buyers, or each one purchases in volumes that are large relative to the size of a single vendor. Large-volume buyers are particularly powerful in industries with high fixed costs, such as telecommunications equipment, offshore drilling, and bulk chemicals. High fixed costs and low marginal costs amplify the pressure on rivals to keep capacity filled through discounting.

- The industry's products are standardized or undifferentiated. If buyers believe they can always find an equivalent product, they tend to play one vendor against another.

- Buyers face few switching costs in changing vendors.

- Buyers can credibly threaten to integrate backward and produce the industry's product themselves if vendors are too profitable. Producers of soft drinks and beer have long controlled the power of packaging manufacturers by threatening to make, and at times actually making, packaging materials themselves.

A buyer group is price sensitive if:

- The product it purchases from the industry represents a significant fraction of its cost structure or procurement budget. Here buyers are likely to shop around and bargain hard, as consumers do for home mortgages. Where the product sold by an industry is a small fraction of buyers' costs or expenditures, buyers are usually less price sensitive.

- The buyer group earns low profits, is strapped for cash, or is otherwise under pressure to trim its purchasing costs. Highly profitable or cash-rich customers, in contrast, are generally less price sensitive (that is, of course, if the item does not represent a large fraction of their costs).

- The quality of buyers' products or services is little affected by the industry's product. Where quality is very much affected by the industry's product, buyers are generally less price sensitive. When purchasing or renting production quality cameras, for instance, makers of major motion pictures opt for highly reliable equipment with the latest features. They pay limited attention to price.

- The industry's product has little effect on the buyer's other costs. Here, buyers focus on price. Conversely, where an industry's product or service can pay for itself many times over by improving performance or reducing labor, material, or other costs, buyers are usually more interested in quality than in price. Examples include products and services like tax accounting or well logging (which measures below-ground conditions of oil wells) that can save or even make the buyer money. Similarly, buyers tend not to be price sensitive in services such as investment banking, where poor performance can be costly and embarrassing.

Most sources of buyer power apply equally to consumers and to business-to-business customers. Like industrial customers, consumers tend to be more price sensitive if they are purchasing products that are undifferentiated, expensive relative to their incomes, and of a sort where product performance has limited consequences. The major difference with consumers is that their needs can be more intangible and harder to quantify.

Intermediate customers, or customers who purchase the product but are not the end user (such as assemblers or distribution channels), can be analyzed the same way as other buyers, with one important addition. Intermediate customers gain significant bargaining power when they can influence the purchasing decisions of customers downstream. Consumer electronics retailers, jewelry retailers, and agricultural-equipment distributors are examples of distribution channels that exert a strong influence on end customers.

Producers often attempt to diminish channel clout through exclusive arrangements with particular distributors or retailers or by marketing directly to end users. Component manufacturers seek to develop power over assemblers by creating preferences for their components with downstream customers. Such is the case with bicycle parts and with sweeteners. DuPont has created enormous clout by advertising its Stainmaster brand of carpet fibers not only to the carpet manufacturers that actually buy them but also to downstream consumers. Many consumers request Stainmaster carpet even though DuPont is not a carpet manufacturer.

The Threat of Substitutes   A substitute performs the same or a similar function as an industry's product by a different means. Video-conferencing is a substitute for travel. Plastic is a substitute for aluminum. E-mail is a substitute for express mail. Sometimes, the threat of substitution is downstream or indirect, when a substitute replaces a buyer industry's product. For example, lawn-care products and services are threatened when multifamily homes in urban areas substitute for single-family homes in the suburbs. Software sold to agents is threatened when airline and travel websites substitute for travel agents.

Substitutes are always present, but they are easy to overlook because they may appear to be very different from the industry's product: To someone searching for a Father's Day gift, neckties and power tools may be substitutes. It is a substitute to do without, to purchase a used product rather than a new one, or to do it yourself (bring the service or product in-house).

When the threat of substitutes is high, industry profitability suffers. Substitute products or services limit an industry's profit potential by placing a ceiling on prices. If an industry does not distance itself from substitutes through product performance, marketing, or other means, it will suffer in terms of profitability—and often growth potential.

Substitutes not only limit profits in normal times, they also reduce the bonanza an industry can reap in good times. In emerging economies, for example, the surge in demand for wired telephone lines has been capped as many consumers opt to make a mobile telephone their first and only phone line.

The threat of a substitute is high if:

- It offers an attractive price-performance trade-off to the industry's product. The better the relative value of the substitute, the tighter is the lid on an industry's profit potential. For example, conventional providers of long-distance telephone service have suffered from the advent of inexpensive internet-based phone services such as Vonage and Skype. Similarly, video rental outlets are struggling with the emergence of cable and satellite video-on-demand services, online video rental services such as Netflix, and the rise of internet video sites like Google's YouTube.

- The buyer's cost of switching to the substitute is low. Switching from a proprietary, branded drug to a generic drug usually involves minimal costs, for example, which is why the shift to generics (and the fall in prices) is so substantial and rapid.

Strategists should be particularly alert to changes in other industries that may make them attractive substitutes when they were not before. Improvements in plastic materials, for example, allowed them to substitute for steel in many automobile components. In this way, technological changes or competitive discontinuities in seemingly unrelated businesses can have major impacts on industry profitability. Of course the substitution threat can also shift in favor of an industry, which bodes well for its future profitability and growth potential.

Rivalry among Existing Competitors   Rivalry among existing competitors takes many familiar forms, including price discounting, new product introductions, advertising campaigns, and service improvements. High rivalry limits the profitability of an industry. The degree to which rivalry drives down an industry's profit potential depends, first, on the *intensity* with which companies compete and, second, on the *basis* on which they compete.

The intensity of rivalry is greatest if:

■ Competitors are numerous or are roughly equal in size and power. In such situations, rivals find it hard to avoid poaching business. Without an industry leader, practices desirable for the industry as a whole go unenforced.

■ Industry growth is slow. Slow growth precipitates fights for market share.

■ Exit barriers are high. Exit barriers, the flip side of entry barriers, arise because of such things as highly specialized assets or management's devotion to a particular business. These barriers keep companies in the market even though they may be earning low or negative returns. Excess capacity remains in use, and the profitability of healthy competitors suffers as the sick ones hang on.

■ Rivals are highly committed to the business and have aspirations for leadership, especially if they have goals that go beyond economic performance in the particular industry. High commitment to a business arises for a variety of reasons. For example, state-owned competitors may have goals that include employment or prestige. Units of larger companies may participate in an industry for image reasons or to offer a full line. Clashes of personality and ego have sometimes exaggerated rivalry to the detriment of profitability in fields such as the media and high technology.

■ Firms cannot read each other's signals well because of lack of familiarity with one another, diverse approaches to competing, or differing goals.

The strength of rivalry reflects not just the intensity of competition but also the basis of competition. The *dimensions* on which competition takes place, and whether rivals converge to compete on the *same dimensions*, have a major influence on profitability.

Rivalry is especially destructive to profitability if it gravitates solely to price because price competition transfers profits directly from an industry to its customers. Price cuts are usually easy for competitors to see and match, making successive rounds of retaliation likely. Sustained price competition also trains customers to pay less attention to product features and service.

Price competition is most liable to occur if:

■ Products or services of rivals are nearly identical and there are few switching costs for buyers. This encourages competitors to cut prices to win new customers. Years of airline price wars reflect these circumstances in that industry.

■ Fixed costs are high and marginal costs are low. This creates intense pressure for competitors to cut prices below their average costs, even close to their marginal costs, to steal incremental customers while still making some contribution to covering fixed costs. Many basic-materials businesses, such as paper and aluminum, suffer from this problem, especially if demand is not growing. So do delivery companies with fixed networks of routes that must be served regardless of volume.

- Capacity must be expanded in large increments to be efficient. The need for large capacity expansions, as in the polyvinyl chloride business, disrupts the industry's supply-demand balance and often leads to long and recurring periods of overcapacity and price cutting.

- The product is perishable. Perishability creates a strong temptation to cut prices and sell a product while it still has value. More products and services are perishable than is commonly thought. Just as tomatoes are perishable because they rot, models of computers are perishable because they soon become obsolete, and information may be perishable if it diffuses rapidly or becomes outdated, thereby losing its value. Services such as hotel accommodations are perishable in the sense that unused capacity can never be recovered.

Competition on dimensions other than price—on product features, support services, delivery time, or brand image, for instance—is less likely to erode profitability because it improves customer value and can support higher prices. Also, rivalry focused on such dimensions can improve value relative to substitutes or raise the barriers facing new entrants. While nonprice rivalry sometimes escalates to levels that undermine industry profitability, this is less likely to occur than it is with price rivalry.

As important as the dimensions of rivalry is whether rivals compete on the *same* dimensions. When all or many competitors aim to meet the same needs or compete on the same attributes, the result is zero-sum competition. Here, one firm's gain is often another's loss, driving down profitability. While price competition runs a stronger risk than nonprice competition of becoming zero sum, this may not happen if companies take care to segment their markets, targeting their low-price offerings to different customers.

Rivalry can be positive sum, or actually increase the average profitability of an industry, when each competitor aims to serve the needs of different customer segments, with different mixes of price, products, services, features, or brand identities. Such competition can not only support higher average profitability but also expand the industry, as the needs of more customer groups are better met. The opportunity for positive-sum competition will be greater in industries serving diverse customer groups. With a clear understanding of the structural underpinnings of rivalry, strategists can sometimes take steps to shift the nature of competition in a more positive direction.

FACTORS, NOT FORCES   **3**

Industry structure, as manifested in the strength of the five competitive forces, determines the industry's long-run profit potential because it determines how the economic value created by the industry is divided—how much is retained by companies in the industry versus bargained away by customers and suppliers, limited by substitutes, or constrained by potential new entrants. By considering all five forces, a strategist keeps overall structure in mind instead of gravitating to any one element. In addition, the strategist's attention remains focused on structural conditions rather than on fleeting factors.

It is especially important to avoid the common pitfall of mistaking certain visible attributes of an industry for its underlying structure. Consider the following:

Industry Growth Rate   A common mistake is to assume that fast-growing industries are always attractive. Growth does tend to mute rivalry, because an expanding pie offers opportunities for all competitors. But fast growth can put suppliers in a powerful position, and high growth with low entry barriers will draw in entrants. Even without new entrants, a high growth rate will not guarantee profitability if customers are powerful or substitutes are attractive. Indeed, some fast-growth businesses, such as personal computers, have been among the least profitable industries in recent years. A narrow focus on growth is one of the major causes of bad strategy decisions.

Technology and Innovation   Advanced technology or innovations are not by themselves enough to make an industry structurally attractive (or unattractive). Mundane, low-technology industries with price-insensitive buyers, high switching costs, or high entry barriers arising from scale economies are often far more profitable than sexy industries, such as software and internet technologies, that attract competitors.[2]

Government   Government is not best understood as a sixth force because government involvement is neither inherently good nor bad for industry profitability. The best way to understand the influence of government on competition is to analyze how specific government policies affect the five competitive forces. For instance, patents raise barriers to entry, boosting industry profit potential. Conversely, government policies favoring unions may raise supplier power and diminish profit potential. Bankruptcy rules that allow failing companies to reorganize rather than exit can lead to excess capacity and intense rivalry. Government operates at multiple levels and through many different policies, each of which will affect structure in different ways.

Complementary Products and Services   Complements are products or services used together with an industry's product. Complements arise when the customer benefit of two products combined is greater than the sum of each product's value in isolation. Computer hardware and software, for instance, are valuable together and worthless when separated.

In recent years, strategy researchers have highlighted the role of complements, especially in high-technology industries where they are most obvious.[3] By no means, however, do complements appear only there. The value of a car, for example, is greater when the driver also has access to gasoline stations, roadside assistance, and auto insurance.

Complements can be important when they affect the overall demand for an industry's product. However, like government policy, complements are not a sixth force determining industry profitability since the presence of strong complements is not necessarily bad (or good) for industry profitability. Complements affect profitability through the way they influence the five forces.

The strategist must trace the positive or negative influence of complements on all five forces to ascertain their impact on profitability. The presence of complements can raise or lower barriers to entry. In application software, for example, barriers to entry were lowered when producers of complementary operating system software, notably Microsoft, provided tool sets making it easier to write applications. Conversely, the need to attract producers of complements can raise barriers to entry, as it does in video game hardware.

---

2 For a discussion of how internet technology improves the attractiveness of some industries while eroding the profitability of others, see Michael E. Porter, "Strategy and the Internet" (HBR, March 2001).

3 See, for instance, Adam M. Brandenburger and Barry J. Nalebuff, *Co-opetition* (Currency Doubleday, 1996).

The presence of complements can also affect the threat of substitutes. For instance, the need for appropriate fueling stations makes it difficult for cars using alternative fuels to substitute for conventional vehicles. But complements can also make substitution easier. For example, Apple's iTunes hastened the substitution from CDs to digital music.

Complements can factor into industry rivalry either positively (as when they raise switching costs) or negatively (as when they neutralize product differentiation). Similar analyses can be done for buyer and supplier power. Sometimes companies compete by altering conditions in complementary industries in their favor, such as when videocassette-recorder producer JVC persuaded movie studios to favor its standard in issuing prerecorded tapes even though rival Sony's standard was probably superior from a technical standpoint.

Identifying complements is part of the analyst's work. As with government policies or important technologies, the strategic significance of complements will be best understood through the lens of the five forces.

CHANGES IN INDUSTRY STRUCTURE

4

So far, we have discussed the competitive forces at a single point in time. Industry structure proves to be relatively stable, and industry profitability differences are remarkably persistent over time in practice. However, industry structure is constantly undergoing modest adjustment—and occasionally it can change abruptly.

Shifts in structure may emanate from outside an industry or from within. They can boost the industry's profit potential or reduce it. They may be caused by changes in technology, changes in customer needs, or other events. The five competitive forces provide a framework for identifying the most important industry developments and for anticipating their impact on industry attractiveness.

Shifting Threat of New Entry   Changes to any of the seven barriers described above can raise or lower the threat of new entry. The expiration of a patent, for instance, may unleash new entrants. On the day that Merck's patents for the cholesterol reducer Zocor expired, three pharmaceutical makers entered the market for the drug. Conversely, the proliferation of products in the ice cream industry has gradually filled up the limited freezer space in grocery stores, making it harder for new ice cream makers to gain access to distribution in North America and Europe.

Strategic decisions of leading competitors often have a major impact on the threat of entry. Starting in the 1970s, for example, retailers such as Wal-Mart, Kmart, and Toys "R" Us began to adopt new procurement, distribution, and inventory control technologies with large fixed costs, including automated distribution centers, bar coding, and point-of-sale terminals. These investments increased the economies of scale and made it more difficult for small retailers to enter the business (and for existing small players to survive).

Changing Supplier or Buyer Power   As the factors underlying the power of suppliers and buyers change with time, their clout rises or declines. In the global appliance industry, for instance, competitors including Electrolux, General Electric, and Whirlpool have been squeezed by the consolidation of retail channels (the decline of appliance specialty stores, for instance, and the rise of big-box retailers like Best Buy and Home Depot in the United States). Another example is travel agents, who depend on airlines as a key supplier. When the internet allowed airlines to sell tickets directly to customers, this significantly increased their power to bargain down agents' commissions.

Shifting Threat of Substitution   The most common reason substitutes become more or less threatening over time is that advances in technology create new substitutes or shift price-performance comparisons in one direction or the other. The earliest microwave ovens, for example, were large and priced above $2,000, making them poor substitutes for conventional ovens. With technological advances, they became serious substitutes. Flash computer memory has improved enough recently to become a meaningful substitute for low-capacity hard-disk drives. Trends in the availability or performance of complementary producers also shift the threat of substitutes.

New Bases of Rivalry   Rivalry often intensifies naturally over time. As an industry matures, growth slows. Competitors become more alike as industry conventions emerge, technology diffuses, and consumer tastes converge. Industry profitability falls, and weaker competitors are driven from the business. This story has played out in industry after industry; televisions, snowmobiles, and telecommunications equipment are just a few examples.

A trend toward intensifying price competition and other forms of rivalry, however, is by no means inevitable. For example, there has been enormous competitive activity in the US casino industry in recent decades, but most of it has been positive-sum competition directed toward new niches and geographic segments (such as riverboats, trophy properties, Native American reservations, international expansion, and novel customer groups like families). Head-to-head rivalry that lowers prices or boosts the payouts to winners has been limited.

The nature of rivalry in an industry is altered by mergers and acquisitions that introduce new capabilities and ways of competing. Or, technological innovation can reshape rivalry. In the retail brokerage industry, the advent of the internet lowered marginal costs and reduced differentiation, triggering far more intense competition on commissions and fees than in the past.

In some industries, companies turn to mergers and consolidation not to improve cost and quality but to attempt to stop intense competition. Eliminating rivals is a risky strategy, however. The five competitive forces tell us that a profit windfall from removing today's competitors often attracts new competitors and backlash from customers and suppliers. In New York banking, for example, the 1980s and 1990s saw escalating consolidations of commercial and savings banks, including Manufacturers Hanover, Chemical, Chase, and Dime Savings. But today the retail-banking landscape of Manhattan is as diverse as ever, as new entrants such as Wachovia, Bank of America, and Washington Mutual have entered the market.

5   IMPLICATIONS FOR STRATEGY

Understanding the forces that shape industry competition is the starting point for developing strategy. Every company should already know what the average profitability of its industry is and how that has been changing over time. The five forces reveal *why* industry profitability is what it is. Only then can a company incorporate industry conditions into strategy.

The forces reveal the most significant aspects of the competitive environment. They also provide a baseline for sizing up a company's strengths and weaknesses: Where does the company stand versus buyers, suppliers, entrants, rivals, and substitutes? Most importantly, an understanding of industry structure guides managers toward fruitful possibilities for strategic action, which may include any or all of the following: positioning the company to better cope with the current competitive forces; anticipating and exploiting shifts in the forces; and shaping the balance of forces to create a new industry structure that is more favorable to the company. The best strategies exploit more than one of these possibilities.

Positioning the Company   Strategy can be viewed as building defenses against the competitive forces or finding a position in the industry where the forces are weakest. Consider, for instance, the position of Paccar in the market for heavy trucks. The heavy-truck industry is structurally challenging. Many buyers operate large fleets or are large leasing companies, with both the leverage and the motivation to drive down the price of one of their largest purchases. Most trucks are built to regulated standards and offer similar features, so price competition is rampant. Capital intensity causes rivalry to be fierce, especially during the recurring cyclical downturns. Unions exercise considerable supplier power. Though there are few direct substitutes for an 18-wheeler, truck buyers face important substitutes for their services, such as cargo delivery by rail.

In this setting, Paccar, a Bellevue, Washington-based company with about 20% of the North American heavy-truck market, has chosen to focus on one group of customers: owner-operators—drivers who own their trucks and contract directly with shippers or serve as subcontractors to larger trucking companies. Such small operators have limited clout as truck buyers. They are also less price sensitive because of their strong emotional ties to and economic dependence on the product. They take great pride in their trucks, in which they spend most of their time.

Paccar has invested heavily to develop an array of features with owner-operators in mind: luxurious sleeper cabins, plush leather seats, noise-insulated cabins, sleek exterior styling, and so on. At the company's extensive network of dealers, prospective buyers use software to select among thousands of options to put their personal signature on their trucks. These customized trucks are built to order, not to stock, and delivered in six to eight weeks. Paccar's trucks also have aerodynamic designs that reduce fuel consumption, and they maintain their resale value better than other trucks. Paccar's roadside assistance program and IT-supported system for distributing spare parts reduce the time a truck is out of service. All these are crucial considerations for an owner-operator. Customers pay Paccar a 10% premium, and its Kenworth and Peterbilt brands are considered status symbols at truck stops.

Paccar illustrates the principles of positioning a company within a given industry structure. The firm has found a portion of its industry where the competitive forces are weaker—where it can avoid buyer power and price-based rivalry. And it has tailored every single part of the value chain to cope well with the forces in its segment. As a result, Paccar has been profitable for 68 years straight and has earned a long-run return on equity above 20%.

In addition to revealing positioning opportunities within an existing industry, the five forces framework allows companies to rigorously analyze entry and exit. Both depend on answering the difficult question: "What is the potential of this business?" Exit is indicated when industry structure is poor or declining and the company has no prospect of a superior positioning. In considering entry into a new industry, creative strategists can use the framework to spot an industry with a good future before this good future is reflected in the prices of acquisition candidates. Five forces analysis may also reveal industries that are not necessarily attractive for the average entrant but in which a company has good reason to believe it can surmount entry barriers at lower cost than most firms or has a unique ability to cope with the industry's competitive forces.

Exploiting Industry Change   Industry changes bring the opportunity to spot and claim promising new strategic positions if the strategist has a sophisticated understanding of the competitive forces and their underpinnings. Consider, for instance, the evolution of the music industry during the past decade. With the advent of the internet and the digital distribution of music, some analysts predicted the birth of thousands of music labels (that is, record companies that develop artists and bring their music to market). This, the analysts argued, would break a pattern that had held since Edison invented the phonograph: Between three and six major record companies had always dominated the industry. The internet would, they predicted, remove distribution as a barrier to entry, unleashing a flood of new players into the music industry.

A careful analysis, however, would have revealed that physical distribution was not the crucial barrier to entry. Rather, entry was barred by other benefits that large music labels enjoyed. Large labels could pool the risks of developing new artists over many bets, cushioning the impact of inevitable failures. Even more important, they had advantages in breaking through the clutter and getting their new artists heard. To do so, they could promise radio stations and record stores access to well-known artists in exchange for promotion of new artists. New labels would find this nearly impossible to match. The major labels stayed the course, and new music labels have been rare.

This is not to say that the music industry is structurally unchanged by digital distribution. Unauthorized downloading created an illegal but potent substitute. The labels tried for years to develop technical platforms for digital distribution themselves, but major companies hesitated to sell their music through a platform owned by a rival. Into this vacuum stepped Apple with its iTunes music store, launched in 2003 to support its iPod music player. By permitting the creation of a powerful new gate-keeper, the major labels allowed industry structure to shift against them. The number of major record companies has actually declined—from six in 1997 to four today—as companies struggled to cope with the digital phenomenon.

When industry structure is in flux, new and promising competitive positions may appear. Structural changes open up new needs and new ways to serve existing needs. Established leaders may overlook these or be constrained by past strategies from pursuing them. Smaller competitors in the industry can capitalize on such changes, or the void may well be filled by new entrants.

Shaping Industry Structure   When a company exploits structural change, it is recognizing, and reacting to, the inevitable. However, companies also have the ability to shape industry structure. A firm can lead its industry toward new ways of competing that alter the five forces for the better. In reshaping structure, a company wants its competitors to follow so that the entire industry will be transformed. While many industry participants may benefit in the process, the innovator can benefit most if it can shift competition in directions where it can excel.

An industry's structure can be reshaped in two ways: by redividing profitability in favor of incumbents or by expanding the overall profit pool. Redividing the industry pie aims to increase the share of profits to industry competitors instead of to suppliers, buyers, substitutes, and keeping out potential entrants. Expanding the profit pool involves increasing the overall pool of economic value generated by the industry in which rivals, buyers, and suppliers can all share.

Redividing profitability.   To capture more profits for industry rivals, the starting point is to determine which force or forces are currently constraining industry profitability and address them. A company can potentially influence all of the competitive forces. The strategist's goal here is to reduce the share of profits that leak to suppliers, buyers, and substitutes or are sacrificed to deter entrants.

To neutralize supplier power, for example, a firm can standardize specifications for parts to make it easier to switch among suppliers. It can cultivate additional vendors, or alter technology to avoid a powerful supplier group altogether. To counter customer power, companies may expand services that raise buyers' switching costs or find alternative means of reaching customers to neutralize powerful channels. To temper profit-eroding price rivalry, companies can invest more heavily in unique products, as pharmaceutical firms have done, or expand support services to customers. To scare off entrants, incumbents can elevate the fixed cost of competing—for instance, by escalating their R&D or marketing expenditures. To limit the threat of substitutes, companies can offer better value through new features or wider product accessibility. When soft-drink producers introduced vending machines and convenience store channels, for example, they dramatically improved the availability of soft drinks relative to other beverages.

Sysco, the largest food-service distributor in North America, offers a revealing example of how an industry leader can change the structure of an industry for the better. Food-service distributors purchase food and related items from farmers and food processors. They then warehouse and deliver these items to restaurants, hospitals, employer cafeterias, schools, and other food-service institutions. Given low barriers to entry, the food-service distribution industry has historically been highly fragmented, with numerous local competitors. While rivals try to cultivate customer relationships, buyers are price sensitive because food represents a large share of their costs. Buyers can also choose the substitute approaches of purchasing directly from manufacturers or using retail sources, avoiding distributors altogether. Suppliers wield bargaining power: They are often large companies with strong brand names that food preparers and consumers recognize. Average profitability in the industry has been modest.

Sysco recognized that, given its size and national reach, it might change this state of affairs. It led the move to introduce private-label distributor brands with specifications tailored to the food-service market, moderating supplier power. Sysco emphasized value-added services to buyers such as credit, menu planning, and inventory management to shift the basis of competition away from just price. These moves, together with stepped-up investments in information technology and regional distribution centers, substantially raised the bar for new entrants while making the substitutes less attractive. Not surprisingly, the industry has been consolidating, and industry profitability appears to be rising.

Industry leaders have a special responsibility for improving industry structure. Doing so often requires resources that only large players possess. Moreover, an improved industry structure is a public good because it benefits every firm in the industry, not just the company that initiated the improvement. Often, it is more in the interests of an industry leader than any other participant to invest for the common good because leaders will usually benefit the most. Indeed, improving the industry may be a leader's most profitable strategic opportunity, in part because attempts to gain further market share can trigger strong reactions from rivals, customers, and even suppliers.

There is a dark side to shaping industry structure that is equally important to understand. Ill-advised changes in competitive positioning and operating practices can *undermine* industry structure. Faced with pressures to gain market share or enamored with innovation for its own sake, managers may trigger new kinds of competition that no incumbent can win. When taking actions to improve their own company's competitive advantage, then, strategists should ask whether they are setting in motion dynamics that will undermine industry structure in the long run. In the early days of the personal computer industry, for instance, IBM tried to make up for its late entry by offering an open architecture that would set industry standards and attract complementary makers of application software and peripherals. In the process, it ceded ownership of the critical components of the PC—the operating system and the microprocessor—to Microsoft and Intel. By standardizing PCs, it encouraged price-based rivalry and shifted power to suppliers. Consequently, IBM became the temporarily dominant firm in an industry with an enduringly unattractive structure.

Expanding the profit pool.   When overall demand grows, the industry's quality level rises, intrinsic costs are reduced, or waste is eliminated, the pie expands. The total pool of value available to competitors, suppliers, and buyers grows. The total profit pool expands, for example, when channels become more competitive or when an industry discovers latent buyers for its product that are not currently being served. When soft-drink producers rationalized their independent bottler networks to make them more efficient and effective, both the soft-drink companies and the bottlers benefited. Overall value can also expand when firms work collaboratively with suppliers to improve coordination and limit unnecessary costs incurred in the supply chain. This lowers the inherent cost structure of the industry, allowing higher profit, greater demand through lower prices, or both. Or, agreeing on quality standards can bring up industrywide quality and service levels, and hence prices, benefiting rivals, suppliers, and customers.

Expanding the overall profit pool creates win-win opportunities for multiple industry participants. It can also reduce the risk of destructive rivalry that arises when incumbents attempt to shift bargaining power or capture more market share. However, expanding the pie does not reduce the importance of industry structure. How the expanded pie is divided will ultimately be determined by the five forces. The most successful companies are those that expand the industry profit pool in ways that allow them to share disproportionately in the benefits.

Defining the Industry   The five competitive forces also hold the key to defining the relevant industry (or industries) in which a company competes. Drawing industry boundaries correctly, around the arena in which competition actually takes place, will clarify the causes of profitability and the appropriate unit for setting strategy. A company needs a separate strategy for each distinct industry. Mistakes in industry definition made by competitors present opportunities for staking out superior strategic positions. (See Box 2, "Defining the Relevant Industry.")

6   COMPETITION AND VALUE

The competitive forces reveal the drivers of industry competition. A company strategist who understands that competition extends well beyond existing rivals will detect wider competitive threats and be better equipped to address them. At the same time, thinking comprehensively about an industry's structure can uncover opportunities: differences in customers, suppliers, substitutes, potential entrants, and rivals that can become the basis for distinct strategies yielding superior performance. In a world of more open competition and relentless change, it is more important than ever to think structurally about competition.

Understanding industry structure is equally important for investors as for managers. The five competitive forces reveal whether an industry is truly attractive, and they help investors anticipate positive or negative shifts in industry structure before they are obvious. The five forces distinguish short-term blips from structural changes and allow investors to take advantage of undue pessimism or optimism. Those companies whose strategies have industry-transforming potential become far clearer. This deeper thinking about competition is a more powerful way to achieve genuine investment success than the financial projections and trend extrapolation that dominate today's investment analysis.

BOX 2 DEFINING THE RELEVANT INDUSTRY

Defining the industry in which competition actually takes place is important for good industry analysis, not to mention for developing strategy and setting business unit boundaries. Many strategy errors emanate from mistaking the relevant industry, defining it too broadly or too narrowly. Defining the industry too broadly obscures differences among products, customers, or geographic regions that are important to competition, strategic positioning, and profitability. Defining the industry too narrowly overlooks commonalities and linkages across related products or geographic markets that are crucial to competitive advantage. Also, strategists must be sensitive to the possibility that industry boundaries can shift.

The boundaries of an industry consist of two primary dimensions. First is the *scope of products or services*. For example, is motor oil used in cars part of the same industry as motor oil used in heavy trucks and stationary engines, or are these different industries? The second dimension is *geographic scope*. Most industries are present in many parts of the world. However, is competition contained within each state, or is it national? Does competition take place within regions such as Europe or North America, or is there a single global industry?

The five forces are the basic tool to resolve these questions. If industry structure for two products is the same or very similar (that is, if they have the same buyers, suppliers, barriers to entry, and so forth), then the products are best treated as being part of the same industry. If industry structure differs markedly, however, the two products may be best understood as separate industries.

In lubricants, the oil used in cars is similar or even identical to the oil used in trucks, but the similarity largely ends there. Automotive motor oil is sold to fragmented, generally unsophisticated customers through numerous and often powerful channels, using extensive advertising. Products are packaged in small containers and logistical costs are high, necessitating local production. Truck and power generation lubricants are sold to entirely different buyers in entirely different ways using a separate supply chain. Industry structure (buyer power, barriers to entry, and so forth) is substantially different. Automotive oil is thus a distinct industry from oil for truck and stationary engine uses. Industry profitability will differ in these two cases, and a lubricant company will need a separate strategy for competing in each area.

Differences in the five competitive forces also reveal the geographic scope of competition. If an industry has a similar structure in every country (rivals, buyers, and so on), the presumption is that competition is global, and the five forces analyzed from a global perspective will set average profitability. A single global strategy is needed. If an industry has quite different structures in different geographic regions, however, each region may well be a distinct industry. Otherwise, competition would have leveled the differences. The five forces analyzed for each region will set profitability there.

The extent of differences in the five forces for related products or across geographic areas is a matter of degree, making industry definition often a matter of judgment. A rule of thumb is that where the differences in any one force are large, and where the differences involve more than one force, distinct industries may well be present.

Fortunately, however, even if industry boundaries are drawn incorrectly, careful five forces analysis should reveal important competitive threats. A closely related product omitted from the industry definition will show up as a substitute, for example, or competitors overlooked as rivals will be recognized as potential entrants. At the same time, the five forces analysis should reveal major differences within overly broad industries that will indicate the need to adjust industry boundaries or strategies.

BOX 3 TYPICAL STEPS IN INDUSTRY ANALYSIS

Define the relevant industry:

- What products are in it? Which ones are part of another distinct industry?
- What is the geographic scope of competition?

Identify the participants and segment them into groups, if appropriate:
Who are

- the buyers and buyer groups?
- the suppliers and supplier groups?
- the competitors?

- the substitutes?
- the potential entrants?

Assess the underlying drivers of each competitive force to determine which forces are strong and which are weak and why.

Determine overall industry structure, and test the analysis for consistency:

- *Why* is the level of profitability what it is?
- Which are the *controlling* forces for profitability?
- Is the industry analysis consistent with actual long-run profitability?
- Are more-profitable players better positioned in relation to the five forces?

Analyze recent and likely future changes in each force, both positive and negative.

Identify aspects of industry structure that might be influenced by competitors, by new entrants, or by your company.

BOX 4 COMMON PITFALLS

In conducting the analysis avoid the following common mistakes:

- Defining the industry too broadly or too narrowly.
- Making lists instead of engaging in rigorous analysis.
- Paying equal attention to all of the forces rather than digging deeply into the most important ones.
- Confusing effect (price sensitivity) with cause (buyer economics).
- Using static analysis that ignores industry trends.
- Confusing cyclical or transient changes with true structural changes.
- Using the framework to declare an industry attractive or unattractive rather than using it to guide strategic choices.

If both executives and investors looked at competition this way, capital markets would be a far more effective force for company success and economic prosperity. Executives and investors would both be focused on the same fundamentals that drive sustained profitability. The conversation between investors and executives would focus on the structural, not the transient. Imagine the improvement in company performance—and in the economy as a whole—if all the energy expended in "pleasing the Street" were redirected toward the factors that create true economic value.

PRACTICE PROBLEMS

The following information relates to Questions 1 and 2

Dynamic Communication dominates a segment of the consumer electronics industry. A small competitor in that segment is Wade Goods & Co. Wade has just introduced a new product, the Carrycom, which will replace the existing Wade product line and could significantly affect the industry segment.

Mike Brandreth is preparing an industry research update that focuses on Wade, including an analysis that makes extensive use of the five competitive forces identified by Porter. As part of his research, Brandreth attends the launch presentation of the Carrycom. Wade's President, Toby White, makes the following statements:

- "Wade has an exclusive three-year production license for Carrycom technology from the patent owners of the new technology. This will provide us a window of opportunity to establish a leading position with this new product before competitors enter the market with similar products."

- "A vital component in all existing competitive products is pari-copper, an enriched form of copper; production of pari-copper is limited and is effectively controlled by Dynamic. The Carrycom is manufactured with ordinary copper, thus overcoming the existing dependence on pari-copper. All other Carrycom components can be purchased from numerous sources."

- "Existing products based on pari-copper are designed to work in a single geographic region that is pre-determined during the manufacturing process. The Carrycom will be the only product on the market that can be reset by the user for use in different regions. We expect other products within our industry segment to incorporate this functionality at the end of our exclusive license period."

- "The Carrycom and similar competitive products have recently added the function of automatic language conversion. This elevates these products to a superior position within the broader electronics market, ahead of personal digital assistants, personal computers, and other consumer electronics. We expect that the broader electronics market will not be able to integrate automatic language conversion for at least one year."

- "We intend to replace Dynamic as the market leader within the next three years. We expect ordinary copper-based products with automatic language conversion to be the industry standard in three years. This will result in a number of similar products and limited pricing power after the three-year license expires."

Brandreth has adequately researched two of Porter's competitive forces—the bargaining power of buyers and the bargaining power of suppliers—and now turns his attention to the remaining competitive forces needed to complete his analysis of Wade.

1 State the *three* remaining competitive forces.

2 Determine, with respect to *each* of the remaining competitive forces, whether Wade's position in the industry is likely to be strong or weak:

          i. One year from now

          ii. Five years from now

Justify *each* of your responses with reference to White's statements.

SOLUTIONS

1   The three remaining competitive forces are the threat of substitute products or services, the threat of new entrants, and rivalry among existing competitors.

2   i. *One year from now.* With respect to all three forces, Wade's position in the industry is likely to be strong one year from now.

   Low threat of substitutes. Carrycom has the only product on the market that can be reset by the user for use in different regions. In addition, the broader electronics market does not yet have Carrycom's automatic language conversion. These two functionalities of Carrycom shield Wade from the threat of substitute products at a one year horizon.

   Low threat of new entrants. Wade faces a low threat of new entrants at a one year horizon because a) Wade has the exclusive ability to manufacture with ordinary copper and b) potential entrants do not have access to the exclusive production license for Carrycom technology.

   Low intensity of rivalry. Wade's exclusive production license for the next three years reduces the potential for competition. However, the broader electronics market may be integrating the automatic language conversion feature into their products after one year so Wade's position is strongest at a one year horizon.

   ii. *Five years from now.* With respect to all three forces, Wade's position in the industry is likely to be weak five years from now.

   High threat of substitutes. White expects other products in the broader consumer electronics industry such as PDAs, PCs, and other consumer electronics will eventually be able to incorporate both of its current market-leading functionalities.

   High threat of new entrants. At time horizons beyond three years the threat of new entrants is high. White expects competitors to market copper-based products, eliminating Carrycom's unique competitive advantage. In addition, the three-year exclusive production license expires.

   High intensity of rivalry. After the license expires in three years White expects other competitors to produce a number of similar products. Those products will limit Wade's pricing power. Limited pricing power is consistent with a high intensity of rivalry.

Your Strategy Needs a Strategy

by Martin Reeves, Claire Love, and Philipp Tillmanns

Martin Reeves (USA). Claire Love (USA). Philipp Tillmanns (Germany).

LEARNING OUTCOMES

Mastery	The candidate should be able to:
☐	a. describe predictability and malleability as factors in assessing an industry;
☐	b. describe how an industry's predictability and malleability are expected to affect the choice of an appropriate corporate strategy (classical, adaptive, visionary, or shaping);
☐	c. evaluate the predictability and malleability of an industry and select an appropriate strategy.

The oil industry holds relatively few surprises for strategists. Things change, of course, sometimes dramatically, but in relatively predictable ways. Planners know, for instance, that global supply will rise and fall as geopolitical forces play out and new resources are discovered and exploited. They know that demand will rise and fall with incomes, GDPs, weather conditions, and the like. Because these factors are outside companies' and their competitors' control and barriers to entry are so high, no one is really in a position to change the game much. A company carefully marshals its unique capabilities and resources to stake out and defend its competitive position in this fairly stable firmament.

The internet software industry would be a nightmare for an oil industry strategist. Innovations and new companies pop up frequently, seemingly out of nowhere, and the pace at which companies can build—or lose—volume and market share is head-spinning. A major player like Microsoft or Google or Facebook can, without much warning, introduce some new platform or standard that fundamentally alters the basis of competition. In this environment, competitive advantage comes from reading and responding to signals faster than your rivals do, adapting quickly to change, or capitalizing on technological leadership to influence how demand and competition evolve.

Clearly, the kinds of strategies that would work in the oil industry have practically no hope of working in the far less predictable and far less settled arena of internet software. And the skill sets that oil and software strategists need are worlds apart as well, because they operate on different time scales, use different tools, and have very different relationships with the people on the front lines who implement their plans. Companies operating in such dissimilar competitive environments should be planning, developing, and deploying their strategies in markedly different ways. But all too often, our research shows, they are not.

That is not for want of trying. Responses from a recent BCG survey of 120 companies around the world in 10 major industry sectors show that executives are well aware of the need to match their strategy-making processes to the specific demands of their competitive environments. Still, the survey found, in practice many rely instead on approaches that are better suited to predictable, stable environments, even when their own environments are known to be highly volatile or mutable.

What's stopping these executives from making strategy in a way that fits their situation? We believe they lack a systematic way to go about it—a strategy for making strategy. Here we present a simple framework that divides strategy planning into four styles according to how predictable your environment is and how much power you have to change it. Using this framework, corporate leaders can match their strategic style to the particular conditions of their industry, business function, or geographic market.

How you set your strategy constrains the kind of strategy you develop. With a clear understanding of the strategic styles available and the conditions under which each is appropriate, more companies can do what we have found that the most successful are already doing—deploying their unique capabilities and resources to better capture the opportunities available to them.

WHEN THE COLD WINDS BLOW

There are circumstances in which none of our strategic styles will work well: when access to capital or other critical resources is severely restricted, by either a sharp economic downturn or some other cataclysmic event. Such a harsh environment threatens the very viability of a company and demands a fifth strategic style—*survival*.

As its name implies, a survival strategy requires a company to focus defensively—reducing costs, preserving capital, trimming business portfolios. It is a short-term strategy, intended to clear the way for the company to live another day. But it does not lead to any long-term growth strategy. Companies in survival mode should therefore look ahead, readying themselves to assess the conditions of the new environment and to adopt an appropriate growth strategy once the crisis ends.

FINDING THE RIGHT STRATEGIC STYLE

Strategy usually begins with an assessment of your industry. Your choice of strategic style should begin there as well. Although many industry factors will play into the strategy you actually formulate, you can narrow down your options by considering just two critical factors: *predictability* (How far into the future and how accurately can you confidently forecast demand, corporate performance, competitive dynamics, and market expectations?) and *malleability* (To what extent can you or your competitors influence those factors?).

Put these two variables into a matrix, and four broad strategic styles—which we label *classical*, *adaptive*, *shaping*, and *visionary*—emerge. (See the exhibit "The Right Strategic Style for Your Environment.") Each style is associated with distinct planning practices and is best suited to one environment. Too often strategists conflate predictability and malleability—thinking that any environment that can be shaped is unpredictable—and thus divide the world of strategic possibilities into only two parts (predictable and immutable or unpredictable and mutable), whereas they ought to consider all four. So it did not surprise us to find that companies that match their strategic style to their environment perform significantly better than those that don't. In our analysis, the three-year total shareholder returns of companies in our survey that use the right style were 4% to 8% higher, on average, than the returns of those that do not.

Let's look at each style in turn.

IDEAS IN BRIEF

Companies that correctly match their strategy-making processes to their competitive circumstances perform better than those that don't. But too many use approaches appropriate only to predictable environments—even in highly volatile situations.

What executives in these cases need is a strategy for setting strategy. The authors present a framework for choosing one, which begins with two questions: How unpredictable is your environment? And how much power do you or others have to change that environment?

The answers give rise to four broad strategic styles, each one particularly suited to a distinct environment.

A classical strategy (the one everyone learned in business school) works well for companies operating in predictable and immutable environments.

A shaping strategy is best in unpredictable environments that you have the power to change.

An adaptive strategy is more flexible and experimental and works far better in immutable environments that are unpredictable.

A visionary strategy (the build-it-and-they-will-come approach) is appropriate in predictable environments that you have the power to change

---

Classical

When you operate in an industry whose environment is predictable but hard for your company to change, a classical strategic style has the best chance of success. This is the style familiar to most managers and business school graduates—five forces, blue ocean, and growth-share matrix analyses are all manifestations of it. A company sets a goal, targeting the most favorable market position it can attain by capitalizing on its particular capabilities and resources, and then tries to build and fortify that position through orderly, successive rounds of planning, using quantitative predictive methods that allow it to project well into the future. Once such plans are set, they tend to stay in place for several years. Classical strategic planning can work well as a stand-alone function because it requires special analytic and quantitative skills, and things move slowly enough to allow for information to pass between departments.

Oil company strategists, like those in many other mature industries, effectively employ the classical style. At a major oil company such as ExxonMobil or Shell, for instance, highly trained analysts in the corporate strategic-planning office spend their days developing detailed perspectives on the long-term economic factors relating to demand and the technological factors relating to supply. These analyses allow them to devise upstream oil-extraction plans that may stretch 10 years into the future and downstream production-capacity plans up to five years out. It could hardly be otherwise, given the time needed to find and exploit new sources of oil, to build production facilities, and to keep them running at optimum capacity. These plans, in turn, inform multiyear financial forecasts, which determine annual targets that are focused on honing the efficiencies required to maintain and bolster the company's market position and performance. Only in the face of something extraordinary—an extended Gulf war; a series of major oil refinery shutdowns—would plans be seriously revisited more frequently than once a year.

Adaptive

The classical approach works for oil companies because their strategists operate in an environment in which the most attractive positions and the most rewarded capabilities today will, in all likelihood, remain the same tomorrow. But that has never been true for some industries, and, as has been noted before in these pages ("Adaptability: The New Competitive Advantage," by Martin Reeves and Mike Deimler, HBR July–August 2011), it's becoming less and less true where global competition, technological innovation, social feedback loops, and economic uncertainty combine to make the environment radically and persistently unpredictable. In such an environment, a carefully crafted classical strategy may become obsolete within months or even weeks.

Companies in this situation need a more adaptive approach, whereby they can constantly refine goals and tactics and shift, acquire, or divest resources smoothly and promptly. In such a fast-moving, reactive environment, when predictions are likely to be wrong and long-term plans are essentially useless, the goal cannot be to optimize efficiency; rather, it must be to engineer flexibility. Accordingly, planning cycles may shrink to less than a year or even become continual. Plans take the form not of carefully specified blueprints but of rough hypotheses based on the best available data. In testing them out, strategy must be tightly linked with or embedded in operations, to best capture change signals and minimize information loss and time lags.

Specialty fashion retailing is a good example of this. Tastes change quickly. Brands become hot (or not) overnight. No amount of data or planning will grant fashion executives the luxury of knowing far in advance what to make. So their best bet is to set up their organizations to continually produce, roll out, and test a variety of products as quickly as they can, constantly adapting production in the light of new learning.

The Spanish retailer Zara uses the adaptive approach. Zara does not rely heavily on a formal planning process; rather, its strategic style is baked into its flexible supply chain. It maintains strong ties with its 1,400 external suppliers, which work closely with its designers and marketers. As a result, Zara can design, manufacture, and ship a garment to its stores in as little as two to three weeks, rather than the industry average of four to six months. This allows the company to experiment with a wide variety of looks and make small bets with small batches of potentially popular styles. If they prove a hit, Zara can ramp up production quickly. If they don't, not much is lost in markdowns. (On average, Zara marks down only 15% of its inventory, whereas the figure for competitors can be as high as 50%.) So it need not predict or make bets on which fashions will capture its customers' imaginations and wallets from month to month. Instead it can respond quickly to information from its retail stores, constantly experiment with various offerings, and smoothly adjust to events as they play out.

Zara's strategic style requires relationships among its planners, designers, manufacturers, and distributors that are entirely different from what a company like ExxonMobil needs. Nevertheless, Exxon's strategists and Zara's designers have one critical thing in common: They take their competitive environment as a given and aim to carve out the best place they can within it.

THE RIGHT STRATEGIC STYLE FOR YOUR ENVIRONMENT

Our research shows that approaches to strategy formulation fall into four buckets, according to how predictable an industry's environment is and how easily companies can change that environment.

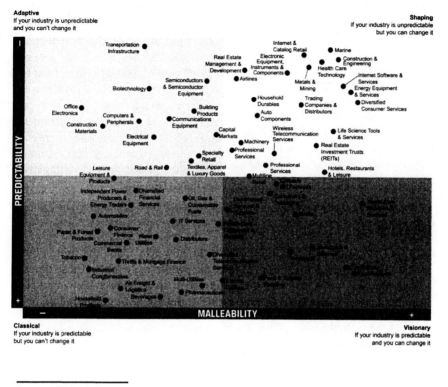

Source: BCG Analysis

Shaping

Some environments, as internet software vendors well know, can't be taken as given. For instance, in new or young high-growth industries where barriers to entry are low, innovation rates are high, demand is very hard to predict, and the relative positions of competitors are in flux, a company can often radically shift the course of industry development through some innovative move. A mature industry that's similarly fragmented and not dominated by a few powerful incumbents, or is stagnant and ripe for disruption, is also likely to be similarly malleable.

In such an environment, a company employing a classical or even an adaptive strategy to find the best possible market position runs the risk of selling itself short, being overrun by events, and missing opportunities to control its own fate. It would do better to employ a strategy in which the goal is to shape the unpredictable environment to its own advantage before someone else does—so that it benefits no matter how things play out.

Like an adaptive strategy, a shaping strategy embraces short or continual planning cycles. Flexibility is paramount, little reliance is placed on elaborate prediction mechanisms, and the strategy is most commonly implemented as a portfolio of experiments. But unlike adapters, shapers focus beyond the boundaries of their own company, often by rallying a formidable ecosystem of customers, suppliers, and/or complementors to their cause by defining attractive new markets, standards, technology platforms, and business practices. They propagate these through marketing, lobbying, and savvy partnerships. In the early stages of the digital revolution, internet software companies frequently used shaping strategies to create new communities, standards, and platforms that became the foundations for new markets and businesses.

That's essentially how Facebook overtook the incumbent MySpace in just a few years. One of Facebook's savviest strategic moves was to open its social-networking platform to outside developers in 2007, thus attracting all manner of applications to its site. Facebook couldn't hope to predict how big or successful any one of them would become. But it didn't need to. By 2008 it had attracted 33,000 applications; by 2010 that number had risen to more than 550,000. So as the industry developed and more than two-thirds of the successful social-networking apps turned out to be games, it was not surprising that the most popular ones—created by Zynga, Playdom, and Playfish—were operating from, and enriching, Facebook's site. What's more, even if the social-networking landscape shifts dramatically as time goes on, chances are the most popular applications will still be on Facebook. That's because by creating a flexible and popular platform, the company actively shaped the business environment to its own advantage rather than merely staking out a position in an existing market or reacting to changes, however quickly, after they'd occurred.

Visionary

Sometimes, not only does a company have the power to shape the future, but it's possible to know that future and to predict the path to realizing it. Those times call for bold strategies—the kind entrepreneurs use to create entirely new markets (as Edison did for electricity and Martine Rothblatt did for XM satellite radio), or corporate leaders use to revitalize a company with a wholly new vision—as Ratan Tata is trying to do with the ultra-affordable Nano automobile. These are the big bets, the build-it-and-they-will-come strategies.

Like a shaping strategist, the visionary considers the environment not as a given but as something that can be molded to advantage. Even so, the visionary style has more in common with a classical than with an adaptive approach. Because the goal is clear, strategists can take deliberate steps to reach it without having to keep many options open. It's more important for them to take the time and care they need to marshal resources, plan thoroughly, and implement correctly so that the vision doesn't fall victim to poor execution. Visionary strategists must have the courage to stay the course and the will to commit the necessary resources.

Back in 1994, for example, it became clear to UPS that the rise of internet commerce was going to be a bonanza for delivery companies, because the one thing online retailers would always need was a way to get their offerings out of cyberspace and onto their customers' doorsteps. This future may have been just as clear to the much younger and smaller FedEx, but UPS had the means—and the will—to make the necessary investments. That year it set up a cross-functional committee drawn from IT, sales, marketing, and finance to map out its path to becoming what the company later called "the enablers of global e-commerce." The committee identified the ambitious initiatives that UPS would need to realize this vision, which involved investing some $1 billion a year to integrate its core package-tracking operations with those of web providers and make acquisitions to expand its global delivery capacity. By 2000 UPS's multibillion-dollar bet had paid off: The company had snapped up a whopping 60% of the e-commerce delivery market.

WHICH STRATEGIC STYLE IS USED MOST?

Our survey found that companies were most often using the two styles best suited to predictable environments—classical and visionary—even when their environments were clearly unpredictable.

9%	Shaping
16%	Adaptive
35%	Classical
40%	Visionary

AVOIDING THE TRAPS

In our survey, fully three out of four executives understood that they needed to employ different strategic styles in different circumstances. Yet judging by the practices they actually adopted, we estimate that the same percentage were using only the two strategic styles—classic and visionary—suited to predictable environments (see the exhibit "Which Strategic Style Is Used the Most?"). That means only one in four was prepared in practice to adapt to unforeseeable events or to seize an opportunity to shape an industry to his or her company's advantage. Given our analysis of how unpredictable their business environments actually are, this number is far too low. Understanding how different the various approaches are and in which environment each best applies can go a long way toward correcting mismatches between strategic style and business environment. But as strategists think through the implications of the framework, they need to avoid three traps we have frequently observed.

Misplaced Confidence

You can't choose the right strategic style unless you accurately judge how predictable and malleable your environment is. But when we compared executives' perceptions with objective measures of their actual environments, we saw a strong tendency to overestimate both factors. Nearly half the executives believed they could control uncertainty in the business environment through their own actions. More than 80% said that achieving goals depended on their own actions more than on things they could not control.

Unexamined Habits

Many executives recognized the importance of building the adaptive capabilities required to address unpredictable environments, but fewer than one in five felt sufficiently competent in them. In part that's because many executives learned only the classical style, through experience or at business school. Accordingly, we weren't surprised to find that nearly 80% said that in practice they begin their strategic planning by articulating a goal and then analyzing how best to get there. What's more, some 70% said that in practice they value accuracy over speed of decisions, even when they are well aware that their environment is fast-moving and unpredictable. As a result, a lot of time is being wasted making untenable predictions when a faster, more iterative, and more experimental approach would be more effective. Executives are also closely attuned to quarterly and annual financial reporting, which heavily influences their strategic-planning cycles. Nearly 90% said they develop strategic plans on an annual basis, regardless of the actual pace of change in their business environments—or even what they perceive it to be.

Culture Mismatches

Although many executives recognize the importance of adaptive capabilities, it can be highly countercultural to implement them. Classical strategies aimed at achieving economies of scale and scope often create company cultures that prize efficiency and the elimination of variation. These can of course undermine the opportunity to experiment and learn, which is essential for an adaptive strategy. And failure is a natural outcome of experimentation, so adaptive and shaping strategies fare poorly in cultures that punish it.

Avoiding some of these traps can be straightforward once the differing requirements of the four strategic styles are understood. Simply being aware that adaptive planning horizons don't necessarily correlate well with the rhythms of financial markets, for instance, might go a long way toward eliminating ingrained planning habits. Similarly, understanding that the point of shaping and visionary strategies is to change the game rather than to optimize your position in the market may be all that's needed to avoid starting with the wrong approach.

Being more thoughtful about metrics is also helpful. Although companies put a great deal of energy into making predictions year after year, it's surprising how rarely they check to see if the predictions they made in the prior year actually panned out. We suggest regularly reviewing the accuracy of your forecasts and also objectively gauging predictability by tracking how often and to what extent companies in your industry change relative position in terms of revenue, profitability, and other performance measures. To get a better sense of the extent to which industry players can change their environment, we recommend measuring industry youthfulness, concentration, growth rate, innovation rate, and rate of technology change—all of which increase malleability.

ARE YOU CLINGING TO THE WRONG STRATEGY STYLE?

A clear estimation of your industry's predictability and malleability is key to picking the right strategy style. But our survey of more than 120 companies in 10 industries showed that companies don't do this well: Their estimates rarely matched our objective measures. They consistently overestimated both predictability and malleability.

OPERATING IN MANY MODES

Matching your company's strategic style to the predictability and malleability of your industry will align overall strategy with the broad economic conditions in which the company operates. But various company units may well operate in differing subsidiary or geographic markets that are more or less predictable and malleable than the industry at large. Strategists in these units and markets can use the same process to select the most effective style for their particular circumstances, asking themselves the same initial questions: How predictable is the environment in which our unit operates? How much power do we have to change that environment? The answers may vary widely. We estimate, for example, that the Chinese business environment overall has been almost twice as malleable and unpredictable as that in the United States, making shaping strategies often more appropriate in China.

Similarly, the functions within your company are likely to operate in environments that call for differing approaches to departmental planning. It's easy to imagine, for instance, that within the auto industry a classical style would work well for optimizing production but would be inappropriate for the digital marketing department, which probably has a far greater power to shape its environment (after all, that's what advertising aims to do) and would hardly benefit from mapping out its campaigns years in advance.

If units or functions within your company would benefit from operating in a strategic style other than the one best suited to your industry as a whole, it follows that you will very likely need to manage more than one strategic style at a time. Executives in our survey are well aware of this: In fact, fully 90% aspired to improve their ability to manage multiple styles simultaneously. The simplest but also the least flexible way to do this is to structure and run functions, regions, or business units that require differing strategic styles separately. Allowing teams within units to select their own styles gives you more flexibility in diverse or fast-changing environments but is generally more challenging to realize. (For an example of a company that has found a systematic way to do it, see the sidebar "The Ultimate in Strategic Flexibility.")

THE ULTIMATE IN STRATEGIC FLEXIBILITY

Haier, a Chinese home-appliance manufacturer, may have taken strategic flexibility just about as far as it can go. The company has devised a system in which units as small as an individual can effectively use differing styles.

How does it manage this? Haier's organization comprises thousands of minicompanies, each accountable for its own P&L. Any employee can start one of them. But there are no cost centers in the company—only profit centers. Each minicompany bears the fully loaded costs of its operations, and each party negotiates with the others for services; even the finance department sells its services to the others. Every employee is held accountable for achieving profits. An employee's salary is based on a simple formula: base salary × % of monthly target achieved + bonus (or deduction) based on individual P&L. In other words, if a minicompany achieves none of its monthly target (0%), the employees in it receive no salary that month.

Operating at this level of flexibility can be as rewarding as it is daunting. Near bankruptcy in 1985, Haier has since become the world's largest home-appliance company—ahead of LG, Samsung, GE, and Whirlpool.

Finally, a company moving into a different stage of its life cycle may well require a shift in strategic style. Environments for start-ups tend to be malleable, calling for visionary or shaping strategies. In a company's growth and maturity phases, when the environment is less malleable, adaptive or classical styles are often best. For companies in a declining phase, the environment becomes more malleable again, generating opportunities for disruption and rejuvenation through either a shaping or a visionary strategy.

Once you have correctly analyzed your environment, not only for the business as a whole but for each of your functions, divisions, and geographic markets, and you have identified which strategic styles should be used, corrected for your own biases, and taken steps to prime your company's culture so that the appropriate styles can successfully be applied, you will need to monitor your environment and be prepared to adjust as conditions change over time. Clearly that's no easy task. But we believe that companies that continually match their strategic styles to their situation will enjoy a tremendous advantage over those that don't.

Industry and Company Analysis

by Matthew L. Coffina, CFA, Anthony M. Fiore, CFA, and
Antonius J. van Ooijen, CFA

Matthew L. Coffina, CFA, is at Morningstar (USA). Anthony M. Fiore, CFA (USA).
Antonius J. van Ooijen, CFA (Netherlands).

LEARNING OUTCOMES

Mastery	The candidate should be able to:
☐	**a.** compare top-down, bottom-up, and hybrid approaches for developing inputs to equity valuation models;
☐	**b.** compare "growth relative to GDP growth" and "market growth and market share" approaches to forecasting revenue;
☐	**c.** evaluate whether economies of scale are present in an industry by analyzing operating margins and sales levels;
☐	**d.** forecast the following costs: cost of goods sold, selling general and administrative costs, financing costs, and income taxes;
☐	**e.** describe approaches to balance sheet modeling;
☐	**f.** describe the relationship between return on invested capital and competitive advantage;
☐	**g.** explain how competitive factors affect prices and costs;
☐	**h.** judge the competitive position of a company based on a Porter's five forces analysis;
☐	**i.** explain how to forecast industry and company sales and costs when they are subject to price inflation or deflation;
☐	**j.** evaluate the effects of technological developments on demand, selling prices, costs, and margins;
☐	**k.** explain considerations in the choice of an explicit forecast horizon;
☐	**l.** explain an analyst's choices in developing projections beyond the short-term forecast horizon;
☐	**m.** demonstrate the development of a sales-based pro forma company model.

1 INTRODUCTION

This reading explores industry and company analysis with a focus on how analysts use industry information and corporate disclosures to forecast a company's future financial results.

Financial forecasts are the basis for fundamental equity valuation based on discounted cash flows and/or market multiples. An effective forecast model must be based on a thorough understanding of a company's business, management, strategy, external environment, and historical results. Thus an analyst begins with a review of the company and its environment—its industry, key products, strategic position, management, competitors, suppliers, and customers. Using this information, an analyst identifies key revenue and cost drivers and assesses the likely impact of relevant trends, such as economic conditions and technological developments. An analyst's understanding of the fundamental drivers of the business and an assessment of future events provides a basis for developing inputs to the forecast model.

This reading begins with an overview of developing a forecast model. Section 2 describes the general approach to forecasting each component of the income statement (revenue, operating costs, and non-operating costs), balance sheet, and cash flow statement. The next sections develop special topics: Sections 3, 4, 5, 6, and 7 describe, respectively, the impact of competitive factors on prices and costs; the effects of inflation and deflation; technological developments; long-term forecasting; and building a company model. Section 8 presents conclusions and a summary.

2 FINANCIAL MODELING: AN OVERVIEW

For most companies, financial modeling begins with the income statement. The income statement is a logical starting point because most companies derive the majority of their value from future cash flow generation, which is primarily determined by the amount of net income generated by the business. Exceptions include banks and insurance companies, for which the value of existing assets and liabilities on the balance sheet may be more relevant to the companies' overall value than projected future income. The income statement also provides a useful starting point for modeling a company's balance sheet and cash flow statement.

2.1 Income Statement Modeling: Revenue

Most companies receive revenue from multiple sources. For analyzing revenue, segment disclosures in companies' financial reports are often the richest source of information. Both International Financial Reporting Standards (IFRS) and US Generally Accepted Accounting Principles (US GAAP) require companies to disclose certain information about business segments, including how segments are defined; segment revenues, expenses, assets, and liabilities; analysis of revenue by geographical area; and reconciliation of segment accounts to the consolidated financial statement. According to accounting standards, separate financial information must be provided for any segment whose revenue, operating income, or assets account for 10% or more of the revenue, operating income, or assets of the combined company. In addition to the interim and annual financial reports issued by the company, important information can often be found in other disclosures, such as regulatory filings, management presentations and conference calls, as well as in external data sources.

Revenue can be analyzed by geographical source, business segment, or product line. In a geographic analysis, the analyst places a company's revenue into various geographic "buckets" (groupings). These buckets may be narrowly defined, such as by individual countries, or more broadly defined, such as by region of the world. A geographic analysis can be particularly useful for global companies operating in multiple countries with different underlying growth rates or competitive dynamics. For example, a company may be experiencing relatively slow growth in one region of the world and relatively fast growth in other regions. By examining each region of the world separately, analysts can enhance their understanding of overall growth.

In a breakdown by segment, the analyst classifies a company's revenue into various business segments. Many companies operate in more than one industry or market niche with widely differing economics. Although information is often available for the different business segments, analysts should make an independent judgment about whether a company's chosen segmentation of its business is relevant and material. Sometimes analysts can regroup reported information in a manner that helps make important points.

Finally, a product line analysis provides the most granular level of detail. A product line analysis is most relevant for a company with a manageably small number of products that behave differently, but when combined, they account for most of the company's sales.

Example 1 introduces the first of more than 50 exhibits in this reading. Many exhibit results have been rounded, so in replicating results based on the numbers given in the text and exhibits, small apparent discrepancies may reflect the rounding error.

EXAMPLE 1

Analysis of Revenue (1)

Novo Nordisk is a Denmark-based biopharmaceutical company with a focus on diabetes drugs. The company provides detailed disclosure of revenue along geographic, business segment, and product lines. All figures are in millions of euros (€).

In its 2011 annual report, Novo Nordisk provided the following geographic breakdown of sales for the previous three years.

Exhibit 1	Novo Nordisk's Sales by Geographic Region (€ millions)		
	2009	**2010**	**2011**
North America	€2,454	€3,170	€3,569
Europe	2,356	2,506	2,573
International	917	1,119	1,257
Japan and Korea	657	760	835
Region China	476	606	671
Total Sales	€6,860	€8,161	€8,905

The company also classified revenue into business segments it defined: diabetes care and biopharmaceuticals. Within each segment, disclosure on several individual product lines was also provided.

Exhibit 2	Novo Nordisk's Sales by Business Segment (€ millions)		
	2009	**2010**	**2011**
Modern insulins	€2,883	€3,572	€3,861
Human insulins	1,520	1,588	1,448
Victoza	12	311	804
Other diabetes products	621	666	656
Total diabetes care	5,036	6,137	6,769
NovoSeven	950	1,078	1,120
Norditropin	591	645	677
Other biopharmaceuticals	283	301	339
Total biopharmaceuticals	1,824	2,024	2,136
Total Sales	€6,860	€8,161	€8,905

Use the data in Exhibits 1 and 2 to answer the following questions:

1   Determine the percentage of Novo Nordisk's sales that came from each geographic region in 2011.

2   Modern insulins provide certain advantages over human insulins, such as having a faster or longer-lasting effect on blood sugar levels. Compare Novo Nordisk's recent sales growth rate of modern insulins with that of human insulins.

3   Which segment was the larger contributor to Novo Nordisk's sales growth over the past two years: diabetes care or biopharmaceuticals?

4   Management only began breaking out revenue for China in 2011. Previously, China had been included in the "International" region. Note that over the past two years, revenue from China has increased 41%, compared with 37% growth for the remainder of the International region. Describe at least two alternative interpretations of why management decided to increase disclosure about China.

Solution to 1:

North America: (3,569/8,905) = 0.401 or 40.1%
Europe: (2,573/8,905) = 0.289 or 28.9%
International: (1,257/8,905) = 0.141 or 14.1%
Japan and Korea: (835/8,905) = 0.094 or 9.4%
Region China: (671/8,905) = 0.075 or 7.5%

Solution to 2:

Between 2009 and 2011, Novo Nordisk's sales of modern insulins increased $3,861/2,883 - 1 \approx 0.339$ or 33.9%, although year-over-year growth has slowed. To calculate a compound annual growth rate, take $(3,861/2,883)^{1/2} - 1 = 0.157$ or 15.7%.

In contrast, sales of human insulins declined modestly. This decline may be explained by the advantages of modern insulins mentioned in the question.

Solution to 3:

In the past two years, Novo Nordisk's total sales increased by €2,045 million (from €6,860 million to €8,905 million). During the same time, diabetes care sales increased by €1,733 million and biopharmaceuticals sales increased by €312 million. The diabetes care segment thus accounted for about 85% (≈ 1,733/2,045) of Novo Nordisk's sales growth between 2009 and 2011.

Solution to 4:

Two possible (but not mutually exclusive) explanations for management's decision to enhance disclosure are: (1) that China is a relatively fast-growing market, so management believes investors will see the company in a more favorable light with this geography broken out, or (2) that China is an area of particular interest to investors and management simply wants to improve investors' understanding of the business by providing extra detail. Because the International region grew almost as quickly as China, the second explanation seems more likely.

Once the analyst has an understanding of the important components of a company's revenue, he must decide whether to use a top-down, bottom-up, or hybrid approach to projecting future revenue. A **top-down approach** usually begins at the level of the overall economy. Forecasts can then be made at more narrowly defined levels, such as sector, industry, and market for a specific product, to arrive at a revenue projection for the individual company. In contrast, a **bottom-up approach** begins at the level of the individual company or a unit within the company, such as individual product lines, locations, or business segments. Analysts then aggregate their projections for the individual products or segments to arrive at a forecast of total revenue for the company. Moreover, analysts also aggregate their revenue projections for individual companies to develop forecasts for a product market, industry, or the overall economy. A **hybrid approach** combines elements of both top-down and bottom-up analysis and can be useful for uncovering implicit assumptions or errors that may arise from using a single approach.

2.1.1 Top-down Approaches to Modeling Revenue

Two common top-down approaches to modeling revenue are "growth relative to GDP growth" and "market growth and market share."

In a growth relative to GDP growth approach, the analyst first forecasts the growth rate of nominal gross domestic product. The analyst then considers how the growth rate of the specific company being examined will compare with nominal GDP growth. The analyst may use a forecast for real GDP growth to project volumes and a forecast for inflation to project prices. Analysts often think in terms of percentage point premiums or discounts derived from a company's position in the industrial life cycle (e.g., embryonic, growth, shakeout, mature, or decline) or business cycle sensitivity. Thus, an analyst's conclusion may be that a health care company's revenue will grow at a rate of 200 bps above the nominal GDP growth rate. The forecast may also be in relative terms. Thus, if GDP is forecast to grow at 4% and the company's revenue is forecast to grow at a 15% faster rate, the forecast percent change in revenue would be 4% × (1 + 0.15) = 4.6%, or 60 bps higher in absolute terms.

In a market growth and market share approach, the analyst first forecasts growth in a particular market. The analyst then considers the company's current market share, and how that share is likely to change over time. For example, if a company is expected to maintain an 8% market share of a given product market and the product market is forecast to grow from €18.75 billion to €20 billion in annual revenue, the forecast growth in company revenue is from a level of 8% × €18.75 billion = €1.5 billion to a level of 8% × €20 billion = €1.6 billion (considering this product market alone). If the product market revenue has a predictable relationship with GDP, regression analysis might be used to estimate the relationship.

2.1.2 Bottom-up Approaches to Modeling Revenue

Examples of bottom-up approaches to modeling revenue include the following:

- *Time series*: forecasts based on historical growth rates or time-series analysis.
- *Return on capital*: forecasts based on balance sheet accounts, for example interest revenue for a bank may be calculated as loans multiplied by the average interest rate.
- *Capacity-based measure:* forecasts (for example, in retailing) based on same-store sales growth and sales related to new stores.[1]

Time-series forecasts are among the simplest. For example, analysts may fit a trend line to historical data and then project sales over the desired timeframe (e.g., using Excel's TREND formula). In such a case, analysts would be projecting historical growth rates to continue, but they might also use different assumptions—for example, they may project growth to decline linearly from current rates to some long-run rate. Note that time-series methods may also be used as tools in executing a top-down analysis, such as projecting GDP growth in a growth relative to GDP growth approach.

2.1.3 Hybrid Approaches to Modeling Revenue

Hybrid approaches combine elements of both top-down and bottom-up analysis, and in practice they are the most commonly used approaches. For example, the analyst may use a market growth and market share approach to model individual product lines or business segments, and then aggregate the individual projections to arrive at a forecast for the overall company because the sum of forecast segment revenue equals the segment market size multiplied by the market share for all segments.

In a volume and price approach, the analyst makes separate projections for volumes (e.g., the number of products sold or the number of customers served) and average selling price. Depending on how these elements are forecast, this approach can be classified as a top-down, bottom-up, or hybrid.

EXAMPLE 2

Analysis of Revenue (2)

Use the data in Example 1 on Novo Nordisk to answer the following questions:

1 Xiaoping Wu is an equity analyst covering European pharmaceutical companies for his clients in China. Wu projects that global nominal GDP will grow 5% annually over the long run, based on 2% real growth and 3% inflation. The incidence of diabetes is escalating globally because of increasingly unhealthy diets and sedentary lifestyles. As a result, Wu believes global sales of diabetes drugs will grow 100 bps faster than nominal GDP over the long run. Wu believes the revenue growth rate of Novo Nordisk's diabetes care segment will decline linearly over the next four years from its growth rate in 2011 to the projected long-run growth rate of the diabetes drug market.

---

[1] Same-store sales growth is the growth rate in sales for stores that have been open at least 12 months.

A Is Wu using a top-down, bottom-up, or hybrid approach to modeling Novo Nordisk's revenue?

B Based on Wu's projections for revenue growth, calculate the estimated revenue growth rate for the diabetes care segment in 2013.

2 Helga Hansen is a buy-side analyst in Denmark. In early 2011, Hansen was investigating Victoza, a recently launched compound in a new class of diabetes drugs called GLP-1 analogs. As of 2011, Victoza has only one direct competitor in its class: Byetta, a drug that is co-marketed by two US-based pharmaceutical companies, Amylin Pharmaceuticals and Eli Lilly. Victoza had a few advantages over Byetta; most notably, it is delivered by injection once a day, rather than twice a day.

Eli Lilly reported global sales of Byetta in US dollars. Hansen converted these figures to euro using the annual average USD/EUR exchange rate and compiled the following table comparing sales of Victoza with sales of Byetta, measured in millions of euros.

	2008	2009	2010
Byetta	513	573	536
Victoza	0	12	311

A What was the growth rate in total GLP-1 analog sales in 2010?

B What percentage of GLP-1 analog sales growth in 2010 was caused by Victoza?

C Hansen projected that the growth rate of the GLP-1 analog market would slow to 28% in 2011. She also expected Victoza to improve its market share by 25 percentage points. What was Hansen's estimate of 2011 Victoza sales? How close was she to the actual result?

D Is Hansen's approach to modeling Novo Nordisk's sales best described as bottom-up, top-down, or hybrid?

Solution to 1A:

Wu's long-run revenue projections are based on Novo Nordisk's growth relative to nominal GDP growth, which is a top-down approach. However, his estimated growth rate is applied to only one of Novo Nordisk's segments (diabetes care), indicating a hybrid approach. Wu's four-year forecasts are also based in part on the historical growth rate of the diabetes care segment, which is a bottom-up approach. Wu is thus using a hybrid approach.

Solution to 1B:

The data in Example 1 indicates that Novo Nordisk's diabetes care segment grew approximately 10% in 2011 (= 6,769/6,137 − 1 ≈ 0.103). Wu projects the long-run growth rate to be in line with the diabetes drug market growth at 6% (100 bps faster than GDP growth of 5%). The difference between the 2011 growth rate and projected long-run growth rate is 4% (= 10% − 6%), and Wu expects the deceleration in growth to occur linearly over four years, implying a reduction of 100 bps per year in the growth rate. The estimated growth rates by year are thus

2012 = 9%

2013 = 8%

2014 = 7%

2015 = 6%

Thereafter, 6%

The estimated revenue growth rate for 2013 is 8%.

Solution to 2A:

Total sales of GLP-1 analogs in 2010 were €847 million (= 536 + 311), compared with total sales of €585 million (= 573 + 12) in 2009. The growth rate was thus around 45% (= 847/585 − 1 ≈ 0.448).

Solution to 2B:

Total GLP-1 analog sales increased by €262 million (from €585 million to €847 million), whereas Victoza sales increased by €299 million (from €12 million to €311 million). So, Victoza accounted for approximately 114% of the growth in sales of this drug class (= 299/262 ≈ 1.14, or 114%). Note that Victoza accounted for more than 100% of the total growth in sales of this drug class because the other drug in the class had a decline in sales.

Solution to 2C:

Based on 2010 sales of €847 million and a projected growth rate of 28%, Hansen projected the total GLP-1 analog market to be worth about €1,084 million in 2011 (= 847 × 1.28 ≈ 1,084.2). Victoza's market share in 2010 was around 37%, which Hansen projected to improve by 25 percentage points, resulting in a 62% market share in 2011. Hansen thus projected 2011 Victoza sales to be around €672 million (= 1,084 × 0.62 ≈ 672). Actual Victoza sales in 2011 were €804 million, so Hansen's estimate was too low by €132 million (= 804 − 672 = 132).

Solution to 2D:

Hansen bases her estimates on market growth and market share, which would normally imply a top-down approach. The analysis, however, is applied to an individual product line, implying a bottom-up approach. Therefore, Hansen is using a hybrid approach.

2.2 Income Statement Modeling: Operating Costs

Disclosure about operating costs is frequently less detailed than disclosure about revenue. If relevant information is available, analysts may consider matching the cost analysis to the revenue analysis. For example, they might model costs separately for different geographic regions, business segments, or product lines. More frequently, analysts will be forced to consider costs at a more aggregated level than the level used to analyze revenue. Analysts should still keep in mind their revenue analysis when deriving cost assumptions. For instance, if a relatively low-margin product is expected to grow faster than a relatively high-margin product, analysts should project some level of overall margin deterioration, even if they are not certain about the precise margins earned on each product.

Once again, analysts can take a top-down, bottom-up, or hybrid view of costs. In a top-down approach, analysts may consider such factors as the overall level of inflation or industry-specific costs before making assumptions about the individual company. In contrast, in a bottom-up approach analysts would start at the company level, considering such factors as segment-level margins, historical cost growth rates, historical margin levels, or the costs of delivering specific products. A hybrid approach would incorporate both top-down and bottom-up elements.

When estimating costs, analysts should pay particular attention to fixed costs. Variable costs are directly linked to revenue growth, and may be best modeled as a percentage of revenue or as projected unit volume multiplied by unit variable costs.

By contrast, increases in fixed costs are not directly related to revenue; rather, they are related to future investment in property, plant, and equipment (PP&E) and to total capacity growth. Practically, fixed costs may be assumed to grow at their own rate, based on an analysis of future PP&E growth. Analysts should determine whether, at its current level of output, the subject company has **economies of scale**, a situation in which average costs per unit of a good or service produced fall as volume rises. Factors that can lead to economies of scale include, at higher levels of production, greater bargaining power with suppliers, lower cost of capital, and lower per unit advertising expenses. Gross and operating margins tend to be positively correlated with sales levels in an industry that enjoys economies of scale.

Analysts must also be aware of any uncertainty surrounding estimates of costs. For example, banks and insurance companies create reserves against estimated future losses, and companies with large pension plans have long-duration liabilities, the true costs of which may not be known for many years. A review of disclosures about reserving practices related to future obligations and pensions can be helpful in assessing whether cost estimates are reasonable. But most of the time it is difficult for the external analyst to anticipate future revisions to cost estimates. Other aspects affecting the uncertainty of cost estimates include competitive factors and technological developments. This impact will be discussed in later sections.

EXAMPLE 3

Approaches to Modeling Operating Costs

Walgreens and Rite Aid are two of the largest retail drugstore chains in the United States. For both companies, around two-thirds of their sales are from prescription pharmaceuticals, with the remaining third coming from front-of-store categories, such as beauty products, over-the-counter drugs, convenience foods, greeting cards, and photofinishing.

Although they are in the same industry, Walgreens and Rite Aid have very different operating margins. There is reason to believe that economies of scale exist in the drugstore business. For example, larger drugstore companies have greater bargaining leverage with suppliers and the ability to negotiate better reimbursement rates with third-party payers. Some relevant data are presented in Exhibit 3. The 2011 column includes results from Walgreens' 2011 fiscal year (ended in August 2011) and Rite Aid's fiscal year 2012 (ended in February 2012).

Exhibit 3 Financial Results for Walgreens and Rite Aid, 2009–2011			
	2009	**2010**	**2011**
Walgreens			
Revenue ($ millions)	63,335	67,420	72,184
Cost of goods sold ($ millions)	45,722	48,444	51,692
Selling, general, and administrative ($ millions)	14,366	15,518	16,561
Operating income ($ millions)	3,247	3,458	3,931
Average selling area square footage (millions sq. ft.)	75.1	81.3	84.7
Same-store sales growth	2.0%	1.6%	3.3%

Rite Aid

(continued)

	2009	**2010**	**2011**
Revenue ($ millions)	25,669	25,215	26,121
Cost of goods sold ($ millions)	18,845	18,522	19,328
Selling, general, and administrative ($ millions)	6,603	6,458	6,531
Operating income ($ millions)	221	235	262
Average selling area square footage (millions sq. ft.)	48.4	47.5	46.9
Same-store sales growth	−0.9%	−0.7%	2.0%

Exhibit 3   (Continued)

Customer service may be one driver of revenue for the retail drug business. Retail analysts commonly use a combination of qualitative and quantitative evidence to assess customer service. Qualitative evidence might come from personal store visits or customer surveys. Quantitative evidence may be based on metrics such as selling, general, and administrative (SG&A) expense per square foot. Too little spending on SG&A might indicate that stores are understaffed. Relatedly, same-store sales growth may be an indicator of customer satisfaction.

Use the data given to answer the following questions:

1 On the basis of the 2011 operating margins for Walgreens and Rite Aid, is there evidence suggesting that economies of scale exist in the retail drugstore business? If so, are economies of scale realized in cost of goods sold or SG&A expenses?

2 Marco Benitez is a US-based equity analyst with an independent research firm. Benitez is researching service levels in the US drugstore industry.

   A Calculate and interpret Walgreens' and Rite Aid's SG&A per average square foot over the past three years.

   B Assuming that customer satisfaction is a driver of sales growth, which company appears to have a more satisfied customer base over the period examined?

   C Benitez projects that Rite Aid's average selling area square footage will decline 2% annually over the next three years. He believes SG&A per average square foot will increase 1% annually during this time. What is Benitez's projection for total SG&A expense in 2014?

3 Jason Lewis is another US-based equity analyst covering the retail drugstore industry. He is considering several approaches to forecasting Walgreens' and Rite Aid's' future costs. Classify each of the following as a bottom-up, top-down, or hybrid approach.

   A Lewis believes government insurance programs in the United States will face budgetary pressures in the future, which will result in lower reimbursements across the retail drugstore industry. Lewis thinks this will lower all drugstores' gross margins.

   B Lewis projects that Walgreens' historical rate of growth in SG&A expenses will continue for the next five years. But in the long-run, he projects SG&A to grow at the rate of inflation.

   C To estimate Rite Aid's future lease expense, Lewis makes assumptions about square footage growth and average rent per square foot, based on past experience.

Solution to 1:

Walgreens' 2011 operating margin (operating income divided by revenue) was 5.4% (= 3,931/72,184 ≈ 0.054). Rite Aid's operating margin in the comparable year was 1.0% (= 262/26,121 ≈ 0.010). Walgreens' much larger size ($72,184 million in sales versus $26,121 million for Rite Aid) combined with its much higher profitability provides evidence suggesting that there are economies of scale in the drugstore industry.

To answer the second part of the question, divide both companies' expense lines by revenue for 2011. Walgreens' cost of goods sold consumed 71.6% (≈ 51,692/72,184) of revenue, whereas Rite Aid's cost of goods sold consumed 74% (≈ 19,328/26,121). Walgreens' SG&A consumed 22.9% (≈ 16,561/72,184) of revenue, whereas Rite Aid's SG&A consumed 25% (≈ 6,531/26,121). The results indicate that there are economies of scale in both cost of goods sold and SG&A.

Solution to 2A:

Walgreen's average SG&A per square foot in 2011 and 2009 were $196 (≈ 16,561/84.7) and $191 (≈ 14,366/75.1), respectively. That is an increase of approximately 2.6%. The same figures for Rite Aid were $139 in 2011 and $136 in 2009, for an increase of 2.2%. This might be evidence of higher service levels at Walgreens. Although Rite Aid spends much less than Walgreen on SG&A per square foot, the trend of the past three years provides little indication that Rite Aid's possible customer service gap relative to Walgreens is increasing.

Solution to 2B:

Walgreens appears to have the more satisfied customer base, considering just same-store sales. Comparing same-store sales growth for the two companies, Walgreens has consistently outperformed Rite Aid in the past three years. This result supports the hypothesis that Rite Aid's customers may be less satisfied than Walgreens' customers over the time period examined.

Solution to 2C:

Benitez projects Rite Aid's average selling area will be around 44.1 million square feet [= 46.9 × $(0.98)^3$] in 2014. He projects SG&A per average square foot will be $143 [= 139 × $(1.01)^3$]. He thus estimates total SG&A to be $6,306.3 million (44.1 × 143) in 2014.

Solution to 3A:

This case describes a top-down approach because Lewis considers the overall industry environment before individual companies.

Solution to 3B:

In this case, Lewis combines a bottom-up approach (projecting the historical rate of growth to continue) with a top-down approach (basing his long-run assumptions on the overall rate of inflation). Therefore, this is a hybrid approach.

Solution to 3C:

This case describes a bottom-up approach because Lewis bases his forecasts on Rite Aid's historical experience.

2.2.1 *Cost of Goods Sold*

The cost of goods sold (COGS) is typically the single largest cost for manufacturing and merchandising companies. For a manufacturer, COGS include raw materials along with the direct labor and overhead used in producing the goods.

Because sales minus COGS equals gross margin, COGS and gross margin vary inversely. Forecasting COGS as a percentage of sales and forecasting gross margin percentage are equivalent in that a value for one implies a value for the other.

Because COGS has a direct link with sales, forecasting this item as a percentage of sales is usually a good approach. Historical data on a company's COGS as a percentage of sales usually provides a useful starting point for estimates. For example, if a company is losing market share in a market in which the emergence of new substitute products are also putting the overall sector under pricing pressure, gross margins are likely to decline. But if the company is gaining market share because it has introduced new competitive and innovative products, especially if it has done so in combination with achieving cost advantages, gross margins are likely to improve.

Because cost of goods sold is relatively a large cost, a small error in this item can have a material impact on the forecasted operating profit. Thus, analysts should consider whether an analysis of these costs (e.g., by segment, by product category, or by volume and price components), when such an analysis is possible, can improve forecasting accuracy. For example, some companies face fluctuating input costs that can be passed on to customers only with a time lag. Particularly for companies that have low gross margins, sudden shocks in input costs can affect operating profit significantly. A good example is the sensitivity of airlines' profits to unhedged changes in jet fuel costs. In these cases, a breakdown of both costs and sales into volume and price components is essential for developing short term forecasts, even if analysts use the overall relationship between sales and input cost for developing longer-term forecasts.

Analysts should also consider the impact of a company's hedging strategy. For example, commodity-driven companies' gross margins almost automatically decline if input prices increase significantly because of variable costs increasing at a faster rate than revenue growth. Assume a company's cost of goods sold as a percent of sales equals 25%. If the input costs double and the company is able to pass the entire increase on to its clients through a 25% price increase, cost of goods sold as a percent of sales will increase (to 40%) because an equal absolute amount has been added to the numerator and to the denominator. Thus, although the absolute amount of gross profit will remain constant, the gross margin will decrease (from 75% to 60%). Through various hedging strategies a company can mitigate the impact on profitability. For example, brewers often hedge the cost of barley, a key raw material needed for brewing beer, one year in advance. Although companies usually do not disclose their hedging positions, their general strategy is often revealed in the footnotes of the annual report. Further, the negative impact of increasing sales prices on sales volume can be mitigated by a policy of gradual sales price increases. For example, if the brewer expects higher barley prices because of a bad harvest, the brewer can slowly increase prices to avoid a strong price jump next year.

Competitors' gross margins can also provide a useful cross check for estimating a realistic gross margin. Gross margin differences among companies within a sector should logically relate to differences in their business operations. For example, in the Netherlands, supermarket chain Albert Heijn has a higher gross margin in the very competitive grocery sector because it can leverage its dominant 34% market share to achieve savings in purchases; it also has an ability to make higher margin private label products. All of these competitive advantages contribute to its structurally higher gross margin within the grocery sector. But if a new large competitor emerges (e.g., through consolidation of the fragmented market), Albert Heijn's above average gross margin could come under pressure. Also note that differences in competitors' gross margins does not always indicate a superior competitive position but instead could simply reflect differences in business models. For example, some companies in the grocery segment own and operate their own retail stores whereas other companies operate as wholesalers with franchised retail operations. In the franchised retailing business model, most of the operating costs are incurred by the franchisee; the wholesaler offers products with only a small markup to these franchisees. Compared with a grocer with its own stores, a supermarket wholesaler will have a much lower gross margin. The grocer with its own stores, however, will have much higher operating costs. Even though differences in business models can complicate direct comparisons, competitors' gross margins can nonetheless offer potentially useful insights.

2.2.2 Selling, General, and Administrative Expenses

Selling, general, and administrative expenses (SG&A) are the other main type of operating costs. In contrast to COGS, SG&A expenses have less of a direct relationship with the revenue of a company. As an illustration of the profit impact of COGS and SG&A, consider French food company Danone. A sampling of its financials is shown in Exhibit 4.

	2010 (€ millions)	2011 (€ millions)	YoY%	Percent of Sales 2010	Percent of Sales 2011
Net sales	17,010	19,318	13.6	100.0	100.0
Cost of goods sold	7,957	9,541	19.9	46.8	49.4
Gross profit	9,053	9,777	8.0	53.2	50.6
Selling expenses	4,663	5,092	9.2	27.4	26.4
General and administrative expense	1,494	1,564	4.7	8.8	8.1
Research and development expense	209	233	11.5	1.2	1.2
Other expense	90	45	50.0	0.5	0.2
Operating income	2,597	2,843	9.5	15.3	14.7

Exhibit 4   Danone Financials

Note: "YoY%" means year-over-year percentage change.
Source: Based on information in Danone's 2011 Annual Report.

As shown in the exhibit, Danone was affected in 2011 by higher input costs that could not immediately be passed on to customers. Consequently, sales growth of 13.6% resulted in only an 8.0% increase in gross profit, and gross margin declined. The company was able to limit its other operating costs; selling expenses grew 9.2% and general and administrative expenses grew 4.7%, but each was less than the 13.6% growth in revenue. Consequently operating income grew 9.5%, which was less than the sales growth of 13.6%, but more than the increase in gross profit of 8.0%.

Danone's income statement illustrates that companies often disclose the different components of SG&A. Danone, for example, shows separate line items for selling expenses and general and administrative expenses. Although SG&A expenses overall are generally less closely linked to revenue than COGS, certain expenses within SG&A are more variable than others. Specifically, selling and distribution expenses often have a large variable component and can be estimated, like COGS, as a percentage of sales. The largest component of selling expenses is often wages and salaries linked to sales. Therefore, selling expenses will usually increase with additional sales people and/or an overall increase in wages and benefits for the sales force.

Other general and administrative expenses are less variable. Overhead costs for employees, for example, are more related to the number of employees at the head office and supporting IT and administrative operations than to short-term changes in the level of sales. Research and development expense is another example of an expense that tends to fluctuate less than sales. Consequently, these expenses are more fixed in nature and tend to increase and decrease gradually over time than do corresponding changes in the company's revenue.

In addition to analyzing the historical relationship between a company's operating expenses and sales, benchmarking a company against its competitors can also be useful. By analyzing the cost structure of a company's competitors, the efficiency potential and margin potential of a specific company can be estimated. As a final measure, performing certain cross checks within a forecast model can be useful too. For example, in the supermarket sector the projected floor square footage (or metric equivalent) underlying the revenue projections should match with the floor space projections underlying the unit selling expense forecasts. Both sales and expense projections may be enhanced if the company provides a breakout of the product and/or geographical segments in the footnotes of the annual report.

EXAMPLE 4

L'Oréal's Operational Cost Structure vs. Competitors

As shown in Exhibit 5, L'Oréal reported an operating margin of 16% in 2011, which makes it the most profitable company among beauty companies. However, the average operating margin of 18% for home and personal goods companies operating in mass markets is even greater than that of L'Oréal. L'Oréal costs are similar to a luxury goods company with high gross margin of 71% that is offset by high "go to market" costs for advertising and promotion (A&P) expenditures. With the exception of Avon, the business model of which is based on direct selling, A&P is substantially greater at the beauty companies than at the mass market producers.

L'Oréal is often considered to be a pure beauty company. But if the underlying business is considered in detail, the company's operations can be split 50/50 between a luxury beauty high-end part and a general consumer part. In the general consumer part, L'Oréal's products compete with such players as Colgate, Proctor & Gamble, and Henkel in the mass market. Exhibit 5[2] presents relevant data.

---

2 The COGS and SG&A expense percentages for some of the companies listed in Exhibit 5 have been adjusted to reflect differences in accounting choices. For example, some of the consumer product companies include shipping and handling expense in cost of sales, whereas others include these costs as a component of SG&A expense. To improve the comparability of gross margins, distribution costs have been included as a component of SG&A expense and removed (when included) from cost of goods sold for all of the companies in this example. Companies affected by this adjustment include Proctor & Gamble, Clorox, and Kimberly-Clark, for which post-adjustment gross margins average about 5.5% higher than the pre-adjustment percentages.

	Sales			Gross		SG&A/	
Company	(€ millions)	Sales	COGS	Margin	A&P	Other	EBIT

Exhibit 5   European and US Home and Personal Care Companies, Beauty vs. Mass Market Companies: Simplified and Common Size Income Statement

Company	Sales (€ millions)	Sales	COGS	Gross Margin	A&P	SG&A/ Other	EBIT
Beauty							
L'Oréal	20,348	100%	29%	71%	31%	24%	16%
Estée Lauder	6,785	100	21	79	27	38	14
Beierdorf Consumer	4,696	100	33	67	30	26	11
Avon	11,292	100	37	63	4	49	10
Average beauty	10,780	100%	30%	70%	23%	34%	13%
Mass market							
Colgate	12,097	100%	43%	57%	12%	22%	23%
Reckitt Benckiser ex-Pharmaceutical	10,051	100	43	57	10	25	22
Proctor & Gamble	60,099	100	45	55	11	26	18
Clorox	3,818	100	52	48	9	21	18
Energizer	3,354	100	54	46	11	20	15
Kimberly-Clark	14,983	100	63	37	3	20	14
Henkel	7,781	100	43	57	15	29	13
Average mass market	16,026	100%	49%	51%	10%	23%	18%

Source: Based on information in company reports, Bernstein, and JPMorgan estimates.

1   Assuming the following information, what will L'Oréal's new operating margin be?

   ● L'Oréal's beauty and mass market operations each represent half of revenues.

   ● L'Oréal will be able to bring the overall costs structure of its mass market operations in line with the average of mass market companies (EBIT = 18%).

   ● The cost structure of L'Oréal's beauty operations will remain stable (EBIT = 16%).

2   What will happen to L'Oréal's operating margin if the company is able to adjust the operating cost structure of its mass market segment (50% of revenues) partly toward the average of its mass markets peers but keep its high gross margin? Assume the following:

   ● The cost structure of half of the business, the beauty operations, will remain stable (EBIT = 16%).

   ● L'Oréal's mass market operations will have a gross margin of 61% (the average of the current gross margin of 71% and the 51% reported by its mass market peers).

   ● L'Oréal's A&P costs will fall half from 31% of sales to 15% of sales and other costs will remain stable.

Solution to 1:

Operating margin will increase from 16% to 17%, which is 50% of 18% (mass market EBIT) plus 50% of 16% (L'Oréal EBIT).

Solution to 2:

Operating margin will increase from 16% to 19%. The operating margin of the mass market operations will improve by 600bps to 22% because a 1,000bps decline in gross margin (from 71% to 61%) will more than offset the 1,600bps of decline in A&P expenditures (from 31% of sales to 15% of sales). The average of the EBIT for beauty (16%) and the new EBIT for mass market operations (22%) is 19%.

Exhibit 6	EBIT for L'Oréal Divisions			
	L'Oréal	**Beauty 50%**	**Mass Market 50%**	**Average**
Sales	100%	100%	100%	100%
Cost of goods sold	29%	29%	39%	34%
Gross margin	71%	71%	61%	66%
A&P	31%	31%	15%	23%
SG&A/Other	24%	24%	24%	24%
EBIT	16%	16%	22%	19%

EXAMPLE 5

Analysis of the Consumer Goods Company Unilever

The consumer goods company Unilever reported an overall operating margin of 14.9% in 2011. As shown in Exhibit 7, the operating margin is higher in the slower growing Western European and Americas regions than in the faster growing Asia, Africa, and Central and Eastern Europe region.

Exhibit 7	Unilever Revenue from Various Regions (€ millions, unless noted)			
	2010	**2011**	**Change**	**USG**
Asia, Africa, Central and Eastern Europe	17,685	18,947	7.14%	10.50%
Americas	14,562	15,251	4.73	6.30
Western Europe	12,015	12,269	2.11	0.70
Total revenues	44,262	46,467	4.98	6.50
Underlying operating profit				
Asia, Africa, Central and Eastern Europe	2,361	2,411	2.12%	
Americas	2,328	2,381	2.28	
Western Europe	1,931	2,109	9.22	
Total underlying operating profit	6,620	6,901	4.24	

Exhibit 7 (Continued)				
	2010	**2011**	**Change**	**USG**
Underlying operating profit margin				
Asia, Africa, Central and Eastern Europe	13.35%	12.72%		
Americas	15.99	15.61		
Western Europe	16.07	17.19		
Total underlying operating profit margin	14.96	14.86		

Notes: USG is "underlying sales growth" or sales growth adjusted for currency, disposals, and acquisitions. USG is the organic sales growth based on volume, price, and mix changes. Underlying profit is operating profit adjusted for exceptional items like restructuring costs
Source: Based on Unilever's 2011 full year and fourth quarter results.

1 Determine the estimated sales, operating profit, and operating profit margin by using the following two approaches: (A) Assume consolidated sales growth of 6.5% and overall stable operating margin of 14.85% for the next five years; and (B) assume each individual region's sales growth and operating margin continue at the same rate reported in 2011. Which approach will result in a higher estimated operating profit after five years?

2 Compare and explain the results under the two alternative approaches described in Question 1 (A and B) with reference to the yearly growth rate in estimated total sales, the yearly growth rate in total operating profit, and the yearly profit margin.

3 Assume Unilever is able to grow revenues the next five years in each region in line with 2011 (Western Europe 0.7%; Americas 6.3%; Asia, Africa, Central and Eastern Europe 10.5%). But operating profit margins in Western Europe will fall 50 bps annually for the next five years (as a result of high competition and limited growth) and operating profit margins in Asia, Africa, and Central and Eastern Europe region will increase 50 bps annually for the next five years (helped by increasing demand for the company's products and better utilization of its factories). Using approach (B), calculate the overall operating profit margin.

Solution to 1:

Operating profit after five years will be €9,455,000,000 under the first approach (A) and €9,388,000,000 under the second approach (B). The results of the calculation are shown in Exhibit 8. Constant sales growth of 6.5% with stable 14.85% margins generates an operating profit of €6,901,000,000 × (1.065)^5. Exhibit 8 shows some of the details.

Exhibit 8 Sales and Operating Profit for Unilever, 2011–2016E (€ millions, unless noted)						
Approach A	**2011**	**2012E**	**2013E**	**2014E**	**2015E**	**2016E**
Sales	46,467	49,487	52,704	56,130	59,778	63,664
YoY %		6.5%	6.5%	6.5%	6.5%	6.5%
Underlying operating profit	6,901	7,350	7,827	8,336	8,878	9,455

(continued)

Exhibit 8	(Continued)					

Approach A	2011	2012E	2013E	2014E	2015E	2016E
YoY %		6.5%	6.5%	6.5%	6.5%	6.5%
Underlying operating profit margin	14.85%	14.85%	14.85%	14.85%	14.85%	14.85%

Approach B	2011	2012E	2013E	2014E	2015E	2016E
Asia, Africa, Central and Eastern Europe	18,947	20,936	23,135	25,564	28,248	31,214
Americas	15,251	16,212	17,233	18,319	19,473	20,700
Western Europe	12,269	12,355	12,441	12,528	12,616	12,704
Total revenues	46,467	49,503	52,809	56,411	60,337	64,618
Asia, Africa, Central and Eastern Europe		10.5%	10.5%	10.5%	10.5%	10.5%
Americas		6.3	6.3	6.3	6.3	6.3
Western Europe		0.7	0.7	0.7	0.7	0.7
YoY revenue		6.5%	6.7%	6.8%	7.0%	7.1%
Asia, Africa, Central and Eastern Europe	2,411	2,664	2,944	3,253	3,595	3,972
Americas	2,381	2,531	2,690	2,860	3,040	3,232
Western Europe	2,109	2,124	2,139	2,154	2,169	2,184
Total underlying operating profit	6,901	7,319	7,773	8,267	8,803	9,388
Asia, Africa, Central and Eastern Europe		10.5%	10.5%	10.5%	10.5%	10.5%
Americas		6.3	6.3	6.3	6.3	6.3
Western Europe		0.7	0.7	0.7	0.7	0.7
YoY underlying profit		6.1%	6.2%	6.3%	6.5%	6.6%
Asia, Africa, Central and Eastern Europe		12.72%	12.72%	12.72%	12.72%	12.72%
Americas		15.61	15.61	15.61	15.61	15.61
Western Europe		17.19	17.19	17.19	17.19	17.19
Total underlying operating margin		14.78%	14.72%	14.65%	14.59%	14.53%

Solution to 2:

Under the first approach (A) a constant 6.5% sales growth rate and a stable 14.85% operating margin are assumed. As a consequence, the operating profit growth rate is in line with the revenue growth rate and constant at 6.5% (see Exhibit 9, Panel A). Under the second approach (see Exhibit 9, Panel B), the high sales growth of

10.5% in the region with the largest amount of sales (Asia, Africa, and Central and Eastern Europe) results in accelerating revenue growth from 6.5% in 2012 to 7.1% in 2016. Because the operating margin in the largest and fastest growing region is less than the overall average, operating margin falls from 14.85% in 2011 to 14.53% in 2016. This comparison illustrates that the higher sales growth in a lower margin region puts the company's operating margin under structural pressure. The rate of operating profit growth continues to be less than the rate of sales growth but gradually improves from 6.1% in 2012 to 6.6% in 2016. As of 2016, the rate of profit growth under (B), which is 6.6%, exceeds the rate under (A), which is 6.5% because the negative operating profit mix effect is offset by the positive sales growth mix effect. Exhibit 9 shows a summary of the sales, operating profit, sales growth, and margin growth.

Exhibit 9	Summary of Results in Exhibit 8					
	2011	**2012E**	**2013E**	**2014E**	**2015E**	**2016E**
A. Sales and operating profit (€ millions)						
Sales A	46,467	49,487	52,704	56,130	59,778	63,664
Sales B	46,467	49,503	52,809	56,411	60,337	64,618
Sales A–B		−16	−105	−281	−559	−955
Sales growth A		6.5%	6.5%	6.5%	6.5%	6.5%
Sales growth B		6.5%	6.7%	6.8%	7.0%	7.1%
Operating profit A	6,901	7,350	7,827	8,336	8,878	9,455
Operating profit B	6,901	7,319	7,773	8,267	8,803	9,388
Operating profit A–B		31	54	70	75	67
B. Growth Rates						
Operating growth A		6.50%	6.50%	6.50%	6.50%	6.50%
Operating profit growth B		6.06%	6.20%	6.35%	6.49%	6.64%
Operating profit margin A	14.85%	14.85%	14.85%	14.85%	14.85%	14.85%
Operating profit margin B	14.85%	14.78%	14.72%	14.65%	14.59%	14.53%

Solution to 3

As shown in Exhibit 10, the overall underlying operating profit margin improves from 14.85% in 2011 to 15.24% in 2016 because the margin decline in Western Europe is offset by the margin increase in the larger and faster growing region of Asia, Africa, and Central and Eastern Europe. Because of the faster revenue growth in Asia, Africa, and Central and Eastern Europe, the trend for the overall margin enhancement is also positive from 2 bps in 2012 (14.87% – 14.85%) to 13 bps in 2016 (15.24% – 15.11%).

Exhibit 10	Sales and Operating Profit for Unilever 2011–2016E (€ millions, unless noted)					
	2011	2012E	2013E	2014E	2015E	2016E
Asia, Africa, Central and Eastern Europe	18,947	20,936	23,135	25,564	28,248	31,214
Americas	15,251	16,212	17,233	18,319	19,473	20,700
Western Europe	12,269	12,355	12,441	12,528	12,616	12,704
Total revenue	46,467	49,503	52,809	56,411	60,337	64,618
Asia, Africa, Central and Eastern Europe		10.5%	10.5%	10.5%	10.5%	10.5%
Americas		6.3%	6.3%	6.3%	6.3%	6.3%
Western Europe		0.7%	0.7%	0.7%	0.7%	0.7%
YoY revenue growth		6.5%	6.7%	6.8%	7.0%	7.1%
Asia, Africa, Central and Eastern Europe	2,411	2,769	3,175	3,636	4,160	4,752
Americas	2,381	2,531	2,690	2,860	3,040	3,232
Western Europe	2,109	2,062	2,014	1,966	1,916	1,866
Total underlying operating profit	6,901	7,362	7,880	8,462	9,116	9,850
Asia, Africa, Central and Eastern Europe		14.8%	14.7%	14.5%	14.4%	14.3%
Americas		6.3%	6.3%	6.3%	6.3%	6.3%
Western Europe		−2.2%	−2.3%	−2.4%	−2.5%	−2.6%
YoY underlying profit growth		6.7%	7.0%	7.4%	7.7%	8.1%
Asia, Africa, Central and Eastern Europe		13.22%	13.72%	14.22%	14.72%	15.22%
Americas		15.61%	15.61%	15.61%	15.61%	15.61%
Western Europe		16.69%	16.19%	15.69%	15.19%	14.69%
Total underlying operating margin		14.87%	14.92%	15.00%	15.11%	15.24%

2.3 Income Statement Modeling: Non-operating Costs

Line items on the income statement that appear below operating profit also need to be modeled. Some of the most important items included here are interest income, interest expense, taxes, minority interest, and income from affiliates, share count, and unusual charges.

Interest income depends on the amount of cash and investments on the balance sheet, as well as the rates of return earned on investments. Interest income is a key component of revenue for banks and insurance companies, but it is relatively less significant to most non-financial companies. Interest expense depends on the level of debt on the balance sheet, as well as the interest rate associated with the debt. Analysts should be aware of the effect of changing interest rates on the market value of company's debt and interest expense in the future.

Taxes are primarily determined by jurisdictional regulations but can also be influenced by the nature of a business. Some companies benefit from special tax treatment, for example from research and development tax credits or accelerated depreciation of fixed assets. Analysts should be aware of any differences between taxes reported on the income statement and cash taxes, which can result in deferred tax assets or liabilities. Analysts should also be aware of any governmental or business changes that can alter tax rates.

The two most significant non-operating expenses in income statement modeling are financing expenses (i.e., interest) and taxes.

2.3.1 Financing Expenses

When forecasting financing expenses, the capital structure of a company is a key determinant. For practical purposes the debt level in combination with the interest rate are the main drivers in forecasting debt financing expenses. Usually the notes to the financial statements provide detail about the maturity structure of the company's debt and the corresponding interest rates. This information can be used to estimate future financing expenses.

EXAMPLE 6

Interest Expense Calculations

Dutch grocer Ahold has a debt structure with a relatively high amount of cash on its balance sheet.

Exhibit 11   Ahold's Debt, Interest Income, and Expense

(€ millions)	2 Jan 2011	1 Jan 2012	Average
Loans	1,851	1,489	1,670
Finance lease liabilities	1,096	1,158	1,127
Cumulative preferred financing shares	497	497	497
Non-current portion of long term debt	3,444	3,144	3,294
Short borrowings and current portion of long-term debt	117	536	327
Gross debt	3,561	3,680	3,621
Less: cash, cash equivalents, and short-term deposits	2,824	2,592	2,708
Net debt	737	1,088	913
Interest income for 2011			20
Interest expense for 2011			245
Net interest expense			225

(continued)

Exhibit 11	(Continued)		
(€ millions)	**2 Jan 2011**	**1 Jan 2012**	**Average**
Other financial expenses			91
Total finance costs			316

Source: Based on information in Ahold's 2011 annual report.

1 Calculate the interest expense on the average gross debt and interest rate on the average cash position.

2 Calculate the interest rate on the average net debt, assuming the other financial income and expenses are not related to the debt or cash balances.

Solution to 1:

Interest expense on average gross debt is calculated as interest expense divided by average gross debt: (€245 million/€3,621 million) = 6.77% or 6.8%. The interest rate on average cash position is interest income divided by the average cash position (€20 million/€2,708 million) = 0.7%.

Solution to 2:

The interest rate on the average net debt is calculated as net interest expense divided by average net debt (€225 million/€913 million) = 24.7%.

2.3.2 *Corporate Income Tax*

The final large non-operating item is the tax expense. This is often a large amount that affects profit substantially. Differences in tax rates can be an important driver of value. Generally, there are three types of tax rates:

■ The statutory tax rate, which is the tax rate applying to what is considered to be a company's domestic tax base.

■ The effective tax rate, which is calculated as the reported tax amount on the income statement divided by the pre-tax income.

■ The cash tax rate, which is the tax actually paid (cash tax) divided by pre-tax income.

Differences between cash taxes and reported taxes typically result from timing differences between accounting and tax calculations and are reflected as a deferred tax asset or a deferred tax liability.

In forecasting tax expense and cash taxes, respectively, the effective tax rate and cash tax rate are key. A good understanding of their operational drivers and the financial structure of a company is useful in forecasting these tax rates.

Differences between the statutory tax rate and the effective tax rate can arise for many reasons. Tax credits, withholding tax on dividends, adjustments to previous years, and expenses not deductible for tax purposes are among the reasons for differences. Effective tax rates can differ when companies are active outside the country in which they are domiciled. The effective tax rate becomes a blend of the different tax rates of the countries in which the activities take place in relation to the profit generated in each country. If a company reports a high profit in a country with a high tax rate and a low profit in a country with a low tax rate, the effective tax rate will be the weighted average of the rates, and higher than the simple average tax rate of both countries. In some cases, companies have also been able to minimize their taxes by using special purposes entities. For example, some companies create specialized financing and holding companies to minimize the amount of taxable profit reported in high tax rate countries. Although such actions could reduce the effective tax rate substantially, they also create risks if, for example, tax laws change. In general, an effective tax rate that is consistently lower than statutory rates or the effective tax rates reported by competitors may warrant additional attention when forecasting future tax expenses. The notes on the financial statements should disclose other types of items, some of which could contribute to a temporarily high or low effective tax rate. The cash tax rate is used for forecasting cash flows and the effective tax rate is relevant for projecting earnings on the income statement. In developing an estimated tax rate for forecasts, analysts should adjust for any one-time events. If the income from equity method investees is a substantial part of pre-tax income and also a volatile component of it, the effective tax rate excluding this amount is likely to be a better estimate for the future tax costs for a company. The tax impact from income from participations is disclosed in the notes on the financial statements.

Often, a good starting point for estimating future tax expense is a tax rate based on normalized operating income, before the results from associates and special items. This normalized tax rate should be a good indication of the future tax expense, adjusted for special items, in an analyst's earnings model.

By building a model, the effective tax amount can be found in the profit and loss projections and the cash tax amount on the cash flow statement.[3] The reconciliation between the profit and loss tax amount and the cash flow tax figures should be the change in the deferred tax asset or liability.

EXAMPLE 7

Tax Rate Estimates

ABC, a hypothetical company, operates in Countries A and B. The tax rate in Country A is 40%, and the tax rate in Country B is 10%. In the first year, the company generates an equal amount of profit before tax in each country.

Exhibit 12 Tax Rates that Differ by Jurisdiction			
	A	**B**	**Total**
Profit before tax	100	100	200
Effective tax rate	40%	10%	25%
Tax	40	10	50
Net profit	60	90	150

1 What will happen to the effective tax rate for the next three years if the profit in Country A is stable but the profit in Country B grows 15% annually?

2 Evaluate the cash tax and effective tax rates for the next three years if the tax authorities in Country A allow some costs (e.g., accelerated depreciation) to be taken sooner for tax purposes. For Country A, the result

---

3 Sometimes shown on the cash flow statement or otherwise given as supplemental information.

will be a 50% reduction in taxes paid in the current year but an increase in taxes paid by the same amount in the following year (this happens each year). Assume stable profit before tax in Country A and 15% annual before-tax-profit growth in Country B.

3 Repeat the exercise of Problem 2, but now assume that it is Country B not Country A that allows some costs to be taken sooner for tax purposes and that the tax effect described applies to Country B. Continue to assume stable profit before tax at Country A and 15% annual profit growth in Country B.

Solution to 1:

The effective tax rate will gradually decline because a higher proportion of profit will be generated in the country with the lower tax rate. In Exhibit 13, the effective tax rate declines from 25% in the beginning to 21.9% in the third year.

Exhibit 13	Worksheet for Problem 1			
	Year			
	0	**1**	**2**	**3**
Profit before tax, Country A	100.0	100.0	100.0	100.0
Profit before tax, Country B	100.0	115.0	132.3	152.1
Total profit before tax	200.0	215.0	232.3	252.1
Tax, Country A (40%)	40.0	40.0	40.0	40.0
Tax, Country B (10%)	10.0	11.5	13.2	15.2
Total tax	50.0	51.5	53.2	55.2
Total tax rate %	25.0%	24.0%	22.9%	21.9%
Net profit	150.0	163.5	179.1	196.9

Solution to 2:

The combined cash tax rate (next to last line in Exhibit 14) will be 15% in the first year and then rebound in subsequent years. Only the rate for the first year will benefit from a tax deferral; in subsequent years the deferral for a given year will be offset by the addition of the amount postponed from the previous year. The combined effective tax rate (last line in Exhibit 14) will be unaffected by the deferral. As shown in Exhibit 14, beginning with the second year, the combined cash tax and effective tax rates decline over time but remain identical to each other.

Exhibit 14	Worksheet for Problem 2			
	Year			
	0	**1**	**2**	**3**
Profit before tax	200.0	215.0	232.3	252.1
Tax per income statement	50.0	51.5	53.2	55.2

Exhibit 14   (Continued)

	Year			
	0	1	2	3
Tax payment, Country A	20.0	20.0	20.0	20.0
Postponed tax payment, Country A		20.0	20.0	20.0
Tax payment Country B	10.0	11.5	13.2	15.2
Total tax payment	30.0	51.5	53.2	55.2
Cash tax rate	15.0%	24.0%	22.9%	21.9%
Tax rate per income statement	25.0%	24.0%	22.9%	21.9%

Solution to 3:

The combined effective tax rate (last line in Exhibit 15) remains unchanged from Exhibits 13 and 14. Because of the growth assumed for Country B, however, the annual tax postponement will result in a lower cash tax rate in Country B than the effective tax rate in Country B. Consequently, as shown in Exhibit 15, the combined cash tax rate will be less than the effective tax rate.

Exhibit 15   Worksheet for Problem 3

	Year			
	0	1	2	3
Profit before tax	200.0	215.0	232.3	252.1
Tax per income statements	50.0	51.5	53.2	55.2
Tax payment, Country A	40.0	40.0	40.0	40.0
Tax payment, Country B	5.0	5.8	6.6	7.6
Postponed tax payment, Country B		5.0	5.8	6.6
Total tax payment	45.0	50.8	52.4	54.2
Cash tax rate	22.5%	23.6%	22.5%	21.5%
Tax rate per income statement	25.0%	24.0%	22.9%	21.9%

The next section addresses several points to note in modeling dividends, share count, and unusual expenses.

2.4 Income Statement Modeling: Other Items

A company's stated dividend policy helps in modeling future dividend growth. Analysts will often assume that dividends grow each year by a certain dollar amount or as a proportion of net income.

If a company shares an ownership interest in a business unit with a third party, the company may report minority interest expense or income from consolidated affiliates on its income statement. If a company owns more than 50% of an affiliate, it will generally consolidate the affiliate's results with its own and report the portion of income that does not belong to the parent company as minority interest. If a company owns less than 50% of an affiliate, it will not consolidate results but will report its share of income from the affiliate under the equity method. If the affiliate is profitable, minority interest would be a deduction from net income, whereas if a consolidated affiliate generates losses, minority interest would be an addition to net income. In either case, income or expense from these jointly owned businesses can be material.

Share count (shares issued and outstanding) is a key input in the calculation of an intrinsic value estimate and earnings per share. Share count changes for three primary reasons: dilution related to stock options, convertible bonds, and similar securities; issuance of new shares; and share repurchases. The market price of a stock is an important determinant of future share count changes, which can complicate their estimation. Projections for share issuance and repurchases should fit within the analyst's broader analysis of a company's capital structure.

Finally, unusual charges can be almost impossible to predict, particularly past the next couple of years. For this reason, analysts typically exclude unusual charges from their forecasts. But if a company has a habit of frequently classifying certain recurring costs as "unusual," analysts should consider some normalized level of charges in their valuation model.

2.5 Balance Sheet and Cash Flow Statement Modeling

Income statement modeling is the starting point for balance sheet and cash flow statement modeling. Analysts normally have a choice of whether to focus on the balance sheet or cash flow statement; the third financial statement will naturally result from the construction of the other two. Here, we focus on the balance sheet.

Some balance sheet line items—such as retained earnings—flow directly from the income statement whereas other lines—such as accounts receivable, accounts payable, and inventory—are very closely linked to income statement projections.

A common way to model working capital accounts is through the use of efficiency ratios. For example, analysts may project future accounts receivable by assuming a number of days sales outstanding and combining that assumption with a sales projection. Days sales outstanding is a measure of the number of days, on average, it takes a company to collect revenue from its customers. For example, if annual revenue (assumed to be all credit sales) is $25 billion and it normally takes 60 days to collect revenue from customers, accounts receivable would be estimated at $4.1 billion ($\approx$ $25 billion $\times$ 60/365). Analysts can project future inventory by assuming an inventory turnover rate and combining that assumption with a cost of goods sold projection. Inventory turnover is a measure of how much inventory a company keeps on hand, or alternatively how quickly a company sells through its inventory. In general, if efficiency ratios are held constant, working capital accounts will grow in line with the related income statement accounts.

Working capital projections can be modified by both top-down and bottom-up considerations. In the absence of a specific opinion about working capital, analysts can look at historical efficiency ratios and project recent performance or a historical average to persist in the future, which would be a bottom-up approach. Conversely, analysts may have a specific view of future working capital. For example, if they project economy-wide retail sales to decline unexpectedly, that could result in slower inventory turnover across the retail sector. Because the analysts began with a forecast for a large sector of the economy, this would be considered a top-down approach.

Projections for long-term assets such as property, plant, and equipment (PP&E) are less directly tied to the income statement for most companies. Net PP&E primarily changes as a result of capital expenditures and depreciation, both of which are important components of the cash flow statement. Depreciation forecasts are usually based on historical depreciation and disclosure about depreciation schedules, whereas capital expenditure forecasts depend on the analysts' judgment of the future need for new PP&E. Capital expenditures can be thought of as including both **maintenance capital expenditures**, which are necessary to sustain the current business, and **growth capital expenditures**, which are needed to expand the business. All else being equal, maintenance capital expenditure forecasts should normally be higher than depreciation because of inflation.

Finally, analysts must make assumptions about a company's future capital structure. Leverage ratios—such as debt-to-capital, debt-to-equity, and debt-to-EBITDA—can be useful for projecting future debt and equity levels. Analysts should consider historical company practice, management's financial strategy, and the capital requirements implied by other model assumptions when projecting the future capital structure.

Once future income statements and balance sheets are constructed, analysts can use them to determine the rate of **return on invested capital** (ROIC) implied by their assumptions. ROIC measures the profitability of the capital invested by the company's shareholders and debt holders. The numerator for ROIC is usually net operating profit less adjusted taxes (NOPLAT). NOPLAT is basically earnings before interest expense (i.e., earnings available to provide a return to both equity holders and debt holders). The denominator for ROIC is invested capital, which is calculated as operating assets less operating liabilities.[4] Invested capital can be measured at the beginning of an accounting period or as an average of the beginning and end of the accounting period. ROIC is a better measure of profitability than return on equity because it is not affected by a company's degree of financial leverage. In general, sustainably high ROIC is a sign of a competitive advantage. To increase ROIC, a company must either increase earnings, reduce invested capital, or both. A closely related measure to ROIC, but focusing on pretax operating profit, is **return on capital employed** (ROCE), which is essentially ROIC before tax.[5] This measure is defined as operating profit divided by capital employed (debt and equity capital). As a pretax measure, ROCE can be useful in several contexts, such as peer comparisons of companies in countries with different tax structures, because comparison of underlying profitability would not be biased in favor of companies benefitting from low tax rate regimes.

---

4 Hawawini and Viallet (2011 p. 628) define invested capital in detail as cash and cash equivalents plus working capital requirement (operating assets minus operating liabilities, where operating assets reflect receivables, inventories, and prepaid expenses and operating liabilities include payables and accrued expenses) plus net fixed assets. There are many variations in practice in the definition of ROIC.

5 This presentation follows one line of analyst practice. But some authorities treat ROCE as identical to ROIC; see Hawawini and Viallet (2011, p. 628). Similar to many financial ratios, there is no single "authoritative" definition.

EXAMPLE 8

Balance Sheet Modeling

1 Management at a restaurant chain intends to maintain a 40% debt-to-capital ratio. Management has a track record of meeting its capital structure targets. The restaurant chain is solidly profitable, but earnings are expected to decline 2% annually over the next five years because of increasing competitive pressure. The company does not pay a dividend or repurchase shares, and all earnings are expected to be retained for the next five years. What is *most likely* to happen to the restaurant chain's total debt over this period?

   A Total debt will increase.

   B Total debt will decrease.

   C Total debt will remain the same.

2 Sophie Moreau, a buy-side analyst, is analyzing a French manufacturing company. Working capital and PP&E account for almost all of the company's assets. Moreau believes that the depreciation schedule used by the company is not reflective of economic reality. Rather, she expects PP&E to last twice as long as what is implied by the depreciation schedule, and as such, she projects capital expenditures to be significantly less than depreciation for the next five years. Moreau projects that both earnings and net working capital will grow at a low single-digit rate during this time. What do Moreau's assumptions *most likely* imply for returns on invested capital during the next five years?

   A ROIC will increase.

   B ROIC will decrease.

   C ROIC will stay the same.

Solution to 1:

A is correct. The restaurant chain is profitable and retains all of its earnings. These facts will lead to rising equity on the balance sheet. To maintain a constant debt-to-capital ratio, management will have to increase its debt.

Solution to 2:

A is correct. Earnings are expected to grow over the next five years. Working capital is expected to grow in line with earnings, which would imply a stable ROIC. But net PP&E is expected to decline because depreciation is expected to exceed capital expenditures. Total invested capital will thus grow more slowly than earnings or even shrink, implying improving returns on invested capital.

   Once projected income statements and balance sheets have been constructed, future cash flow statements can be projected. Analysts will normally make assumptions about how a company will use its future cash flows, whether for share repurchases, dividends, additional capital expenditures, acquisitions, and so on.

2.6 Scenario Analysis and Sensitivity Analysis

Regardless of the approach used, equity valuation involves a significant degree of uncertainty. Valuing businesses requires making assumptions about the future, which is inherently uncertain. Recognizing this uncertainty, effective analysis should always consider scenarios in addition to the most likely "base case" result.

Sensitivity analysis involves changing one assumption at a time to see the effect on the estimate of intrinsic value. For example, analysts might examine the impact of a different revenue growth rate on the company's valuation. **Scenario analysis** has the same goal, but involves changing multiple assumptions at the same time. For example, analysts might simultaneously change assumptions for revenue growth, operating margin, and capital investment. Either sensitivity analysis or scenario analysis can be used to determine a range of potential intrinsic value estimates based on a variety of different assumptions about the future. Analysts can use either tool to estimate the effect on a company's valuation of different assumptions for economic growth, for inflation, for the success of a particular product, and so on.

Value estimates for companies involve varying degrees of uncertainty. Large, mature, slow growing, non-cyclical businesses with well-capitalized balance sheets may be relatively easy to value. In this case, intrinsic value estimates from upside and downside scenarios may be close to the base case. Conversely, for new ventures, companies exposed to technological or regulatory change, companies with significant operating or financial leverage, and so on, the range of potential intrinsic value estimates could be much wider. In this case, analysts may hesitate to make an investment recommendation without substantial confidence that intrinsic value differs markedly from market price.

Analysts should normally think of their valuations as a range of possibilities, rather than an estimate at a single point. For most companies, the range will be approximately symmetrical and might be imagined as a bell curve. The base case estimate of intrinsic value would be at the middle of the distribution, with (depending on the judgment of the analysts) similar probabilities of upside and downside outcomes as shown in Exhibit 16. The width of the tails will depend on the level of uncertainty pertaining to forecasts. For example, the large, mature, slow-growing company would have a steep distribution with relatively thin tails, representing a relatively low likelihood of extreme values.[6]

---

6 Note that the probability distribution of estimates need not be symmetrical. In addition, technically, a distribution of security values would be bounded on the left by zero.

Exhibit 16   Distribution of Intrinsic Value Estimates

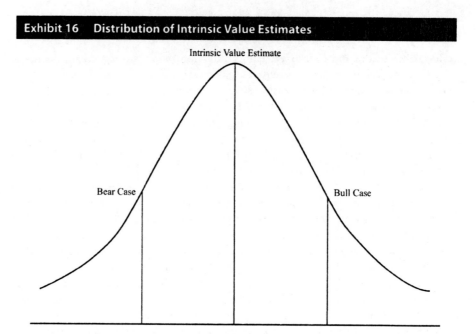

For some companies, the range of potential outcomes might be skewed or highly irregular. For example, there might be a relatively high probability that a debt-laden company will have insufficient cash flow to cover interest and principal payments, in which case the value of the equity could be zero. A company with a single untested product may be worth very little or a lot, depending on whether the product turns out to be a success. Scenario analysis can be particularly useful in these cases, because there may not be a meaningful "base case." A common approach is for analysts to value such companies by using a probability-weighted average of the various scenarios.

<table>
<tr><td>3</td><td></td></tr>
</table>

THE IMPACT OF COMPETITIVE FACTORS ON PRICES AND COSTS

Incorporating competition into financial forecasting can be a challenging task. Most of the items that analysts must forecast—including revenues, profit margin, and capital expenditures—are linked to the competitive environment, and competition can affect these items both separately and collectively. Analysts can use various conceptual tools in thinking about how competition will affect forecasts. Such tools provide a way to organize data and ideas, and although there are no "rules" for incorporating competitive analysis in forecasts, it is arguably the analysts' most important job. Analysts' projections for revenue growth, margin development, capital expenditures, and working capital investment, are all based on an estimate of a company's future competitive strength.

One of the tools that analysts can use to think about how competition will affect financial results is Michael Porter's widely used "five forces" framework.[7] The framework identifies five forces that affect the intensity of a company's competitive environment

---

7 See Porter (1980).

and thus costs and price projections. These forces include the following: threat of substitute products, intensity of rivalry among incumbent companies, bargaining power of suppliers, bargaining power of customers, and threat of new entrants.

The first force is the threat of substitute products. If numerous substitutes exist and switching costs are low, companies have limited pricing power. Conversely if few substitutes exist and/or switching costs are high, companies have greater pricing power.

The second force is the intensity of rivalry among incumbent companies. Pricing power is limited in industries that are fragmented, have limited growth, high exit barriers, high fixed costs, and have more or less identical product offerings.

The third force is the bargaining power of suppliers. Companies (and overall industries) whose suppliers have greater ability to increase prices and/or limit the quality and quantity of inputs face downward pressure on profitability. Suppliers' bargaining power is generally a function of relative size, the relative importance the supplier places on a particular product, and the availability of alternatives.

The fourth force is the bargaining power of customers. Companies (and overall industries) whose customers have greater ability to demand lower prices and/or control the quality and quantity of end products face downward pressure on profitability. Buyer power is the reverse of supplier power. Bargaining power of customers is generally lower in markets with a fragmented customer base, a non-standardized product, and high switching costs for the customer.

The fifth force is the threat of new entrants. Companies in industries in which the threat of new entrants is high because of the presence of above-market returns face downward pressure on profitability. In contrast, if there are barriers to entry, it may be costly for new competitors to enter a market. It is easier for incumbents to raise prices and defend their market position when barriers to entry are high.

ANALYSIS OF ANHEUSER-BUSCH INBEV USING PORTER'S FIVE FORCES

The competitive structure a company faces can vary among countries, with implications for modeling revenue growth, profit margins, capital expenditures, and return on investments. For example, Anheuser-Busch (AB) InBev, the largest global brewer, operates in many countries, two of which are Brazil and the United Kingdom. AB InBev's competitive position and prospects in the highly consolidated and growing Brazilian market are much more favorable than in the fragmented and declining UK market.

The Brazilian beer market is divided among four players. In Brazil, AmBev (AB InBev's local subsidiary) is the dominant brewer with a 69% market share in 2011 versus 11% for Petropolis, 10% for Grupo Schincariol, and 9% for Heineken. Helped by its dominant market position and strong distribution network, AmBev was able to report an operating margin of nearly 49% in 2011, the highest in the global beer industry. In the still-growing Brazilian beer market, the industry participants focus less on price competition and more on expanding distribution and "premiumization" (i.e., selling more expensive beers.) In this environment, an analyst would likely forecast solid revenue growth for AmBev. Exhibit 17 presents an analysis of the Brazilian beer market using Porter's five forces framework. Most of the competitive forces represent a low threat to profitability (consistent with AmBev's historical profitability), implying that analysts would most likely forecast continued above-average profitability.

Exhibit 17	Analysis of the Brazilian Beer Market Using Porter's Five Forces	
Force	**Degree**	**Factors to Consider**
Threat of substitutes	Medium	■ Beer consumers do not easily shift to other beverages, but such alternatives as wine and spirits are available.
		■ Unlike many other countries, the range of beers is relatively limited.
Rivalry	Low	■ AmBev dominates the market with a 69% market share. Its economies of scale in production and distribution yield significant cost advantages relative to competition.
		■ Price competition is limited because of AmBev's cost advantages and because of overall increasing beer volumes.
Bargaining power of suppliers	Low	■ The primary inputs (water, hops, barley, and packaging) are basically commodities.
Bargaining power of buyers	Low	■ Beer is mostly, 65% of volume, consumed in bars and restaurants. The owners of these outlets represent a large and highly fragmented group of beer buyers.
		■ The supermarket industry in Brazil is relatively fragmented, and supermarkets are less likely to offer alternatives, such as private labels.
Threat of new entrants	Low	■ Barriers to entry are relatively high because of the high costs of building a brewery, establishing a national distribution network, and establishing a nationally known brand name.

The UK beer market is also divided among four players, but the competitive structure is totally different in the United Kingdom than in Brazil. According to beer market data specialist Plato Logic, Heineken, MolsonCoors, AB InBev, and Carlsberg had market shares of 24%, 19%, 18%, and 14%, respectively, in 2011. Consequently, the British market has no dominant brewer. Given the high fixed costs of a brewery, declining UK beer consumption, and the highly consolidated customer base, which provides the clients with substantial purchasing power (particularly in the retail channels), price competition has been intense in recent years. Profitability is less than the beer industry's global average; operating margins are less than 10%. In this kind of environment, analysts would most likely forecast only very cautious revenue growth, if any. Exhibit 18 presents an analysis of the UK beer market using Porter's five forces framework.

Exhibit 18	Analysis of the UK Beer Market Using Porter's Five Forces	
Force	**Degree**	**Factors to Consider**
Threat of substitutes	Medium	■ Beer consumers do not easily shift to other beverages, but such alternatives as wine, spirits, and cider are available.
Rivalry	High	■ The market is relatively fragmented with no dominant market leader.
		■ Declining beer volumes make price wars more likely.[a]
		■ Brand loyalty is less developed because of the extensive range of alternative beers.
Bargaining power of supplier	Low	■ The primary inputs (water, hops, barley, and packaging) are basically commodities.
Bargaining power of buyers	High	■ The large supermarket chains that dominate the grocery sector have significant bargaining power.
		■ Large pub organisations in the on trade[b] also have strong bargaining power.
Threat of new entrants	Low	■ Barriers to entry are relatively high because of the high costs of building a brewery, establishing a national distribution network (particularly given the history of brewers owning bars), and establishing a nationally known brand.
		■ Because the United Kingdom consists of islands, companies with breweries in other countries face higher transportation costs than existing participants.

[a] In some declining markets, companies focus on increasing prices to offset declining volumes. But in the case of beer, the market is very fragmented and without price leadership, making price increases less viable.
[b] In the United Kingdom, drinks sold in a pub are known as "on trade;" drinks sold through a shop are known as "off trade."

There is a distinction between Porter's five forces and other factors that can affect profitability, such as government regulation and taxes:

> Industry structure, as manifested in the strength of the five competitive forces, determines the industry's long-run profit potential because it determines how the economic value created by the industry is divided... Government is not best understood as a sixth force because government involvement is neither inherently good nor bad for industry profitability. The best way to understand the influence of government on competition is to analyze how specific government policies affect the five competitive forces.[8]

---

8 Porter (2008), page 10.

EXAMPLE 9

Russian Beer Market

Carlsberg is the smallest of the global brewers, but it is the dominant beer company in Russia. In 2011, Carlsberg's subsidiary Baltika was the market leader in Russia with a 37% market share, followed by AB InBev with 16%, Heineken with 12%, Efes with 11%, and SAB Miller with 7%. The Russian market is considered a growth market because of its low per capita consumption of beer but high overall alcohol consumption.

In 2010, the Russian government, in its fight to curb alcohol consumption, tripled the excise duty on beer from RUB3 per liter to RUB9 and announced that excise duty will further increase by RUB1 per liter for each of the next two years.

In 2011, Baltika made significant efforts to strengthen the position of the more expensive brands in its portfolio. These efforts led to a 28% increase in selling costs. Similar to most consumer staple companies, Baltika experienced higher production costs. Poor grain harvests put price pressure on buyers of almost all feedstocks, and rising oil prices resulted in higher packaging costs. In 2011, competing companies were much more cautious with advertising and promotional spending than Baltika.

Two analysts research Baltika. In making their Baltika forecasts, both analysts use the separate published annual report from Baltika (see Exhibit 19). Based on the data on Baltika's selling costs, Exhibit 19, and the assumption of no cost inflation, the two analysts have arrived at distinctly different conclusions. Analyst A thinks Baltika has a weak competitive position in Russia and should exit. But Analyst B is enthusiastic about Baltika's prospects despite Baltika's 8% lower operating profit in 2011.

Exhibit 19   Baltika Key Financial and Operational Data

(RUB millions)	2011	2010	2009	Change 2011/2010	Change 2010/2009
Retail revenues	162,200	144,607	142,915	12%	1%
Excise duty	38,600	33,840	12,810	14	164
Excise duty of retail price	23.8%	23.4%	9.0%		
VAT (18%)	18,854	16,897	19,847	12	−15
Net sales consumers	104,746	93,870	110,259	12	−15
Profit for distributors[a]	14,951	14,563	16,539	3	−12
Profit margin–trade	14.3%	15.5%	15.0%		

Baltika Key Financial Performance Indicators (RUB millions, unless noted)

	2011	2010	2009	Change 2011/2010	Change 2010/2009
Volume (million hectoliters)	38.6	37.6	42.7	3%	−12%
Net revenue	89,795	79,307	93,720	13	−15
Cost of sales	42,116	34,162	42,466	23	−20
Gross profit	47,679	45,145	51,254	6	−12
Selling expenses	23,752	18,552	19,150	28	−3
Administrative expenses	2,439	2,429	2,529	0	−4
Adjustments	+182	−533	+43		

Exhibit 19   (Continued)

Baltika Key Financial Performance Indicators (RUB millions, unless noted)

	2011	2010	2009	Change 2011/2010	Change 2010/2009
Operating profit	21,670	23,631	29,618	−8	−20
Gross margin %	53.1%	56.9%	54.7%	−3.8	2.2
Selling expenses	26.5%	23.4%	20.4%		
Operating margin %	24.1%	29.8%	31.6%	−5.7	−1.8
ROCE %	38.7%	43.9%	50.8%	−5.2	−6.9
Capital Employed	55,995	53,829	58,303	4	−8

[RUB per hectoliter (hl)]	2011	2010	2009	Change 2011/2010	Change 2010/2009
Retail price/hl	4,202	3,846	3,347	9%	15%
Excise duty/hl	1,000	900	300	11	200
Margin for retailer sales	387	387	387	0	0
Net revenue	2,326	2,109	2,195	10	−4
Cost of sales	1,091	909	995	20	−9
Gross profit	1,235	1,201	1,200	3	0
Selling expenses	615	493	448	25	10
Administrative expenses	63	65	59	−2	9
Adjustments	5	−14	1		
Operating profit	561	628	694	−11%	−9%

Note: Capital employed includes debt and equity capital.
[a] This is the profit for all companies who buy beer direct from the manufacturers (brewers) for sale to any end user.
Source: Based on information from Baltika annual reports.

1   Both analysts believe there will be an increase in the excise duty (special tax on beer) in Russia; it should result in an approximate 10% increase in selling prices. Assume that half the cost of sales is fixed per hectoliter (hl) and half is variable based on volume, that selling expenses are a stable percentage of sales, and that administrative expenses are fixed. Also assume that Baltika will pass on the 10% excise duty increase to its customers without lowering its own net sales prices.

   A   Analyst A expects a price elasticity of 0.8, indicating that volume will fall by 8% given the 10% retail price increase. Calculate the impact on operating profit and operating profit margin in 2012 using Exhibit 20.

   B   Analyst B expects a price elasticity of 0.5, indicating that volume will fall by 5% given the 10% retail price increase. Calculate the impact on operating profit and operating profit margin in 2012 using Exhibit 20.

Exhibit 20   Baltika's Costs Structure for 2011–2012E (RUB millions, unless noted)

		Analyst A		Analyst B	
	2011	2012E	YoY%	2012E	YoY%
Volume (million hl)	38.6	35.5	−8.0%	36.7	−5.0%
Net revenue per hl	2.326				
Revenues	89,795				
Cost of sales	42,116				
Gross profit	47,679				
Gross margin	53.1%				
Selling expenses	23,752				
Administrative expenses	2,439	2,439		2,439	
Operating profit	21,488				
Operating profit %	23.9%				
Cost of sales (fixed)	21,058	21,058		21,058	
Cost of sales (variable)	21,058				
Cost of sales (variable)/hl	546	546		546	
Selling expenses as % of sales	26.5%	26.5%		26.5%	

Note: "YoY%" means year-over-year percent change

2   Gross margin improved in 2010 (56.9%) but fell in 2011 (53.1%). Cost of sales was relatively high in 2011 because of high barley costs, an important input for brewing beer. Assume that in 2011 half of the cost of sales is fixed and half is based on volume. Of the variable part of the cost of sales, assume that half of the amount is related to the barley price in 2011. Barley prices increased 33% in 2011. For 2012, assume that revenues will remain stable and that barley prices will return to their previous 2010 level. Calculate Baltika's estimated gross margin for 2012.

3   Baltika's selling expenses increased from 23.4% of sales in 2010 to 26.5% of sales in 2011. Which competitive forces most likely influenced Baltika's significant increase in selling expenses?

4   Retailers are the direct customers of brewers. They buy directly from the brewer and sell to the ultimate consumer. Analyst A expects that the increase in mass retailers in Russia will cause brewers' margins to decline. He expects Baltika's operating margin will decrease from 24.1% in 2011 to 15% in 2015 with stable sales (RUB89,795) and an unchanged amount of invested capital (RUB55,995). Analyst B also sees the increasing importance of the larger food retailers but expects that Baltika can offset potential pricing pressure by offering more attractive trade credit (e.g., allowing the retailers longer payment terms). He thinks operating margin can remain stable at 24.1% with no sales growth. Capital employed (RUB 55,995), however, will double because of the extra investments in inventory and receivables. Describe the analysts' expectations about the impact of large retailers on brewers in terms of Porter's five forces and ROCE. Which of the two scenarios would be better for Baltika?

Solution to 1:

In Exhibit 21, the results for both analysts' projections are shown. Analyst A predicts that operating profit will decrease by 16.7% to RUB17,889 in 2012, resulting in an operating margin decline from 23.9% in 2011 to 21.7% in 2012. Analyst A calculates a revenue decline of 8% to RUB82,611 based on volume dropping by 8% and a constant price per hl of RUB2,326. The decrease in volume reflects the price elasticity of 0.8 and the price increase of 10% as a result of the excise duty increase. Cost of goods sold fell only 4% because part of the costs are fixed. Cost of goods as the sum of fixed and variable costs is RUB21,058 + [35.51 (hl volume) × RUB545.5 (hl cost)] = RUB21,058 + RUB19,373 (ignoring rounding error) or RUB40,431. Analyst A predicts selling expenses will decline in line with sales by 8% and administrative costs will remain unchanged because of their fixed character in the short term.

Analyst B forecasts that operating profit will decline by 10.5% to RUB19.239. Analyst B's calculations follow the same pattern as those of Analyst A, but Analyst B predicts a smaller, 5%, decline in volume. Analyst A's estimates are more pessimistic than those of Analyst B, which corresponds to their opinions of the Russian beer market. Note that the net price/hl for the brewer is held constant although the price for the consumer increased 10% as a result of the excise duty increase. Because of Analyst B's more optimistic volume forecast, fixed costs are spread over a higher level of sales than is the case for Analyst A. Consequently, Analyst B will have a higher operating margin estimate than Analyst A. However, both analysts are predicting a decline in operating margin in 2012.

Exhibit 21   Analysts' Results for Baltika's Cost Structure and Projection (RUB millions, unless noted)

	2011	Analyst A		Analyst B	
		2012E	YoY%	2012E	YoY%
Volume	38.6	35.5	−8.0%	36.7	−5.0%
Net revenue per hl	2,326	2,326	0.0	2,326	0.0
Net revenues	89,795	82,611	−8.0	85,305	−5.0
Cost of sales	42,116	40,431	−4.0	41,063	−2.5
Gross profit	47,679	42,180	−11.5	44,242	−7.2
Gross margin	53.1%	51.1%		51.9%	
Selling expenses	23,752	21,852	−8.0	22,564	−5.0
Administrative expenses	2,439	2,439	0.0	2,439	0.0
Operating profit	21,488	17,889	−16.7%	19,239	−10.5%
Operating profit (%)	23.9%	21.7%		22.6%	
Costs of sales (fixed)	21,058	21,058		21,058	
Costs of sales (variable)	21,058	19,373		20,005	
Costs of sales (per hl)	546	546		546	
Selling expenses as % of sales	26.5%	26.5%		26.5%	

Solution to 2:

If barley prices return to their 2010 level, they will decline 25% in 2012. Because volumes are assumed to remain constant, other variable costs will not change. Gross profit in 2011 was 53.1% of sales which indicates the cost of sales was 46.9% (100% – 53.1%). Barley is 25% of the cost of sales (because barley represents half of variable costs and variable cost of sales represents half of total cost of sales). Cost of sales is predicted to decline by 25% × 25% = 6.25%. New costs of sales will be 46.9% – (6.25% × 46.9%) or 43.97%. Consequently, gross margin is predicted to be 100% – 43.97% = 56.03% in 2012. Compared with the gross margin of 53.10% in 2011, gross margin is predicted to increase by 293 bps.

Exhibit 22	Percent of Sales		
	2011	**2012E**	**YoY%**
Revenues	100.00	100.00	0.0
– Barley costs	11.73	8.79	–25.0
– Other costs	11.73	11.73	0.0
Variable cost of sales	23.45	20.52	–12.5
Fixed cost of sales	23.45	23.45	0.0
Total cost of sales	46.90	43.97	–6.2
Gross profit	53.10	56.03	5.5

Solution to 3:

Intra-industry rivalry and threat of substitutes most likely influenced Baltika's significant increase in selling costs. By spending more on advertising, Baltika wanted to enhance the brand loyalty of its products thus improving its competitive position versus its brewer rivals and makers of other alcoholic beverages. Furthermore, buyers' bargaining power probably also influenced Baltika's increased spending to the extent that advertising creates demand by the ultimate consumer. Strong demand at the ultimate consumer level for Baltika's specific brands could enhance the company's bargaining position with its direct customers, the distributors who serve as intermediaries.

Solution to 4:

The increase in mass retailers in Russia is expected to strengthen the bargaining power of buyers relative to brewers. According to Analyst A, this stronger bargaining power of buyers may result in lower prices. Analyst B also expects price pressure to come from larger buyers, as well as increased demand for more favorable credit terms. Analyst A expects operating profit on capital employed to fall from 38.6% (24.1% × RUB89,795/RUB55,995) to 24.1% (15% × RUB89,795/RUB55,995). Analyst B's assumptions indicate that the ROCE (operating profit divided by capital employed) in 2011 of 38.7% will fall by half to 19.4% as the operating result is earned on double the amount of invested capital. The scenario envisioned by Analyst A is better for Baltika.

In summary, Porter's five forces framework and similar analytical tools can help analysts assess the relative profit potential of a company by helping them understand the company's industry and its position within that industry. Understanding the industry and competitive contexts of a company helps analysts estimate whether, for example, sales growth is likely to be relatively high or low (relative to history, relative to the overall growth in the economy or a sector, and/or relative to competing companies) and whether profit margins are likely to be relatively high or low (relative to historical profit margins and relative to competing companies). The process of incorporating an industry and competitive analysis into expectations for future financial performance requires judgment. Suppose analysts observe that a given company is the market leader in a moderately competitive industry with limited buyer and supplier power and relatively high barriers to entry. In broad terms, analysts might project that the company's future revenue growth will be in line with that of the overall industry and that its profit margins and ROIC might be somewhat higher than those of other companies in the industry. But there is no mechanical link between the analysts' observations and projecting the company's future sales growth and profit margin. Instead, the link is more subjective and probabilistic.

INFLATION AND DEFLATION

4

Inflation and deflation (i.e., the overall increase and decrease in the prices of goods and services) can significantly affect the accuracy of forecasts for a company's future revenue, profit, and cash flow. The impact of inflation or deflation on revenue and expenses differs from company to company. Even within a single company, the impact of inflation or deflation is generally different for revenue and expenses categories.

Some companies are better able to pass on higher input costs by raising the prices at which they sell their output. The ability to pass on price increases can be the result of, for example, strong branding (Coca-Cola) or proprietary technology (Apple). Companies that are well positioned to pass on price increases are, in turn, more likely to have higher and more stable profits and cash flow, relative to competitors.

We first consider the impact of inflation on sales and then on costs.

4.1 Sales Projections with Inflation and Deflation

The following analysis addresses the projection of industry sales and company sales in the presence of inflation.

4.1.1 Industry Sales and Inflation or Deflation

Most increases in the cost of inputs, such as commodities or labor, will eventually result in higher prices for end products. Industry structure can be an important factor in determining the relationship between increases in input costs and increases in the price of end products. For example, in the United States, the beer market is an oligopoly, with one player, AB InBev, controlling almost half of the market. Moreover, the three-tier structure of the US beer market, in which the producers (the brewers) have to use a third party (the wholesalers) to get the their products (beer) to the consumers (café, restaurants, and retailers) results in a fragmented customer base because brewers are not allowed to deliver directly to the end consumer but rather must use wholesale distributors. These wholesalers often differ state by state. Large nationwide retailers, such as Wal-Mart, still have to negotiate with several different wholesalers instead of using their dominant national market position to negotiate directly with the brewers. The industry structure in the United States has likely contributed to increases in beer prices roughly in line with the US Consumer Price Index (CPI). In other words, beer prices have generally risen during years of inflation in input costs and decreased when costs have eased. If necessary, US brewers have been able to increase prices to compensate for costs inflation. In contrast, European beer companies distribute through a more concentrated customer base, namely dominant retail outlets, such as Carrefour, Tesco, and Ahold, which results in a weaker pricing position for the brewers. Also, the European market lacks an overall dominant brewer. As a result of the industry structure and the lack of underlying volume growth, changes in beer prices in Europe have been on average 100bps less than CPI.

Exhibit 23   US General Inflation and Inflation in Beer Prices

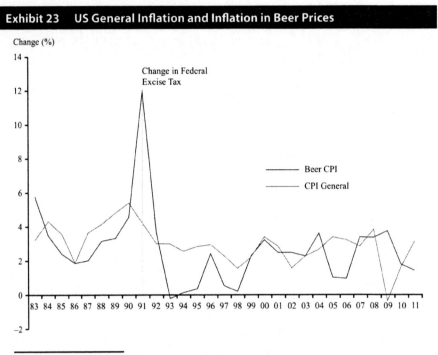

Source: Based on data from the US Bureau of Labor Statistics.

A company's efforts to pass on inflation through higher prices can have a negative impact on volume if the demand is price elastic, which would be the case if there are cheaper substitutes available. If selling prices could be increased 10% while maintaining unit sales volume to offset an increase of 10% in input costs, gross profit margin percentage would decrease but the absolute amount of gross profit would be maintained. In the short term, however, volumes will usually decline as result of a price increase. The decline would depend not only on the price elasticity of demand, but also on the reaction of competitors and the availability of substitutes. Lower input costs also make lower consumer prices possible. The first competitor to lower prices will usually benefit with an uptick in volume. Competitors react quickly, however, resulting in a short-term benefit. The price–volume trade-off can make accurate revenue projections difficult. In an inflationary environment, raising prices too late will result in a profit margin squeeze but acting too soon could result in volume losses. In a deflationary environment, lowering prices too soon will result in a lower gross margin but waiting too long will result in volume losses.

In the highly competitive consumer goods market, pricing is strongly influenced by movements in input prices, which can account for half of the cost of goods sold. In recent years, customers' price sensitivity has resulted in a strong inverse relationship between volume and pricing. For example, increased input prices for packaging, wheat, and milk forced Anglo-Dutch consumer staple company Unilever to increase prices for its products in 2008 and into 2009. Consequently, volumes deteriorated. But as raw material prices fell in late 2009 and early 2010, the company's prices were lowered and volumes recovered strongly. As the company started to increase prices in 2011, volume growth once again slowed. Exhibit 24 illustrates the inverse relationship between Unilever's volume and price.

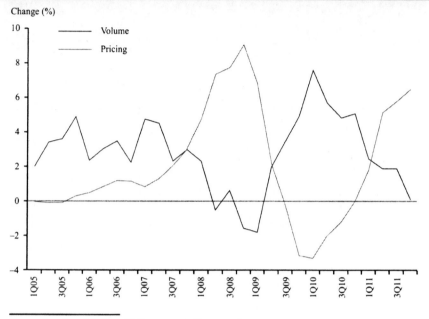

Exhibit 24   Unilever Overall Revenue Growth by Percentage Change in Volume and Price, 1Q2005–4Q2011

Source: Based on data from Unilever quarterly press releases.

4.1.2 *Company Sales and Inflation or Deflation*

Revenue projections in a model are based on the expected volume and price development. Forecasting revenue for a company faced with inflation in input costs requires some understanding of the price elasticity of the products, the different rates of cost inflation in the countries where the company is active, and if possible the likely inflation in costs relevant to a company's individual product categories. Also important is pricing strategy and market position.

The impact of higher prices on volume depends on the price elasticity of demand (i.e., how the quantity demanded varies with price). If demand is relatively price inelastic, revenues will benefit from inflation. If demand is relatively price elastic,[9] revenue can decline even if unit prices are raised. For example, a regression of volume on food inflation in UK food stores (shown in Exhibit 25) gives a regression slope coefficient of –0.398. (For every increase by 1 percentage point in year-on-year food prices, year-on-year sales decreased by about 0.4%.)

An analyst covering the UK food retailers can use this information when building forecast profit models. By assuming an expected level of food inflation, volume growth can be estimated and revenue calculated.

---

9 Technically, the condition is greater than unit price elasticity.

Exhibit 25   UK Relationship between Food Inflation and Volume,
              January 1989–February 2012

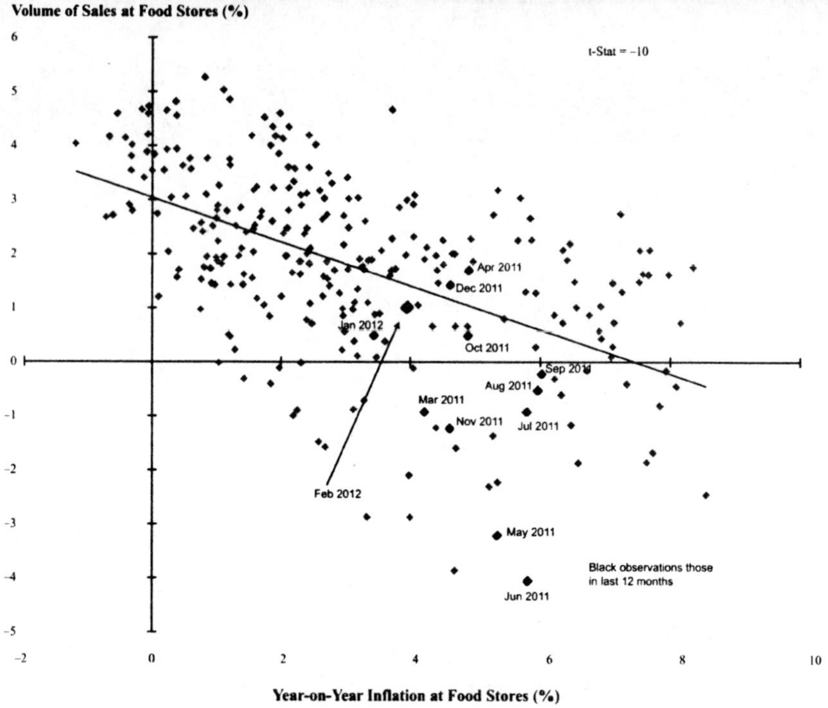

Source: Based on data from Datastream. Analysis is the authors'.

The expected pricing component for an international company should take into account the geographic mix of its operations to reflect different rates of the cost of inflation among countries. Of course, strategy and competitive factors, in addition to inflation in input costs, play roles in price setting.

AB InBev's volume growth and pricing has been more robust in emerging markets, for example, thanks to strong demand for its new beer products. The impact of inflation is also an important factor. In its Latin America South division, which mainly consists of Argentina, the brewer reported strong 24.7% organic revenue growth in 2011, of which only 2.1% was driven by volume and the remainder by price. As costs increased in line with revenues, operating margin remained more or less stable and organic operating profit growth was high at 27%. With only a limited negative currency impact, reported operating profit increased 24% in US dollars.

High inflation in a company's export market relative to a company's domestic inflation rate generally implies that the export country's currency will come under pressure and any pricing gain may be wiped out by the currency losses. The strong pricing increases AB InBev reported in its Latin America South division were clearly driven by input price inflation. The absence of a negative currency impact should be seen as a positive surprise but not as a typical outcome. A country's currency will usually come under pressure and depreciate if high rates of inflation persist for an extended period of time.

Most analysts adjust for recent high inflation in foreign countries by assuming a normalized growth rate for both revenues and costs after one or two years. This constant currency growth rate is based on an underlying growth rate assumption for the business. This approach can understate revenues in the short term. Other analysts reflect in their forecasts the high impact of inflation on revenues and expense and adjust growth rates for the expected currency (interest rate parity) impact. This approach is also imperfect given the difficulty in projecting currency rates.

Identifying a company's major input costs provides an indication of likely pricing. For a specialist retail bakery chain, for example, the impact of increased grain prices will be more significant than for a diversified standard supermarket chain. Consequently, it seems logical that the bakery is likely to increase its prices by a higher percentage than the grocer in response to increased grain prices.

Company strategy is also an important factor. Faced with rising input prices, a company may decide to preserve its margins by passing on the costs to its customers, or it may decide to accept some margin reduction to increase its market share. In other words, the company may try to gain market share by not fully increasing prices to reflect increased costs. Many analysts think Sysco Company, the largest food distributor to restaurants and institutions in North America, has sometimes not passed on food price increases in recessionary conditions from a concern of not financially weakening already recession-affected customers (restaurants, private clubs, schools, nursing homes, etc.). On the other hand, in 2011 and 2012, the large French cognac houses increased the prices for their products substantially in China to reduce strong demand. Because older cognac generates a higher price, it can be more profitable to build an inventory of vintage cognac instead of maximizing short-term volumes.

EXAMPLE 10

Passing on Input Cost Increases or Not

Global supermarket chain Carrefour is likely to be confronted with 5% inflation in its cost of goods sold (with stable volume). Four analysts have their own expectations about how the company will react. Exhibit 26 shows Carrefour's 2011 results and Exhibit 27 shows the four analysts' estimates of input prices, volume growth, and pricing.

Exhibit 26 Carrefour Data (€ millions, unless noted)	
	2011
Sales	81,271
Cost of goods sold	64,912
Gross profit	16,359
Gross margin	20.1%

Source: Based on data from Carrefour's annual report for 2011.

Exhibit 27 Four Analysts' Estimates of Carrefour's Reaction to Inflation				
	A	**B**	**C**	**D**
Price increase for revenues	0.0%	2.0%	4.0%	5.0%
Volume growth	8.0%	4.0%	1.0%	−7.0%

(continued)

Exhibit 27	(Continued)			
	A	**B**	**C**	**D**
Total revenue growth	8.0%	6.1%	5.0%	−2.4%
Input costs increase	5.0%	5.0%	5.0%	5.0%

1   What are each analyst's predictions for gross profit and gross margin?
2   Who has the highest gross margin in his model?
3   Who has the highest absolute gross profit in his model?

Solution to 1:

The results for each analyst are shown in Exhibit 28. For Analyst B revenues increase 6.1% [= (1.02 × 1.04) − 1] and cost of goods sold 9.2% [= (1.04 × 1.05) − 1]. The difference between the calculated revenue and cost of goods sold is the new gross profit.

Exhibit 28	Results for Analysts' Predictions (€ millions, unless noted)								
	2011	**Analyst A**	**YoY%**	**Analyst B**	**YoY%**	**Analyst C**	**YoY%**	**Analyst D**	**YoY%**
Carrefour									
Sales	81,271	87,773	8.0%	86,212	6.1%	85,367	5.0%	79,361	−2.4%
Cost of goods sold	64,912	73,610	13.4%	70,884	9.2%	68,839	6.1%	63,387	−2.4%
Gross profit	16,359	14,162	−13.4%	15,328	−6.3%	16,528	1.0%	15,975	−2.4%
Gross margin	20.1%	16.1%		17.8%		19.4%		20.1%	

Note: "YoY%" means year-over-year percent change

Solution to 2:

The highest gross margin is projected by Analyst D, who increased prices at 5% to keep gross margin stable.

Solution to 3:

The highest gross profit is projected by Analyst C, who expects a margin decline that is more than offset by volume growth.

4.2 Cost Projections with Inflation and Deflation

The following analysis addresses the forecasting of industry and company costs in the presence of inflation and deflation.

4.2.1 *Industry Costs and Inflation or Deflation*

Familiarity with the specific purchasing characteristics of an industry can also be useful in forecasting costs. For example, long-term price-fixed forward contracts and hedges can delay the impact of price increases. Thus, an analyst forecasting costs for an industry in which companies customarily use such purchasing practices would incorporate any expected input price fluctuations more slowly than for an industry in which the participants do not use long-term contracts or hedges.

Monitoring the underlying drivers of input prices can also be useful in forecasting costs. For example, weather conditions can have a dramatic impact on the price of agricultural products and consequently on the cost base of industries that rely on them. An analyst observing a particular weather pattern may thus be able to incorporate this information into forecasts of costs.

How inflation or deflation affects an industry's cost structure depends on its competitive environment. For example, if the participants within the industry have access to alternative inputs or are vertically integrated, the impact of volatility in input costs can be mitigated. DE Masterblenders is a coffee company that has been facing high and volatile coffee prices. However, its coffee is a blend of different kinds of beans. By shifting the mix slightly, DE can keep both taste and costs constant by reducing the amount of the more expensive types of coffee beans in the blend. But if all supplier countries significantly increase the price of coffee simultaneously, DE cannot play the blending game anymore and will be confronted with overall higher input costs. To sustain its profitability, DE will have to increase its prices to its clients. But if competition from other companies, such as Nestlé (Nespresso, Dolce Gusto, Nescafe) or Mondelez International (Jacobs coffee, Carte Noir), makes it difficult to increase prices, DE will have to look for alternatives if it wants to keep its profit margins stable. An easy solution for the short term could be reducing advertising and promotional spending. This approach usually has not an immediate negative effect on revenues and improves profit. For the longer term, however, it could be harmful because the company's brand position could be weakened.

For example, the 2010 Russian heat wave destroyed large parts of that country's grain harvest, causing prices for malting barley, one input for beer, to shoot up. Carlsberg, as the largest Russian brewer, was particularly hard hit because it had to pay more for its Russian barley and also needed to import grain into the country, incurring additional transportation costs. By increasing imports from Western Europe, Carlsberg also pushed up barley prices in this region, affecting the cost base of other Western European brewers.

4.2.2 *Company Costs and Inflation or Deflation*

In forecasting a company's costs, it is often helpful to segment the cost structure by category and geography. For each item of cost, an assessment should be made about the impact of potential inflation and deflation on input prices. This assessment should take into account the company's ability to substitute cheaper alternatives for expensive inputs or to increase efficiency to offset the impact of increases in input prices. For example, although a jump in raw material prices in 2011 caused Unilever's and Nestlé's gross margins to fall sharply (by 110–170 bps), increases in operational efficiencies, such as reducing advertising spending, enabled both companies to achieve slightly higher overall operating profit margins that year. Example 11 shows the use of common size (percent-of-sales) analysis of inflation in input costs.

EXAMPLE 11

Inflation in Input Costs

Two consumer staple companies—Swiss chocolate specialist Lindt and global food producer Nestlé—have costs that are constantly affected by inflation and deflation. Exhibit 29 presents a common size analysis.

Exhibit 29	Common Size Analysis for Nestlé and Lindt	
	Nestlé	**Lindt**
Net sales	100%	100%
COGS	50%	36%
Gross margin	50%	64%
SG&A	31%	47%
Depreciation	3%	4%
EBIT	16%	13%
Raw materials	22%	22%
Packaging	12%	10%
Other COGS	16%	4%
Total COGS	50%	36%

Source: Based on information in companies' annual reports.

1 Assume inflation of 10% for all costs (except depreciation) and that the companies are not able to pass on this increase through higher prices (total revenues will remain constant).

   A Calculate the gross profit margin for each company. Which company will experience the greatest reduction in gross profit margin?

   B Calculate the operating profit margin for each company. Which company will experience the greatest reduction in operating profit (EBIT) margin?

2 Assume inflation of 10% only for the raw material costs (reflected in COGS) and that the companies are not able to pass on this increase through higher prices. Which company will be most affected negatively in terms of gross profit margin and operating profit margin?

Solutions:

Exhibit 30	Effect of Cost Inflation			
	All Costs (Except Depreciation) + 10%		**Raw Materials + 10%**	
	Nestlé	**Lindt**	**Nestlé**	**Lindt**
Net sales	100%	100%	100%	100%
COGS	55%	40%	52%	38%
Gross margin	45%	60%	48%	62%
SG&A	34%	52%	31%	47%
Depreciation	3%	4%	3%	4%
EBIT	8%	5%	14%	11%

Solution to 1A:

The company with the highest COGS as a percent of net sales—equivalently, the lowest gross margin—will experience the greatest negative impact. Nestlé has a lower gross margin than Lindt: 50% compared with 64%, as shown in Exhibit 29. After the 10% increase in COGS to $1.10 \times 50\% = 55\%$, Nestlé's gross margin will fall to 45% as shown in Exhibit 30. Nestlé's resulting gross margin of 45% represents a proportional decline of 10% from the initial value of 50%. In contrast, the proportional decline in Lindt's gross margin is approximately $4\%/64\% = 6\%$.

Solution to 1B:

Lindt has higher overall costs than Nestlé, primarily as a consequence of its high SG&A expenses. Lindt's operating profit margin will drop to approximately 5% as shown in Exhibit 30, representing a proportional decline of about 62% compared with a proportional decline of about $8\%/16\% = 50\%$ for Nestlé.

Solution to 2:

The company with the highest raw material expense component will experience the most negative effect. In this case, raw materials represent 22% of net sales for both Nestlé and Lindt. Gross margin and operating margin will decline by 220 bps for both. This impact is more severe on gross margin on a relative basis for Nestlé ($2.2\%/50\% = 4.4\%$ decline) than for Lindt ($2.2\%/64\% = 3.4\%$ decline). But the relative effect on operating margin will be more severe for Lindt ($2.2\%/13\% = 16.9\%$ decline) than for Nestlé ($2.2\%/16\% = 13.8\%$).

TECHNOLOGICAL DEVELOPMENTS

5

Technological developments have the potential to change the economics of individual businesses and entire industries. Quantifying the potential impact of such developments on an individual company's earnings involves making certain assumptions about future demand. Such assumptions should be explored through scenario and/or sensitivity analysis so that a range of potential earnings outcomes may be considered. When a technological development results in a new product that threatens to cannibalize demand for an existing product, a unit forecast for the new product combined with an expected cannibalization factor may be used to estimate the impact on future demand for the existing product. When developing an estimate of the cannibalization factor, it may be useful to segment the market if the threat of substitution differs across segments.

Technological developments can affect demand for a product, the quantity supplied of a product, or both. When changes in technology lead to lower manufacturing costs, the supply curve will shift to the right as suppliers produce more of the product at the same price. Conversely, if technology results in the development of attractive substitute products, the demand curve will shift to the left. Consider the following example.

EXAMPLE 12

Quantifying the Tablet Market's Potential to Cannibalize Demand for Personal Computers

The worldwide tablet market experienced a major technological development with the introduction of the Apple iPad in April 2010, which has important implications for the personal computer (PC) industry. A tablet can be thought of as a portable personal computer with a touchscreen interface instead of a keyboard, which is commonly used as the input device in traditional PCs. Another distinguishing feature of tablets is that, unlike the majority of PCs that run on the Microsoft Windows platform, most tablets run on a non-Microsoft operating system, including Apple's iOS and Google's Android. Given the tablet's ability to perform many of the most common tasks of a PC, including e-mailing, browsing the web, sharing photos, playing music, watching movies, playing games, keeping a calendar, managing contacts, and so on, an analyst might reasonably wonder to what extent sales of tablets might cannibalize demand for PCs and the potential impact that might have on Microsoft's sales and earnings. Exhibit 31 presents one approach to answering these questions.

Exhibit 31   Unit and Revenue Projections (thousands, unless noted)

PRE-CANNIBALIZATION PC PROJECTIONS	FY2011	FY2012E	FY2013E	FY2014E	3-Year CAGR
Consumer PC shipments	170,022	174,430	184,120	193,811	4.5%
Non-consumer PC shipments	180,881	185,570	195,880	206,189	4.5%
Total global PC shipments	350,903	360,000	380,000	400,000	4.5%
% of which is consumer	48%	48%	48%	48%	
% of which is non-consumer	52%	52%	52%	52%	
Consumer tablet shipments	36,785	82,800	111,250	148,750	59.3%
Non-consumer tablet shipments	1,686	7,200	13,750	26,250	149.7%
Global tablet shipments	38,471	90,000	125,000	175,000	65.7%
% of which is consumer	96%	92%	89%	85%	
% of which is non-consumer	4%	8%	11%	15%	
Cannibalization factor, consumer	30%	30%	30%	30%	
Cannibalization factor, non-consumer	10%	10%	10%	10%	
# of consumer PCs cannibalized by tablets	11,036	24,840	33,375	44,625	
# of non-consumer PCs cannibalized by tablets	169	720	1,375	2,625	
Total PCs cannibalized by tablets	11,204	25,560	34,750	47,250	
% of total PCs cannibalized by tablets	3.2%	7.1%	9.1%	11.8%	
POST-CANNIBALIZATION PC PROJECTIONS					
Consumer PC shipments	158,986	149,590	150,745	149,186	−2.1%
Non-consumer PC shipments	180,712	184,850	194,505	203,564	4.0%
Total global PC shipments	339,698	334,440	345,250	352,750	1.3%

Microsoft implied average selling price
(ASP)

Exhibit 31 (Continued)				
POST-CANNIBALIZATION PC PROJECTIONS				
Consumer	$85	$85	$85	$85
Non-consumer	155	155	155	155
Revenue impact for Microsoft ($ millions)				
Consumer	938	2,111	2,837	3,793
Non-consumer	26	112	213	407
Total revenue impact	964	2,223	3,050	4,200

Notes: CAGR is compound annual growth rate. Non-consumer includes enterprise, education, and government purchasers.
Source: Based on data from Gartner, JPMorgan, Microsoft, and authors' analysis.

To begin, worldwide market shipments of PCs in FY2011 were 350.9 million units and worldwide shipments of tablets were 38.5 million units.[10] Shipments of tablets to consumers represented 96% of total shipments during fiscal year 2011. Next, we estimate the magnitude of the potential substitution effect, or cannibalization factor, that tablets will have on the PC market. Because the cannibalization factor depends on many different variables, including user preferences, end-use application, and whether the purchaser already owns a PC, just to name a few, we use a range of potential estimates. Moreover, we also divide the worldwide PC market into consumer and non-consumer (enterprise, education, and government purchasers) because the degree of substitution is likely to differ between the two. For purposes of illustration, we assume a cannibalization factor of 30% for the consumer market and 10% for the non-consumer market in our base case scenario.

In addition, the base case scenario assumes that non-consumer adoption of tablets increases to 15% of the market from 4% in 2011. Moreover, although the composition of the global PC market is roughly evenly divided between consumers and non-consumers (48% and 52% in fiscal 2011, respectively), the non-consumer segment is significantly more profitable for Microsoft because approximately 80% of the company's Office products are sold to enterprise, education, and government institutions. The average selling price (ASP) estimates are derived by dividing Microsoft's estimated average revenue for the prior three years by customer type by Microsoft's estimated PC shipments for each type of customer. By multiplying the projected number of PCs cannibalized by tablets by the estimated ASP, we are able to derive an estimate of the revenue impact for Microsoft. For example, in FY2012 it is projected that 24.8 million consumer PCs will be cannibalized by sales of tablets. With an average consumer ASP of $85, this cannibalization implies a revenue loss for Microsoft of $2.1 billion (24.8 million units × $85 ASP per unit = $2.1 billion).

Once the revenue impact has been projected, the next step is to estimate the impact of lower PC unit volumes on operating costs and margins. We begin by analyzing the cost structure of Microsoft, and more specifically, the breakdown between fixed and variable costs. Most software companies have a cost structure with a relatively high proportion of fixed costs and a low proportion of variable costs because costs related to product development and marketing (mostly fixed)

---

10 Information is from Gartner Personal Computer Quarterly Statistics Worldwide Database.

are sunk and unrecoverable whereas the cost of producing an additional copy of the software (mostly variable) is relatively low. Because very few, if any, companies provide an explicit breakdown of fixed versus variable costs, an estimate almost always needs to be made. One method is to use the formula

$$\%\Delta \text{ (Cost of revenue + Operating expense)}/\%\Delta \text{ revenue}$$

where $\%\Delta$ is "percent change in," as a proxy for variable cost percentage. Another approach is to assign an estimate of the percentage of fixed and variable costs to the various components of operating expenses. Both approaches are illustrated in Exhibits 32 and 33.

Exhibit 32   Estimation of Variable Costs for Microsoft, Method 1 ($ millions)

Selected Operating Segments	FY2009	FY2010	FY2011	FY2011/FY2009 Percent Change
Windows and Windows Live	15,563	18,792	18,778	
Microsoft business division	19,211	19,345	21,986	
Total segment revenue	34,774	38,137	40,764	17%
Windows and Windows Live	6,191	6,539	6,810	
Microsoft business division	8,058	7,703	8,159	
Total operating expense	14,249	14,242	14,969	5%

%Variable cost ≈ %Δ (Cost of revenue + Operating expense)/%Δ revenue ≈ 5%/17% ≈ **29%**
%Fixed cost ≈ 1 − %Variable cost ≈ 1 − 29% ≈ **71%**

Exhibit 33   Estimation of Variable Costs for Microsoft, Method 2 ($ millions)

Operating Expenses	FY2009	FY2010	FY2011	FY2009–FY2011 Average	% of Total Op Expense	Estimated % of Cost Fixed	Fixed Cost Contribution
Cost of revenue (excl. depreciation)	10,455	10,595	13,577	11,542	29%	20%	6%
Depreciation expense	1,700	1,800	2,000	1,833	5%	100%	5%
Total cost of revenue	12,155	12,395	15,577	13,376	34%		11%
Research and development	9,010	8,714	9,043	8,922	22%	100%	22%
Sales and marketing	12,879	13,214	13,940	13,344	34%	80%	27%
General and admin.	4,030	4,063	4,222	4,105	10%	100%	10%
Total operating expenses	38,074	38,386	42,782	39,747	66%		60%

Exhibit 33	(Continued)						

Operating Expenses	FY2009	FY2010	FY2011	FY2009–FY2011 Average	% of Total Op Expense	Estimated % of Cost Fixed	Fixed Cost Contribution
Estimated percentage of Microsoft's total cost structure that is fixed:							70%

Note: Fiscal year ends in June.
Source of data: Microsoft 2011 Form 10-K and authors' analysis.

As can be seen, Microsoft's cost structure appears to consist of approximately 70% fixed costs and 30% variable costs. Note, however, that a growing company like Microsoft will typically re-invest in property, plant, and equipment to support future growth, so even those expenses that appear to be "fixed" will increase over time. To adjust for this expected growth in fixed costs, this example includes an assumption that the change in fixed costs will be half the rate of the change in sales. Variable costs are projected to change at the same rate as sales. As shown in Exhibit 34, after incorporating these assumptions into the projections, an assumed 7.0% compound annual growth rate (CAGR) in revenue through FY2014 would translate into a 10.6% CAGR in operating income [$(36,757/27,161)^{1/3} - 1 = 0.106$, or 10.6%]. In addition, these assumptions would result in an operating margin expansion of 410 bps over the same period (42.9% – 38.8% = 4.1%, or 410 bps) because of the significant amount of operating leverage that exists as a result of a relatively large fixed cost base. With the further assumptions of no change in other income, a constant effective tax rate, and no change in shares outstanding, the pre-cannibalization model Exhibit 34 results in projected revenue of $85.7 billion, operating income of $36.8 billion, an operating margin of 42.9%, and earnings per share (EPS) that increases at a CAGR of 10.3% to $3.62 in FY2014.

Exhibit 34	Microsoft Pre-Cannibalization EPS Projections ($ millions)				
	FY2011	FY2012E	FY2013E	FY2014E	3-Year CAGR
Revenue	69,943	74,839	80,078	85,683	7.0%
Year-over-year percent change		7.0%	7.0%	7.0%	
Operating Expenses					
Fixed (70%)	29,947	30,996	32,080	33,203	3.5%
Variable (30%)	12,835	13,733	14,694	15,723	7.0%
Total operating expenses	42,782	44,729	46,775	48,926	4.6%
Operating income	27,161	30,110	33,303	36,757	10.6%
Operating margin	38.83%	40.23%	41.59%	42.90%	
Other income (Expense)	910	910	910	910	
Pretax Income	28,071	31,020	34,213	37,6678	

(continued)

Exhibit 34   (Continued)

	FY2011	FY2012E	FY2013E	FY2014E	3-Year CAGR
Provision for income taxes	4,921	5,438	5,998	6,603	
Effective tax rate	17.53%	17.53%	17.53%	17.53%	
Net income	23,150	25,582	28,215	31,064	
Weighted average shares outstanding, diluted	8,593	8,593	8,593	8,593	
Estimated EPS pre-cannibalization	$2.69	$2.98	$3.28	$3.62	10.3%

In the post-cannibalization scenario, as shown in Exhibit 35, revenue is reduced each year to reflect the expected impact from cannibalization. The expected impact of cannibalization results in a decrease in the CAGR of revenue over the period to 5.2%, down from 7.0% in the pre-cannibalization scenario. Given the reduction in revenue growth, and holding the cost structure constant at 70/30 fixed versus variable costs, operating income growth slows to a CAGR of 8.0%, down from 10.6% in the pre-cannibalization scenario. Operating margin at the end of the period is reduced by approximately 100 bps from 42.9% to 41.9% because the company is unable to leverage its fixed cost base to the same degree as a result of slower revenue growth. Overall, in the post-cannibalization scenario, Microsoft is expected to generate revenue of $81.5 billion, operating income of $34.2 billion, an operating margin of 41.9%, and EPS that increase at a CAGR of 7.8% to $3.37 in FY2014. Thus, the cannibalization of PCs as a result of projected growth in the tablet market is expected to reduce the company's annual revenues in FY2014 by $4.2 billion, operating income by $2.6 billion, operating margins by 96 bps, and EPS by $0.25.

Exhibit 35   Microsoft Post-Cannibalization EPS Projections, Base Case Scenario ($ millions, unless noted)

	FY2011	FY2012E	FY2013E	FY2014E	3-Year CAGR
Revenue	69,943	72,616	77,028	81,483	5.2%
Year-over-year percent change		3.8%	6.1%	5.8%	
Operating Expenses					
Fixed (70%)	29,947	30,520	31,447	32,356	2.6%
Variable (30%)	12,835	13,325	14,135	14,952	5.2%
Total operating expenses	42,782	43,845	45,581	47,308	3.4%
Operating income	27,161	28,771	31,446	34,175	8.0%
Operating margin	38.83%	39.62%	40.82%	41.94%	
Other income (Expense)	910	910	910	910	
Pretax income	28,071	29,681	32,356	35,085	

	FY2011	FY2012E	FY2013E	FY2014E	3-Year CAGR
Exhibit 35 (Continued)					
Provision for income taxes	4,921	5,203	5,672	6,151	
Effective tax rate	17.53%	17.53%	17.53%	17.53%	
Net income	23,150	24,478	26,684	28,934	
Weighted average shares outstanding, diluted	8,593	8,593	8,593	8,593	
Estimated EPS post-cannibalization	$2.69	$2.85	$3.11	$3.37	7.8%
Estimated impact on operating margin		−61 bps	−76 bps	−96 bps	
Estimated impact on EPS		($0.13)	($0.18)	($0.25)	−2.6%

Example 13 addresses questions related to the text discussion on cannibalization.

EXAMPLE 13

Estimating the Impact of Cannibalization

Answer the following questions using Exhibits 31 through 35 on Microsoft:

1 Estimate post-cannibalization global PC shipments in FY2012 assuming a cannibalization factor for consumers of 40% and 15% for non-consumers.

2 Using the results derived in Question 1, estimate the post-cannibalization revenue in FY2012 for Microsoft.

3 Using the estimate for post-cannibalization revenue derived in Question 2 and the cost structure provided, estimate post-cannibalization operating income and operating margin in FY2012 for Microsoft. Assume that fixed costs change at half the rate of the change in sales.

4 Using the estimate for operating income derived in Question 3 and the data in the exhibits, calculate the expected post-cannibalization EPS in FY2012 for Microsoft. Assume that other income (expense), the effective tax rate, and the diluted weighted average shares outstanding provided for FY2011 remain constant in FY2012.

Solution to 1:

The number of PCs cannibalized by tablets is equal to the product of the expected number of global tablet shipments, the percentage representation of each category, and the cannibalization factor for the category. Exhibit 31 shows that tablet shipments in FY2012 are projected to be 90 million units. (90 million tablets × 92% consumer representation × 40% consumer cannibalization factor

= 33.12 million consumer PCs cannibalized by tablets) + (90 million tablets × 8% non-consumer representation × 15% cannibalization = 1.08 million non-consumer PCs cannibalized by tablets) = 34.2 million total PCs cannibalized by tablets. Post-cannibalization shipments is equal to pre-cannibalization shipments minus expected cannibalization, or 360 million − 34.2 million = 325.8 million.

Solution to 2:

The estimated impact on revenue is equal to the product of the number of PCs cannibalized and the average selling price. Using the results obtained in Question 1 and the ASP data contained in Exhibit 31, the expected revenue impact can be calculated as (33.12 million consumer PCs cannibalized by tablets × $85 ASP = $2.815 billion) + (1.08 million non-consumer PCs cannibalized by tablets × $155 ASP = $167.4 million) = $2.983 billion total impact on revenue for Microsoft. Post-cannibalization revenue is equal to pre-cannibalization revenue minus the estimated impact on revenue from cannibalization, or $74.839 billion − $2.983 billion = $71.856 billion.

Solution to 3:

Exhibit 36   Solution to Problem 3 ($ millions)

	FY2011	FY2012E	Notes:
Revenue	69,943	71,856	Derived from Question 2
YoY %		2.74%	Rate of change in sales used to estimate operating expenses
Operating Expenses			
Fixed (70%)	29,947	30,357	Fixed costs change at half the rate of the change in sales, or 29,947 × (1 + 2.74%/2)
Variable (30%)	12,835	13,186	Variable costs change at the same rate as the change in sales, or 12,835 × (1 + 2.74%)
Total operating expenses	42,782	43,543	Although not shown, operating expenses include cost of goods sold.
Operating income	27,161	28,313	Revenue minus total operating expense, or 71,856 − 43,543 = 28,313
Operating margin	38.8%	39.4%	Operating income divided by revenue, or 28,313/71,856 = 39.4%

Post-cannibalization operating income and operating margin in FY2012 for Microsoft is $28,313 million and 39.4%, respectively.

Solution to 4:

Exhibit 37	Solution to Problem 4 ($ millions, unless noted)		
	FY2011	**FY2012E**	**Notes:**
Revenue	69,943	71,856	
YoY %		2.74%	
Operating Expenses			
Fixed (70%)	29,947	30,357	
Variable (30%)	12,835	13,186	
Total operating expenses	42,782	43,543	
Operating income	27,161	28,313	
Operating margin	38.8%	39.4%	
Other income (expense)	910	910	
Pretax income	28,071	29,224	Operating income + Other income (expense), or 28,314 + 910 = 29,224
Provision for income taxes	4,921	5,123	Pretax Income × Effective tax rate, or 29,224 × 17.53% = 5,123
Effective tax rate	17.53%	17.53%	
Net income	23,150	24,101	Pretax Income – Provision for income taxes, or 29,224 – 5,123 = 24,101
Weighted average shares outstanding, diluted	8,593	8,593	
EPS post-cannibalization	**$2.69**	**$2.80**	Net income/Wtd Avg Shs Out, or 24,101/8,593 = $2.80

Whenever one is estimating something that depends on many different variables that are difficult to measure, we recommend altering some of the assumptions to generate a range of estimates based on various scenarios. Thus, having developed a forecast under a base case cannibalization scenario, we are able to analyze the sensitivity of the results by altering the cannibalization assumptions. The base case scenario corresponds to the assumptions in the boxed center of the table in Exhibit 38. Exhibit 39 summarizes the results of bull and bear case scenarios, showing the estimated FY2014 EPS under alternative estimated cannibalization factors.

Exhibit 38   Estimated 2014 EPS Sensitivity to Changes in Cannibalization Rates

		Non-consumer Cannibalization				
		0.0%	5.0%	10.0%	15.0%	20.0%
	15%	$0.11	$0.12	$0.14	$0.15	$0.16
	20%	$0.15	$0.16	$0.17	$0.19	$0.20
	25%	$0.19	$0.20	$0.21	$0.22	$0.23
Consumer Cannibalization	30%	$0.22	$0.24	$0.25	$0.26	$0.27
	35%	$0.26	$0.27	$0.28	$0.30	$0.31
	40%	$0.30	$0.31	$0.32	$0.33	$0.35
	45%	$0.34	$0.35	$0.36	$0.37	$0.38

Exhibit 39   Post-Cannibalization EPS Projections for Bull and Bear Scenarios ($ millions, unless noted)

Bull Case Scenario (Cannibalization Factor: 15% Consumer/5% Non-Consumer)

	FY2011	FY2012E	FY2013E	FY2014E	3-Year CAGR
Revenue	69,943	73,728	78,553	83,583	6.1%
YoY %		5.4%	6.5%	6.4%	
Operating Expenses					
Fixed (70%)	29,947	30,758	31,764	32,781	3.1%
Variable (30%)	12,835	13,529	14,414	15,338	6.1%
Total operating expenses	42,782	44,287	46,179	48,119	4.0%
Operating income	27,161	29,441	32,374	35,464	9.3%
Operating margin	38.83%	39.93%	41.21%	42.43%	
Other income (expense)	910	910	910	910	
Pretax income	28,071	30,351	33,284	36,374	
Provision for income taxes	4,921	5,321	5,835	6,377	
Effective tax rate	17.53%	17.53%	17.53%	17.53%	
Net income	23,150	25,030	27,449	29,998	
Weighted average shares outstanding, diluted	8,593	8,593	8,593	8,593	
Estimated EPS post-cannibalization	**$2.69**	**$2.91**	**$3.19**	**$3.49**	**9.0%**
Estimated impact on operating margin		−30 bps	−38 bps	−47 bps	
Estimated impact on EPS		($0.06)	($0.09)	($0.12)	−1.3%

Exhibit 39   (Continued)

Bear Case Scenario (Cannibalization Factor: 40% Consumer/20% Non-Consumer)

	FY2011	FY2012E	FY2013E	FY2014E	3-Year CAGR
Revenue	69,943	71,801	75,869	79,812	4.5%
YoY %		2.7%	5.7%	5.2%	
Operating Expenses					
Fixed (70%)	29,947	30,345	31,205	32,016	2.3%
Variable (30%)	12,835	13,175	13,922	14,646	4.5%
Total operating expenses	42,782	43,521	45,127	46,661	2.9%
Operating income	27,161	28,280	30,742	33,151	6.9%
Operating margin	38.83%	39.39%	40.52%	41.54%	
Other income (Expense)	910	910	910	910	
Pretax income	28,071	29,190	31,652	34,061	
Provision for income taxes	4,921	5,117	5,549	5,971	
Effective tax rate	17.53%	17.53%	17.53%	17.53%	
Net income	23,150	24,073	26,103	28,090	
Weighted average shares outstanding, diluted	8,593	8,593	8,593	8,593	
Estimated EPS post-cannibalization	**$2.69**	**$2.80**	**$3.04**	**$3.27**	**6.7%**
Estimated impact on operating margin		**−85 bps**	**−107 bps**	**−136 bps**	
Estimated impact on EPS		**($0.18)**	**($0.25)**	**($0.35)**	**−3.6%**

LONG-TERM FORECASTING

6

The choice of the forecast time horizon may be influenced by certain factors, including the investment strategy for which the stock is being considered, cyclicality of the industry, company specific factors, and the analyst's employer's preferences. Most professionally managed equity investment strategies describe the investment timeframe, or average holding period for a stock, in the stated investment objectives of the strategy; the timeframe should ideally correspond with average annual turnover of the portfolio. For example, a stated investment time horizon of 3–5 years would imply average annual portfolio turnover between 20–33%.[11] Cyclicality of the industry may

---

11 The average holding period is calculated as one/portfolio turnover.

also influence the analyst's choice of timeframe, because the forecast period should be long enough to allow the business to reach an expected mid-cycle level of sales and profitability. Similar to cyclicality, various company specific factors, including recent acquisition or restructuring activity, may influence the selection of the forecast period to allow enough time for the realization of the expected benefits from such activity to be reflected in the financial statements. In other cases, there may be no individual analyst choice in the sense that the analyst's employer has specified a particular discounted cash flow (DCF) model with more or less fixed parameters. Much of the discussion so far has focused on various methods of forecasting a company's income statement, balance sheet, and cash flow for an explicit short-term forecast period. Although the underlying principles remain the same if one extends the time horizon, there are certain considerations and choices available to the analyst when developing longer-term projections.

Longer-term projections often provide a better representation of the normalized earnings potential of a company than a short-term forecast, especially when certain temporary factors are present. **Normalized earnings** are the expected level of mid-cycle earnings for a company in the absence of any unusual or temporary factors that impact profitability (either positively or negatively). For example, at any given point in time there are a number of temporary factors that may impact a company's profitability, including the stage in the business cycle, recent merger and acquisition activity, restructuring activity, and so on. Similarly, normalized free cash flow can be defined as the expected level of mid-cycle cash flow from operations adjusted for unusual items just described less recurring capital expenditures. By extending the forecast period, an analyst is able to adjust for these unusual or temporary factors and derive an estimate of earnings that the company is likely to earn in a normal year. We will consider various alternatives for two aspects of long-term forecasting: revenue forecasts and terminal value.

As with most income statement projections, a long-term forecast begins with a revenue projection with most of the remaining income statement items subsequently derived from the level or change in revenue. Revenue projection methods were covered earlier.

Case Study: Estimating Normalized Revenue

Exhibit 40 contains 10 years of historical revenue data and four years of estimated normalized data for 3M, a globally diversified manufacturer of technology, health care, and industrial products. The accompanying bar chart in Exhibit 41 graphically depicts the data and includes a trendline based on a linear regression of the data. The numerical values for each point along the trend line can be found by using the TREND formula in Microsoft Excel. The TREND formula uses observations on the dependent variable (in this case revenue) and observations on the explanatory (time) variable to perform a linear regression by using least squares criterion to find the best fit. After computing the best fit regression model, the TREND formula returns predicted values associated with new points in time.[12]

---

12 See http://support.microsoft.com/kb/828801 for more information on how to use the TREND formula.

Exhibit 40	Historical and Estimated Revenue Data for 3M, 2002–2015E ($ millions)						
	2002	**2003**	**2004**	**2005**	**2006**	**2007**	**2008**
Revenue	16,332	18,232	20,011	21,167	22,923	24,462	25,269
Normalized revenue	17,108	18,368	19,630	20,890	22,149	23,408	24,671
Percent above/ below trend	−4.5%	−0.7%	1.9%	1.3%	3.5%	4.5%	2.4%
	2009	**2010**	**2011**	**2012E**	**2013E**	**2014E**	**2015E**
Revenue	23,123	26,662	29,611				
Normalized revenue	25,930	27,190	28,449	29,712	30,971	32,230	33,489
Percent above/ below trend	−10.8%	−1.9%	4.1%				

Source: Based on data from FactSet Research.

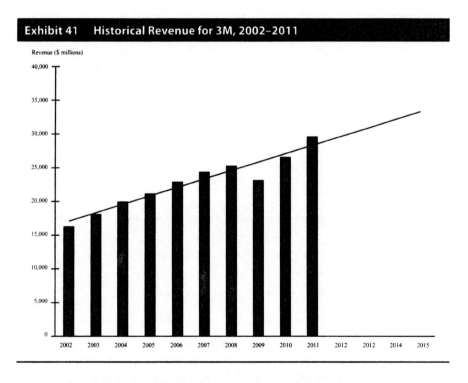

Exhibit 41   Historical Revenue for 3M, 2002–2011

The "growth relative to GDP growth" and "market growth and market share" methods discussed in section 2.1.1 can also be applied to developing longer-term projections. Once a revenue projection has been established, previously described methods of forecasting costs can be used to complete the income statement, balance sheet, and cash flow statement.

After a financial forecast has been established for the explicit forecast period, an analyst typically estimates a terminal value. There are certain considerations to keep in mind when deriving the terminal value based on long-term projections. For example, when using an historical multiples–based approach to derive the terminal value of a company, an analyst is implicitly assuming that the past is relevant to the future in terms of growth expectations and required rates of return. If a multiple is used to derive the terminal value (TV), the choice of the multiple should be consistent with the long-run expectations for growth and required return. It is common for an analyst to use a historical average multiple as the basis for the target multiple in the terminal value calculation. For example, as of the mid-2012 date of the analysis, 3M had traded at a median P/E multiple that was 15% higher than that of the S&P 500 Index over the previous 10 years. Thus, an analyst could forecast a terminal value in the year 2015 as the product of 1.15 and the current next 12 months (NTM) P/E of the S&P 500, times forecasted EPS for 3M in 2016.[13] But in estimating the TV of a company, historical multiples are only relevant to the extent that the future growth and profitability is expected to resemble the past. If the future growth or profitability of the company is likely to differ significantly from the historical average, then the target multiple should reflect an expected premium or discount to the historical multiple to reflect this difference in growth and/or profitability.

EXAMPLE 14

Historical Valuation Multiples

Long-term historical average valuation multiples are frequently used in equity analysis as a reference point or as justification of a target multiple at which the shares are expected to trade in the future. Such widespread use is predicated on a belief in mean reversion, the idea that over time the valuation of a stock will revert to its long-term historical average. Of course, this implicitly assumes that the future growth and profitability of the company will resemble the past. If the future outlook differs significantly from the past, the historical average multiple might not be relevant. The multiple may not be computed in the same manner by all analysts. The underlying financial data can be trailing, forward, or current year.

Answer the following assumptions about a hypothetical company with premium, discount, or not applicable on the basis of how you would expect the stock's future multiple to compare with its long-term historical average, keeping all other factors constant. Assumptions:

1 The company is likely to earn higher returns on invested capital in the future.

2 Earnings growth is likely to accelerate in the future.

3 The intensity of competition is likely to increase in the future.

4 The company makes a major acquisition or divestiture.

Solution to 1:

If a company is likely to earn higher returns on invested capital in the future than it has historically, then the company's shares are likely to trade at a premium to their historical average multiple to reflect the expected improvement in profitability.

---

13 According to data obtained from FactSet Research, shares of 3M have traded at a median premium of 15% to the S&P 500 over the past 10 years on the basis of P/E. NTM P/E is the P/E based on an estimate of next 12 months earnings per share.

Solution to 2:

If a company is likely to generate faster EPS growth in the future than it has historically, then the company's shares are likely to trade at a premium to their historical average multiple to reflect the faster expected growth rate.

Solution to 3:

If competition in the industry is expected to intensify in the future, then the company's shares are likely to trade at a discount to their historical average multiple to reflect the likely degradation in profitability.

Solution to 4:

If either the future growth or profitability of a company is expected to change significantly as a result of a major acquisition or divesture, then the historical valuation multiple of the company should no longer be relied on as either a reference point or as justification of a target multiple at which the shares are expected to trade in the future. The historical valuation multiple would be considered not applicable.

When using a DCF approach to developing terminal value, an analyst should avoid mechanically applying a long-term growth rate to a terminal year free cash flow projection. First, an analyst should consider whether the terminal year free cash flow projection should be normalized before that cash flow is incorporated into a long-term projection. For example, if the explicitly forecasted terminal year free cash flow is "low" (e.g., because of business cycle reasons or capital investment projects), an adjustment to normalize the amount may be warranted. Second, an analyst should consider whether and how the future long-term growth rate will differ from the historical growth rate. For example, even some mature companies may be able to accelerate their long-term growth rate through product innovation and/or market expansion (e.g., Apple), whereas other seemingly well-protected "growers" may experience an unanticipated decline in their business as a result of technological change (e.g., Kodak).

One of the greatest challenges facing the analyst is anticipating inflection points, when the future will look significantly different from the recent past. Most discounted cash flow models rely on some kind of perpetuity calculation. A perpetuity calculation assumes that the cash flows from the last year of an explicit forecast grow at a constant rate forever. Because the perpetuity can account for a relatively large portion of the overall valuation of the company, it is critical that the cash flow used is representative of a "normalized" or "mid-cycle" result. If the analyst is examining a cyclical company, using a boom year as the starting point for the perpetuity could result in a grossly overstated intrinsic value estimate. Similarly, using a trough year could result in an intrinsic value estimate that is much too low.

Another important consideration is economic disruption, such as occurred in the 2008 global financial crisis. The economy can occasionally experience sudden, unprecedented changes that affect a wide variety of companies. Even a company with a sound strategy and solid operations can be thrown far off course by a sudden economic disruption, particularly if the company has a high degree of financial leverage.

Regulation and technology are also potential drivers of inflection points, and it is important for the analyst to keep a close eye on both. Government actions can have extreme, sudden, and unpredictable impacts on some businesses. Technological advances can turn fast-growing innovators into obsolete dinosaurs in a matter of months. Both regulation and technology affect some industries more than others. Utilities experience intense regulation, but may not see a significant technological change for decades. Semiconductor manufacturers must constantly keep up with new technology, but experience relatively light regulation. Medical device manufacturers are heavily exposed to both regulation and technological advances.

Finally, long-term growth is a key input in the perpetuity calculation. Some companies and industries can grow faster than the overall economy for long periods of time, causing them to account for an increasing share of the economic pie. Current examples include certain smartphone manufacturers, such as Apple and Samsung, and some internet-related companies, such as Amazon and Google. Other companies, such as the New York Times or Kodak, are likely to grow slower than the overall economy or even shrink over time. Using an unrealistic long-term growth rate can put the analyst's estimate of intrinsic value far off the mark.

EXAMPLE 15

Important Considerations When Making Assumptions

1   Air France-KLM operates in the highly cyclical airline industry. Operating margins for the last nine years are shown in the following table.

	2003	2004	2005	2006	2007	2008	2009	2010	2011
Operating Margin (%)	1.5	1.1	2.6	6.8	5.3	5.3	−0.8	−6.1	3.8

On the basis of only the information in the table, which of the following operating margins would *most likely* be appropriate to use in a perpetuity calculation for Air France-KLM to arrive at a reasonable intrinsic value estimate?

A   2.2%

B   3.8%

C   5.3%

For each of the companies in the following problems, indicate which of the choices is *least likely* to cause an inflection point in the company's outlook.

2   Nokia, a manufacturer of cell phones and mobile network equipment.

A   Pricing of technology components has been steadily falling, consistent with past experience, and this decline is expected to continue over the next several years.

B   Consumers have been rapidly adopting smartphones, threatening Nokia's historic strength in lower-end devices.

C   Nokia has formed a partnership with Microsoft to supply phones with a potentially important new operating system.

3   Abbott Laboratories, a diversified manufacturer of health care products, including pharmaceuticals and medical devices.

A   It has become more difficult for medical device manufacturers to receive regulatory approval for new products because of heightened safety concerns.

B   A competitor has demonstrated favorable efficacy data on a drug candidate that will compete with an important Abbott product.

C   Management reiterates its long-standing approach to capital deployment.

4   Grupo Aeroportuario del Sureste, operator of nine airports in Mexico, especially in the tourist-heavy southeast.

   A   A technological advance will allow airlines to save 5% on fuel costs, but it is not expected to meaningfully alter passenger volumes. Similar developments in the past have benefited airlines but not airports, whose price per passenger is regulated.

   B   Global economic disruption has caused a sharp decline in international travel.

   C   Regulators will allow the construction of a new airport by a competitor in Grupo Aeroportuario del Sureste's service territory.

5   LinkedIn, operator of an online social network for professionals, with low investment needs and no debt.

   A   Facebook, another online social network, announces a plan to enhance its offerings in the professional category.

   B   Regulators announce an investigation of LinkedIn's privacy practices, which could result in significant changes to the service.

   C   The US Federal Reserve has just increased interest rates. Although this will raise borrowing costs, the rate increase is not expected to have a negative impact on the economy.

Solution to 1:

A is correct. Because the airline industry is cyclical, an estimate of "mid-cycle" or "normalized" operating margin is necessary to estimate a perpetuity value. The nine-year average operating margin was 19.5/9 = 2.2%.

Solution to 2:

A is correct. Although it is important that pricing of technology components has been falling, this decline is consistent with past experience and so does not represent an inflection point.

Solution to 3:

C is correct. Management is sticking with its historical approach to capital deployment, so this does not represent an inflection point.

Solution to 4:

A is correct. Although the technological advance is good for the airlines, it will not have a meaningful effect on passenger volumes, which will likely prevent the airports from sharing in that benefit. In contrast, both B and C could have a significant impact on the long-run earnings power of Mexican airports.

Solution to 5:

C is correct. Because LinkedIn carries no debt, it is unlikely that the new interest rates will create an inflection point in the company's outlook.

7 BUILDING A MODEL

This section provides an example of building a company model.[14] The subject company is the Rémy Cointreau Group (Rémy), a French company that sells wines and spirits. After providing a brief overview of the company and industry, we will focus primarily on the mechanics of constructing pro forma income statements, statements of cash flows, and balance sheets.

7.1 Industry Overview

This industry overview will focus on the cognac industry because it is Rémy's most important business segment, accounting for 75% of total operating profit. (In practice, an analyst would also perform a similar industry analysis for the company's other major segments.) An important feature of the cognac market is that supply is limited and demand is growing. Supply is limited because cognac production, similar to champagne, is highly regulated, in this case through the Bureau National Interprofessionnel du Cognac (BNIC). By regulation, cognac can only be produced in a limited geographic area, located around the town of Cognac in southwest France. Furthermore, within the region, production volume is capped each year. The cognac market is highly concentrated, with the top four players controlling 78% of world volume and 84% of global value. Rémy's market share is 14% and 18% of global volume and value, respectively. Demand for cognac is growing because of increased demand from China. From 2000 to 2010, global cognac volumes grew at a 2% CAGR, driven by demand from Asia, most of which originated from China. The Chinese market grew at a 16% CAGR on a volume basis. Simultaneously, Rémy has also seen a product mix improvement because Chinese consumers increasingly prefer superior quality and more expensive cognac. Exhibit 42 summarizes a Porter's five forces analysis of the cognac industry.

Exhibit 42	Porter's Five Forces Analysis for Cognac Industry	
Force	**Degree**	**Factors to Consider**
Threat of substitutes	Low	■ Cognac consumers show brand loyalty and do not easily shift to other beverages or high-end spirits.
Rivalry	Low	■ Market is consolidated with four players controlling 78% of the world market in volume and 84% of global value.
		■ Only the European market is fragmented with slightly more than half of the market not controlled by the top four.
Bargaining power of suppliers	Low/medium	■ Large number of small independent vineyards supply inputs.
		■ Most of the distillation is carried out by a large body of independent distillers who sell to the big houses.

---

14 Data sources for this example include the company's fiscal 2012 annual report, the company's interim reports, and corresponding investor presentations for additional information on the underlying results of the respective divisions.

Exhibit 42   (Continued)

Force	Degree	Factors to Consider
Bargaining power of buyers	Low	■ Premium beverages are mostly sold to wine and spirits retail outlets that do not coordinate purchasing.
		■ Premium beverages are mostly consumed in small and fragmented on-premises outlets (restaurants, etc.).
Threat of new entrants	Low	■ Producers have long-term contracts with suppliers in the Cognac area.
		■ Barriers to entry are high.
		• Building brands is difficult because they must have heritage/pedigree.
		• Large capital investment is required to build an inventory with "aged" cognac and set up a distribution network.

In summary, the cognac market, Rémy's largest and most profitable operating segment, exhibits a favorable profitability profile. In addition to limited supply and growing demand, the industry faces a generally favorable situation with respect to substitutes, rivalry, suppliers, buyers, and potential new entrants.

7.2 Company Overview

Rémy, whose reporting year ends 31 March, operates three business segments:

1 Cognac. This division, which is named after its main brand Rémy Martin, represented about 58% of FY2012 revenue and 75% of total operating profits.

2 Liqueurs & Spirits. The main brands in this segment are Cointreau, Passoa, Metaxa, Saint Rémy, and Mount Gay, and they represented about 21% of FY2012 revenue and operating profits.

3 Partner Brands. This division includes other companies' brands that are marketed through Rémy's distribution network, and they represented about 21% of FY2012 revenue and less than 2% of operating profits.

Segment financial information is summarized in Exhibit 43. As shown, the company's largest business segment is also its most profitable: the Cognac segment earned an operating profit margin of around 29% (= €173million/€593million) in fiscal 2012.

Exhibit 43   Analysis of Rémy's Turnover and Operating Profit

	FY2010	FY2011	FY2012
Rémy Martin (€ millions)	406	486	593
Liqueurs & Spirits (€ millions)	207	208	216
Partner Brands (€ millions)	196	214	218
Total revenues (€ millions)	808	908	1,026

Operating Profit (€ millions)

(continued)

	FY2010	FY2011	FY2012
Exhibit 43　(Continued)			
Rémy Martin	106	141	173
Liqueurs & Spirits	52	43	53
Partner Brands	2	2	4
Holding costs[a]	18	18	22
Champagne (disposed)	0	0	0
Total operating profit	142	167	208
Operating Profit as % of Revenue			
Rémy Martin	26.1%	28.9%	29.2%
Liqueurs & Spirits	25.0%	20.5%	24.4%
Partner Brands	1.0%	1.0%	1.9%
Holding costs as % of total revenue	−2.2%	−2.0%	−2.2%
Operating margin	17.6%	18.4%	20.2%

[a] Holding costs are a deduction.

Source: Based on information in consolidated financial statements of the Rémy Cointreau Group on 31 March 2012, Note 15.1.

7.3 Construction of Pro Forma Income Statement

This section will illustrate the construction of pro forma income statements. The forecasts of revenue follow the structure of the company's operating segments. Rémy's 2012 reporting year ends on 31 March.

7.3.1 *Revenue Forecast*

The revenue forecasts use primarily a hybrid approach because trends in the individual segments (bottom-up) are combined with the economic development in the relevant regions (top-down). For each segment, the change in revenue is driven by volume, price, and foreign currency estimates, based on historical trends as adjusted for expected deviations from trend. Price changes refer not only to price changes for a single product but to changes in price/mix, which is defined as changes in average price that result from selling a different mix of higher and lower priced products. Changes in revenue attributable to volume or price/mix are considered to be organic growth and are shown separately from the impact of foreign exchange (forex impact in the model).

In the Cognac segment, historical volume growth accelerated from 4.2% in 2010 to 10.8% in 2012. For future years, volume growth is expected to remain robust but to be somewhat slower than in 2012, given the global economic slowdown at the time of this projection. The growing number of affluent Chinese consumers will likely keep demand high, although developed market consumption is likely to be rather flat. In the model, the assumption is for 8% volume growth in 2013, gradually declining by 1 percentage point a year to a more stable 5% in 2016.

Price/mix contributed around 8%, 23%, 5%, and 13% to the Cognac segment revenue growth in 2009, 2010, 2011, and 2012, respectively. Although the impact of price/mix on revenue growth has fluctuated in recent years, it is likely that price/mix will remain a relatively significant contributor to revenue growth in the future given the favorable structure of the industry. A 10% price/mix contribution to revenue growth is assumed in 2013, and then it slows 2 percentage points a year to 6% by 2015. The combined projections for 2013 of 8% volume growth and 10% price/mix impact results in overall organic revenue growth of 18.8%, calculated as [(1 + 0.08) × (1 + 0.10) = 1.188] − 1 = 0.188, or 18.8%.

In addition to the impact of volume and price/mix, Rémy's revenues are affected by movements in exchange rates. Company disclosures indicate that around 70% of revenues are realized outside the eurozone, whereas most of Rémy's production occurs in the eurozone. On the basis of the current financial situation, the model results forecast a positive foreign currency impact on revenue in 2012 and 2013, with major currencies strengthening against the euro.

Exhibit 44 summarizes historical and projected information for the Cognac segment's revenue.

Exhibit 44	Historical and Projected Information for Rémy Martin (Cognac) Segment Revenue							
	2008	**2009**	**2010**	**2011**	**2012**	**2013E**	**2014E**	**2015E**
Revenues (€ million)	362	312	406	486	593	739	854	960
YoY %	4.2%	−13.9%	30.1%	19.8%	21.9%	24.8%	15.6%	12.4%
Volume growth %	6.7	−19.6	4.2	6.5	10.8	8.0	7.0	6.0
Price/mix %	4.5	7.6	23.0	5.3	12.9	10.0	8.0	6.0
Organic growth %	11.5	−13.5	28.2	12.1	25.1	18.8	15.6	12.4
Forex impact %	−7.3	−0.3	1.9	7.7	−3.2	6.0	0.0	0.0
Scope change %	0.0	0.0	0.0	0.0	0.0	0.0	0.0	0.0
YoY %	4.2	−13.8	30.1	19.8	21.9	24.8	15.6	12.4

Source: Based on data from Rémy Cointreau and authors' analysis.

A similar analysis can be performed to project revenue for the other segments, and then the amounts can be summed to derive projected revenue for the company as a whole.

7.3.2 Cost of Goods Sold

Rémy's gross margin improved 4.3 percentage points from 57.1% in 2011 to 61.4% in 2012. The strong price/mix effect in the Rémy Martin division was the key driver. The strong price/mix effect and corresponding gross margin improvement was the underlying driver for the gross margin improvement in the previous year as a result of the strong growth in the high margin region of Asia. Because Asia, with its appetite for expensive Cognac, is expected to be the main driver for the volume growth, price/mix will also continue to rise, which will consequently drive the gross margin enhancement in future years. The limited supply of the cognac category and the strong demand for premium spirits, particular in Asia, justify a high price/mix (see Section 7.3.1 Revenue Forecast) and corresponding higher gross margin in future periods. As the contribution effect of price/mix on revenue slows over time, the pace of gross margin improvement will also decelerate.

7.3.3 Selling, General, and Administrative Expenses

Distribution costs jumped from 26.1% of revenue in 2009 to 33.6% in 2012 because of higher advertising and promotion (A&P) costs and expansion of the owned distribution network. In particular, the setup of Rémy's distribution network in Asia increased the cost base. Rémy is very committed to its brand building and also wants to diversify geographically. We estimate a further increase in distribution costs as a percentage of revenue, albeit at a slower growth rate. Administrative costs as a percentage of revenue are kept constant at 7.7%, in line with 2012.

Exhibit 45 provides a consolidated income statement for Rémy.

Exhibit 45	Consolidated Historical and Projected Income Statement for Rémy Cointreau (€ millions, unless noted)						
	2009	**2010**	**2011**	**2012**	**2013E**	**2014E**	**2015E**
Sales	710	808	908	1,026	1,206	1,337	1,461
Cost of sales	337	362	390	396	442	471	500
Gross profit	373	446	518	630	764	866	961
Gross margin	52.6%	55.2%	57.1%	61.4%	63.4%	64.8%	65.8%
Change in gross margin		2.6%	1.9%	4.3%	2.0%	1.4%	1.0%
Distribution costs	185	239	284	345	417	473	524
Distribution costs as % of sales	26.1%	29.6%	31.3%	33.6%	34.6%	35.3%	35.8%
Administrative expenses	68	70	73	79	93	103	112
Administrative expenses as % of sales	9.6%	8.7%	8.0%	7.7%	7.7%	7.7%	7.7%
Other income from operations	4	5	6	2	0	0	0
EBIT	124	142	167	208	254	290	325
EBIT %	17.5%	17.6%	18.4%	20.2%	21.1%	21.7%	22.2%
Depreciation and amortization (add-back)	12	14	14	15	22	26	30
Depreciation and amortization as % of sales	1.6%	1.7%	1.6%	1.4%	1.8%	1.9%	2.1%
EBITDA	136	156	181	222	276	316	355
EBITDA margin	19.1%	19.2%	20.0%	21.7%	22.9%	23.7%	24.3%
Other operating income/expenses	11	−2	−47	−3	0	0	0
EBIT including other income/costs	135	140	121	205	254	290	325
Finance costs	17	22	27	27	17	17	17
Other financial expenses	6	3	2	8	0	0	0
Total financial expenses	23	19	30	35	17	17	17
Profit before tax	113	121	91	169	237	273	308
Income tax	35	33	22	47	66	76	86
Tax rate	30.7%	27.0%	23.9%	27.9%	28.0%	28.0%	28.0%

Exhibit 45	(Continued)						
	2009	**2010**	**2011**	**2012**	**2013E**	**2014E**	**2015E**
Income from associates	3	5	4	0	0	0	−1
Profit from continuing operations	81	93	73	122	170	196	221
Profit/loss from discontinued operations	5	−4	−3	−11	0	0	0
Net profit for the year	86	89	71	111	170	196	221
Non-controlling interest	0	3	0	0	0	0	0
Owners of the company	86	86	71	111	170	196	221
EPS basic continuing operations in €	1.73	1.94	1.50	2.47	3.53	4.05	4.56
EPS diluted continuing operations in €	1.72	1.93	1.49	2.46	3.44	3.96	4.47
EPS basic total in €	1.84	1.80	1.44	2.25	3.52	4.05	4.55
EPS diluted total in €	1.83	1.79	1.43	2.24	3.44	3.96	4.46
Reported group profit	86	86	71	111	170	196	221
Adjusted net profit for one-offs	76	92	108	136	170	196	221
YoY %			16.7%	26.4%	25.0%	15.2%	12.7%
EPS adjusted basic in €	1.63	1.92	2.19	2.76	3.52	4.05	4.55
EPS adjusted diluted in €	1.62	1.91	2.18	2.75	3.44	3.96	4.46
YoY basic %		18.1%	14.3%	25.6%	27.8%	14.9%	12.5%
Average number of shares, basic in millions	46.9	48.0	49.0	49.3	48.3	48.4	48.5
Average number of shares, diluted in millions	47.1	48.2	49.2	49.5	49.5	49.5	49.5

Source: Based on information from Rémy Cointreau and authors' analysis.

7.3.4 Operating Profit by Division

In this section, we estimate operating profit by division for Rémy. If the cost of goods sold, selling, general, and administrative costs, and other income from operations are subtracted from revenue, the result is EBIT (a proxy for operating profit). This number for consolidated operations should match the cumulative EBIT of the individual segments. For the Cognac segment (Rémy Martin), the forecast of higher revenue growth assumes an improving product mix that will also result in a higher gross margin. But the benefit to gross margin will be somewhat mitigated by higher advertising and distribution costs. For 2013, we estimate an operating margin improvement of 0.4 percentage points to 29.6%. In the following years, the expectation is that the Cognac segment's operating margin will increase at a slightly slower pace. By 2015, its operating margin is forecast to be 30.1%. As a benchmark, this forecast can be compared with the financial results reported by Hennessy, another Cognac brand. Hennessy's operating margin in recent years was 30–32%.

For the other segments, there is not much upside. In the Liqueurs & Spirits division, we assume that a gradual recovery in operating margin to 24.9% by 2015 should be achievable because of improvements in distribution. In total, Rémy Cointreau's consolidated operating margin is forecast to improve from 20.2% in 2012 to 21.1% in 2013 and ultimately to 22.2% in 2015, largely as a result of growth in the Cognac segment, the most profitable division.

Exhibit 46   Historical and Projected Operating Profit by Segment for Rémy Cointreau

	2009	2010	2011	2012	2013E	2014E	2015E
Revenues (€ millions)							
Rémy Martin	312	406	486	593	739	854	960
Liqueurs & Spirits	196	207	208	216	231	239	249
Partner Brands	80	99	214	218	235	244	252
Champagne (disposed)	126	97	0	0	0	0	0
Total revenues	714	808	908	1,026	1,206	1,337	1,461
Operating profit (€ millions)							
Rémy Martin	80	106	141	173	219	255	289
Liqueurs & Spirits	58	52	43	53	57	59	62
Partner Brands	2	2	2	4	5	5	5
Holding costs	15	18	18	22	26	29	31
Champagne (disposed)							
Total operating profit	124	142	167	208	254	290	325
Operating profit as % of revenue							
Rémy Martin	25.7	26.1	28.9	29.2	29.6	29.9	30.1
Liqueurs & Spirits	29.4	25.0	20.5	24.4	24.5	24.7	24.9
Partner Brands	1.9	2.4	1.0	1.9	1.9	1.9	1.9
Holding costs	2.1	2.2	2.0	2.2	2.2	2.2	2.2
Operating margin	17.4	17.6	18.4	20.2	21.1	21.7	22.2
Operating margin change (%)							
Rémy Martin	−0.1	0.4	2.8	0.3	0.4	0.3	0.2
Liqueurs & Spirits	4.3	−4.4	−4.5	3.9	0.2	0.2	0.2
Partner Brands			−1.4	0.9	0.0	0.0	0.0
Operating margin change			0.8	1.8	0.8	0.6	0.5

Source: Based on information from Rémy Cointreau and authors' analysis.

7.3.5 *Non-operating Expenses*

Two types of non-operating expenses are included in the model: finance expenses (i.e., interest expenses) and income taxes.

Exhibit 47 shows the computation of finance costs. Finance costs require estimating the debt and cash position. Companies usually pay a fixed or variable interest rate on debt. If the interest rate is variable, the rate would be determined from existing market rates. A credit spread is normally applied to an estimate of the benchmark (e.g., Libor, Euribor) being used. In Exhibit 47, finance costs are fixed and calculated as 5% incurred on gross debt at the beginning of the period minus 1% earned on the cash position at the beginning of the period. Other financial expenses are assumed to be zero. Estimated finance costs for fiscal year 2013 total €19 million, calculated as €379 million gross debt times the 5% assumed interest rate. Estimated interest income is €2 million, calculated as €190 million cash position times 1% interest.

Exhibit 47	Debt Position and Financial Costs and Income for Rémy (€ millions, unless noted)						
	2009	**2010**	**2011**	**2012**	**2013E**	**2014E**	**2015E**
Long-term financial debt	592	538	378	340	340	340	340
Short-term financial debt and accrued interest	29	50	32	39	39	39	39
Gross debt	621	588	410	379	379	379	379
Cash and cash equivalents	−89	−86	−81	−190	−146	−202	−286
Net debt	532	501	329	189	232	177	93
Average gross debt		605	499	394	379	379	379
Average net debt		517	415	259	210	205	135
Finance costs	17	22	27	24	19	19	19
Adjusted one-offs	0	0	4	7	0	0	0
Finance costs	17	22	24	17	19	19	19
Interest income		0	0	2	2	1	2
Finance costs excludes one-offs		22	24	15	17	17	17
Finance costs/Average net debt		4.3%	5.7%	6.7%	9.0%	9.2%	14.0%
Finance costs/Average gross debt		3.6%	4.7%	4.4%	5.0%	5.0%	5.0%
Finance costs/Gross debt begin		3.5%	5.8%	4.6%	5.0%	5.0%	5.0%
Interest income/Cash (beginning)				2.9%	1.0%	1.0%	1.0%

Source: Based on information from Rémy Cointreau and authors' analysis.

7.3.6 *Corporate Income Tax Forecast*

In line with 2012, the tax rate is set at 28% for the future periods. Because it is also the average rate for past three years, this is not an extraordinary percentage. Rémy Cointreau has no significant minority interests in any of its subsidiaries.

7.4 Construction of Pro Forma Cash Flow Statement and Balance Sheet

To calculate the balance sheet for the end of the year, combine the projections made for the income statement with the expected cash flows during the year. These cash flows could be a direct result of the operational activities, cash proceeds from revenues, and cash outflows from costs. Based on the expected volume trends, the necessary production capacity and corresponding capital investments and cash outlays for the coming years can be budgeted. Dividend payments, share repurchases, and debt redemptions are financial cash flows that will affect the balance sheet and also need to be taken into account.

7.4.1 Capital Investments and Depreciation Forecasts

Capital investment, or capex, as a percentage of revenue was 1.7% in FY2012. In the previous three years capex as a percentage of sales was 3.2%, on average. Given the strong growth prospects, we expect capex to be at the high end of the historical level. Therefore, 3% of sales for capex is used in the model. With Rémy's growing fixed asset base, it is logical that depreciation will increase. A gradual growth of depreciation as a percentage of sales with annual increases of 0.125 percentage points is assumed for the next three years. The breakdown of capex, depreciation, and amortization is shown in Exhibit 48.

Exhibit 48	Capex, Depreciation, and Amortization Breakdown						
	2009	**2010**	**2011**	**2012**	**2013E**	**2014E**	**2015E**
Depreciation and amortization (€ millions)	12	14	14	15	22	26	30
as % of sales	1.6%	1.7%	1.6%	1.5%	1.8%	1.9%	2.1%
as % of fixed assets	5.9%	6.5%	10.1%	10.2%	13.6%	14.8%	16.0%
Capex (€ millions)	27	23	27	17	36	40	44
Capex as % of sales	3.8%	2.8%	3.0%	1.7%	3.0%	3.0%	3.0%
as % of fixed assets	13.7%	10.8%	19.4%	11.6%	22.5%	22.9%	23.2%
Capex/(depreciation and amortization)	2.3	1.7	1.9	1.1	1.7	1.5	1.5

Source: Based on information from Rémy Cointreau and authors' analysis.

7.4.2 Working Capital Forecasts

We have assumed that working capital as a percentage of sales will remain constant. In Exhibit 49, we include only the relevant balance sheet items related to revenues and costs (i.e., inventories, trade and other receivables, and trade and other payables) and keep the other items constant. Rémy Cointreau had positive working capital of more than half of its sales in fiscal year 2012. The largest working capital component is inventory, which accounts for almost 77% of annual revenues. Given the strong sales growth, working capital also increases rapidly. This has a negative impact on operational cash flow. Note that we have taken the balance sheet amount of the working capital items at the end of the year. The reported change of the working capital in the cash flow statement does not automatically correspond with the figures calculated further on because of acquisitions and divestments. In particular, the sale of Champagne activities announced in 2011 and carried out in 2012, complicates the forecasting of working capital at Rémy Cointreau. In Exhibit 49, this results in a large change in working capital from 2010 to 2011. Working capital before 2011 still includes the Champagne division, but working capital as of 2011 excludes the Champagne working capital. On the 2011 balance sheet, a large amount of €485 million for assets held for sale consisted of the Champagne stocks that were previously reported under inventories.

Exhibit 49	Working Capital Development for Rémy						
	2009	**2010**	**2011**	**2012**	**2013E**	**2014E**	**2015E**
Inventories (€ millions)	958	970	699	793	931	1,033	1,129
Trade and other receivables	282	248	214	208	244	271	296
Trade and other payables	−453	−439	−407	−468	−549	−609	−666
Working capital	788	779	506	533	626	695	759
Inventories at year end as % of sales	135	120	77	77	77	77	77
Trade and other receivables at year end as % of sales	40	31	24	20	20	20	20
Trade and other payables at year end as % of sales	−64	−54	−45	−46	−46	−46	−46
Working capital at year end as % of sales	111	96	56	52	52	52	52
Inventories as % of sales at year end change		14.9	43.0	0.2	0.0	0.0	0.0
Trade and other receivables at year end as % of sales change		9.0	7.2	3.3	0.0	0.0	0.0
Trade and other payables at year end as % of sales change		9.4	9.6	0.8	0.0	0.0	0.0
Working capital as % at year end of sales change		14.5	40.6	3.8	0.0	0.0	0.0
Absolute change in inventories at year end (€ millions)		11	271	94	139	102	96
Absolute change in trade and other receivables at year end		34	35	6	36	27	25
Absolute change in trade and other payables at year end		14	33	61	82	60	56
Absolute change in working capital at year end		9	272	27	93	68	64

Source: Based on information from Rémy Cointreau and authors' analysis.

7.4.3 *Forecasted Cash Flow Statement*

With the operating profit, capex, and working capital estimates already in place, the cash flow statement is almost automatically generated. Although in 2011 and 2012 Rémy paid a €1 per share special dividend, raising the total payout to €2.30, we keep the expected dividend for the next years constant at €1.30 per share. Consequently, we see a high dividend outflow of €111 million (48.2 million shares get €2,30 for 2012) in 2013 and a lower dividend outflow of €63 million (48.2 million shares receive €1,30) in the years thereafter. (Note that despite the same dividend per share of €2,30 in 2011 and 2012 the amount of dividend paid to the shareholders in 2012 for 2011 was higher than we estimate for 2013 because the number of outstanding shares declined as a result of a share buy-back).

Exhibit 50	Projected Statement of Cash Flows for Rémy (€ millions)						
	2009	**2010**	**2011**	**2012**	**2013E**	**2014E**	**2015E**
Current operating profit	124	142	167	208	254	290	324
Adjustment for depreciation, amortization, and impairments	12	14	14	15	22	26	30
Adjustment for share based payments	4	3	3	4	4	4	4
Dividends received from associates	1	2	3	2	0	0	0
EBITDA	141	161	187	229	280	320	359
Change in inventories	−37	−20	−11	−40	−139	−102	−96
Change in trade receivables	37	−39	27	4	−6	−27	−25
Change in trade payables	82	23	3	6	82	60	56
Change in other receivables and payables	−54	51	22	23	0	0	0
Change in working capital	28	15	40	−7	−93	−68	−64
Net cash flow from operations	169	176	227	222	187	252	294
Other operating cash flows	−185	−1	−2	0	0	0	0
Net financial income	−9	−25	−20	−17	−17	−17	−17
Net income tax	29	−54	−31	−104	−66	−76	−86
Total other operating cash flow	−165	−80	−53	−121	−83	−94	−103
Net cash flow from operating activities, continuing operations	4	96	173	101	103	158	191
Impact from discontinued operations	−67	−7	8	12	0	0	0
Net cash flow from operating activities	−62	88	182	113	103	158	191
Capital expenditures	−27	−23	−27	−17	−36	−40	−44
Net other cash flow from investing	56	−13	62	1	0	0	0
Net cash flow from investment, continuing operations	31	−35	34	−16	−36	−40	−44
Impact of discontinued operations	−3	4	1	71	0	0	0
Net cash flow from investment activities	29	−31	35	56	−36	−40	−44
Capital increase	1	1	7	3	0	0	0
Treasury shares	−2	2	0	−95	0	0	0
Increase in financial debt	137	2	330	25	0	0	0
Repayment of financial debt	−2	−30	−517	−58	0	0	0
Dividends paid to shareholders	−39	−39	−41	−114	−111	−63	−63
Net cash flow from financing activities, continuing operations	94	−64	−222	−239	−111	−63	−63
Impact from discontinued operations	0	0	0	173	0	0	0

Exhibit 50   (Continued)

	2009	2010	2011	2012	2013E	2014E	2015E
Net cash flow from financing activities	94	−64	−222	−67	−111	−63	−63
Translation differences cash	−8	3	−1	8	0	0	0
Change in cash and cash equivalents	52	−3	−6	110	−44	55	84
Cash at the beginning	37	89	86	81	190	146	202
Cash at the end	89	86	81	190	146	202	286

Note: Apparent small discrepancies in addition reflect the effects of rounding error.
Source: Based on information from Rémy Cointreau and authors' analysis.

7.4.4 Forecasted Balance Sheet

The forecasted balance sheet is given in Exhibit 51 and is based on the combination of the projected income statement (Exhibit 45), the projected statement of cash flows (Exhibit 50), and the historical starting balance sheet. The balance sheet items that were not specifically discussed are held constant.

Exhibit 51   Projected Balance Sheet for Rémy (€ millions)

	2009	2010	2011	2012	2013E	2014E	2015E
Brands and other intangible assets	630	630	447	443	443	443	443
Property, plant, and equipment	197	209	141	146	161	175	189
Investments in associates	62	64	65	68	68	68	68
Other financial assets	61	71	11	87	87	87	87
Deferred tax assets	22	27	30	44	44	44	44
Total non-current assets	972	1,001	694	789	803	817	831
Inventories	958	970	699	793	931	1,033	1,129
Trade and other receivables	282	248	214	208	244	271	296
Cash and cash equivalents	89	86	81	190	146	202	286
Other current assets	17	11	503	10	10	10	10
Total current assets	1,347	1,316	1,497	1,200	1,332	1,515	1,720
Total assets	2,319	2,317	2,191	1,989	2,135	2,332	2,551
Share capital	76	78	79	79	84	88	92
Share premium	686	708	736	738	738	738	738
Treasury shares	−2	0	−1	−96	−96	−96	−96
Consolidated reserves	127	152	178	134	134	241	374
Net profit to owners of the company	86	86	71	111	170	196	221

(continued)

Exhibit 51   (Continued)

	2009	2010	2011	2012	2013E	2014E	2015E
Translation reserve	−1	0	−8	9	9	9	9
Profit and loss recorded in equity	−1	−5	8	0	0	0	0
Equity attributable to shareholders	971	1,018	1,063	975	1,038	1,175	1,337
Non-controlling interest	−2	1	1	1	2	2	2
Equity	969	1,019	1,064	976	1,040	1,177	1,340
Long-term financial debt	592	538	378	340	340	340	340
Provision for employee benefits	19	24	21	22	22	22	22
Long-term provisions for liabilities and charges	12	5	7	7	7	7	7
Deferred tax liabilities	199	200	122	98	98	98	98
Total non-current liabilities	823	766	527	467	467	467	467
Short-term financial debt and accrued interest	29	50	32	39	39	39	39
Trade and other payables	453	439	407	468	549	609	666
Income tax payable	33	12	39	13	13	13	13
Short-term provisions for liabilities and charges	6	20	10	2	2	2	2
Derivative financial instruments	7	11	5	25	25	25	25
Liabilities held for sale	0	0	109	0	0	0	0
Current liabilities	528	532	601	546	628	688	744
Total equity and liabilities	2,319	2,317	2,191	1,989	2,135	2,332	2,551

Source: Based on information from Rémy Cointreau and authors' analysis.

7.5 Valuation Inputs

In the previous sections, we have built a model that projects the future profit and loss, cash flow statement, and balance sheet for Rémy Cointreau. This model is the starting point for valuation. Most company-specific metrics can be found in the model. Valuation estimates can be made based on a variety of metrics, including free cash flow, earnings per share, EBITDA, or EBIT. The company-specific inputs needed to build a discounted cash flow model are shown in Exhibit 52. The first line in Exhibit 52 is from Exhibit 45, excluding other operating expenses. Depreciation and amortization are from Exhibit 48. The remaining data are from Exhibit 50.

Exhibit 52   Calculating Free Cash Flow as Basis for a DCF Valuation (€ millions)

	2012	2013E	2014E	2015E
Normalized operating profit	208	254	290	324
Taxes (28% tax rate)	58	71	81	91
Normalized operating profit after tax	150	183	209	233

Exhibit 52	(Continued)			
	2012	**2013E**	**2014E**	**2015E**
Depreciation and amortization	15	22	26	30
	165	205	235	263
Change in working capital	−7	−93	−68	−64
Capital expenditures	−17	−36	−40	−44
Free cash flow to the firm	141	75	127	155

Source: Based on the authors' analysis.

CONCLUSIONS AND SUMMARY

8

Industry and company analysis are essential tools of fundamental analysis. Among the points made in this reading, the key points include the following.

- Analysts can use a top-down, bottom-up, or a hybrid approach to forecasting income and expenses. Top-down approaches usually begin at the level of the overall economy. Bottom-up approaches begin at the level of the individual company or unit within the company (e.g., business segment). Time-series approaches are considered bottom-up, although time-series analysis can be a tool used in top-down approaches. Hybrid approaches include elements of top-down and bottom-up approaches.

- In a "growth relative to GDP growth" approach to forecasting revenue, the analyst forecasts the growth rate of nominal gross domestic product and industry and company growth relative to GDP growth.

- In a "market growth and market share" approach to forecasting revenue, the analyst combines forecasts of growth in particular markets with forecasts of a company's market share in the individual markets.

- Operating margins that are positively correlated with sales provide evidence of economies of scale in an industry.

- Some balance sheet line items, such as retained earnings, flow directly from the income statement, whereas accounts receivable, accounts payable, and inventory are very closely linked to income statement projections.

- A common way to model working capital accounts is to use efficiency ratios.

- Return on invested capital (ROIC), defined as net operating profit less adjusted taxes divided by the difference between operating assets and operating liabilities, is an after-tax measure of the profitability of investing in a company. High and persistent levels of ROIC are often associated with having a competitive advantage.

- Competitive factors affect a company's ability to negotiate lower input prices with suppliers and to raise prices for products and services. Porter's five forces framework can be used as a basis for identifying such factors.

- Inflation (deflation) affects pricing strategy depending on industry structure, competitive forces, and the nature of consumer demand.

- When a technological development results in a new product that threatens to cannibalize demand for an existing product, a unit forecast for the new product combined with an expected cannibalization factor can be used to estimate the impact on future demand for the existing product.

- Factors influencing the choice of the explicit forecast horizon include the projected holding period, an investor's average portfolio turnover, cyclicality of an industry, company specific factors, and employer preferences.

REFERENCES

Hawawini, Gabriel, and Claude Viallet. 2011. *Finance for Executives: Managing for Value Creation*, 4th edition. Mason, Ohio: South-Western Cengage Learning.

Porter, Michael E. 1980. *Competitive Strategy: Techniques for Analyzing Industries and Competitors*. New York, NY: The Free Press.

Porter, Michael E. 2008. "The Five Competitive Forces That Shape Strategy." *Harvard Business Review*, (January).

PRACTICE PROBLEMS

The following information relates to Questions 1–6

Angela Green, an investment manager at Horizon Investments, intends to hire a new investment analyst. After conducting initial interviews, Green has narrowed the pool to three candidates. She plans to conduct second interviews to further assess the candidates' knowledge of industry and company analysis.

Prior to the second interviews, Green asks the candidates to analyze Chrome Network Systems, a company that manufactures internet networking products. Each candidate is provided Chrome's financial information presented in Exhibit 1.

Exhibit 1	Chrome Network Systems Selected Financial Information (in millions of $)		
	Year Ended:		
	2010	**2011**	**2012**
Net sales	46.8	50.5	53.9
Cost of sales	18.2	18.4	18.8
Gross profit	28.6	32.1	35.1
Selling, general, and administrative (SG&A) expenses	19.3	22.5	25.1
Operating income	9.3	9.6	10.0
Interest expense	0.5	0.7	0.6
Income before provision for income tax	8.8	8.9	9.4
Provision for income taxes	2.8	2.8	3.1
Net income	6.0	6.1	6.3

Green asks each candidate to forecast the 2013 income statement for Chrome and to outline the key assumptions used in their analysis. The job candidates are told to include Horizon's economic outlook for 2013 in their analysis, which assumes nominal GDP growth of 3.6%, based on expectations of real GDP growth of 1.6% and inflation of 2.0%.

Green receives the models from each of the candidates and schedules second interviews. To prepare for the interviews, Green compiles a summary of the candidates' key assumptions in Exhibit 2.

Exhibit 2	Summary of Key Assumptions Used in Candidates' Models		
Metric	**Candidate A**	**Candidate B**	**Candidate C**
Net sales	Net sales will grow at the average annual growth rate in net sales over the 2010–2012 time period.	Industry sales will grow at the same rate as nominal GDP, but Chrome will have a 2 percentage points decline in market share.	Net sales will grow 50 basis points slower than nominal GDP.
Cost of sales	2013 gross margin will be same as the average annual gross margin over the 2010–2012 time period.	2013 gross margin will decline as costs increase by expected inflation.	2013 gross margin will increase by 20 basis points from 2012.
Selling, general, and administrative (SG&A) expenses	2013 SG&A/net sales ratio will be the same as the average ratio over the 2010–2012 time period.	2013 SG&A will grow at the rate of inflation.	2013 SG&A/net sales ratio will be the same as the 2012 ratio.
Interest expense	2013 interest expense assumes the effective interest rate will be the same as the 2012 rate.	2013 interest expense will be the same as the 2012 interest expense.	2013 interest expense will be the same as the average expense over the 2010–2012 time period.
Income taxes	2013 effective tax rate will be the same as the 2012 rate.	2013 effective tax rate will equal the blended statutory rate of 30%.	2013 effective tax rate will be the same as the average effective tax rate over the 2010–2012 time period.

1 Based on Exhibit 1, which of the following provides the strongest evidence that Chrome displays economies of scale?

   A   Increasing net sales

   B   Profit margins that are increasing with net sales

   C   Gross profit margins that are increasing with net sales

2 Based on Exhibit 2, the job candidate *most likely* using a bottom-up approach to model net sales is:

   A   Candidate A.

   B   Candidate B.

   C   Candidate C.

3 Based on Exhibit 2, the modeling approach used by Candidate B to project future net sales is *most accurately* classified as a:

   A   hybrid approach.

   B   top-down approach.

   C   bottom-up approach.

4 Based on Exhibits 1 and 2, Candidate C's forecast for cost of sales in 2013 is *closest* to:

A $18.3 million.

B $18.9 million.

C $19.3 million.

5 Based on Exhibits 1 and 2, Candidate A's forecast for selling, general, and administrative expenses in 2013 is *closest* to:

A $23.8 million.

B $25.5 million.

C $27.4 million.

6 Based on Exhibit 2, forecasted interest expense will reflect changes in Chrome's debt level under the forecast assumptions used by:

A Candidate A.

B Candidate B.

C Candidate C.

The following information relates to Questions 7–12

Nigel French, an analyst at Taurus Investment Management, is analyzing Archway Technologies, a manufacturer of luxury electronic auto equipment, at the request of his supervisor, Lukas Wright. French is asked to evaluate Archway's profitability over the past five years relative to its two main competitors, which are located in different countries with significantly different tax structures.

French begins by assessing Archway's competitive position within the luxury electronic auto equipment industry using Porter's five forces framework. A summary of French's industry analysis is presented in Exhibit 3.

Exhibit 3	Analysis of Luxury Electronic Auto Equipment Industry Using Porter's Five Forces Framework
Force	**Factors to Consider**
Threat of substitutes	Customer switching costs are high
Rivalry	Archway holds 60% of world market share; each of its two main competitors holds 15%
Bargaining power of suppliers	Primary inputs are considered basic commodities, and there are a large number of suppliers
Bargaining power of buyers	Luxury electronic auto equipment is very specialized (non-standardized)
Threat of new entrants	High fixed costs to enter industry

French notes that for the year just ended (2014), Archway's cost of goods sold was 30% of sales. To forecast Archway's income statement for 2015, French assumes that all companies in the industry will experience an inflation rate of 8% on the cost of goods sold. Exhibit 4 shows French's forecasts relating to Archway's price and volume changes.

Exhibit 4	Archway's 2015 Forecasted Price and Volume Changes
Average price increase per unit	5.00%
Volume growth	−3.00%

After putting together income statement projections for Archway, French forecasts Archway's balance sheet items; he uses Archway's historical efficiency ratios to forecast the company's working capital accounts.

Based on his financial forecast for Archway, French estimates a terminal value using a valuation multiple based on the company's average price-to-earnings multiple (P/E) over the past five years. Wright discusses with French how the terminal value estimate is sensitive to key assumptions about the company's future prospects. Wright asks French:

> "What change in the calculation of the terminal value would you make if a technological development that would adversely affect Archway was forecast to occur sometime beyond your financial forecast horizon?"

7 Which return metric should French use to assess Archway's five-year historic performance relative to its competitors?

   A Return on equity

   B Return on invested capital

   C Return on capital employed

8 Based on the current competitive landscape presented in Exhibit 3, French should conclude that Archway's ability to:

   A pass along price increases is high.

   B demand lower input prices from suppliers is low.

   C generate above-average returns on invested capital is low.

9 Based on the current competitive landscape presented in Exhibit 3, Archway's operating profit margins over the forecast horizon are *least likely* to:

   A decrease.

   B remain constant.

   C increase.

10 Based on Exhibit 4, Archway's forecasted gross profit margin for 2015 is *closest* to:

   A 62.7%.

   B 67.0%.

   C 69.1%.

11 French's approach to forecasting Archway's working capital accounts would be *most likely* classified as a:

   A hybrid approach.

   B top-down approach.

   C bottom-up approach.

12 The *most appropriate* response to Wright's question about the technological development is to:

   A increase the required return.

B decrease the price-to-earnings multiple.

C decrease the perpetual growth rate.

The following information relates to Questions 13–18

Gertrude Fromm is a transportation sector analyst at Tucana Investments. She is conducting an analysis of Omikroon, N.V., a publicly traded European transportation company that manufactures and sells scooters and commercial trucks.

Omikroon's petrol scooter division is the market leader in its sector and has two competitors. Omikroon's petrol scooters have a strong brand-name and a well-established distribution network. Given the strong branding established by the market leaders, the cost of entering the industry is high. But Fromm anticipates that inexpensive imported small petrol-fueled motorcycles may become substitutes for Omikroon's petrol scooters.

Fromm uses return on invested capital as the metric to assess Omikroon's performance.

Omikroon has just introduced the first electric scooter to the market at year-end 2014. The company's expectations are as follows:

- Competing electric scooters will reach the market in 2016.
- Electric scooters will not be a substitute for petrol scooters.
- The important research costs in 2015 and 2016 will lead to more efficient electric scooters.

Fromm decides to use a five-year forecast horizon for Omikroon after considering the following factors:

Factor 1   The annual portfolio turnover at Tucana investments is 30%.

Factor 2   The electronic scooter industry is expected to grow rapidly over the next 10 years.

Factor 3   Omikroon has announced it would acquire a light truck manufacturer that will be fully integrated to its truck division by 2016 and will add 2% to its total revenues.

Fromm uses the base case forecast for 2015 shown in Exhibit 5 to perform the following sensitivity analysis:

- The price of an imported specialty metal used for engine parts increases by 20%.
- This metal constitutes 4% of Omikroon's cost of sales.
- Omikroon will not be able to pass on the higher metal expense to its customers.

Exhibit 5	Omikroon's Selected Financial Forecasts for 2015 Base Case (€ millions)			
	Petrol Scooter Division	Commercial Truck Division	Electric Scooter Division	Total
Sales	99.05	45.71	7.62	152.38
Cost of sales				105.38

(continued)

	Petrol Scooter Division	Commercial Truck Division	Electric Scooter Division	Total
Gross profit				47.00
Operating profit				9.20

Exhibit 5   (Continued)

Omikroon will initially outsource its electric scooter parts. But manufacturing these parts in-house beginning in 2016 will imply changes to an existing factory. This factory cost €7 million three years ago and had an estimated useful life of 10 years. Fromm is evaluating two scenarios:

Scenario 1   Sell the existing factory for €5 million. Build a new factory costing €30 million with a useful life of 10 years.

Scenario 2   Refit the existing factory for €27 million.

13 Using Porter's five forces analysis, which of the following competitive factors is likely to have the *greatest* impact on Omikroon's petrol scooter pricing power?

A   Rivalry

B   Threat of substitutes

C   Threat of new entrants

14 The metric used by Fromm to assess Omikroon's performance takes into account:

A   degree of financial leverage.

B   operating liabilities relative to operating assets.

C   competitiveness relative to companies in other tax regimes.

15 Based on Omikroon's expectations, the gross profit margin of Omikroon's electric scooter division in 2016 is *most likely* to be affected by:

A   competition.

B   research costs.

C   cannibalization by petrol scooters.

16 Which factor *best* justifies the five-year forecast horizon for Omikroon selected by Fromm?

A   Factor 1

B   Factor 2

C   Factor 3

17 Fromm's sensitivity analysis will result in a decrease in the 2015 base case gross profit margin *closest to*:

A   0.55 percentage points.

B   0.80 percentage points.

C   3.32 percentage points.

18 Fromm's estimate of growth capital expenditure included in Omikroon's property, plant, and equipment under Scenario 2 should be:

A   lower than under Scenario 1.

B the same as under Scenario 1.

C higher than under Scenario 1.

SOLUTIONS

1 C is correct. Economies of scale are a situation in which average costs decrease with increasing sales volume. Chrome's gross margins have been increasing with net sales. Gross margins that increase with sales levels provide evidence of economies of scale, assuming that higher levels of sales reflect increased unit sales. Gross margin more directly reflects the cost of sales than does profit margin.

Metric	2010	2011	2012
Net sales	$46.8	$50.5	$53.9
Gross profit	28.6	32.1	35.1
Gross margin (gross profit/net sales)	61.11%	63.56%	65.12%

2 A is correct. A bottom-up approach for developing inputs to equity valuation models begins at the level of the individual company or a unit within the company. By modeling net sales using the average annual growth rate, Candidate A is using a bottom-up approach. Both Candidate B and Candidate C are using a top-down approach, which begins at the level of the overall economy.

3 B is correct. A top-down approach usually begins at the level of the overall economy. Candidate B assumes industry sales will grow at the same rate as nominal GDP but that Chrome will have a 2 percentage points decline in market share. Candidate B is not using any elements of a bottom-up approach; therefore, a hybrid approach is not being employed.

4 C is correct. Candidate C assumes that the 2013 gross margin will increase by 20 bps from 2012 and that net sales will grow at 50 bps slower than nominal GDP (nominal GDP = Real GDP + Inflation = 1.6% + 2.0% = 3.6%). Accordingly, the 2013 forecasted costs of sales are $19.27 million, rounded to $19.3 million.

Metric	Calculation	Result
2013 gross margin = 2012 gm + 20 bps	$35.1/$53.9 = 65.12% + 0.20% =	65.32%
2013 CoS/net sales = 100% − gross margin	100% − 65.32% =	34.68%
2013 net sales = 2012 net sales × (1 + Nominal GDP − 0.50%)	$53.9 million × (1 + 0.036 − 0.005) = $53.9 million × 1.031 =	$55.57 million
2013 cost of sales = 2013 net sales × CoS/net sales	$55.57 × 34.68% =	$19.27 million

5 B is correct. Candidate A assumes that the 2013 SG&A/net sales ratio will be the same as the average SG&A/net sales ratio over the 2010–2012 time period, and that net sales will grow at the annual average growth rate in net sales over the 2010–2012 time period. Accordingly, the 2013 forecasted selling, general, and administrative expenses are $25.5 million.

Metric	Calculation	Result
Average SG&A/net sales, 2010–2012*	(41.24% + 44.55% + 46.57%)/3 =	44.12%
Average annual growth sales in net sales, 2010–2012**	(7.91% + 6.73%)/2 =	7.32%

Metric	Calculation	Result
2013 net sales = 2012 net sales × (1 + Average annual growth rate in net sales)	$53.9 million × 1.0732 =	$57.85 million
2013 SG&A = 2013 net sales × Average SG&A/net sales	$57.85 million × 44.12% =	$25.52 million

* SG&A/net sales ratios are calculated as follows:

Metric	2010	2011	2012
Net Sales	$46.8	$50.5	$53.9
SG&A expenses	10.3	22.5	25.1
SG&A-to-sales ratio	41.24%	44.55%	46.57%

** Growth rate in net sales is calculated as follows:

Year	Calculation
2011	($50.5/$46.8) − 1 = 7.91%
2012	($53.9/$50.5) − 1 = 6.73%

6 A is correct. In forecasting financing costs such as interest expense, the debt/equity structure of a company is a key determinant. Accordingly, a method that recognizes the relationship between the income statement account (interest expense) and the balance sheet account (debt) would be a preferable method for forecasting interest expense when compared with methods that forecast based solely on the income statement account. By using the effective interest rate (interest expense divided by average gross debt), Candidate A is taking the debt/equity structure into account whereas Candidate B (who forecasts 2013 interest expense to be the same as 2012 interest expense) and Candidate C (who forecasts 2013 interest expense to be the same as the 2010–2012 average interest expense) are not taking the balance sheet into consideration.

7 C is correct. The return on capital employed (ROCE) is a pre-tax return measure that can be useful in the peer comparison of companies in countries with different tax structures. Archway's two main competitors are located in different countries with significantly different tax structures, and therefore, a pre-tax measure of return on capital is better than an after-tax measure.

8 A is correct. Porter's five forces framework in Exhibit 3 describes an industry with high barriers to entry, high customer switching costs (suggesting a low threat of substitutes), and a specialized product (suggesting low bargaining power of buyers). Furthermore, the primary production inputs from the large group of suppliers are considered basic commodities (suggesting low bargaining power of suppliers). These favorable industry characteristics will likely enable Archway to pass along price increases and generate above-average returns on invested capital.

9 A is correct. The current favorable characteristics of the industry (high barriers to entry, low bargaining power of suppliers and buyers, low threat of substitutes), coupled with Archway's dominant market share position, is likely to lead to Archway's profit margins being at least equal to or greater than current levels over the forecast horizon.

10 C is correct. The calculation of Archway's gross profit margin for 2015, which reflects the industry-wide 8% inflation on cost of goods sold (COGS), is calculated as follows:

Revenue growth	1.85%
Cost of goods sold increase	4.76%
Forecasted revenue (Base revenue = 100)	101.85
Forecasted COGS (Base COGS = 30)	31.43
Forecasted gross profit	70.42
Forecasted gross profit margin	69.14%

Revenue growth = (1 + Price increase for revenue) × (1 + Volume growth) − 1

Revenue growth = (1.05) × (0.97) − 1 = 1.85%

COGS increase = (1 + Price increase for COGS) × (1 + Volume growth) − 1

COGS increase = (1.08) × (0.97) − 1 = 4.76%

Forecasted revenue = Base revenue × Revenue growth increase

Forecasted revenue = 100 × 1.0185 = 101.85

Forecasted COGS = Base COGS × COGS increase

Forecasted COGS = 30 × 1.0476 = 31.43

Forecasted gross profit = Forecasted revenue − Forecasted COGS

Forecasted gross profit = 101.85 − 31.43 = 70.42

Forecasted gross profit margin = Forecasted gross profit/Forecasted revenue

Forecasted gross profit margin = 70.42/101.85 = 69.14%

11 C is correct. French is using a bottom-up approach to forecast Archway's working capital accounts by using the company's historical efficiency ratios to project future performance.

12 B is correct. If the future growth or profitability of a company is likely to be lower than the historical average (in this case, because of a potential technological development), then the target multiple should reflect a discount to the historical multiple to reflect this difference in growth and/or profitability. If a multiple is used to derive the terminal value of a company, the choice of the multiple should be consistent with the long-run expectations for growth and required return. French tells Wright he believes that such a technological development may have an adverse impact on Archway beyond the forecast horizon.

13 B is correct. Inexpensive, small imported motorcycles are substitutes for petrol scooters and may increasingly have an impact on Omikroon's petrol scooter pricing power.

14 B is correct. Return on invested capital is net operating profit minus adjusted taxes divided by invested capital, where invested capital is defined as operating assets minus operating liabilities.

15 A is correct. Competition from other electric scooter manufacturers is expected to begin in one year. After this time, competing electric scooters could lead to lower demand for Omikroon's electric scooters and affect Omikroon's gross profit margin.

16 B is correct. The electric scooter industry is new and growing and the contribution of Omikroon's electric scooter division is forecast to expand over 10 years.

17 A is correct. The sensitivity analysis consists of an increase of 20% in the price of an input that constitutes 4% of cost of sales. Change in gross profit margin because of that increase is calculated as the change in cost of sales because of price increase divided by sales:

= (Cost of sales × 0.04 × 0.2)/Sales

= (105.38 × 0.04 × 0.2)/152.38

= 0.0055

18 C is correct. In Scenario 2, growth capital expenditure of €27 million for the refit of the existing idle factory is higher than the growth capital expenditure in Scenario 1 of €25 million. The €25 million is the cost of building a new factory for €30 million less the proceeds from the sale of the existing idle factory of €5 million.

Discounted Dividend Valuation

**by Jerald E. Pinto, PhD, CFA, Elaine Henry, PhD, CFA,
Thomas R. Robinson, PhD, CFA, and John D. Stowe, PhD, CFA**

*Jerald E. Pinto, PhD, CFA, is at CFA Institute (USA). Elaine Henry, PhD, CFA, is at
Fordham University (USA). Thomas R. Robinson, PhD, CFA, is at CFA Institute (USA).
John D. Stowe, PhD, CFA, is at Ohio University (USA).*

LEARNING OUTCOMES

Mastery	The candidate should be able to:
☐	a. compare dividends, free cash flow, and residual income as inputs to discounted cash flow models and identify investment situations for which each measure is suitable;
☐	b. calculate and interpret the value of a common stock using the dividend discount model (DDM) for single and multiple holding periods;
☐	c. calculate the value of a common stock using the Gordon growth model and explain the model's underlying assumptions;
☐	d. calculate and interpret the implied growth rate of dividends using the Gordon growth model and current stock price;
☐	e. calculate and interpret the present value of growth opportunities (PVGO) and the component of the leading price-to-earnings ratio (P/E) related to PVGO;
☐	f. calculate and interpret the justified leading and trailing P/Es using the Gordon growth model;
☐	g. calculate the value of noncallable fixed-rate perpetual preferred stock;
☐	h. describe strengths and limitations of the Gordon growth model and justify its selection to value a company's common shares;
☐	i. explain the assumptions and justify the selection of the two-stage DDM, the H-model, the three-stage DDM, or spreadsheet modeling to value a company's common shares;
☐	j. explain the growth phase, transitional phase, and maturity phase of a business;

(continued)

The data and examples for this reading were updated in 2014 by Professor Stephen Wilcox, CFA.

Equity Asset Valuation, Second Edition, by Jerald E. Pinto, CFA, Elaine Henry, CFA, Thomas R. Robinson,
CFA, and John D. Stowe, CFA. Copyright © 2009 by CFA Institute.

LEARNING OUTCOMES

Mastery	The candidate should be able to:
☐	k. describe terminal value and explain alternative approaches to determining the terminal value in a DDM;
☐	l. calculate and interpret the value of common shares using the two-stage DDM, the H-model, and the three-stage DDM;
☐	m. estimate a required return based on any DDM, including the Gordon growth model and the H-model;
☐	n. explain the use of spreadsheet modeling to forecast dividends and to value common shares;
☐	o. calculate and interpret the sustainable growth rate of a company and demonstrate the use of DuPont analysis to estimate a company's sustainable growth rate;
☐	p. evaluate whether a stock is overvalued, fairly valued, or undervalued by the market based on a DDM estimate of value.

1   INTRODUCTION

Common stock represents an ownership interest in a business. A business in its operations generates a stream of cash flows, and as owners of the business, common stockholders have an equity ownership claim on those future cash flows. Beginning with John Burr Williams (1938), analysts have developed this insight into a group of valuation models known as discounted cash flow (DCF) valuation models. DCF models—which view the intrinsic value of common stock as the present value of its expected future cash flows—are a fundamental tool in both investment management and investment research. This reading is the first of several that describe DCF models and address how to apply those models in practice.

Although the principles behind discounted cash flow valuation are simple, applying the theory to equity valuation can be challenging. Four broad steps in applying DCF analysis to equity valuation are:

■ choosing the class of DCF model—equivalently, selecting a specific definition of cash flow;

■ forecasting the cash flows;

■ choosing a discount rate methodology; and

■ estimating the discount rate.

In this reading, we take the perspective that dividends—distributions to shareholders authorized by a company's board of directors—are an appropriate definition of cash flows. The class of models based on this idea is called dividend discount models, or DDMs. The basic objective of any DDM is to value a stock. The variety of implementations corresponds to different ways to model a company's future stream of dividend payments. The steps of choosing a discount rate methodology and estimating the discount rate involve the same considerations for all DCF models, so they have been presented separately in a reading on return concepts.

The reading is organized as follows: Section 2 provides an overview of present value models. A general statement of the dividend discount model follows in Section 3. Forecasting dividends, individually and in detail, into the indefinite future is not generally practicable, so the dividend-forecasting problem is usually simplified. One approach is to assign dividends to a stylized growth pattern. The simplest pattern—dividends growing at a constant rate forever—is the constant growth (or Gordon growth) model, discussed in Section 4. For some companies, it is more appropriate to view earnings and dividends as having multiple stages of growth; multistage dividend discount models are presented in Section 5 along with spreadsheet modeling. Section 6 lays out the determinants of dividend growth rates, and the final section summarizes the reading.

PRESENT VALUE MODELS

2

Present value models as a group constitute a demanding and rigorous approach for valuing assets. In this section, we discuss the economic rationale for valuing an asset as the present value of its expected future cash flows. We also discuss alternative definitions of cash flows and present the major alternative methods for estimating the discount rate.

2.1 Valuation Based on the Present Value of Future Cash Flows

The value of an asset must be related to the benefits or returns we expect to receive from holding it. Those returns are called the asset's future cash flows (we will define *cash flow* more concretely and technically later). We also need to recognize that a given amount of money received in the future is worth less than the same amount of money received today. Money received today gives us the option of immediately spending and consuming it, so money has a time value. Therefore, when valuing an asset, before adding up the estimated future cash flows, we must **discount** each cash flow back to the present: the cash flow's value is reduced with respect to how far away it is in time. The two elements of discounted cash flow valuation—estimating the cash flows and discounting the cash flows to account for the time value of money—provide the economic rationale for discounted cash flow valuation. In the simplest case, in which the timing and amounts of future cash flows are known with certainty, if we invest an amount equal to the present value of future cash flows at the given discount rate, that investment will replicate all of the asset's cash flows (with no money left over).

For some assets, such as government debt, cash flows may be essentially known with certainty—that is, they are default risk free. The appropriate discount rate for such a risk-free cash flow is a risk-free rate of interest. For example, if an asset has a single, certain cash flow of $100 to be received in two years, and the risk-free interest rate is 5 percent a year, the value of the asset is the present value of $100 discounted at the risk-free rate, $100/(1.05)^2 = $90.70.

In contrast to risk-free debt, future cash flows for equity investments are not known with certainty—they are risky. Introducing risk makes applying the present value approach much more challenging. The most common approach to dealing with risky cash flows involves two adjustments relative to the risk-free case. First, discount the *expected* value of the cash flows, viewing the cash flows as random variables.[1] Second, adjust the discount rate to reflect the risk of the cash flows.

---

[1] The expected value of a random quantity is the mean, or average, value of its possible outcomes, in which each outcome's weight in the average is its probability of occurrence. See DeFusco, McLeavey, Pinto, and Runkle (2004) for all statistical concepts used in this reading.

The following equation expresses the concept that an asset's value is the present value of its (expected) future cash flows:

$$V_0 = \sum_{t=1}^{n} \frac{CF_t}{(1+r)^t} \tag{1}$$

where

V_0 = the value of the asset at time $t = 0$ (today)

n = number of cash flows in the life of the asset (n is set equal to ∞ for equities)

CF_t = the cash flow (or the expected cash flow, for risky cash flows) at time t

r = the discount rate or required rate of return

For simplicity, the discount rate in Equation 1 is represented as the same for all time periods (i.e., a flat term structure of discount rates is assumed). The analyst has the latitude in this model, however, to apply different discount rates to different cash flows.[2]

Equation 1 gives an asset's value from the perspective of today ($t = 0$). Likewise, an asset's value at some point in the future equals the value of all subsequent cash flows discounted back to that point in time. Example 1 illustrates these points.

EXAMPLE 1

Value as the Present Value of Future Cash Flows

An asset is expected to generate cash flows of $100 in one year, $150 in two years, and $200 in three years. The value of this asset today, using a 10 percent discount rate, is

$$V_0 = \frac{100}{(1.10)^1} + \frac{150}{(1.10)^2} + \frac{200}{(1.10)^3}$$

$$= 90.909 + 123.967 + 150.263 = \$365.14$$

The value at $t = 0$ is $365.14. The same logic is used to value an asset at a future date. The value of the asset at $t = 1$ is the present value, discounted back to $t = 1$, of all cash flows after this point. This value, V_1, is

$$V_1 = \frac{150}{(1.10)^1} + \frac{200}{(1.10)^2}$$

$$= 136.364 + 165.289 = \$301.65$$

At any point in time, the asset's value is the value of future cash flows (CF) discounted back to that point. Because V_1 represents the value of CF_2 and CF_3 at $t = 1$, the value of the asset at $t = 0$ is also the present value of CF_1 and V_1:

$$V_0 = \frac{100}{(1.10)^1} + \frac{301.653}{(1.10)^1}$$

$$= 90.909 + 274.23 = \$365.14$$

---

2 Different discount rates could reflect different degrees of cash flow riskiness or different risk-free rates at different time horizons. Differences in cash flow riskiness may be caused by differences in business risk, operating risk (use of fixed assets in production), or financial risk or leverage (use of debt in the capital structure). The simple expression given, however, is adequate for this discussion.

Finding V_0 as the present value of CF_1, CF_2, and CF_3 is logically equivalent to finding V_0 as the present value of CF_1 and V_1.

In the next section, we present an overview of three alternative definitions of cash flow. The selected cash flow concept defines the type of DCF model we can use: the dividend discount model, the free cash flow model, or the residual income model. We also broadly characterize the types of valuation problems for which analysts often choose a particular model. (Further details are supplied when each model is discussed individually.)

2.2 Streams of Expected Cash Flows

In present value models of stock valuation, the three most widely used definitions of returns are dividends, free cash flow, and residual income. We discuss each definition in turn.

The dividend discount model defines cash flows as dividends. The basic argument for using this definition of cash flow is that an investor who buys and holds a share of stock generally receives cash returns only in the form of dividends.[3] In practice, analysts usually view investment value as driven by earnings. Does the definition of cash flow as dividends ignore earnings not distributed to shareholders as dividends? Reinvested earnings should provide the basis for increased future dividends. Therefore, the DDM accounts for reinvested earnings when it takes all future dividends into account. Because dividends are less volatile than earnings and other return concepts, the relative stability of dividends may make DDM values less sensitive to short-run fluctuations in underlying value than alternative DCF models. Analysts often view DDM values as reflecting long-run intrinsic value.

A stock either pays dividends or does not pay dividends. A company might not pay dividends on its stock because the company is not profitable and has no cash to distribute. Also, a company might not pay dividends for the opposite reason: because it is very profitable. For example, a company may reinvest all earnings—paying no dividends—to take advantage of profitable growth opportunities. As the company matures and faces fewer attractive investment opportunities, it may initiate dividends. Generally, mature, profitable companies tend to pay dividends and are reluctant to reduce the level of dividends.[4]

Dividend policy practices have international differences and change through time, even in one market. Typically, a lower percentage of companies in a given US stock market index have paid dividends than have companies in a comparable European stock market index. Wanger (2007) noted a much higher propensity for European and Asian small-cap companies to pay dividends compared with US companies. In addition, the following broad trends in dividend policy have been observed:

- The fraction of companies paying cash dividends has been in long-term decline in most developed markets (e.g., the United States, Canada, the European Union, the United Kingdom, and Japan).[5] For example, Fama and French (2001) found that although 66.5 percent of US stocks paid dividends in 1978, only 20.8 percent did in 1999, with later research documenting a small rebound since 2001.[6] In the United States, the decline was caused by a reduced propensity to

---

3 Corporations can also effectively distribute cash to stockholders through stock repurchases (also called buybacks). This fact, however, does not affect the argument.
4 See Lintner (1956) and Grullon, Paye, Underwood, and Weston (2007).
5 See von Eije and Megginson (2008) and references therein.
6 Julio and Ikenberry (2004).

pay dividends (controlling for differences in profitability and growth opportunities) and by growth in the number of smaller, publicly traded companies with low profitability and large growth opportunities.[7]

▪ Since the early 1980s in the United States[8] and the early 1990s in the United Kingdom and continental Europe,[9] the fraction of companies engaging in share repurchases (an alternative way to distribute cash to shareholders) has trended upwards.

Analysts will frequently need to value non-dividend-paying shares. Can the DDM be applied to non-dividend-paying shares? In theory it can, as is illustrated later, but in practice it generally is not.

Predicting the timing of dividend initiation and the magnitude of future dividends without any prior dividend data or specifics about dividend policy to guide the analysis is generally not practical. For a non-dividend-paying company, analysts usually prefer a model that defines returns at the company level (as free cash flow or residual income—these concepts are defined shortly) rather than at the stockholder level (as dividends). Another consideration in the choice of models relates to ownership perspective. An investor purchasing a small ownership share does not have the ability to meaningfully influence the timing or magnitude of the distribution of the company's cash to shareholders. That perspective is the one taken in applying a dividend discount model. The only access to the company's value is through the receipt of dividends, and dividend policy is taken as a given. If dividends do not bear an understandable relation to value creation in the company, applying the DDM to value the stock is prone to error.

Generally, the definition of returns as dividends, and the DDM, is most suitable when:

▪ the company is dividend-paying (i.e., the analyst has a dividend record to analyze);

▪ the board of directors has established a dividend policy that bears an understandable and consistent relationship to the company's profitability; and

▪ the investor takes a noncontrol perspective.

Often, companies with established dividends are seasoned companies, profitable but operating outside the economy's fastest-growing subsectors. Professional analysts often apply a dividend discount model to value the common stock of such companies.

EXAMPLE 2

Coca-Cola Bottling Company and Hormel Foods: Is the DDM an Appropriate Choice?

As director of equity research at a brokerage, you have final responsibility in the choice of valuation models. An analyst covering consumer/noncyclicals has approached you about the use of a dividend discount model for valuing the equity of two companies: Coca-Cola Bottling Company Consolidated (NASDAQ:

---

7 Fama and French (2001).
8 Important in the United States was the adoption of Securities and Exchange Commission Rule 10b-18 in 1982, which relieved companies from concerns of stock manipulation in repurchasing shares so long as companies follow certain guidelines.
9 See von Eije and Megginson (2008).

COKE) and Hormel Foods (NYSE: HRL). Exhibit 1 gives the most recent 15 years of data. (In the table, EPS is earnings per share, DPS is dividends per share, and payout ratio is DPS divided by EPS.)

Exhibit 1   COKE and HRL: The Earnings and Dividends Record

Year	COKE			HRL		
	EPS ($)	DPS ($)	Payout Ratio (%)	EPS ($)	DPS ($)	Payout Ratio (%)
2012	3.08	1.00	32	1.86	0.60	32
2011	3.08	1.00	32	1.74	0.51	29
2010	3.94	1.00	25	1.51	0.42	28
2009	3.56	1.00	28	1.27	0.38	30
2008	1.77	1.00	56	1.04	0.37	36
2007	2.17	1.00	46	1.07	0.30	28
2006	2.55	1.00	39	1.03	0.28	27
2005	2.53	1.00	40	0.91	0.26	29
2004	2.41	1.00	41	0.78	0.23	29
2003	3.40	1.00	29	0.67	0.21	31
2002	2.56	1.00	39	0.68	0.20	29
2001	1.07	1.00	93	0.65	0.19	29
2000	0.71	1.00	141	0.61	0.18	30
1999	0.37	1.00	270	0.54	0.17	31
1998	1.75	1.00	57	0.41	0.16	39

Source: The Value Line Investment Survey, sec.edgar-online.com.

Answer the following questions based on the information in Exhibit 1:

1   State whether a dividend discount model is an appropriate choice for valuing COKE. Explain your answer.

2   State whether a dividend discount model is an appropriate choice for valuing HRL. Explain your answer.

Solution to 1:

Based only on the data given in Exhibit 1, a DDM does not appear to be an appropriate choice for valuing COKE. COKE's dividends have been $1.00 per share since 1998. In 1998, COKE's EPS was $1.75 but fell sharply to $0.37 in 1999. EPS recovered to $2.56 in 2002 but has varied from $1.77 to $3.94 since with a value of $3.08 in 2012. In short, during the ten year period of 2002–2012, COKE achieved compound annual growth of just 1.9 percent with considerable variability while DPS were flat. Based on the record presented, it is hard to discern an understandable and consistent relationship of dividends to earnings. Because dividends do not appear to adjust to reflect changes in profitability, applying a DDM to COKE is probably inappropriate. Valuing COKE on another basis, such as a company-level definition of cash flows, appears to be more appropriate.

Solution to 2:

The historical earnings of HRL show a long-term upward trend, with the exception of 2003 and 2008. Although you might want to research those divergent payout ratios, HRL's dividends have generally followed its growth in earnings.

Earnings per share and dividends per share grew at comparable compound annual growth rates of 11.4 percent and 9.9 percent during the entire period. During the most recent four year period, EPS and DPS also grew at comparable rates, reflecting a dividend payout ratio varying only between 28 percent and 32 percent. In summary, because HRL is dividend-paying and dividends bear an understandable and consistent relationship to earnings, using a DDM to value HRL is appropriate.

Valuation is a forward-looking exercise. In practice, the analyst would check for public disclosures concerning changes in dividend policy going forward.

A second definition of returns is free cash flow. The term *cash flow* has been given many meanings in different contexts. Earlier the term was used informally, referring to returns to ownership (equity). We now want to give it a more technical meaning, related to accounting usage. Over a given period of time, a company can add to cash (or use up cash) by selling goods and services. This money is cash flow from operations (for that time period). Cash flow from operations is the critical cash flow concept addressing a business's underlying economics. Companies can also generate (or use up) cash in two other ways. First, a company affects cash through buying and selling assets, including investment and disinvestment in plant and equipment. Second, a company can add to or reduce cash through its financing activities. Financing includes debt and equity. For example, issuing bonds increases cash, and buying back stock decreases cash (all else equal).[10]

Assets supporting current sales may need replacement because of obsolescence or wear and tear, and the company may need new assets to take advantage of profitable growth opportunities. The concept of free cash flow responds to the reality that, for a going concern, some of the cash flow from operations is not "free" but rather needs to be committed to reinvestment and new investment in assets. **Free cash flow to the firm** (FCFF) is cash flow from operations minus capital expenditures. Capital expenditures—reinvestment in new assets, including working capital—are needed to maintain the company as a going concern, so only that part of cash flow from operations remaining after such reinvestment is "free." (This definition is conceptual; a later reading defines free cash flow concepts in detail.) FCFF is the part of the cash flow generated by the company's operations that can be withdrawn by bondholders and stockholders without economically impairing the company. Conceptually, the value of common equity is the present value of expected future FCFF—the total value of the company—minus the market value of outstanding debt.

Another approach to valuing equity works with free cash flow to equity. **Free cash flow to equity** (FCFE) is cash flow from operations minus capital expenditures, or FCFF, from which we net all payments to debtholders (interest and principal repayments net of new debt issues). Debt has a claim on the cash of the company that must be satisfied before any money can be paid to stockholders, so money paid on debt is not available to common stockholders. Conceptually, common equity can be valued as the present value of expected FCFE. FCFF is a predebt free cash flow concept; FCFE is a postdebt free cash flow concept. The FCFE model is the baseline free cash

---

10 Internationally, accounting definitions may not be fully consistent with the presented concepts in distinguishing between types of sources and uses of cash. Although the implementation details are not the focus here, an example can be given. US generally accepted accounting principles include a financing item, net interest payments, in *cash flow from operating activities.* So, careful analysts working with US accounting data often add back after-tax net interest payments to cash flow from operating activities when calculating cash flow from operations. Under International Accounting Standards, companies may or may not include interest expense as an operating cash flow.

flow valuation model for equity, but the FCFF model may be easier to apply in several cases, such as when the company's leverage (debt in its capital structure) is expected to change significantly over time.

Valuation using a free cash flow concept is popular in current investment practice. Free cash flow (FCFF or FCFE) can be calculated for any company. The record of free cash flows can also be examined even for a non-dividend-paying company. FCFE can be viewed as measuring what a company can afford to pay out in dividends. Even for dividend-paying companies, a free cash flow model valuation may be preferred when dividends exceed or fall short of FCFE by significant amounts.[11] FCFE also represents cash flow that can be redeployed outside the company without affecting the company's capital investments. A controlling equity interest can effect such redeployment. As a result, free cash flow valuation is appropriate for investors who want to take a control perspective. (Even a small shareholder may want to take such a perspective when potential exists for the company to be acquired, because stock price should reflect the price an acquirer would pay.)

Just as there are cases in which an analyst would find it impractical to apply the DDM, applying the free cash flow approach is a problem in some cases. Some companies have intense capital demands and, as a result, have negative expected free cash flows far into the future. As one example, a retailer may be constantly constructing new outlets and be far from saturating even its domestic market. Even if the retailer is currently very profitable, free cash flow may be negative indefinitely because of the level of capital expenditures. The present value of a series of negative free cash flows is a negative number: The use of a free cash flow model may entail a long forecast horizon to capture the point at which expected free cash flow turns positive. The uncertainty associated with distant forecasts may be considerable. In such cases, the analyst may have more confidence using another approach, such as residual income valuation.

Generally, defining returns as free cash flow and using the FCFE (and FCFF) models are most suitable when:

- the company is not dividend-paying;
- the company is dividend-paying but dividends significantly exceed or fall short of free cash flow to equity;
- the company's free cash flows align with the company's profitability within a forecast horizon with which the analyst is comfortable; and
- the investor takes a control perspective.

The third and final definition of returns that we will discuss in this overview is residual income. Conceptually, **residual income** for a given time period is the earnings for that period in excess of the investors' required return on beginning-of-period investment (common stockholders' equity). Suppose shareholders' initial investment is $200 million, and the required rate of return on the stock is 8 percent. The required rate of return is investors' **opportunity cost** for investing in the stock: the highest expected return available from other equally risky investments, which is the return that investors forgo when investing in the stock. The company earns $18 million in the course of a year. How much value has the company added for shareholders? A return of 0.08 × $200 million = $16 million just meets the amount investors could have earned in an equivalent-risk investment (by the definition of opportunity cost). Only the residual or excess amount of $18 million – $16 million = $2 million represents value added, or an economic gain, to shareholders. So, $2 million is the company's residual income for the period. The residual income approach attempts to match

---

11 In theory, when period-by-period dividends equal FCFE, the DDM and FCFE models should value stock identically, if all other assumptions are consistent. See Miller and Modigliani (1961), a classic reference for the mathematics and theory of present value models of stock value.

profits to the time period in which they are earned (but not necessarily realized as cash). In contrast to accounting net income (which has the same matching objective in principle), however, residual income attempts to measure the value added in excess of opportunity costs.

The residual income model states that a stock's value is book value per share plus the present value of expected future residual earnings. (**Book value per share** is common stockholders' equity divided by the number of common shares outstanding.) In contrast to the dividend and free cash flow models, the residual income model introduces a stock concept, book value per share, into the present value expression. Nevertheless, the residual income model can be viewed as a restatement of the dividend discount model, using a company-level return concept. Dividends are paid out of earnings and are related to earnings and book value through a simple expression.[12] The residual income model is a useful addition to an analyst's toolbox. Because the record of residual income can always be calculated, a residual income model can be used for both dividend-paying and non-dividend-paying stocks. Analysts may choose a residual income approach for companies with negative expected free cash flows within their comfortable forecast horizon. In such cases, a residual income valuation often brings the recognition of value closer to the present as compared with a free cash flow valuation, producing higher value estimates.

The residual income model has an attractive focus on profitability in relation to opportunity costs.[13] Knowledgeable application of the residual income model requires a detailed knowledge of accrual accounting; consequently, in cases for which the dividend discount model is suitable, analysts may prefer it as the simpler choice. Management sometimes exercises its discretion within allowable accounting practices to distort the accuracy of its financials as a reflection of economic performance. If the quality of accounting disclosure is good, the analyst may be able to calculate residual income by making appropriate adjustments (to reported net income and book value, in particular). In some cases, the degree of distortion and the quality of accounting disclosure can be such that the application of the residual income model is error-prone.

Generally, the definition of returns as residual income, and the residual income model, is most suitable when:

- the company is not paying dividends, as an alternative to a free cash flow model, or
- the company's expected free cash flows are negative within the analyst's comfortable forecast horizon.

In summary, the three most widely used definitions of returns to investors are dividends, free cash flow, and residual income. Although claims are often made that one cash flow definition is inherently superior to the rest—often following changing fashions in investment practice—a more flexible viewpoint is practical. The analyst may find that one model is more suitable to a particular valuation problem. The analyst may also develop more expertise in applying one type of model. In practice, skill in application—in particular, the quality of forecasts—is frequently decisive for the usefulness of the analyst's work.

---

12 Book value of equity at t = (Book value of equity at $t - 1$) + (Earnings over $t - 1$ to t) − (Dividends paid at t), as long as anything that goes through the balance sheet (affecting book value) first goes through the income statement (reflected in earnings), apart from ownership transactions. The condition that all changes in the book value of equity other than transactions with owners are reflected in income is known as **clean surplus accounting**. US and international accounting standards do not always follow clean surplus accounting; the analyst, therefore, in using this expression, must critically evaluate whether accounting-based results conform to clean surplus accounting and, if they do not, adjust them appropriately.

13 Executive compensation schemes are sometimes based on a residual income concept, including branded variations such as Economic Value Added (EVA®) from Stern Stewart & Co.

In the next section, we present the general form of the dividend discount model as a prelude to discussing the particular implementations of the model that are suitable for different sets of attributes of the company being valued.

THE DIVIDEND DISCOUNT MODEL

3

Investment analysts use a wide range of models and techniques to estimate the value of common stock, including present value models. In Section 2.2, we discussed three common definitions of returns for use in present value analysis: dividends, free cash flow, and residual income. In this section, we develop the most general form of the dividend discount model.

The DDM is the simplest and oldest present value approach to valuing stock. In a survey of CFA Institute[14] members by Block (1999), 42 percent of respondents viewed the DDM as "very important" or "moderately important" for determining the value of individual stocks. Beginning in 1989, the *Merrill Lynch Institutional Factor Survey* has assessed the popularity of 23 valuation factors and methods among a group of institutional investors. The highest recorded usage level of the DDM was in the first survey in 1989, when more than 50 percent of respondents reported using the DDM. Since 1993, reported usage has been in the 25 to 40 percent range with usage increasing to over 35 percent in 2012. Besides its continuing significant position in practice, the DDM has an important place in both academic and practitioner equity research. The DDM is, for all these reasons, a basic tool in equity valuation.

3.1 The Expression for a Single Holding Period

From the perspective of a shareholder who buys and holds a share of stock, the cash flows he or she will obtain are the dividends paid on it and the market price of the share when he or she sells it. The future selling price should in turn reflect expectations about dividends subsequent to the sale. In this section, we will show how this argument leads to the most general form of the dividend discount model. In addition, the general expression developed for a finite holding period corresponds to one practical approach to DDM valuation; in that approach, the analyst forecasts dividends over a finite horizon, as well as the terminal sales price.

If an investor wishes to buy a share of stock and hold it for one year, the value of that share of stock today is the present value of the expected dividend to be received on the stock plus the present value of the expected selling price in one year:

$$V_0 = \frac{D_1}{\left(1+r\right)^1} + \frac{P_1}{\left(1+r\right)^1} = \frac{D_1 + P_1}{\left(1+r\right)^1} \tag{2}$$

where

V_0 = the value of a share of stock today, at $t = 0$

P_1 = the expected price per share at $t = 1$

D_1 = the expected dividend per share for Year 1, assumed to be paid at the end of the year at $t = 1$

r = the required rate of return on the stock

---

14 Then called and referred to in the Block (1999) paper as the Association for Investment Management and Research. The name was changed to CFA Institute in 2004.

Equation 2 applies, to a single holding period, the principle that an asset's value is the present value of its future cash flows. In this case, the expected cash flows are the dividend in one year (for simplicity, assumed to be received as one payment at the end of the year)[15] and the price of the stock in one year.

EXAMPLE 3

DDM Value with a Single Holding Period

Suppose that you expect Carrefour SA (NYSE Euronext Paris: CA) to pay a €0.58 dividend next year. You expect the price of CA stock to be €27.00 in one year. The required rate of return for CA stock is 9 percent. What is your estimate of the value of CA stock?

Discounting the expected dividend of €0.58 and the expected sales price of €27.00 at the required return on equity of 9 percent, we obtain

$$V_0 = \frac{D_1 + P_1}{(1+r)^1} = \frac{0.58 + 27.00}{(1 + 0.09)^1} = \frac{27.58}{1.09} = 25.30$$

3.2 The Expression for Multiple Holding Periods

If an investor plans to hold a stock for two years, the value of the stock is the present value of the expected dividend in Year 1, plus the present value of the expected dividend in Year 2, plus the present value of the expected selling price at the end of Year 2.

$$V_0 = \frac{D_1}{(1+r)^1} + \frac{D_2}{(1+r)^2} + \frac{P_2}{(1+r)^2} = \frac{D_1}{(1+r)^1} + \frac{D_2 + P_2}{(1+r)^2} \qquad (3)$$

The expression for the DDM value of a share of stock for any finite holding period is a straightforward extension of the expressions for one-year and two-year holding periods. For an n-period model, the value of a stock is the present value of the expected dividends for the n periods plus the present value of the expected price in n periods (at $t = n$).

$$V_0 = \frac{D_1}{(1+r)^1} + \cdots + \frac{D_n}{(1+r)^n} + \frac{P_n}{(1+r)^n} \qquad (4)$$

If we use summation notation to represent the present value of the first n expected dividends, the general expression for an n-period holding period or investment horizon can be written as

$$V_0 = \sum_{t=1}^{n} \frac{D_t}{(1+r)^t} + \frac{P_n}{(1+r)^n} \qquad (5)$$

Equation 5 is significant in DDM application because analysts may make individual forecasts of dividends over some finite horizon (often two to five years) and then estimate the terminal price, P_n, based on one of a number of approaches. (We will discuss valuation using a finite forecasting horizon in Section 5.) Example 4 reviews the mechanics of this calculation.

---

15 Throughout the discussion of the DDM, we assume that dividends for a period are paid in one sum at the end of the period.

EXAMPLE 4

Finding the Stock Price for a Five-Year Forecast Horizon

For the next five years, the annual dividends of a stock are expected to be $2.00, $2.10, $2.20, $3.50, and $3.75. In addition, the stock price is expected to be $40.00 in five years. If the required return on equity is 10 percent, what is the value of this stock?

The present values of the expected future cash flows can be written out as

$$V_0 = \frac{2.00}{(1.10)^1} + \frac{2.10}{(1.10)^2} + \frac{2.20}{(1.10)^3} + \frac{3.50}{(1.10)^4} + \frac{3.75}{(1.10)^5} + \frac{40.00}{(1.10)^5}$$

Calculating and summing these present values gives a stock value of $V_0 = 1.818 + 1.736 + 1.653 + 2.391 + 2.328 + 24.837 = \$34.76$.

The five dividends have a total present value of $9.926 and the terminal stock value has a present value of $24.837, for a total stock value of $34.76.

With a finite holding period, whether one, two, five, or some other number of years, the dividend discount model finds the value of stock as the sum of 1) the present values of the expected dividends during the holding period, and 2) the present value of the expected stock price at the end of the holding period. As the holding period is increased by one year, we have an extra expected dividend term. In the limit (i.e., if the holding period extends into the indefinite future), the stock's value is the present value of all expected future dividends.

$$V_0 = \frac{D_1}{(1+r)^1} + \ldots + \frac{D_n}{(1+r)^n} + \ldots \qquad \textbf{(6)}$$

This value can be expressed with summation notation as

$$V_0 = \sum_{t=1}^{\infty} \frac{D_t}{(1+r)^t} \qquad \textbf{(7)}$$

Equation 7 is the general form of the dividend discount model, first presented by John Burr Williams (1938). Even from the perspective of an investor with a finite investment horizon, the value of stock depends on all future dividends. For that investor, stock value today depends *directly* on the dividends the investor expects to receive before the stock is sold and *indirectly* on the expected dividends after the stock is sold, because those future dividends determine the expected selling price.

Equation 7, by expressing the value of stock as the present value of expected dividends into the indefinite future, presents a daunting forecasting challenge. In practice, of course, analysts cannot make detailed, individual forecasts of an infinite number of dividends. To use the DDM, the forecasting problem must be simplified. Two broad approaches exist, each of which has several variations:

1 Future dividends can be forecast by assigning the stream of future dividends to one of several stylized growth patterns. The most commonly used patterns are:

- constant growth forever (the Gordon growth model);
- two distinct stages of growth (the two-stage growth model and the H-model); and
- three distinct stages of growth (the three-stage growth model).

The DDM value of the stock is then found by discounting the dividend streams back to the present. We present the Gordon growth model in Section 4, and the two-stage, H-model, and three-stage growth models are presented in Section 5.

2 A finite number of dividends can be forecast individually up to a terminal point, by using pro forma financial statement analysis, for example. Typically, such forecasts extend from 3 to 10 years into the future. Although some analysts apply the same horizon to all companies under analysis, the horizon selected often depends on the perceived predictability (sometimes called the **visibility**) of the company's earnings. We can then forecast either:

- the remaining dividends from the terminal point forward by assigning those dividends to a stylized growth pattern, or
- the share price at the terminal point of our dividend forecasts (**terminal share price**), by using some method (such as taking a multiple of forecasted book value or earnings per share as of that point, based on one of several methods for estimating such multiples).

The stock's DDM value is then found by discounting the dividends (and forecasted price, if any) back to the present.

Spreadsheets are particularly convenient tools for implementing a DDM with individual dividend forecasts, but are useful in all cases. We address spreadsheet modeling in Section 5.

Whether analysts are using dividends or some other definition of cash flow, they generally use one of the above forecasting approaches when valuing stock. The challenge in practice is to choose an appropriate model for a stock's future dividends and to develop quality inputs to that model.

4   THE GORDON GROWTH MODEL

The Gordon growth model, developed by Gordon and Shapiro (1956) and Gordon (1962), assumes that dividends grow indefinitely at a constant rate. This assumption, applied to the general dividend discount model (Equation 7), leads to a simple and elegant valuation formula that has been influential in investment practice. This section explores the development of the Gordon growth model and illustrates its uses.

4.1 The Gordon Growth Model Equation

The simplest pattern that can be assumed in forecasting future dividends is growth at a constant rate. In mathematical terms, this assumption can be stated as

$$D_t = D_{t-1}(1 + g)$$

where g is the expected constant growth rate in dividends and D_t is the expected dividend payable at time t. Suppose, for example, that the most recent dividend, D_0, was €10. Then, if a 5 percent dividend growth rate is forecast, the expected dividend at $t = 1$ is $D_1 = D_0(1 + g) = €10 \times 1.05 = €10.5$. For any time t, D_t also equals the $t = 0$ dividend, compounded at g for t periods:

$$D_t = D_0(1 + g)^t \qquad (8)$$

To continue the example, at the end of five years the expected dividend is $D_5 = D_0(1 + g)^5 = €10 \times (1.05)^5 = €10 \times 1.276282 = €12.76$. If $D_0(1 + g)^t$ is substituted into Equation 7 for D_t, it gives the Gordon growth model. If all of the terms are written out, they are

$$V_0 = \frac{D_0(1 + g)}{(1 + r)} + \frac{D_0(1 + g)^2}{(1 + r)^2} + \ldots + \frac{D_0(1 + g)^n}{(1 + r)^n} + \ldots \qquad (9)$$

Equation 9 is a geometric series; that is, each term in the expression is equal to the previous term times a constant, which in this case is $(1 + g)/(1 + r)$. This equation can be simplified algebraically into a much more compact equation:[16]

$$V_0 = \frac{D_0(1 + g)}{r - g}, \text{ or } V_0 = \frac{D_1}{r - g} \qquad (10)$$

Both equations are equivalent because $D_1 = D_0(1 + g)$. In Equation 10, it must be specified that the required return on equity must be greater than the expected growth rate: $r > g$. If $r = g$ or $r < g$, Equation 10 as a compact formula for value assuming constant growth is not valid. If $r = g$, dividends grow at the same rate at which they are discounted, so the value of the stock (as the undiscounted sum of all expected future dividends) is infinite. If $r < g$, dividends grow faster than they are discounted, so the value of the stock is infinite. Of course, infinite values do not make economic sense; so constant growth with $r = g$ or $r < g$ does not make sense.

To illustrate the calculation, suppose that an annual dividend of €5 has just been paid ($D_0 = $ €5). The expected long-term growth rate is 5 percent and the required return on equity is 8 percent. The Gordon growth model value per share is $D_0(1 + g)/(r - g) = $ (€5 × 1.05)/(0.08 − 0.05) = €5.25/0.03 = €175. When calculating the model value, be careful to use D_1 and not D_0 in the numerator.

The Gordon growth model (Equation 10) is one of the most widely recognized equations in the field of security analysis. Because the model is based on indefinitely extending future dividends, the model's required rate of return and growth rate should reflect long-term expectations. Further, model values are very sensitive to both the required rate of return, r, and the expected dividend growth rate, g. In this model and other valuation models, it is helpful to perform a sensitivity analysis on the inputs, particularly when an analyst is not confident about the proper values.

Earlier we stated that analysts typically apply DDMs to dividend-paying stocks when dividends bear an understandable and consistent relation to the company's profitability. The same qualifications hold for the Gordon growth model. In addition, the Gordon growth model form of the DDM is most appropriate for companies with earnings expected to grow at a rate comparable to or lower than the economy's nominal growth rate. Businesses growing at much higher rates than the economy often grow at lower rates in maturity, and the horizon in using the Gordon growth model is the entire future stream of dividends.

To determine whether the company's growth rate qualifies it as a candidate for the Gordon growth model, an estimate of the economy's nominal growth rate is needed. This growth rate is usually measured by the growth in **gross domestic product** (GDP). (GDP is a money measure of the goods and services produced within a country's borders.) National government agencies as well as the World Bank (www.worldbank.org) publish GDP data, which are also available from several secondary sources. Exhibit 2 shows the recent real GDP growth record for a number of major developed markets.

Exhibit 2   Average Annual Real GDP Growth Rates: 1983–2012 (in Percent)

Country	Time Period		
	1983–1992	1993–2002	2003–12
Australia	3.4%	3.8%	2.4%
Canada	2.7	3.5	1.9

(continued)

---

16 The simplification involves the expression for the sum of an infinite geometric progression with the first term equal to a and the growth factor equal to m with $|m| < 1$ [i.e., the sum of $a + am + am^2 + \dots$ is $a/(1 - m)$]. Setting $a = D_1/(1 + r)$ and $m = (1 + g)/(1 + r)$, gives the Gordon growth model.

Exhibit 2   (Continued)

Country	Time Period		
	1983–1992	**1993–2002**	**2003–12**
Denmark	2.1	2.4	0.6
France	2.3	2.0	1.1
Germany	3.0	1.4	1.2
Italy	2.5	1.6	0.0
Japan	4.3	0.8	0.9
Netherlands	2.9	3.0	1.1
Sweden	1.9	2.7	2.3
Switzerland	2.1	1.3	1.9
United Kingdom	2.6	3.4	1.4
United States	3.5	3.4	1.7

Source: OECD.

Based on historical and/or forward-looking information, nominal GDP growth can be estimated as the sum of the estimated real growth rate in GDP plus the expected long-run inflation rate. For example, an estimate of the underlying real growth rate of the Canadian economy is 1.2 percent as of early 2013. By using the Bank of Canada's inflation target of 2 percent as the expected inflation rate, an estimate of the Canadian economy's nominal annual growth rate is 1.2 percent + 2 percent = 3.2 percent. Publicly traded companies constitute varying amounts of the total corporate sector, but always less than 100 percent. As a result, the overall growth rate of the public corporate sector can diverge from the nominal GDP growth rate during a long horizon; furthermore, within the public corporate sector, some subsectors may experience persistent growth rate differentials. Nevertheless, an earnings growth rate far above the nominal GDP growth rate is not sustainable in perpetuity.

When forecasting an earnings growth rate far above the economy's nominal growth rate, analysts should use a multistage DDM in which the final-stage growth rate reflects a growth rate that is more plausible relative to the economy's nominal growth rate, rather than using the Gordon growth model.

EXAMPLE 5

Valuation Using the Gordon Growth Model (1)

Joel Williams follows Sonoco Products Company (NYSE: SON), a manufacturer of paper and plastic packaging for both consumer and industrial use. SON appears to have a dividend policy of recognizing sustainable increases in the level of earnings with increases in dividends, keeping the dividend payout ratio within a range of 40 percent to 60 percent. Williams also notes:

- SON's most recent quarterly dividend (ex-dividend date: 14 August 2013) was $0.31, consistent with a current annual dividend of 4 × $0.31 = $1.24 per year.

- A forecasted dividend growth rate of 4.0 percent per year.
- With a beta (β_i) of 0.95, given an equity risk premium (expected excess return of equities over the risk-free rate, $E(R_M) - R_F$) of 4.5 percent and a risk-free rate (R_F) of 3 percent, SON's required return on equity is $r = R_F + \beta_i[E(R_M) - R_F] = 3.0 + 0.95(4.5) = 7.3$ percent, using the capital asset pricing model (CAPM).

Williams believes the Gordon growth model may be an appropriate model for valuing SON.

1 Calculate the Gordon growth model value for SON stock.

2 The current market price of SON stock is $38.10. Using your answer to Question 1, judge whether SON stock is fairly valued, undervalued, or overvalued.

Solution to 1:

Using Equation 10,

$$V_0 = \frac{D_0(1 + g)}{r - g} = \frac{\$1.24 \times 1.04}{0.073 - 0.04} = \frac{\$1.2896}{0.033} = \$39.08$$

Solution to 2:

The market price of $38.10 is $0.98 or approximately 2.5 percent less than the Gordon growth model intrinsic value estimate of $39.08. SON appears to be slightly undervalued, based on the Gordon growth model estimate.

The next example illustrates a Gordon growth model valuation introducing some problems the analyst might face in practice. The example refers to adjusted beta; the most common calculation adjusts raw historical beta toward the overall mean value of one for beta.

EXAMPLE 6

Valuation Using the Gordon Growth Model (2)

As an analyst for a US domestic equity–income mutual fund, Roberta Kim is evaluating Middlesex Water Company (NASDAQ: MSEX), a publicly traded water utility, for possible inclusion in the approved list of investments. Kim is conducting the analysis in mid-2013.

Not all countries have traded water utility stocks. In the United States, about 85 percent of the population gets its water from government entities. A group of investor-owned water utilities, however, also supplies water to the public. With a market capitalization of about $327 million as of mid-2013, MSEX is among the ten largest publicly traded US water utilities. MSEX's historical base is the Middlesex System, serving residential, industrial, and commercial customers in a well-developed area of central New Jersey. Through various subsidiaries, MSEX also provides water and wastewater collection and treatment services to areas of southern New Jersey and Delaware.

Hampered by a decline in earnings during the recent recession, net income growth during the past five years has been somewhat less than 2 percent. During the last five years, MSEX's return on equity averaged 7.8 percent with relatively little variation, and its profit margins are above industry averages. Because MSEX obtains most of its revenue from the regulated business providing an important staple, water, to a relatively stable population, Kim feels confident in forecasting future earnings and dividend growth. MSEX appears to have a policy of small annual increases in the dividend rate, maintaining an average dividend payout ratio of approximately 80 percent. Other facts and forecasts include the following:

- MSEX's per-share dividends for 2012 (D_0) were $0.74.

- Kim forecasts a long-term earnings growth rate of 3.5 percent per year, somewhat above the 2.7 percent consensus 3–5-year earnings growth rate forecast reported by Zacks Investment Research (based on two analysts).

- MSEX's raw beta and adjusted beta are, respectively, 0.70 and 0.80 based on 60 monthly returns. The R^2 associated with beta, however, is under 20 percent.

- Kim estimates that MSEX's pretax cost of debt is 5.6 percent based on Standard & Poor's issuer rating for MSEX of A– and the current corporate yield curve.

- Kim's estimate of MSEX's required return on equity is 7.00 percent.

- MSEX's current market price is $20.50.

1 Calculate the Gordon growth model estimate of value for MSEX using Kim's required return on equity estimate.

2 State whether MSEX appears to be overvalued, fairly valued, or undervalued based on the Gordon growth model estimate of value.

3 Justify the selection of the Gordon growth model for valuing MSEX.

4 Calculate the CAPM estimate of the required return on equity for MSEX under the assumption that beta regresses to the mean. (Assume an equity risk premium of 4.5 percent and a risk-free rate of 3 percent as of the price quotation date.)

5 Calculate the Gordon growth estimate of value using A) the required return on equity from your answer to Question 4, and B) a bond-yield-plus-risk-premium approach with a risk premium of 2.5 percent.

6 Evaluate the effect of uncertainty in MSEX's required return on equity on the valuation conclusion in Question 2.

Solution to 1:

From Equation 10,

$$V_0 = \frac{D_0(1 + g)}{r - g} = \frac{\$0.74(1.035)}{0.07 - 0.035} = \$21.88$$

Solution to 2:

Because the Gordon growth model estimate of $21.88 is $1.38 or about 6.7 percent higher than the market price of $20.50, MSEX appears to be undervalued.

Solution to 3:

The Gordon growth model, which assumes that dividends grow at a stable rate in perpetuity, is a realistic model for MSEX for the following reasons:

- MSEX profitability is stable as reflected in its return on equity. This stability reflects predictable demand and regulated prices for its product, water.

- Dividends bear an understandable and consistent relationship to earnings, as evidenced by the company's policy of annual increases and predictable dividend payout ratios.

- Historical earnings growth, at 2.5 percent a year, is somewhat below the long-term nominal annual GDP growth for the United States (3.2 percent for 1947–2013, according to the US Bureau of Economic Analysis).

- Forecasted earnings growth of 3.5 percent seems attainable, given a plausible forecast for nominal GDP growth, and does not include a period of forecasted very high or very low growth.

Solution to 4:

The assumption of regression to the mean is characteristic of adjusted historical beta. The required return on equity as given by the CAPM is 3 percent + 0.80(4.5 percent) = 6.6 percent using adjusted beta, which assumes reversion to the mean of 1.0.

Solution to 5:

A The Gordon growth value of MSEX using a required return on equity of 6.6 percent is

$$V_0 = \frac{D_0(1+g)}{r-g} = \frac{\$0.74(1.035)}{0.066 - 0.035} = \$24.71$$

B The bond-yield-plus-risk-premium estimate of the required return on equity is 5.6 percent + 2.5 percent = 8.1 percent.

$$V_0 = \frac{D_0(1+g)}{r-g} = \frac{\$0.74(1.035)}{0.081 - 0.035} = \$16.65$$

Solution to 6:

Using the CAPM estimate of the required return on equity (Question 5A), MSEX appears to be definitely undervalued. Beta explains less than 20 percent of the variation in MSEX's returns, however, according to the fact given concerning R^2. Using a bond-yield-plus-risk-premium approach, MSEX appears to be overvalued ($16.65 is less than the market price of $20.50 by more than 18 percent). No specific evidence, however, supports the particular value of the risk premium selected in the bond-yield-plus-risk-premium approach. In this case, because of the uncertainty in the required return on equity estimate, one has less confidence that MSEX is overvalued. Given the results of the other two approaches, the analyst may view MSEX as undervalued.

As mentioned earlier, an analyst needs to be aware that Gordon growth model values can be very sensitive to small changes in the values of the required rate of return and expected dividend growth rate. Example 7 illustrates a format for a sensitivity analysis.

EXAMPLE 7

Valuation Using the Gordon Growth Model (3)

In Example 6, the Gordon growth model value for MSEX was estimated as $21.88 based on a current dividend of $0.74, an expected dividend growth rate of 3.5 percent, and a required return on equity of 7.00 percent. What if the estimates of r and g can each vary by 25 basis points? How sensitive is the model value to changes in the estimates of r and g? Exhibit 3 provides information on this sensitivity.

Exhibit 3	Estimated Price Given Uncertain Inputs		
	g = 3.25%	**g = 3.50%**	**g = 3.75%**
r = 6.75%	$21.83	$23.57	$25.59
r = 7.00%	$20.37	**$21.88**	$23.62
r = 7.25%	$19.10	$20.42	$21.94

A point of interest following from the mathematics of the Gordon growth model is that when the spread between r and g is the widest (r = 7.25 percent and g = 3.25 percent), the Gordon growth model value is the smallest ($19.10), and when the spread is the narrowest (r = 6.75 percent and g = 3.75 percent), the model value is the largest ($25.59). As the spread goes to zero, in fact, the model value increases without bound. The largest value in Exhibit 3, $25.59, is almost 34 percent larger than the smallest value, $19.10. Two-thirds of the values in Exhibit 3 exceed MSEX's current market price of $20.50, tending to support the conclusion that MSEX is undervalued. In summary, the best estimate of the value of MSEX given the assumptions is $21.88, bolded in Exhibit 3, but the estimate is quite sensitive to rather small changes in inputs.

Examples 6 and 7 illustrate the application of the Gordon growth model to a utility, a traditional source for such illustrations because of the stability afforded by providing an essential service in a regulated environment. Before applying any valuation model, however, analysts need to know much more about a company than industry membership. For example, as of mid-2013, another water utility, Aqua America Inc. (NYSE: WTR), was expected to grow at 6.4 percent for the next five years as a result of an aggressive growth-by-acquisition strategy. Furthermore, many utility holding companies in the United States have major, nonregulated business subsidiaries so the traditional picture of steady and slow growth often does not hold.

In addition to individual stocks, analysts have often used the Gordon growth model to value broad equity market indices, especially in developed markets. Because the value of publicly traded issues typically represents a large fraction of the overall corporate sector in developed markets, such indices reflect average economic growth rates. Furthermore, in such economies, a sustainable trend value of growth may be identifiable.

The Gordon growth model can also be used to value the noncallable form of a traditional type of preferred stock, **fixed-rate perpetual preferred stock** (stock with a specified dividend rate that has a claim on earnings senior to the claim of common stock, and no maturity date). Perpetual preferred stock has been used particularly by financial institutions such as banks to obtain permanent equity capital while diluting the interests of common equity. Generally, such issues have been callable by the issuer after a certain period, so valuation must take account of the issuer's call option. Valuation of the noncallable form, however, is straightforward.

If the dividend on such preferred stock is D, because payments extend into the indefinite future a **perpetuity** (a stream of level payments extending to infinity) exists in the constant amount of D. With $g = 0$, which is true because dividends are fixed for such preferred stock, the Gordon growth model becomes

$$V_0 = \frac{D}{r} \tag{11}$$

The discount rate, r, capitalizes the amount D, and for that reason is often called a **capitalization rate** in this expression and any other expression for the value of a perpetuity.

EXAMPLE 8

Valuing Noncallable Fixed-Rate Perpetual Preferred Stock

Kansas City Southern Preferred 4% (NYSE: KSU-P), issued 2 January 1963, has a par value of $25 per share. Thus, a share pays 0.04($25) = $1.00 in annual dividends. The required return on this security is estimated at 5.5 percent. Estimate the value of this issue.

Solution:

According to the model in Equation 11, KSU-P preferred stock is worth $D/r = 1.00/0.055 = \$18.18$.

A perpetual preferred stock has a level dividend, thus a dividend growth rate of zero. Another case is a declining dividend—a negative growth rate. The Gordon growth model also accommodates this possibility, as illustrated in Example 9.

EXAMPLE 9

Gordon Growth Model with Negative Growth

Afton Mines is a profitable company that is expected to pay a $4.25 dividend next year. Because it is depleting its mining properties, the best estimate is that dividends will decline forever at a rate of 4 percent. The required rate of return on Afton stock is 9 percent. What is the value of Afton shares?

Solution:

For Afton, the value of the stock is

$$V_0 = \frac{4.25}{\left[0.09 - (-0.04)\right]}$$

$$= \frac{4.25}{0.13} = \$32.69$$

The negative growth results in a $32.69 valuation for the stock.

4.2 The Links Among Dividend Growth, Earnings Growth, and Value Appreciation in the Gordon Growth Model

The Gordon growth model implies a set of relationships for the growth rates of dividends, earnings, and stock value. With dividends growing at a constant rate g, stock value also grows at g as well. The current stock value is $V_0 = D_1/(r - g)$. Multiplying both sides by $(1 + g)$ gives $V_0(1 + g) = D_1(1 + g)/(r - g)$, which is $V_1 = D_2/(r - g)$. So, both dividends and value have grown at a rate of g (holding r constant).[17] Given a constant payout ratio—a constant, proportional relationship between earnings and dividends—dividends and earnings grow at g.

To summarize, g in the Gordon growth model is the rate of value or capital appreciation (sometimes also called the capital gains yield). Some textbooks state that g is the rate of price appreciation. If prices are efficient (price equals value), price is indeed expected to grow at a rate of g. If there is mispricing (price is different from value), however, the actual rate of capital appreciation depends on the nature of the mispricing and how fast it is corrected, if at all. This topic is discussed in the reading on return concepts.

Another characteristic of the constant growth model is that the components of total return (dividend yield and capital gains yield) will also stay constant through time, given that price tracks value exactly. The dividend yield, which is D_1/P_0 at $t = 0$, will stay unchanged because both the dividend and the price are expected to grow at the same rate, leaving the dividend yield unchanged through time. For example, consider a stock selling for €50.00 with a **forward dividend yield** (a dividend yield based on the anticipated dividend during the next 12 months) of 2 percent based on an expected dividend of €1. The estimate of g is 5.50 percent per year. The dividend yield of 2 percent, the capital gains yield of 5.50 percent, and the total return of 7.50 percent are expected to be the same at $t = 0$ and at any future point in time.

4.3 Share Repurchases

An issue of increasing importance in many developed markets is share repurchases. Companies can distribute free cash flow to shareholders in the form of share repurchases (also called buybacks) as well as dividends. In the United States currently, more than half of dividend-paying companies also make regular share repurchases.[18] Clearly, analysts using DDMs need to understand share repurchases. Share repurchases and cash dividends have several distinctive features:

▪ Share repurchases involve a reduction in the number of shares outstanding, all else equal. Selling shareholders see their relative ownership position reduced compared to nonselling shareholders.

▪ Whereas many corporations with established cash dividends are reluctant to reduce or omit cash dividends, corporations generally do not view themselves as committed to maintain share repurchases at any specified level.

▪ Cash dividends tend to be more predictable in money terms and more predictable as to timing.[19] Although evidence from the United States suggests that, for companies with active repurchase programs, the amount of repurchases during two-year intervals bears a relationship to earnings, companies appear to be opportunistic in timing exactly when to repurchase.[20] Thus, share repurchases are generally harder to forecast than the cash dividends of companies with an identifiable dividend policy.

▪ As a baseline case, share repurchases are neutral in their effect on the wealth of ongoing shareholders if the repurchases are accomplished at market prices.

---

17 More formally, the fact that the value grows at a rate equal to g is demonstrated as follows:

$$\frac{V_{t+1} - V_t}{V_t} = \frac{D_{t+2}/(r-g) - D_{t+1}/(r-g)}{D_{t+1}/(r-g)} = \frac{D_{t+2} - D_{t+1}}{D_{t+1}} = 1 + g - 1 = g$$

18 See Skinner (2008), who also finds evidence that this group of companies increasingly has tended to distribute earnings increases via share repurchases rather than cash dividends.
19 As discussed by Wanger (2007).
20 See Skinner (2008).

The analyst could account for share repurchases directly by forecasting the total earnings, total distributions to shareholders (via either cash dividends or share repurchases), and shares outstanding. Experience and familiarity with such models is much less than for DDMs. Focusing on cash dividends, however, DDMs supply accurate valuations consistent with such an approach if the analyst takes account of the effect of expected repurchases on the per-share growth rates of dividends. Correctly applied, the DDM is a valid approach to common stock valuation even when the company being analyzed engages in share repurchases.

4.4 The Implied Dividend Growth Rate

Because the dividend growth rate affects the estimated value of a stock using the Gordon growth model, differences between estimated values of a stock and its actual market value might be explained by different growth rate assumptions. Given price, the expected next-period dividend, and an estimate of the required rate of return, the dividend growth rate reflected in price can be inferred assuming the Gordon growth model. (Actually, it is possible to infer the market-price-implied dividend growth based on other DDMs as well.) An analyst can then judge whether the implied dividend growth rate is reasonable, high, or low, based on what he or she knows about the company. In effect, the calculation of the implied dividend growth rate provides an alternative perspective on the valuation of the stock (fairly valued, overvalued, or undervalued). Example 10 shows how the Gordon growth model can be used to infer the market's implied growth rate for a stock.

EXAMPLE 10

The Growth Rate Implied by the Current Stock Price

Suppose a company has a beta of 1.1. The risk-free rate is 5.6 percent and the equity risk premium is 6 percent. The current dividend of $2.00 is expected to grow at 5 percent indefinitely. The price of the stock is $40.

1 Estimate the value of the company's stock.

2 Determine the constant dividend growth rate that would be required to justify the market price of $40.

Solution to 1:

The required rate of return is 5.6 percent + 1.1(6 percent) = 12.2 percent. The value of one share, using the Gordon growth model, is

$$V_0 = \frac{D_0(1 + g)}{r - g}$$

$$= \frac{2.00(1.05)}{0.122 - 0.05}$$

$$= \frac{2.10}{0.072} = \$29.17$$

Solution to 2:

The valuation estimate of the model ($29.17) is less than the market value of $40.00, thus the market price must be forecasting a growth rate above the assumed 5 percent. Assuming that the model and the required return assumption are appropriate, the growth rate in dividends required to justify the $40 stock price can be calculated by substituting all known values into the Gordon growth model equation except for g:

$$40 = \frac{2.00(1 + g)}{0.122 - g}$$

$$4.88 - 40g = 2 + 2g$$

$$42g = 2.88$$

$$g = 0.0686$$

An expected dividend growth rate of 6.86 percent is required for the stock price to be correctly valued at the market price of $40.

4.5 The Present Value of Growth Opportunities

The value of a stock can be analyzed as the sum of 1) the value of the company without earnings reinvestment, and 2) the **present value of growth opportunities** (PVGO). PVGO, also known as the **value of growth**, sums the expected value today of opportunities to profitably reinvest future earnings.[21] In this section, we illustrate this decomposition and discuss how it may be interpreted to gain insight into the market's view of a company's business and prospects.

Earnings growth may increase, leave unchanged, or reduce shareholder wealth depending on whether the growth results from earning returns in excess of, equal to, or less than the opportunity cost of funds. Consider a company with a required return on equity of 10 percent that has earned €1 per share. The company is deciding whether to pay out current earnings as a dividend or to reinvest them at 10 percent and distribute the ending value as a dividend in one year. If it reinvests, the present value of investment is €1.10/1.10 = €1.00, equaling its cost, so the decision to reinvest has a net present value (NPV) of zero. If the company were able to earn more than 10 percent by exploiting a profitable growth opportunity, reinvesting would have a positive NPV, increasing shareholder wealth. Suppose the company could reinvest earnings at 25 percent for one year: The per-share NPV of the growth opportunity would be €1.25/1.10 − €1 ≈ €0.14. Note that any reinvestment at a positive rate below 10 percent, although increasing EPS, is not in shareholders' interests. Increases in shareholder wealth occur only when reinvested earnings earn more than the opportunity cost of funds (i.e., investments are in positive net present value projects).[22] Thus, investors actively assess whether and to what degree companies will have opportunities to invest in profitable projects. In principle, companies without prospects for investing in positive NPV projects should distribute most or all earnings to shareholders as dividends so the shareholders can redirect capital to more attractive areas.

A company without positive expected NPV projects is defined as a **no-growth company** (a term for a company without opportunities for *profitable* growth). Such companies should distribute all their earnings in dividends because earnings cannot be reinvested profitably and earnings will be flat in perpetuity, assuming a constant return on equity (ROE). This flatness occurs because earnings equal ROE × Equity, and equity is constant because retained earnings are not added to it. E_1 is $t = 1$ earnings,

---

21 More technically, PVGO can be defined as the forecasted total net present value of future projects. See Brealey, Myers, and Allen (2006), p. 259.

22 We can interpret this condition of profitability as ROE > r with ROE calculated with the *market* value of equity (rather than the book value of equity) in the denominator. Book value based on historical cost accounting can present a distorted picture of the value of shareholders' investment in the company. The condition that ROE = r would be consistent with an equilibrium in which investment opportunities were such that a company could just earn its opportunity cost of capital.

which is the constant level of earnings or the average earnings of a no-growth company if return on equity is viewed as varying about its average level. The **no-growth value per share** is defined as E_1/r, which is the present value of a perpetuity in the amount of E_1 where the capitalization rate, r, is the required rate of return on the company's equity. E_1/r can also be interpreted as the per-share value of assets in place because of the assumption that the company is making no new investments because none are profitable. For any company, the actual value per share is the sum of the no-growth value per share and the present value of growth opportunities (PVGO):

$$V_0 = \frac{E_1}{r} + \text{PVGO} \qquad\qquad (12)$$

If prices reflect value ($P_0 = V_0$), P_0 less E_1/r gives the market's estimate of the company's value of growth, PVGO. Referring back to Example 6, suppose that MSEX is expected to have average EPS of $0.79 if it distributed all earnings as dividends. Its required return of 9.25 percent and a current price of $18.39 gives

$$\$18.39 = (\$0.79/0.0925) + \text{PVGO}$$
$$= \$8.54 + \text{PVGO}$$

where PVGO = $18.39 − $8.54 = $9.85. So, 54 percent ($9.85/$18.39 = 0.54) of the company's value, as reflected in the market price, is attributable to the value of growth.

Exhibit 4, based on data from early August 2013, illustrates that the value of growth represented about 44 percent of the market value of technology company Google and a much smaller percentage of McDonald's value and Macy's value. The low value for McDonald's PVGO could be explained in several ways. The value could reflect increased competition in the fast food business, commodity cost pressures, and/or unfavorable foreign exchange (foreign operations contribute over 65 percent of revenues); it could reflect that the company has a much higher payout ratio than Google or Macy's (53 percent in 2012 versus zero and 23 percent for Google and Macy's) and, therefore, future growth is expected to be slower; or it might indicate that the estimated no-growth value per share was too high because the earnings estimate was too high and/or the required return on equity estimate was too low.

Exhibit 4	Estimated PVGO as a Percentage of Price						
Company	β	r	E_1	Price	E_1/r	PVGO	PVGO/Price
Google, Inc.	0.90	7.1%	$35.80	$896.57	$504.23	$392.34	43.8%
McDonald's Corp	0.60	5.7	5.70	102.14	100.00	2.14	2.1
Macy's Inc.	1.35	9.1	4.00	48.79	43.96	4.83	9.9

Source: Value Line Investment Survey for beta, earnings estimate, and price of each.
Note: The required rate of return is estimated using the CAPM with the following inputs: the beta from the Value Line Investment Survey, 3.0 percent (20-year US T-bond rate) for the risk-free rate of return, and 4.5 percent for the equity risk premium.

What determines PVGO? One determinant is the value of a company's options to invest, captured by the word "opportunities." In addition, the flexibility to adapt investments to new circumstances and information is valuable. Thus, a second determinant of PVGO is the value of the company's options to time the start, adjust the scale, or even abandon future projects. This element is the value of the company's **real options** (options to modify projects, in this context). Companies that have good business opportunities and/or a high level of managerial flexibility in responding to changes in the marketplace should tend to have higher values of PVGO than companies that do not have such advantages. This perspective on what contributes to PVGO can provide additional understanding of the results in Exhibit 4.

As an additional aid to an analyst, Equation 12 can be restated in terms of the familiar P/E ratio based on forecasted earnings:

$$\frac{V_0}{E_1} \text{ or } \frac{P_0}{E_1} \text{ or P/E} = \frac{1}{r} + \frac{\text{PVGO}}{E_1} \tag{13}$$

The first term, $1/r$, is the value of the P/E for a no-growth company. The second term is the component of the P/E value that relates to growth opportunities. For MSEX, the P/E is \$18.39/\$0.79 = 23.3. The no-growth P/E is 1/0.0925 = 10.8 and is the multiple the company should sell at if it has no growth opportunities. The growth component of \$9.85/\$0.79 = 12.5 reflects anticipated growth opportunities. Leibowitz and Kogelman (1990) and Leibowitz (1997) have provided elaborate analyses of the drivers of the growth component of P/E as a franchise-value approach.

As analysts, the distinction between no-growth and growth values is of interest because the value of growth and the value of assets in place generally have different risk characteristics (as the interpretation of PVGO as incorporating the real options suggests).

4.6 Gordon Growth Model and the Price-to-Earnings Ratio

The price-to-earnings ratio (P/E) is perhaps the most widely recognized valuation indicator, familiar to readers of newspaper financial tables and institutional research reports. Using the Gordon growth model, an expression for P/E in terms of the fundamentals can be developed. This expression has two uses:

▪ When used with forecasts of the inputs to the model, the analyst obtains a **justified (fundamental) P/E**—the P/E that is fair, warranted, or justified on the basis of fundamentals (given that the valuation model is appropriate). The analyst can then state his or her view of value in terms not of the Gordon growth model value but of the justified P/E. Because P/E is so widely recognized, this method may be an effective way to communicate the analysis.

▪ The analyst may also use the expression for P/E to weigh whether the forecasts of earnings growth built into the current stock price are reasonable. What expected earnings growth rate is implied by the actual market P/E? Is that growth rate plausible?

The expression for P/E can be stated in terms of the current (or trailing) P/E (today's market price per share divided by trailing 12 months' earnings per share) or in terms of the leading (or forward) P/E (today's market price per share divided by a forecast of the next 12 months' earnings per share, or sometimes the next fiscal year's earnings per share).

Leading and trailing justified P/E expressions can be developed from the Gordon growth model. Assuming that the model can be applied for a particular stock's valuation, the dividend payout ratio is considered fixed. Define b as the retention rate, the fraction of earnings reinvested in the company rather than paid out in dividends. The dividend payout ratio is then, by definition, $(1 - b)$ = Dividend per share/Earnings per share = D_t/E_t. If $P_0 = D_1/(r - g)$ is divided by next year's earnings per share, E_1, we have

$$\frac{P_0}{E_1} = \frac{D_1/E_1}{r - g} = \frac{1 - b}{r - g} \tag{14}$$

This represents a leading P/E, which is current price divided by next year's earnings. Alternatively, if $P_0 = D_0(1 + g)/(r - g)$ is divided by the current-year's earnings per share, E_0, the result is

$$\frac{P_0}{E_0} = \frac{D_0(1 + g)/E_0}{r - g} = \frac{(1 - b)(1 + g)}{r - g} \qquad \textbf{(15)}$$

This expression is for trailing P/E, which is current price divided by trailing (current year) earnings.

EXAMPLE 11

The Justified P/E Based on the Gordon Growth Model

Harry Trice wants to use the Gordon growth model to find a justified P/E for the French company Carrefour SA (NYSE Euronext: CA), a global food retailer specializing in hypermarkets and supermarkets. Trice has assembled the following information:

- Current stock price = €23.84.
- Trailing annual earnings per share = €1.81
- Current level of annual dividends = €0.58.
- Dividend growth rate = 3.5 percent.
- Risk-free rate = 2.8 percent.
- Equity risk premium = 4.00 percent.
- Beta versus the CAC index = 0.80.

1 Calculate the justified trailing and leading P/Es based on the Gordon growth model.

2 Based on the justified trailing P/E and the actual P/E, judge whether CA is fairly valued, overvalued, or undervalued.

Solution to 1:

For CA, the required rate of return using the CAPM is

$$r_i = 2.80\% + 0.80(4.00\%)$$
$$= 6.0\%$$

The dividend payout ratio is

$$(1 - b) = D_0/E_0$$
$$= 0.58/1.81$$
$$= 0.32$$

The justified leading P/E (based on next year's earnings) is

$$\frac{P_0}{E_1} = \frac{1 - b}{r - g} = \frac{0.32}{0.06 - 0.035} = 12.8$$

The justified trailing P/E (based on trailing earnings) is

$$\frac{P_0}{E_0} = \frac{(1 - b)(1 + g)}{r - g} = \frac{0.32(1.035)}{0.06 - 0.035} = 13.2$$

Solution to 2:

Based on a current price of €23.84 and trailing earnings of €1.81, the trailing P/E is €23.84/€1.81 = 13.2. Because the actual P/E of 13.2 is the same as the justified trailing P/E of 13.2 (to one decimal place), the conclusion is that CA appears to be fairly valued. The result can also be expressed in terms of price using the Gordon growth model. Using Trice's assumptions, the Gordon growth model assigns a value of 0.58(1.035)/(0.06 − 0.035) = €24.01, which is about the same as the current market value of €23.84.

Later in the reading, we will present multistage DDMs. Expressions for the P/E can be developed in terms of the variables of multistage DDMs, but the usefulness of these expressions is not commensurate with their complexity. For multistage models, the simple way to calculate a justified leading P/E is to divide the model value directly by the first year's expected earnings. In all cases, the P/E is explained in terms of the required return on equity, expected dividend growth rate(s), and the dividend payout ratio(s). All else equal, higher prices are associated with higher anticipated dividend growth rates.

4.7 Estimating a Required Return Using the Gordon Growth Model

Under the assumption of efficient prices, the Gordon growth model has been used to estimate a stock's required rate of return, or equivalently, the market-price-implied expected return. The Gordon growth model solved for r is

$$r = \frac{D_0(1+g)}{P_0} + g = \frac{D_1}{P_0} + g \tag{16}$$

As explained in the reading on return concepts, r in Equation 16 is technically an internal rate of return (IRR). The rate r is composed of two parts; the dividend yield (D_1/P_0) and the capital gains (or appreciation) yield (g).

EXAMPLE 12

Finding the Expected Rate of Return with the Gordon Growth Model

Bob Inguigiatto, CFA, has been given the task of developing mean return estimates for a list of stocks as preparation for a portfolio optimization. On his list is NextEra Energy, Inc. (NYSE: NEE), formerly FPL Group, Inc. On analysis, he decides that it is appropriate to model NEE using the Gordon growth model, and he takes prices as reflecting value. The company paid dividends of $2.40 in 2012, and the current stock price is $80.19. The growth rates of dividends and earnings per share have been 7.5 percent and 10.0 percent, respectively, for the past five years. Analysts' consensus estimate of the five-year earnings growth rate is 5.0 percent. Based on his own analysis, Inguigiatto has decided to use

5.50 percent as his best estimate of the long-term earnings and dividend growth rate. Next year's projected dividend, D_1, should be $2.40(1.055) = $2.532. Using the Gordon growth model, NEE's expected rate of return should be

$$r = \frac{D_1}{P_0} + g$$

$$= \frac{2.532}{80.19} + 0.055$$

$$= 0.0316 + 0.055$$

$$= 0.0866 = 8.66\%$$

The expected rate of return can be broken into two components, the dividend yield (D_1/P_0 = 3.16 percent) and the capital gains yield (g = 5.50 percent).

4.8 The Gordon Growth Model: Concluding Remarks

The Gordon growth model is the simplest practical implementation of discounted dividend valuation. The Gordon growth model is appropriate for valuing the equity of dividend-paying companies when its key assumption of a stable future dividend and earnings growth rate is expected to be satisfied. Broad equity market indices of developed markets frequently satisfy the conditions of the model fairly well; as a result, analysts have used it to judge whether an equity market is fairly valued or not and for estimating the equity risk premium associated with the current market level. In the multistage models discussed in the next section, the Gordon growth model has often been used to model the last growth stage, when a previously high growth company matures and the growth rate drops to a long-term sustainable level. In any case in which the model is applied, the analyst must be aware that the output of the model is typically sensitive to small changes in the assumed growth rate and required rate of return.

The Gordon growth model is a single-stage DDM because all future periods are grouped into one stage characterized by single growth rate. For many or even the majority of companies, however, future growth can be expected to consist of multiple stages. Multistage DDMs are the subject of the next section.

MULTISTAGE DIVIDEND DISCOUNT MODELS

5

Earlier we noted that the basic expression for the DDM (Equation 7) is too general for investment analysts to use in practice because one cannot forecast individually more than a relatively small number of dividends. The strongest simplifying assumption—a stable dividend growth rate from now into the indefinite future, leading to the Gordon growth model—is not realistic for many or even most companies. For many publicly traded companies, practitioners assume growth falls into three stages (see Sharpe, Alexander, and Bailey 1999):

- **Growth phase.** A company in its growth phase typically enjoys rapidly expanding markets, high profit margins, and an abnormally high growth rate in earnings per share (**supernormal growth**). Companies in this phase often have negative free cash flow to equity because the company invests heavily in expanding operations. Given high prospective returns on equity, the dividend payout ratios of growth-phase companies are often low or even zero. As the company's markets mature or as unusual growth opportunities attract competitors, earnings growth rates eventually decline.

▪ **Transition phase.** In this phase, which is a transition to maturity, earnings growth slows as competition puts pressure on prices and profit margins or as sales growth slows because of market saturation. In this phase, earnings growth rates may be above average but declining toward the growth rate for the overall economy. Capital requirements typically decline in this phase, often resulting in positive free cash flow and increasing dividend payout ratios (or the initiation of dividends).

▪ **Mature phase.** In maturity, the company reaches an equilibrium in which investment opportunities on average just earn their opportunity cost of capital. Return on equity approaches the required return on equity, and earnings growth, the dividend payout ratio, and the return on equity stabilize at levels that can be sustained long term. The dividend and earnings growth rate of this phase is called the **mature growth rate**. This phase, in fact, reflects the stage in which a company can properly be valued using the Gordon growth model, and that model is one tool for valuing this phase of a current high-growth company's future.

A company may attempt and succeed in restarting the growth phase by changing its strategic focuses and business mix. Technological advances may alter a company's growth prospects for better or worse with surprising rapidity. Nevertheless, this growth-phase picture of a company is a useful approximation. The growth-phase concept provides the intuition for multistage discounted cash flow (DCF) models of all types, including multistage dividend discount models. Multistage models are a staple valuation discipline of investment management firms using DCF valuation models.

In the following sections, we present three popular multistage DDMs: the two-stage DDM, the H-model (a type of two-stage model), and the three-stage DDM. Keep in mind that all these models represent stylized patterns of growth; they are attempting to identify the pattern that most accurately approximates an analyst's view of the company's future growth.

5.1 Two-Stage Dividend Discount Model

Two common versions of the two-stage DDM exist. Both versions assume constant growth at a mature growth rate (for example, 7 percent) in Stage 2. In the first version ("the general two-stage model"), the whole of Stage 1 represents a period of abnormal growth—for example, growth at 15 percent. The transition to mature growth in Stage 2 is generally abrupt.

In the second version, called the H-model, the dividend growth rate is assumed to decline from an abnormal rate to the mature growth rate during the course of Stage 1. For example, the growth rate could begin at 15 percent and decline continuously in Stage 1 until it reaches 7 percent. The second model will be presented after the general two-stage model.

The first two-stage DDM provides for a high growth rate for the initial period, followed by a sustainable and usually lower growth rate thereafter. The two-stage DDM is based on the multiple-period model

$$V_0 = \sum_{t=1}^{n} \frac{D_t}{(1+r)^t} + \frac{V_n}{(1+r)^n}$$

(17)

where V_n is used as an estimate of P_n. The two-stage model assumes that the first n dividends grow at an extraordinary short-term rate, g_S:

$$D_t = D_0(1+g_S)^t$$

After time n, the annual dividend growth rate changes to a normal long-term rate, g_L. The dividend at time $n + 1$ is $D_{n+1} = D_n(1 + g_L) = D_0(1 + g_S)^n(1 + g_L)$, and this dividend continues to grow at g_L. Using D_{n+1}, an analyst can use the Gordon growth model to find V_n:

$$V_n = \frac{D_0(1 + g_S)^n(1 + g_L)}{r - g_L}$$ (18)

To find the value at $t = 0$, V_0, simply find the present value of the first n dividends and the present value of the projected value at time n

$$V_0 = \sum_{t=1}^{n} \frac{D_0(1 + g_S)^t}{(1 + r)^t} + \frac{D_0(1 + g_S)^n(1 + g_L)}{(1 + r)^n(r - g_L)}$$ (19)

EXAMPLE 13

Valuing a Stock Using the Two-Stage Dividend Discount Model

Carl Zeiss Meditec AG (Deutsche Börse XETRA: AFX), 65 percent owned by the Carl Zeiss Group, provides screening, diagnostic, and therapeutic systems for the treatment of ophthalmologic (vision) problems. Reviewing the issue as of mid-August 2013, when it is trading for €23.37, Hans Mattern, a buy-side analyst covering Meditec, forecasts that the current dividend of €0.40 will grow by 9 percent per year during the next 10 years. Thereafter, Mattern believes that the growth rate will decline to 5 percent and remain at that level indefinitely.

Mattern estimates Meditec's required return on equity as 7.1 percent based on a beta of 0.90 against the DAX, a 2.4 percent risk-free rate, and his equity risk premium estimate of 5.2 percent.

Exhibit 5 shows the calculations of the first ten dividends and their present values discounted at 7.1 percent. The terminal stock value at $t = 10$ is

$$V_{10} = \frac{D_0(1 + g_S)^n(1 + g_L)}{r - g_L}$$

$$= \frac{0.40(1.09)^{10}(1.05)}{0.071 - 0.05}$$

$$= 47.3473$$

The terminal stock value and its present value are also given.

Exhibit 5	Carl Zeiss Meditec AG			
Time	Value	Calculation	D_t or V_t	Present Values $D_t/(1.071)^t$ or $V_t/(1.071)^t$
1	D_1	€0.40(1.09)	€0.4360	€0.4071
2	D_2	0.40(1.09)^2	0.4752	0.4143
3	D_3	0.40(1.09)^3	0.5180	0.4217
4	D_4	0.40(1.09)^4	0.5646	0.4291
5	D_5	0.40(1.09)^5	0.6154	0.4368
6	D_6	0.40(1.09)^6	0.6708	0.4445
7	D_7	0.40(1.09)^7	0.7312	0.4524

(continued)

		Exhibit 5 (Continued)		

Time	Value	Calculation	D_t or V_t	Present Values $D_t/(1.071)^t$ or $V_t/(1.071)^t$
8	D_8	$0.40(1.09)^8$	0.7970	0.4604
9	D_9	$0.40(1.09)^9$	0.8688	0.4686
10	D_{10}	$0.40(1.09)^{10}$	0.9469	0.4769
10	V_{10}	$0.40(1.09)^{10}(1.05)/(0.071 - 0.05)$	47.3473	23.8452
Total				€28.2570

In this two-stage model, the dividends are forecast during the first stage and then their present values are calculated. The Gordon growth model is used to derive the terminal value (the value of the dividends in the second stage as of the beginning of that stage). As shown in Exhibit 5, the terminal value is $V_{10} = D_{11}/(r - g_L)$. Ignoring rounding errors, the Period 11 dividend is €0.9943 ($= D_{10} \times 1.05 = €0.9479 \times 1.05$). By using the standard Gordon growth model, $V_{10} = €47.3473 = €0.9943/(0.071 - 0.05)$. The present value of the terminal value is €23.8452 = €47.3473/1.071^{10}. The total estimated value of Meditec is €28.26 using this model. Notice that approximately 84 percent of this value, €23.85, is the present value of V_{10}, and the balance, €28.26 – €23.85 = €4.41, is the present value of the first ten dividends. Recalling the discussion of the sensitivity of the Gordon growth model to changes in the inputs, an interval for the intrinsic value of Meditec could be calculated by varying the mature growth rate through the range of plausible values.

The two-stage DDM is useful because many scenarios exist in which a company can achieve a supernormal growth rate for a few years, after which time the growth rate falls to a more sustainable level. For example, a company may achieve supernormal growth through possession of a patent, first-mover advantage, or another factor that provides a temporary lead in a specific marketplace. Subsequently, earnings will most likely descend to a level that is more consistent with competition and growth in the overall economy. Accordingly, that is why in the two-stage model, extraordinary growth is often forecast for a few years and normal growth is forecast thereafter. A possible limitation of the two-stage model is that the transition between the initial abnormal growth period and the final steady-state growth period is abrupt.

The accurate estimation of V_n, the **terminal value of the stock** (also known as its **continuing value**) is an important part of the correct use of DDMs. In practice, analysts estimate the terminal value either by applying a multiple to a projected terminal value of a fundamental, such as earnings per share or book value per share, or they estimate V_n using the Gordon growth model. In the reading on market multiples, we will discuss using price–earnings multiples in this context.

In the examples, a single discount rate, r, is used for all phases, reflecting both a desire for simplicity and lack of a clear objective basis for adjusting the discount rate for different phases. Some analysts, however, use different discount rates for different growth phases.

The following example values E. I. DuPont de Nemours and Company by combining the dividend discount model and a P/E valuation model.

Combining a DDM and P/E Model to Value a Stock

An analyst is reviewing the valuation of DuPont (NYSE: DD) as of the beginning of July 2013 when DD is selling for $52.72. In the previous year, DuPont paid a $1.70 dividend that the analyst expects to grow at a rate of 4 percent annually for the next four years. At the end of Year 4, the analyst expects the dividend to equal 35 percent of earnings per share and the trailing P/E for DD to be 13. If the required return on DD common stock is 9.0 percent, calculate the per-share value of DD common stock.

Exhibit 6 summarizes the relevant calculations. When the dividends are growing at 4 percent, the expected dividends and the present value of each (discounted at 9.0 percent) are shown. The terminal stock price, V_4, deserves some explanation. As shown in the table, the Year 4 dividend is $1.70(1.04)^4 = 1.9888$. Because dividends at that time are assumed to be 35 percent of earnings, the EPS projection for Year 4 is $EPS_4 = D_4/0.35 = 1.9888/0.35 = 5.6822$. With a trailing P/E of 13.0, the value of DD at the end of Year 4 should be $13.0(5.6822) = \$73.8682$. Discounted at 9 percent for four years, the present value of V_4 is $52.3301.

Exhibit 6		Value of DuPont Common Stock		
Time	**Value**	**Calculation**	**D_t or V_t**	**Present Values** $D_t/(1.09)^t$ **or** $V_t/(1.09)^t$
1	D_1	$\$1.70(1.04)^1$	$1.7680	$1.6220
2	D_2	$1.70(1.04)^2$	1.8387	1.5476
3	D_3	$1.70(1.04)^3$	1.9123	1.4766
4	D_4	$1.70(1.04)^4$	1.9888	1.4089
4	V_4	$13 \times [1.70(1.04)^4/0.35]$ $= 13 \times [1.9888/0.35]$ $= 13 \times 5.6822$	73.8682	52.3301
Total				$58.3852

The present values of the dividends for Years 1 through 4 sum to $6.06. The present value of the terminal value of $73.87 is $52.33. The estimated total value of DD is the sum of these, or $58.39 per share.

5.2 Valuing a Non-Dividend-Paying Company

The fact that a stock is currently paying no dividends does not mean that the principles of the dividend discount model do not apply. Even though D_0 and/or D_1 may be zero, and the company may not begin paying dividends for some time, the present value of future dividends may still capture the value of the company. Of course, if a company pays no dividends and will never be able to distribute cash to shareholders, the stock is worthless.

To value a non-dividend-paying company using a DDM, generally an analyst can use a multistage DDM model in which the first-stage dividend equals zero. Example 15 illustrates the approach.

Valuing a Non-Dividend-Paying Stock

Assume that a company is currently paying no dividend and will not pay one for several years. If the company begins paying a dividend of $1.00 five years from now, and the dividend is expected to grow at 5 percent thereafter, this future dividend stream can be discounted back to find the value of the company. This company's required rate of return is 11 percent. Because the expression

$$V_n = \frac{D_{n+1}}{r - g}$$

values a stock at period n using the next period's dividend, the $t = 5$ dividend is used to find the value at $t = 4$:

$$V_4 = \frac{D_5}{r - g} = \frac{1.00}{0.11 - 0.05} = \$16.67$$

To find the value of the stock today, simply discount V_4 back for four years:

$$V_0 = \frac{V_4}{(1 + r)^4} = \frac{16.67}{(1.11)^4} = \$10.98$$

The value of this stock, even though it will not pay a dividend until Year 5, is $10.98.

If a company is not paying a dividend but is very profitable, an analyst might be willing to forecast its future dividends. Of course, for non-dividend-paying, unprofitable companies, such a forecast would be very difficult. Furthermore, as discussed in Section 2.2 (Streams of Expected Cash Flows), it is usually difficult for the analyst to estimate the timing of the initiation of dividends and the dividend policy that will then be established by the company. Thus, the analyst may prefer a free cash flow or residual income model for valuing such companies.

5.3 The H-Model

The basic two-stage model assumes a constant, extraordinary rate for the supernormal growth period that is followed by a constant, normal growth rate thereafter. The difference in growth rates may be substantial. For instance, in Example 13, the growth rate for Carl Zeiss Meditec was 15 percent annually for 10 years, followed by a drop to 8 percent growth in Year 11 and thereafter. In some cases, a smoother transition to the mature phase growth rate would be more realistic. Fuller and Hsia (1984) developed a variant of the two-stage model in which growth begins at a high rate and declines linearly throughout the supernormal growth period until it reaches a normal rate at the end. The value of the dividend stream in the H-model is

$$V_0 = \frac{D_0(1 + g_L)}{r - g_L} + \frac{D_0 H(g_S - g_L)}{r - g_L} \qquad (20)$$

or

$$V_0 = \frac{D_0(1 + g_L) + D_0 H(g_S - g_L)}{r - g_L}$$

Where

V_0 = value per share at $t = 0$

D_0 = current dividend

r = required rate of return on equity

H = half-life in years of the high-growth period (i.e., high-growth period = $2H$ years)

g_S = initial short-term dividend growth rate

g_L = normal long-term dividend growth rate after Year $2H$

The first term on the right-hand side of Equation 20 is the present value of the company's dividend stream if it were to grow at g_L forever. The second term is an approximation of the extra value (assuming $g_S > g_L$) accruing to the stock because of its supernormal growth for Years 1 through $2H$ (see Fuller and Hsia 1984, for technical details).[23] Logically, the longer the supernormal growth period (i.e., the larger the value of H, which is one-half the length of the supernormal growth period) and the larger the extra growth rate in the supernormal growth period (measured by g_S minus g_L), the higher the share value, all else equal. To illustrate the expression, if the analyst in Example 13 had forecast a linear decline of the growth rate from 15 percent to 8 percent over the next 10 years, his estimate of value using the H-model would have been €11.78 (rather than €16.09 as in Example 13):

$$
\begin{aligned}
V_0 &= \frac{D_0(1 + g_L) + D_0 H(g_S - g_L)}{r - g_L} \\
&= \frac{0.14(1.08) + 0.14(5)(0.15 - 0.08)}{0.097 - 0.08} \\
&= \frac{0.1512 + 0.0490}{0.017} \\
&= 11.78
\end{aligned}
$$

Note that an H of 5 corresponds to the 10-year high-growth period of Example 13. Example 16 provides another illustration of the H-model.

EXAMPLE 16

Valuing a Stock with the H-Model

Françoise Delacour, a portfolio manager of a US-based diversified global equity portfolio, is researching the valuation of Vinci SA (NYSE Euronext: DG). Vinci is the world's largest construction company, operating chiefly in France (approximately two-thirds of revenue) and the rest of Europe (approximately one-quarter of revenue). Through 2003, DG paid a single regular cash dividend per fiscal year. Since 2004 it has paid two dividends per (fiscal) year, an interim dividend in December and a final dividend in May. Although during the past five years total annual dividends grew at less than 3 percent per year, Delacour foresees faster future growth.

---

23 We can provide some intuition on the expression. On average, the expected excess growth rate in the supernormal period will be $(g_S - g_L)/2$. Through $2H$ periods, a total excess amount of dividends (compared with the level given g_L) of $2HD_0(g_S - g_L)/2 = D_0H(g_S - g_L)$ is expected. This term is the H-model upward adjustment to the first dividend term, reflecting the extra expected dividends as growth declines from g_S to g_L during the first period. Note, however, that the timing of the individual dividends in the first period is not reflected by individually discounting them; the expression is thus an approximation.

Having decided to compute the H-model value estimate for DG, Delacour gathers the following facts and forecasts:

- The share price as of mid-August 2013 was €41.70.
- The current dividend is €1.77.
- The initial dividend growth rate is 7 percent, declining linearly during a 10-year period to a final and perpetual growth rate of 4 percent.
- Delacour estimates DG's required rate of return on equity as 9.5 percent.

1 Using the H-model and the information given, estimate the per-share value of DG.

2 Estimate the value of DG shares if its normal growth period began immediately.

3 Evaluate whether DG shares appear to be fairly valued, overvalued, or undervalued.

Solution to 1:

Using the H-model expression gives

$$
\begin{aligned}
V_0 &= \frac{D_0(1 + g_L)}{r - g_L} + \frac{D_0 H(g_S - g_L)}{r - g_L} \\
&= \frac{1.77(1.04)}{0.095 - 0.04} + \frac{1.77(5)(0.07 - 0.04)}{0.095 - 0.04} \\
&= 33.47 + 4.83 = €38.30
\end{aligned}
$$

Solution to 2:

If DG experienced normal growth starting now, its estimated value would be the first component of the H-model estimate, €33.47. Note that the faster initial growth assumption adds €4.83 to its value, resulting in an estimate of €38.30 for the value of a DG share.

Solution to 3:

€38.30 is approximately 8 percent less than DG's current market price. Thus DG appears to be overvalued.

The H-model is an approximation model that estimates the valuation that would result from discounting all of the future dividends individually. In many circumstances, this approximation is very close. For a long extraordinary growth period (a high H) or for a large difference in growth rates (the difference between g_S and g_L), however, the analyst might abandon the approximation model for the more exact model. Fortunately, the many tedious calculations of the exact model are made fairly easy using a spreadsheet program.

5.4 Three-Stage Dividend Discount Models

There are two popular versions of the three-stage DDM, distinguished by the modeling of the second stage. In the first version ("the general three-stage model"), the company is assumed to have three distinct stages of growth and the growth rate of the second stage is typically constant. For example, Stage 1 could assume 20 percent growth for three years, Stage 2 could have 10 percent growth for four years, and Stage 3 could have 5 percent growth thereafter. In the second version, the growth rate in the middle (second) stage is assumed to decline linearly to the mature growth rate: essentially, the second and third stages are treated as an H-model.

The example below shows how the first type of the three-stage model can be used to value a stock, in this case IBM.

EXAMPLE 17

The Three-Stage DDM with Three Distinct Stages

IBM (as of early 2013) pays a dividend of $3.30 per year. A current price is $194.98. An analyst makes the following estimates:

- the current required return on equity for IBM is 9 percent, and

- dividends will grow at 14 percent for the next two years, 12 percent for the following five years, and 6.75 percent thereafter.

Based only on the information given, estimate the value of IBM using a three-stage DDM approach.

Solution:

Exhibit 7 gives the calculations.

Exhibit 7   Estimated Value of IBM

Time	Value	Calculation	D_t or V_t	Present Values $D_t/(1.09)^t$ or $V_t/(1.09)^t$
1	D_1	$3.30(1.14)$	$3.7620	$3.4514
2	D_2	$3.30(1.14)^2$	4.2887	3.6097
3	D_3	$3.30(1.14)^2(1.12)$	4.8033	3.7090
4	D_4	$3.30(1.14)^2(1.12)^2$	5.3797	3.8111
5	D_5	$3.30(1.14)^2(1.12)^3$	6.0253	3.9160
6	D_6	$3.30(1.14)^2(1.12)^4$	6.7483	4.0238
7	D_7	$3.30(1.14)^2(1.12)^5$	7.5581	4.1346
7	V_7	$3.30(1.14)^2(1.12)^5(1.0675)/$ $(0.09 - 0.0675)$	$358.5908	196.161
Total				$222.8171

Given these assumptions, the three-stage model indicates that a fair price should be $222.82, which is above the current market price by over 14 percent. Characteristically, the present value of the terminal value of $196.16 constitutes the overwhelming portion (here, about 88 percent) of total estimated value.

A second version of the three-stage DDM has a middle stage similar to the first stage in the H-model. In the first stage, dividends grow at a high, constant (supernormal) rate for the whole period. In the second stage, dividends decline linearly as they do in the H-model. Finally, in Stage 3, dividends grow at a sustainable, constant growth rate. The process of using this model involves four steps:

- Gather the required inputs:

- the current dividend;
- the lengths of the first, second, and third stages;
- the expected growth rates for the first and third stages; and
- an estimate of the required return on equity.

■ Compute the expected dividends in the first stage and find the sum of their present values.

■ Apply the H-model expression to the second and third stages to obtain an estimate of their value as of the beginning of the second stage. Then find the present value of this H-value as of today ($t = 0$).

■ Sum the values obtained in the second and third steps.

In the first step, analysts often investigate the company more deeply, making explicit, individual earnings and dividend forecasts for the near future (often 3, 5, or 10 years), rather than applying a growth rate to the current level of dividends.

EXAMPLE 18

The Three-Stage DDM with Declining Growth Rates in Stage 2

Elaine Bouvier is evaluating Energen (NYSE: EGN) for possible inclusion in a small-cap growth oriented portfolio. Headquartered in Alabama, EGN is a diversified energy company involved in oil and gas exploration through its subsidiary, Energen Resources, and in natural gas distribution through its Alabama Gas Corporation subsidiary. In light of EGN's aggressive program of purchasing oil and gas producing properties, Bouvier expects above average growth for the next five years. Bouvier establishes the following facts and forecasts (as of the beginning of August 2013):

■ The current market price is $56.18.

■ The current dividend is $0.56.

■ Bouvier forecasts an initial 5-year period of 11 percent per year earnings and dividend growth.

■ Bouvier anticipates that EGN can grow 6.5 percent per year as a mature company, and allows 10 years for the transition to the mature growth period.

■ To estimate the required return on equity using the CAPM, Bouvier uses an adjusted beta of 1.2 based on 2 years of weekly observations, an estimated equity risk premium of 4.2 percent, and a risk-free rate based on the 20-year Treasury bond yield of 3 percent.

■ Bouvier considers any security trading within a band of ± 20 percent of her estimate of intrinsic value to be within a "fair value range."

1 Estimate the required return on EGN using the CAPM. (Use only one decimal place in stating the result.)

2 Estimate the value of EGN using a three-stage dividend discount model with a linearly declining dividend growth rate in Stage 2.

3 Calculate the percentages of the total value represented by the first stage and by the second and third stages considered as one group.

4 Judge whether EGN is undervalued or overvalued according to Bouvier's perspective.

5 Some analysts are forecasting essentially flat EPS and dividends in the second year. Estimate the value of EGN making the assumption that EPS is flat in the second year and that 11 percent growth resumes in the third year.

Solution to 1:

The required return on equity is r = 3 percent + 1.2(4.2 percent) = 8 percent.

Solution to 2:

The first step is to compute the five dividends in Stage 1 and find their present values at 8 percent. The dividends in Stages 2 and 3 can be valued with the H-model, which estimates their value at the beginning of Stage 2. This value is then discounted back to find the dividends' present value at $t = 0$.

The calculation of the five dividends in Stage 1 and their present values are given in Exhibit 8. The H-model for calculating the value of the Stage 2 and Stage 3 dividends at the beginning of Stage 2 ($t = 5$) would be

$$V_5 = \frac{D_5(1 + g_L)}{r - g_L} + \frac{D_5 H(g_S - g_L)}{r - g_L}$$

where

$D_5 = D_0(1 + g_S)^5 = 0.56(1.11)^5 = \$0.9436$

$g_S = 11.0\%$

$g_L = 6.5\%$

$r = 8.0\%$

$H = 5$ (the second stage lasts $2H$ = 10 years)

Substituting these values into the equation for the H-model gives V_5 as:

$$V_5 = \frac{0.9436(1.065)}{0.08 - 0.065} + \frac{0.9463(5)(0.11 - 0.065)}{0.08 - 0.065}$$

$$= 66.9979 + 14.1545$$

$$= \$81.1524$$

The present value of V_5 is $\$81.1524/(1.08)^5 = \$55.2310$.

Exhibit 8	Energen			
Time	D_t or V_t	Explanation of D_t or V_t	Value of D_t or V_t	PV at 8%
1	D_1	$0.564(1.11)^1$	$0.6216	$0.5756
2	D_2	$0.564(1.11)^2$	0.6900	0.5915
3	D_3	$0.564(1.11)^3$	0.7659	0.6080
4	D_4	$0.564(1.11)^4$	0.8501	0.6249
5	D_5	$0.564(1.11)^5$	0.9436	0.6422
5	V_5	H-model explained above	$81.1524	55.2310
Total				$58.2731

According to the three-stage DDM model, the total value of EGN is $58.27.

Solution to 3:

The sum of the first five present value amounts in the last column of Exhibit 8 is $3.0422. Thus, the first stage represents $3.0422/$58.2731 = 5.2 percent of total value. The second and third stages together represent 100% − 5.2% = 94.8 percent of total value (check: $55.2310/$58.2731 = 94.8 percent).

Solution to 4:

The band Bouvier is looking at is $58.27 ± 0.20($58.27), which runs from $58.27 + $11.65 = $69.92 on the upside to $58.27 − $11.65 = $46.62 on the downside. Because $58.27 is between $46.62 and $69.92, Bouvier would consider EGN to be fairly valued.

Solution to 5:

The estimated value becomes $52.56 with no growth in Year 2 as shown in Exhibit 9. The value of the second and third stages are given by

$$V_5 = \frac{0.8501(1.065)}{0.08 - 0.065} + \frac{0.8501(5)(0.11 - 0.065)}{0.08 - 0.065} = \$73.1103$$

Exhibit 9	Energen with No Growth in Year 2			
Time	D_t or V_t	Explanation of D_t or V_t	Value of D_t or V_t	PV at 8%
1	D_1	$0.564(1.11)^1$	$0.6216	$0.5756
2	D_2	No growth in Year 2	0.6216	0.5329
3	D_3	$0.564(1.11)^2$	0.6900	0.5477
4	D_4	$0.564(1.11)^3$	0.7659	0.5629
5	D_5	$0.564(1.11)^4$	0.8501	0.5786
5	V_5	H-model explained above	$73.1103	49.7576
Total				$52.5553

In Problem 5 of Example 18, the analyst examined the consequences of 11 percent growth in Year 1 and no growth in Year 2, with 11 percent growth resuming in Years 3, 4, and 5. In the first stage, analysts may forecast earnings and dividends individually for a certain number of years.

The three-stage DDM with declining growth in Stage 2 has been widely used among companies using a DDM approach to valuation. An example is the DDM adopted by Bloomberg L.P., a financial services company that provides "Bloomberg terminals" to professional investors and analysts. The Bloomberg DDM is a model that provides an estimated value for any stock that the user selects. The DDM is a three-stage model with declining growth in Stage 2. The model uses fundamentals about the company for assumed Stage 1 and Stage 3 growth rates, and then assumes that the Stage 2 rate is a linearly declining rate between the Stage 1 and Stage 3 rates. The model also makes estimates of the required rate of return and the lengths of the three stages, assigning higher growth companies shorter growth periods (i.e., first stages) and longer transition periods, and slower growth companies longer growth periods and shorter transition periods. Fixing the total length of the growth and transition phases together at 17 years, the growth stage/transition stage durations for Bloomberg's four growth classifications are 3 years/14 years for "explosive growth" equities, 5 years/12 years for "high growth" equities, 7 years/10 years for "average growth" equities, and 9 years/8 years for "slow/mature growth" equities. Analysts, by tailoring stage specifications to their understanding of the specific company being valued, should be able to improve on the accuracy of valuations compared to a fixed specification.

5.5 Spreadsheet (General) Modeling

DDMs, such as the Gordon growth model and the multistage models presented earlier, assume stylized patterns of dividend growth. With the computational power of personal computers, calculators, and personal digital assistants, however, *any* assumed dividend pattern is easily valued.

Spreadsheets allow the analyst to build complicated models that would be very cumbersome to describe using algebra. Furthermore, built-in spreadsheet functions (such as those for finding rates of return) use algorithms to get a numerical answer when a mathematical solution would be impossible or extremely challenging. Because of the widespread use of spreadsheets, several analysts can work together or exchange information by sharing their spreadsheet models. The following example presents the results of using a spreadsheet to value a stock with dividends that change substantially through time.

EXAMPLE 19

Finding the Value of a Stock Using a Spreadsheet Model

Yang Co. is expected to pay a $21.00 dividend next year. The dividend will decline by 10 percent annually for the following three years. In Year 5, Yang will sell off assets worth $100 per share. The Year 5 dividend, which includes a distribution of some of the proceeds of the asset sale, is expected to be $60. In Year 6, the dividend is expected to decrease to $40 and will be maintained at $40 for one additional year. The dividend is then expected to grow by 5 percent annually thereafter. If the required rate of return is 12 percent, what is the value of one share of Yang?

Solution:

The value is shown in Exhibit 10. Each dividend, its present value discounted at 12 percent, and an explanation are included in the table. The final row treats the dividends from $t = 8$ forward as a Gordon growth model because after Year 7, the dividend grows at a constant 5 percent annually. V_7 is the value of these dividends at $t = 7$.

Exhibit 10	Value of Yang Co. Stock			
Year	D_t or V_t	Value of D_t or V_t	Present Value at 12%	Explanation of D_t or V_t
1	D_1	$21.00	$18.75	Dividend set at $21
2	D_2	18.90	15.07	Previous dividend × 0.90
3	D_3	17.01	12.11	Previous dividend × 0.90
4	D_4	15.31	9.73	Previous dividend × 0.90
5	D_5	60.00	34.05	Set at $60
6	D_6	40.00	20.27	Set at $40
7	D_7	40.00	18.09	Set at $40

(continued)

			Present	
		Value of	Value at	
Year	D_t or V_t	D_t or V_t	12%	Explanation of D_t or V_t
7	V_7	600.00	271.41	$V_7 = D_8/(r-g)$
				$V_7 = (40.00 \times 1.05)/(0.12 - 0.05)$
Total			\$399.48	

Exhibit 10   (Continued)

As the table in Example 19 shows, the total present value of Yang Co.'s dividends is \$399.48. In this example, the terminal value of the company (V_n) at the end of the first stage is found using the Gordon growth model and a mature growth rate of 5 percent. Several alternative approaches to estimating g are available in this context:

- Use the formula g = (b in the mature phase) × (ROE in the mature phase). We will discuss the expression $g = b \times$ ROE in Section 6. Analysts estimate mature-phase ROE in several ways, such as:

  - The DuPont decomposition of ROE based on forecasts for the components of the DuPont expression.

  - Setting ROE = r, the required rate of return on equity, based on the assumption that in the mature phase companies can do no more than earn investors' opportunity cost of capital.

  - Setting ROE in the mature phase equal to the median industry ROE.

- The analyst may estimate the growth rate, g, with other models by relating the mature growth rate to macroeconomic, including industry, growth projections.

When the analyst uses the sustainable growth expression, the earnings retention ratio, b, may be empirically based. For example, Bloomberg L.P.'s model assumes that b = 0.55 in the mature phase, equivalent to a dividend payout ratio of 45 percent, a long-run average payout ratio for mature dividend-paying companies in the United States. In addition, sometimes analysts project the dividend payout ratio for the company individually.

EXAMPLE 20

A Sustainable Growth Rate Calculation

In Example 17, the analyst estimated the dividend growth rate of IBM in the final stage of a three-stage model as 6.75 percent. This value was based on the expression

g = (b in the mature phase) × (ROE in the mature phase)

IBM's payout ratio has increased from 16.5 percent to 22.7 percent over the last 10 years. Assuming that in the final stage IBM has a payout ratio of 25 percent and achieves a ROE equal to its estimated required return on equity of 9 percent, the calculation is:

g = 0.75(9%) = 6.75%

5.6 Estimating a Required Return Using Any DDM

This reading has focused on finding the value of a security using assumptions for dividends, required rates of return, and expected growth rates. Given current price and all inputs to a DDM except for the required return, an IRR can be calculated. Such an IRR has been used as a required return estimate (although reusing it in a DDM is not appropriate because it risks circularity). This IRR can also be interpreted as the expected return on the issue implied by the market price—essentially, an efficient market expected return. In the following discussion, keep in mind that if price does not equal intrinsic value, the expected return will need to be adjusted to reflect the additional component of return that accrues when the mispricing is corrected, as discussed earlier.

In some cases, finding the IRR is very easy. In the Gordon growth model, $r = D_1/P_0 + g$. The required return estimate is the dividend yield plus the expected dividend growth rate. For a security with a current price of $10, an expected dividend of $0.50, and expected growth of 8 percent, the required return estimate is 13 percent.

For the H-model, the expected rate of return can be derived as[24]

$$r = \left(\frac{D_0}{P_0}\right)\left[(1 + g_L) + H(g_S - g_L)\right] + g_L \qquad (21)$$

When the short- and long-term growth rates are the same, this model reduces to the Gordon growth model. For a security with a current dividend of $1, a current price of $20, and an expected short-term growth rate of 10 percent declining over 10 years ($H = 5$) to 6 percent, the expected rate of return would be

$$r = \left(\frac{\$1}{\$20}\right)\left[(1 + 0.06) + 5(0.10 - 0.06)\right] + 0.06 = 12.3\%$$

For multistage models and spreadsheet models, finding a single equation for the rate of return can be more difficult. The process generally used is similar to that of finding the IRR for a series of varying cash flows. Using a computer or trial and error, the analyst must find the rate of return such that the present value of future expected dividends equals the current stock price.

EXAMPLE 21

Finding the Expected Rate of Return for Varying Expected Dividends

An analyst expects JNJ's (Johnson & Johnson) dividend of $2.40 for 2012 to grow by 7.5 percent for six years and then grow by 6 percent into perpetuity. A recent price for JNJ as of late-August 2013 is $86.97. What is the IRR on an investment in JNJ's stock?

In performing trial and error with the two-stage model to estimate the expected rate of return, having a good initial guess is important. In this case, the expected rate of return formula from the Gordon growth model and JNJ's long-term growth rate can be used to find a first approximation: $r = (\$2.40 \times 1.075)/\$86.97 + 0.06 = 9$ percent. Because the growth rate in the first six years is more than the long-term growth rate of 6 percent, the estimated rate of return must be above 9 percent. Exhibit 11 shows the value estimate of JNJ for two discount rates, 9 percent and 10 percent.

---

[24] Fuller and Hsia (1984).

		Present Value of D_t and V_6 at r = 9%	**Present Value of D_t and V_6 at r = 10%**
Time	D_t		
1	$2.5800	$2.3670	$2.3455
2	2.7735	2.3344	2.2921
3	2.9815	2.3023	2.2401
4	3.2051	2.2706	2.1891
5	3.4455	2.2393	2.1394
6	3.7039	2.2085	2.0908
7	3.9262		
Subtotal 1	(t = 1 to 6)	$13.7221	$13.2970
Subtotal 2	(t = 7 to ∞)	$78.0347	$55.4054
Total		$91.76	$68.70
Market Price		$86.97	$86.97

Exhibit 11   Johnson & Johnson

In the exhibit, the first subtotal is the present value of the expected dividends for Years 1 through 6. The second subtotal is the present value of the terminal value, $V_6/(1 + r)^6 = [D_7/(r - g)]/(1 + r)^6$. For r = 9 percent, that present value is $[3.9262/(0.09 - 0.06)]/(1.09)^6 = \$78.0347$. The present value for other values of r is found similarly.

Using 9 percent as the discount rate, the value estimate for JNJ is $91.76, which is about 5.5 percent larger than JNJ's market price of $86.97. This fact indicates that the IRR is greater than 9 percent. With a 10 percent discount rate, the present value of $68.72 is significantly less than the market price. Thus, the IRR is slightly more than 9 percent. The IRR can be determined to be 9.16 percent, using a calculator or spreadsheet.

5.7 Multistage DDM: Concluding Remarks

Multistage dividend discount models can accommodate a variety of patterns of future streams of expected dividends.

In general, multistage DDMs make stylized assumptions about growth based on a lifecycle view of business. The first stage of a multistage DDM frequently incorporates analysts' individual earnings and dividend forecasts for the next two to five years (sometimes longer). The final stage is often modeled using the Gordon growth model based on an assumption of the company's long-run sustainable growth rate. In the case of the H-model, the transition to the mature growth phase happens smoothly during the first stage. In the case of the standard two-stage model, the growth rate typically transitions immediately to mature growth rate in the second period. In three-stage models, the middle stage is a stage of transition. Using a spreadsheet, an analyst can model an almost limitless variety of cash flow patterns.

Multistage DDMs have several limitations. Often, the present value of the terminal stage represents more than three-quarters of the total value of shares. Terminal value can be very sensitive to the growth and required return assumptions. Furthermore, technological innovation can make the lifecycle model a crude representation.

THE FINANCIAL DETERMINANTS OF GROWTH RATES

6

In a number of examples earlier in this reading, we have implicitly used the relationship that the dividend growth rate (g) equals the earning retention ratio (b) times the return on equity (ROE). In this section, we explain this relationship and show how it can be combined with a method of analyzing return on equity, called DuPont analysis, as a simple tool for forecasting dividend growth rates.

6.1 Sustainable Growth Rate

We define the **sustainable growth rate** as the rate of dividend (and earnings) growth that can be sustained for a given level of return on equity, assuming that the capital structure is constant through time and that additional common stock is not issued. The reason for studying this concept is that it can help in estimating the stable growth rate in a Gordon growth model valuation, or the mature growth rate in a multistage DDM in which the Gordon growth formula is used to find the terminal value of the stock.

The expression to calculate the sustainable growth rate is

$$g = b \times \text{ROE} \qquad \textbf{(22)}$$

where

> g = dividend growth rate
> b = earnings retention rate (1 − Dividend payout ratio)
> ROE = return on equity

More precisely, in Equation 22 the retention rate should be multiplied by the rate of return expected to be earned on new investment. Analysts commonly assume that the rate of return is well approximated by the return on equity, as shown in Equation 22; however, whether that is actually the case should be investigated by the analyst on a case-by-case basis.

Example 22 is an illustration of the fact that growth in shareholders' equity is driven by reinvested earnings alone (no new issues of equity and debt growing at the rate g).[25]

EXAMPLE 22

Example Showing $g = b \times$ ROE

Suppose that a company's ROE is 25 percent and its retention rate is 60 percent. According to the expression for the sustainable growth rate, the dividends should grow at $g = b \times \text{ROE} = 0.60 \times 25$ percent = 15 percent.

To demonstrate the working of the expression, suppose that, in the year just ended, a company began with shareholders' equity of $1,000,000, earned $250,000 net income, and paid dividends of $100,000. The company begins the next year with $1,000,000 + 0.60($250,000) = $1,000,000 + $150,000 = $1,150,000 of shareholders' equity. No additions to equity are made from the sale of additional shares.

If the company again earns 25 percent on equity, net income will be $0.25 \times \$1,150,000 = \$287,500$, which is a $287,500 − $250,000 = $37,500 or a $37,500/$250,000 = 0.15 percent increase from the prior year level. The company retains 60 percent of earnings, 60 percent × $287,500 = $172,500, and pays out

---

[25] With debt growing at the rate g, the capital structure is constant. If the capital structure is not constant, ROE would not be constant in general because ROE depends on leverage.

the other 40 percent, 40 percent × $287,500 = $115,000 as dividends. Dividends for the company grew from $100,000 to $115,000, which is exactly a 15 percent growth rate. With the company continuing to earn 25 percent each year on the 60% of earnings that is reinvested in the company, dividends would continue to grow at 15 percent.

Equation 22 implies that the higher the return on equity, the higher the dividend growth rate, all else constant. That relation appears to be reliable. Another implication of the expression is that the lower (higher) the earnings retention ratio, the lower (higher) the growth rate in dividends, holding all else constant; this relationship has been called *the dividend displacement of earnings*.[26] Of course, all else may not be equal—the return on reinvested earnings may not be constant at different levels of investment, or companies with changing future growth prospects may change their dividend policy. Arnott and Asness (2003) and Zhou and Ruland (2006), in providing US-based evidence that dividend-paying companies had higher future growth rates during the period studied, indicate that caution is appropriate in assuming that dividends displace earnings.

A practical logic for defining *sustainable* in terms of growth through internally generated funds (retained earnings) is that external equity (secondary issues of stock) is considerably more costly than internal equity (reinvested earnings), for several reasons including the investment banker fees associated with secondary equity issues. In general, continuous issuance of new stock is not a practical funding alternative for companies.[27] Growth of capital through issuance of new debt, however, can sometimes be sustained for considerable periods. Further, if a company manages its capital structure to a target percentage of debt to total capital (debt and common stock), it will need to issue debt to maintain that percentage as equity grows through reinvested earnings. (This approach is one of a variety of observed capital structure policies.) In addition, the earnings retention ratio nearly always shows year-to-year variation in actual companies. For example, earnings may have transitory components that management does not want to reflect in dividends. The analyst may thus observe actual dividend growth rates straying from the growth rates predicted by Equation 22 because of these effects, even when his or her input estimates are unbiased. Nevertheless, the equation can be useful as a simple expression for approximating the average rate at which dividends can grow over a long horizon.

---

26 ROE is a variable that reflects underlying profitability as well as the use of leverage or debt. The retention ratio or dividend policy, in contrast, is not a fundamental variable in the same sense as ROE. A higher dividend growth rate through a higher retention ratio (lower dividend payout ratio) is neutral for share value in and of itself. Holding investment policy (capital projects) constant, the positive effect on value from an increase in *g* will be offset by the negative effect from a decrease in dividend payouts in the expression for the value of the stock in any DDM. Sharpe, Alexander, and Bailey (1999) discuss this concept in more detail.
27 As a long-term average, about 2 percent of US publicly traded companies issue new equity in a given year, which corresponds to a secondary equity issue once every 50 years, on average. Businesses may be rationed in their access to secondary issues of equity because of the costs associated with informational asymmetries between management and the public. Because management has more information on the future cash flows of the company than the general public, and equity is an ownership claim to those cash flows, the public may react to additional equity issuance as possibly motivated by an intent to "share (future) misery" rather than "share (future) wealth."

6.2 Dividend Growth Rate, Retention Rate, and ROE Analysis

Thus far we have seen that a company's sustainable growth, as defined in Section 6.1, is a function of its ability to generate return on equity (which depends on investment opportunities) and its retention rate. We now expand this model by examining what drives ROE. Remember that ROE is the return (net income) generated on the equity invested in the company:

$$ROE = \frac{\text{Net income}}{\text{Shareholders' equity}} \qquad (23)$$

If a company has a ROE of 15 percent, it generates $15 of net income for every $100 invested in stockholders' equity. For purposes of analyzing ROE, it can be related to several other financial ratios. For example, ROE can be related to return on assets (ROA) and the extent of financial leverage (equity multiplier):

$$ROE = \frac{\text{Net income}}{\text{Total assets}} \times \frac{\text{Total assets}}{\text{Shareholders' equity}} \qquad (24)$$

Therefore, a company can increase its ROE either by increasing ROA or the use of leverage (assuming the company can borrow at a rate lower than it earns on its assets).

This model can be expanded further by breaking ROA into two components, profit margin and turnover (efficiency):

$$ROE = \frac{\text{Net income}}{\text{Sales}} \times \frac{\text{Sales}}{\text{Total assets}} \times \frac{\text{Total assets}}{\text{Shareholders' equity}} \qquad (25)$$

The first term is the company's profit margin. A higher profit margin will result in a higher ROE. The second term measures total asset turnover, which is the company's efficiency. A turnover of one indicates that a company generates $1 in sales for every $1 invested in assets. A higher turnover will result in higher ROE. The last term is the equity multiplier, which measures the extent of leverage, as noted earlier. This relationship is widely known as the DuPont model or analysis of ROE. Although ROE can be analyzed further using a five-way analysis, the three-way analysis will provide insight into the determinants of ROE that are pertinent to our understanding of the growth rate. By combining Equations 22 and 25, it shows that the dividend growth rate is equal to the retention rate multiplied by ROE:

$$g = \frac{\text{Net income} - \text{Dividends}}{\text{Net income}} \times \frac{\text{Net income}}{\text{Sales}}$$
$$\times \frac{\text{Sales}}{\text{Total assets}} \times \frac{\text{Total assets}}{\text{Shareholders' equity}} \qquad (26)$$

This expansion of the sustainable growth expression has been called the PRAT model (Higgins 2007). Growth is a function of profit margin (P), retention rate (R), asset turnover (A), and financial leverage (T). The profit margin and asset turnover determine ROA. The other two factors, the retention rate and financial leverage, reflect the company's financial policies. So, the growth rate in dividends can be viewed as determined by the company's ROA and financial policies. Analysts may use Equation 26 to forecast a company's dividend growth rate in the mature growth phase.

Theoretically, the sustainable growth rate expression and this expansion of it based on the DuPont decomposition of ROE hold exactly only when ROE is calculated using beginning-of-period shareholders' equity, as illustrated in Example 22. Such calculation assumes that retained earnings are not available for reinvestment until the end of the period. Analysts and financial databases more frequently prefer to use average total assets in calculating ROE and, practically, DuPont analysis is frequently performed using that definition.[28] The example below illustrates the logic behind this equation.

EXAMPLE 23

ROA, Financial Policies, and the Dividend Growth Rate

Baggai Enterprises has an ROA of 10 percent, retains 30 percent of earnings, and has an equity multiplier of 1.25. Mondale Enterprises also has an ROA of 10 percent, but it retains two-thirds of earnings and has an equity multiplier of 2.00.

1   What are the sustainable dividend growth rates for (A) Baggai Enterprises and (B) Mondale Enterprises?

2   Identify the drivers of the difference in the sustainable growth rates of Baggai Enterprises and Mondale Enterprises.

Solution to 1:

A   Baggai's dividend growth rate should be $g = 0.30 \times 10\% \times 1.25 = 3.75\%$.

B   Mondale's dividend growth rate should be $g = (2/3) \times 10\% \times 2.00 = 13.33\%$.

Solution to 2:

Because Mondale has the higher retention rate and higher financial leverage, its dividend growth rate is much higher.

If growth is being forecast for the next five years, an analyst should use the expectations of the four factors driving growth during this five-year period. If growth is being forecast into perpetuity, an analyst should use very long-term forecasts for these variables.

To illustrate the calculation and implications of the sustainable growth rate using the expression for ROE given by the DuPont formula, assume the growth rate is $g = b \times ROE = 0.60$ (15 percent) = 9 percent. The ROE of 15 percent was based on a profit margin of 5 percent, an asset turnover of 2.0, and an equity multiplier of 1.5. Given fixed ratios of sales-to-assets and assets-to-equity, sales, assets, and debt will also be growing at 9 percent. Because dividends are fixed at 40 percent of income, dividends will grow at the same rate as income, or 9 percent. If the company increases dividends faster than 9 percent, this growth rate would not be sustainable using internally generated funds. Earning retentions would be reduced, and the company would not be able to finance the assets required for sales growth without external financing.

An analyst should be careful in projecting historical financial ratios into the future when using this analysis. Although a company may have grown at 25 percent a year for the last five years, this rate of growth is probably not sustainable indefinitely. Abnormally high ROEs, which may have driven that growth, are unlikely to persist indefinitely because of competitive forces and possibly other reasons, such as adverse changes in technology or demand. In the following example, an above average terminal growth rate is plausibly forecasted because the company has positioned itself in businesses that may have relatively high margins on an ongoing basis.

---

28 See Robinson, van Greuning, Henry, and Broihahn (2006).

EXAMPLE 24

Forecasting Growth with the PRAT Formula

International Business Machines (NYSE: IBM), which currently pays a dividend of $3.40 per share, has been the subject of two other examples in this reading. In one example, an analyst estimated IBM's mature phase growth rate at 6.75 percent, based on its mature phase ROE exactly equaling its estimated required return on equity of 9 percent. Another estimate can be made using the DuPont decomposition of ROE.

An analysis of IBM's ROE for the past ten years is shown in Exhibit 12. During the period shown, EPS grew at a compound annual rate of about 16 percent. IBM's retention ratio has declined from 83.5 percent in 2003 to 77.3 percent in 2012. Annual nominal investment in property, plant, and equipment has also declined from $4.4 billion in 2003 to $4.1 billion in 2012.

Exhibit 12	IBM Corporation			
Year	ROE (%)	Profit Margin (%)	Asset Turnover	Financial Leverage
2012	87.5 =	15.89	× 0.88	× 6.28
2011	78.4 =	14.83	× 0.92	× 5.75
2010	64.0 =	14.85	× 0.88	× 4.90
2009	59.0 =	14.02	× 0.88	× 4.79
2008	90.8 =	11.90	× 0.95	× 8.06
2007	36.6 =	10.55	× 0.82	× 4.23
2006	33.3 =	10.38	× 0.89	× 3.62
2005	24.0 =	8.71	× 0.86	× 3.19
2004	23.6 =	7.77	× 0.87	× 3.50
2003	22.2 =	7.36	× 0.84	× 3.59

IBM's ROE has been much higher the last five years than it was in the preceding five year period. This change can largely be attributed to improved profit margins and a significant increase in leverage. However, it is unrealistic to assume that sustainable earnings growth (growth in perpetuity) will be equal to a recent average ROE (75.9 percent over the last five years) times a plausible assumption for the future retention rate (most recently 77.3 percent) given that world-wide economic growth is typically in the mid-single digits. That sort of estimate is also totally inconsistent with the noted historical EPS growth rate of 16.0 percent.

Profit margins are strongly mean-reverting. Suppose the analyst believes that IBM's recent superiority in profit margin in comparison to peers will be much reduced in the mature phase. The analyst forecasts a peer mean pretax profit margin of 5 percent during IBM's mature phase. With its strategy of searching for high-margined growth and its strong ability to compete in integrated hardware–software solutions for businesses, the analyst forecasts a long-run pretax profit margin of 6 percent for IBM, equal to a profit margin (after tax) of about 4.2 percent based on an effective tax rate of about 30 percent.

The analyst also believes that capital investment will continue to decline as IBM matures, and cash flow that was previously used for investment will be used to retire debt and pay dividends. The analyst forecasts a financial leverage ratio of 3.5, consistent with 2003–2007 values, but well below the ratio of 6.28 in 2012. The analyst also sees the dividend payout ratio continuing its recent rise and ultimately reaching a level of 40 percent.

Based on an asset turnover ratio of 0.88 (the mean value in Exhibit 12), but using a profit margin estimate of 4.2, a forecast of ROE in the maturity phase is (4.2 percent)(0.88)(3.5) = 12.9 percent. Therefore, based on this analysis, the estimate of the sustainable growth rate for IBM would be g = (0.60)(12.9 percent) = 7.7 percent.

6.3 Financial Models and Dividends

Analysts can also forecast dividends by building more complex models of the company's total operating and financial environment. Because there can be so many aspects to such a model, a spreadsheet is used to build pro forma income statements and balance sheets. The company's ability to pay dividends in the future can be predicted using one of these models. The example below shows the dividends that a highly profitable and rapidly growing company can pay when its growth rates and profit margins decline because of increasing competition over time.

EXAMPLE 25

A Spreadsheet Model for Forecasting Dividends

An analyst is preparing a forecast of dividends for Hoshino Distributors for the next five years. He uses a spreadsheet model with the following assumptions:

- Sales are $100 million in Year 1. They grow by 20 percent in Year 2, 15 percent in Year 3, and 10 percent in Years 4 and 5.

- Operating profits (earnings before interest and taxes, or EBIT) are 20 percent of sales in Years 1 and 2, 18 percent of sales in Year 3, and 16 percent of sales in Years 4 and 5.

- Interest expenses are 10 percent of total debt for the current year.

- The income tax rate is 40 percent.

- Hoshino pays out 20 percent of earnings in dividends in Years 1 and 2, 30 percent in Year 3, 40 percent in Year 4, and 50 percent in Year 5.

- Retained earnings are added to equity in the next year.

- Total assets are 80 percent of the current year's sales in all years.

- In Year 1, debt is $40 million and shareholders' equity is $40 million. Debt equals total assets minus shareholders' equity. Shareholders' equity will equal the previous year's shareholders' equity plus the addition to retained earnings from the previous year.

- Hoshino has 4 million shares outstanding.

- The required return on equity is 15 percent.

- The value of the company at the end of Year 5 is expected to be 10.0 times earnings.

The analyst wants to estimate the current value per share of Hoshino. Exhibit 13 adheres to the modeling assumptions above. Total dividends and earnings are found at the bottom of the income statement.

Exhibit 13 Hoshino Distributors Pro Forma Financial Statements (in Millions)

	Year 1	Year 2	Year 3	Year 4	Year 5
Income statement					
Sales	$100.00	$120.00	$138.00	$151.80	$166.98
EBIT	20.00	24.00	24.84	24.29	26.72
Interest	4.00	4.83	5.35	5.64	6.18
EBT	16.00	19.17	19.49	18.65	20.54
Taxes	6.40	7.67	7.80	7.46	8.22
Net income	9.60	11.50	11.69	11.19	12.32
Dividends	1.92	2.30	3.51	4.48	6.16
Balance sheet					
Total assets	$80.00	$96.00	$110.40	$121.44	$133.58
Total debt	40.00	48.32	53.52	56.38	61.81
Equity	40.00	47.68	56.88	65.06	71.77

Dividing the total dividends by the number of outstanding shares gives the dividend per share for each year shown below. The present value of each dividend, discounted at 15 percent, is also shown.

	Year 1	Year 2	Year 3	Year 4	Year 5	Total
DPS	$0.480	$0.575	$0.877	$1.120	$1.540	$4.59
PV	0.417	0.435	0.577	0.640	0.766	2.84

The earnings per share in Year 5 are $12.32 million divided by 4 million shares, or $3.08 per share. Given a P/E of 10, the market price in Year 5 is predicted to be $30.80. Discounted at 15 percent, the required return on equity by assumption, the present value of this price is $15.31. Adding the present values of the five dividends, which sum to $2.84, gives a total stock value today of $18.15 per share.

SUMMARY

This reading provided an overview of DCF models of valuation, discussed the estimation of a stock's required rate of return, and presented in detail the dividend discount model.

- In DCF models, the value of any asset is the present value of its (expected) future cash flows

$$V_0 = \sum_{t=1}^{n} \frac{CF_t}{(1+r)^t}$$

where V_0 is the value of the asset as of $t = 0$ (today), CF_t is the (expected) cash flow at time t, and r is the discount rate or required rate of return. For infinitely lived assets such as common stocks, n runs to infinity.

- Several alternative streams of expected cash flows can be used to value equities, including dividends, free cash flow, and residual income. A discounted dividend approach is most suitable for dividend-paying stocks in which the company has a discernible dividend policy that has an understandable relationship to the company's profitability, and the investor has a noncontrol (minority ownership) perspective.

- The free cash flow approach (FCFF or FCFE) might be appropriate when the company does not pay dividends, dividends differ substantially from FCFE, free cash flows align with profitability, or the investor takes a control (majority ownership) perspective.

- The residual income approach can be useful when the company does not pay dividends (as an alternative to a FCF approach) or free cash flow is negative.

- The DDM with a single holding period gives stock value as

$$V_0 = \frac{D_1}{(1+r)^1} + \frac{P_1}{(1+r)^1} = \frac{D_1 + P_1}{(1+r)^1}$$

  where D_1 is the expected dividend at time 1 and V_0 is the stock's (expected) value at time 0. Assuming that V_0 is equal to today's market price, P_0, the expected holding-period return is

$$r = \frac{D_1 + P_1}{P_0} - 1 = \frac{D_1}{P_0} + \frac{P_1 - P_0}{P_0}$$

- The expression for the DDM for any given finite holding period n and the general expression for the DDM are, respectively,

$$V_0 = \sum_{t=1}^{n} \frac{D_t}{(1+r)^t} + \frac{P_n}{(1+r)^n} \text{ and } V_0 = \sum_{t=1}^{\infty} \frac{D_t}{(1+r)^t}$$

- There are two main approaches to the problem of forecasting dividends. First, an analyst can assign the entire stream of expected future dividends to one of several stylized growth patterns. Second, an analyst can forecast a finite number of dividends individually up to a terminal point and value the remaining dividends either by assigning them to a stylized growth pattern or by forecasting share price as of the terminal point of the dividend forecasts.

- The Gordon growth model assumes that dividends grow at a constant rate g forever, so that $D_t = D_{t-1}(1 + g)$. The dividend stream in the Gordon growth model has a value of

$$V_0 = \frac{D_0(1+g)}{r-g}, \text{ or } V_0 = \frac{D_1}{r-g} \text{ where } r > g$$

- The value of noncallable fixed-rate perpetual preferred stock is $V_0 = D/r$, where D is the stock's (constant) annual dividend.

- Assuming that price equals value, the Gordon growth model estimate of a stock's expected rate of return is

$$r = \frac{D_0(1+g)}{P_0} + g = \frac{D_1}{P_0} + g$$

- Given an estimate of the next-period dividend and the stock's required rate of return, the Gordon growth model can be used to estimate the dividend growth rate implied by the current market price (making a constant growth rate assumption).

- The present value of growth opportunities (PVGO) is the part of a stock's total value, V_0, that comes from profitable future growth opportunities in contrast to the value associated with assets already in place. The relationship is $V_0 = E_1/r +$ PVGO, where E_1/r is defined as the no-growth value per share.

- The leading price-to-earnings ratio (P_0/E_1) and the trailing price-to-earnings ratio (P_0/E_0) can be expressed in terms of the Gordon growth model as, respectively,

$$\frac{P_0}{E_1} = \frac{D_1/E_1}{r - g} = \frac{1 - b}{r - g} \text{ and } \frac{P_0}{E_0} = \frac{D_0(1 + g)/E_0}{r - g} = \frac{(1 - b)(1 + g)}{r - g}$$

The above expressions give a stock's justified price-to-earnings ratio based on forecasts of fundamentals (given that the Gordon growth model is appropriate).

- The Gordon growth model may be useful for valuing broad-based equity indices and the stock of businesses with earnings that are expected to grow at a stable rate comparable to or lower than the nominal growth rate of the economy.

- Gordon growth model values are very sensitive to the assumed growth rate and required rate of return.

- For many companies, growth falls into phases. In the growth phase, a company enjoys an abnormally high growth rate in earnings per share, called supernormal growth. In the transition phase, earnings growth slows. In the mature phase, the company reaches an equilibrium in which such factors as earnings growth and the return on equity stabilize at levels that can be sustained long term. Analysts often apply multistage DCF models to value the stock of a company with multistage growth prospects.

- The two-stage dividend discount model assumes different growth rates in Stage 1 and Stage 2

$$V_0 = \sum_{t=1}^{n} \frac{D_0(1 + g_S)^t}{(1 + r)^t} + \frac{D_0(1 + g_S)^n(1 + g_L)}{(1 + r)^n(r - g_L)}$$

where g_S is the expected dividend growth rate in the first period and g_L is the expected growth rate in the second period.

- The terminal stock value, V_n, is sometimes found with the Gordon growth model or with some other method, such as applying a P/E multiplier to forecasted EPS as of the terminal date.

- The H-model assumes that the dividend growth rate declines linearly from a high supernormal rate to the normal growth rate during Stage 1, and then grows at a constant normal growth rate thereafter:

$$V_0 = \frac{D_0(1 + g_L)}{r - g_L} + \frac{D_0 H(g_S - g_L)}{r - g_L} = \frac{D_0(1 + g_L) + D_0 H(g_S - g_L)}{r - g_L}$$

- There are two basic three-stage models. In one version, the growth rate in the middle stage is constant. In the second version, the growth rate declines linearly in Stage 2 and becomes constant and normal in Stage 3.

- Spreadsheet models are very flexible, providing the analyst with the ability to value any pattern of expected dividends.

- In addition to valuing equities, the IRR of a DDM, assuming assets are correctly priced in the marketplace, has been used to estimate required returns. For simpler models (such as the one-period model, the Gordon growth model, and the H-model), well-known formulas may be used to calculate these rates of return.

For many dividend streams, however, the rate of return must be found by trial and error, producing a discount rate that equates the present value of the forecasted dividend stream to the current market price.

■ Multistage DDM models can accommodate a wide variety of patterns of expected dividends. Even though such models may use stylized assumptions about growth, they can provide useful approximations.

■ Dividend growth rates can be obtained from analyst forecasts, statistical forecasting models, or company fundamentals. The sustainable growth rate depends on the ROE and the earnings retention rate, b: $g = b \times$ ROE. This expression can be expanded further, using the DuPont formula, as

$$g = \frac{\text{Net income} - \text{Dividends}}{\text{Net income}} \times \frac{\text{Net income}}{\text{Sales}}$$
$$\times \frac{\text{Sales}}{\text{Total assets}} \times \frac{\text{Total assets}}{\text{Shareholders' equity}}$$

REFERENCES

Arnott, Robert D., and Clifford S. Asness. 2003. "Surprise! Higher Dividends = Higher Earnings Growth." *Financial Analysts Journal*, vol. 59, no. 1:70–87.

Block, Stanley B. 1999. "A Study of Financial Analysts: Practice and Theory." *Financial Analysts Journal*, vol. 55, no. 4:86–95.

Brealey, Richard A., Stewart C. Myers, and Franklin Allen. 2006. *Principles of Corporate Finance*. New York: McGraw-Hill/Irwin.

DeFusco, Richard, Dennis McLeavey, Jerald Pinto, and David Runkle. 2004. *Quantitative Methods for Investment Analysis*, 2nd edition. Charlottesville, VA: CFA Institute.

Fama, Eugene F., and Kenneth R. French. 2001. "Disappearing Dividends: Changing Firm Characteristics or Lower Propensity to Pay?" *Journal of Financial Economics*, vol. 60, no. 1:3–43.

Fuller, Russell J., and Chi-Cheng Hsia. 1984. "A Simplified Common Stock Valuation Model." *Financial Analysts Journal*, vol. 40, no. 5:49–56.

Gordon, Myron J. 1962. *The Investment, Financing, and Valuation of the Corporation*. Homeward, IL: Richard D. Irwin.

Gordon, Myron J., and Eli Shapiro. 1956. "Capital Equipment Analysis: The Required Rate of Profit." *Management Science*, vol. 3, no. 1:102–110.

Grullon, Gustavo, Bradley S. Paye, Shane Underwood, and James Weston. 2007. "Has the Propensity to Pay Out Declined?" Working Paper.

Julio, Brandon, and David L. Ikenberry. 2004. "Reappearing Dividends." *Journal of Applied Corporate Finance*, vol. 16, no. 4:89–100.

Leibowitz, Martin L. 1997. "Sales-Driven Franchise Value." Charlottesville, VA: Research Foundation of the ICFA.

Leibowitz, Martin L., and Stanley Kogelman. 1990. "Inside the P/E Ratio: The Franchise Factor." *Financial Analysts Journal*, vol. 46, no. 6:17–35.

Lintner, John. 1956. "Distribution of Incomes of Corporations among Dividends, Retained Earnings, and Taxes." *American Economic Review*, vol. 46:97–113.

Miller, Merton, and Franco Modigliani. 1961. "Dividend Policy, Growth, and the Valuation of Shares." *Journal of Business*, vol. 34, no. 4:411–433.

Robinson, Thomas, Hennie van Greuning, Elaine Henry, and Michael Broihahn. 2006. "Financial Analysis Techniques." *International Financial Statement Analysis*. Hoboken, NJ: John Wiley & Sons.

Sharpe, William, Gordon Alexander, and Jeffery Bailey. 1999. *Investments*. Upper Saddle River, NJ: Prentice Hall.

Skinner, Douglas J. 2008. "The Evolving Relation between Earnings, Dividends, and Stock Repurchases." *Journal of Financial Economics*, vol. 87, no. 3:582–609.

von Eije, J. Henk, and William L. Megginson. 2008. "Dividends and Share Repurchases in the European Union." *Journal of Financial Economics*, vol. 89:347–374.

Wanger, Ralph. 2007. "More Dividends, Please." *CFA Magazine*, vol. 18, no. 2:8–11.

Williams, John Burr. 1938. *The Theory of Investment Value*. Cambridge, MA: Harvard University Press.

Zhou, Ping, and William Ruland. 2006. "Dividend Payout and Future Earnings Growth." *Financial Analysts Journal*, vol. 62, no. 3:58–69.

PRACTICE PROBLEMS

1 Amy Tanner is an analyst for a US pension fund. Her supervisor has asked her to value the stocks of General Electric (NYSE: GE) and General Motors (NYSE: GM). Tanner wants to evaluate the appropriateness of the dividend discount model (DDM) for valuing GE and GM and has compiled the following data for the two companies for 2000 through 2007.

	GE			GM		
Year	EPS ($)	DPS ($)	Payout Ratio	EPS ($)	DPS ($)	Payout Ratio
2007	2.17	1.15	0.53	−68.45	1.00	−0.01
2006	1.99	1.03	0.52	−3.50	1.00	−0.29
2005	1.76	0.91	0.52	−18.50	2.00	−0.11
2004	1.61	0.82	0.51	4.94	2.00	0.40
2003	1.55	0.77	0.50	5.03	2.00	0.40
2002	1.51	0.73	0.48	3.35	2.00	0.60
2001	1.41	0.66	0.47	1.77	2.00	1.13
2000	1.27	0.57	0.45	6.68	2.00	0.30

Source: Compustat.

For each of the stocks, explain whether the DDM is appropriate for valuing the stock.

2 Vincent Nguyen, an analyst, is examining the stock of British Airways (London Stock Exchange: BAY) as of the beginning of 2008. He notices that the consensus forecast by analysts is that the stock will pay a £4 dividend per share in 2009 (based on 21 analysts) and a £5 dividend in 2010 (based on 10 analysts). Nguyen expects the price of the stock at the end of 2010 to be £250. He has estimated that the required rate of return on the stock is 11 percent. Assume all dividends are paid at the end of the year.

   A Using the DDM, estimate the value of BAY stock at the end of 2009.

   B Using the DDM, estimate the value of BAY stock at the end of 2008.

3 Justin Owens is an analyst for an equity mutual fund that invests in British stocks. At the beginning of 2008, Owens is examining domestic stocks for possible inclusion in the fund. One of the stocks that he is analyzing is British Sky Broadcasting Group (London Stock Exchange: BSY). The stock has paid dividends per share of £9, £12.20, and £15.50 at the end of 2005, 2006, and 2007, respectively. The consensus forecast by analysts is that the stock will pay a dividend per share of £18.66 at the end of 2008 (based on 19 analysts) and £20.20 at the end of 2009 (based on 17 analysts). Owens has estimated that the required rate of return on the stock is 11 percent.

   A Compare the compound annual growth rate in dividends from 2005 to 2007 inclusive (i.e., from a beginning level of £9 to an ending level of £15.50) with the consensus predicted compound annual growth rate in dividends from 2007 to 2009, inclusive.

Practice Problems and Solutions: *Equity Asset Valuation*, Second Edition, by Jerald E. Pinto, CFA, Elaine Henry, CFA, Thomas R. Robinson, CFA, and John D. Stowe, CFA. Copyright © 2009 by CFA Institute

B Owens believes that BSY has matured such that the dividend growth rate will be constant going forward at half the consensus compound annual growth rate from 2007 to 2009, inclusive, computed in Part A. Using the growth rate forecast of Owens as the constant growth rate from 2007 onwards, estimate the value of the stock as of the end of 2007 given an 11 percent required rate of return on equity.

C State the relationship between estimated value and *r* and estimated value and *g*.

4 During the period 1960–2007, earnings of the S&P 500 Index companies have increased at an average rate of 8.18 percent per year and the dividends paid have increased at an average rate of 5.9 percent per year. Assume that:

- Dividends will continue to grow at the 1960–2007 rate.
- The required return on the index is 8 percent.
- Companies in the S&P 500 Index collectively paid $246.6 billion in dividends in 2007.

Estimate the aggregate value of the S&P 500 Index component companies at the beginning of 2008 using the Gordon growth model.

5 Great Plains Energy is a public utility holding company that listed its 4.5 percent cumulative perpetual preferred stock series E on the NYSE Euronext in March 1952 (Ticker: GXPPrE). The par value of the preferred stock is $100. If the required rate of return on this stock is 5.6 percent, estimate the value of the stock.

6 German Resources is involved in coal mining. The company is currently profitable and is expected to pay a dividend of €4 per share next year. The company has suspended exploration, however, and because its current mature operations exhaust the existing mines, you expect that the dividends paid by the company will decline forever at an 8 percent rate. The required return on German Resource's stock is 11 percent. Using the DDM, estimate the value of the stock.

7 Maspeth Robotics shares are currently selling for €24 and have paid a dividend of €1 per share for the most recent year. The following additional information is given:

- The risk-free rate is 4 percent;
- The shares have an estimated beta of 1.2; and
- The equity risk premium is estimated at 5 percent.

Based on the above information, determine the constant dividend growth rate that would be required to justify the market price of €24.

8 You believe the Gordon (constant) growth model is appropriate to value the stock of Reliable Electric Corp. The company had an EPS of $2 in 2008. The retention ratio is 0.60. The company is expected to earn an ROE of 14 percent on its investments and the required rate of return is 11 percent. Assume that all dividends are paid at the end of the year.

A Calculate the company's sustainable growth rate.

B Estimate the value of the company's stock at the beginning of 2009.

C Calculate the present value of growth opportunities.

D Determine the fraction of the company's value which comes from its growth opportunities.

9 Stellar Baking Company in Australia has a trailing P/E of 14. Analysts predict that Stellar's dividends will continue to grow at its recent rate of 4.5 percent per year into the indefinite future. Given a current dividend and EPS of A$0.7 per share and A$2.00 per share, respectively, and a required rate of return on equity of 8 percent, determine whether Stellar Baking Company is undervalued, fairly valued, or overvalued. Justify your answer.

10 Mohan Gupta is the portfolio manager of an India-based equity fund. He is analyzing the value of Tata Chemicals Ltd. (Bombay Stock Exchange: TATACHEM). Tata Chemicals is India's leading manufacturer of inorganic chemicals, and also manufactures fertilizers and food additives. Gupta has concluded that the DDM is appropriate to value Tata Chemicals.

During the last five years (fiscal year ending 31 March 2004 to fiscal year ending 31 March 2008), the company has paid dividends per share of Rs. 5.50, 6.50, 7.00, 8.00, and 9.00, respectively. These dividends suggest an average annual growth rate in DPS of just above 13 percent. Gupta has decided to use a three-stage DDM with a linearly declining growth rate in Stage 2. He considers Tata Chemicals to be an average growth company, and estimates Stage 1 (the growth stage) to be 6 years and Stage 2 (the transition stage) to be 10 years. He estimates the growth rate to be 14 percent in Stage 1 and 10 percent in Stage 3. Gupta has estimated the required return on equity for Tata Chemicals to be 16 percent. Estimate the current value of the stock.

11 You are analyzing the stock of Ansell Limited (Australian Stock Exchange: ANN), a healthcare company, as of late June 2008. The stock price is A$9.74. The company's dividend per share for the fiscal year ending 30 June 2008 was A$0.27. You expect the dividend to increase by 10 percent for the next three years and then increase by 8 percent per year forever. You estimate the required return on equity of Ansell Limited to be 12 percent.

A Estimate the value of ANN using a two-stage dividend discount model.

B Judge whether ANN is undervalued, fairly valued, or overvalued.

12 Sime Natural Cosmetics Ltd. has a dividend yield of 2 percent based on the current dividend and a mature phase dividend growth rate of 5 percent a year. The current dividend growth rate is 10 percent a year, but the growth rate is expected to decline linearly to its mature phase value during the next six years.

A If Sime Natural Cosmetics is fairly priced in the marketplace, what is the expected rate of return on its shares?

B If Sime were in its mature growth phase right now, would its expected return be higher or lower, holding all other facts constant?

13 Kazuo Uto is analyzing the stock of Brother Industries, Ltd. (Tokyo Stock Exchange: 64480), a diversified Japanese company that produces a wide variety of products. Brother distributes its products under its own name and under original-equipment manufacturer agreements with other companies. Uto has concluded that a multistage DDM is appropriate to value the stock of Brother Industries and the company will reach a mature stage in four years. The ROE of the company has declined from 16.7 percent in the fiscal year ending in 2004 to 12.7 percent in the fiscal year ending in 2008. The dividend payout ratio has increased from 11.5 percent in 2004 to 22.3 percent in 2008. Uto has estimated that in the mature phase Brother's ROE will be 11 percent, which is approximately equal to estimated required return on equity. He has also estimated that the payout ratio in the mature phase will be 40 percent, which is significantly greater than its payout ratio in 2008 but less than the average payout of about 50 percent for Japanese companies.

A Calculate the sustainable growth rate for Brother in the mature phase.

B With reference to the formula for the sustainable growth rate, a colleague of Uto asserts that the greater the earnings retention ratio, the greater the sustainable growth rate because g is a positive function of b. The colleague argues that Brother should decrease payout ratio. Explain the flaw in that argument.

14 An analyst following Chevron Corp. (NYSE Euronext: CVX) wants to estimate the sustainable growth rate for the company by using the PRAT model. For this purpose, the analyst has compiled the data in the following table. Assets and equity values are for the end of the year; the analyst uses averages of beginning and ending balance sheet values in computing ratios based on total assets and shareholders' equity. For example average total assets for 2007 would be computed as (148,786 + 132,628)/2 = $140,707. *Note*: All numbers except for EPS and DPS are in $ millions.

Item	2007	2006	2005	2004
Net income	$18,688	$17,138	$14,099	$13,328
Sales	214,091	204,892	193,641	150,865
Total assets	148,786	132,628	125,833	93,208
Shareholders' equity	77,088	68,935	62,676	45,230
EPS	8.77	7.80	6.54	6.28
DPS	2.26	2.01	1.75	1.53

Source: Financial statements from Chevron's website.

A Compute the average value of each PRAT component during 2005–2007.

B Using the overall mean value of the average component values calculated in Part A, estimate the sustainable growth rate for Chevron.

C Judge whether Chevron has reached a mature growth stage.

15 Casey Hyunh is trying to value the stock of Resources Limited. To easily see how a change in one or more of her assumptions affects the estimated value of the stock, she is using a spreadsheet model. The model has projections for the next four years based on the following assumptions.

- Sales will be $300 million in Year 1.
- Sales will grow at 15 percent in Years 2 and 3 and 10 percent in Year 4.
- Operating profits (EBIT) will be 17 percent of sales in each year.
- Interest expense will be $10 million per year.
- Income tax rate is 30 percent.
- Earnings retention ratio would stay at 0.60.
- The per-share dividend growth rate will be constant from Year 4 forward and this final growth rate will be 200 basis points less than the growth rate from Year 3 to Year 4.

The company has 10 million shares outstanding. Hyunh has estimated the required return on Resources' stock to be 13 percent.

A Estimate the value of the stock at the end of Year 4 based on the above assumptions.

B Estimate the current value of the stock using the above assumptions.

C Hyunh is wondering how a change in the projected sales growth rate would affect the estimated value. Estimate the current value of the stock if the sales growth rate in Year 3 is 10 percent instead of 15 percent.

The following information relates to Questions 16–21

Jacob Daniel is the chief investment officer at a US pension fund sponsor, and Steven Rae is an analyst for the pension fund who follows consumer/noncyclical stocks. At the beginning of 2009, Daniel asks Rae to value the equity of Tasty Foods Company for its possible inclusion in the list of approved investments. Tasty Foods Company is involved in the production of frozen foods that are sold under its own brand name to retailers.

Rae is considering if a dividend discount model would be appropriate for valuing Tasty Foods. He has compiled the information in the following table for the company's EPS and DPS during the last five years. The quarterly dividends paid by the company have been added to arrive at the annual dividends. Rae has also computed the dividend payout ratio for each year as DPS/EPS and the growth rates in EPS and DPS.

Year	EPS ($)	DPS ($)	Payout Ratio	Growth in EPS (%)	Growth in DPS (%)
2008	2.12	0.59	0.278	2.9	3.5
2007	2.06	0.57	0.277	2.5	5.6
2006	2.01	0.54	0.269	6.3	5.9
2005	1.89	0.51	0.270	6.2	6.3
2004	1.78	0.48	0.270		

Rae notes that the EPS of the company has been increasing at an average rate of 4.48 percent per year. The dividend payout ratio has remained fairly stable and dividends have increased at an average rate of 5.30 percent. In view of a history of dividend payments by the company and the understandable relationship dividend policy bears to the company's earnings, Rae concludes that the DDM is appropriate to value the equity of Tasty Foods. Further, he expects the moderate growth rate of the company to persist and decides to use the Gordon growth model.

Rae uses the CAPM to compute the return on equity. He uses the annual yield of 4 percent on the 10-year Treasury bond as the risk-free return. He estimates the expected US equity risk premium, with the S&P 500 Index used as a proxy for the market, to be 6.5 percent per year. The estimated beta of Tasty Foods against the S&P 500 Index is 1.10. Accordingly, Rae's estimate for the required return on equity for Tasty Foods is 0.04 + 1.10(0.065) = 0.1115 or 11.15 percent.

Using the past growth rate in dividends of 5.30 percent as his estimate of the future growth rate in dividends, Rae computes the value of Tasty Foods stock. He shows his analysis to Alex Renteria, his colleague at the pension fund who specializes in the frozen foods industry. Renteria concurs with the valuation approach used by Rae but disagrees with the future growth rate he used. Renteria believes that the stock's current price of $8.42 is the fair value of the stock.

16 Which of the following is *closest* to Rae's estimate of the stock's value?

A $10.08.

B $10.54.

C $10.62.

17 What is the stock's justified trailing P/E based on the stock's value estimated by Rae?

A   5.01.

B   5.24.

C   5.27.

18 Rae considers a security trading within a band of ±10 percent of his estimate of intrinsic value to be within a "fair value range." By that criterion, the stock of Tasty Foods is:

A   undervalued.

B   fairly valued.

C   overvalued.

19 The beta of Tasty Foods stock of 1.10 used by Rae in computing the required return on equity was based on monthly returns for the last 10 years. If Rae uses daily returns for the last 5 years, the beta estimate is 1.25. If a beta of 1.25 is used, what would be Rae's estimate of the value of the stock of Tasty Foods?

A $8.64.

B $9.10.

C $20.13.

20 Alex Renteria has suggested that the market price of Tasty Foods stock is its fair value. What is the implied growth rate of dividends given the stock's market price? Use the required return on equity based on a beta of 1.10.

A   3.87%.

B   5.30%.

C   12.1%.

21 If Alex Renteria is correct that the current price of Tasty Foods stock is its fair value, what is expected capital gains yield on the stock?

A   3.87%.

B   4.25%.

C   5.30%.

The following information relates to Questions 22–27

Assorted Fund, a UK-based globally diversified equity mutual fund, is considering adding Talisman Energy Inc. (Toronto Stock Exchange: TLM) to its portfolio. Talisman is an independent upstream oil and gas company headquartered in Calgary, Canada. It is one of the largest oil and gas companies in Canada and has operations in several countries. Brian Dobson, an analyst at the mutual fund, has been assigned the task of estimating a fair value of Talisman. Dobson is aware of several approaches that could be used for this purpose. After carefully considering the characteristics of the company and its competitors, he believes the company will have extraordinary growth for the next few years and normal growth thereafter. So, he has concluded that a two-stage DDM is the most appropriate for valuing the stock.

Talisman pays semi-annual dividends. The total dividends during 2006, 2007, and 2008 have been C$0.114, C$0.15, and C$0.175, respectively. These imply a growth rate of 32 percent in 2007 and 17 percent in 2008. Dobson believes that the growth rate will be 14 percent in the next year. He has estimated that the first stage will include the next eight years.

Dobson is using the CAPM to estimate the required return on equity for Talisman. He has estimated that the beta of Talisman, as measured against the S&P/TSX Composite Index (formerly TSE 300 Composite Index), is 0.84. The Canadian risk-free rate, as measured by the annual yield on the 10-year government bond, is 4.1 percent. The equity risk premium for the Canadian market is estimated at 5.5 percent. Based on these data, Dobson has estimated that the required return on Talisman stock is 0.041 + 0.84(0.055) = 0.0872 or 8.72 percent. Dobson is doing the analysis in January 2009 and the stock price at that time is C$17.

Dobson realizes that even within the two-stage DDM, there could be some variations in the approach. He would like to explore how these variations affect the valuation of the stock. Specifically, he wants to estimate the value of the stock for each of the following approaches separately.

I. The dividend growth rate will be 14 percent throughout the first stage of eight years. The dividend growth rate thereafter will be 7 percent.

II. Instead of using the estimated stable growth rate of 7 percent in the second stage, Dobson wants to use his estimate that eight years later Talisman's stock will be worth 17 times its earnings per share (trailing P/E of 17). He expects that the earnings retention ratio at that time will be 0.70.

III. In contrast to the first approach above in which the growth rate declines abruptly from 14 percent in the eighth year to 7 percent in the ninth, the growth rate would decline linearly from 14 percent in the first year to 7 percent in the ninth.

22 What is the terminal value of the stock based on the first approach?

  A C$17.65.

  B C$31.06.

  C C$33.09.

23 In the first approach, what proportion of the total value of the stock is represented by the value of second stage?

  A 0.10.

  B 0.52.

  C 0.90.

24 What is the terminal value of the stock based on the second approach (earnings multiple)?

  A C$12.12.

  B C$28.29.

  C C$33.09.

25 What is the current value of the stock based on the second approach?

  A C$16.24.

  B C$17.65.

  C C$28.29.

26 Based on the third approach (the H-model), the stock is:

  A undervalued.

  B fairly valued.

    C overvalued.

27 Dobson is wondering what the consequences would be if the duration of the first stage was assumed to be 11 years instead of 8, with all the other assumptions/estimates remaining the same. Considering this change, which of the following is true?

    A In the second approach, the proportion of the total value of the stock represented by the second stage would not change.

    B The total value estimated using the third approach would increase.

    C Using this new assumption and the first approach will lead Dobson to conclude that the stock is overvalued.

SOLUTIONS

1   Both companies are dividend-paying and have an established history of dividend payments that can provide some help in forecasting future dividends. In the case of GE, EPS has been increasing steadily from 2000 to 2007 and DPS has shown increases consistent with this trend. For example, EPS increased by $0.23 from 2005 to 2006 and DPS increased by $0.12. Then EPS increased by $0.18 from 2006 to 2007 and DPS increased by $0.12. The payout ratios have also been increasing gradually during the period examined. Dividends appear to be at least somewhat predictable given earnings forecasts. Overall, the DDM seems to be an appropriate model for valuing GE. In the case of GM, however, dividends do not have a discernable relationship to the company's profitability. For example, DPS was $2 in 2000 when GM was doing well and had an EPS of $6.68, but DPS continued to be $2 in 2005 when EPS was –$18.50. The company continued to pay dividends in 2007, which was the third consecutive year of a negative EPS: in 2007, EPS had fallen to –$68.45. The lack of a clear relationship of dividends to operating results suggests that the DDM is not appropriate for valuing GM.

2   **A**   Discounting the expected dividend of £5 in 2010 and the expected stock price of £250 at the end of 2010,

$$V_1 = \frac{D_2 + P_2}{(1+r)^1} = \frac{5 + 250}{(1+0.11)^1} = \frac{255}{1.11} = 229.73$$

B   One way to answer this question is to use a DDM for two holding periods. Accordingly, discounting the expected dividend of £5 in 2010 and the expected stock price of £250 at the end of 2010 for two periods, and discounting the expected dividend of £4 in 2009 for one period,

$$V_0 = \frac{D_1}{(1+r)^1} + \frac{D_2 + P_2}{(1+r)^2} = \frac{4}{(1+0.11)^1} + \frac{5+250}{(1+0.11)^2}$$

$$= \frac{4}{1.11} + \frac{255}{1.11^2} = 3.60 + 206.96 = 210.57$$

based on full precision, or £210.56 with intermediate rounding. Another way to answer this question is to use the answer to Part A and a DDM for one holding period. Accordingly, discounting the expected dividend of £4 in 2009 and the expected stock price of £229.73 at the end of 2009 for one period,

$$V_0 = \frac{D_1 + V_1}{(1+r)^1} = \frac{4 + 229.73}{(1+0.11)^1} = \frac{233.73}{1.11} = 210.57$$

3   **A**   The growth rate from 2005 to 2007 is $(15.50/9)^{1/2} - 1 = 0.312$ or 31.2 percent. The consensus predicted growth rate from 2007 to 2009 is $(20.20/15.50)^{1/2} - 1 = 0.142$ or 14.2 percent. Thus, the consensus forecast is for a sharp decline in the dividend growth rate for 2008 to 2009.

B   Half of the growth rate computed in Part A = 14.2/2 = 7.1 percent. Based on this growth rate, $D_1 = £15.50(1.071) = £16.60$, rounded. Using the Gordon growth model,

$$V_0 = \frac{D_1}{r-g} = \frac{16.60}{0.11 - 0.071} = 425.64$$

or 425.65 based on not rounding the numerator.

C The estimated value of BSY would decrease as r increases and increase as g increases, all else equal.

4 Applying the Gordon growth model with the assumed 5.9 percent dividend growth rate results in an estimated value of $12,435.7 billion for the S&P 500 Index.

$$V_0 = \frac{D_1}{r - g} = \frac{246.6(1 + 0.059)}{0.08 - 0.059} = \$12{,}435.7 \text{ billion}$$

5 The preferred stock pays 4.5 percent of $100 or $4.50 in annual dividends. The dividend is fixed; so $g = 0$. Therefore, using the Gordon growth model with zero growth,

$$V_0 = \frac{D_1}{r} = \frac{4.50}{0.056} = \$80.36$$

6 This problem can be addressed using the Gordon growth model with constant expected negative growth. The estimated value of the stock is

$$V_0 = \frac{D_1}{r - g} = \frac{4}{0.11 - (-0.08)} = 21.05$$

7 Using the CAPM, the required rate of return on Maspeth Robotics shares is 4 percent + 1.2(5%) = 10 percent. Therefore, the constant dividend growth rate implied by a market price of €24 is 5.6 percent as shown below:

$$V_0 = \frac{D_0(1 + g)}{r - g}$$

$$24 = \frac{1.00(1 + g)}{0.10 - g}$$

$$2.4 - 24g = 1.00 + g$$

$$25g = 1.4$$

$$g = 0.056 \text{ or } 5.6 \text{ percent}$$

8 A With $b = 0.60$, the dividend payout ratio = $1 - b = 1 - 0.60 = 0.40$. Sustainable growth rate $g = b(\text{ROE}) = 0.60(0.14) = 0.084$ or 8.4 percent.

B The company paid a dividend per share of $1 - b(\text{EPS}) = 0.40(\$2) = \$0.80$ in 2008. The estimated value at the beginning of 2009 is

$$V_0 = \frac{D_1}{r - g} = \frac{0.80(1 + 0.0840)}{0.1100 - 0.0840} = \$33.35$$

C If the company was a no-growth company, that is it paid out all its earnings and did not reinvest any, its earnings would stay the same. The value of such a company would be the value of a perpetuity, which is $D/r = E/r = \$2/0.11 = \$18.18$. This amount is the no-growth value per share. So, PVGO = $33.35 - $18.18 = $15.17.

D The fraction of the company's value that comes from its growth opportunities is 15.17/33.35 = 0.4549 or 45.49 percent.

9 The payout ratio is A\$0.70/A\$2.00 = 0.35 = 1 − b, where b is the earnings retention ratio. Therefore, the justified trailing P/E based on fundamentals is 10.45, as shown below:

$$\frac{P_0}{E_0} = \frac{(1-b)(1+g)}{r-g}$$

$$= \frac{0.35(1+0.045)}{0.08 - 0.045}$$

$$= 10.45$$

Because the market trailing P/E of 14 is greater than 10.45, Stellar Baking Company shares appear to be overvalued (i.e., selling at a higher than warranted P/E).

10 The dividends in Stages 2 and 3 can be valued with the H-model, which estimates their value at the beginning of Stage 2. In this case, V_6 would capture the value of Stages 2 and 3 dividends. V_6 would then be discounted to the present. Also, the present values of dividends D_1 through D_6 need to be added to the present value of V_6.

$$V_6 = \frac{D_6(1 + g_L) + D_6 H(g_S - g_L)}{r - g_L}$$

where

$$D_6 = D_0(1 + g_S)^6 = 9(1.14)^6 = 19.7548$$

$$r = 0.16$$

$$H = 10/2 = 5$$

$$g_S = 0.14$$

$$g_L = 0.10$$

$$V_6 = \frac{19.7548(1.10) + 19.7548(5)(0.14 - 0.10)}{0.16 - 0.10} = 428.02$$

PV of $V_6 = 428.02/1.16^6 = 175.68$

PV of $D_1 = 9(1.14) / 1.16 = 8.8448$

PV of $D_2 = 9(1.14)^2 / 1.16^2 = 8.6923$

PV of $D_3 = 9(1.14)^3 / 1.16^3 = 8.5425$

PV of $D_4 = 9(1.14)^4 / 1.16^4 = 8.3952$

PV of $D_5 = 9(1.14)^5 / 1.16^5 = 8.2504$

PV of $D_6 = 9(1.14)^6 / 1.16^6 = 8.1082$

Value of stock = 8.8448 + 8.6923 + 8.5425 + 8.3952 + 8.2504 + 8.1082 +

175.68 = Rs. 226.51

11 A Let r be the required rate of return. Also let $t = 0$ indicate the middle of 2008. Because the dividend growth rate becomes constant from the middle of 2011 ($t = 3$), the value of the mature phase can be expressed as

$$V_3 = D_4/(r - g) = D_4/(r - 0.08)$$

Also,

$$D_1 = 0.27(1.10) = 0.2970$$

$$D_2 = 0.27(1.10)^2 = 0.3267$$

$$D_3 = 0.27(1.10)^3 = 0.3594$$

$$D_4 = D_3(1.08) = 0.3594(1.08) = 0.3881$$

V_0 can be expressed as

$$V_0 = 9.74 = \frac{D_1}{1+r} + \frac{D_2}{(1+r)^2} + \frac{D_3}{(1+r)^3} + \frac{V_3}{(1+r)^3}$$

$$= \frac{0.2970}{1+0.12} + \frac{0.3267}{(1+0.12)^2} + \frac{0.3594}{(1+0.12)^3} + \frac{0.3881}{(0.12-0.08)(1+0.12)^3}$$

$$= 0.2652 + 0.2604 + 0.2558 + 6.9064$$

$$A\$ = 7.69$$

B   Because ANN's estimated value of A\$7.69 is less than the market price of A\$9.74, ANN appears to be overvalued at the market price.

12 A   Use the H-model expression, with $H = 6/2 = 3$ and long-term and short-term dividend growth rates of 0.05 and 0.10, respectively, which gives an expected return of 7.4 percent as shown below:

$$r = \left(\frac{D_0}{P_0}\right)\left[(1+g_L) + H(g_S - g_L)\right] + g_L$$

$$= 0.02\left[(1+0.05) + 3(0.10 - 0.05)\right] + 0.05$$

$$= 0.024 + 0.05$$

$$= 0.074$$

B   In this case the long- and short-term dividend growth rates are identical and the expected return is lower:

$$r = \left(\frac{D_0}{P_0}\right)\left[(1+g_L) + H(g_S - g_L)\right] + g_L$$

$$= 0.02\left[(1+0.05) + 3(0.05 - 0.05)\right] + 0.05$$

$$= 0.021 + 0.05$$

$$= 0.071$$

It is intuitive that a higher dividend growth rate is associated with a higher expected return if all the other facts (such as the assumed required rate of return) are held constant.

13 A   The formula for sustainable growth rate is

$g = (b$ in the mature phase$) \times ($ROE in the mature phase$)$

Because the dividend payout ratio in the mature phase is estimated to be 40 percent or 0.40, the retention ratio b is expected to $1 - 0.40 = 0.60$. Therefore, given the 11 percent per year forecasted ROE,

$g = 0.60(11\%) = 6.6\%$

B   Based on the formula for sustainable growth rate, as b increases, growth rate increases, holding all else constant. However, all else may not be constant. In particular, the return accruing to additional investments may be lower, leading to a lower overall ROE. If that is the case and Brother lowers the payout ratio to below 0.40 (thus increasing b to above 0.60), ROE would be expected to decline, which may lead to a lower growth rate.

14 A The four components of PRAT are computed for 2007 as follows:

$$P \text{ (Profit margin)} = \text{NI/Sales} = 18,688/214,091 = 0.0873$$

$$R \text{ (Retention)} = b = (\text{EPS} - \text{DPS})/\text{EPS} = (8.77 - 2.26)/8.77$$
$$= 0.7423$$

$$A \text{ (Asset turnover)} = \text{Sales/Average total assets}$$
$$= 214,091/0.5(148,786) + 132,628) = 1.5215$$

$$T \text{ (Leverage)} = \text{Average total assets/Average shareholders' equity}$$
$$= (148,786 + 132,628)/(77,088 + 68,935) = 1.9272$$

The components are similarly computed for the other years and summarized in the following table. Their average values are also included.

	Needed for Solution to B	Solution to A		
Item	**Average**	**2007**	**2006**	**2005**
P (Profit margin)	0.0812	0.0873	0.0836	0.0728
R (Retention)	0.7390	0.7423	0.7423	0.7324
A (Asset turnover)	1.6250	1.5215	1.5855	1.7681
T (Leverage)	1.9736	1.9272	1.9638	2.0299

B Using the average values for each component,

$$g = \text{PRAT} = (0.0812)(0.7390)(1.6250)(1.9736) = 0.1924 \text{ or } 19.2 \text{ percent}$$

The sustainable growth rate for Chevron based on the PRAT expression is 19.2 percent.

C Given that the high value of g does not seem sustainable indefinitely, it appears that the company has not reached the mature phase yet.

15 A The following table provides the details from the spreadsheet model. The constant growth rate after Year 4 is 2 percent less than that in Year 4. So,

$$g = 0.1180 - 0.0200 = 0.098 \text{ or } 9.8 \text{ percent.}$$
$$V_4 = D_4(1 + g)/(r - g) = 1.80(1.098)/(0.13 - 0.098) = \$61.76$$

Year	**1**	**2**	**3**	**4**
Sales ($ millions)	300.00	345.00	396.75	436.43
EBIT	51.00	58.65	67.45	74.19
Interest ($ millions)	10.00	10.00	10.00	10.00
EBT	41.00	48.65	57.45	64.19
Taxes (30%)	12.30	14.60	17.23	19.26
Net income	28.70	34.06	40.21	44.93
Dividends	11.48	13.62	16.09	17.97
DPS	1.15	1.36	1.61	1.80
Growth rate of DPS		18.26%	18.38%	11.80%
PV of DPS	1.02	1.07	1.12	1.10
$V_4 = D_4(1 + g)/(r - g)$				61.76
PV of V_4				$37.87

B V_0 = Sum of PV of DPS and PV of V_4 = 1.02 + 1.07 + 1.12 + 1.10 + 61.76/$(1 + 0.13)^4$ = $42.18

C The following table provides the details if the sales growth rate in Year 3 is 10 percent:

Year	1	2	3	4
Sales ($ millions)	300.00	345.00	379.50	417.45
EBIT	51.00	58.65	64.52	70.97
Interest ($ millions)	10.00	10.00	10.00	10.00
EBT	41.00	48.65	54.52	60.97
Taxes (%)	12.30	14.60	16.35	18.29
Net income	28.70	34.06	38.16	42.68
Dividends	11.48	13.62	15.26	17.07
DPS	1.15	1.36	1.53	1.71
Growth rate of DPS		18.26%	12.50%	11.76%
PV of DPS	1.02	1.07	1.06	1.05
$V_4 = D_4(1 + g)/(r - g)$				57.93
PV of V_4				$35.53

V_0 = Sum of PV of DPS and PV of V_4

= 1.02 + 1.07 + 1.06 + 1.05 + 35.53

= $39.73

16 C is correct. Using the Gordon growth model,

$$V_0 = \frac{D_1}{r - g} = \frac{0.59(1 + 0.0530)}{0.1115 - 0.0530} = \$10.62$$

17 A is correct. The justified trailing P/E or P_0/E_0 is V_0/E_0, where V_0 is the fair value based on the stock's fundamentals. The fair value V_0 computed earlier is $10.62 and E_0 is $2.12. So, the justified trailing P/E is 10.62/2.12 = 5.01.

18 A is correct. Rae's estimate of the intrinsic value is $10.62. So, the band Rae is looking at is $10.62 ± 0.10($10.62), which runs from $10.62 + $1.06 = $11.68 on the upside to $10.62 − $1.06 = $9.56 on the downside. Because $8.42 is below $9.56, Rae would consider Tasty Foods to be undervalued.

19 B is correct. Using a beta of 1.25, Rae's estimate for the required return on equity for Tasty Foods is 0.04 + 1.25(0.065) = 0.1213 or 12.13 percent. The estimated value of the stock is

$$V_0 = \frac{D_1}{r - g} = \frac{0.59 \times (1 + 0.0530)}{0.1213 - 0.0530} = \$9.10$$

20 A is correct. The price of the stock is $8.42. If this price is also the fair value of the stock,

$$V_0 = 8.42 = \frac{D_1}{r - g} = \frac{0.59 \times (1 + g)}{0.1115 - g}$$

0.9388 − 8.42g = 0.59 + 0.59g

9.01g = 0.3488

g = 0.0387 or 3.87 percent

21 A is correct. If the stock is fairly priced in the market as per the Gordon growth model, the stock price is expected to increase at g, the expected growth rate in dividends. The implied growth rate in dividends, if price is the fair value, is 3.87 percent. Therefore, the expected capital gains yield is 3.87 percent.

22 B is correct. The following table provides the calculations needed to compute the value of the stock using the first approach, including the calculations for the terminal value V_8. As the table shows, the terminal value V_8 = C$31.0550.

Time	Value	Calculation	D_t or V_t	Present Values $D_t/(1.0872)^t$ or $V_t/(1.0872)^t$
1	D_1	C$0.175(1.14)	C$0.1995	C$0.1835
2	D_2	0.175(1.14)^2	0.2274	0.1924
3	D_3	0.175(1.14)^3	0.2593	0.2018
4	D_4	0.175(1.14)^4	0.2956	0.2116
5	D_5	0.175(1.14)^5	0.3369	0.2218
6	D_6	0.175(1.14)^6	0.3841	0.2326
7	D_7	0.175(1.14)^7	0.4379	0.2439
8	D_8	0.175(1.14)^8	0.4992	0.2557
8	V_8	0.175(1.14)^8(1.07)/(0.0872 – 0.07)	31.0550	15.9095
Total				C$17.6528

23 C is correct. As shown in the above table, the value of the second stage = PV of V_8 = C$15.9095. The total value is C$17.6528. As a proportion, the second stage represents 15.9095/17.6528 = 0.90 of the total value.

24 B is correct.

$$V_8/E_8 = 17$$
$$D_8/E_8 = 1 - 0.70 = 0.30$$

From the table with the calculation details for the solution to Problem 22, D_8 = C$0.4992. So, 0.4992/ E_8 = 0.30, which means that E_8 = 0.4992/0.30 = 1.6640.

V_8/E_8 = 17 implies that $V_8/1.6640$ = 17, which gives V_8 = 17(1.6640)

= C$28.2880.

25 A is correct. As computed earlier, V_8 = 17(1.6640) = C$28.2880.

PV of V_8 = 28.2880/1.0872^8 = 14.4919

From the table with the calculation details for the solution to Problem 22,

Sum of PV of D_1 through D_8 = 1.7433

So, the value of stock V_0 = 14.4919 + 1.7433 = C$16.2352.

26 C is correct. Using the H-model

$$V_0 = \frac{D_0(1 + g_L) + D_0 H(g_S - g_L)}{r - g_L}$$

where

$$D_0 = 0.175$$
$$r = 0.0872$$
$$H = 4$$
$$g_S = 0.14$$
$$g_L = 0.07$$

$$V_0 = \frac{0.175(1.07) + 0.175(4)(0.14 - 0.07)}{0.0872 - 0.07} = 13.7355$$

The market price is C\$17, which is greater than C\$13.7355. So, the stock is overvalued in the market.

27 B is correct. If the extraordinary growth rate of 14 percent is expected to continue for a longer duration, the stock's value would increase. Choice A is false because given that the first stage is longer (11 years instead of 8), the terminal value is being calculated at a later point in time. So, its present value would be smaller. Moreover, the first stage has more years and contributes more to the total value. Overall, the proportion contributed by the second stage would be smaller. Choice C is false because the intrinsic value of the stock would be higher and the appropriate conclusion would be that the stock would be undervalued to a greater extent based on the first approach.

12

Equity Investments

Valuation Models

This study session presents additional valuation methods for estimating a company's intrinsic value. The dividend discount model discussed in Study Session 11 remains a baseline model. The free cash flow approach to valuation is an important alternative to the dividend discount model when dividends are not the best representation of a company's value. Price and enterprise multiples are among the most familiar and widely used valuation measures because of the relative ease with which they can be used and communicated. Residual income models represent an approach to valuation in which accounting income is adjusted to reflect a deduction for the opportunity cost of capital. The final reading is an introduction to how companies without readily marketable shares are valued.

READING ASSIGNMENTS

Reading 35	Free Cash Flow Valuation by Jerald E. Pinto, PhD, CFA, Elaine Henry, PhD, CFA, Thomas R. Robinson, PhD, CFA, and John D. Stowe, PhD, CFA
Reading 36	Market-Based Valuation: Price and Enterprise Value Multiples by Jerald E. Pinto, PhD, CFA, Elaine Henry, PhD, CFA, Thomas R. Robinson, PhD, CFA, and John D. Stowe, PhD, CFA

(continued)

Reading 37   Residual Income Valuation
                               by Jerald E. Pinto, PhD, CFA, Elaine Henry, PhD, CFA,
                               Thomas R. Robinson, PhD, CFA, and John D. Stowe, PhD,
                               CFA

Reading 38   Private Company Valuation
                               by Raymond D. Rath, ASA, CFA

READING

35

Free Cash Flow Valuation

by Jerald E. Pinto, PhD, CFA, Elaine Henry, PhD, CFA,
Thomas R. Robinson, PhD, CFA, and John D. Stowe, PhD, CFA

*Jerald E. Pinto, PhD, CFA, is at CFA Institute (USA). Elaine Henry, PhD, CFA, is at
Fordham University (USA). Thomas R. Robinson, PhD, CFA, is at CFA Institute (USA).
John D. Stowe, PhD, CFA, is at Ohio University (USA).*

LEARNING OUTCOMES

Mastery	The candidate should be able to:
☐	a. compare the free cash flow to the firm (FCFF) and free cash flow to equity (FCFE) approaches to valuation;
☐	b. explain the ownership perspective implicit in the FCFE approach;
☐	c. explain the appropriate adjustments to net income, earnings before interest and taxes (EBIT), earnings before interest, taxes, depreciation, and amortization (EBITDA), and cash flow from operations (CFO) to calculate FCFF and FCFE;
☐	d. calculate FCFF and FCFE;
☐	e. describe approaches for forecasting FCFF and FCFE;
☐	f. compare the FCFE model and dividend discount models;
☐	g. explain how dividends, share repurchases, share issues, and changes in leverage may affect future FCFF and FCFE;
☐	h. evaluate the use of net income and EBITDA as proxies for cash flow in valuation;
☐	i. explain the single-stage (stable-growth), two-stage, and three-stage FCFF and FCFE models and select and justify the appropriate model given a company's characteristics;
☐	j. estimate a company's value using the appropriate free cash flow model(s);
☐	k. explain the use of sensitivity analysis in FCFF and FCFE valuations;
☐	l. describe approaches for calculating the terminal value in a multistage valuation model;
☐	m. evaluate whether a stock is overvalued, fairly valued, or undervalued based on a free cash flow valuation model.

The data and examples for this reading were updated in 2014 by Professor Stephen Wilcox, CFA.

Equity Asset Valuation, Second Edition, by Jerald E. Pinto, CFA, Elaine Henry, CFA, Thomas R. Robinson, CFA, and John D. Stowe, CFA. Copyright © 2009 by CFA Institute.

1 INTRODUCTION TO FREE CASH FLOWS

Discounted cash flow (DCF) valuation views the intrinsic value of a security as the present value of its expected future cash flows. When applied to dividends, the DCF model is the discounted dividend approach or dividend discount model (DDM). This reading extends DCF analysis to value a company and its equity securities by valuing free cash flow to the firm (FCFF) and free cash flow to equity (FCFE). Whereas dividends are the cash flows actually paid to stockholders, free cash flows are the cash flows *available* for distribution to shareholders.

Unlike dividends, FCFF and FCFE are not readily available data. Analysts need to compute these quantities from available financial information, which requires a clear understanding of free cash flows and the ability to interpret and use the information correctly. Forecasting future free cash flows is also a rich and demanding exercise. The analyst's understanding of a company's financial statements, its operations, its financing, and its industry can pay real "dividends" as he or she addresses that task. Many analysts consider free cash flow models to be more useful than DDMs in practice. Free cash flows provide an economically sound basis for valuation.

Analysts like to use free cash flow as the return (either FCFF or FCFE) whenever one or more of the following conditions is present:

- The company does not pay dividends.
- The company pays dividends but the dividends paid differ significantly from the company's capacity to pay dividends.
- Free cash flows align with profitability within a reasonable forecast period with which the analyst is comfortable.
- The investor takes a "control" perspective. With control comes discretion over the uses of free cash flow. If an investor can take control of the company (or expects another investor to do so), dividends may be changed substantially; for example, they may be set at a level approximating the company's capacity to pay dividends. Such an investor can also apply free cash flows to uses such as servicing the debt incurred in an acquisition.

Common equity can be valued directly by using FCFE or indirectly by first using a FCFF model to estimate the value of the firm and then subtracting the value of non-common-stock capital (usually debt) from FCFF to arrive at an estimate of the value of equity. The purpose of this reading is to develop the background required to use the FCFF or FCFE approaches to value a company's equity.

Section 2 defines the concepts of free cash flow to the firm and free cash flow to equity and then presents the two valuation models based on discounting of FCFF and FCFE. We also explore the constant-growth models for valuing FCFF and FCFE, which are special cases of the general models, in this section. After reviewing the FCFF and FCFE valuation process in Section 2, we turn in Section 3 to the vital task of calculating and forecasting FCFF and FCFE. Section 4 explains multistage free cash flow valuation models and presents some of the issues associated with their application. Analysts usually value operating assets and nonoperating assets separately and then combine them to find the total value of the firm, an approach described in Section 5.

FCFF AND FCFE VALUATION APPROACHES

2

The purpose of this section is to provide a conceptual understanding of free cash flows and the valuation models based on them. A detailed accounting treatment of free cash flows and more-complicated valuation models follow in subsequent sections.

2.1 Defining Free Cash Flow

Free cash flow to the firm is the cash flow available to the company's suppliers of capital after all operating expenses (including taxes) have been paid and necessary investments in working capital (e.g., inventory) and fixed capital (e.g., equipment) have been made. FCFF is the cash flow from operations minus capital expenditures. A company's suppliers of capital include common stockholders, bondholders, and sometimes, preferred stockholders. The equations analysts use to calculate FCFF depend on the accounting information available.

Free cash flow to equity is the cash flow available to the company's holders of common equity after all operating expenses, interest, and principal payments have been paid and necessary investments in working and fixed capital have been made. FCFE is the cash flow from operations minus capital expenditures minus payments to (and plus receipts from) debtholders.

The way in which free cash flow is related to a company's net income, cash flow from operations, and measures such as EBITDA (earnings before interest, taxes, depreciation, and amortization) is important: The analyst must understand the relationship between a company's reported accounting data and free cash flow in order to forecast free cash flow and its expected growth. Although a company reports cash flow from operations (CFO) on the statement of cash flows, CFO is *not* free cash flow. Net income and CFO data can be used, however, in determining a company's free cash flow.

The advantage of FCFF and FCFE over other cash-flow concepts is that they can be used directly in a DCF framework to value the firm or to value equity. Other cash-flow- or earnings-related measures, such as CFO, net income, EBIT, and EBITDA, do not have this property because they either double-count or omit cash flows in some way. For example, EBIT and EBITDA are before-tax measures, and the cash flows available to investors (in the firm or in the equity of the firm) must be after tax. From the stockholders' perspective, EBITDA and similar measures do not account for differing capital structures (the after-tax interest expenses or preferred dividends) or for the funds that bondholders supply to finance investments in operating assets. Moreover, these measures do not account for the reinvestment of cash flows that the company makes in capital assets and working capital to maintain or maximize the long-run value of the firm.

Using free cash flow in valuation is more challenging than using dividends because in forecasting free cash flow, the analyst must integrate the cash flows from the company's operations with those from its investing and financing activities. Because FCFF is the after-tax cash flow going to all suppliers of capital to the firm, the value of the firm is estimated by discounting FCFF at the weighted average cost of capital (WACC). An estimate of the value of equity is then found by subtracting the value of debt from the estimated value of the firm. The value of equity can also be estimated directly by discounting FCFE at the required rate of return for equity (because FCFE is the cash flow going to common stockholders, the required rate of return on equity is the appropriate risk-adjusted rate for discounting FCFE).

The two free cash flow approaches, indirect and direct, for valuing equity should theoretically yield the same estimates if all inputs reflect identical assumptions. An analyst may prefer to use one approach rather than the other, however, because of the characteristics of the company being valued. For example, if the company's capital structure is relatively stable, using FCFE to value equity is more direct and simpler than using FCFF. The FCFF model is often chosen, however, in two other cases:

- *A levered company with negative FCFE.* In this case, working with FCFF to value the company's equity might be easiest. The analyst would discount FCFF to find the present value of operating assets (adding the value of excess cash and marketable securities and of any other significant nonoperating assets[1] to get total firm value) and then subtract the market value of debt to obtain an estimate of the intrinsic value of equity.

- *A levered company with a changing capital structure.* First, if historical data are used to forecast free cash flow growth rates, FCFF growth might reflect fundamentals more clearly than does FCFE growth, which reflects fluctuating amounts of net borrowing. Second, in a forward-looking context, the required return on equity might be expected to be more sensitive to changes in financial leverage than changes in the WACC, making the use of a constant discount rate difficult to justify.

Specialized DCF approaches are also available to facilitate the equity valuation when the capital structure is expected to change.[2]

In the following, we present the general form of the FCFF valuation model and the FCFE valuation model.

2.2 Present Value of Free Cash Flow

The two distinct approaches to using free cash flow for valuation are the FCFF valuation approach and the FCFE valuation approach. The general expressions for these valuation models are similar to the expression for the general dividend discount model. In the DDM, the value of a share of stock equals the present value of forecasted dividends from Time 1 through infinity discounted at the required rate of return for equity.

2.2.1 Present Value of FCFF

The FCFF valuation approach estimates the value of the firm as the present value of future FCFF discounted at the weighted average cost of capital:

$$\text{Firm value} = \sum_{t=1}^{\infty} \frac{\text{FCFF}_t}{(1 + \text{WACC})^t} \tag{1}$$

Because FCFF is the cash flow available to all suppliers of capital, using WACC to discount FCFF gives the total value of all of the firm's capital. The value of equity is the value of the firm minus the market value of its debt:

$$\text{Equity value} = \text{Firm value} - \text{Market value of debt} \tag{2}$$

Dividing the total value of equity by the number of outstanding shares gives the value per share.

---

1 Adjustments for excess cash and marketable securities and for other nonoperating assets are discussed further in Section 5. "Excess" means excess in relation to operating needs.

2 The **adjusted present value** (APV) approach is one example of such models. In the APV approach, firm value is calculated as the sum of 1) the value of the company under the assumption that debt is not used (i.e., unlevered firm value) and 2) the net present value of any effects of debt on firm value (such as any tax benefits of using debt and any costs of financial distress). In this approach, the analyst estimates unlevered company value by discounting FCFF (under the assumption of no debt) at the unlevered cost of equity (the cost of equity given that the firm does not use debt). For details, see Ross, Westerfield, and Jaffe (2005), who explain APV in a capital budgeting context.

The cost of capital is the required rate of return that investors should demand for a cash flow stream like that generated by the company being analyzed. WACC depends on the riskiness of these cash flows. The calculation and interpretation of WACC were discussed in the reading on return concepts—that is, WACC is the weighted average of the after (corporate) tax required rates of return for debt and equity, where the weights are the proportions of the firm's total market value from each source, debt and equity. As an alternative, analysts may use the weights of debt and equity in the firm's target capital structure when those weights are known and differ from market value weights. The formula for WACC is

$$\text{WACC} = \frac{\text{MV}(\text{Debt})}{\text{MV}(\text{Debt}) + \text{MV}(\text{Equity})} r_d (1 - \text{Tax rate})$$
$$+ \frac{\text{MV}(\text{Equity})}{\text{MV}(\text{Debt}) + \text{MV}(\text{Equity})} r \tag{3}$$

MV (Debt) and MV (Equity) are the current market values of debt and equity, not their book or accounting values, and the ratios of MV(Debt) and MV(Equity) to the total market value of debt plus equity define the weights in the WACC formula. The quantities $r_d (1 - \text{Tax rate})$ and r are, respectively, the after-tax cost of debt and the after-tax cost of equity (in the case of equity, one could just write "cost of equity" because net income, the income belonging to equity, is after tax). In Equation 3, the tax rate is in principle the marginal corporate income tax rate.

2.2.2 Present Value of FCFE

The value of equity can also be found by discounting FCFE at the required rate of return on equity, r:

$$\text{Equity value} = \sum_{t=1}^{\infty} \frac{\text{FCFE}_t}{(1 + r)^t} \tag{4}$$

Because FCFE is the cash flow remaining for equity holders after all other claims have been satisfied, discounting FCFE by r (the required rate of return on equity) gives the value of the firm's equity. Dividing the total value of equity by the number of outstanding shares gives the value per share.

2.3 Single-Stage (Constant-Growth) FCFF and FCFE Models

In the DDM approach, the Gordon (constant- or stable-growth) model makes the assumption that dividends grow at a constant rate. The assumption that free cash flows grow at a constant rate leads to a single-stage (stable-growth) FCFF or FCFE model.[3]

2.3.1 Constant-Growth FCFF Valuation Model

Assume that FCFF grows at a constant rate, g, such that FCFF in any period is equal to FCFF in the previous period multiplied by $(1 + g)$:

$$\text{FCFF}_t = \text{FCFF}_{t-1}(1 + g)$$

If FCFF grows at a constant rate,

$$\text{Firm value} = \frac{\text{FCFF}_1}{\text{WACC} - g} = \frac{\text{FCFF}_0(1 + g)}{\text{WACC} - g} \tag{5}$$

Subtracting the market value of debt from the firm value gives the value of equity.

---

3 In the context of private company valuation, these constant-growth free cash flow models are often referred to as **capitalized cash flow models**.

EXAMPLE 1

Using the Constant-Growth FCFF Valuation Model

Cagiati Enterprises has FCFF of 700 million Swiss francs (CHF) and FCFE of CHF620 million. Cagiati's before-tax cost of debt is 5.7 percent, and its required rate of return for equity is 11.8 percent. The company expects a target capital structure consisting of 20 percent debt financing and 80 percent equity financing. The tax rate is 33.33 percent, and FCFF is expected to grow forever at 5.0 percent. Cagiati Enterprises has debt outstanding with a market value of CHF2.2 billion and has 200 million outstanding common shares.

1 What is Cagiati's weighted average cost of capital?

2 What is the value of Cagiati's equity using the FCFF valuation approach?

3 What is the value per share using this FCFF approach?

Solution to 1:

From Equation 3, WACC is

$$\text{WACC} = 0.20(5.7\%)(1 - 0.3333) + 0.80(11.8\%) = 10.2\%$$

Solution to 2:

The firm value of Cagiati Enterprises is the present value of FCFF discounted by using WACC. For FCFF growing at a constant 5 percent rate, the result is

$$\text{Firm value} = \frac{\text{FCFF}_1}{\text{WACC} - g} = \frac{\text{FCFF}_0(1 + g)}{\text{WACC} - g} = \frac{700(1.05)}{0.102 - 0.05}$$

$$= \frac{735}{0.052} = \text{CHF14,134.6 million}$$

The value of equity is the value of the firm minus the value of debt:

$$\text{Equity value} = 14{,}134.6 - 2{,}200 = \text{CHF11,934.6 million}$$

Solution to 3:

Dividing CH11,934.6 million by the number of outstanding shares gives the estimated value per share, V_0:

$$V_0 = \text{CHF11,934.6 million}/200 \text{ million shares}$$
$$= \text{CHF59.67 per share}$$

2.3.2 Constant-Growth FCFE Valuation Model

The constant-growth FCFE valuation model assumes that FCFE grows at constant rate g. FCFE in any period is equal to FCFE in the preceding period multiplied by $(1 + g)$:

$$\text{FCFE}_t = \text{FCFE}_{t-1}(1 + g)$$

The value of equity if FCFE is growing at a constant rate is

$$\text{Equity value} = \frac{\text{FCFE}_1}{r - g} = \frac{\text{FCFE}_0(1 + g)}{r - g} \qquad \textbf{(6)}$$

The discount rate is r, the required rate of return on equity. Note that the growth rate of FCFF and the growth rate of FCFE need not be and frequently are not the same.

In this section, we presented the basic ideas underlying free cash flow valuation and the simplest implementation, single-stage free cash flow models. The next section examines the precise definition of free cash flow and introduces the issues involved in forecasting free cash flow.

FORECASTING FREE CASH FLOW 3

Estimating FCFF or FCFE requires a complete understanding of the company and its financial statements. To provide a context for the estimation of FCFF and FCFE, we first use an extensive example to show the relationship between free cash flow and accounting measures of income.

For most of this section, we assume that the company has two sources of capital, debt and common stock. Once the concepts of FCFF and FCFE are understood for a company financed by using only debt and common stock, it is easy to incorporate preferred stock for the relatively small number of companies that actually use it (in Section 3.8 we incorporate preferred stock as a third source of capital).

3.1 Computing FCFF from Net Income

FCFF is the cash flow available to the company's suppliers of capital after all operating expenses (including taxes) have been paid and operating investments have been made. The company's suppliers of capital include bondholders and common shareholders (plus, occasionally, holders of preferred stock, which we ignore until later). Keeping in mind that a noncash charge is a charge or expense that does not involve the outlay of cash, we can write the expression for FCFF as follows[4]:

FCFF = Net income available to common shareholders (NI)

　　Plus: Net noncash charges (NCC)

　　Plus: Interest expense $\times (1 - \text{Tax rate})$

　　Less: Investment in fixed capital (FCInv)

　　Less: Investment in working capital (WCInv)

This equation can be written more compactly as

$$\text{FCFF} = \text{NI} + \text{NCC} + \text{Int}(1 - \text{Tax rate}) - \text{FCInv} - \text{WCInv} \qquad (7)$$

Consider each component of FCFF. The starting point in Equation 7 is net income available to common shareholders—the bottom line in an income statement. It represents income after depreciation, amortization, interest expense, income taxes, and the payment of dividends to preferred shareholders (but not payment of dividends to common shareholders).

Net noncash charges represent an adjustment for noncash decreases and increases in net income. This adjustment is the first of several that analysts generally perform on a net basis. If noncash decreases in net income exceed the increases, as is usually the case, the adjustment is positive. If noncash increases exceed noncash decreases, the adjustment is negative. The most common noncash charge is depreciation expense. When a company purchases fixed capital, such as equipment, the balance sheet reflects a cash outflow at the time of the purchase. In subsequent periods, the company records depreciation expense as the asset is used. The depreciation expense reduces net income but is not a cash outflow. Depreciation expense is thus one (the most

---

4 In this reading, when we refer to "investment in fixed capital" or "investment in working capital," we are referring to the investments made in the specific period for which the free cash flow is being calculated.

common) noncash charge that must be added back in computing FCFF. In the case of intangible assets, there is a similar noncash charge, amortization expense, which must be added back. Other noncash charges vary from company to company and are discussed in Section 3.3.

After-tax interest expense must be added back to net income to arrive at FCFF. This step is required because interest expense net of the related tax savings was deducted in arriving at net income and because interest is a cash flow available to one of the company's capital providers (i.e., the company's creditors). In the United States and many other countries, interest is tax deductible (reduces taxes) for the company (borrower) and taxable for the recipient (lender). As we explain later, when we discount FCFF, we use an after-tax cost of capital. For consistency, we thus compute FCFF by using the after-tax interest paid.[5]

Similar to after-tax interest expense, if a company has preferred stock, dividends on that preferred stock are deducted in arriving at net income available to common shareholders. Because preferred stock dividends are also a cash flow available to one of the company's capital providers, this item is added back to net income available to common shareholders in deriving FCFF. Further discussion of the effects of preferred stock is in Section 3.8.

Investments in fixed capital represent the outflows of cash to purchase fixed capital necessary to support the company's current and future operations. These investments are capital expenditures for long-term assets, such as the property, plant, and equipment (PP&E) necessary to support the company's operations. Necessary capital expenditures may also include intangible assets, such as trademarks. In the case of cash acquisition of another company instead of a direct acquisition of PP&E, the cash purchase amount can also be treated as a capital expenditure that reduces the company's free cash flow (note that this treatment is conservative because it reduces FCFF). In the case of large acquisitions (and all noncash acquisitions), analysts must take care in evaluating the impact on future free cash flow. If a company receives cash in disposing of any of its fixed capital, the analyst must deduct this cash in calculating investment in fixed capital. For example, suppose we had a sale of equipment for $100,000. This cash inflow would reduce the company's cash outflows for investments in fixed capital.

The company's statement of cash flows is an excellent source of information on capital expenditures as well as on sales of fixed capital. Analysts should be aware that some companies acquire fixed capital without using cash—for example, through an exchange for stock or debt. Such acquisitions do not appear in a company's statement of cash flows but, if material, must be disclosed in the footnotes. Although noncash exchanges do not affect historical FCFF, if the capital expenditures are necessary and may be made in cash in the future, the analyst should use this information in forecasting future FCFF.

The final point to cover is the important adjustment for net increases in working capital. This adjustment represents the net investment in current assets (such as accounts receivable) less current liabilities (such as accounts payable). Analysts can find this information by examining either the company's balance sheet or its statement of cash flows.

Although working capital is often defined as current assets minus current liabilities, working capital for cash flow and valuation purposes is defined to exclude cash and short-term debt (which includes notes payable and the current portion of long-term debt). When finding the net increase in working capital for the purpose of calculating free cash flow, we define working capital to exclude cash and cash equivalents as well as notes payable and the current portion of long-term debt. Cash and cash equivalents

---

5 Note that we could compute WACC on a pretax basis and compute FCFF by adding back interest paid with no tax adjustment. Whichever approach is adopted, the analyst must use mutually consistent definitions of FCFF and WACC.

are excluded because a change in cash is what we are trying to explain. Notes payable and the current portion of long-term debt are excluded because they are liabilities with explicit interest costs that make them financing items rather than operating items.

Example 2 shows all of the adjustments to net income required to find FCFF.

EXAMPLE 2

Calculating FCFF from Net Income

Cane Distribution, Inc., incorporated on 31 December 2009 with initial capital infusions of $224,000 of debt and $336,000 of common stock, acts as a distributor of industrial goods. The company managers immediately invested the initial capital in fixed capital of $500,000 and working capital of $60,000. Working capital initially consisted solely of inventory. The fixed capital consisted of nondepreciable property of $50,000 and depreciable property of $450,000. The depreciable property has a 10-year useful life with no salvage value. Exhibits 1, 2, and 3 provide Cane's financial statements for the three years following incorporation. Starting with net income, calculate Cane's FCFF for each year.

Exhibit 1 Cane Distribution, Inc. Income Statement (in Thousands)			
	Years Ending 31 December		
	2010	**2011**	**2012**
Earnings before interest, taxes, depreciation, and amortization (EBITDA)	$200.00	$220.00	$242.00
Depreciation expense	45.00	49.50	54.45
Operating income	155.00	170.50	187.55
Interest expense (at 7 percent)	15.68	17.25	18.97
Income before taxes	139.32	153.25	168.58
Income taxes (at 30 percent)	41.80	45.97	50.58
Net income	$97.52	$107.28	$118.00

Exhibit 2 Cane Distribution, Inc. Balance Sheet (in Thousands)				
	Years Ending 31 December			
	2009	**2010**	**2011**	**2012**
Cash	$0.00	$108.92	$228.74	$360.54
Accounts receivable	0.00	100.00	110.00	121.00
Inventory	60.00	66.00	72.60	79.86
Current assets	60.00	274.92	411.34	561.40
Fixed assets	500.00	500.00	550.00	605.00
Less: Accumulated depreciation	0.00	45.00	94.50	148.95
Total assets	$560.00	$729.92	$866.84	$1,017.45
Accounts payable	$0.00	$50.00	$55.00	$60.50
Current portion of long-term debt	0.00	0.00	0.00	0.00
Current liabilities	0.00	50.00	55.00	60.50

(continued)

Exhibit 2   (Continued)

	Years Ending 31 December			
	2009	2010	2011	2012
Long-term debt	224.00	246.40	271.04	298.14
Common stock	336.00	336.00	336.00	336.00
Retained earnings	0.00	97.52	204.80	322.80
Total liabilities and equity	$560.00	$729.92	$866.84	$1,017.45

Exhibit 3   Cane Distribution, Inc. Working Capital (in Thousands)

	Years Ending 31 December			
	2009	2010	2011	2012
Current assets excluding cash				
Accounts receivable	$0.00	$100.00	$110.00	$121.00
Inventory	60.00	66.00	72.60	79.86
Total current assets excluding cash	60.00	166.00	182.60	200.86
Current liabilities excluding short-term debt				
Accounts payable	0.00	50.00	55.00	60.50
Working capital	$60.00	$116.00	$127.60	$140.36
Increase in working capital		$56.00	$11.60	$12.76

Solution:

Following the logic in Equation 7, we calculate FCFF from net income as follows: We add noncash charges (here, depreciation) and after-tax interest expense to net income, then subtract the investment in fixed capital and the investment in working capital. The format for presenting the solution follows the convention that parentheses around a number indicate subtraction. The calculation follows (in thousands):

	Years Ending 31 December		
	2010	2011	2012
Net income	$97.52	$107.28	$118.00
Noncash charges – Depreciation	45.00	49.50	54.45
Interest expense × (1 – Tax rate)	10.98	12.08	13.28
Investment in fixed capital	(0.00)	(50.00)	(55.00)
Investment in working capital	(56.00)	(11.60)	(12.76)
Free cash flow to the firm	$97.50	$107.26	$117.97

3.2 Computing FCFF from the Statement of Cash Flows

FCFF is cash flow available to all providers of capital (debt and equity). Analysts frequently use cash flow from operations, taken from the statement of cash flows, as a starting point to compute free cash flow because CFO incorporates adjustments for noncash expenses (such as depreciation and amortization) as well as for net investments in working capital.

In a statement of cash flows, cash flows are separated into three components: cash flow from operating activities (or cash flow from operations), cash flow from investing activities, and cash flow from financing activities. Cash flow from operations is the net amount of cash provided by the company's operating activities. The operating section of the statement of cash flows shows such cash flows as cash received from customers and cash paid to suppliers. Cash flow from investing activities includes the company's investments in (or sales of) long-term assets—for example, PP&E and long-term investments in other companies. Cash flow from financing activities relates to the company's activities in raising or repaying capital. International Financial Reporting Standards (IFRS) allow the company to classify interest paid as either an operating or financing activity. Furthermore, IFRS allow dividends paid to be classified as either an operating or financing activity. Interestingly, under US generally accepted accounting principles (GAAP), interest expense paid to providers of debt capital must be classified as part of cash flow from operations (as is interest income) but payment of dividends to providers of equity capital is classified as a financing activity.

Exhibit 4 summarizes IFRS and US GAAP treatment of interest and dividends.

Exhibit 4	IFRS versus US GAAP Treatment of Interest and Dividends	
	IFRS	**US GAAP**
Interest received	Operating or Investing	Operating
Interest paid	Operating or Financing	Operating
Dividends received	Operating or Investing	Operating
Dividends paid	Operating or Financing	Financing

To estimate FCFF by starting with CFO, we must recognize the treatment of interest paid. If the after-tax interest expense was taken out of net income and out of CFO, as with US GAAP, then after-tax interest expense must be added back to get FCFF. In the case of US GAAP, FCFF can be estimated as follows:

Free cash flow to the firm = Cash flow from operations

Plus: Interest expense $\times (1 - \text{Tax rate})$

Less: Investment in fixed capital

or

$$FCFF = CFO + Int(1 - \text{Tax rate}) - FCInv \qquad (8)$$

To reiterate, the after-tax interest expense is added back because it was previously taken out of net income. The investment in working capital does not appear in Equation 8 because CFO already includes investment in working capital. Example 3 illustrates the use of CFO to calculate FCFF. In this example, the calculation of CFO begins with calculating net income, an approach known as the "indirect" method.[6]

---

6 See Robinson, Henry, Pirie, and Broihahn (2011) for a discussion of the indirect and direct cash flow statement formats.

EXAMPLE 3

Calculating FCFF from CFO

Use the information from the statement of cash flows given in Exhibit 5 to calculate FCFF for the three years 2010–2012. The tax rate (as given in Exhibit 1) is 30 percent.

Exhibit 5	Cane Distribution, Inc. Statement of Cash Flows: Indirect Method (in Thousands)		
	Years Ending 31 December		
	2010	**2011**	**2012**
Cash flow from operations			
Net income	$97.52	$107.28	$118.00
Plus: Depreciation	45.00	49.50	54.45
Increase in accounts receivable	(100.00)	(10.00)	(11.00)
Increase in inventory	(6.00)	(6.60)	(7.26)
Increase in accounts payable	50.00	5.00	5.50
Cash flow from operations	86.52	145.18	159.69
Cash flow from investing activities			
Purchases of PP&E	0.00	(50.00)	(55.00)
Cash flow from financing activities			
Borrowing (repayment)	22.40	24.64	27.10
Total cash flow	108.92	119.82	131.80
Beginning cash	0.00	108.92	228.74
Ending cash	$108.92	$228.74	$360.54
Notes:			
Cash paid for interest	($15.68)	($17.25)	($18.97)
Cash paid for taxes	($41.80)	($45.98)	($50.57)

Solution:

As shown in Equation 8, FCFF equals CFO plus after-tax interest minus the investment in fixed capital:

	Years Ending 31 December		
	2010	**2011**	**2012**
Cash flow from operations	$86.52	$145.18	$159.69
Interest expense × (1 – Tax rate)	10.98	12.08	13.28
Investment in fixed capital	(0.00)	(50.00)	(55.00)
Free cash flow to the firm	$97.50	$107.26	$117.97

3.3 Noncash Charges

The best place to find historical noncash charges is in the company's statement of cash flows. If an analyst wants to use an add-back method, as in FCFF = NI + NCC + Int(1 – Tax rate) – FCInv – WCInv, the analyst should verify the noncash charges to ensure that the FCFF estimate provides a reasonable basis for forecasting. For example, restructuring charges may involve cash expenditures and noncash charges. Severance pay for laid-off employees could be a cash restructuring charge, but a write-down in the value of assets as part of a restructuring charge is a noncash item. Example 4 illustrates noncash restructuring charges that must be added back to net income to obtain CFO.

<hr>

EXAMPLE 4

An Examination of Noncash Charges

Syngenta AG (SWX: SYNN), a company domiciled and incorporated in Switzerland, is a world-leading agribusiness operating in the Crop Protection, Seeds and Lawn and Garden markets. Crop Protection chemicals include herbicides, insecticides, fungicides and seed treatments to control weeds, insects and diseases in crops and are essential inputs enabling growers around the world to improve agricultural productivity and food quality. In Seeds, Syngenta operates in the high value commercial sectors of field crops (including corn, oilseeds, cereals and sugar beet) and vegetables. The Lawn and Garden business provides professional growers and consumers with flowers, turf and landscape products.

Syngenta's financial statements are presented in United States dollars as it is the major currency in which revenues are denominated. Jane Everett wants to value Syngenta by using the FCFF method. She collects information from the company's 10-K for the fiscal year ended 31 December 2012. The 2011 and 2012 cash flow from operating activities section from the consolidated statements of cash flow appear in Exhibit 6.

Exhibit 6	Consolidated Statements of Cash Flow for Syngenta AG and Subsidiaries (in US$ millions)	
	2012	**2011**
Income before taxes	2,152	1,901
Reversal of non-cash items	984	801
Cash (paid)/received in respect of:		
Interest received	135	96
Interest paid	(162)	(174)
Other financial receipts	62	216
Other financial payments	(260)	(252)
Income taxes	(378)	(282)
Restructuring costs	(55)	(71)
Contributions to pension plans, excluding restructuring costs	(78)	(198)
Other provisions	(182)	(116)
Cash flow before change in net working capital	2,218	1,921
Change in net working capital:		

(continued)

Exhibit 6   (Continued)

	2012	2011
Change in inventories	(555)	(478)
Change in trade and other working capital assets	(814)	(120)
Change in trade and other working capital liabilities	510	548
Cash flow from operating activities	1,359	1,871

Everett notices that the reconciliation amount in the 2012 cash flow statement for restructuring costs of $55 differs significantly from the $241 restructuring expense that was reflected in the income statement. She finds the following discussion of provisions in Note 19 of the financial statements (Exhibit 7).

Exhibit 7   Movement in Provisions for Year Ended 31 December 2012 (in US$ millions)

	1 January	Charges to income	Release of provisions credited to income	Payments	Actuarial gains and losses	Transfers offset in defined benefit pension assets	Currency translation effects	31 December
Restructuring provisions								
Employee termination costs	75	10	(2)	(44)	—	—	6	45
Other third party costs	23	3	—	(11)	—	—	(1)	14
Employee benefits:								
Pensions	288	81	—	(78)	131	(127)	7	302
Other post retirement benefits	101	3	(54)	(11)	22	—	—	61
Other long-term employee benefits	57	14	(1)	(15)		—	6	61
Environmental provisions	369	4	(3)	(33)		—	6	343
Provisions for legal and product liability settlements	189	86	(10)	(112)		—	(5)	148
Other provisions	98	40	(24)	(11)		—	—	103
Total	1,200	241	(94)	(315)	153	(127)	19	1,077

Using the provided information, answer the following questions:

1 Why is there a difference in the amount shown for restructuring expenses in the income statement and the amount shown for restructuring costs in the cash flow statement?

2 How should the restructuring costs be treated when forecasting future cash flows?

Solution to 1:

The difference between restructuring expenses in the income statement and restructuring costs in the cash flow statement is due to two reasons. First, restructuring expenses in the income statement were more broadly defined than restructuring costs were in the cash flow statement. Note from Exhibit 7 that the $241 that was included in net income reflects restructuring charges as well as changes to benefit and other provisional accounts. Second, the cash flow statement reflects the fact that some of the charges were paid in cash and some were not. In the cash flow statement, non-cash restructuring charges would be included as part of the $984 million reversal of non-cash items that is added back to net income.

Reconciling Exhibit 6 and Exhibit 7, the $55 appearing as restructuring costs in Exhibit 6 matches with the sum of employee termination costs, $44, and other third party costs, $11, as noted in the Payments column in Exhibit 7. The $78 appearing as contributions to pension plans, excluding restructuring costs, in Exhibit 6 matches with the $78 entry in the Payments column for pensions in Exhibit 7. Finally, the $182 appearing as other provisions in Exhibit 6 matches with the remaining entries ($11 + $15 + $33 + $112 + $11) appearing in the Payments column in Exhibit 7.

Solution to 2:

Restructuring charges are generally unpredictable and are frequently left out of a forecast. As Exhibit 7 shows, Syngenta AG still has provisional accounts set aside for restructuring. The amounts in these accounts and the history of past charges could be considered when attempting to forecast future cash flows.

Noncash restructuring charges may also cause an increase in net income in some circumstances—for example when a company reverses part or all of a previous accrual. Gains and losses (e.g., of operating assets) are another noncash item that may increase or decrease net noncash charges. If a company sells a piece of equipment with a book value of €60,000 for €100,000, it reports the €40,000 gain as part of net income. The €40,000 gain is not a cash flow, however, and must be subtracted in arriving at FCFF. Note that the €100,000 *is* a cash flow and is part of the company's net investment in fixed capital. A loss reduces net income and thus must be added back in arriving at FCFF. Aside from depreciation, gains and losses are the most commonly seen noncash charges that require an adjustment to net income. Analysts should examine the company's statement of cash flows to identify items particular to a company and to determine what adjustments the analyst might need to make for the accounting numbers to be useful for forecasting purposes.

Exhibit 8 summarizes the common noncash charges that affect net income and indicates for each item whether to add it to or subtract it from net income in arriving at FCFF.

Exhibit 8	Noncash Items and FCFF
Noncash Item	**Adjustment to NI to Arrive at FCFF**
Depreciation	Added back
Amortization and impairment of intangibles	Added back
Restructuring charges (expense)	Added back
Restructuring charges (income resulting from reversal)	Subtracted
Losses	Added back
Gains	Subtracted
Amortization of long-term bond discounts	Added back
Amortization of long-term bond premiums	Subtracted
Deferred taxes	Added back but calls for special attention

The item deferred taxes requires special attention because deferred taxes result from differences in the timing of reporting income and expenses in the company's financial statements and the company's tax return. The income tax expense deducted in arriving at net income for financial reporting purposes is not the same as the amount of cash taxes paid. Over time, these differences between book income and taxable income should offset each other and have no impact on aggregate cash flows. Generally, if the analyst's purpose is forecasting and, therefore, identifying the persistent components of FCFF, then the analyst should not add back deferred tax changes that are expected to reverse in the near future. In some circumstances, however, a company may be able to consistently defer taxes until a much later date. If a company is growing and has the ability to indefinitely defer its tax liability, adding back deferred taxes to net income is warranted. Nevertheless, an acquirer must be aware that these taxes may be payable at some time in the future.

Companies often record expenses (e.g., restructuring charges) for financial reporting purposes that are not deductible for tax purposes. In this case, current tax payments are higher than taxes reported in the income statement, resulting in a deferred tax *asset* and a subtraction from net income to arrive at cash flow in the statement of cash flows. If the deferred tax asset is expected to reverse in the near future (e.g., through tax depreciation deductions), to avoid underestimating future cash flows, the analyst should not subtract the deferred tax asset in a cash flow forecast. If the company is expected to have these charges on a continual basis, however, a subtraction that will lower the forecast of future cash flows is warranted.

Employee share-based compensation (stock options) provides another challenge to the forecaster. Under IFRS and US GAAP, companies must record in the income statement an expense for options provided to employees. The granting of options themselves does not result in a cash outflow and is thus a noncash charge; however, the granting of options has long-term cash flow implications. When the employee exercises the option, the company receives some cash related to the exercise price of the option at the strike price. This cash flow is considered a financing cash flow. Also, in some cases, a company receives a tax benefit from issuing options, which could increase operating cash flow but not net income. Both IFRS and US GAAP require that a portion of the tax effect be recorded as a financing cash flow rather than an operating cash flow in the statement of cash flows. Analysts should review the statement of cash flows and footnotes to determine the impact of options on operating cash flows. If these cash flows are not expected to persist in the future, analysts should not include them in their forecasts of cash flows. Analysts should also consider the impact of stock options on the number of shares outstanding. When computing equity value, analysts may want to use the number of shares *expected* to be outstanding (based on the exercise of employee stock options) rather than the number currently outstanding.

Example 5 illustrates that when forecasting cash flows for valuation purposes, analysts should consider the sustainability of historical working capital effects on free cash flow.

EXAMPLE 5

Sustainability of Working Capital Effects on Free Cash Flow

Ryanair Holdings PLC (LSE: RYA) operates a low-fare scheduled passenger airline serving short-haul, point-to-point routes between Ireland, the United Kingdom, Continental Europe, and Morocco. The operating activities section of its statement of cash flows and a portion of the investing activities section are presented in Exhibit 9. The statement of cash flows was prepared in accordance with IFRS.

Exhibit 9 Ryanair Holdings PLC Excerpt from Statement of Cash Flows (Euros in Millions)			
	Year Ended 31 March		
	2012	2011	2010
Operating activities			
Profit before tax	633.0	420.9	341.0
Adjustments to reconcile profits before tax to net cash provided by operating activities			
Depreciation	309.2	277.7	235.4
Increase in inventories	(0.1)	(0.2)	(0.4)
Increase in trade receivables	(0.9)	(6.3)	(2.5)
Decrease (increase) in other current assets	34.5	(20.9)	11.6
Increase (decrease) in trade payables	30.4	(3.2)	21.3
Increase in accrued expenses	11.6	135.0	189.7
Increase (decrease) in other creditors	19.7	(10.0)	30.1
Increase (decrease) in maintenance provisions	6.6	(7.9)	30.7
Gain on disposal of property, plant, and equipment	(10.4)	—	(2.0)
Loss on impairment of available-for-sale financial asset	—	—	13.5
Decrease (increase) in interest receivable	—	1.6	(1.2)
Increase (decrease) in interest payable	1.1	2.3	(0.5)
Retirement costs	(0.1)	(0.1)	(0.1)
Share based payments	(0.7)	3.3	4.9
Income tax paid	(13.6)	(5.9)	—
Net cash provided by operating activities	1,020.3	786.3	871.5
Investing activities			
Capital expenditure (purchase of property, plant, and equipment)	(317.6)	(897.2)	(997.8)

Analysts predict that as Ryanair grows in coming years, depreciation expense will increase substantially. Based on the information given, address the following:

1   Contrast reported depreciation expense to reported capital expenditures and describe the implications of future growth in depreciation expense (all else being equal) for future net income and future cash from operating activities.

2   Explain the effects on free cash flow to equity of changes in 2012 in working capital accounts, such as inventory, accounts receivable, and accounts payable, and comment on the long-term sustainability of such changes.

Solution to 1:

In the 2010–2012 period, the amount of depreciation expense relative to the amount of capital expenditures changed significantly. For example, in 2012, capital expenditures of €317.6 million were just slightly more than the €309.2 million depreciation expense. In 2010, capital expenditures of €997.8 million were over 4 times more than depreciation charges of €235.4 million. The rate of growth in depreciation expense will be highly dependent on future capital expenditures.

In calculating net income, depreciation is a deduction. Therefore, as depreciation expense increases in coming years, net income will decrease. Specifically, net income will be reduced by (depreciation expense) × (1 − Tax rate). In calculating CFO, however, depreciation is added back in full to net income. The difference between depreciation expense—the amount added back to net income to calculate CFO—and the amount by which net income is reduced by depreciation expense is (tax rate) × (depreciation expense), which represents a positive increment to CFO. Thus, the projected increase in depreciation expense is a negative for future net income but a positive for future CFO. (At worst, if the company operates at a loss, depreciation is neutral for CFO.)

Solution to 2:

In 2012, the increases in inventory and accounts receivable ("trade receivables") resulted in negative adjustments to net income (i.e., the changes reduced cash flow relative to net income). The adjustments are negative because increases in these accounts are a use of cash. On the current liabilities side, the increase in trade payables, accrued expenses, and "other creditors" are added back to net income and are sources of cash because such increases represent increased amounts for which cash payments have yet to be made. Because CFO is a component of FCFE, the items that had a positive (negative) effect on CFO also have a positive (negative) effect on FCFE.

Although not the case here, declining balances for assets, such as inventory, or for liabilities, such as accounts payable, are not sustainable indefinitely. In the extreme case, the balance declines to zero and no further reduction is possible. Given the growth in its net income and the expansion of PP&E evidenced by capital expenditures, Ryanair appears to be growing and investors should expect its working capital requirements to grow accordingly.

3.4 Computing FCFE from FCFF

FCFE is cash flow available to equity holders only. To find FCFE, therefore, we must reduce FCFF by the after-tax value of interest paid to debtholders and add net borrowing (which is debt issued less debt repaid over the period for which one is calculating free cash flow):

Free cash flow to equity = Free cash flow to the firm

Less: Interest expense $\times (1 - \text{Tax rate})$

Plus: Net borrowing

or

FCFE = FCFF – Int(1 – Tax rate) + Net borrowing   **(9)**

As Equation 9 shows, FCFE is found by starting from FCFF, subtracting after-tax interest expenses, and adding net new borrowing. The analyst can also find FCFF from FCFE by making the opposite adjustments—by adding after-tax interest expenses and subtracting net borrowing: FCFF = FCFE + Int(1 – Tax rate) – Net borrowing.

Exhibit 10 uses the values for FCFF for Cane Distribution calculated in Example 3 to show the calculation of FCFE when starting with FCFF. To calculate FCFE in this manner, we subtract after-tax interest expense from FCFF and then add net borrowing (equal to new debt borrowing minus debt repayment).

Exhibit 10 Calculating FCFE from FCFF			
	Years Ending 31 December		
	2010	**2011**	**2012**
Free cash flow to the firm	97.50	107.26	117.97
Interest paid × (1 – Tax rate)	(10.98)	(12.08)	(13.28)
New debt borrowing	22.40	24.64	27.10
Debt repayment	(0)	(0)	(0)
Free cash flow to equity	108.92	119.82	131.79

To reiterate, FCFE is the cash flow available to common stockholders—the cash flow remaining after all operating expenses (including taxes) have been paid, capital investments have been made, and other transactions with other suppliers of capital have been carried out. The company's other capital suppliers include creditors, such as bondholders, and preferred stockholders. The cash flows (net of taxes) that arise from transactions with creditors and preferred stockholders are deducted from FCFF to arrive at FCFE.

FCFE is the amount that the company can afford to pay out as dividends. In actuality, for various reasons companies often pay out substantially more or substantially less than FCFE, so FCFE often differs from dividends paid. One reason for this difference is that the dividend decision is a discretionary decision of the board of directors. Most corporations "manage" their dividends; they prefer to raise them gradually over time, partly because they do not want to cut dividends. Many companies raise dividends slowly even when their earnings are increasing rapidly, and companies often maintain their current dividends even when their profitability has declined. Consequently, earnings are much more volatile than dividends.

In Equations 7 and 8, we show the calculation of FCFF starting with, respectively, net income and cash flow from operations. As Equation 9 shows, FCFE = FCFF − Int(1 − Tax rate) + Net borrowing. By subtracting after-tax interest expense and adding net borrowing to Equations 7 and 8, we have equations to calculate FCFE starting with, respectively, net income and CFO:

$$\text{FCFE} = \text{NI} + \text{NCC} - \text{FCInv} - \text{WCInv} + \text{Net borrowing} \tag{10}$$

$$\text{FCFE} = \text{CFO} - \text{FCInv} + \text{Net borrowing} \tag{11}$$

Example 6 illustrates how to adjust net income or CFO to find FCFF and FCFE.

EXAMPLE 6

Adjusting Net Income or CFO to Find FCFF and FCFE

The balance sheet, income statement, and statement of cash flows for the Pitts Corporation are shown in Exhibit 11. Note that the statement of cash flows follows a convention according to which the positive numbers of $400 million and $85 million for "cash *used for* investing activities" and "cash *used for* financing activities," respectively, indicate outflows and thus amounts to be *subtracted*. Analysts will also encounter a convention in which the value "(400)" for "cash provided by (used for) investing activities" would be used to indicate a subtraction of $400.

Exhibit 11   Financial Statements for Pitts Corporation (in Millions, except for Per-Share Data)

	Year Ended 31 December	
Balance Sheet	2011	2012
Assets		
Current assets		
Cash and equivalents	$190	$200
Accounts receivable	560	600
Inventory	410	440
Total current assets	1,160	1,240
Gross fixed assets	2,200	2,600
Accumulated depreciation	(900)	(1,200)
Net fixed assets	1,300	1,400
Total assets	$2,460	$2,640
Liabilities and shareholders' equity		
Current liabilities		
Accounts payable	$285	$300
Notes payable	200	250
Accrued taxes and expenses	140	150
Total current liabilities	625	700
Long-term debt	865	890
Common stock	100	100
Additional paid-in capital	200	200
Retained earnings	670	750

Exhibit 11 (Continued)

Balance Sheet	Year Ended 31 December	
	2011	**2012**
Total shareholders' equity	970	1,050
Total liabilities and shareholders' equity	$2,460	$2,640

Statement of Income Year Ended 31 December	2012
Total revenues	$3,000
Operating costs and expenses	2,200
EBITDA	800
Depreciation	300
Operating income (EBIT)	500
Interest expense	100
Income before tax	400
Taxes (at 40 percent)	160
Net income	240
Dividends	160
Change in retained earnings	80
Earnings per share (EPS)	$0.48
Dividends per share	$0.32

Statement of Cash Flows Year Ended 31 December	2012
Operating activities	
Net income	$240
Adjustments	
Depreciation	300
Changes in working capital	
Accounts receivable	(40)
Inventories	(30)
Accounts payable	15
Accrued taxes and expenses	10
Cash provided by operating activities	$495
Investing activities	
Purchases of fixed assets	400
Cash used for investing activities	$400
Financing activities	
Notes payable	(50)
Long-term financing issuances	(25)
Common stock dividends	160
Cash used for financing activities	$85

(continued)

Statement of Cash Flows Year Ended 31 December	2012
Cash and equivalents increase (decrease)	10
Cash and equivalents at beginning of year	190
Cash and equivalents at end of year	$200
Supplemental cash flow disclosures	
Interest paid	$100
Income taxes paid	$160

Exhibit 11 (Continued)

Note that the Pitts Corporation had net income of $240 million in 2012. In the following, show the calculations required to do each of the following:

1 Calculate FCFF starting with the net income figure.
2 Calculate FCFE starting from the FCFF calculated in Part 1.
3 Calculate FCFE starting with the net income figure.
4 Calculate FCFF starting with CFO.
5 Calculate FCFE starting with CFO.

Solution to 1:

The analyst can use Equation 7 to find FCFF from net income (amounts are in millions):

Net income available to common shareholders	$240
Plus: Net noncash charges	300
Plus: Interest expense × (1 – Tax rate)	60
Less: Investment in fixed capital	400
Less: Investment in working capital	45
Free cash flow to the firm	$155

In the format shown and throughout the solutions, "Less: . . . x" is interpreted as "subtract x."
This equation can also be written as

$$FCFF = NI + NCC + Int(1 - Tax\ rate) - FCInv - WCInv$$
$$= 240 + 300 + 60 - 400 - 45 = \$155\ million$$

Some of these items need explanation. Capital spending is $400 million, which is the increase in gross fixed assets shown on the balance sheet and in capital expenditures shown as an investing activity in the statement of cash flows. The increase in working capital is $45 million, which is the increase in accounts receivable of $40 million ($600 million – $560 million) plus the increase in inventories of $30 million ($440 million – $410 million) minus the increase in accounts payable of $15 million ($300 million – $285 million) minus the increase in accrued taxes and expenses of $10 million ($150 million – $140 million). When finding the increase in working capital, we ignore cash because the change in cash is what we are calculating. We also ignore short-term debt, such as notes payable, because such debt is part of the capital provided to the company and is not considered an operating item. The after-tax interest cost is the interest expense times (1 − Tax rate): $100 million × (1 − 0.40) = $60 million. The values of the remaining items in Equation 7 can be taken directly from the financial statements.

Solution to 2:

Finding FCFE from FCFF can be done with Equation 9:

Free cash flow to the firm	$155
Less: Interest expense × (1 − Tax rate)	60
Plus: Net borrowing	75
Free cash flow to equity	$170

Or by using the equation

$$\text{FCFE} = \text{FCFF} - \text{Int}(1 - \text{Tax rate}) + \text{Net borrowing}$$
$$= 155 - 60 + 75 = \$170 \text{ million}$$

Solution to 3:

The analyst can use Equation 10 to find FCFE from NI.

Net income available to common shareholders	$240
Plus: Net noncash charges	300
Less: Investment in fixed capital	400
Less: Investment in working capital	45
Plus: Net borrowing	75
Free cash flow to equity	$170

Or by using the equation

$$\text{FCFE} = \text{NI} + \text{NCC} - \text{FCInv} - \text{WCInv} + \text{Net borrowing}$$
$$= 240 + 300 - 400 - 45 + 75 = \$170 \text{ million}$$

Because notes payable increased by $50 million ($250 million − $200 million) and long-term debt increased by $25 million ($890 million − $865 million), net borrowing is $75 million.

Solution to 4:

Equation 8 can be used to find FCFF from CFO:

Cash flow from operations	$495
Plus: Interest expense × (1 − Tax rate)	60
Less: Investment in fixed capital	400
Free cash flow to the firm	$155

or

$$\text{FCFF} = \text{CFO} + \text{Int}(1 - \text{Tax rate}) - \text{FCInv}$$
$$= 495 + 60 - 400 = \$155 \text{ million}$$

Solution to 5:

Equation 11 can be used to find FCFE from CFO:

Cash flow from operations	$495
Less: Investment in fixed capital	400
Plus: Net borrowing	75
Free cash flow to equity	$170

or

$$FCFE = CFO - FCInv + \text{Net borrowing}$$
$$= 495 - 400 + 75 = \$170 \text{ million}$$

FCFE is usually less than FCFF. In this example, however, FCFE ($170 million) exceeds FCFF ($155 million) because external borrowing was large during this year.

3.5 Finding FCFF and FCFE from EBIT or EBITDA

FCFF and FCFE are most frequently calculated from a starting basis of net income or CFO (as shown in Sections 3.1 and 3.2). Two other starting points are EBIT and EBITDA from the income statement.

To show the relationship between EBIT and FCFF, we start with Equation 7 and assume that the only noncash charge (NCC) is depreciation (Dep):

$$FCFF = NI + Dep + Int(1 - \text{Tax rate}) - FCInv - WCInv$$

Net income (NI) can be expressed as

$$NI = (EBIT - Int)(1 - \text{Tax rate}) = EBIT(1 - \text{Tax rate}) - Int(1 - \text{Tax rate})$$

Substituting this equation for NI in Equation 7, we have

$$FCFF = EBIT(1 - \text{Tax rate}) + Dep - FCInv - WCInv \qquad (12)$$

To get FCFF from EBIT, we multiply EBIT by (1 − Tax rate), add back depreciation, and then subtract the investments in fixed capital and working capital.

The relationship between FCFF and EBITDA can also be easily shown. Net income can be expressed as

$$NI = (EBITDA - Dep - Int)(1 - \text{Tax rate})$$
$$= EBITDA(1 - \text{Tax rate}) - Dep(1 - \text{Tax rate}) - Int(1 - \text{Tax rate})$$

Substituting this equation for NI in Equation 7 results in

$$FCFF = EBITDA(1 - \text{Tax rate}) + Dep(\text{Tax rate}) - FCInv - WCInv \qquad (13)$$

FCFF equals EBITDA times (1 − Tax rate) plus depreciation times the tax rate minus investments in fixed capital and working capital. In comparing Equations 12 and 13, note the difference in how depreciation is handled.

Many adjustments for noncash charges that are required to calculate FCFF when starting from net income are not required when starting from EBIT or EBITDA. In the calculation of net income, many noncash charges are made after computing EBIT or EBITDA, so they do not need to be added back when calculating FCFF based on EBIT or EBITDA. Another important consideration is that some noncash charges, such as depreciation, are tax deductible. A noncash charge that affects taxes must be accounted for.

In summary, in calculating FCFF from EBIT or EBITDA, whether an adjustment for a noncash charge is needed depends on where in the income statement the charge has been deducted; furthermore, the form of any needed adjustment depends on whether the noncash charge is a tax-deductible expense.

We can also calculate FCFE (instead of FCFF) from EBIT or EBITDA. An easy way to obtain FCFE based on EBIT or EBITDA is to use Equation 12 (the expression for FCFF in terms of EBIT) or Equation 13 (the expression for FCFF in terms of EBITDA), respectively, and then subtract Int(1 − Tax rate) and add net borrowing because FCFE is related to FCFF as follows (see Equation 9):

$$FCFE = FCFF - Int(1 - \text{Tax rate}) + \text{Net borrowing}$$

Example 7 uses the Pitts Corporation financial statements to find FCFF and FCFE from EBIT and EBITDA.

Adjusting EBIT and EBITDA to Find FCFF and FCFE

The Pitts Corporation (financial statements provided in Example 6) had EBIT of $500 million and EBITDA of $800 million in 2012. Show the adjustments that would be required to find FCFF and FCFE:

1 Starting from EBIT.

2 Starting from EBITDA.

Solution to 1:

To get FCFF from EBIT using Equation 12, we carry out the following (in millions):

EBIT(1 − Tax rate) = 500(1 − 0.40)	$300
Plus: Net noncash charges	300
Less: Net investment in fixed capital	400
Less: Net increase in working capital	45
Free cash flow to the firm	$155

or

$$FCFF = EBIT(1 - Tax\ rate) + Dep - FCInv - WCInv$$
$$= 500(1 - 0.40) + 300 - 400 - 45 = \$155\ million$$

To obtain FCFE, make the appropriate adjustments to FCFF:

$$FCFE = FCFF - Int(1 - Tax\ rate) + Net\ borrowing$$
$$= 155 - 100(1 - 0.40) + 75 = \$170\ million$$

Solution to 2:

To obtain FCFF from EBITDA using Equation 13, we do the following (in millions):

EBITDA(1 − Tax rate) = $800(1 − 0.40)	$480
Plus: Dep(Tax rate) = $300(0.40)	120
Less: Net investment in fixed capital	400
Less: Net increase in working capital	45
Free cash flow to the firm	$155

or

$$FCFF = EBITDA(1 - Tax\ rate) + Dep(Tax\ rate) - FCInv - WCInv$$
$$= 800(1 - 0.40) + 300(0.40) - 400 - 45 = \$155\ million$$

Again, to obtain FCFE, make the appropriate adjustments to FCFF:

$$FCFE = FCFF - Int(1 - Tax\ rate) + Net\ borrowing$$
$$= 155 - 100(1 - 0.40) + 75 = \$170\ million$$

3.6 FCFF and FCFE on a Uses-of-Free-Cash-Flow Basis

Prior sections illustrated the calculation of FCFF and FCFE from various income or cash flow starting points (e.g., net income or cash flow from operations). Those approaches to calculating free cash flow can be characterized as showing the *sources* of free cash flow. An alternative perspective examines the *uses* of free cash flow. In the context of calculating FCFF and FCFE, analyzing free cash flow on a uses basis serves as a consistency check on the sources calculation and may reveal information relevant to understanding a company's capital structure policy or cash position.

In general, a firm has the following alternative uses of positive FCFF: 1) retain the cash and thus increase the firm's balances of cash and marketable securities; 2) use the cash for payments to providers of debt capital (i.e., interest payments and principal payments in excess of new borrowings); and 3) use the cash for payments to providers of equity capital (i.e., dividend payments and/or share repurchases in excess of new share issuances). Similarly, a firm has the following general alternatives for covering negative free cash flows: draw down cash balances, borrow additional cash, or issue equity.

The effects on the company's capital structure of its transactions with capital providers should be noted. For a simple example, assume that free cash flows are zero and that the company makes no change to its cash balances. Obtaining cash via net new borrowings and using the cash for dividends or net share repurchases will increase the company's leverage, whereas obtaining cash from net new share issuances and using that cash to make principal payments in excess of new borrowings will reduce leverage.

We calculate uses of FCFF as follows:

Uses of FCFF =

Increases (or minus decreases) in cash balances

Plus: Net payments to providers of debt capital, which are calculated as:

- Plus: Interest expense × (1 – Tax rate).
- Plus: Repayment of principal in excess of new borrowing (or minus new borrowing in excess of debt repayment if new borrowing is greater).

Plus: Payments to providers of equity capital, which are calculated as:

- Plus: Cash dividends.
- Plus: Share repurchases in excess of share issuance (or minus new share issuance in excess of share repurchases if share issuance is greater).

Uses of FCFF must equal sources of FCFF as previously calculated.

Free cash flows to equity reflect free cash flows to the firm net of the cash used for payments to providers of debt capital. Accordingly, we can calculate FCFE as follows:

Uses of FCFE =

Plus: Increases (or minus decreases) in cash balances

Plus: Payments to providers of equity capital, which are calculated as:

- Plus: Cash dividends.
- Plus: Share repurchases in excess of share issuance (or minus new share issuance in excess of share repurchases if share issuance is greater).

Again, the uses of FCFE must equal the sources of FCFE (calculated previously).

To illustrate the equivalence of sources and uses of FCFF and FCFE for the Pitts Corporation, whose financial statements are given in Exhibit 11 in Example 6, note the following for 2012:

- The increase in the balance of cash and equivalents was $10, calculated as $200 − $190.

- After-tax interest expense was $60, calculated as interest expense × (1 − Tax rate) = $100 × (1 − 0.40).

- Net borrowing was $75, calculated as increase in borrowing minus repayment of debt = $50 (increase in notes payable) + $25 (increase in long-term debt).

- Cash dividends totaled $160.

- Share repurchases and issuance both equaled $0.

FCFF, previously calculated, was $155. Pitts Corporation used the FCFF as follows:[7]

Increase in balance of cash and cash equivalents		$10
Plus:	After-tax interest payments to providers of debt capital	$60
Minus:	New borrowing	($75)
Plus:	Payments of dividends to providers of equity capital	$160
Plus:	Share repurchases in excess of share issuances (or minus new share issuance in excess of share repurchases)	$0
Total uses of FCFF		$155

FCFE, previously calculated, was $170. Pitts Corporation used the FCFE as follows:

Increase in balance of cash and cash equivalents		$10
Plus:	Payments of dividends to providers of equity capital	$160
Plus:	Share repurchases in excess of share issuances (or minus new share issuance in excess of share repurchases)	$0
Total uses of FCFE		$170

In summary, an analysis of the uses of free cash flows shows that Pitts Corporation was using free cash flows to manage its capital structure by increasing debt. The additional debt was not needed to cover capital expenditures; the statement of cash flows showed that the company's operating cash flows of $495 were more than adequate to cover its capital expenditures of $400. Instead, the additional debt was used, in part, to make dividend payments to the company's shareholders.

3.7 Forecasting FCFF and FCFE

Computing FCFF and FCFE from historical accounting data is relatively straightforward. In some cases, these data are used directly to extrapolate free cash flow growth in a single-stage free cash flow valuation model. On other occasions, however, the analyst may expect that the future free cash flows will not bear a simple relationship to the past. The analyst who wishes to forecast future FCFF or FCFE directly for such a company must forecast the individual components of free cash flow. This section extends our previous presentation on *computing* FCFF and FCFE to the more complex task of *forecasting* FCFF and FCFE.

---

[7] Payments of principal to providers of debt capital in excess of new borrowings are a use of free cash flow. Here, the corporation did not use its free cash flow to repay debt; rather, it borrowed new debt, which increased the cash flows available to be used for providers of equity capital.

One method for forecasting free cash flow involves applying some constant growth rate to a current level of free cash flow (possibly adjusted). The simplest basis for specifying the future growth rate is to assume that a historical growth rate will also apply to the future. This approach is appropriate if a company's free cash flow has tended to grow at a constant rate and if historical relationships between free cash flow and fundamental factors are expected to continue. Example 8 asks that the reader apply this approach to the Pitts Corporation based on 2012 FCFF of $155 million as calculated in Examples 6 and 7.

EXAMPLE 8

Constant Growth in FCFF

Use Pitts Corporation data to compute its FCFF for the next three years. Assume that growth in FCFF remains at the historical levels of 15 percent a year. The answer is (in millions):

	2012 Actual	2013 Estimate	2014 Estimate	2015 Estimate
FCFF	155.00	178.25	204.99	235.74

A more complex approach is to forecast the components of free cash flow. This approach is able to capture the complex relationships among the components. One popular method[8] is to forecast the individual components of free cash flow—EBIT(1–Tax rate), net noncash charges, investment in fixed capital, and investment in working capital. EBIT can be forecasted directly or by forecasting sales and the company's EBIT margin based on an analysis of historical data and the current and expected economic environment. Similarly, analysts can base forecasts of capital needs on historical relationships between increases in sales and investments in fixed and working capital.

In this discussion, we illustrate a simple sales-based forecasting method for FCFF and FCFE based on the following major assumption:

> Investment in fixed capital in excess of depreciation (FCInv – Dep) and investment in working capital (WCInv) both bear a constant relationship to forecast increases in the size of the company as measured by increases in sales.

In addition, for FCFE forecasting, we assume that the capital structure represented by the debt ratio (DR)—debt as a percentage of debt plus equity—is constant. Under that assumption, DR indicates the percentage of the investment in fixed capital in excess of depreciation (also called "net new investment in fixed capital") and in working capital that will be financed by debt. This method involves a simplification because it considers depreciation as the only noncash charge, so the method does not work well when that approximation is not a good assumption.

If depreciation reflects the annual cost for maintaining the existing capital stock, the difference between fixed capital investment and depreciation—incremental FCInv—should be related to the capital expenditures required for growth. In this case, the following inputs are needed:

■ forecasts of sales growth rates;

■ forecasts of the after-tax operating margin (for FCFF forecasting) or profit margin (for FCFE forecasting);

---

8 See Rappaport (1997) for a variation of this model.

- an estimate of the relationship of incremental FCInv to sales increases;
- an estimate of the relationship of WCInv to sales increases; and
- an estimate of DR.

In the case of FCFF forecasting, FCFF is calculated by forecasting EBIT(1 − Tax rate) and subtracting incremental fixed capital expenditures and incremental working capital expenditures.[9] To estimate FCInv and WCInv, we multiply their past proportion to sales increases by the forecasted sales increases. Incremental fixed capital expenditures as a proportion of sales increases are computed as follows:

$$\frac{\text{Capital expenditures} - \text{Depreciation expense}}{\text{Increase in sales}}$$

Similarly, incremental working capital expenditures as a proportion of sales increases are

$$\frac{\text{Increase in working capital}}{\text{Increase in sales}}$$

When depreciation is the only significant net noncash charge, this method yields the same results as the previous equations for estimating FCFF or FCFE. Rather than adding back all depreciation and subtracting all capital expenditures when starting with EBIT(1 − Tax rate), this approach simply subtracts the net capital expenditures in excess of depreciation.

Although the recognition may not be obvious, this approach recognizes that capital expenditures have two components: those expenditures necessary to maintain existing capacity (fixed capital replacement) and those incremental expenditures necessary for growth. In forecasting, the expenditures to maintain capacity are likely to be related to the current level of sales and the expenditures for growth are likely to be related to the forecast of sales growth.

When forecasting FCFE, analysts often make an assumption that the financing of the company involves a "target" debt ratio. In this case, they assume that a specified percentage of the sum of 1) net new investment in fixed capital (new fixed capital minus depreciation expense) and 2) increase in working capital is financed based on a target DR. This assumption leads to a simplification of FCFE calculations. If we assume that depreciation is the only noncash charge, Equation 10, which is FCFE = NI + NCC − FCInv − WCInv + Net borrowing, becomes

$$\text{FCFE} = \text{NI} - (\text{FCInv} - \text{Dep}) - \text{WCInv} + \text{Net borrowing} \tag{14}$$

Note that FCInv − Dep represents the incremental fixed capital expenditure net of depreciation. By assuming a target DR, we eliminated the need to forecast net borrowing and can use the expression

$$\text{Net borrowing} = \text{DR}(\text{FCInv} - \text{Dep}) + \text{DR}(\text{WCInv})$$

By using this expression, we do not need to forecast debt issuance and repayment on an annual basis to estimate net borrowing. Equation 14 then becomes

$$\text{FCFE} = \text{NI} - (\text{FCInv} - \text{Dep}) - \text{WCInv} + (\text{DR})(\text{FCInv} - \text{Dep}) + (\text{DR})(\text{WCInv})$$

or

$$\text{FCFE} = \text{NI} - (1 - \text{DR})(\text{FCInv} - \text{Dep}) - (1 - \text{DR})(\text{WCInv}) \tag{15}$$

Equation 15 says that FCFE equals NI minus the amount of fixed capital expenditure (net of depreciation) and working capital investment that is financed by equity. Again for Equation 15, we have assumed that the only noncash charge is depreciation.

---

9 See Rappaport (1997).

Examples 9 and 10 illustrate this sales-based method for forecasting free cash flow to the firm.

EXAMPLE 9

Free Cash Flow Tied to Sales

Carla Espinosa is an analyst following Pitts Corporation at the end of 2012. From the data in Example 6, she can see that the company's sales for 2012 were $3,000 million, and she assumes that sales grew by $300 million from 2011 to 2012. Espinosa expects Pitts Corporation's sales to increase by 10 percent a year thereafter. Pitts Corporation is a fairly stable company, so Espinosa expects it to maintain its historical EBIT margin and proportions of incremental investments in fixed and working capital. Pitts Corporation's EBIT for 2012 is $500 million; its EBIT margin is 16.67 percent (500/3,000), and its tax rate is 40 percent.

Note from Pitts Corporation's 2012 statement of cash flows (Exhibit 11) the amount for "purchases of fixed assets" (i.e., capital expenditures) of $400 million and depreciation of $300 million. Thus, incremental fixed capital investment in 2012 was

$$\frac{\text{Capital expenditures} - \text{Depreciation expense}}{\text{Increase in sales}}$$

$$= \frac{400 - 300}{300} = 33.33\%$$

Incremental working capital investment in the past year was

$$\frac{\text{Increase in working capital}}{\text{Increase in sales}} = \frac{45}{300} = 15\%$$

So, for every $100 increase in sales, Pitts Corporation invests $33.33 in new equipment in addition to replacement of depreciated equipment and $15 in working capital. Espinosa forecasts FCFF for 2013 as follows (dollars in millions):

Sales	$3,300	Up 10 percent
EBIT	550	16.67 percent of sales
EBIT(1 – Tax rate)	330	Adjusted for 40 percent tax rate
Incremental FC	(100)	33.33 percent of sales increase
Incremental WC	(45)	15 percent of sales increase
FCFF	$185	

This model can be used to forecast multiple periods and is flexible enough to allow varying sales growth rates, EBIT margins, tax rates, and rates of incremental capital increases.

EXAMPLE 10

Free Cash Flow Growth Tied to Sales Growth

Continuing her work, Espinosa decides to forecast FCFF for the next five years. She is concerned that Pitts Corporation will not be able to maintain its historical EBIT margin and that the EBIT margin will decline from the current 16.67 percent to 14.5 percent in the next five years. Exhibit 12 summarizes her forecasts.

Exhibit 12	Free Cash Flow Growth for Pitts Corporation (Dollars in Millions)				
	Year 1	**Year 2**	**Year 3**	**Year 4**	**Year 5**
Sales growth	10.00%	10.00%	10.00%	10.00%	10.00%
EBIT margin	16.67%	16.00%	15.50%	15.00%	14.50%
Tax rate	40.00%	40.00%	40.00%	40.00%	40.00%
Incremental FC investment	33.33%	33.33%	33.33%	33.33%	33.33%
Incremental WC investment	15.00%	15.00%	15.00%	15.00%	15.00%
Prior-year sales	$3,000.00				
Sales forecast	$3,300.00	$3,630.00	$3,993.00	$4,392.30	$4,831.53
EBIT forecast	550.00	580.80	618.92	658.85	700.57
EBIT(1 − Tax rate)	330.00	348.48	371.35	395.31	420.34
Incremental FC	(100.00)	(110.00)	(121.00)	(133.10)	(146.41)
Incremental WC	(45.00)	(49.50)	(54.45)	(59.90)	(65.88)
FCFF	$185.00	$188.98	$195.90	$202.31	$208.05

The model need not begin with sales; it could start with net income, cash flow from operations, or EBITDA.

A similar model can be designed for FCFE, as shown in Example 11. In the case of FCFE, the analyst should begin with net income and must also forecast any net new borrowing or net preferred stock issue.

EXAMPLE 11

Finding FCFE from Sales Forecasts

Espinosa decides to forecast FCFE for the year 2013. She uses the same expectations derived in Example 9. Additionally, she expects the following:

- the profit margin will remain at 8 percent (= 240/3,000), and
- the company will finance incremental fixed and working capital investments with 50 percent debt—the target DR. Espinosa's forecast for 2013 is as follows (dollars in millions):

Sales	$3,300	Up 10 percent
NI	264	8.0 percent of sales
Incremental FC	(100)	33.33 percent of sales increase
Incremental WC	(45)	15 percent of sales increase
Net borrowing	72.50	(100 FCInv + 45 WCInv) × 50%
FCFE	$191.50	

When the company being analyzed has significant noncash charges other than depreciation expense, the approach we have just illustrated will result in a less accurate estimate of FCFE than one obtained by forecasting all the individual components of FCFE. In some cases, the analyst will have specific forecasts of planned components, such as capital expenditures. In other cases, the analyst will study historical relationships, such as previous capital expenditures and sales levels, to develop a forecast.

3.8 Other Issues in Free Cash Flow Analysis

We have already presented a number of practical issues that arise in using free cash flow valuation models. Other issues relate to analyst adjustments to CFO, the relationship between free cash flow and dividends, and valuation with complicated financial structures.

3.8.1 Analyst Adjustments to CFO

Although many corporate financial statements are straightforward, some are not transparent (i.e., the quality of the reported numbers and of disclosures is not high). Sometimes, difficulties in analysis arise because the companies and their transactions are more complicated than the Pitts Corporation example we just provided.

For instance, in many corporate financial statements, the changes in balance sheet items (the increase in an asset or the decrease in a liability) differ from the changes reported in the statement of cash flows. Similarly, depreciation in the statement of cash flows may differ from depreciation expense in the income statement. How do such problems arise?

Factors that can cause discrepancies between changes in balance sheet accounts and the changes reported in the statement of cash flows include acquisitions or divestitures and the presence of nondomestic subsidiaries. For example, an increase in an inventory account may result from purchases from suppliers (which is an operating activity) or from an acquisition or merger with another company that has inventory on its balance sheet (which is an investing activity). Discrepancies may also occur from currency translations of the earnings of nondomestic subsidiaries.

Because the CFO figure from the statement of cash flows may be contaminated by cash flows arising from financing and/or investing activities, when analysts use CFO in a valuation context, ideally they should remove such contaminations. The resulting analyst-adjusted CFO is then the starting point for free cash flow calculations.

3.8.2 Free Cash Flow versus Dividends and Other Earnings Components

Many analysts have a strong preference for free cash flow valuation models over dividend discount models. Although one type of model may have no theoretical advantage over another type, legitimate reasons to prefer one model can arise in the process of applying free cash flow models versus DDMs. First, many corporations pay no, or very low, cash dividends. Using a DDM to value these companies is difficult because they require forecasts about when dividends will be initiated, the level of dividends at initiation, and the growth rate or rates from that point forward. Second, dividend payments are at the discretion of the corporation's board of directors. Therefore, they may imperfectly signal the company's long-run profitability. Some corporations clearly pay dividends that are substantially less than their free cash flow, and others pay dividends that are substantially more. Finally, as mentioned earlier, dividends are the cash flow actually going to shareholders whereas free cash flow to equity is the cash flow available to be distributed to shareholders without impairing the company's value. If a company is being analyzed because it is a target for takeover, free cash flow is the appropriate cash flow measure; once the company is taken over, the new owners will have discretion over how free cash flow is used (including its distribution in the form of dividends).

We have defined FCFF and FCFE and presented alternative (equivalent) ways to calculate both of them. So, the reader should have a good idea of what is included in FCFF or FCFE but may wonder why some cash flows are not included. Specifically, what role do dividends, share repurchases, share issuance, or changes in leverage have on FCFF and FCFE? The simple answer is: not much. Recall the formulas for FCFF and FCFE:

$$FCFF = NI + NCC + Int(1 - Tax\ rate) - FCInv - WCInv$$

and

$$FCFE = NI + NCC - FCInv - WCInv + Net\ borrowing$$

Notice that dividends and share repurchases and issuance are absent from the formulas. The reason is that FCFF and FCFE are the cash flows *available* to investors or to stockholders; dividends and share repurchases are *uses* of these cash flows. So, the simple answer is that transactions between the company and its shareholders (through cash dividends, share repurchases, and share issuances) do not affect free cash flow. Leverage changes, such as the use of more debt financing, have some impact because they increase the interest tax shield (reduce corporate taxes because of the tax deductibility of interest) and reduce the cash flow available to equity. In the long run, the investing and financing decisions made today will affect future cash flows.

If all the inputs were known and mutually consistent, a DDM and a FCFE model would result in identical valuations for a stock. One possibility would be that FCFE equals cash dividends each year. Then, both cash flow streams would be discounted at the required return for equity and would have the same present value.

Generally, however, FCFE and dividends will differ, but the same economic forces that lead to low (high) dividends lead to low (high) FCFE. For example, a rapidly growing company with superior investment opportunities will retain a high proportion of earnings and pay low dividends. This same company will have high investments in fixed capital and working capital and have a low FCFE (which is clear from the expression FCFE = NI + NCC – FCInv – WCInv + Net borrowing). Conversely, a mature company that is investing relatively little might have high dividends and high FCFE. In spite of this tendency, however, FCFE and dividends will usually differ.

FCFF and FCFE, as defined in this reading, are measures of cash flow designed for valuation of the firm or its equity. Other definitions of "free cash flow" frequently appear in textbooks, articles, and vendor-supplied databases of financial information on public companies. In many cases, these other definitions of free cash flow are not designed for valuation purposes and thus should not be used for valuation. Using numbers supplied by others without knowing exactly how they are defined increases the likelihood of making errors in valuation. As consumers and producers of research, analysts should understand (if consumers) or make clear (if producers) the definition of free cash flow being used.

Because using free cash flow analysis requires considerable care and understanding, some practitioners erroneously use earnings components such as NI, EBIT, EBITDA, or CFO in a discounted cash flow valuation. Such mistakes may lead the practitioner to systematically overstate or understate the value of a stock. Shortcuts can be costly.

A common shortcut is to use EBITDA as a proxy for the cash flow to the firm. Equation 13 clearly shows the differences between EBITDA and FCFF:

$$FCFF = EBITDA(1 - Tax\ rate) + Dep(Tax\ rate) - FCInv - WCInv$$

Depreciation charges as a percentage of EBITDA differ substantially for different companies and industries, as does the depreciation tax shield (the depreciation charge times the tax rate). Although FCFF captures this difference, EBITDA does not. EBITDA also does not account for the investments a company makes in fixed capital or working capital. Hence, EBITDA is a poor measure of the cash flow available to the company's investors. Using EBITDA (instead of free cash flow) in a DCF model has another important aspect as well: EBITDA is a before-tax measure, so the discount rate applied to EBITDA would be a before-tax rate. The WACC used to discount FCFF is an after-tax cost of capital.

EBITDA is a poor proxy for free cash flow to the firm because it does not account for the depreciation tax shield and the investment in fixed capital and working capital, but it is an even poorer proxy for free cash flow to equity. From a stockholder's perspective, additional defects of EBITDA include its failure to account for the after-tax interest costs or cash flows from new borrowing or debt repayments. Example 12 shows the mistakes sometimes made in discussions of cash flows.

EXAMPLE 12

The Mistakes of Using Net Income for FCFE and EBITDA for FCFF

A recent job applicant made some interesting comments about FCFE and FCFF: "I don't like the definitions for FCFE and FCFF because they are unnecessarily complicated and confusing. The best measure of FCFE, the funds available to pay dividends, is simply net income. You take the net income number straight from the income statement and don't need to make any further adjustments. Similarly, the best measure of FCFF, the funds available to the company's suppliers of capital, is EBITDA. You can take EBITDA straight from the income statement, and you don't need to consider using anything else."

How would you respond to the job applicant's definition of 1) FCFE and 2) FCFF?

Solution to 1:

The FCFE is the cash generated by the business's operations less the amount it must reinvest in additional assets plus the amounts it is borrowing. Equation 10, which starts with net income to find FCFE, shows these items:

Free cash flow to equity   =   Net income available to common shareholders

                                        Plus: Net noncash charges

                                        Less: Investment in fixed capital

                                        Less: Investment in working capital

                                        Plus: Net borrowing

Net income does not include several cash flows. So, net income tells only part of the overall story. Investments in fixed or working capital reduce the cash available to stockholders, as do loan repayments. New borrowing increases the cash available. FCFE, however, includes the cash generated from operating the business and also accounts for the investing and financing activities of the company. Of course, a special case exists in which net income and FCFE are the same. This case occurs when new investments exactly equal depreciation and the company is not investing in working capital or engaging in any net borrowing.

Solution to 2:

Assuming that EBITDA equals FCFF introduces several possible mistakes. Equation 13 highlights these mistakes:

Free cash flow to the firm   =   EBITDA (1 − Tax rate)

                                          Plus: Depreciation (Tax rate)

                                        Less: Investment in fixed capital

                                        Less: Investment in working capital

The applicant is ignoring taxes, which obviously reduce the cash available to the company's suppliers of capital.

3.8.3 *Free Cash Flow and Complicated Capital Structures*

For the most part, the discussion of FCFF and FCFE so far has assumed the company has a simple capital structure with two sources of capital, namely, debt and equity. Including preferred stock as a third source of capital requires the analyst to add terms to the equations for FCFF and FCFE to account for the dividends paid on preferred stock and for the issuance or repurchase of preferred shares. Instead of including those terms in all of the equations, we chose to leave preferred stock out because only a few corporations use preferred stock. For companies that do have preferred stock, however, the effects of the preferred stock can be incorporated in the valuation models.

For example, in Equation 7, which calculates FCFF starting with net income available to common shareholders, preferred dividends paid would be added to the cash flows to obtain FCFF. In Equation 10 which calculates FCFE starting with net income available to common shareholders, if preferred dividends were already subtracted when arriving at net income, no further adjustment for preferred dividends would be required. Issuing (redeeming) preferred stock increases (decreases) the cash flow available to common stockholders, however, so this term would have to be added in. The existence of preferred stock in the capital structure has many of the same effects as the existence of debt, except that unlike interest payments on debt, preferred stock dividends paid are not tax deductible.

Example 13 shows how to calculate WACC, FCFE, and FCFF when the company has preferred stock.

EXAMPLE 13

FCFF Valuation with Preferred Stock in the Capital Structure

Welch Corporation uses bond, preferred stock, and common stock financing. The market value of each of these sources of financing and the before-tax required rates of return for each are given in Exhibit 13:

Exhibit 13	Welch Corporation Capital Structure (Dollars in Millions)	
	Market Value ($)	**Required Return (%)**
Bonds	400	8.0
Preferred stock	100	8.0
Common stock	500	12.0
Total	1,000	

Other financial information (dollars in millions):

- Net income available to common shareholders = $110.
- Interest expenses = $32.
- Preferred dividends = $8.
- Depreciation = $40.
- Investment in fixed capital = $70.
- Investment in working capital = $20.
- Net borrowing = $25.
- Tax rate = 30 percent.

- Stable growth rate of FCFF = 4.0 percent.
- Stable growth rate of FCFE = 5.4 percent.

1   Calculate Welch Corporation's WACC.
2   Calculate the current value of FCFF.
3   Based on forecasted Year 1 FCFF, what is the total value of Welch Corporation and the value of its equity?
4   Calculate the current value of FCFE.
5   Based on forecasted Year 1 FCFE, what is the value of equity?

Solution to 1:

Based on the weights and after-tax costs of each source of capital, the WACC is

$$\text{WACC} = \frac{400}{1,000} 8\%(1 - 0.30) + \frac{100}{1,000} 8\% + \frac{500}{1,000} 12\% = 9.04\%$$

Solution to 2:

If the company did not issue preferred stock, FCFF would be

$$\text{FCFF} = \text{NI} + \text{NCC} + \text{Int}(1 - \text{Tax rate}) - \text{FCInv} - \text{WCInv}$$

If preferred stock dividends have been paid (and net income is income available to common shareholders), the preferred dividends must be added back just as after-tax interest expenses are. The modified equation (including preferred dividends) for FCFF is

$$\text{FCFF} = \text{NI} + \text{NCC} + \text{Int}(1 - \text{Tax rate}) + \text{Preferred dividends}$$
$$- \text{FCInv} - \text{WCInv}$$

For Welch Corporation, FCFF is

$$\text{FCFF} = 110 + 40 + 32(1 - 0.30) + 8 - 70 - 20 = \$90.4 \text{ million}$$

Solution to 3:

The total value of the firm is

$$\text{Firm value} = \frac{\text{FCFF}_1}{\text{WACC} - g} = \frac{90.4(1.04)}{0.0904 - 0.04}$$
$$= \frac{94.016}{0.0504} = \$1,865.40 \text{ million}$$

The value of (common) equity is the total value of the company minus the value of debt and preferred stock:

$$\text{Equity} = 1,865.40 - 400 - 100 = \$1,365.40 \text{ million}$$

Solution to 4:

With no preferred stock, FCFE is

$$\text{FCFE} = \text{NI} + \text{NCC} - \text{FCInv} - \text{WCInv} + \text{Net borrowing}$$

If the company has preferred stock, the FCFE equation is essentially the same. Net borrowing in this case is the total of new debt borrowing and net issuances of new preferred stock. For Welch Corporation, FCFE is

$$\text{FCFE} = 110 + 40 - 70 - 20 + 25 = \$85 \text{ million}$$

Solution to 5:

Valuing FCFE, which is growing at 5.4 percent, produces a value of equity of

$$\text{Equity} = \frac{\text{FCFE}_1}{r - g} = \frac{85(1.054)}{0.12 - 0.054} = \frac{89.59}{0.066} = \$1,357.42 \text{ million}$$

Paying cash dividends on common stock does not affect FCFF or FCFE, which are the amounts of cash *available* to all investors or to common stockholders. It is simply a use of the available cash. Share repurchases of common stock also do not affect FCFF or FCFE. Share repurchases are, in many respects, a substitute for cash dividends. Similarly, issuing shares of common stock does not affect FCFF or FCFE.

Changing leverage, however (changing the amount of debt financing in the company's capital structure), does have some effects on FCFE particularly. An increase in leverage will not affect FCFF (although it might affect the calculations used to arrive at FCFF). An increase in leverage affects FCFE in two ways. In the year the debt is issued, it increases the FCFE by the amount of debt issued. After the debt is issued, FCFE is then reduced by the after-tax interest expense.

In Section 3, we have discussed the concepts of FCFF and FCFE and their estimation. The next section presents additional valuation models that use forecasts of FCFF or FCFE to value the firm or its equity. These free cash flow models are similar in structure to dividend discount models, although the analyst must face the reality that estimating free cash flows is more time-consuming than estimating dividends.

FREE CASH FLOW MODEL VARIATIONS

4

Section 4 presents several extensions of the free cash flow models presented earlier. In many cases, especially when inflation rates are volatile, analysts will value real cash flows instead of nominal values. As with dividend discount models, free cash flow models are sensitive to the data inputs, so analysts routinely perform sensitivity analyses of their valuations.

In Section 2.3, we presented the single-stage free cash flow model, which has a constant growth rate. In the following, we use the single-stage model to address selected valuation issues; we then present multistage free cash flow models.

4.1 An International Application of the Single-Stage Model

Valuation by using real (inflation-adjusted) values instead of nominal values has much appeal when inflation rates are high and volatile. Many analysts use this adaptation for both domestic and nondomestic stocks, but the use of real values is especially helpful for valuing international stocks. Special challenges to valuing equities from multiple countries include 1) incorporating economic factors—such as interest rates, inflation rates, and growth rates—that differ among countries and 2) dealing with varied accounting standards. Furthermore, performing analyses in multiple countries challenges the analyst—particularly a team of analysts—to use *consistent* assumptions for all countries.

Several securities firms have adapted the single-stage FCFE model to address some of the challenges of international valuation. They choose to analyze companies by using real cash flows and real discount rates instead of nominal values. To estimate real discount rates, they use a modification of the build-up method mentioned in the reading on return concepts. Starting with a "country return," which is a real required rate of return for stocks from a particular country, they then make adjustments to the country return for the stock's industry, size, and leverage:

Country return (real)	x.xx%
+ / – Industry adjustment	x.xx%
+ / – Size adjustment	x.xx%
+ / – Leverage adjustment	x.xx%
Required rate of return (real)	x.xx%

The adjustments in the model should have sound economic justification. They should reflect factors expected to affect the relative risk and return associated with an investment.

The securities firms making these adjustments predict the growth rate of FCFE also in real terms. The firms supply their analysts with estimates of the real economic growth rate for each country, and each analyst chooses a real growth rate for the stock being analyzed that is benchmarked against the real country growth rate. This approach is particularly useful for countries with high or variable inflation rates.

The value of the stock is found with an equation essentially like Equation 6 except that all variables in the equation are stated in real terms:

$$V_0 = \frac{FCFE_0(1 + g_{real})}{r_{real} - g_{real}}$$

Whenever real discount rates and real growth rates can be estimated more reliably than nominal discount rates and nominal growth rates, this method is worth using. Example 14 shows how this procedure can be applied.

EXAMPLE 14

Using Real Cash Flows and Discount Rates for International Stocks

YPF Sociedad Anonima (NYSE: YPF) is an integrated oil and gas company headquartered in Buenos Aires, Argentina. Although the company's cash flows have been volatile, an analyst has estimated a per share normalized FCFE of 7.05 Argentine pesos (ARS) for the year just ended. The real country return for Argentina is 7.30 percent; adjustments to the country return for YPF S.A. are an industry adjustment of + 0.80 percent, a size adjustment of –0.33 percent, and a leverage adjustment of –0.12 percent. The long-term real growth rate for Argentina is estimated to be 3.0 percent, and the real growth rate of YPF S.A. is expected to be about 0.5 percent below the country rate. The real required rate of return for YPF S.A. is

Country return (real)	7.30%
Industry adjustment	+ 0.80%
Size adjustment	– 0.33%
Leverage adjustment	– 0.12%
Required rate of return	7.65%

The real growth rate of FCFE is expected to be 2.5 percent (3.0 percent – 0.5 percent), so the value of one share is

$$V_0 = \frac{\text{FCFE}_0(1 + g_{\text{real}})}{r_{\text{real}} - g_{\text{real}}} = \frac{7.05(1.025)}{0.0765 - 0.025} = \frac{7.22625}{0.0515} = \text{ARS}140.32$$

4.2 Sensitivity Analysis of FCFF and FCFE Valuations

In large measure, growth in FCFF and in FCFE depends on a company's future profitability. Sales growth and changes in net profit margins dictate future net profits. Sales growth and profit margins depend on the growth phase of the company and the profitability of the industry. A highly profitable company in a growing industry can enjoy years of profit growth. Eventually, however, its profit margins are likely to be eroded by increased competition; sales growth is also likely to abate because of fewer opportunities for expansion of market size and market share. Growth rates and the duration of growth are difficult to forecast.

The base-year values for the FCFF or FCFE growth models are also critical. Given the same required rates of return and growth rates, the value of the firm or the value of equity will increase or decrease proportionately with the initial value of FCFF or FCFE used.

To examine how sensitive the final valuation is to changes in each of a valuation model's input variables, analysts can perform a sensitivity analysis. Some input variables have a much larger impact on stock valuation than others. Example 15 shows the sensitivity of the valuation of Petroleo Brasileiro to four input variables.

EXAMPLE 15

Sensitivity Analysis of a FCFE Valuation

Steve Bono is valuing the equity of Petroleo Brasileiro (NYSE: PBR), commonly known as Petrobras, in early 2013 (before the release of 2012 financial results) by using the single-stage (constant-growth) FCFE model. Estimated FCFE for 2012 is 1.05 Brazilian reais (BRL). Bono's best estimates of input values for the analysis are as follows:

- The FCFE growth rate is 6.0 percent.
- The risk-free rate is 5.2 percent.
- The equity risk premium is 5.5 percent.
- Beta is 1.2.

Using the capital asset pricing model (CAPM), Bono estimates that the required rate of return for Petrobras is

$$r = E(R_i) = R_F + \beta_i[E(R_M) - R_F] = 5.2\% + 1.2(5.5\%) = 11.8\%$$

The estimated value per share is

$$V_0 = \frac{\text{FCFE}_0(1 + g)}{r - g} = \frac{1.05(1.06)}{0.118 - 0.06} = \text{BRL}19.19$$

Exhibit 14 shows Bono's base case and the highest and lowest reasonable alternative estimates. The column "Valuation with Low Estimate" gives the estimated value of Petrobras based on the low estimate for the variable on the same row of the first column and the base-case estimates for the remaining three variables. "Valuation with High Estimate" performs a similar exercise based on the high estimate for the variable at issue.

	Base-Case Estimate	Low Estimate	High Estimate	Valuation with Low Estimate	Valuation with High Estimate
Variable					
Beta	1.2	1.0	1.4	BRL23.68	BRL16.13
Risk-free rate	5.20%	4.20%	6.20%	BRL23.19	BRL16.37
Equity risk premium	5.50%	4.50%	6.50%	BRL24.20	BRL15.90
FCFE growth rate	6.0%	4.00%	8.00%	BRL14.00	BRL29.84

Exhibit 14   Sensitivity Analysis for Petrobras Valuation

As Exhibit 14 shows, the value of Petrobras is very sensitive to the inputs. Of the four variables presented, the stock valuation is least sensitive to the range of estimates for the risk-free rate and beta. The range of estimates for these variables produces the smallest ranges of stock values (from BRL16.37 to BRL23.19 for the risk-free rate and from BRL16.13 to BRL23.68 for beta). The stock value is most sensitive to the extreme values for the FCFE growth rate and, to a lesser degree, the equity risk premium. Of course, the variables to which a stock price is most sensitive vary from case to case. A sensitivity analysis gives the analyst a guide as to which variables are most critical to the final valuation.

4.3 Two-Stage Free Cash Flow Models

Several two-stage and multistage models exist for valuing free cash flow streams, just as several such models are available for valuing dividend streams. The free cash flow models are much more complex than the dividend discount models because to find FCFF or FCFE, the analyst usually incorporates sales, profitability, investments, financing costs, and new financing.

In two-stage free cash flow models, the growth rate in the second stage is a long-run sustainable growth rate. For a declining industry, the second-stage growth rate could be slightly below the GDP growth rate. For an industry that is expected to grow in the future faster than the overall economy, the second-stage growth rate could be slightly greater than the GDP growth rate.

The two most popular versions of the two-stage FCFF and FCFE models are distinguished by the pattern of the growth rates in Stage 1. In one version, the growth rate is constant in Stage 1 before dropping to the long-run sustainable rate in Stage 2. In the other version, the growth rate declines in Stage 1 to reach the sustainable rate at the beginning of Stage 2. This second type of model is like the H-model for discounted dividend valuation, in which dividend growth rates decline in Stage 1 and are constant in Stage 2.

Unlike multistage DDMs, in which the growth rates are consistently dividend growth rates, in free cash flow models, the "growth rate" may refer to different variables (which variables should be stated or should be clear from the context). The growth rate could be the growth rate for FCFF or FCFE, the growth rate for income (either net income or operating income), or the growth rate for sales. If the growth rate is for net income, the changes in FCFF or FCFE also depend on investments in operating assets and the financing of these investments. When the growth rate in income declines, such as between Stage 1 and Stage 2, investments in operating assets probably decline at the same time. If the growth rate is for sales, changes in net profit margins as well as investments in operating assets and financing policies will determine FCFF and FCFE.

A general expression for the two-stage FCFF valuation model is

$$\text{Firm value} = \sum_{t=1}^{n} \frac{\text{FCFF}_t}{(1 + \text{WACC})^t} + \frac{\text{FCFF}_{n+1}}{(\text{WACC} - g)} \frac{1}{(1 + \text{WACC})^n} \qquad \textbf{(16)}$$

The summation gives the present value of the first n years of FCFF. The terminal value of the FCFF from Year $n + 1$ forward is $\text{FCFF}_{n+1}/(\text{WACC} - g)$, which is discounted at the WACC for n periods to obtain its present value. Subtracting the value of outstanding debt gives the value of equity. The value per share is then found by dividing the total value of equity by the number of outstanding shares.

The general expression for the two-stage FCFE valuation model is

$$\text{Equity value} = \sum_{t=1}^{n} \frac{\text{FCFE}_t}{(1 + r)^t} + \frac{\text{FCFE}_{n+1}}{r - g} \frac{1}{(1 + r)^n} \qquad \textbf{(17)}$$

In this case, the summation is the present value of the first n years of FCFE and the terminal value of $\text{FCFE}_{n+1}/(r - g)$ is discounted at the required rate of return on equity for n years. The value per share is found by dividing the total value of equity by the number of outstanding shares.

In Equation 17, the terminal value of the stock at $t = n$, TV_n, is found by using the constant-growth FCFE model. In this case, $\text{TV}_n = \text{FCFE}_{n+1}/(r - g)$. (Of course, the analyst might choose to estimate terminal value another way, such as using a P/E multiplied by the company's forecasted EPS.) The terminal value estimation is critical for a simple reason: The present value of the terminal value is often a substantial portion of the total value of the stock. For example, in Equation 17, when the analyst is calculating the total present value of the first n cash flows (FCFE) and the present value of the terminal value, the present value of the terminal value is often substantial. In the examples that follow, the terminal value usually represents a substantial part of total estimated value. The same is true in practice.

4.3.1 *Fixed Growth Rates in Stage 1 and Stage 2*

The simplest two-stage FCFF or FCFE growth model has a constant growth rate in each stage. Example 16 finds the value of a firm that has a 20 percent sales growth rate in Stage 1 and a 6 percent sales growth rate in Stage 2.

EXAMPLE 16

A Two-Stage FCFE Valuation Model with a Constant Growth Rate in Each Stage

Uwe Henschel is doing a valuation of TechnoSchaft on the basis of the following information:

- Year 0 sales per share = €25.
- Sales growth rate = 20 percent annually for three years and 6 percent annually thereafter.
- Net profit margin = 10 percent forever.
- Net investment in fixed capital (net of depreciation) = 50 percent of the sales increase.
- Annual increase in working capital = 20 percent of the sales increase.

- Debt financing = 40 percent of the net investments in capital equipment and working capital.
- TechnoSchaft beta = 1.20; the risk-free rate of return = 7 percent; the equity risk premium = 4.5 percent.

The required rate of return for equity is

$$r = E(R_i) = R_F + \beta_i\left[E(R_M) - R_F\right] = 7\% + 1.2(4.5\%) = 12.4\%$$

Exhibit 15 shows the calculations for FCFE.

Exhibit 15   FCFE Estimates for TechnoSchaft (in Euros)

	Year					
	1	2	3	4	5	6
Sales growth rate	20%	20%	20%	6%	6%	6%
Sales per share	30.000	36.000	43.200	45.792	48.540	51.452
Net profit margin	10%	10%	10%	10%	10%	10%
EPS	3.000	3.600	4.320	4.579	4.854	5.145
Net FCInv per share	2.500	3.000	3.600	1.296	1.374	1.456
WCInv per share	1.000	1.200	1.440	0.518	0.550	0.582
Debt financing per share	1.400	1.680	2.016	0.726	0.769	0.815
FCFE per share	0.900	1.080	1.296	3.491	3.700	3.922
Growth rate of FCFE		20%	20%	169%	6%	6%

In Exhibit 15, sales are shown to grow at 20 percent annually for the first three years and then at 6 percent thereafter. Profits, which are 10 percent of sales, grow at the same rates. The net investments in fixed capital and working capital are, respectively, 50 percent of the increase in sales and 20 percent of the increase in sales. New debt financing equals 40 percent of the total increase in net fixed capital and working capital. FCFE is EPS minus the net investment in fixed capital per share minus the investment in working capital per share plus the debt financing per share.

Notice that FCFE grows by 20 percent annually for the first three years (i.e., between $t = 0$ and $t = 3$). Then, between Year 3 and Year 4, when the sales growth rate drops from 20 percent to 6 percent, FCFE increases substantially. In fact, FCFE increases by 169 percent from Year 3 to Year 4. This large increase in FCFE occurs because profits grow at 6 percent but the investments in capital equipment and working capital (and the increase in debt financing) drop substantially from the previous year. In Years 5 and 6 in Exhibit 15, sales, profit, investments, financing, and FCFE are all shown to grow at 6 percent.

The stock value is the present value of the first three years' FCFE plus the present value of the terminal value of the FCFE from Years 4 and later. The terminal value is

$$TV_3 = \frac{FCFE_4}{r - g} = \frac{3.491}{0.124 - 0.06} = €54.55$$

The present values are

$$V_0 = \frac{0.900}{1.124} + \frac{1.080}{(1.124)^2} + \frac{1.296}{(1.124)^3} + \frac{54.55}{(1.124)^3}$$

$$= 0.801 + 0.855 + 0.913 + 38.415 = \text{€}40.98$$

The estimated value of this stock is €40.98 per share.

As mentioned previously, the terminal value may account for a large portion of the value of a stock. In the case of TechnoSchaft, the present value of the terminal value is €38.415 out of a total value of €40.98. The present value (PV) of the terminal value is almost 94 percent of the total value of TechnoSchaft stock.

4.3.2 Declining Growth Rate in Stage 1 and Constant Growth in Stage 2

Growth rates usually do not drop precipitously as they do between the stages in the two-stage model just described, but growth rates can decline over time for many reasons. Sometimes, a small company has a high growth rate that is not sustainable as its market share increases. A highly profitable company may attract competition that makes it harder for the company to sustain its high profit margins.

In this section, we present two examples of the two-stage model with declining growth rates in Stage 1. In the first example, the growth rate of EPS declines during Stage 1. As a company's profitability declines and the company is no longer generating high returns, the company will usually reduce its net new investment in operating assets. The debt financing accompanying the new investments will also decline. Many highly profitable, growing companies have negative or low free cash flows. Later, when growth in profits slows, investments will tend to slow and the company will experience positive cash flows. Of course, the negative cash flows incurred in the high-growth stage help determine the cash flows that occur in future years.

Example 17 models FCFE per share as a function of EPS that declines constantly during Stage 1. Because of declining earnings growth rates, the company in the example also reduces its new investments over time. The value of the company depends on these free cash flows, which are substantial after the high-growth (and high-profitability) period has largely elapsed.

EXAMPLE 17

A Two-Stage FCFE Valuation Model with Declining Net Income Growth in Stage 1

Vishal Noronha needs to prepare a valuation of Sindhuh Enterprises. Noronha has assembled the following information for his analysis. It is now the first day of 2013.

- EPS for 2012 is $2.40.
- For the next five years, the growth rate in EPS is given in the following table. After 2017, the growth rate will be 7 percent.

	2013	2014	2015	2016	2017
Growth rate for EPS	30%	18%	12%	9%	7%

- Net investments in fixed capital (net of depreciation) for the next five years are given in the following table. After 2017, capital expenditures are expected to grow at 7 percent annually.

	2013	2014	2015	2016	2017
Net capital expenditure per share	$3.00	$2.50	$2.00	$1.50	$1.00

- The investment in working capital each year will equal 50 percent of the net investment in capital items.
- Thirty percent of the net investment in fixed capital and investment in working capital will be financed with new debt financing.
- Current market conditions dictate a risk-free rate of 6.0 percent, an equity risk premium of 4.0 percent, and a beta of 1.10 for Sindhuh Enterprises.

1 What is the per-share value of Sindhuh Enterprises on the first day of 2013?

2 What should be the trailing P/E on the first day of 2013 and the first day of 2017?

Solution to 1:

The required return for Sindhuh should be

$$r = E(R_i) = R_F + \beta_i \left[E(R_M) - R_F \right] = 6\% + 1.1(4\%) = 10.4\%$$

The FCFEs for the company for years 2013 through 2017 are given in Exhibit 16.

Exhibit 16   FCFE Estimates for Sindhuh Enterprises (Per-Share Data in US Dollars)

			Year		
	2013	2014	2015	2016	2017
Growth rate for EPS	30%	18%	12%	9%	7%
EPS	3.120	3.682	4.123	4.494	4.809
Net FCInv per share	3.000	2.500	2.000	1.500	1.000
WCInv per share	1.500	1.250	1.000	0.750	0.500
Debt financing per share[a]	1.350	1.125	0.900	0.675	0.450
FCFE per share[b]	−0.030	1.057	2.023	2.919	3.759
PV of FCFE discounted at 10.4%	−0.027	0.867	1.504	1.965	

[a] 30 percent of (Net FCInv + WCInv).
[b] EPS − Net FCInv per share − WCInv per share + Debt financing per share.

Earnings are $2.40 in 2012. Earnings increase each year by the growth rate given in the table. Net capital expenditures (capital expenditures minus depreciation) are the amounts that Noronha assumed. The increase in working capital each year is 50 percent of the increase in net capital expenditures. Debt financing is 30 percent of the total outlays for net capital expenditures and working capital each year. The FCFE each year is net income minus net capital expenditures minus increase in working capital plus new debt financing. Finally, for years 2013 through 2016, the present value of FCFE is found by discounting FCFE by the 10.4 percent required rate of return for equity.

After 2017, FCFE will grow by a constant 7 percent annually, so the constant growth FCFE valuation model can be used to value this cash flow stream. At the end of 2016, the value of the future FCFE is

$$V_{2016} = \frac{FCFE_{2017}}{r - g} = \frac{3.759}{0.104 - 0.07} = \$110.56 \text{ per share}$$

To find the present value of V_{2016} as of the end of 2012, V_{2012}, we discount V_{2016} at 10.4 percent for four years:

$$PV = 110.56/(1.104)^4 = \$74.425 \text{ per share}$$

The total present value of the company is the present value of the first four years' FCFE plus the present value of the terminal value, or

$$V_{2012} = -0.027 + 0.867 + 1.504 + 1.965 + 74.42 = \$78.73 \text{ per share}$$

Solution to 2:

Using the estimated \$78.73 stock value, we find that the trailing P/E at the beginning of 2013 is

$$P/E = 78.73/2.40 = 32.8$$

At the beginning of 2017, the expected stock value is \$110.56 and the previous year's EPS is \$4.494, so the trailing P/E at this time would be

$$P/E = 110.56/4.494 = 24.6$$

After its high-growth phase has ended, the P/E for the company declines substantially.

The FCFE in Example 17 was based on forecasts of future EPS. Analysts often model a company by forecasting future sales and then estimating the profits, investments, and financing associated with those sales levels. For large companies, analysts may estimate the sales, profitability, investments, and financing for each division or large subsidiary. Then, they aggregate the free cash flows for all of the divisions or subsidiaries to get the free cash flow for the company as a whole.

Example 18 is a two-stage FCFE model with declining sales growth rates in Stage 1, with profits, investments, and financing keyed to sales. In Stage 1, the growth rate of sales and the profit margin on sales both decline as the company matures and faces more competition and slower growth.

EXAMPLE 18

A Two-Stage FCFE Valuation Model with Declining Sales Growth Rates

Medina Werks, a manufacturing company headquartered in Canada, has a competitive advantage that will probably deteriorate over time. Analyst Flavio Torino expects this deterioration to be reflected in declining sales growth rates as well as declining profit margins. To value the company, Torino has accumulated the following information:

■ Current sales are C\$600 million. Over the next six years, the annual sales growth rate and the net profit margin are projected to be as follows:

	Year 1 (%)	Year 2 (%)	Year 3 (%)	Year 4 (%)	Year 5 (%)	Year 6 (%)
Sales growth rate	20	16	12	10	8	7
Net profit margin	14	13	12	11	10.5	10

Beginning in Year 6, the 7 percent sales growth rate and 10 percent net profit margin should persist indefinitely.

▪ Capital expenditures (net of depreciation) in the amount of 60 percent of the sales increase will be required each year.

▪ Investments in working capital equal to 25 percent of the sales increase will also be required each year.

▪ Debt financing will be used to fund 40 percent of the investments in net capital items and working capital.

▪ The beta for Medina Werks is 1.10; the risk-free rate of return is 6.0 percent; the equity risk premium is 4.5 percent.

▪ The company has 70 million outstanding shares.

1 What is the estimated total market value of equity?

2 What is the estimated value per share?

Solution to 1:

The required return for Medina is

$$r = E(R_i) = R_F + \beta_i \left[E(R_M) - R_F \right] = 6\% + 1.10(4.5\%) = 10.95\%$$

The annual sales and net profit can be readily found as shown in Exhibit 17.

Exhibit 17   FCFE Estimates for Medina Werks (C$ in Millions)

	Year					
	1	**2**	**3**	**4**	**5**	**6**
Sales growth rate	20%	16%	12%	10%	8%	7%
Net profit margin	14%	13%	12%	11%	10.50%	10%
Sales	720.000	835.200	935.424	1028.966	1111.284	1189.074
Net profit	100.800	108.576	112.251	113.186	116.685	118.907
Net FCInv	72.000	69.120	60.134	56.125	49.390	46.674
WCInv	30.000	28.800	25.056	23.386	20.579	19.447
Debt financing	40.800	39.168	34.076	31.804	27.988	26.449
FCFE	39.600	49.824	61.137	65.480	74.703	79.235
PV of FCFE at 10.95%	35.692	40.475	44.763	43.211	44.433	

As can be seen, sales are expected to increase each year by a declining sales growth rate. Net profit each year is the year's net profit margin times the year's sales. Capital investment (net of depreciation) equals 60 percent of the sales increase from the previous year. The investment in working capital is 25 percent of the sales increase from the previous year. The debt financing each year is equal to 40 percent of the total net investment in capital items and working capital for that year. FCFE is net income minus the net capital investment minus the working capital investment plus the debt financing. The present value of each year's FCFE is found by discounting FCFE at the required rate of return for equity, 10.95 percent.

In Year 6 and beyond, Torino predicts sales to increase at 7 percent annually. Net income will be 10 percent of sales, so net profit will also grow at a 7 percent annual rate. Because they are pegged to the 7 percent sales increase, the investments in capital items and working capital and debt financing will also grow at the same 7 percent rate. The amounts in Year 6 for net income, investment in capital items, investment in working capital, debt financing, and FCFE will grow at 7 percent.

The terminal value of FCFE in Year 6 and beyond is

$$TV_5 = \frac{FCFE_6}{r - g} = \frac{79.235}{0.1095 - 0.07} = C\$2{,}005.95 \text{ million}$$

The present value of this amount is

$$PV \text{ of } TV_5 = \frac{2{,}005.95}{(1.1095)^5} = C\$1{,}193.12 \text{ million}$$

The estimated total market value of the firm is the present value of FCFE for Years 1 through 5 plus the present value of the terminal value:

$$MV = 35.692 + 40.475 + 44.763 + 43.211 + 44.433 + 1{,}193.12$$
$$= C\$1{,}401.69 \text{ million}$$

Solution to 2:

Dividing C\$1,401.69 million by the 70 million outstanding shares gives the estimated value per share of C\$20.02.

4.4 Three-Stage Growth Models

Three-stage models are a straightforward extension of the two-stage models. One common version of a three-stage model is to assume a constant growth rate in each of the three stages. The growth rates could be for sales, profits, and investments in fixed and working capital; external financing could be a function of the level of sales or changes in sales. A simpler model would apply the growth rate to FCFF or FCFE.

A second common model is a three-stage model with constant growth rates in Stages 1 and 3 and a declining growth rate in Stage 2. Again, the growth rates could be applied to sales or to FCFF or FCFE. Although future FCFF and FCFE are unlikely to follow the assumptions of either of these three-stage growth models, analysts often find such models to be useful approximations.

Example 19 is a three-stage FCFF valuation model with declining growth rates in Stage 2. The model directly forecasts FCFF instead of deriving FCFF from a more complicated model that estimates cash flow from operations and investments in fixed and working capital.

EXAMPLE 19

A Three-Stage FCFF Valuation Model with Declining Growth in Stage 2

Charles Jones is evaluating Reliant Home Furnishings by using a three-stage growth model. He has accumulated the following information:

- Current FCFF = $745 million.
- Outstanding shares = 309.39 million.
- Equity beta = 0.90, risk-free rate = 5.04 percent; equity risk premium = 5.5 percent.
- Cost of debt = 7.1 percent.
- Marginal tax rate = 34 percent.
- Capital structure = 20 percent debt, 80 percent equity.
- Long-term debt = $1.518 billion.
- Growth rate of FCFF =
  - 8.8 percent annually in Stage 1, Years 1–4.
  - 7.4 percent in Year 5, 6.0 percent in Year 6, 4.6 percent in Year 7.
  - 3.2 percent in Year 8 and thereafter.

From the information that Jones has accumulated, estimate the following:

1 WACC.
2 Total value of the firm.
3 Total value of equity.
4 Value per share.

Solution to 1:

The required return for equity is

$$r = E(R_i) = R_F + \beta_i \left[E(R_M) - R_F \right] = 5.04\% + 0.9(5.5\%) = 9.99\%$$

WACC is

$$\text{WACC} = 0.20(7.1\%)(1 - 0.34) + 0.80(9.99\%) = 8.93\%$$

Solution to 2:

Exhibit 18 displays the projected FCFF for the next eight years and the present value of each FCFF discounted at 8.93 percent:

Exhibit 18   Forecasted FCFF for Reliant Home Furnishings

	Year							
	1	2	3	4	5	6	7	8
Growth rate	8.80%	8.80%	8.80%	8.80%	7.40%	6.00%	4.60%	3.20%
FCFF	811	882	959	1,044	1,121	1,188	1,243	1,283
PV at 8.93%	744	743	742	741	731	711	683	

The terminal value at the end of Year 7 is

$$TV_7 = \frac{FCFF_8}{WACC - g} = \frac{1,283}{0.0893 - 0.032} = \$22,391 \text{ million}$$

The present value of this amount discounted at 8.93 percent for seven years is

$$PV \text{ of } TV_7 = \frac{22,391}{(1.0893)^7} = \$12,304 \text{ million}$$

The total present value of the first seven years of FCFF is \$5,097 million. The total value of the firm is 12,304 + 5,097 = \$17,401 million.

Solution to 3:

The value of equity is the value of the firm minus the market value of debt:

17,401 − 1,518 = \$15,833 million

Solution to 4:

Dividing the equity value by the number of shares yields the value per share:

\$15,833 million/309.39 million = \$51.34

The next section discusses an important technical issue, the treatment of nonoperating assets in valuation.

NONOPERATING ASSETS AND FIRM VALUE

5

Free cash flow valuation focuses on the value of assets that generate or are needed to generate operating cash flows. If a company has significant nonoperating assets, such as excess cash,[10] excess marketable securities, or land held for investment, then analysts often calculate the value of the firm as the value of its operating assets (e.g., as estimated by FCFF valuation) plus the value of its nonoperating assets:

Value of firm = Value of operating assets

+Value of nonoperating assets

(18)

In general, if any company asset is excluded from the set of assets being considered in projecting a company's future cash flows, the analyst should add that omitted asset's estimated value to the cash-flows-based value estimate. Some companies have substantial noncurrent investments in stocks and bonds that are not operating subsidiaries but, rather, financial investments. These investments should be reflected at their current market value. Those securities reported at book values on the basis of accounting conventions should be revalued to market values.

---

10 In this case, "excess" is in relation to what is needed for generating operating cash flows. Estimating what constitutes excess cash may be difficult; for example, an analyst could consider as excess cash any amount in excess of the amount predicted by multiplying total assets by the industry median level of the ratio of cash to total assets.

SUMMARY

Discounted cash flow models are widely used by analysts to value companies.

- Free cash flow to the firm (FCFF) and free cash flow to equity (FCFE) are the cash flows available to, respectively, all of the investors in the company and to common stockholders.

- Analysts like to use free cash flow (either FCFF or FCFE) as the return:
  - if the company is not paying dividends;
  - if the company pays dividends but the dividends paid differ significantly from the company's capacity to pay dividends;
  - if free cash flows align with profitability within a reasonable forecast period with which the analyst is comfortable; or
  - if the investor takes a control perspective.

- The FCFF valuation approach estimates the value of the firm as the present value of future FCFF discounted at the weighted average cost of capital:

$$\text{Firm value} = \sum_{t=1}^{\infty} \frac{\text{FCFF}_t}{(1 + \text{WACC})^t}$$

The value of equity is the value of the firm minus the value of the firm's debt:

$$\text{Equity Value} = \text{Firm value} - \text{Market value of debt}$$

Dividing the total value of equity by the number of outstanding shares gives the value per share.

The WACC formula is

$$\text{WACC} = \frac{\text{MV}(\text{Debt})}{\text{MV}(\text{Debt}) + \text{MV}(\text{Equity})} r_d (1 - \text{Tax rate})$$
$$+ \frac{\text{MV}(\text{Equity})}{\text{MV}(\text{Debt}) + \text{MV}(\text{Equity})} r$$

- The value of the firm if FCFF is growing at a constant rate is

$$\text{Firm value} = \frac{\text{FCFF}_1}{\text{WACC} - g} = \frac{\text{FCFF}_0(1 + g)}{\text{WACC} - g}$$

- With the FCFE valuation approach, the value of equity can be found by discounting FCFE at the required rate of return on equity, r:

$$\text{Equity value} = \sum_{t=1}^{\infty} \frac{\text{FCFE}_t}{(1 + r)^t}$$

Dividing the total value of equity by the number of outstanding shares gives the value per share.

- The value of equity if FCFE is growing at a constant rate is

$$\text{Equity value} = \frac{\text{FCFE}_1}{r - g} = \frac{\text{FCFE}_0(1 + g)}{r - g}$$

- FCFF and FCFE are frequently calculated by starting with net income:

$$\text{FCFF} = \text{NI} + \text{NCC} + \text{Int}(1 - \text{Tax rate}) - \text{FCInv} - \text{WCInv}$$

$$FCFE = NI + NCC - FCInv - WCInv + Net\ borrowing$$

- FCFF and FCFE are related to each other as follows:

$$FCFE = FCFF - Int(1 - Tax\ rate) + Net\ borrowing$$

- FCFF and FCFE can be calculated by starting from cash flow from operations:

$$FCFF = CFO + Int(1 - Tax\ rate) - FCInv$$

$$FCFE = CFO - FCInv + Net\ borrowing$$

- FCFF can also be calculated from EBIT or EBITDA:

$$FCFF = EBIT(1 - Tax\ rate) + Dep - FCInv - WCInv$$

$$FCFF = EBITDA(1 - Tax\ rate) + Dep(Tax\ rate) - FCInv - WCInv$$

FCFE can then be found by using $FCFE = FCFF - Int(1 - Tax\ rate) + Net$ borrowing.

- Finding CFO, FCFF, and FCFE may require careful interpretation of corporate financial statements. In some cases, the needed information may not be transparent.

- Earnings components such as net income, EBIT, EBITDA, and CFO should not be used as cash flow measures to value a firm. These earnings components either double-count or ignore parts of the cash flow stream.

- FCFF or FCFE valuation expressions can be easily adapted to accommodate complicated capital structures, such as those that include preferred stock.

- A general expression for the two-stage FCFF valuation model is

$$\text{Firm value} = \sum_{t=1}^{n} \frac{FCFF_t}{(1 + WACC)^t} + \frac{FCFF_{n+1}}{(WACC - g)} \frac{1}{(1 + WACC)^n}$$

- A general expression for the two-stage FCFE valuation model is

$$\text{Equity value} = \sum_{t=1}^{n} \frac{FCFE_t}{(1 + r)^t} + \frac{FCFE_{n+1}}{r - g} \frac{1}{(1 + r)^n}$$

- One common two-stage model assumes a constant growth rate in each stage, and a second common model assumes declining growth in Stage 1 followed by a long-run sustainable growth rate in Stage 2.

- To forecast FCFF and FCFE, analysts build a variety of models of varying complexity. A common approach is to forecast sales, with profitability, investments, and financing derived from changes in sales.

- Three-stage models are often considered to be good approximations for cash flow streams that, in reality, fluctuate from year to year.

- Nonoperating assets, such as excess cash and marketable securities, noncurrent investment securities, and nonperforming assets, are usually segregated from the company's operating assets. They are valued separately and then added to the value of the company's operating assets to find total firm value.

REFERENCES

Rappaport, Alfred. 1997. *Creating Shareholder Value: A Guide for Managers and Investors.* Revised and Updated. New York: The Free Press.

Robinson, Thomas, Elaine Henry, Wendy Pirie, and Michael Broihahn. 2011. "Understanding the Cash Flow Statement." *International Financial Statement Analysis*, 2nd edition. Hoboken, NJ: John Wiley & Sons.

Ross, Stephen, Randolph Westerfield, and Jeffrey Jaffe. 2005. *Corporate Finance*, 7th edition. McGraw-Hill/Irwin.

PRACTICE PROBLEMS

1 Indicate the effect on this period's FCFF and FCFE of a change in each of the items listed here. Assume a $100 increase in each case and a 40 percent tax rate.

   A   Net income.

   B   Cash operating expenses.

   C   Depreciation.

   D   Interest expense.

   E   EBIT.

   F   Accounts receivable.

   G   Accounts payable.

   H   Property, plant, and equipment.

   I   Notes payable.

   J   Cash dividends paid.

   K   Proceeds from issuing new common shares.

   L   Common shares repurchased.

2 LaForge Systems, Inc. has net income of $285 million for the year 2008. Using information from the company's financial statements given here, show the adjustments to net income that would be required to find:

   A   FCFF.

   B   FCFE.

   C   In addition, show the adjustments to FCFF that would result in FCFE.

LaForge Systems, Inc. Balance Sheet (in Millions)		
Years Ended 31 December	**2007**	**2008**
Assets		
Current assets		
Cash and equivalents	$210	$248
Accounts receivable	474	513
Inventory	520	564
Total current assets	1,204	1,325
Gross fixed assets	2,501	2,850
Accumulated depreciation	(604)	(784)
Net fixed assets	1,897	2,066
Total assets	$3,101	$3,391
Liabilities and shareholders' equity		
Current liabilities		
Accounts payable	$295	$317
Notes payable	300	310

(continued)

Practice Problems and Solutions: *Equity Asset Valuation*, Second Edition, by Jerald E. Pinto, CFA, Elaine Henry, CFA, Thomas R. Robinson, CFA, and John D. Stowe, CFA. Copyright © 2009 by CFA Institute.

(Continued)

Years Ended 31 December	2007	2008
Accrued taxes and expenses	76	99
Total current liabilities	671	726
Long-term debt	1,010	1,050
Common stock	50	50
Additional paid-in capital	300	300
Retained earnings	1,070	1,265
Total shareholders' equity	1,420	1,615
Total liabilities and shareholders' equity	$3,101	$3,391

Statement of Income In Millions, except Per-Share Data	31 December 2008
Total revenues	$2,215
Operating costs and expenses	1,430
EBITDA	785
Depreciation	180
EBIT	605
Interest expense	130
Income before tax	475
Taxes (at 40 percent)	190
Net income	285
Dividends	90
Addition to retained earnings	195

Statement of Cash Flows In Millions	31 December 2008
Operating activities	
Net income	$285
Adjustments	
Depreciation	180
Changes in working capital	
Accounts receivable	(39)
Inventories	(44)
Accounts payable	22
Accrued taxes and expenses	23
Cash provided by operating activities	$427
Investing activities	
Purchases of fixed assets	349
Cash used for investing activities	$349
Financing activities	
Notes payable	$(10)

(Continued)	
Statement of Cash Flows In Millions	**31 December 2008**
Long-term financing issuances	(40)
Common stock dividends	90
Cash used for financing activities	$40
Cash and equivalents increase (decrease)	38
Cash and equivalents at beginning of year	210
Cash and equivalents at end of year	$248
Supplemental cash flow disclosures	
Interest paid	$130
Income taxes paid	$190

Note: The statement of cash flows shows the use of a convention by which the positive numbers of $349 and $40 for cash used for investing activities and cash used for financing activities, respectively, are understood to be subtractions, because "cash used" is an outflow.

3   For LaForge Systems, whose financial statements are given in Problem 2, show the adjustments from the current levels of CFO (which is $427 million), EBIT ($605 million), and EBITDA ($785 million) to find:

A   FCFF.

B   FCFE.

4   The term "free cash flow" is frequently applied to cash flows that differ from the definition for FCFF that should be used to value a firm. Two such definitions of free cash flow are given below. Compare these two definitions for free cash flow with the technically correct definition of FCFF used in the reading.

A   FCF = Net income + Depreciation and amortization – Cash dividends – Capital expenditures.

B   FCF = Cash flow from operations (from the statement of cash flows) – Capital expenditures.

5   Proust Company has FCFF of $1.7 billion and FCFE of $1.3 billion. Proust's WACC is 11 percent, and its required rate of return for equity is 13 percent. FCFF is expected to grow forever at 7 percent, and FCFE is expected to grow forever at 7.5 percent. Proust has debt outstanding of $15 billion.

A   What is the total value of Proust's equity using the FCFF valuation approach?

B   What is the total value of Proust's equity using the FCFE valuation approach?

6   Quinton Johnston is evaluating TMI Manufacturing Company, Ltd., which is headquartered in Taiwan. In 2008, when Johnston is performing his analysis, the company is unprofitable. Furthermore, TMI pays no dividends on its common shares. Johnston decides to value TMI Manufacturing by using his forecasts of FCFE. Johnston gathers the following facts and assumptions:

● The company has 17.0 billion shares outstanding.

- Sales will be $5.5 billion in 2009, increasing at 28 percent annually for the next four years (through 2013).
- Net income will be 32 percent of sales.
- Investment in fixed assets will be 35 percent of sales; investment in working capital will be 6 percent of sales; depreciation will be 9 percent of sales.
- 20 percent of the net investment in assets will be financed with debt.
- Interest expenses will be only 2 percent of sales.
- The tax rate will be 10 percent. TMI Manufacturing's beta is 2.1; the risk-free government bond rate is 6.4 percent; the equity risk premium is 5.0 percent.
- At the end of 2013, Johnston projects TMI terminal stock value at 18 times earnings.

What is the value of one ordinary share of TMI Manufacturing Company?

7   Do Pham is evaluating Phaneuf Accelerateur by using the FCFF and FCFE valuation approaches. Pham has collected the following information (currency in euros):

- Phaneuf has net income of €250 million, depreciation of €90 million, capital expenditures of €170 million, and an increase in working capital of €40 million.
- Phaneuf will finance 40 percent of the increase in net fixed assets (capital expenditures less depreciation) and 40 percent of the increase in working capital with debt financing.
- Interest expenses are €150 million. The current market value of Phaneuf's outstanding debt is €1,800 million.
- FCFF is expected to grow at 6.0 percent indefinitely, and FCFE is expected to grow at 7.0 percent.
- The tax rate is 30 percent.
- Phaneuf is financed with 40 percent debt and 60 percent equity. The before-tax cost of debt is 9 percent, and the before-tax cost of equity is 13 percent.
- Phaneuf has 10 million outstanding shares.

A   Using the FCFF valuation approach, estimate the total value of the firm, the total market value of equity, and the per-share value of equity.

B   Using the FCFE valuation approach, estimate the total market value of equity and the per-share value of equity.

8   PHB Company currently sells for $32.50 per share. In an attempt to determine whether PHB is fairly priced, an analyst has assembled the following information:

- The before-tax required rates of return on PHB debt, preferred stock, and common stock are, respectively, 7.0 percent, 6.8 percent, and 11.0 percent.
- The company's target capital structure is 30 percent debt, 15 percent preferred stock, and 55 percent common stock.
- The market value of the company's debt is $145 million, and its preferred stock is valued at $65 million.
- PHB's FCFF for the year just ended is $28 million. FCFF is expected to grow at a constant rate of 4 percent for the foreseeable future.
- The tax rate is 35 percent.
- PHB has 8 million outstanding common shares.

What is PHB's estimated value per share? Is PHB's stock underpriced?

9 Watson Dunn is planning to value BCC Corporation, a provider of a variety of industrial metals and minerals. Dunn uses a single-stage FCFF approach. The financial information Dunn has assembled for his valuation is as follows:

- The company has 1,852 million shares outstanding.
- The market value of its debt is $3.192 billion.
- The FCFF is currently $1.1559 billion.
- The equity beta is 0.90; the equity risk premium is 5.5 percent; the risk-free rate is 5.5 percent.
- The before-tax cost of debt is 7.0 percent.
- The tax rate is 40 percent.
- To calculate WACC, he will assume the company is financed 25 percent with debt.
- The FCFF growth rate is 4 percent.

Using Dunn's information, calculate the following:

A WACC.

B Value of the firm.

C Total market value of equity.

D Value per share.

10 Kenneth McCoin is valuing McInish Corporation and performing a sensitivity analysis on his valuation. He uses a single-stage FCFE growth model. The base-case values for each of the parameters in the model are given, together with possible low and high estimates for each variable, in the following table.

Variable	Base-Case Value	Low Estimate	High Estimate
Normalized $FCFE_0$	$0.88	$0.70	$1.14
Risk-free rate	5.08%	5.00%	5.20%
Equity risk premium	5.50%	4.50%	6.50%
Beta	0.70	0.60	0.80
FCFE growth rate	6.40%	4.00%	7.00%

A Use the base-case values to estimate the current value of McInish Corporation.

B Calculate the range of stock prices that would occur if the base-case value for $FCFE_0$ were replaced by the low estimate and the high estimate for $FCFE_0$. Similarly, using the base-case values for all other variables, calculate the range of stock prices caused by using the low and high values for beta, the risk-free rate, the equity risk premium, and the growth rate. Based on these ranges, rank the sensitivity of the stock price to each of the five variables.

11 An aggressive financial planner who claims to have a superior method for picking undervalued stocks is courting one of your clients. The planner claims that the best way to find the value of a stock is to divide EBITDA by the risk-free bond rate. The planner is urging your client to invest in NewMarket, Inc. The planner says that NewMarket's EBITDA of $1,580 million divided by the long-term government bond rate of 7 percent gives a total value of $22,571.4 million. With 318 million outstanding shares, NewMarket's value per share found by using this method is $70.98. Shares of NewMarket currently trade for $36.50.

A Provide your client with an alternative estimate of NewMarket's value per share based on a two-stage FCFE valuation approach. Use the following assumptions:

- Net income is currently $600 million. Net income will grow by 20 percent annually for the next three years.

- The net investment in operating assets (capital expenditures less depreciation plus investment in working capital) will be $1,150 million next year and grow at 15 percent for the following two years.

- Forty percent of the net investment in operating assets will be financed with net new debt financing.

- NewMarket's beta is 1.3; the risk-free bond rate is 7 percent; the equity risk premium is 4 percent.

- After three years, the growth rate of net income will be 8 percent and the net investment in operating assets (capital expenditures minus depreciation plus increase in working capital) each year will drop to 30 percent of net income.

- Debt is, and will continue to be, 40 percent of total assets.

- NewMarket has 318 million shares outstanding.

B Criticize the valuation approach that the aggressive financial planner used.

12 Bron has EPS of $3.00 in 2002 and expects EPS to increase by 21 percent in 2003. EPS are expected to grow at a decreasing rate for the following five years, as shown in the following table.

	2003	2004	2005	2006	2007	2008
Growth rate for EPS	21%	18%	15%	12%	9%	6%
Net capital expenditures per share	$5.00	$5.00	$4.50	$4.00	$3.50	$1.50

In 2008, the growth rate will be 6 percent and is expected to stay at that rate thereafter. Net capital expenditures (capital expenditures minus depreciation) will be $5.00 per share in 2002 and then follow the pattern predicted in the table. In 2008, net capital expenditures are expected to be $1.50 and will then grow at 6 percent annually. The investment in working capital parallels the increase in net capital expenditures and is predicted to equal 25 percent of net capital expenditures each year. In 2008, investment in working capital will be $0.375 and is predicted to grow at 6 percent thereafter. Bron will use debt financing to fund 40 percent of net capital expenditures and 40 percent of the investment in working capital. The required rate of return for Bron is 12 percent.

Estimate the value of a Bron share using a two-stage FCFE valuation approach.

13 The management of Telluride, an international diversified conglomerate based in the United States, believes that the recent strong performance of its wholly owned medical supply subsidiary, Sundanci, has gone unnoticed. To realize Sundanci's full value, Telluride has announced that it will divest Sundanci in a tax-free spin-off.

Sue Carroll, CFA, is director of research at Kesson and Associates. In developing an investment recommendation for Sundanci, Carroll has gathered the information shown in Exhibits 1 and 2.

Exhibit 1	Sundanci Actual 2007 and 2008 Financial Statements for Fiscal Years Ending 31 May (Dollars in Millions except Per-Share Data)

Income Statement	2007	2008
Revenue	$474	$598
Depreciation	20	23
Other operating costs	368	460
Income before taxes	86	115
Taxes	26	35
Net income	60	80
Dividends	18	24
EPS	$0.714	$0.952
Dividends per share	$0.214	$0.286
Common shares outstanding	84.0	84.0

Balance Sheet	2007	2008
Current assets (includes $5 cash in 2007 and 2008)	$201	$326
Net property, plant, and equipment	474	489
Total assets	675	815
Current liabilities (all non-interest-bearing)	57	141
Long-term debt	0	0
Total liabilities	57	141
Shareholders' equity	618	674
Total liabilities and equity	675	815
Capital expenditures	34	38

Exhibit 2	Selected Financial Information

Required rate of return on equity	14%
Industry growth rate	13%
Industry P/E	26

Abbey Naylor, CFA, has been directed by Carroll to determine the value of Sundanci's stock by using the FCFE model. Naylor believes that Sundanci's FCFE will grow at 27 percent for two years and at 13 percent thereafter. Capital expenditures, depreciation, and working capital are all expected to increase proportionately with FCFE.

A Calculate the amount of FCFE per share for 2008 by using the data from Exhibit 1.

B Calculate the current value of a share of Sundanci stock based on the two-stage FCFE model.

C Describe limitations that the two-stage DDM and FCFE models have in common.

14 John Jones, CFA, is head of the research department of Peninsular Research. One of the companies he is researching, Mackinac Inc., is a US-based manufacturing company. Mackinac has released the June 2007 financial statements shown in Exhibits 1, 2, and 3.

Exhibit 1 Mackinac Inc. Annual Income Statement 30 June 2007 (in Thousands, except Per-Share Data)

Sales	$250,000
Cost of goods sold	125,000
Gross operating profit	125,000
Selling, general, and administrative expenses	50,000
EBITDA	75,000
Depreciation and amortization	10,500
EBIT	64,500
Interest expense	11,000
Pretax income	53,500
Income taxes	16,050
Net income	$37,450
Shares outstanding	13,000
EPS	$2.88

Exhibit 2 Mackinac Inc. Balance Sheet 30 June 2007 (in Thousands)

Current Assets		
Cash and equivalents	$20,000	
Receivables	40,000	
Inventories	29,000	
Other current assets	23,000	
Total current assets		$112,000
Noncurrent Assets		
Property, plant, and equipment	$145,000	
Less: Accumulated depreciation	43,000	
Net property, plant, and equipment		102,000

Exhibit 2 (Continued)

Investments	70,000	
Other noncurrent assets	36,000	
Total noncurrent assets		208,000
Total assets		$320,000
Current Liabilities		
Accounts payable	$41,000	
Short-term debt	12,000	
Other current liabilities	17,000	
Total current liabilities		$ 70,000
Noncurrent Liabilities		
Long-term debt	100,000	
Total noncurrent liabilities		100,000
Total liabilities		170,000
Shareholders' Equity		
Common equity	40,000	
Retained earnings	110,000	
Total equity		150,000
Total liabilities and equity		$320,000

Exhibit 3 Mackinac Inc. Statement of Cash Flows
30 June 2007 (in Thousands)

Cash Flow from Operating Activities		
Net income		$37,450
Depreciation and amortization		10,500
Change in Working Capital		
(Increase) decrease in receivables	($5,000)	
(Increase) decrease in inventories	(8,000)	
Increase (decrease) in payables	6,000	
Increase (decrease) in other current liabilities	1,500	
Net change in working capital		(5,500)
Net cash from operating activities		$42,450
Cash Flow from Investing Activities		
Purchase of property, plant, and equipment	($15,000)	
Net cash from investing activities		($15,000)
Cash Flow from Financing Activities		
Change in debt outstanding	$4,000	
Payment of cash dividends	(22,470)	
Net cash from financing activities		(18,470)
Net change in cash and cash equivalents		$8,980

(continued)

Exhibit 3   (Continued)

Cash at beginning of period	11,020
Cash at end of period	$20,000

Mackinac has announced that it has finalized an agreement to handle North American production of a successful product currently marketed by a company headquartered outside North America. Jones decides to value Mackinac by using the DDM and FCFE models. After reviewing Mackinac's financial statements and forecasts related to the new production agreement, Jones concludes the following:

- Mackinac's earnings and FCFE are expected to grow 17 percent a year over the next three years before stabilizing at an annual growth rate of 9 percent.
- Mackinac will maintain the current payout ratio.
- Mackinac's beta is 1.25.
- The government bond yield is 6 percent, and the market equity risk premium is 5 percent.

A   Calculate the value of a share of Mackinac's common stock by using the two-stage DDM.

B   Calculate the value of a share of Mackinac's common stock by using the two-stage FCFE model.

C   Jones is discussing with a corporate client the possibility of that client acquiring a 70 percent interest in Mackinac. Discuss whether the DDM or FCFE model is more appropriate for this client's valuation purposes.

15 SK Telecom Company is a cellular telephone paging and computer communication services company in Seoul, South Korea. The company is traded on the Korea, New York, and London stock exchanges (NYSE: SKM). Sol Kim has estimated the normalized FCFE for SK Telecom to be 1,300 Korean won (per share) for the year just ended. The real country return for South Korea is 6.50 percent. To estimate the required return for SK Telecom, Kim makes the following adjustments to the real country return: an industry adjustment of +0.60 percent, a size adjustment of −0.10 percent, and a leverage adjustment of +0.25 percent. The long-term real growth rate for South Korea is estimated to be 3.5 percent, and Kim expects the real growth rate of SK Telecom to track the country rate.

A   What is the real required rate of return for SK Telecom?

B   Using the single-stage FCFE valuation model and real values for the discount rate and FCFE growth rate, estimate the value of one share of SK Telecom.

16 Lawrence McKibben is preparing a valuation of QuickChange Auto Centers, Inc. McKibben has decided to use a three-stage FCFE valuation model and the following estimates. The FCFE per share for the current year is $0.75. The FCFE is expected to grow at 10 percent for next year, then at 26 percent annually for the following three years, and then at 6 percent in Year 5 and thereafter. QuickChange's estimated beta is 2.00, and McKibben believes that current

market conditions dictate a 4.5 percent risk-free rate of return and a 5.0 percent equity risk premium. Given McKibben's assumptions and approach, estimate the value of a share of QuickChange.

17 Clay Cooperman has valued the operating assets of Johnson Extrusion at $720 million. The company also has short-term cash and securities with a market value of $60 million that are not needed for Johnson's operations. The noncurrent investments have a book value of $30 million and a market value of $45 million. The company also has an overfunded pension plan, with plan assets of $210 million and plan liabilities of $170 million. Johnson Extrusion has $215 million of notes and bonds outstanding and 100 million outstanding shares. What is the value per share of Johnson Extrusion stock?

The following information relates to Questions 18–23

Ryan Leigh is preparing a presentation that analyzes the valuation of the common stock of two companies under consideration as additions to his firm's recommended list, Emerald Corporation and Holt Corporation. Leigh has prepared preliminary valuations of both companies using a FCFE model and is also preparing a value estimate for Emerald using a dividend discount model. Holt's 2007 and 2008 financial statements, contained in Exhibits 1 and 2, are prepared in accordance with US GAAP.

Exhibit 1	Holt Corporation Consolidated Balance Sheets (US$ Millions)			
		As of 31 December		
		2008		2007
Assets				
Current assets				
Cash and cash equivalents		$ 372		$315
Accounts receivable		770		711
Inventories		846		780
Total current assets		1,988		1,806
Gross fixed assets	4,275		3,752	
Less: Accumulated depreciation	1,176	3,099	906	2,846
Total assets		$5,087		$4,652
Liabilities and shareholders' equity				
Current liabilities				
Accounts payable		$ 476		$443
Accrued taxes and expenses		149		114
Notes payable		465		450
Total current liabilities		1,090		1,007
Long-term debt		1,575		1,515
Common stock		525		525

(continued)

Exhibit 1   (Continued)

Retained earnings	1,897	1,605
Total liabilities and shareholders' equity	**$5,087**	**$4,652**

Exhibit 2   Holt Corporation Consolidated Income Statement for the Year Ended 31 December 2008 (US$ Millions)

Total revenues	$3,323
Cost of goods sold	1,287
Selling, general, and administrative expenses	858
Earnings before interest, taxes, depreciation, and amortization (EBITDA)	1,178
Depreciation expense	270
Operating income	908
Interest expense	195
Pretax income	713
Income tax (at 32 percent)	228
Net income	$ 485

Leigh presents his valuations of the common stock of Emerald and Holt to his supervisor, Alice Smith. Smith has the following questions and comments:

1   "I estimate that Emerald's long-term expected dividend payout rate is 20 percent and its return on equity is 10 percent over the long term."

2   "Why did you use a FCFE model to value Holt's common stock? Can you use a DDM instead?"

3   "How did Holt's FCFE for 2008 compare with its FCFF for the same year? I recommend you use a FCFF model to value Holt's common stock instead of using a FCFE model because Holt has had a history of leverage changes in the past."

4   "In the last three years, about 5 percent of Holt's growth in FCFE has come from decreases in inventory."

Leigh responds to each of Smith's points as follows:

1   "I will use your estimates and calculate Emerald's long-term, sustainable dividend growth rate."

2   "There are two reasons why I used the FCFE model to value Holt's common stock instead of using a DDM. The first reason is that Holt's dividends have differed significantly from its capacity to pay dividends. The second reason is that Holt is a takeover target and once the company is taken over, the new owners will have discretion over the uses of free cash flow."

3 "I will calculate Holt's FCFF for 2008 and estimate the value of Holt's common stock using a FCFF model."

4 "Holt is a growing company. In forecasting either Holt's FCFE or FCFF growth rates, I will not consider decreases in inventory to be a long-term source of growth."

18 Which of the following long-term FCFE growth rates is *most* consistent with the facts and stated policies of Emerald?

A 5 percent or lower.

B 2 percent or higher.

C 8 percent or higher.

19 Do the reasons provided by Leigh support his use of the FCFE model to value Holt's common stock instead of using a DDM?

A Yes.

B No, because Holt's dividend situation argues in favor of using the DDM.

C No, because FCFE is not appropriate for investors taking a control perspective.

20 Holt's FCFF (in millions) for 2008 is *closest* to:

A $308.

B $370.

C $422.

21 Holt's FCFE (in millions) for 2008 is *closest* to:

A $175.

B $250.

C $364.

22 Leigh's comment about not considering decreases in inventory to be a source of long-term growth in free cash flow for Holt is:

A inconsistent with a forecasting perspective.

B mistaken because decreases in inventory are a use rather than a source of cash.

C consistent with a forecasting perspective because inventory reduction has a limit, particularly for a growing firm.

23 Smith's recommendation to use a FCFF model to value Holt is:

A logical, given the prospect of Holt changing capital structure.

B not logical because a FCFF model is used only to value the total firm.

C not logical because FCFE represents a more direct approach to free cash flow valuation.

SOLUTIONS

1

For a $100 increase in:	Change in FCFF (in US Dollars)	Change in FCFE (in US Dollars)
A. Net income	+100	+100
B. Cash operating expenses	−60	−60
C. Depreciation	+40	+40
D. Interest expense	0	−60
E. EBIT	+60	+60
F. Accounts receivable	−100	−100
G. Accounts payable	+100	+100
H. Property, plant, and equipment	−100	−100
I. Notes payable	0	+100
J. Cash dividends paid	0	0
K. Proceeds from new shares issued	0	0
L. Share repurchases	0	0

2 A   Free cash flow to the firm, found with Equation 7, is

$$FCFF = NI + NCC + Int(1 - \text{Tax rate}) - FCInv - WCInv$$
$$FCFF = 285 + 180 + 130(1 - 0.40) - 349 - (39 + 44 - 22 - 23)$$
$$FCFF = 285 + 180 + 78 - 349 - 38 = \$156 \text{ million}$$

B   Free cash flow to equity, found with Equation 10, is

$$FCFE = NI + NCC - FCInv - WFCInv + \text{Net borrowing}$$
$$FCFE = 285 + 180 - 349 - (39 + 44 - 22 - 23) + (10 + 40)$$
$$FCFE = 285 + 180 - 349 - 38 + 50 = \$128 \text{ million}$$

C   To find FCFE from FCFF, one uses the relationship in Equation 9:

$$FCFE = FCFF - Int(1 - \text{Tax rate}) + \text{Net borrowing}$$
$$FCFE = 156 - 130(1 - 0.40) + (10 + 40)$$
$$FCFE = 156 - 78 + 50 = \$128 \text{ million}$$

3 A   To find FCFF from CFO, EBIT, or EBITDA, the analyst can use Equations 8, 12, and 13.

To find FCFF from CFO:

$$FCFF = CFO + Int(1 - \text{Tax rate}) - FCInv$$
$$FCFF = 427 + 130(1 - 0.40) - 349 = 427 + 78 - 349 = \$156 \text{ million}$$

To find FCFF from EBIT:

$$FCFF = EBIT(1 - \text{Tax rate}) + Dep - FCInv - WCInv$$
$$FCFF = 605(1 - 0.40) + 180 - 349 - 38$$
$$FCFF = 363 + 180 - 349 - 38 = \$156 \text{ million}$$

Finally, to obtain FCFF from EBITDA:

$$FCFF = EBITDA(1 - Tax\ rate) + Dep(Tax\ rate) - FCInv - WCInv$$
$$FCFF = 785(1 - 0.40) + 180(0.40) - 349 - 38$$
$$FCFF = 471 + 72 - 349 - 38 = \$156\ million$$

B The simplest approach is to calculate FCFF from CFO, EBIT, or EBITDA as was done in Part A and then to find FCFE by making the appropriate adjustments to FCFF:

$$FCFE = FCFF - Int(1 - Tax\ rate) + Net\ borrowing.$$
$$FCFE = 156 - 130(1 - 0.40) + 50 = 156 - 78 + 50 = \$128\ million$$

The analyst can also find FCFE by using CFO, EBIT, or EBITDA directly. Starting with CFO and using Equation 11, FCFE is found to be

$$FCFE = CFO - FCInv + Net\ borrowing$$
$$FCFE = 427 - 349 + 50 = \$128\ million$$

Starting with EBIT, on the basis of Equations 9 and 12, FCFE is

$$FCFE = EBIT(1 - Tax\ rate) + Dep - Int(1 - Tax\ rate) - FCInv$$
$$- WCInv + Net\ borrowing$$
$$FCFE = 605(1 - 0.40) + 180 - 130(1 - 0.40) - 349 - 38 + 50$$
$$FCFE = 363 + 180 - 78 - 349 - 38 + 50 = \$128\ million$$

Finally, starting with EBITDA, on the basis of Equations 9 and 13, FCFE is

$$FCFE = EBITDA(1 - Tax\ rate) + Dep(Tax\ rate)$$
$$- Int(1 - Tax\ rate) - FCInv - WCInv + Net\ borrowing$$
$$FCFE = 785(1 - 0.40) + 180(0.40) - 130(1 - 0.40) - 349 - 38 + 50$$
$$FCFE = 471 + 72 - 78 - 349 - 38 + 50 = \$128\ million$$

4 A FCF = Net income + Depreciation and amortization − Cash dividends − Capital expenditures. This definition of free cash flow is sometimes used to determine how much "discretionary" cash flow management has at its disposal. Management discretion concerning dividends is limited by investor expectations that dividends will be maintained. Comparing this definition with Equation 7, FCFF = NI + NCC + Int(1 − Tax rate) − FCInv − WCInv, we find that FCFF includes a reduction for investments in working capital and the addition of after-tax interest expense. Common stock dividends are not subtracted from FCFF because dividends represent a distribution of the cash available to investors. (If a company pays preferred dividends and they were previously taken out when net income available to common shareholders was calculated, they are added back in Equation 7 to include them in FCFF.)

B FCF = Cash flow from operations (from the statement of cash flows) − Capital expenditures. Comparing this definition of free cash flow with Equation 8, FCFF = CFO + Int(1 − Tax rate) − FCInv, highlights the relationship of CFO to FCFF: The primary point is that when Equation 8 is used, after-tax interest is added back to CFO to arrive at the cash flow to all investors. Then FCInv is subtracted to arrive at the amount of that cash flow that is "free" in the sense of available for distribution to those investors after taking care of capital investment needs. If preferred dividends were subtracted to obtain net income (in CFO), they would also have to be added back in. This definition is commonly used to approximate FCFF, but it generally understates the actual FCFF by the amount of after-tax interest expense.

5 A The firm value is the present value of FCFF discounted at the WACC, or

$$\text{Firm value} = \frac{\text{FCFF}_1}{\text{WACC} - g} = \frac{\text{FCFF}_0(1 + g)}{\text{WACC} - g} = \frac{1.7(1.07)}{0.11 - 0.07}$$

$$= \frac{1.819}{0.04} = \$45.475 \text{ billion}$$

The market value of equity is the value of the firm minus the value of debt:

Equity = 45.475 − 15 = $30.475 billion

B Using the FCFE valuation approach, we find the present value of FCFE discounted at the required rate of return on equity to be

$$\text{PV} = \frac{\text{FCFE}_1}{r - g} = \frac{\text{FCFE}_0(1 + g)}{r - g} = \frac{1.3(1.075)}{0.13 - 0.075} = \frac{1.3975}{0.055}$$

$$= \$25.409 \text{ billion}$$

The value of equity using this approach is $25.409 billion.

6 The required rate of return found with the CAPM is

$$r = E(R_i) = R_F + \beta_i \big[E(R_M) - R_F \big] = 6.4\% + 2.1(5.0\%) = 16.9\%$$

The following table shows the values of sales, net income, capital expenditures less depreciation, and investments in working capital. FCFE equals net income less the investments financed with equity:

$$\text{FCFE} = \text{Net income} - (1 - \text{DR})(\text{Capital expenditures} - \text{Depreciation})$$

$$- (1 - \text{DR})(\text{Investment in working capital})$$

where DR is the debt ratio (debt financing as a percentage of debt and equity). Because 20 percent of net new investments are financed with debt, 80 percent of the investments are financed with equity, which reduces FCFE by 80 percent of (Capital expenditures − Depreciation) and 80 percent of the investment in working capital.

(All Data in Billions of Taiwan Dollars)	2009	2010	2011	2012	2013
Sales (growing at 28%)	5.500	7.040	9.011	11.534	14.764
Net income = 32% of sales	1.760	2.253	2.884	3.691	4.724
FCInv − Dep = (35% − 9%) × Sales	1.430	1.830	2.343	2.999	3.839
WCInv = (6% of Sales)	0.330	0.422	0.541	0.692	0.886
0.80 × (FCInv − Dep + WCInv)	1.408	1.802	2.307	2.953	3.780
FCFE = NI − 0.80 × (FCInv − Dep + WCInv)	0.352	0.451	0.577	0.738	0.945
PV of FCFE discounted at 16.9%	0.301	0.330	0.361	0.395	0.433
Terminal stock value		85.032			
PV of terminal value discounted at 16.9%		38.950			
Total PV of FCFE		1.820			
Total value of equity		40.770			

The terminal stock value is 18.0 times the earnings in 2013, or $18 \times 4.724 =$ \$85.03 billion. The present value of the terminal value (\$38.95 billion) plus the present value of the first five years' FCFE (\$1.82 billion) is \$40.77 billion. Because TMI Manufacturing has 17 billion outstanding shares, the value per ordinary share is \$2.398.

7 **A** The FCFF is (in euros)

$$FCFF = NI + NCC + Int(1 - \text{Tax rate}) - FCInv - WCInv$$
$$FCFF = 250 + 90 + 150(1 - 0.30) - 170 - 40$$
$$FCFF = 250 + 90 + 105 - 170 - 40 = 235 \text{ million}$$

The weighted-average cost of capital is

$$WACC = 9\%(1 - 0.30)(0.40) + 13\%(0.60) = 10.32\%$$

The value of the firm (in euro) is

$$\text{Firm value} = \frac{FCFF_1}{WACC - g} = \frac{FCFF_0(1 + g)}{WACC - g} = \frac{235(1.06)}{0.1032 - 0.06}$$
$$= \frac{249.1}{0.0432} = 5{,}766.20 \text{ million}$$

The total value of equity is the total firm value minus the value of debt, Equity = €5,766.20 million − €1,800 million = €3,966.20 million. Dividing by the number of shares gives the per share estimate of V_0 = €3,966.20 million/10 million = €396.62 per share.

B The free cash flow to equity is

$$FCFE = NI + NCC - FCInv - WCInv + \text{Net borrowing}$$
$$FCFE = 250 + 90 - 170 - 40 + 0.40(170 - 90 + 40)$$
$$FCFE = 250 + 90 - 170 - 40 + 48 = €178 \text{ million}$$

Because the company is borrowing 40 percent of the increase in net capital expenditures (170 − 90) and working capital (40), net borrowing is €48 million.

The total value of equity is the FCFE discounted at the required rate of return of equity,

$$\text{Equity value} = \frac{FCFE_1}{r - g} = \frac{FCFE_0(1 + g)}{r - g} = \frac{178(1.07)}{0.13 - 0.07}$$
$$= \frac{190.46}{0.06} = €3{,}174.33 \text{ million}$$

The value per share is V_0 = €3,174.33 million/10 million = €317.43 per share.

8 The WACC for PHB Company is

$$WACC = 0.30(7.0\%)(1 - 0.35) + 0.15(6.8\%) + 0.55(11.0\%) = 8.435\%$$

The firm value is

Firm value = $FCFF_0(1 + g)/(WACC - g)$
Firm value = $28(1.04)/(0.08435 - 0.04) = 29.12/0.04435$
$$= \$656.60 \text{ million}$$

The value of equity is the firm value minus the value of debt minus the value of preferred stock: Equity = 656.60 − 145 − 65 = $446.60 million. Dividing this amount by the number of shares gives the estimated value per share of $446.60 million/8 million shares = $55.82.

The estimated value for the stock is greater than the market price of $32.50, so the stock appears to be undervalued.

9 A The required return on equity is

$$r = E(R_i) = R_F + \beta_i\left[E(R_M) - R_F\right] = 5.5\% + 0.90(5.5\%) = 10.45\%$$

The weighted-average cost of capital is

$$\text{WACC} = 0.25(7.0\%)(1 - 0.40) + 0.75(10.45\%) = 8.89\%$$

B

$$\text{Firm value} = \frac{\text{FCFF}_0(1 + g)}{\text{WACC} - g}$$

$$\text{Firm value} = \frac{1.1559(1.04)}{0.0889 - 0.04} = \$24.583$$

C Equity value = Firm value − Market value of debt

Equity value = 24.583 − 3.192 = $21.391 billion

D Value per share = Equity value/Number of shares

Value per share = $21.391 billion/1.852 billion = $11.55

10 A The required rate of return for McInish found with the CAPM is

$$r = E(R_i) = R_F + \beta_i\left[E(R_M) - R_F\right] = 5.08\% + 0.70(5.50\%) = 8.93\%$$

The value per share is

$$V_0 = \frac{\text{FCFE}_0(1 + g)}{r - g} = \frac{0.88(1.064)}{0.0893 - 0.064} = \$37.01$$

B The following table shows the calculated price for McInish based on the base-case values for all values except the variable being changed from the base-case value.

Variable	Estimated Price with Low Value ($)	Estimated Price with High Value ($)	Range (Rank) ($)
Normalized FCFE$_0$	29.44	47.94	18.50 (3)
Risk-free rate	38.22	35.33	2.89 (5)
Equity risk premium	51.17	28.99	22.18 (2)
Beta	47.29	30.40	16.89 (4)
FCFE growth rate	18.56	48.79	30.23 (1)

As the table shows, the value of McInish is most sensitive to the changes in the FCFE growth rate, with the price moving over a wide range. McInish's stock price is least sensitive to alternative values of the risk-free rate. Alternative values of beta, the equity risk premium, or the initial FCFE value also have a large impact on the value of the stock, although the effects of these variables are smaller than the effect of the growth rate.

11 A Using the CAPM, the required rate of return for NewMarket is

$$r = E(R_i) = R_F + \beta_i \big[E(R_M) - R_F \big] = 7\% + 1.3(4\%) = 12.2\%$$

To estimate FCFE, we use Equation 15:

$$\text{FCFE} = \text{Net income} - (1 - \text{DR})(\text{FCInv} - \text{Depreciation})$$
$$- (1 - \text{DR})(\text{WCInv})$$

which can be written

$$\text{FCFE} = \text{Net income} - (1 - \text{DR})(\text{FCInv} - \text{Depreciation} + \text{WCInv})$$
$$= \text{Net income} - (1 - \text{DR})(\text{Net investment in operating assets})$$

The following table shows that net income grows at 20 percent annually for Years 1, 2, and 3 and then grows at 8 percent for Year 4. The net investment in operating assets is \$1,150 million in Year 1 and grows at 15 percent annually for Years 2 and 3. Debt financing is 40 percent of this investment. FCFE is NI − Net investment in operating assets + New debt financing. Finally, the present value of FCFE for Years 1, 2, and 3 is found by discounting at 12.2 percent.

		Year		
(in $ Millions)	**1**	**2**	**3**	**4**
Net income	720.00	864.00	1,036.80	1,119.74
Net investment in operating assets	1,150.00	1,322.50	1,520.88	335.92
New debt financing	460.00	529.00	608.35	134.37
FCFE	30.00	70.50	124.27	918.19
PV of FCFE discounted at 12.2%	26.74	56.00	87.98	

In Year 4, net income is 8 percent larger than in Year 3. In Year 4, the investment in operating assets is 30 percent of net income and debt financing is 40 percent of this investment. The FCFE in Year 4 is \$918.19 million. The value of FCFE after Year 3 is found by using the constant-growth model:

$$V_3 = \frac{\text{FCFE}_4}{r - g} = \frac{918.19}{0.122 - 0.08} = \$21,861.67 \text{ million}$$

The present value of V_3 discounted at 12.2 percent is \$15,477.64 million. The total value of equity, the present value of the first three years' FCFE plus the present value of V_3, is \$15,648.36 million. Dividing this by the number of outstanding shares (318 million) gives a value per share of \$49.21. For the first three years, NewMarket has a small FCFE because of the large investments it is making during the high-growth phase. In the normal-growth phase, FCFE is much larger because the investments required are much smaller.

B The planner's estimate of the share value of \$70.98 is much higher than the FCFE model estimate of \$49.21 for several reasons. First, taxes and interest expenses have a prior claim to the company's cash flow and should be taken out of the cash flows used in estimating the value of equity because these amounts are not available to equityholders. The planner did not do this.

Second, EBITDA does not account for the company's reinvestments in operating assets. So, EBITDA overstates the funds available to stockholders if reinvestment needs exceed depreciation charges, which is the case for growing companies such as NewMarket.

Third, EBITDA does not account for the company's capital structure. Using EBITDA to represent a benefit to stockholders (as opposed to stockholders and bondholders combined) is a mistake.

Finally, dividing EBITDA by the bond rate commits a major error. The risk-free bond rate is an inappropriate discount rate for risky equity cash flows; the proper measure is the required rate of return on the company's equity. Dividing by a fixed rate also assumes, erroneously, that the cash flow stream is a fixed perpetuity. EBITDA cannot be a perpetual stream because if it were distributed, the stream would eventually decline to zero (lacking capital investments). NewMarket is actually a growing company, so assuming it to be a nongrowing perpetuity is a mistake.

12 The following table develops the information to calculate FCFE per share (amounts are in US dollars).

	2003	2004	2005	2006	2007	2008
Growth rate for EPS	21%	18%	15%	12%	9%	6%
EPS	3.630	4.283	4.926	5.517	6.014	6.374
Capital expenditure per share	5.000	5.000	4.500	4.000	3.500	1.500
Investment in WC per share	1.250	1.250	1.125	1.000	0.875	0.375
New debt financing = 40% of (Capital expenditure + WCInv)	2.500	2.500	2.250	2.000	1.750	0.750
FCFE = NI – Capital expenditure – WCInv + New debt financing	–0.120	0.533	1.551	2.517	3.389	5.249
PV of FCFE discounted at 12%	–0.107	0.425	1.104	1.600	1.923	

Earnings per share for 2002 are $3.00, and the EPS estimates for 2003 through 2008 in the table are found by increasing the previous year's EPS by that year's growth rate. The net capital expenditures each year were specified by the analyst. The increase in working capital per share is equal to 25 percent of net capital expenditures. Finally, debt financing is 40 percent of that year's total net capital expenditures and investment in working capital. For example, in 2003, the per-share amount for net capital expenditures plus investment in working capital is $5.00 + $1.25 = $6.25. Debt financing is 40 percent of $6.25, or $2.50. Debt financing for 2004 through 2008 is found in the same way.

FCFE equals net income minus net capital expenditures minus investment in working capital plus new debt financing. Notice that FCFE is negative in 2003 because of large capital investments and investments in working capital. As these investments decline relative to net income, FCFE becomes positive and substantial.

The present values of FCFE from 2003 through 2007 are given in the bottom row of the table. These five present values sum to $4.944 per share. Because FCFE from 2008 onward will grow at a constant 6 percent, the constant-growth model can be used to value these cash flows.

$$V_{2007} = \frac{FCFE_{2008}}{r - g} = \frac{5.249}{0.12 - 0.06} = \$87.483$$

The present value of this stream is $87.483/(1.12)^5 = $49.640. The value per share is the present value of the first five FCFEs (2003–2007) plus the present value of the FCFE after 2007, or $4.944 + $ 49.640 = $54.58.

13 A FCFE is defined as the cash flow remaining after the company meets all financial obligations, including debt payment, and covers all capital expenditure and working capital needs. Sundanci's FCFE for the year 2008 is calculated as follows:

Net income	= $80 million
Plus: Depreciation expense	= 23
Less: Capital expenditures	= 38
Less: Investment in WC	= 41
Equals: FCFE	= $24 million

Thus, FCFE per share equals ($24 million)/(84 million shares) = $0.286.

B The FCFE model requires forecasts of FCFE for the high-growth years (2009 and 2010) plus a forecast for the first year of stable growth (2011) to allow for an estimate of the terminal value in 2010 based on constant perpetual growth. Because all of the components of FCFE are expected to grow at the same rate, the values can be obtained by projecting the FCFE at the common rate. (Alternatively, the components of FCFE can be projected and aggregated for each year.)

The following table provides the process for estimating Sundanci's current value on a per-share basis.

Free Cash Flow to Equity					
Base assumptions:					
Shares outstanding (millions)	84				
Required return on equity, r	14%				

			Projected 2009	Projected 2010	Projected 2011
			$g = 27\%$	$g = 27\%$	$g = 13\%$
	Total	Per share			
Earnings after tax	$80	$0.952	$1.2090	$1.5355	$1.7351
Plus: Depreciation expense	$23	$0.274	$0.3480	$0.4419	$0.4994
Less: Capital expenditures	$38	$0.452	$0.5740	$0.7290	$0.8238
Less: Increase in net working capital	$41	$0.488	$0.6198	$0.7871	$0.8894
Equals: FCFE	$24	$0.286	$0.3632	$0.4613	$0.5213
Terminal value[a]				$52.1300	
Total cash flows to equity[b]			$0.3632	$52.5913	
Discounted value[c]			$0.3186	$40.4673	
Current value per share[d]	$40.7859				

[a] Projected 2010 terminal value = Projected 2011 FCFE/$(r - g)$.
[b] Projected 2010 total cash flows to equity = Projected 2010 FCFE + Projected 2010 terminal value.
[c] Discounted values obtained by using $r = 14$ percent.
[d] Current value per share = Discounted value 2009 + Discounted value 2010.

C The following limitations of the DDM *are* addressed by the FCFE model: The DDM uses a strict definition of cash flow to equity; that is, cash flows to equity are the dividends on the common stock. The FCFE model expands the definition of cash flow to include the balance of residual cash flows after all financial obligations and investment needs have been met. Thus, the FCFE model explicitly recognizes the company's investment and financing policies as well as its dividend policy. In instances of a change of corporate control, and thus the possibility of changing dividend policy, the FCFE model provides a better estimate of value.

Both two-stage valuation models allow for two distinct phases of growth—an initial finite period when the growth is abnormal followed by a stable growth period that is expected to last forever. These two-stage models share the same limitations with respect to the growth assumptions:

First, the analyst must confront the difficulty of defining the duration of the extraordinary growth period. A long period of high growth will produce a higher valuation, and the analyst may be tempted to assume an unrealistically long period of extraordinary growth.

Second, the analyst must realize that assuming a sudden shift from high growth to lower, stable growth is unrealistic. The transformation is more likely to occur gradually over time.

Third, because value is quite sensitive to the steady-state growth assumption, overestimating or underestimating this rate can lead to large errors in value.

The two models also share other limitations—notably, difficulties in accurately estimating required rates of return.

14 A   When a two-stage DDM is used, the value of a share of Mackinac, dividends per share (DPS), is calculated as follows:

$$DPS_0 = \text{Cash dividends/Shares outstanding} = \$22{,}470/13{,}000$$
$$= \$1.7285$$
$$DPS_1 = DPS_0 \times 1.17 = \$2.0223$$
$$DPS_2 = DPS_0 \times 1.17^2 = \$2.3661$$
$$DPS_3 = DPS_0 \times 1.17^3 = \$2.7683$$
$$DPS_4 = DPS_0 \times 1.17^3 \times 1.09 = \$3.0175$$

When the CAPM is used, the required return on equity, r, is

$$r = \text{Government bond rate} + (\text{Beta} \times \text{Equity risk premium})$$
$$= 0.06 + (1.25 \times 0.05) = 0.1225 \text{ or } 12.25 \text{ percent}$$

$$\text{Value per share} = DPS_1/(1 + r) + DPS_2/(1 + r)^2 + DPS_3/(1 + r)^3$$
$$+ \left[DPS_4/(r - g_{\text{stable}})\right]/(1 + r)^3$$

$$\text{Value per share} = \$2.0223/1.1225 + \$2.3661/1.1225^2$$
$$+ \$2.7683/1.1225^3$$
$$+ \left[\$3.0175/(0.1225 - 0.09)\right]/1.1225^3$$
$$= \$1.8016 + \$1.8778 + \$1.9573 + \$65.6450$$
$$= \$71.28$$

B When the two-stage FCFE model is used, the value of a share of Mackinac is calculated as follows (in $ thousands except per-share data):

Net income = $37,450

Depreciation = $10,500

Capital expenditures = $15,000

Change in working capital = $5,500

New debt issuance – Principal repayments = Change in debt outstanding = $4,000

$FCFE_0$ = Net income + Depreciation – Capital expenditures – Change in working capital – Principal repayments + New debt issues

$FCFE_0$ = $37,450 + $10,500 – $15,000 – $5,500 + $4,000

   = $31,450

$FCFE_0$ per share = $31,450/13,000 = $2.4192

$FCFE_1 = FCFE_0 \times 1.17 = \$2.8305$

$FCFE_2 = FCFE_0 \times 1.17^2 = \$3.3117$

$FCFE_3 = FCFE_0 \times 1.17^3 = \$3.8747$

$FCFE_4 = FCFE_0 \times 1.17^3 \times 1.09 = \$4.2234$

From the answer to A, r = 12.25 percent.

$$\text{Value per share} = FCFE_1/(1+r) + FCFE_2/(1+r)^2 + FCFE_3/(1+r)^3 + \left[FCFE_4/(r - g_{stable})\right]/(1+r)^3$$

$$\begin{aligned}\text{Value per share} &= \$2.8305/1.1225 + \$3.3117/1.1225^2 \\ &\quad + \$3.8747/1.1225^3 \\ &\quad + \left[\$4.2234/(0.1225 - 0.09)\right]/1.1225^3 \\ &= \$2.5216 + \$2.6283 + \$2.7395 + \$91.8798 \\ &= \$99.77\end{aligned}$$

C The FCFE model is best for valuing companies for takeovers or in situations that have a reasonable chance of a change in corporate control. Because controlling stockholders can change the dividend policy, they are interested in estimating the maximum residual cash flow after meeting all financial obligations and investment needs. The DDM is based on the premise that the only cash flows received by stockholders are dividends. FCFE uses a more expansive definition to measure what a company can afford to pay out as dividends.

15 A The real required rate of return for SK Telecom is

Country return (real)	6.50%
Industry adjustment	+0.60%
Size adjustment	−0.10%
Leverage adjustment	+0.25%
Required rate of return	7.25%

B The real growth rate of FCFE is expected to be the same as the country rate of 3.5 percent. The value of one share is

$$V_0 = \frac{FCFE_0(1 + g_{real})}{r_{real} - g_{real}} = \frac{1,300(1.035)}{0.0725 - 0.035} = 35,880 \text{ Korean won}$$

16 The required return for QuickChange, found by using the CAPM, is $r = E(R_i) = R_F + \beta_i[E(R_M) - R_F] = 4.5\% + 2.0(5.0\%) = 14.5\%$. The estimated future values of FCFE are given in the following exhibit (amounts in US dollars):

Year t	Variable	Calculation	Value in Year t	Present Value at 14.5%
1	$FCFE_1$	0.75(1.10)	0.825	0.721
2	$FCFE_2$	0.75(1.10)(1.26)	1.040	0.793
3	$FCFE_3$	$0.75(1.10)(1.26)^2$	1.310	0.873
4	$FCFE_4$	$0.75(1.10)(1.26)^3$	1.650	0.960
4	TV_4	$FCFE_5/ (r - g)$ $= 0.75(1.10)(1.26)^3(1.06)/(0.145 - 0.06)$ $= 1.749/0.085$	20.580	11.974
0	Total value =	PV of FCFE for Years 1–4 + PV of Terminal value		15.32

The FCFE grows at 10 percent for Year 1 and then at 26 percent for Years 2–4. These calculated values for FCFE are shown in the exhibit. The present values of the FCFE for the first four years discounted at the required rate of return are given in the last column of the table. After Year 4, FCFE will grow at 6 percent forever, so the constant-growth FCFE model is used to find the terminal value at Time 4, which is $TV_4 = FCFE_5/(r - g)$. TV_4 is discounted at the required return for four periods to find its present value, as shown in the table. Finally, the total value of the stock, $15.32, is the sum of the present values of the first four years' FCFE per share plus the present value of the terminal value per share.

17 The total value of nonoperating assets is

    $60 million short-term securities

    $45 million market value of noncurrent assets

    $40 million pension fund surplus

    $145 million nonoperating assets

The total value of the firm is the value of the operating assets plus the value of the nonoperating assets, or $720 million plus $145 million = $865 million. The equity value is the value of the firm minus the value of debt, or $865 million – $215 million = $650 million. The value per share is $650 million/100 million shares = $6.50 per share.

18 C is correct. The sustainable growth rate is return on equity (ROE) multiplied by the retention ratio. ROE is 10 percent, and the retention ratio is 1 – Payout ratio, or 1.0 – 0.2 = 0.8. The sustainable growth rate is 0.8 × 10% = 8%. FCFE growth should be at least 8 percent per year in the long term.

19 A is correct. Justifications for choosing the FCFE model over the DDM include:

● The company pays dividends but its dividends differ significantly from the company's capacity to pay dividends (the first reason given by Leigh).

● The investor takes a control perspective (the second reason given by Leigh).

20 A is correct. FCFF = NI + NCC + Interest expense (1 – Tax rate) – FCInv – WCInv. In this case:

NI = $485 million

NCC = Depreciation expense = $270 million

Interest expense (1 − Tax rate) = 195 (1 − 0.32) = $132.6 million

FCInv = Net purchase of fixed assets = Increase in gross fixed assets

= 4,275 − 3,752 = $523 million

WCInv = Increase in accounts receivable + Increase in inventory − Increase in accounts payable − Increase in accrued liabilities

= (770 − 711) + (846 − 780) − (476 − 443) − (149 − 114)

= $57 million

FCFF = 485 + 270 + 132.6 − 523 − 57 = 307.6, or $308 million

21 B is correct. FCFE = NI + NCC − FCInv − WCInv + Net borrowing. In this case:

NI = $485 million

NCC = Depreciation expense = $270 million

FCInv = Net purchase of fixed assets = Increase in gross fixed assets

= 4,275 − 3,752 = $523 million

WCInv = Increase in accounts receivable + Increase in inventory − Increase in accounts payable − Increase in accrued liabilities

= (770 − 711) + (846 − 780) − (476 − 443) − (149 − 114)

= $57 million

Net borrowing = Increase in notes payable + Increase in long-term debt

= (465 − 450) + (1,575 − 1,515) = $75 million

FCFE = 485 + 270 − 523 − 57 + 75 = $250 million

An alternative calculation is

FCFE = FCFF − Int(1 − Tax rate) + Net borrowing

FCFE = 307.6 − 195(1 − 0.32) + (15 +60) = $250 million

22 C is correct. Inventory cannot be reduced below zero. Furthermore, sales growth tends to increase inventory.

23 A is correct. The FCFF model is often selected when the capital structure is expected to change because FCFF estimation may be easier than FCFE estimation in the presence of changing financial leverage.

Market-Based Valuation: Price and Enterprise Value Multiples

by Jerald E. Pinto, PhD, CFA, Elaine Henry, PhD, CFA,
Thomas R. Robinson, PhD, CFA, and John D. Stowe, PhD, CFA

Jerald E. Pinto, PhD, CFA, is at CFA Institute (USA). Elaine Henry, PhD, CFA, is at Fordham University (USA). Thomas R. Robinson, PhD, CFA, is at CFA Institute (USA). John D. Stowe, PhD, CFA, is at Ohio University (USA).

LEARNING OUTCOMES

Mastery	The candidate should be able to:
☐	a. distinguish between the method of comparables and the method based on forecasted fundamentals as approaches to using price multiples in valuation, and explain economic rationales for each approach;
☐	b. calculate and interpret a justified price multiple;
☐	c. describe rationales for and possible drawbacks to using alternative price multiples and dividend yield in valuation;
☐	d. calculate and interpret alternative price multiples and dividend yield;
☐	e. calculate and interpret underlying earnings, explain methods of normalizing earnings per share (EPS), and calculate normalized EPS;
☐	f. explain and justify the use of earnings yield (E/P);
☐	g. describe fundamental factors that influence alternative price multiples and dividend yield;
☐	h. calculate and interpret the justified price-to-earnings ratio (P/E), price-to-book ratio (P/B), and price-to-sales ratio (P/S) for a stock, based on forecasted fundamentals;
☐	i. calculate and interpret a predicted P/E, given a cross-sectional regression on fundamentals, and explain limitations to the cross-sectional regression methodology;
☐	j. evaluate a stock by the method of comparables and explain the importance of fundamentals in using the method of comparables;

(continued)

The data and examples for this reading were updated in 2014 by Professor Stephen Wilcox, CFA.

Equity Asset Valuation, Second Edition, by Jerald E. Pinto, CFA, Elaine Henry, CFA, Thomas R. Robinson, CFA, and John D. Stowe, CFA. Copyright © 2009 by CFA Institute.

LEARNING OUTCOMES

Mastery	The candidate should be able to:
☐	**k.** calculate and interpret the P/E-to-growth ratio (PEG) and explain its use in relative valuation;
☐	**l.** calculate and explain the use of price multiples in determining terminal value in a multistage discounted cash flow (DCF) model;
☐	**m.** explain alternative definitions of cash flow used in price and enterprise value (EV) multiples and describe limitations of each definition;
☐	**n.** calculate and interpret EV multiples and evaluate the use of EV/EBITDA;
☐	**o.** explain sources of differences in cross-border valuation comparisons;
☐	**p.** describe momentum indicators and their use in valuation;
☐	**q.** explain the use of the arithmetic mean, the harmonic mean, the weighted harmonic mean, and the median to describe the central tendency of a group of multiples;
☐	**r.** evaluate whether a stock is overvalued, fairly valued, or undervalued based on comparisons of multiples.

1 INTRODUCTION

Among the most familiar and widely used valuation tools are price and enterprise value multiples. **Price multiples** are ratios of a stock's market price to some measure of fundamental value per share. **Enterprise value multiples**, by contrast, relate the total market value of all sources of a company's capital to a measure of fundamental value for the entire company.

The intuition behind price multiples is that investors evaluate the price of a share of stock—judge whether it is fairly valued, overvalued, or undervalued—by considering what a share buys in terms of per share earnings, net assets, cash flow or some other measure of value (stated on a per share basis). The intuition behind enterprise value multiples is similar; investors evaluate the market value of an entire enterprise relative to the amount of earnings before interest, taxes, depreciation, and amortization (EBITDA), sales, or operating cash flow it generates. As valuation indicators (measures or indicators of value), multiples have the appealing qualities of simplicity in use and ease in communication. A multiple summarizes in a single number the relationship between the market value of a company's stock (or of its total capital) and some fundamental quantity, such as earnings, sales, or **book value** (owners' equity based on accounting values).

Among the questions we will study in this reading for answers that will help in making correct use of multiples as valuation tools are the following:

- What accounting issues affect particular price and enterprise value multiples, and how can analysts address them?

- How do price multiples relate to fundamentals, such as earnings growth rates, and how can analysts use this information when making valuation comparisons among stocks?

- For which types of valuation problems is a particular price or enterprise value multiple appropriate or inappropriate?
- What challenges arise in applying price and enterprise value multiples internationally?

Multiples may be viewed as valuation indicators relating to individual securities. Another type of valuation indicator used in securities selection is **momentum indicators**. They typically relate either price or a fundamental (such as earnings) to the time series of its own past values or, in some cases, to its expected value. The logic behind the use of momentum indicators is that such indicators may provide information on future patterns of returns over some time horizon. Because the purpose of momentum indicators is to identify potentially rewarding investment opportunities, they can be viewed as a class of valuation indicators with a focus that is different from and complementary to the focus of price and enterprise value multiples.

This reading is organized as follows. In Section 2, we put the use of price and enterprise value multiples in an economic context and present certain themes common to the use of any price or enterprise value multiple. Section 3 presents price multiples; a subsection is devoted to each multiple. The treatment of each multiple follows a common format: usage considerations, the relationship of the multiple to investors' expectations about fundamentals, and using the multiple in valuation based on comparables. Section 4 presents enterprise value multiples and is organized similarly to Section 3. Section 5 presents international considerations in using multiples. A treatment of momentum indicators follows in Section 6. Section 7 discusses several practical issues that arise in using valuation indicators. We then summarize the reading, and the reading concludes with practice problems.

PRICE AND ENTERPRISE VALUE MULTIPLES IN VALUATION

2

In practice, two methods underpin analysts' use of price and enterprise value multiples: the method of comparables and the method based on forecasted fundamentals. Each of these methods relates to a definite economic rationale. In this section, we introduce the two methods and their associated economic rationales.

2.1 The Method of Comparables

The **method of comparables** refers to the valuation of an asset based on multiples of comparable (similar) assets—that is, valuation based on multiples benchmarked to the multiples of similar assets. The similar assets may be referred to as the **comparables**, the **comps**, or the **guideline assets** (or in the case of equity valuation, **guideline companies**). For example, multiplying a benchmark value of the price-to-earnings (P/E) multiple by an estimate of a company's earnings per share (EPS) provides a quick estimate of the value of the company's stock that can be compared with the stock's market price. Equivalently, comparing a stock's actual price multiple with a relevant benchmark multiple should lead the analyst to the same conclusion on whether the stock is relatively fairly valued, relatively undervalued, or relatively overvalued.

The idea behind price multiples is that a stock's price cannot be evaluated in isolation. Rather, it needs to be evaluated in relation to what it buys in terms of earnings, net assets, or some other measure of value. Obtained by dividing price by a measure of value per share, a price multiple gives the price to purchase one unit of value in whatever way value is measured. For example, a P/E of 20 means that it takes 20 units of currency (for example, €20) to buy one unit of earnings (for example, €1 of earnings). This scaling of price per share by value per share also makes possible comparisons among various stocks. For example, an investor pays more for a unit of earnings for a stock with a P/E of 25 than for another stock with a P/E of 20. Applying the method of comparables, the analyst would reason that if the securities are otherwise closely similar (if they have similar risk, profit margins, and growth prospects, for example), the security with the P/E of 20 is undervalued relative to the one with the P/E of 25.

The word *relative* is necessary. An asset may be undervalued relative to a comparison asset or group of assets, and an analyst may thus expect the asset to outperform the comparison asset or assets on a relative basis. If the comparison asset or assets themselves are not efficiently priced, however, the stock may not be undervalued—it could be fairly valued or even overvalued (on an absolute basis, i.e., in relation to its intrinsic value). Example 1 presents the method of comparables in its simplest application.

EXAMPLE 1

The Method of Comparables at Its Simplest

Company A's EPS is $1.50. Its closest competitor, Company B, is trading at a P/E of 22. Assume the companies have a similar operating and financial profile.

1   If Company A's stock is trading at $37.50, what does that indicate about its value relative to Company B?

2   If we assume that Company A's stock should trade at about the same P/E as Company B's stock, what will we estimate as an appropriate price for Company A's stock?

Solution to 1:

If Company A's stock is trading at $37.50, its P/E will be 25 ($37.50 divided by $1.50). If the companies are similar, this P/E would indicate that Company A is overvalued relative to Company B.

Solution to 2:

If we assume that Company A's stock should trade at about the same P/E as Company B's stock, we will estimate that an appropriate price for Company A's stock is $33 ($1.50 times 22).

The method of comparables applies also to enterprise value multiples. In this application, we would evaluate the market value of an entire company in relation to some measure of value relevant to all providers of capital, not only providers of equity capital. For example, multiplying a benchmark multiple of enterprise value (EV) to earnings before interest, taxes, depreciation, and amortization (EBITDA) times an estimate of a company's EBITDA provides a quick estimate of the value of the entire company. Similarly, comparing a company's actual enterprise value multiple with a relevant benchmark multiple allows an assessment of whether the company is relatively fairly valued, relatively undervalued, or relatively overvalued.

Many choices for the benchmark value of a multiple have appeared in valuation methodologies, including the multiple of a closely matched individual stock and the average or median value of the multiple for the stock's industry peer group. The economic rationale underlying the method of comparables is the **law of one** price—the economic principle that two identical assets should sell at the same price.[1] The method of comparables is perhaps the most widely used approach for analysts *reporting* valuation judgments on the basis of price multiples. For this reason, the use of multiples in valuation is sometimes viewed solely as a type of relative-valuation approach; however, multiples can also be derived from, and expressed in terms of, fundamentals, as discussed in the next section.

2.2 The Method Based on Forecasted Fundamentals

The **method based on forecasted fundamentals**[2] refers to the use of multiples that are derived from forecasted fundamentals—characteristics of a business related to profitability, growth, or financial strength. Fundamentals drive cash flows, and we can relate multiples to company fundamentals through a discounted cash flow (DCF) model. Algebraic expressions of price multiples in terms of fundamentals facilitate an examination of how valuation differences among stocks relate to different expectations for those fundamentals. We illustrated this concept in the reading on discounted dividend valuation, where we explained P/E in terms of perhaps the simplest DCF model, the Gordon growth dividend discount model, in an expression that includes (among other variables) the expected dividend growth rate.

One process for relating multiples to forecasted fundamentals begins with a valuation based on a DCF model. Recall that DCF models estimate the intrinsic value of a firm or its equity as the present value of expected cash flows, and that fundamentals drive cash flows. Multiples are stated with respect to a single value of a fundamental, but any price or enterprise value multiple relates to the entire future stream of expected cash flows through its DCF value.

We can illustrate this concept by first taking the present value of the stream of expected future cash flows and then expressing the result relative to a forecasted fundamental. For example, if the DCF value of a UK stock is £10.20 and its forecasted EPS is £1.2, the forward P/E multiple consistent with the DCF value is £10.20/£1.2 = 8.5. (The term **forward P/E** refers to a P/E calculated on the basis of a forecast of EPS and is discussed in further detail later in this reading.) This exercise of relating a valuation to a price multiple applies to any definition of price multiple and any DCF model or residual income model.[3]

In summary, we can approach valuation by using multiples from two perspectives. First, we can use the method of comparables, which involves comparing an asset's multiple to a standard of comparison. Similar assets should sell at similar prices. Second, we can use the method based on forecasted fundamentals, which involves forecasting the company's fundamentals rather than making comparisons with other companies. The price multiple of an asset should be related to its expected future cash flows. We can also incorporate the insights from the method based on forecasted fundamentals in explaining valuation differences based on comparables, because we seldom (if ever) find exact comparables. In the sections covering each multiple, we will present the method based on forecasted fundamentals first so we can refer to it when using the method of comparables.

---

1 In practice, analysts can match characteristics among companies or across time only approximately. Nevertheless, the law of one price is the idea driving the method of comparables. To keep our classification simple, we will discuss comparisons with a market index or with historical values of a stock's multiple under the rubric of the method of comparables.

2 For brevity, we sometimes use the phrase "based on fundamentals" in describing multiples derived using this approach.

3 Recall that residual income models estimate the intrinsic value of a share of common stock as the sum of book value per share and the present value of expected future per-share residual income. Residual income equals net income minus a deduction for the cost of equity capital.

Using either method, how can an analyst communicate a view about the value of a stock? Of course, the analyst can offer simply a qualitative judgment about whether the stock appears to be fairly valued, overvalued, or undervalued (and offer specific reasons for the view). The analyst may also be more precise by communicating a **justified price multiple** for the stock. The justified price multiple is the estimated fair value of that multiple, which can be justified on the basis of the method of comparables or the method of forecasted fundamentals.

For an example of a justified multiple based on the method of comparables, suppose we use the price-to-book (P/B) multiple in a valuation and find that the median P/B for the company's peer group, which would be the standard of comparison, is 2.2.[4] The stock's justified P/B based on the method of comparables is 2.2 (without making any adjustments for differences in fundamentals). We can compare the justified P/B with the actual P/B based on market price to form an opinion about value. If the justified P/B is larger (smaller) than the actual P/B, the stock may be undervalued (overvalued). We can also, on the assumption that the comparison assets are fairly priced, translate the justified P/B based on comparables into an estimate of absolute fair value of the stock. If the current book value per share is $23, then the fair value of the stock is 2.2 × $23 = $50.60, which can be compared with its market price.

For an example of a justified multiple based on fundamentals, suppose that we are using a residual income model and estimate that the value of the stock is $46. Then, the justified P/B based on forecasted fundamentals is $46/$23 = 2.0, which we can again compare with the actual value of the stock's P/B. We can also state our estimate of the stock's absolute fair value as 2 × $23 = $46. (Note that the analyst could report valuation judgments related to a DCF model in terms of the DCF value directly; price multiples are a familiar form, however, in which to state valuations.) Furthermore, we can incorporate the insights from the method based on fundamentals to explain differences from results based on comparables.

In the next section, we begin a discussion of specific price and enterprise value multiples used in valuation.

3 PRICE MULTIPLES

In this section, we first discuss the most familiar price multiple, the price-to-earnings ratio. In the context of that discussion, we introduce a variety of practical issues that have counterparts for most other multiples. These issues include analyst adjustments to the denominator of the ratio for accuracy and comparability and the use of inverse price multiples. Then, we discuss four other major price multiples from the same practical perspective.

3.1 Price to Earnings

In the first edition of *Security Analysis* (Graham and Dodd, 1934, p. 351), Benjamin Graham and David L. Dodd described common stock valuation based on P/Es as the standard method of that era, and the P/E is still the most familiar valuation measure today.

---

4 Note we are using the median, rather than the mean, value of the peer group's multiple to avoid distortions by outliers. This issue is often important when dealing with peer groups because they frequently consist of a small number of companies. An alternative is to use the harmonic mean, which we describe and illustrate in a later section.

We begin our discussion with rationales offered by analysts for the use of P/E and with the possible drawbacks of its use. We then define the two chief variations of the P/E: the trailing P/E and the forward P/E (also called the "leading P/E"). The multiple's numerator, market price, is (as in other multiples) definitely determinable; it presents no special problems of interpretation. But the denominator, EPS, is based on the complex rules of accrual accounting and presents significant interpretation issues. We discuss those issues and the adjustments analysts can make to obtain more-meaningful P/Es. Finally, we conclude the section by examining how analysts use P/Es to value a stock using the method of forecasted fundamentals and the method of comparables. As mentioned earlier, we discuss fundamentals first so that we can draw insights from that discussion when using comparables.

Several rationales support the use of P/E multiples in valuation:

- Earning power is a chief driver of investment value, and EPS, the denominator in the P/E ratio, is perhaps the chief focus of security analysts' attention.[5] In a 2007 survey of CFA Institute members, P/E ranked first among price multiples used in market-based valuation.[6] According to the 2012 BofA *Merrill Lynch Institutional Factor Survey*, 81 percent of respondents considered P/E when making investment decisions, making it the most popular valuation metric surveyed.

- The P/E ratio is widely recognized and used by investors.

- Differences in stocks' P/Es may be related to differences in long-run average returns on investments in those stocks, according to empirical research.[7]

Potential drawbacks to using P/Es derive from the characteristics of EPS:

- EPS can be zero, negative, or insignificantly small relative to price, and P/E does not make economic sense with a zero, negative, or insignificantly small denominator.

- The ongoing or recurring components of earnings that are most important in determining intrinsic value can be practically difficult to distinguish from transient components.

- The application of accounting standards requires corporate managers to choose among acceptable alternatives and to use estimates in reporting. In making such choices and estimates, managers may distort EPS as an accurate reflection of economic performance. Such distortions may affect the comparability of P/Es among companies.

Methods to address these potential drawbacks will be discussed later in the reading. In the next section, we discuss alternative definitions of P/E based on alternative specifications of earnings.

---

5 US-based empirical research tends to show that valuations derived from earnings-based multiples are closer to actual market prices than valuations derived from multiples based on other fundamentals (Liu, Nissim, and Thomas 2002, 2007). If shares are efficiently priced on average, such findings support the importance of earnings in the pricing of common shares.

6 See Pinto, Marmorstein, Robinson, Stowe, and McLeavey (2008) for more details.

7 Chan and Lakonishok (2004) summarize and update academic empirical evidence of superior returns to value investing—that is, investing focused on stocks with low price multiples (e.g., P/E)—in most of the 13 countries they examined. O'Shaughnessy (2005) provides empirical evidence of superior returns to long-term value investing in the US market since 1951, although returns to a low-P/E strategy were dominated by returns to low-P/B, low price-to-sales, and low price-to-cash-flow strategies. In general, debate continues about whether long-run average superior returns to value investing are attributable to higher risk in value than in growth stocks and about other elements in the interpretation of the evidence.

3.1.1 *Alternative Definitions of P/E*

In calculating a P/E, the numerator most commonly used is the current price of the common stock, which is generally easily obtained and unambiguous for publicly traded companies. Selecting the appropriate EPS figure to be used in the denominator is not as straightforward. The following two issues must be considered:

- the time horizon over which earnings are measured, which results in alternative definitions of P/E, and

- adjustments to accounting earnings that the analyst may make so that P/Es for various companies can be compared.

Common alternative definitions of P/E are trailing P/E and forward P/E.

- A stock's **trailing P/E** (sometimes referred to as a current P/E[8]) is its current market price divided by the most recent four quarters' EPS. In such calculations, EPS is sometimes referred to as "trailing 12 month (TTM) EPS."

- The **forward P/E** (also called the **leading P/E** or **prospective P/E**) is a stock's current price divided by next year's expected earnings. Trailing P/E is the P/E usually presented first in stock profiles that appear in financial databases, but most databases also provide the forward P/E. In practice, the forward P/E has a number of important variations that depend on how "next year" is defined, as discussed in Section 3.1.3.

Other names and time-horizon definitions for P/E exist. For example, Thomson First Call[9] provides various P/Es, including ratios that have as the denominator a stock's trailing twelve months EPS, last reported annual EPS, and EPS forecasted for one year to three years ahead. Another example is Value Line's company reports which display a median P/E, which is a rounded average of the four middle values of the range of annual average P/Es over the past 10 years.

In using the P/E, an analyst should apply the same definition to all companies and time periods under examination. Otherwise, the P/Es are not comparable, for a given company over time or for various companies at a specific point in time. One reason is that the differences in P/Es calculated by different methods may be systematic (as opposed to random). For example, for companies with rising earnings, the forward P/E will be smaller than the trailing P/E because the denominator in the forward P/E calculation will be larger.

Valuation is a forward-looking process, so analysts usually focus on the forward P/E when earnings forecasts are available. For large public companies, an analyst can develop earnings forecasts and/or obtain consensus earnings forecasts from a commercial database. When earnings are not readily predictable, however, a trailing P/E (or another valuation metric) may be more appropriate than forward P/E. Furthermore, logic sometimes indicates that a particular definition of the P/E is not relevant. For example, a major acquisition or divestiture or a significant change in financial leverage may change a company's operating or financial risk so much that the trailing P/E based on past EPS is not informative about the future and thus not relevant to a valuation. In such a case, the forward P/E is the appropriate measure. In the following sections, we address issues that arise in calculating trailing and forward P/Es.

---

8 However, *The Value Line Investment Survey* uses "current P/E" to mean a P/E based on EPS for the most recent six months plus the projected EPS for the coming six months. That calculation blends historical and forward looking elements.

9 Thomson First Call is now part of Reuters; the Reuters and Thomson First Call databases are separate, however, so these estimates continue to be referred to as Thomson First Call estimates.

Trailing P/Es and forward P/Es are based on a single year's EPS. If that number is negative or viewed as unrepresentative of a company's earning power, however, an analyst may base the P/E calculation on a longer run expected average EPS value. P/Es based on such normalized EPS data may be called **normalized P/Es**. Because the denominators in normalized P/Es are typically based on historical information, they are covered in the next section on calculating the trailing P/E.

3.1.2 *Calculating the Trailing P/E*

When using trailing earnings to calculate a P/E, the analyst must take care in determining the EPS to be used in the denominator. The analyst must consider the following:

- potential dilution of EPS;[10]
- transitory, nonrecurring components of earnings that are company specific;
- transitory components of earnings ascribable to cyclicality (business or industry cyclicality); and
- differences in accounting methods (when different companies' stocks are being compared).

Among the considerations mentioned, potential dilution of EPS generally makes the least demands on analysts' accounting expertise because companies are themselves required to present both basic EPS and diluted EPS. **Basic earnings per share** data reflect total earnings divided by the weighted average number of shares actually outstanding during the period. **Diluted earnings per share** reflects division by the number of shares that would be outstanding if holders of securities such as executive stock options, equity warrants, and convertible bonds exercised their options to obtain common stock. The diluted EPS measure also reflects the effect of such conversion on the numerator, earnings.[11] Because companies present both EPS numbers, the analyst does not need to make the computation. Companies also typically report details of the EPS computation in a footnote to the financial statements. Example 2, illustrating the first bullet point, shows the typical case in which the P/E based on diluted EPS is higher than the P/E based on basic EPS.

EXAMPLE 2

Basic versus Diluted EPS

For the fiscal year ended 31 December 2012, WPP Group PLC (London: WPP) reported basic EPS of £66.2 and diluted EPS of £62.8. Based on a closing stock price of £1058.0 on 1 February 2013, the day on which the company issued its earnings press release, WPP's trailing P/E is 16.0 if basic EPS is used and 16.8 if diluted EPS is used.

When comparing companies, analysts generally prefer to use diluted EPS so that the EPS of companies with differing amounts of dilutive securities are on a comparable basis. The other bulleted considerations frequently lead to analyst adjustments to reported earnings numbers and are discussed in order below.

---

10 Dilution refers to a reduction in proportional ownership interest as a result of the issuance of new shares.
11 For example, conversion of a convertible bond affects both the numerator (earnings) and the denominator (number of shares) in the EPS calculation. If the holder of a convertible bond exercises the option to convert the bond into common shares, the issuer no longer has an obligation to pay interest on the bond, which affects the amount of earnings, and the issuer issues the required number of shares, which, all else being equal, increases the total number of shares outstanding.

3.1.2.1 Analyst Adjustments for Nonrecurring Items   Items in earnings that are not expected to recur in the future are generally removed by analysts because valuation concentrates on future cash flows. The analyst's focus is on estimating **underlying earnings** (other names for this concept include **persistent earnings**, **continuing earnings**, and **core earnings**)—that is, earnings that exclude nonrecurring items. An increase in underlying earnings reflects an increase in earnings that the analyst expects to persist into the future. Companies may disclose adjusted earnings, which may be called non-IFRS earnings (because they differ, as a result of adjustments, from earnings as reportable under International Financial Reporting Standards), non-GAAP earnings (because they differ, as a result of adjustments, from earnings as reportable under US generally accepted accounting principles), pro forma earnings, adjusted earnings, or, as in Example 3, core earnings. All of these terms indicate that the earnings number differs in some way from that presented in conformity with accounting standards. Example 3 shows the calculation of EPS and P/E before and after analyst adjustments for nonrecurring items.

EXAMPLE 3

Calculating Trailing 12 Months EPS and Adjusting EPS for Nonrecurring Items

You are calculating a trailing P/E for AstraZeneca PLC (NYSE, LSE: AZN) as of 1 April 2013, when the share price closed at $50.11 in New York (£28.25 in London). In its first quarter of 2013, ended 31 March, AZN reported basic and diluted EPS according to IFRS of $0.81, which included $0.34 of restructuring costs and $0.26 of amortization of intangibles arising from acquisitions. Adjusting for all of these items, AZN reported "core EPS" of $1.41 for the first quarter of 2013, compared with core EPS of $1.87 for the first quarter of 2012. Because the core EPS differed from the EPS calculated under IFRS, the company provided a reconciliation of the two EPS figures.

Other data for AZN as of 31 March 2013 are given below. The trailing 12 months diluted EPS for 31 March 2013 includes one quarter in 2013 and three quarters in 2012.

Measure	Full Year 2012 (a)	Less 1st Quarter 2012 (b)	Three Quarters of 2012 (c = a − b)	Plus 1st Quarter 2013 (d)	Trailing 12 Months EPS (e = c + d)
Reported diluted EPS	$4.98	$1.27	$3.71	$0.81	$4.52
Core EPS	$6.41	$1.81	$4.60	$1.41	$6.01
EPS excluding 2012 legal provisions	$5.07	$1.28	$3.79	$0.81	$4.60

Based on the table and information about AZN, address the following:

1   Based on the company's reported EPS, determine the trailing P/E of AZN as of 31 March 2013.

2   Determine the trailing P/E of AZN as of 31 March 2013 using core earnings as determined by AZN.

Suppose you expect the amortization charges to continue for some years and note that, although AZN excluded restructuring charges from its core earnings calculation, AZN has reported restructuring charges in previous years. After reviewing all relevant data, you conclude that, in this instance, only the legal provision related to a previously disclosed legal matter should be viewed as clearly nonrecurring.

3   Determine the trailing P/E based on your adjustment to EPS.

Solution to 1:

Based on reported EPS and without any adjustments for nonrecurring items, the trailing P/E is $50.11/$4.52 = 11.1.

Solution to 2:

Using the company's reported core earnings, you find that the trailing EPS would be $4.59 and the trailing P/E would be $50.11/$6.01 = 8.3.

Solution to 3:

The trailing EPS excluding only what you consider to be nonrecurring items is $4.60 and the trailing P/E on that basis is $50.11/$4.60 = 10.9.

Example 3 makes several important points:

- By any of its various names, underlying earnings or core earnings is a non-IFRS concept without prescribed rules for its calculation.

- An analyst's calculation of underlying earnings may well differ from that of the company supplying the earnings numbers. Company-reported core earnings may not be comparable among companies because of differing bases of calculation. Analysts should thus always carefully examine the calculation and, generally, should not rely on such company-reported core earnings numbers.

- In general, the P/E that an analyst uses in valuation should reflect the analyst's judgment about the company's underlying earnings and should be calculated on a consistent basis among all stocks under review.

The identification of nonrecurring items often requires detailed work—in particular, examination of the income statement, the footnotes to the income statement, and the management discussion and analysis section. The analyst cannot rely on income statement classifications alone to identify nonrecurring components of earnings. Nonrecurring items (for example, gains and losses from the sale of assets, asset write-downs, goodwill impairment, provisions for future losses, and changes in accounting estimates) often appear in the income from continuing operations portion of a business's income statement.[12] An analyst may decide not to exclude income/loss from discontinued operations when assets released from discontinued operations are redirected back into the company's earnings base. An analyst who takes income statement classifications at face value may draw incorrect conclusions in a valuation.

---

12 An asset **write-down** is a reduction in the value of an asset as stated in the balance sheet. The timing and amount of write-downs often are, at least in part, discretionary. **Accounting estimates** are numerous. Some examples include the useful (depreciable) lives of assets, salvage value of assets, warranty costs, product returns, and the amount of uncollectible receivables.

This discussion does not exhaust the analysis that may be necessary to distinguish earnings components that are expected to persist into the future from those that are not. For example, earnings may be decomposed into cash flow and accrual components.[13] Some research indicates that the cash flow component of earnings should receive a greater weight than the accrual component of earnings in valuation,[14] and analysts may attempt to reflect that conclusion in the earnings used in calculating P/Es.

3.1.2.2 Analyst Adjustments for Business-Cycle Influences
In addition to company-specific effects, such as restructuring costs, transitory effects on earnings can come from business-cycle or industry-cycle influences. These effects are somewhat different from company-specific effects. Because business cycles repeat, business-cycle effects, although transitory, can be expected to recur in subsequent cycles.

Because of cyclical effects, the most recent four quarters of earnings may not accurately reflect the average or long-term earning power of the business, particularly for **cyclical businesses**—those with high sensitivity to business- or industry-cycle influences, such as automobile and steel manufacturers. Trailing EPS for such stocks are often depressed or negative at the bottom of a cycle and unusually high at the top of a cycle. Empirically, P/Es for cyclical companies are often highly volatile over a cycle even without any change in business prospects: High P/Es on depressed EPS at the bottom of the cycle and low P/Es on unusually high EPS at the top of the cycle reflect the countercyclical property of P/Es known as the **Molodovsky effect**.[15] Analysts address this problem by normalizing EPS—that is, estimating the level of EPS that the business could be expected to achieve under mid-cyclical conditions (**normalized EPS** or **normal EPS**).[16] Two of several available methods to calculate normalized EPS are as follows:

■ The method of *historical average EPS*, in which normalized EPS is calculated as average EPS over the most recent full cycle.

■ The method of *average return on equity*, in which normalized EPS is calculated as the average return on equity (ROE) from the most recent full cycle, multiplied by current book value per share.

The first method is one of several possible statistical approaches to the problem of cyclical earnings; however, this method does not account for changes in a business's size. The second alternative, by using recent book value per share, reflects more accurately the effect on EPS of growth or shrinkage in the company's size. For that reason, the method of average ROE is sometimes preferred.[17] When reported current book value does not adequately reflect company size in relation to past values (because of items

---

13 See Richardson and Tuna (2008) summarizing research by Sloan (1996) and others. The accrual component of earnings is the difference between a cash measure of earnings and a measure of earnings under the relevant set of accounting standards (e.g., IFRS or US GAAP). For example, a cash measure of revenues for a period equals only those amounts collected during the period. In contrast, an accrual measure of revenues includes all revenues earned during the period (both the amounts collected during the period and amounts expected to be collected in future periods, which are, therefore, still in the accounts receivable section at the end of the period.) Additionally, accrual revenues are adjusted for estimated returns and allowances, and accounts receivable are adjusted for estimated uncollectibles.

14 See Richardson and Tuna (2008).

15 This effect was named after Nicholas Molodovsky, who wrote on this subject in the 1950s and referred to using averaged earnings as a simple starting point for understanding a company's underlying earning power. We can state the Molodovsky effect another way: P/Es may be negatively related to the recent earnings growth rate but positively related to the anticipated future growth rate because of expected rebounds in earnings.

16 Here, we are using the term "normalized earnings" to refer to earnings adjusted for the effects of a business cycle. Some sources use the term "normalized earnings" also to refer to earnings adjusted for nonrecurring items.

17 This approach has appeared in valuation research; for example, Michaud (1999) calculated a normalized earnings yield (that is, EPS divided by price) rather than a normalized P/E.

such as large write-downs), the analyst can make appropriate accounting adjustments. The analyst can also estimate normalized earnings by multiplying total assets by an estimate of the long-run return on total assets[18] or by multiplying shareholders' equity by an estimate of the long-run return on total shareholders' equity. These methods are particularly useful for a period in which a cyclical company has reported a loss.

Example 4 illustrates this concept. The example uses data for an **American Depositary Receipt** (ADR) but is applicable to any equity security. An ADR is intended to facilitate US investment in non-US companies. It is a negotiable certificate issued by a depositary bank that represents ownership in a non-US company's deposited equity (i.e., equity held in custody by the depositary bank in the company's home market). One ADR may represent one, more than one, or fewer than one, deposited share. The number of, or fraction of, deposited securities represented by one ADR is referred to as the "ADR ratio."

EXAMPLE 4

Normalizing EPS for Business-Cycle Effects

You are researching the valuation of Taiwan Semiconductor Manufacturing Company (NYSE: TSM, TAIEX: 2330), the world's largest dedicated semiconductor foundry (www.tsmc.com). Your research is for a US investor who is interested in the company's ADRs rather than the company's shares listed on the Taiwan Stock Exchange. On 5 July 2013, the closing price of TSM, the NYSE listed ADR, was $18.21. The semiconductor industry is notably cyclical, so you decide to normalize earnings as part of your analysis. You believe that data from 2006 reasonably captures the beginning of the most recent business cycle, and you want to evaluate a normalized P/E. Exhibit 1 supplies data on EPS (based on Republic of China GAAP) for one TSM ADR, book value per share (BVPS) for one ADR, and the company's ROE.[19]

Exhibit 1	Taiwan Semiconductor Manufacturing Company (Currency in US Dollars)						
Measure	2006	2007	2008	2009	2010	2011	2012
EPS (ADR)	$0.74	$0.63	$0.61	$0.54	$1.07	$0.88	$1.08
BVPS (ADR)	$3.00	$2.93	$2.85	$2.99	$3.80	$4.03	$4.82
ROE	24.7%	22.4%	21.8%	18.0%	28.1%	21.3%	22.9%

Source: The Value Line Investment Survey.

---

18 An example of the application of this method is the study of the intrinsic value of the Dow Jones Industrial Average (the US equities index) by Lee, Myers, and Swaminathan (1999). The authors used 6 percent of total assets as a proxy for normal earnings to estimate a payout ratio for periods in which a company's earnings were negative. According to the authors, the long-run return on total assets in the United States is approximately 6 percent.

19 This example involves a single company. When the analyst compares multiple companies on the basis of P/Es based on normalized EPS and uses this normalization approach, the analyst should be sure that the ROEs are being calculated consistently by the subject companies. In this example, ROE for each year is being calculated by using ending BVPS and, essentially, trailing earnings are being normalized.

Using the data in Exhibit 1:

1   Calculate a normalized EPS for TSM by the method of historical average EPS and then calculate the P/E based on that estimate of normalized EPS.

2   Calculate a normalized EPS for TSM by the method of average ROE and the P/E based on that estimate of normalized EPS.

3   Explain the source of the differences in the normalized EPS calculated by the two methods, and contrast the impact on the estimate of a normalized P/E.

Solution to 1:

Averaging EPS over the 2006–2012 period, you would find it to be ($0.74 + $0.63 + $0.61 + $0.54 + $1.07 + $0.88 + $1.08)/7 = $0.79. Thus, according to the method of historical average EPS, TSM's normalized EPS is $0.79. The P/E based on this estimate is $18.21/$0.79 = 23.1.

Solution to 2:

Average ROE over the 2006–2012 period is (24.7% + 21.5% + 21.4% + 18.1% + 28.2% + 21.8% + 22.4%)/7 = 22.6%. Based on the current BVPS of $4.82, the method of average ROE gives 0.226 × $4.82 = $1.09 as normalized EPS. The P/E based on this estimate is $18.21/$1.09 = 16.7.

Solution to 3:

From 2006 to 2012, BVPS increased from $3.00 to $4.82, an increase of about 161 percent. The estimate of normalized EPS of $1.09 from the average ROE method reflects the use of information on the current size of the company better than does the $0.79 calculated from the historical average EPS method. Because of that difference, TSM appears more conservatively valued (as indicated by a lower P/E) when the method based on average ROE is used.

3.1.2.3 Analyst Adjustments for Comparability with Other Companies   Analysts adjust EPS for differences in accounting methods between the company and companies it is being compared with so that the P/Es will be comparable. For example, if an analyst is comparing a company that uses the last-in, first-out (LIFO) method of inventory accounting as permitted by US GAAP (but not by IFRS) with another company that uses the first-in, first-out (FIFO) method, the analyst should adjust earnings to provide comparability in all ratio and valuation analyses. In general, any adjustment made to a company's reported financials for purposes of financial statement analysis should be incorporated into an analysis of P/E and other multiples.

3.1.2.4 Dealing with Extremely Low, Zero, or Negative Earnings   Having addressed the challenges that arise to calculating P/E because of nonrecurring items, business-cycle influences, and for comparability among companies, we present in this section the methods analysts have developed for dealing with extremely low, zero, or negative earnings.

Stock selection disciplines that use P/Es or other price multiples often involve ranking stocks from highest value of the multiple to lowest value of the multiple. The security with the lowest positive P/E has the lowest purchase cost per currency unit of earnings among the securities ranked. Zero earnings and negative earnings pose a problem if the analyst wishes to use P/E as the valuation metric. Because division by zero is undefined, P/Es cannot be calculated for zero earnings.

A P/E can technically be calculated in the case of negative earnings. Negative earnings, however, result in a negative P/E. A negative-P/E security will rank below the lowest positive-P/E security but, because earnings are negative, the negative-P/E security is actually the most costly in terms of earnings purchased. Thus, negative P/Es are not meaningful.

In some cases, an analyst might handle negative EPS by using normalized EPS instead. Also, when trailing EPS are negative, the year-ahead EPS and thus the forward P/E may be positive. An argument in favor of either of these approaches based on positive earnings is that if a company is appropriately treated as a going concern, losses cannot be the usual operating result.

If the analyst is interested in a ranking, however, one solution (applicable to any ratio involving a quantity that can be negative or zero) is the use of an **inverse price ratio**—that is, the reciprocal of the original ratio, which places price in the denominator. The use of inverse price multiples addresses the issue of consistent ranking because price is never negative.[20] In the case of the P/E, the inverse price ratio is earnings to price (E/P), known as the **earnings yield**. Ranked by earnings yield from highest to lowest, the securities are correctly ranked from cheapest to most costly in terms of the amount of earnings one unit of currency buys.

Exhibit 2 illustrates these points for a group of beer companies, one of which has a negative EPS. When reporting a P/E based on negative earnings, analysts should report such P/Es as "NM" (not meaningful).

Exhibit 2	P/E and E/P for Five Beer Companies (as of 5 September 2013; in US Dollars)			
Company	Current Price	Diluted EPS (TTM)	P/E (TTM)	E/P (%)
Molson Coors Brewing Co. (NYSE: TAP)	49.19	3.14	15.7	6.38
Anheuser-Busch Cos. (NYSE: BUD)	94.73	8.04	11.8	8.49
Boston Beer Co. (NYSE: SAM)	223.57	4.73	47.3	2.12
Craft Brew Alliance, Inc. (NASDAQ GM: BREW)	12.30	0.02	615.0	0.16
Mendocino Brewing Company, Inc (OTC Markets: MENB)	0.29	−0.02	NM	−6.90

Source: Yahoo! Finance.

In addition to zero and negative earnings, extremely low earnings can pose problems when using P/Es—particularly for evaluating the distribution of P/Es of a group of stocks under review. In this case, again, inverse price ratios can be useful. The P/E of a stock with extremely low earnings may, nevertheless, be extremely high because an earnings rebound is anticipated. An extremely high P/E—an outlier P/E—can overwhelm the effect of the other P/Es in the calculation of the mean P/E. Although

---

20 Earnings yield can be based on normalized EPS, expected next-year EPS, or trailing EPS. In these cases also, earnings yield provides a consistent ranking.

the use of median P/Es and other techniques can mitigate the problem of skewness caused by outliers, the distribution of inverse price ratios is inherently less susceptible to outlier-induced skewness.

As mentioned, earnings yield is but one example of an inverse price ratio—that is, the reciprocal of a price ratio. Exhibit 3 summarizes inverse price ratios for all the price ratios we discuss in this reading.

Exhibit 3	Summary of Price and Inverse Price Ratios	
Price Ratio	**Inverse Price Ratio**	**Comments**
Price-to-earnings (P/E)	Earnings yield (E/P)	Both forms commonly used.
Price-to-book (P/B)	Book-to-market (B/P)*	Book value is less commonly negative than EPS. Book-to-market is favored in research but not common in practitioner usage.
Price-to-sales (P/S)	Sales-to-price (S/P)	S/P is rarely used except when all other ratios are being stated in the form of inverse price ratios; sales is not zero or negative in practice for going concerns.
Price-to-cash flow (P/CF)	Cash flow yield (CF/P)	Both forms are commonly used.
Price-to-dividends (P/D)	Dividend yield (D/P)	Dividend yield is much more commonly used because P/D is not calculable for non-dividend-paying stocks, but both D/P and P/D are used in discussing index valuation.

* "Book-to-*market*" is probably more common usage than "book-to-*price*." Book-to-market is variously abbreviated B/M, BV/MV (for "book value" and "market value"), or B/P.
Note: B, S, CF, and D are in per-share terms.

3.1.3 *Forward P/E*

The forward P/E is a major and logical alternative to the trailing P/E because valuation is naturally forward looking. In the definition of forward P/E, analysts have interpreted "next year's expected earnings" as expected EPS for:

- the next four quarters;
- the next 12 months; or
- the next fiscal year.

In this section, unless otherwise stated, we use the first definition of forward P/E (i.e., the next four quarters), which is closest to how cash flows are dated in our discussion of DCF valuation.[21] To illustrate the calculation, suppose the current market price of a stock is $15 as of 1 March 2013 and the most recently reported quarterly EPS (for the quarter ended 31 December 2012) is $0.22. Our forecasts of EPS are as follows:

- $0.15 for the quarter ending 31 March 2013;
- $0.18 for the quarter ending 30 June 2013;
- $0.18 for the quarter ending 30 September 2013; and
- $0.24 for the quarter ending 31 December 2013.

The sum of the forecasts for the next four quarters is $0.15 + $0.18 + $0.18 + $0.24 = $0.75, and the forward P/E for this stock is $15/$0.75 = 20.0.

---

21 Analysts have developed DCF expressions that incorporate fractional time periods. In practice, uncertainty in forecasts reduces accuracy more than any other factor in estimating justified P/Es.

Another important concept related to the forward P/E is the next twelve month (NTM) P/E, which corresponds in a forward-looking sense to the TTM P/E concept of trailing P/E. A stock's **NTM P/E** is its current market price divided by an estimated next twelve months EPS, which typically combines the annual EPS estimates from two fiscal years, weighted to reflect the relative proximity of the fiscal year. For example, assume that in August 2013, an analyst is looking at Microsoft Corporation (NASDAQ GS: MSFT). Microsoft has a June fiscal year end, so at the time of the analyst's scrutiny, there were 10 months remaining until the end of the company's 2014 fiscal year (i.e., September 2013 through June 2014, inclusive). The estimated next twelve months EPS for Microsoft would be calculated as $[(10/12) \times \text{FY14E EPS}] + [(2/12) \times \text{FY15E EPS}]$. NTM P/E is useful because it facilitates comparison of companies with different fiscal year-ends without the need to use quarterly estimates, which for many companies are not available.

Applying the fiscal-year concept, Thomson First Call reports a stock's "forward P/E" in two ways: first, based on the mean of analysts' *current fiscal year* (FY1 = Fiscal Year 1) forecasts, for which analysts may have actual EPS in hand for some quarters; second, based on analysts' *following fiscal year* (FY2 = Fiscal Year 2) forecasts, which must be based entirely on forecasts. For Thomson First Call, "forward P/E" contrasts with "current P/E," which is based on the last reported annual EPS.

Clearly, analysts must be consistent in the definition of forward P/E when comparing stocks. Examples 5 and 6 illustrate two ways of calculating forward P/E.

EXAMPLE 5

Calculating a Forward P/E (1)

A market price for the common stock of IBM (NYSE: IBM) in early-September 2013 was $184.15. IBM's fiscal year coincides with the calendar year. According to data from Thomson First Call, the consensus EPS forecast for 2013 (FY1) as of September 2013 was $16.19. The consensus EPS forecast for 2014 (FY2) as of September 2013 was $18.35.

1　Calculate IBM's forward P/E based on a fiscal-year definition per Thomson First Call and FY1 consensus forecasted EPS.

2　Calculate IBM's forward P/E based on a fiscal-year definition and FY2 consensus forecasted EPS.

Solution to 1:

IBM's forward P/E is $184.15/$16.19 = 11.4 based on FY1 forecasted EPS. Note that this EPS number involves the forecast of two remaining quarters as of early-September 2013.

Solution to 2:

IBM's forward P/E is $184.15/$18.35 = 10.0 based on FY2 forecasted EPS.

In Example 5, the company's EPS was expected to increase by slightly more than 13 percent, so the forward P/Es based on the two different EPS specifications differed from one another somewhat but not dramatically. Example 6 presents the calculation of forward P/Es for a company with volatile earnings.

EXAMPLE 6

Calculating a Forward P/E (2)

In this example, we use alternative definitions of "forward" to compute forward P/Es. Exhibit 4 presents actual and forecasted EPS for Boyd Gaming Corp. (NYSE: BYD) that owns and operates 21 gaming entertainment properties in Nevada, Mississippi, Illinois, New Jersey, Indiana, Kansas, Iowa, and Louisiana.

Exhibit 4	Quarterly EPS for BYD (in US Dollars; Excluding Nonrecurring Items and Discontinued Operations)				
Year	31 March	30 June	30 September	31 December	Annual Estimate
2013	0.01	0.00	E(0.01)	E(0.05)	(0.05)
2014	E0.07	E0.08	E0.03	E(0.03)	0.15

Source: The Value Line Investment Survey.

On 9 August 2013, BYD closed at $12.20. BYD's fiscal year ends on 31 December. As of 9 August 2013, solve the following problems by using the information in Exhibit 4:

1 Calculate BYD's forward P/E based on the next four quarters of forecasted EPS.

2 Calculate BYD's NTM P/E.

3 Calculate BYD's forward P/E based on a fiscal-year definition and current fiscal year (2013) forecasted EPS.

4 Calculate BYD's forward P/E based on a fiscal-year definition and next fiscal year (2014) forecasted EPS.

Solution to 1:

We sum forecasted EPS as follows:

3Q:2013 EPS (estimate)	($0.01)
4Q:2013 EPS (estimate)	($0.05)
1Q:2014 EPS (estimate)	$0.07
2Q:2014 EPS (estimate)	$0.08
Sum	$0.09

The forward P/E by this definition is $12.20/$0.09 = 135.6.

Solution to 2:

As of 9 August 2013, approximately five months remained in FY2013. Therefore, the estimated next twelve months EPS for BYD would be based on annual estimates in the last column of Exhibit 4: $[(5/12) \times \text{FY13E EPS}] + [(7/12) \times \text{FY14E EPS}] = (5/12)(-0.05) + (7/12)(0.15) = 0.067$. The NTM P/E would be $12.20/$0.067 = 182.1.

Solution to 3:

We sum EPS as follows:

1Q:2013 EPS (actual)	$0.01
2Q:2013 EPS (actual)	$0.00
3Q:2013 EPS (estimate)	($0.01)
4Q:2013 EPS (estimate)	($0.05)
Sum	($0.05)

The forward P/E is $12.20/($0.05) = −244.0, which is not meaningful.

Solution to 4:

We sum EPS as follows:

1Q:2014 EPS (estimate)	$0.07
2Q:2014 EPS (estimate)	$0.08
3Q:2014 EPS (estimate)	$0.03
4Q:2014 EPS (estimate)	($0.03)
Sum	$0.15

The forward P/E by this definition is $12.20/$0.15 = 81.3.

As illustrated in Example 6, for companies with volatile earnings, forward P/Es and thus valuations based on forward P/Es can vary dramatically depending on the definition of earnings. The analyst would probably be justified in normalizing EPS for BYD. The gaming industry is highly sensitive to discretionary spending; thus, BYD's earnings are strongly procyclical.

Having explored the issues involved in calculating P/Es, we turn to using them in valuation.

3.1.4 *Valuation Based on Forecasted Fundamentals*

The analyst who understands DCF valuation models can use them not only in developing an estimate of the justified P/E for a stock but also to gain insight into possible sources of valuation differences when the method of comparables is used. Linking P/Es to a DCF model helps us address what value the market should place on a dollar of EPS when we are given a particular set of expectations about the company's profitability, growth, and cost of capital.

3.1.4.1 Justified P/E The simplest of all DCF models is the Gordon (constant) growth form of the dividend discount model (DDM). Presentations of discounted dividend valuation commonly show that the P/E of a share can be related to the value of a stock as calculated in the Gordon growth model through the expressions

$$\frac{P_0}{E_1} = \frac{D_1/E_1}{r-g} = \frac{1-b}{r-g} \qquad (1)$$

for the forward P/E, and for the trailing P/E,

$$\frac{P_0}{E_0} = \frac{D_0(1+g)/E_0}{r-g} = \frac{(1-b)(1+g)}{r-g} \qquad (2)$$

where

P = price

E = earnings

D = dividends

r = required rate of return

g = dividend growth rate

b = retention rate

Under the assumption of constant dividend growth, the first expression gives the justified forward P/E and the second gives the justified trailing P/E. Note that both expressions state P/E as a function of two fundamentals: the stock's required rate of return, r, which reflects its risk, and the expected (stable) dividend growth rate, g. The dividend payout ratio, $1 - b$, also enters into the expressions.

A particular value of the P/E is associated with a set of forecasts of the fundamentals and the dividend payout ratio. This value is the stock's **justified (fundamental) P/E** based on forecasted fundamentals (that is, the P/E justified by fundamentals). All else being equal, the higher the expected dividend growth rate or the lower the stock's required rate of return, the higher the stock's intrinsic value and the higher its justified P/E.

This intuition carries over to more-complex DCF models. Using any DCF model, all else being equal, justified P/E is:

■ inversely related to the stock's required rate of return, and

■ positively related to the growth rate(s) of future expected cash flows, however defined.

We illustrate the calculation of a justified forward P/E in Example 7.

EXAMPLE 7

Forward P/E Based on Fundamental Forecasts (1)

BP p.l.c. (London: BP) is one of the world's largest integrated oil producers. As of early September 2013, the company continued to deal with litigation concerns surrounding its role in a 2010 drilling rig accident. Jan Unger, an energy analyst, forecasts a long-term earnings retention rate, b, for BP of 10 percent and a long-term growth rate of 3 percent. Given the significant legal uncertainties still facing BP shareholders, Unger estimates a required rate of return of 12.5 percent. Based on Unger's forecasts of fundamentals and Equation 1, BP's justified forward P/E is

$$\frac{P_0}{E_1} = \frac{1-b}{r-g} = \frac{1-0.10}{0.125-0.03} = 9.5$$

When using a complex DCF model to value the stock (e.g., a model with varying growth rates and varying assumptions about dividends), the analyst may not be able to express the P/E as a function of fundamental, constant variables. In such cases, the analyst can still calculate a justified P/E by dividing the value per share (that results from a DCF model) by estimated EPS, as illustrated in Example 8. Approaches similar to this one can be used to develop other justified multiples.

EXAMPLE 8

Forward P/E Based on Fundamental Forecasts (2)

Toyota Motor Corporation (TYO: 7203; NYSE: TM) is one of the world's largest vehicle manufacturers. The company's most recent fiscal year ended on 31 March 2013. In early September 2013, you are valuing Toyota stock, which closed at ¥6,340 on the previous day. You have used a free cash flow to equity (FCFE) model to value the company stock and have obtained a value of ¥6,722 for the stock. For ease of communication, you want to express your valuation in terms of a forward P/E based on your forecasted fiscal year 2014 EPS of ¥600. Toyota's fiscal year 2014 is from 1 April 2013 through 31 March 2014.

1 What is Toyota's justified P/E based on forecasted fundamentals?

2 Based on a comparison of the current price of ¥6,340 with your estimated intrinsic value of ¥6,722, the stock appears to be undervalued by approximately 6 percent. Use your answer to Part 1 to state this evaluation in terms of P/Es.

Solution to 1:

Value of the stock derived from FCFE = ¥6,722
  Forecasted 2014 EPS = ¥600
  ¥6,722/¥600 = 11.2 is the justified forward P/E.

Solution to 2:

The justified P/E of 11.2 is about 6 percent higher than the forward P/E based on current market price, ¥6,340/¥600 = 10.6.

The next section illustrates another, but less commonly used, approach to relating price multiples to fundamentals.

3.1.4.2 Predicted P/E Based on Cross-Sectional Regression   A predicted P/E, which is conceptually similar to a justified P/E, can be estimated from cross-sectional regressions of P/E on the fundamentals believed to drive security valuation. Kisor and Whitbeck (1963) and Malkiel and Cragg (1970) pioneered this approach. The studies measured P/Es for a group of stocks and the characteristics thought to determine P/E: growth rate in earnings, payout ratio, and a measure of volatility, such as standard deviation of earnings changes or beta. An analyst can conduct such cross-sectional regressions by using any set of explanatory variables considered to determine investment value; the analyst must bear in mind, however, potential distortions that can be introduced by multicollinearity among independent variables. Example 9 illustrates the prediction of P/E using cross-sectional regression.

EXAMPLE 9

Predicted P/E Based on a Cross-Sectional Regression

You are valuing a food company with a beta of 0.9, a dividend payout ratio of 0.45, and an earnings growth rate of 0.08. The estimated regression for a group of other stocks in the same industry is

Predicted P/E = 12.12 + (2.25 × DPR) − (0.20 × Beta) + (14.43 × EGR)

where DPR is the dividend payout ratio and EGR is the five-year earnings growth rate.

1 Based on this cross-sectional regression, what is the predicted P/E for the food company?

2 If the stock's actual trailing P/E is 18, is the stock fairly valued, overvalued, or undervalued?

Solution to 1:

Predicted P/E = 12.12 + (2.25 × 0.45) − (0.20 × 0.9) + (14.43 × 0.08) = 14.1. The predicted P/E is 14.1.

Solution to 2:

Because the predicted P/E of 14.1 is less than the actual P/E of 18, the stock appears to be overvalued. That is, it is selling at a higher multiple than is justified by its fundamentals.

A cross-sectional regression summarizes a large amount of data in a single equation and can provide a useful additional perspective on a valuation. It is not frequently used as a main tool, however, because it is subject to at least three limitations:

■ The method captures valuation relationships only for the specific stock (or sample of stocks) over a particular time period. The predictive power of the regression for a different stock and different time period is not known.

■ The regression coefficients and explanatory power of the regressions tend to change substantially over a number of years. The relationships between P/E and fundamentals may thus change over time. Empirical evidence suggests that the relationships between P/Es and such characteristics as earnings growth, dividend payout, and beta are not stable over time (Damodaran 2012). Furthermore, because distributions of multiples change over time, the predictive power of results from a regression at any point in time can be expected to diminish with the passage of time (Damodaran 2012).

■ Because regressions based on this method are prone to the problem of multicollinearity (correlation within linear combinations of the independent variables), interpreting individual regression coefficients is difficult.

Overall, rather than examining the relationship between a stock's P/E multiple and economic variables, the bulk of capital market research examines the relationship between companies' stock prices (and returns on the stock) and explanatory variables, one of which is often earnings (or unexpected earnings). A classic example of such research is the Fama and French (1992) study showing that, used alone, a number of factors explained cross-sectional stock returns in the 1963–1990 period; the factors were E/P, size, leverage, and the book-to-market multiples. When these variables were used in combination, however, size and book-to-market had explanatory power that absorbed the roles of the other variables in explaining cross-sectional stock returns. Research building on that study eventually resulted in the Fama–French three-factor model (with the factors of size, book-to-market, and beta). Another classic academic study providing evidence that accounting variables appear to have predictive power for stock returns is Lakonishok, Shleifer, and Vishny (1994), which also provided evidence that value strategies—buying stocks with low prices relative to earnings, book value, cash flow, and sales growth—produced superior five-year buy-and-hold returns in the 1968–1990 period without involving greater fundamental risk than a strategy of buying growth stocks.

3.1.5 *Valuation Based on Comparables*

The most common application of the P/E approach to valuation is to estimate the value of a company's stock by applying a benchmark multiple to the company's actual or forecasted earnings. An essentially equivalent approach is to compare a stock's actual price multiple with a benchmark value of the multiple. This section explores these comparisons for P/Es. Using any multiple in the method of comparables involves the following steps:

- Select and calculate the price multiple that will be used in the comparison.
- Select the comparison asset or assets and calculate the value of the multiple for the comparison asset(s). For a group of comparison assets, calculate a median or mean value of the multiple for the assets. The result in either case is the **benchmark value of the multiple**.
- Use the benchmark value of the multiple, possibly subjectively adjusted for differences in fundamentals, to estimate the value of a company's stock. (Equivalently, compare the subject stock's actual multiple with the benchmark value.)
- When feasible, assess whether differences between the estimated value of the company's stock and the current price of the company's stock are explained by differences in the fundamental determinants of the price multiple and modify conclusions about relative valuation accordingly. (An essentially equivalent approach is to assess whether differences between a company's actual multiple and the benchmark value of the multiple can be explained by differences in fundamentals.)

These bullet points provide the structure for this reading's presentation of the method of comparables. The first price multiple that will be used in the comparison is the P/E. Practitioners' choices for the comparison assets and the benchmark value of the P/E derived from these assets include the following:

- the average or median value of the P/E for the company's peer group of companies within an industry, including an average past value of the P/E for the stock relative to this peer group;
- the average or median value of the P/E for the company's industry or sector, including an average past value of the P/E for the stock relative to the industry or sector;
- the P/E for a representative equity index, including an average past value of the P/E for the stock relative to the equity index; and
- an average past value of the P/E for the stock.

To illustrate the first bullet point, the company's P/E (say, 15) may be compared to the median P/E for the peer companies currently (say, 10), or the ratio 15/10 = 1.5 may be compared to its average past value. The P/E of the most closely matched individual stock can also be used as a benchmark; because of averaging, however, using a group of stocks or an equity index is typically expected to generate less valuation error than using a single stock. In Section 3.3, we illustrate a comparison with a single closely matched individual stock.

Economists and investment analysts have long attempted to group companies by similarities and differences in their business operations. A country's economy overall is typically grouped most broadly into **economic sectors** or large industry groupings. These groupings differ depending on the source of the financial information, and an analyst should be aware of differences among data sources. Classifications often attempt to group companies by what they supply (e.g., energy, consumer goods), by demand characteristics (e.g., consumer discretionary), or by financial market or economic "theme" (e.g., consumer cyclical, consumer noncyclical).

Two classification systems that are widely used in equity analysis are the Global Industry Classification System (GICS) sponsored by Standard & Poor's and MSCI, and the Industrial Classification Benchmark (ICB) originally developed by Dow Jones and FTSE, which in 2006 replaced the FTSE Global Classification System. Many other classification schemes developed by commercial and governmental organizations and by academics are also in use.[22]

The GICS structure assigns each company to one of 154 subindustries, an industry (68 in total), an industry group (24 in total), and an economic sector (10 in total: consumer discretionary, consumer staples, energy, financials, health care, industrials, information technology, materials, telecommunication services, and utilities).[23] The assignment is made by a judgment as to the company's principal business activity, which is based primarily on sales. Because a company is classified on the basis of one business activity, a given company appears in just one group at each level of the classification. A classification ("industrial conglomerates") is available under the capital goods sector of industrials for companies that cannot be assigned to a principal business activity.

The ICB, like GICS, has four levels, but the terminology of ICB uses "sector" and "industry" in nearly opposite senses. At the bottom of the four levels are 114 subsectors, each of which belongs to one of 41 sectors; each sector belongs to one of 19 supersectors; and each supersector belongs to one of 10 industries at the highest level of classification.[24] The industries are oil and gas, basic materials, industrials, consumer goods, health care, consumer services, telecommunications, utilities, financials, and technology.[25]

For these classification systems, analysts often choose the narrowest grouping (i.e., subindustry for GICS and subsector for ICB) as an appropriate starting point for comparison asset identification. For example, the company Continental AG (Xetra Level 1: 543900, also traded as an ADR; OTC Pink: CTTAY), an auto parts manufacturer headquartered in Hanover, Germany, appears in the ICB subsector "tires." This subsector also includes Michelin (NYSE Euronext Paris: ML), Goodyear Tire & Rubber Company (NYSE: GT), Bridgestone (Tokyo Stock Exchange: 5108; also traded as an ADR with ticker BRDCY), and Cooper Tire and Rubber (NYSE: CTB). One level up, the sector automobiles and parts includes, in addition to tire companies, such disparate companies as automobile manufacturers and their nontire parts suppliers. To narrow the list of comparables in the subsector, an analyst might use information on company size (as measured by revenue or market value of equity) and information on the specific markets served.

Analysts should be aware that, although different organizations often group companies in a broadly similar fashion, sometimes they differ sharply. For example, Reuters Company Research places GATX Corporation (NYSE: GMT), which has several distinct business units, under miscellaneous transportation (within a transportation sector),

---

22 The most notable academic industrial classification was developed by Fama and French. Bhojraj, Lee, and Oler (2003) and Chan, Lakonishok, and Swaminathan (2007) provide some information of the relative performance of these various systems in an investments context.

23 The numbers in the groups are current as of 8 August 2008; changes are made to the classifications from time to time. See www.gics.standardandpoors.com for details.

24 The numbers in the groups are current as of 8 August 2008; changes are made to the classification from time to time. See www.icbenchmark.com for details.

25 One of the chief contrasts between the ICB and GICS systems is that the ICB makes a distinction between goods and services (in GICS, both consumer discretionary and consumer staples include both goods and services components). The two systems also have some similarities that they do not share with other systems—for example, 10 groups at the highest level and an avoidance of a cyclical versus noncyclical distinction in their nomenclature.

GICS places it under trading companies and distributors (within its industrials sector), and Yahoo! Finance places it under rental and leasing services (in the services sector); the lists of peer companies or competitors given by each are, as a result, quite distinct.

The comparable companies—selected by using any of the choices described previously—provide the basis for calculating a benchmark value of the multiple. In analyzing differences between the subject company's multiple and the benchmark value of the multiple, financial ratio analysis serves as a useful tool. Financial ratios can point out:

- a company's ability to meet short-term financial obligations (liquidity ratios);
- the efficiency with which assets are being used to generate sales (asset turnover ratios);
- the use of debt in financing the business (leverage ratios);
- the degree to which fixed charges, such as interest on debt, are being met by earnings or cash flow (coverage ratios); and
- profitability (profitability ratios).

With this understanding of terms in hand, we turn to using the method of comparables. We begin with cross-sectional P/Es derived from industry peer groups and move to P/Es derived from comparison assets that are progressively less closely matched to the stock. We then turn to using historical P/Es—that is, P/Es derived from the company's own history. Finally, we sketch how both fundamentals- and comparables-driven models for P/Es can be used to calculate the terminal value in a multistage DCF valuation.

3.1.5.1 Peer-Company Multiples   Companies operating in the same industry as the subject company (i.e., its peer group) are frequently used as comparison assets. The advantage of using a peer group is that the constituent companies are typically similar in their business mix to the company being analyzed. This approach is consistent with the idea underlying the method of comparables—that similar assets should sell at similar prices. The subject stock's P/E is compared with the median or mean P/E for the peer group to arrive at a relative valuation. Equivalently, multiplying the benchmark P/E by the company's EPS provides an estimate of the stock's value that can be compared with the stock's market price. The value estimated in this way represents an estimate of intrinsic value if the comparison assets are efficiently (fairly) priced.

In practice, analysts often find that the stock being valued has some significant differences from the median or mean fundamental characteristics of the comparison assets. In applying the method of comparables, analysts usually attempt to judge whether differences from the benchmark value of the multiple can be explained by differences in the fundamental factors believed to influence the multiple. The following relationships for P/E hold, all else being equal:

- If the subject stock has higher-than-average (or higher-than-median) expected earnings growth, a higher P/E than the benchmark P/E is justified.
- If the subject stock has higher-than-average (or higher-than-median) risk (operating or financial), a lower P/E than the benchmark P/E is justified.

Another perspective on these two points is that for a group of stocks with comparable relative valuations, the stock with the greatest expected growth rate (or the lowest risk) is, all else equal, the most attractively valued. Example 10 illustrates a simple comparison of a company with its peer group.

EXAMPLE 10

A Simple Peer-Group Comparison

As a telecommunications industry analyst at a brokerage firm, you are valuing Verizon Communications, Inc. (NYSE: VZ), one of the world's leading telecommunications companies. The valuation metric that you have selected is the trailing P/E. You are evaluating the P/E using the median trailing P/E of peer-group companies as the benchmark value. According to GICS, VZ is in the telecommunications services sector and, within it, the integrated telecommunication services subindustry. Exhibit 5 presents the relevant data. (Note that although BCE Inc. is a Canadian company, it is classified in this peer group.)

Exhibit 5	Trailing P/Es of Telecommunications Services Companies (as of 11 September 2013)
Company	**Trailing P/E**
AT&T (NYSE: T)	25.73
BCE Inc. (NYSE: BCE; TSX: BCE)	14.49
Centurytel (NYSE: CTL)	18.86
Equinix (NASDAQGS: EQIX)	131.28
Frontier Communications Corp. (NASDAQ GS: FTR)	43.30
Verizon Communications (NYSE: VZ)	86.06
Windstream Corp. (NYSE: WIN)	36.91
Mean	50.95
Median	36.91

Source: Thomson Financial.

Based on the data in Exhibit 5, address the following:

1 Given the definition of the benchmark stated above, determine the most appropriate benchmark value of the P/E for VZ.

2 State whether VZ is relatively fairly valued, relatively overvalued, or relatively undervalued, assuming no differences in fundamentals among the peer group companies. Justify your answer.

3 Identify the stocks in this group of telecommunication companies that appear to be relatively undervalued when the median trailing P/E is used as a benchmark. Explain what further analysis might be appropriate to confirm your answer.

Solution to 1:

As stated earlier, the use of median values mitigates the effect of outliers on the valuation conclusion. In this instance, the P/E for EQIX is clearly an outlier. Therefore, the median trailing P/E for the group, 36.91, is more appropriate than the mean trailing P/E of 50.95 for use as the benchmark value of the P/E. *Note:* When a group includes an odd number of companies, as here, the median value will be the middle value when the values are ranked (in either ascending or descending order). When the group includes an even number of companies, the median value will be the average of the two middle values.

Solution to 2:

If you assume no differences in fundamentals among the peer group companies, VZ appears to be overvalued because its P/E is greater than the median P/E of 36.91.

Solution to 3:

T, BCE, and CTL appear to be undervalued relative to their peers because their trailing P/Es are lower than the median P/E. WIN appears to be relatively fairly valued because its P/E equals the median P/E. VZ, FTR, and EQIX appear to be overvalued.

To confirm this valuation conclusion, you should look at other metrics. One issue for this particular industry is that earnings may differ significantly from cash flow. These companies invest considerable amounts of money to build out their networks—whether it be landlines or increasing bandwidth capacity for mobile users. Because telecommunication service providers are frequently required to take large non-cash charges on their infrastructure, reported earnings are typically very volatile and frequently much lower than cash flow.

A metric that appears to address the impact of earnings growth on P/E is the P/E-to-growth (**PEG**) ratio. PEG is calculated as the stock's P/E divided by the expected earnings growth rate (in percentage terms). The ratio, in effect, is a calculation of a stock's P/E per percentage point of expected growth. Stocks with lower PEGs are more attractive than stocks with higher PEGs, all else being equal. Some consider that a PEG ratio less than 1 is an indicator of an attractive value level. PEG is useful but must be used with care for several reasons:

- PEG assumes a linear relationship between P/E and growth. The model for P/E in terms of the DDM shows that, in theory, the relationship is not linear.

- PEG does not factor in differences in risk, an important determinant of P/E.

- PEG does not account for differences in the duration of growth. For example, dividing P/Es by short-term (five-year) growth forecasts may not capture differences in long-term growth prospects.

The way in which fundamentals can add insight to comparables is illustrated in Example 11.

EXAMPLE 11

A Peer-Group Comparison Modified by Fundamentals

Continuing with the valuation of telecommunication service providers, you gather information on selected fundamentals related to risk (beta), profitability (five-year earnings growth forecast), and valuation (trailing and forward P/Es).[26] These data are reported in Exhibit 6, which lists companies in order of descending earnings growth forecast. The use of forward P/Es recognizes that differences in trailing P/Es could be the result of transitory effects on earnings.

---

[26] In comparables work, analysts may also use other measures of risk, such as financial leverage, and of profitability, such as return on assets.

Exhibit 6	Valuation Data for Telecommunications Services Companies (as of 11 September 2013)				
Company	Trailing P/E	Forward P/E	Five-Year EPS Growth Forecast	Forward PEG	Beta
EQIX	131.28	43.97	25.30%	1.74	1.26
FTR	43.30	18.83	21.80	0.86	0.78
VZ	86.06	14.40	10.22	1.41	0.38
T	25.73	12.62	6.46	1.95	0.40
BCE	14.49	14.12	3.00	4.71	0.76
CTL	18.86	12.04	1.35	8.92	0.89
WIN	36.91	18.66	−11.55	NM	0.89
Mean	50.95	19.23	8.08%	3.27	0.77
Median	36.91	14.40	6.46	1.85	0.78

Notes: NM = not meaningful. The five-year EPS growth forecast for WIN is a negative number which would result in a negative PEG.
Source: www.finviz.com.

Based on the data in Exhibit 6, answer the following questions:

1   In Example 10, Part 3, T, BCE, and CTL were identified as possibly relatively undervalued compared with the peer group as a whole, and WIN was identified as relatively fairly valued. What does the additional information in Exhibit 6 relating to profitability and risk suggest about the relative valuation of these stocks?

2   T has a consensus year-ahead EPS forecast of $2.69. Suppose the median P/E of 14.40 for the peer group is subjectively adjusted upward to 15.00 to reflect T's superior profitability and below-average risk. Estimate T's intrinsic value.

3   T's current market price is $33.99. State whether T appears to be fairly valued, overvalued, or undervalued when compared with the intrinsic value estimated in answer to Part 2 above.

Solution to 1:

According to the profitability data and PEG given in Exhibit 6, EQIX, FTR, and VZ appear to represent the greatest undervaluation. Of the three stocks, FTR has:

■   the second highest five-year consensus earnings growth forecast, and
■   the lowest PEG based on forward P/E.

Of the three stocks, EQIX has the highest beta by far, which is consistent with studies that have shown that growth stocks tend to have higher beta values than those of value stocks. Based on the high trailing and forward P/E ratios, it appears that investors in EQIX have high expectations concerning the company's future earnings potential. However, the high beta value is likely reflective of the uncertainty surrounding the earnings forecast and the possibility that actual future earnings may be less than expected.

Some analysts consider a PEG ratio below 1 to be a signal of undervaluation implying that FTR is attractive when judged by this ratio. However, one limitation of the PEG ratio is that it does not account for the overall growth rate of an industry or the economy as a whole. Hence, it is typically a good idea for an investor to compare a stock's PEG ratio to an average or median PEG ratio for the industry, as well as the entire market, to get an accurate sense of how fairly valued a stock is. The PEG ratio of FTR is not only below 1, but it is significantly lower than the PEG ratios for the other telecommunication companies—further indicating that FTR is relatively undervalued.

Solution to 2:

$2.69 × 15.0 = $40.35 is an estimate of intrinsic value.

Solution to 3:

Because the estimated intrinsic value of $40.35 is greater than the current market price of $33.99, T appears to be undervalued by the market on an absolute basis.

In Problem 2 of the above example, a peer median P/E of 14.40 was subjectively adjusted upward to 15.00. Depending on the context, the justification for using the specific value of 15.00 as the relevant benchmark rather than some other value, such as 13.75, 14.80, or 15.40, could be raised. To avoid that issue, one way to express the analysis and results would be as follows: Given its similar growth and lower risk, T should trade at a premium to the median P/E (14.40) of its peer group.

Analysts frequently compare a stock's multiple with the median or mean value of the multiple for larger sets of assets than a company's peer group. The next sections examine comparisons with these larger groups.

3.1.5.2 Industry and Sector Multiples Median or mean P/Es for industries and for economic sectors are frequently used in relative valuations. Although median P/Es have the advantage that they are insensitive to outliers, some databases report only mean values of multiples for industries.

The mechanics of using industry multiples are identical to those used for peer-group comparisons. Taking account of relevant fundamental information, we compare a stock's multiple with the median or mean multiple for the company's industry.

Using industry and sector data can help an analyst explore whether the peer-group comparison assets are themselves appropriately priced. Comparisons with broader segments of the economy can potentially provide insight about whether the relative valuation based on comparables accurately reflects intrinsic value. For example, Value Line reports a relative P/E that is calculated as the stock's current P/E divided by the median P/E of all issues under Value Line review. The less closely matched the stock is to the comparison assets, the more dissimilarities are likely to be present to complicate the analyst's interpretation of the data. Arguably, however, the larger the number of comparison assets, the more likely that mispricing of individual assets cancel out. In some cases, we may be able to draw inferences about an industry or sector overall. For example, during the 1998–2000 internet bubble, comparisons of an individual internet stock's value with the overall market would have been more likely to point to overvaluation than comparisons of relative valuation only among internet stocks.

3.1.5.3 Overall Market Multiple Although the logic of the comparables approach suggests the use of industry and peer companies as comparison assets, equity market indices also have been used as comparison assets. The mechanics of using the method of comparables do not change in such an approach, although the user should be cognizant of any size differences between the subject stock and the stocks in the selected index.

The question of whether the overall market is fairly priced has captured analyst interest throughout the entire history of investing. We mentioned one approach to market valuation (using a DDM) in an earlier reading.

Example 12 shows a valuation comparison to the broad equity market on the basis of P/E.

EXAMPLE 12

Valuation Relative to the Market

You are analyzing three large-cap US stock issues with approximately equal earnings growth prospects and risk. As one step in your analysis, you have decided to check valuations relative to the S&P 500 Composite Index. Exhibit 7 provides the data.

Exhibit 7	Comparison with an Index Multiple (Prices and EPS in US Dollars; as of 31 March 2013)			
Measure	**Stock A**	**Stock B**	**Stock C**	**S&P 500**
Current price	23	50	80	1569.19
P/E	12.5	25.5	12.5	17.9
Five-year average P/E (as percent of S&P 500 P/E)	80	120	105	

Source: www.us.spindices.com for S&P 500 data.

Based only on the data in Exhibit 7, address the following:

1 Explain which stock appears relatively undervalued when compared with the S&P 500.

2 State the assumption underlying the use of five-year average P/E comparisons.

Solution to 1:

Stock C appears to be undervalued when compared to the S&P 500. Stock A and Stock C are both trading at a P/E of 12.5 relative to trailing earnings, versus a P/E of 17.9 for the S&P 500. But the last row of Exhibit 7 indicates that Stock A has historically traded at a P/E reflecting a 20 percent discount to the S&P 500 (which, based on the current level of the S&P 500, would imply a P/E of 0.8 × 17.9 = 14.3). In contrast, Stock C has usually traded at a premium to the S&P 500 P/E but now trades at a discount to it. Stock B is trading at a high P/E, even higher than its historical relationship to the S&P 500's P/E (1.2 × 17.9 = 21.5).

Solution to 2:

Using historical relative-value information in investment decisions relies on an assumption of stable underlying economic relationships (that is, that the past is relevant for the future).

Because many equity indices are market-capitalization weighted, financial databases often report the average market P/E with the individual P/Es weighted by the company's market capitalization. As a consequence, the largest constituent stocks heavily influence the calculated P/E. If P/Es differ systematically by market capitalization, however, differences in a company's P/E multiple from the index's multiple may be explained by that effect. Therefore, particularly for stocks in the middle-cap range, the analyst should favor using the median P/E for the index as the benchmark value of the multiple.

As with other comparison assets, the analyst may be interested in whether the equity index itself is efficiently priced. A common comparison is the index's P/E in relation to historical values. Siegel (2002) noted that P/Es in 2001 were more than twice as high as the average P/E for US stocks over a 130-year period (1871–2001) of 14.5. Potential justifications for a higher-than-average P/E include lower-than-average interest rates and/or higher-than-average expected growth rates. An alternative hypothesis in a situation such as that noted by Siegel is that the market as a whole is overvalued (and in 2002 a sharp downturn in US equities did occur) or, alternatively, that earnings are abnormally low.

The time frame for comparing average multiples is important. For example, at the end of the second quarter of 2008, the P/E for the S&P 500, based on 2008 earnings estimates, was 17.6. That value, although higher than the 15.8 historical average since 1935, fell below the historical average for the previous 5-, 10-, and 20-year time periods, when the P/E ranged between 20 and 26. The use of past data relies on the key assumption that the past (sometimes the distant past) is relevant for the future.

We end this section with an introduction to valuation of the equity market itself on the basis of P/E. A well-known comparison is the earnings yield (the E/P) on a group of stocks and the interest yield on a bond. The so-called Fed Model, based on a paper written by three analysts at the US Federal Reserve, predicts the return on the S&P 500 on the basis of the relationship between forecasted earnings yields and yields on bonds (Lander, Orphanides, and Douvogiannis 1997). Example 13 illustrates the Fed Model.

EXAMPLE 13

The Fed Model

One of the main drivers of P/E for the market as a whole is the level of interest rates. The inverse relationship between value and interest rates can be seen from the expression of P/E in terms of fundamentals, because the risk-free rate is one component of the required rate of return that is inversely related to value. The Fed Model relates the earnings yield on the S&P 500 to the yield to maturity on 10-year US Treasury bonds. As we have defined it, the earnings yield (E/P) is the inverse of the P/E; the Fed Model uses expected earnings for the next 12 months in calculating the ratio.

Based on the premise that the two yields should be closely linked, on average, the trading rule based on the Fed Model considers the stock market to be overvalued when the market's current earnings yield is less than the 10-year Treasury bond (T-bond) yield. The intuition is that when risk-free T-bonds offer a yield that is higher than stocks—which are a riskier investment—stocks are an unattractive investment.

According to the model, the justified or fair-value P/E for the S&P 500 is the reciprocal of the 10-year T-bond yield. As of 11 September 2013, according to the model, with a 10-year T-bond yielding 2.93 percent, the justified P/E on the S&P 500 was 1/0.0293 = 34.1. The forward P/E based on 2014 reported earnings estimates for the S&P 500 as of same date was 16.1.

We previously presented an expression for the justified P/E in terms of the Gordon growth model. That expression indicates that the expected growth rate in dividends or earnings is a variable that enters into the intrinsic value of a stock (or an index of stocks). A concern in considering the Fed Model is that this variable is lacking in the model.[27] Example 14 presents a valuation model for the equity market that incorporates the expected growth rate in earnings.

EXAMPLE 14

The Yardeni Model

Yardeni (2000) developed a model that incorporates the expected growth rate in earnings—a variable that is missing in the Fed Model.[28] Yardeni's model is

$$\text{CEY} = \text{CBY} - b \times \text{LTEG} + \text{Residual}$$

where CEY is the current earnings yield on the market index, CBY is the current Moody's Investors Service A-rated corporate bond yield, and LTEG is the consensus five-year earnings growth rate forecast for the market index. The coefficient b measures the weight the market gives to five-year earnings projections. (Recall that the expression for P/E in terms of the Gordon growth model is based on the long-term sustainable growth rate and that five-year forecasts of growth may not be sustainable.) Although CBY incorporates a default risk premium relative to T-bonds, it does not incorporate an equity risk premium per se. For example, in the bond yield plus risk premium model for the cost of equity, an analyst typically adds 300–400 basis points to a corporate bond yield.

Yardeni found that, prior to publication of the model in 2000, the coefficient b had averaged 0.10. In recent years, he has reported valuations based on growth weights of 0.10, 0.20, and 0.25. Noting that CEY is E/P and taking the inverse of both sides of this equation, Yardeni obtained the following expression for the justified P/E on the market:

$$\frac{P}{E} = \frac{1}{\text{CBY} - b \times \text{LTEG}}$$

Consistent with valuation theory, in Yardeni's model, higher current corporate bond yields imply a lower justified P/E and higher expected long-term growth results in a higher justified P/E.

Critics of the Fed Model point out that it ignores the equity risk premium (Stimes and Wilcox 2011). The model also inadequately reflects the effects of inflation and incorrectly incorporates the differential effects of inflation on earnings and interest payments (e.g., Siegel 2002). Some empirical evidence has shown that prediction of future returns based on simple P/E outperforms prediction based on the Fed Model's differential with bond yields (for the US market, see Arnott and Asness 2003; for nine other markets, see Aubert and Giot 2007).

Another drawback to the Fed Model is that the relationship between interest rates and earnings yields is not a linear one. This drawback is most noticeable at low interest rates; Example 13 provided an example of this limitation of the model. Furthermore, small changes in interest rates and/or corporate profits can significantly alter the justified P/E predicted by the model. Overall, an analyst should look to the

---

27 The earnings yield is, in fact, the expected rate of return on a no-growth stock (under the assumption that price equals value). With PVGO the present value of growth opportunities and setting price equal to value, we obtain $P_0 = E_1/r + \text{PVGO}$. Setting the present value of growth opportunities equal to zero and rearranging, we obtain $r = E_1/P_0$.

28 This model is presented as one example of more-complex models than the Fed Model. Economic analysts at many investment firms have their own models that incorporate growth and historical relationships of market indices with government bonds.

Fed Model only as one tool for calibrating the overall value of the stock market and should avoid overreliance on the model as a predictive method, particularly in periods of low inflation and low interest rates.

3.1.5.4 Own Historical P/E As an alternative to comparing a stock's valuation with that of other stocks, one traditional approach uses past values of the stock's own P/E as a basis for comparison. Underlying this approach is the idea that a stock's P/E may regress to historical average levels.

An analyst can obtain a benchmark value in a variety of ways with this approach. Value Line reports as a "P/E median" a rounded average of four middle values of a stock's average annual P/E for the previous 10 years. The five-year average trailing P/E is another reasonable metric. In general, trailing P/Es are more commonly used than forward P/Es in such computations. In addition to "higher" and "lower" comparisons with this benchmark, justified price based on this approach may be calculated as follows:

$$\text{Justified price} = (\text{Benchmark value of own historical P/Es}) \times (\text{Most recent EPS}) \tag{3}$$

Normalized EPS replaces most recent EPS in this equation when EPS is negative and whenever otherwise appropriate.

Example 15 illustrates the use of past values of the stock's own P/E as a basis for reaching a valuation conclusion.

EXAMPLE 15

Valuation Relative to Own Historical P/Es

As of mid-September 2013, you are valuing Honda Motor Company (TSE: 7267; NYSE ADR: HMC), among the market leaders in Japan's auto manufacturing industry. You are applying the method of comparables using HMC's five-year average P/E as the benchmark value of the multiple. Exhibit 8 presents the data.

Exhibit 8	Historical P/Es for HMC					
2012	**2011**	**2010**	**2009**	**2008**	**Mean**	**Median**
15.8	23.1	10.0	19.8	35.8	20.9	19.8

Sources: The Value Line Investment Survey for average annual P/Es; calculations for mean and median P/Es.

---

1 State a benchmark value for Honda's P/E.
2 Given EPS for fiscal year 2013 (ended 31 March) of ¥203.71, calculate and interpret a justified price for Honda.
3 Compare the justified price with the stock's recent price of ¥3,815.

Solution to 1:

From Exhibit 8, the benchmark value based on the median P/E value is 19.8 and based on the mean P/E value is 20.9.

Solution to 2:

The calculation is 19.8 × ¥203.71 = ¥4,033 when the median-based benchmark P/E is used and 20.9 × ¥203.71 = ¥4,258 when the mean-based benchmark P/E is used.

Solution to 3:

The stock's recent price is 5.4 percent (calculated as 3,815/4,033 − 1) less than the justified price of the stock based on median historical P/E but 10.4 percent (calculated as 3,815/4,258 − 1) less than the justified price of the stock based on mean historical P/Es. The stock may be undervalued but misvaluation, if present, appears slight. Reaching a conclusion from these results is complicated by the fact that the time period of the analysis reflects the effects of the financial crisis of 2007–2009. Prior to the crisis, the P/E for HMC was much lower than the mean and median values used in this analysis. In particular, history suggests that the P/E ratio of 35.8 in 2008 should be considered an outlier.

In using historical P/Es for comparisons, analysts should be alert to the impact on P/E levels of changes in a company's business mix and leverage over time. If the company's business has changed substantially within the time period being examined, the method based on a company's own past P/Es is prone to error. Shifts in the use of financial leverage may also impair comparability based on average own past P/E.

Changes in the interest rate environment and economic fundamentals over different time periods can be another limitation to using an average past value of P/E for a stock as a benchmark. A specific caution is that inflation can distort the economic meaning of reported earnings. Consequently, if the inflationary environments reflected in current P/E and average own past P/E are different, a comparison between the two P/Es may be misleading. Changes in a company's ability to pass through cost inflation to higher prices over time may also affect the reliability of such comparisons, as illustrated in Example 16 in the next section.

3.1.6 *P/Es in Cross-Country Comparisons*

When comparing the P/Es of companies in different countries, the analyst should be aware of the following effects that may influence the comparison:

- the effect on EPS of differences in accounting standards. Comparisons (without analyst adjustments) among companies preparing financial statements based on different accounting standards may be distorted. Such distortions may occur when, for example, the accounting standards differ as to permissible recognition of revenues, expenses, or gains.

- the effect on market wide benchmarks of differences in their macroeconomic contexts. Differences in macroeconomic contexts may distort comparisons of benchmark P/E levels among companies operating in different markets.

A specific case of the second bullet point is differences in inflation rates and in the ability of companies to pass through inflation in their costs in the form of higher prices to their customers. For two companies with the same pass-through ability, the company operating in the environment with higher inflation will have a lower justified P/E; if the inflation rates are equal but pass-through rates differ, the justified P/E should be lower for the company with the lower pass-through rate. Example 16 provides analysis in support of these conclusions.

EXAMPLE 16

An Analysis of P/Es and Inflation[29]

Assume a company with no real earnings growth, such that its earnings growth can result only from inflation, will pay out all its earnings as dividends. Based on the Gordon (constant growth) DDM, the value of a share is:

$$P_0 = \frac{E_0(1 + I)}{r - I}$$

where:

P_0 = current price, which is substituted for the intrinsic value, V_0, for purposes of analyzing a justified P/E

E_0 = current EPS, which is substituted for current dividends per share, D_0, because the assumption in this example is that all earnings are paid out as dividends

I = rate of inflation, which is substituted for expected growth, g, because of the assumption in this example that the company's only growth is from inflation

r = required return

Suppose the company has the ability to pass on some or all inflation to its customers and let λ represent the percentage of inflation in costs that the company can pass through to revenue. The company's earnings growth may then be expressed as λI and the equation becomes

$$P_0 = \frac{E_0(1 + \lambda I)}{r - \lambda I} = \frac{E_1}{r - \lambda I}$$

Now, introduce a real rate of return, defined here as r minus I and represented as ρ. The value of a share and the justified forward P/E can now be expressed, respectively, as follows:[30]

$$P_0 = \frac{E_1}{\rho + (1 - \lambda)I}$$

and

$$\frac{P_0}{E_1} = \frac{1}{\rho + (1 - \lambda)I}$$

If a company can pass through all inflation, so that $\lambda = 1$ (100 percent), then the P/E is equal to $1/\rho$. But if the company can pass through no inflation, so that $\lambda = 0$, then the P/E is equal to $1/(\rho + I)$—that is, $1/r$.

You are analyzing two companies, Company M and Company P. The real rate of return required on the shares of Company M and Company P is 3 percent per year. Using the analytic framework provided, address the following:

1 Suppose both Company M and Company P can pass through 75 percent of cost increases. Cost inflation is 6 percent for Company M but only 2 percent for Company P.

   A Estimate the justified P/E for each company.

   B Interpret your answer to Part A.

---

29 This example follows the analysis of Solnik and McLeavey (2004, pp. 289–290).

30 The denominator of this equation is derived from the previous equation as follows: $r - \lambda I = r - I + I - I\lambda = (r - I) + (1 - \lambda)I = \rho + (1 - \lambda)I$.

2 Suppose both Company M and Company P face 6 percent a year inflation. Company M can pass through 90 percent of cost increases, but Company P can pass through only 70 percent.

  A Estimate the justified P/E for each company.

  B Interpret your answer to Part A.

Solution to 1:

A For Company M, $\dfrac{1}{0.03 + (1 - 0.75)0.06} = 22.2$

  For Company P, $\dfrac{1}{0.03 + (1 - 0.75)0.02} = 28.6$

B With less than 100 percent cost pass-through, the justified P/E is inversely related to the inflation rate.

Solution to 2:

A For Company M, $\dfrac{1}{0.03 + (1 - 0.90)0.06} = 27.8$

  For Company P, $\dfrac{1}{0.03 + (1 - 0.70)0.06} = 20.8$

B For equal inflation rates, the company with the higher pass-through rate has a higher justified P/E.

Example 16 illustrates that with less than 100 percent cost pass-through, the justified P/E is inversely related to the inflation rate (with complete cost pass-through, the justified P/E should not be affected by inflation). The higher the inflation rate, the greater the impact of incomplete cost pass-through on P/E. From Example 16, one can also infer that the higher the inflation rate, the more serious the effect on justified P/E of a pass-through rate that is less than 100 percent.

3.1.7 Using P/Es to Obtain Terminal Value in Multistage Dividend Discount Models

In using a DDM to value a stock, whether applying a multistage model or modeling within a spreadsheet (forecasting specific cash flows individually up to some horizon), estimation of the terminal value of the stock is important. The key condition that must be satisfied is that terminal value reflects earnings growth that the company can sustain in the long run. Analysts frequently use price multiples—in particular, P/Es and P/Bs—to estimate terminal value. We can call such multiples **terminal price multiples**. Choices for the terminal multiple, with a terminal P/E multiple used as the example, include the following:

Terminal Price Multiple Based on Fundamentals   As illustrated earlier, analysts can restate the Gordon growth model as a multiple by, for example, dividing both sides of the model by EPS. For terminal P/E multiples, dividing both sides of the Gordon growth model by EPS at time n, where n is the point in time at which the final stage begins (i.e., E_n), gives a trailing terminal price multiple; dividing both sides by EPS at time $n + 1$ (i.e., E_{n+1}) gives a leading terminal price multiple. Of course, an analyst can use the Gordon growth model to estimate terminal value and need not go through the process of deriving a terminal price multiple and then multiplying by the same value of the fundamental to estimate terminal value. Because of their familiarity, however, multiples may be useful in communicating an estimate of terminal value.

Terminal Price Multiple Based on Comparables   Analysts have used various choices for the benchmark value, including:

- median industry P/E;
- average industry P/E; and
- average of own past P/Es.

Having selected a terminal multiple, the expression for terminal value when using a terminal P/E multiple is

$$V_n = \text{Benchmark value of trailing terminal P/E} \times E_n$$

or

$$V_n = \text{Benchmark value of forward terminal P/E} \times E_{n+1}$$

where

V_n = terminal value at time n

The use of a comparables approach has the strength that it is entirely grounded in market data. In contrast, the Gordon growth model calls for specific estimates (the required rate of return, the dividend payout ratio, and the expected mature growth rate), and the model's output is very sensitive to changes in those estimates. A possible disadvantage to the comparables approach is that when the benchmark value reflects mispricing (over- or undervaluation), so will the estimate of terminal value. Example 17 illustrates the use of P/Es and the Gordon growth model to estimate terminal value.

EXAMPLE 17

Using P/Es and the Gordon Growth Model to Value the Mature Growth Phase

As an energy analyst, you are valuing the stock of an oil exploration company. You have projected earnings and dividends three years out (to $t = 3$), and you have gathered the following data and estimates:

- Required rate of return = 0.10.
- Average dividend payout rate for mature companies in the market = 0.45.
- Industry average ROE = 0.13.
- E_3 = $3.00.
- Industry average P/E = 14.3.

On the basis of this information, carry out the following:

1   Calculate terminal value based on comparables, using your estimated industry average P/E as the benchmark.

2   Contrast your answer in Part 1 to an estimate of terminal value using the Gordon growth model.

Solution to 1:

V_n = Benchmark value of P/E $\times E_n$ = 14.3 $\times$ $3.00 = $42.90.

Solution to 2:

Recall that the Gordon growth model expresses intrinsic value, V, as the present value of dividends divided by the required rate of return, r, minus the growth rate, g: $V_0 = D_0(1 + g)/(r - g)$. Here we are estimating terminal value, so the relevant expression is $V_n = D_n(1 + g)/(r - g)$. You would estimate that the dividend at $t =$

3 will equal earnings in Year 3 of $3.00 times the average payout ratio of 0.45, or $D_n = \$3.00 \times 0.45 = \$1.35$. Recall also the sustainable growth rate expression—that is, $g = b \times \text{ROE}$, where b is the retention rate and equivalent to 1 minus the dividend payout ratio. In this example, $b = (1 - 0.45) = 0.55$, and you can use $\text{ROE} = 0.13$ (the industry average). Therefore, $g = b \times \text{ROE} = 0.55 \times 0.13 = 0.0715$. Given the required rate of return of 0.10, you obtain the estimate $V_n = (\$1.35)$ $(1 + 0.0715)/(0.10 - 0.0715) = \$50.76$. In this example, therefore, the Gordon growth model estimate of terminal value is 18.3 percent higher than the estimate based on comparables calculated in Part 1 (i.e., $0.1832 = \$50.76/\$42.90 - 1$).

3.2 Price to Book Value

The ratio of market price per share to book value per share (P/B), like P/E, has a long history of use in valuation practice (as discussed in Graham and Dodd 1934). According to the 2012 BofA *Merrill Lynch Institutional Factor Survey*, 53 percent of respondents considered P/B when making investment decisions.

In the P/E multiple, the measure of value (EPS) in the denominator is a flow variable relating to the income statement. In contrast, the measure of value in the P/B's denominator (book value per share) is a stock or level variable coming from the balance sheet. (*Book* refers to the fact that the measurement of value comes from accounting records or books, in contrast to market value.) Intuitively, therefore, we note that book value per share attempts to represent, on a per-share basis, the investment that common shareholders have made in the company. To define book value per share more precisely, we first find **shareholders' equity** (total assets minus total liabilities). Because our purpose is to value common stock, we subtract from shareholders' equity any value attributable to preferred stock to obtain common shareholders' equity, or the **book value of equity** (often called simply **book value**).[31] Dividing book value by the number of common stock shares outstanding, we obtain **book value per share**, the denominator in P/B.

In the balance of this section, we present the reasons analysts have offered for using P/B and possible drawbacks to its use. We then illustrate the calculation of P/B and discuss the fundamental factors that drive P/B. We end the section by showing the use of P/B based on the method of comparables.

Analysts have offered several rationales for the use of P/B; some specifically compare P/B with P/E:

- Because book value is a cumulative balance sheet amount, book value is generally positive even when EPS is zero or negative. An analyst can generally use P/B when EPS is zero or negative, whereas P/E based on a zero or negative EPS is not meaningful.

- Because book value per share is more stable than EPS, P/B may be more meaningful than P/E when EPS is abnormally high or low or is highly variable.

- As a measure of net asset value per share, book value per share has been viewed as appropriate for valuing companies composed chiefly of liquid assets, such as finance, investment, insurance, and banking institutions (Wild, Bernstein, and Subramanyam 2001, p. 233). For such companies, book values of assets may approximate market values. When information on individual corporate assets is available, analysts may adjust reported book values to market values where they differ.

---

[31] If we were to value a company as a whole, rather than value only the common stock, we would not exclude the value of preferred stock from the computation.

- Book value has also been used in the valuation of companies that are not expected to continue as a going concern (Martin 1998, p. 22).
- Differences in P/Bs may be related to differences in long-run average returns, according to empirical research.[32]

Possible drawbacks of P/Bs in practice include the following:

- Assets in addition to those recognized in financial statements may be critical operating factors. For example, in many service companies, **human capital**— the value of skills and knowledge possessed by the workforce—is more important than physical capital as an operating factor, but it is not reflected as an asset on the balance sheet. Similarly, the good reputation that a company develops by consistently providing high-quality goods and services is not reflected as an asset on the balance sheet.

- P/B may be misleading as a valuation indicator when the levels of assets used by the companies under examination differ significantly. Such differences may reflect differences in business models.

- Accounting effects on book value may compromise how useful book value is as a measure of the shareholders' investment in the company. In general, intangible assets that are generated internally (as opposed to being acquired) are not shown as assets on a company's balance sheet. For example, companies account for advertising and marketing as expenses, so the value of internally generated brands, which are created and maintained by advertising and marketing activities, do not appear as assets on a company's balance sheet under IFRS or US GAAP. Similarly, when accounting standards require that research and development (R&D) expenditures be treated as expenses, the value of internally developed patents do not appear as assets. Certain R&D expenditures can be capitalized, although rules vary among accounting standards. Accounting effects such as these may impair the comparability of P/B among companies and countries unless appropriate analyst adjustments are made.

- Book value reflects the reported value of assets and liabilities. Some assets and liabilities, such as some financial instruments, may be reported at fair value as of the balance sheet date; other assets, such as property, plant, and equipment, are generally reported at historical cost, net of accumulated depreciation, amortization, depletion, and/or impairment. It is important to examine the notes to the financial statements to identify how assets and liabilities are measured and reported. For assets measured at net historical cost, inflation and technological change can eventually result in significant divergence between the book value and the market value of assets. As a result, book value per share often does not accurately reflect the value of shareholders' investments. When comparing companies, significant differences in the average age of assets may lessen the comparability of P/Bs.

- Share repurchases or issuances may distort historical comparisons.

As an example of the effects of share repurchases, consider Colgate-Palmolive Company (NYSE: CL). As of 13 September 2013, CL's trailing P/E and P/B were, respectively, 24.84 and 36.01. Five years earlier, CL's trailing P/E and P/B were 23.55 and 15.94. In other words, the company's P/E widened by 5.5 percent (= 24.84/23.55 − 1) while its P/B widened by 125.9 percent (= 36.01/15.94 − 1). The majority of the difference in changes in these two multiples can be attributed to the substantial amount of shares that CL repurchased over those five years, as reflected by book value (i.e., total common equity) declining from $2.48 billion as of 30 June 2008 to $1.53 billion

---

32 See Bodie, Kane, and Marcus (2008) for a brief summary of the empirical research.

as of 30 June 2013. Because of those share repurchases, CL's book value declined at an annual rate of 9.2 percent. In summary, when a company repurchases shares at a price higher than the current book value per share, it lowers the overall book value per share for the company. All else being equal, the effect is to make the stock appear more expensive if the current P/B is compared to its historical values.

Example 18 illustrates another potential limitation to using P/B in valuation.

EXAMPLE 18

Differences in Business Models Reflected in Differences in P/Bs

As of late 2013, few sectors had a wider range of P/B ratios than the US banking industry. Much of these differences in P/B ratios can be attributed to differences in company-specific business models. Exhibit 9 presents P/B ratios for three major US banks as of 13 September 2013.

Exhibit 9	P/B Ratios For Selected US Banks
Entity	**P/B**
Citigroup, Inc. (NYSE: C)	0.77
Wells Fargo & Company (NYSE: WFC)	1.46
US Bancorp (NYSE: USB)	1.93

Source: S&P Capital IQ

Citigroup's low P/B versus its peers is a reflection of the troubled "one-stop shopping" business model it and some other mega-banks pursued in the 1990s. Citigroup suffered huge losses during the global financial crisis and had to be rescued in November 2008 by the US government.

Wells Fargo derives most of its revenue from loans and service fees. Its business model focuses on cross-selling multiple products and in 2012 it was responsible for originating close to a third of all US home loans. Wells Fargo is also predominantly a domestic business, whereas other large banks are much more exposed to overseas markets.

US Bancorp's relatively risk-averse business model is focused on consumer and business banking as well as trusts and payment processing. Compared with other mega-banks, US Bancorp has a much smaller presence in investment banking and capital markets. Another reason for the bank's relatively high P/B was its acquisition activity, which has helped it grow its business considerably since the economic downturn.

3.2.1 *Determining Book Value*

In this section, we illustrate how to calculate book value and how to adjust book value to improve the comparability of P/Bs among companies. To compute book value per share, we need to refer to the business's balance sheet, which has a shareholders' (or stockholders') equity section. The computation of book value is as follows:

- (Shareholders' equity) – (Total value of equity claims that are senior to common stock) = Common shareholders' equity.

- (Common shareholders' equity)/(Number of common stock shares outstanding) = Book value per share.

Possible claims senior to the claims of common stock, which would be subtracted from shareholders' equity, include the value of preferred stock and the dividends in arrears on preferred stock.[33] Example 19 illustrates the calculation.

EXAMPLE 19

Computing Book Value per Share

Headquartered in Toronto, Canada, The Toronto-Dominion Bank and its subsidiaries are collectively known as TD Bank Group (TSX: TD and NYSE: TD). With operations organized into four segments (Canadian Personal and Commercial Banking, US Personal and Commercial Banking, Wholesale Banking, and Wealth and Insurance), in 2012 TD provided financial products and services to approximately 22 million customers. Exhibit 10 presents data from the equity section of TD's consolidated balance sheets for the years 2010–2012.

Exhibit 10 Equity Data for TD Bank Group (millions of Canadian dollars)			
	31 October 2012	**31 October 2011**	**1 November 2010**
Equity			
Common shares	CAD18,691	CAD17,491	CAD15,804
Millions of shares issued and outstanding:			
2012: 918.2			
2011: 902.4			
2010: 879.7			
Preferred shares	3,395	3,395	3,395
Millions of shares issued and outstanding:			
2012: 135.8			
2011: 135.8			
2010: 135.8			
Treasury shares-common	(166)	(116)	(91)
Millions of shares held:			
2012: 2.1			
2011: 1.4			

(continued)

---

[33] Some preferred stock issues have the right to premiums (liquidation premiums) if they are liquidated. If present, these premiums should also be deducted.

Exhibit 10	**(Continued)**		
	31 October 2012	**31 October 2011**	**1 November 2010**
2010: 1.2			
Treasury shares-preferred	(1)	—	(1)
2012: nil			
2011: nil			
2010: nil			
Contributed surplus	196	212	235
Retained earnings	21,763	18,213	14,781
Accumulated and other comprehensive income	3,645	3,326	4,256
	47,523	42,521	38,379
Non-controlling interests in subsidiaries	1,477	1,483	1,493
Total equity	**CAD49,000**	**CAD44,004**	**CAD39,872**

Source: TD Bank Group 2012 annual report

1 Using the data in Exhibit 10, calculate book value per share for 2010, 2011, and 2012.

2 Given a closing price of CAD81.23 on 31 October 2012, calculate TD's 2012 P/B ratio.

Solution to 1:

Because preferred shareholders have a claim on income and assets that is senior to that of the common shareholders, total equity must be adjusted by the value of outstanding and repurchased preferred shares. The divisor is the number of common shares outstanding.

2012: Book value per share = (49,000 − 3,395 + 1)/918.2 = CAD49.67

2011: Book value per share = (44,004 − 3,395)/902.4 = CAD45.00

2010: Book value per share = (39,872 − 3,395 + 1)/879.7 = CAD41.46.

Solution to 2:

P/B = CAD81.23/CAD49.67 = 1.64

Example 19 illustrated the calculation of book value per share without any adjustments. Adjusting P/B has two purposes: 1) to make the book value per share more accurately reflect the value of shareholders' investment and 2) to make P/B more useful for making comparisons among different stocks. Some adjustments are as follows:

■ Some services and analysts report a **tangible book value per share**. Computing tangible book value per share involves subtracting reported intangible assets on the balance sheet from common shareholders' equity. The analyst should be familiar with the calculation. From the viewpoint of financial theory, however, the general exclusion of all intangibles may not be warranted. In the case of individual intangible assets, such as patents, which can be separated from the entity and sold, exclusion may not be justified. Exclusion may be appropriate, however, for goodwill from acquisitions, particularly for comparative purposes. **Goodwill** represents the excess of the purchase price of an acquisition beyond the fair value of acquired tangible assets and specifically identifiable intangible assets. Many analysts believe that goodwill does not represent an asset because it is not separable and may reflect overpayment for an acquisition.

■ Certain adjustments may be appropriate for enhancing comparability. For example, one company may use FIFO whereas a peer company uses LIFO, which in an inflationary environment will generally understate inventory values. To accurately assess the relative valuation of the two companies, the analyst should restate the book value of the company using LIFO to what it would be based on FIFO. For a more complete discussion of adjustments to balance sheet amounts, refer to readings on financial statement analysis.

■ For book value per share to most accurately reflect current values, the balance sheet should be adjusted for significant off-balance sheet assets and liabilities. An example of an off-balance sheet liability is a guarantee to pay a debt of another company in the event of that company's default. US accounting standards require companies to disclose off-balance sheet liabilities.

Example 20 illustrates adjustments an analyst might make to a financial firm's P/B to obtain an accurate firm value.

EXAMPLE 20

Adjusting Book Value

Edward Stavos is a junior analyst at a major US pension fund. Stavos is researching Barclays PLC (LSE: BARC and NYSE: BCS) for his fund's Credit Services Portfolio and is preparing background information prior to an upcoming meeting with the company. Headquartered in London, United Kingdom, Barclays is a major global financial services provider engaged in personal banking, credit cards, corporate and investment banking, and wealth and investment management with an extensive international presence in Europe, the Americas, Africa, and Asia.

Stavos is particularly interested in Barclays' P/B and how adjusting asset and liability accounts to their current fair value impacts the ratio. He gathers the condensed 2012 balance sheet (as of 31 December) and footnote data from Barclay's website as shown in Exhibit 11.

Exhibit 11	Barclays PLC 2012 Condensed Consolidated Balance Sheet and Footnote Data (£ in millions)
	2012
Assets	
Cash and balances at central banks	£86,175
Items in the course of collection from other banks	1,456
Trading portfolio assets	145,030
Financial assets designated at fair value	46,061
Derivative financial instruments	469,146
Available for sale investments	75,109
Loans and advances to banks	40,489
Loans and advances to customers	425,729

(continued)

Exhibit 11 (Continued)	
	2012
Reverse repurchase agreements and other similar secured lending	176,956
Prepayments, accrued income and other assets	4,360
Investments in associates and joint ventures	570
Property, plant and equipment	5,754
Goodwill and intangible assets	7,915
Current tax assets	252
Deferred tax assets	3,016
Retirement benefit assets	2,303
Total assets	£1,490,321
Liabilities	
Deposits from banks	77,010
Items in the course of collection due to other banks	1,573
Customer accounts	385,707
Repurchase agreements and other similar secured borrowing	217,342
Trading portfolio liabilities	44,794
Financial liabilities designated at fair value	78,280
Derivative financial instruments	462,468
Debt securities in issue	119,581
Subordinated liabilities	24,018
Accruals, deferred income and other liabilities	12,232
Provisions	2,766
Current tax liabilities	621
Deferred tax liabilities	719
Retirement benefit liabilities	253
Total liabilities	1,427,364
Shareholders' equity	
Shareholders' equity excluding non-controlling interests	53,586
Non-controlling interests	9,371
Total shareholders' equity	62,957
Total liabilities and shareholders' equity	£1,490,321

	2012	
	Carrying amount	Fair value
Excerpt from Footnotes to the Barclays Financial Statements **Financial Assets and Liabilities at Carrying Amount and Fair Value**		
Financial assets		
Loans and advances to banks	£40,489	£40,489
Loans and advances to customers:		
– Home loans	174,988	164,608
– Credit cards, unsecured and other retail lending	66,414	65,357
– Corporate loans	184,327	178,492
Reverse repurchase agreements and other similar secured lending	176,956	176,895
	£643,174	£625,841
Financial liabilities		
Deposits from banks	77,010	77,023
Customer accounts:		
– Current and demand accounts	127,819	127,819
– Savings accounts	99,875	99,875
– Other time deposits	158,013	158,008
Debt securities in issue	119,581	119,725
Repurchase agreements and other similar secured borrowing	217,342	217,342
Subordinated liabilities	24,018	23,467
	£823,658	£823,259

Source: Barclays' 2012 annual report

The 31 December 2012 share price for Barclays was £2.4239 and the diluted weighted average number of shares was 12,614 million. Stavos computes book value per share initially by dividing total shareholders' equity by the by the share count and arrives at a book value per share of £4.9910 (£62,957/12,614) and a P/B of 0.52 (£2.4239/£4.9910).

Stavos then computes tangible book value per share as £4.3636 (calculated as £62,957 minus £7,915 of goodwill and intangible assets, which is then divided by 12,614 shares). The P/B ratio based on tangible book value per share is 0.49 (£2.5975/£4.3636).

Stavos then turns to the footnotes to examine the fair value data. He notes the fair value of financial assets is £17,333 million less than their carrying amount (£643,174 – £625,841) and the fair value of financial liabilities is £399 million less than their carrying amount (£823,658 – £823,259). Including these adjustments to tangible book value results in an adjusted book value per share of £3.0211 [(£62,957 – £7,915 – £17,333 + £399)/12,614]. Stavos' adjusted P/B ratio is 0.80 (£2.4239/£3.0211).

Stavos is concerned about the wide range in his computed P/B ratios. He knows that if quoted prices are not available for financial assets and liabilities, IAS 39 allows for the use of valuation models to estimate fair value. He decides to question management regarding their use of models to value assets, liabilities, and derivatives and the sensitivity of these accounts to changes in interest rates and currency values.

An analyst should also be aware of differences in accounting standards related to how assets and liabilities are valued in financial statements. Accounting standards currently require companies to report some assets and liabilities at fair value[34] and others at historical cost (with some adjustments).

Financial assets, such as investments in marketable securities, are usually reported at fair value. Investments classified as "held to maturity" and reported on a historical cost basis are an exception. (Instead of the term "held-to-maturity," IFRS refers to this category of investments as financial assets measured at amortised cost.) Some financial liabilities also are reported at fair value.

Nonfinancial assets, such as land and equipment, are generally reported at their historical acquisition costs, and in the case of equipment, the assets are depreciated over their useful lives. The value of these assets may have increased over time, however, or the value may have decreased more than is reflected in the accumulated depreciation. When the reported amount of an asset—i.e., its carrying value—exceeds its recoverable amount, both international accounting (IFRS) and US accounting standards (GAAP) require companies to reduce the reported amount of the asset and show the reduction as an impairment loss.[35] US GAAP, however, prohibit subsequent reversal of impairment losses, whereas IFRS permit subsequent reversals. In addition, as mentioned above, IFRS allow companies to measure fixed assets using either the historical cost model or a revaluation model, under which the assets are reported at their current value. When assets are reported at fair value, P/Bs become more comparable among companies; for this reason, P/Bs are considered to be more comparable for companies with significant amounts of financial assets.

3.2.2 Valuation Based on Forecasted Fundamentals

We can use forecasts of a company's fundamentals to estimate a stock's justified P/B. For example, assuming the Gordon growth model and using the expression $g = b \times$ ROE for the sustainable growth rate, the expression for the justified P/B based on the most recent book value (B_0) is[36]

$$\frac{P_0}{B_0} = \frac{\text{ROE} - g}{r - g} \tag{4}$$

For example, if a business's ROE is 12 percent, its required rate of return is 10 percent, and its expected growth rate is 7 percent, then its justified P/B based on fundamentals is $(0.12 - 0.07)/(0.10 - 0.07) = 1.67$.

---

[34] **Fair value** is defined as "the price that would be received to sell an asset or paid to transfer a liability in an orderly transaction between market participants at the measurement date." The definition is identical in IFRS and US GAAP.

[35] The two sets of standards differ in the measurement of impairment losses.

[36] According to the Gordon growth model, $V_0 = E_1 \times (1 - b)/(r - g)$. Defining ROE as E_1/B_0 so $E_1 = B_0 \times$ ROE and substituting for E_1 into the prior expression, we have $V_0 = B_0 \times \text{ROE} \times (1 - b)/(r - g)$, giving $V_0/B_0 = \text{ROE} \times (1 - b)/(r - g)$. The sustainable growth rate expression is $g = b \times$ ROE. Substituting $b = g/\text{ROE}$ into the expression just given for V_0/B_0, we have $V_0/B_0 = (\text{ROE} - g)/(r - g)$. Because justified price is intrinsic value, V_0, we obtain Equation 4.

Equation 4 states that the justified P/B is an increasing function of ROE, all else equal. Because the numerator and denominator are differences of, respectively, ROE and r from the same quantity, g, what determines the justified P/B in Equation 4 is ROE in relation to the required rate of return r. The larger ROE is in relation to r, the higher is the justified P/B based on fundamentals.[37]

A practical insight from Equation 4 is that we cannot conclude whether a particular value of the P/B reflects undervaluation without taking into account the business's profitability. Equation 4 also suggests that if we are evaluating two stocks with the same P/B, the one with the higher ROE is relatively undervalued, all else equal. These relationships have been confirmed through cross-sectional regression analyses.[38]

Further insight into P/B comes from the residual income model, which is discussed in detail in another reading. The expression for the justified P/B based on the residual income valuation is[39]

$$\frac{P_0}{B_0} = 1 + \frac{\text{Present value of expected future residual earnings}}{B_0} \qquad (5)$$

Equation 5, which makes no special assumptions about growth, states the following:

- If the present value of expected future residual earnings is zero—for example, if the business just earns its required return on investment in every period—the justified P/B is 1.

- If the present value of expected future residual earnings is positive (negative), the justified P/B is greater than (less than) 1.

3.2.3 Valuation Based on Comparables

To use the method of comparables for valuing stocks using a P/B, we follow the steps given in Section 3.1.5. In contrast to EPS, however, analysts' forecasts of book value are not aggregated and widely disseminated by financial data vendors; in practice, most analysts use trailing book value in calculating P/Bs.[40] Evaluation of relative P/Bs should consider differences in ROE, risk, and expected earnings growth. The use of P/Bs in the method of comparables is illustrated in Example 21.

---

37 This relationship can be seen clearly if we set g equal to 0 (the no-growth case): $P_0/B_0 = \text{ROE}/r$.

38 Harris and Marston (1994) performed a regression of book value to market value (MV), which is the inverse of P/B, against variables for growth (mean analyst forecasts) and risk (beta) for a large sample of companies over the period July 1982 through December 1989. The estimated regression was B/P = 1.172 − 4.15 × Growth + 0.093 × Risk (with R^2 = 22.9%). The coefficient of −4.15 indicates that expected growth was negatively related to B/P and, as a consequence, positively related to P/B. Risk was positively related to B/P and thus negatively related to P/B. Both variables were statistically significant, with growth having the greatest impact. Fairfield (1994) also found that P/Bs are related to future expectations of ROE in the predicted fashion.

39 Noting that (ROE − r) × B_0 would define a level residual income stream, we can show that Equation 4 is consistent with Equation 5 (a general expression) as follows. In P_0/B_0 = (ROE − g)/(r − g), we can successively rewrite the numerator (ROE − g) + r − r = (r − g) + (ROE − r), so P_0/B_0 = [(r − g) + (ROE − r)]/(r − g) = 1 + (ROE − r)/(r − g), which can be written P_0/B_0 = 1 + [(ROE − r)/(r − g)] × B_0/B_0 = 1 + [(ROE − r) × $B_0/(r$ − g)]/B_0; the second term in the final expression is the present value of residual income divided by B_0 as in Equation 5.

40 Because equity in successive balance sheets is linked by net income from the income statement, however, the analyst could, given dividend forecasts, translate EPS forecasts into corresponding book value forecasts while taking account of any anticipated ownership transactions.

EXAMPLE 21

P/B Comparables Approach

You are working on a project to value an independent securities brokerage firm. You know the industry had a significant decline in valuations during the 2007–2009 financial crisis. You decide to perform a time series analysis on three firms: E*TRADE Financial Corp. (NASDAQ: ETFC), The Charles Schwab Corporation (NASDAQ: SCHW), and TD Ameritrade Holding Corp. (NYSE: AMTD). Exhibit 12 presents information on these firms.

Exhibit 12	Price-to-Book Comparables								
	Price-to Book Value Ratio								
Entity	2006	2007	2008	2009	2010	2011	2012	As of 19 July 2013	Mean
ETFC	2.37	2.38	0.68	0.88	0.84	0.74	0.54	0.65	1.14
Forecasted growth in book value: 1.5%									
Forecasted growth in revenues: −1.0%									
Beta: 1.65									
SCHW	4.23	6.69	6.14	3.54	3.15	2.50	1.96	2.31	3.81
Forecasted growth in book value: 10.5%									
Forecasted growth in revenues: 5.0%									
Beta: 1.20									
AMTD	6.96	4.85	3.33	2.60	2.68	2.44	2.20	2.53	3.45
Forecasted growth in book value: 9.0%									
Forecasted growth in revenues: 3.5%									
Beta: 1.10									

Source: The Value Line Investment Survey. Price-to-book value ratio is based on average of the annual high and low price and end-of-year book value.

Based only on the information in Exhibit 12, discuss the relative valuation of ETFC relative to the other two companies.

Solution:

ETFC is currently selling at a P/B that is less than 30 percent of the P/B for either SCHW and AMTD. It is also selling at a P/B that is less than 60 percent of its average P/B for the time period noted in the exhibit. The likely explanation for ETFC's low P/B is that its growth forecasts for book value and revenues are lower and its beta higher than for those for SCH and AMTD. In deciding whether ETFC is overvalued or undervalued, an analyst would likely decide how his or her growth forecast and the uncertainty surrounding that forecast compare to the market consensus.

3.3 Price to Sales

Certain types of privately held companies, including investment management companies and many types of companies in partnership form, have long been valued by a multiple of annual revenues. In recent decades, the ratio of price to sales has become well known as a valuation indicator for the equity of publicly traded companies as well. Based on US data, O'Shaughnessy (2005) characterized P/S as the best ratio for selecting undervalued stocks.

According to the 2012 BofA *Merrill Lynch Institutional Factor Survey*, about 30 percent of respondents consistently used P/S in their investment process. Analysts have offered the following rationales for using P/S:

- Sales are generally less subject to distortion or manipulation than are other fundamentals, such as EPS or book value. For example, through discretionary accounting decisions about expenses, company managers can distort EPS as a reflection of economic performance. In contrast, total sales, as the top line in the income statement, is prior to any expenses.

- Sales are positive even when EPS is negative. Therefore, analysts can use P/S when EPS is negative, whereas the P/E based on a zero or negative EPS is not meaningful.

- Because sales are generally more stable than EPS, which reflects operating and financial leverage, P/S is generally more stable than P/E. P/S may be more meaningful than P/E when EPS is abnormally high or low.

- P/S has been viewed as appropriate for valuing the stocks of mature, cyclical, and zero-income companies (Martin 1998).

- Differences in P/S multiples may be related to differences in long-run average returns, according to empirical research.[41]

Possible drawbacks of using P/S in practice include the following:

- A business may show high growth in sales even when it is not operating profitably as judged by earnings and cash flow from operations. To have value as a going concern, a business must ultimately generate earnings and cash.

- Share price reflects the effect of debt financing on profitability and risk. In the P/S multiple, however, price is compared with sales, which is a prefinancing income measure—a logical mismatch. For this reason, some experts use a ratio of enterprise value to sales because enterprise value incorporates the value of debt.

- P/S does not reflect differences in cost structures among different companies.

- Although P/S is relatively robust with respect to manipulation, revenue recognition practices have the potential to distort P/S.

Despite the contrasts between P/S to P/E, the ratios have a relationship with which analysts should be familiar. The fact that (Sales) × (Net profit margin) = Net income means that (P/E) × (Net profit margin) = P/S. For two stocks with the same positive P/E, the stock with the higher P/S has a higher (actual or forecasted) net profit margin, calculated as the ratio of P/S to P/E.

---

41 Nathan, Sivakumar, and Vijayakumar (2001); O'Shaughnessy (2005); Senchack and Martin (1987).

3.3.1 *Determining Sales*

P/S is calculated as price per share divided by annual net sales per share (net sales is total sales minus returns and customer discounts). Analysts usually use annual sales from the company's most recent fiscal year in the calculation, as illustrated in Example 22. Because valuation is forward looking in principle, the analyst may also develop and use P/S multiples based on forecasts of next year's sales.

EXAMPLE 22

Calculating P/S

Stora Enso Oyj (Helsinki Stock Exchange: STERV) is an integrated paper, packaging, and forest products company headquartered in Finland. In its fiscal year ended 31 December 2012, Stora Enso reported net sales of €10,814.8 million and had 788.6 million shares outstanding. Calculate the P/S for Stora Enso based on a closing price of €6.72 on 16 September 2013.

Solution:

Sales per share = €10,814.8 million/788.6 million shares = €13.71. So, P/S = €6.72/€13.71 = 0.490.

Although the determination of sales is more straightforward than the determination of earnings, the analyst should evaluate a company's revenue recognition practices—in particular those tending to speed up the recognition of revenues—before relying on the P/S multiple. An analyst using a P/S approach who does not also assess the quality of accounting for sales may place too high a value on the company's shares. Example 23 illustrates the problem.

EXAMPLE 23

Revenue Recognition Practices (1)

Analysts label stock markets "bubbles" when market prices appear to lose contact with intrinsic values. To many analysts, the run-up in the prices of internet stocks in the US market in the 1998–2000 period represented a bubble. During that period, many analysts adopted P/S as a metric for valuing the many internet stocks that had negative earnings and cash flow. Perhaps at least partly as a result of this practice, some internet companies engaged in questionable revenue recognition practices to justify their high valuations. To increase sales, some companies engaged in bartering website advertising with other internet companies. For example, InternetRevenue.com might barter $1,000,000 worth of banner advertising with RevenueIsUs.com. Each could then show $1,000,000 of revenue and $1,000,000 of expenses. Although neither had any net income or cash flow, each company's revenue growth and market valuation was enhanced (at least temporarily). In addition the value placed on the advertising was frequently questionable.

As a result of these and other questionable activities, the US SEC issued a stern warning to companies and formalized revenue recognition practices for barter in Staff Accounting Bulletin No. 101. Similarly, international accounting standard setters issued Standing Interpretations Committee Interpretation 31 to define revenue recognition principles for barter transactions involving advertising services. The analyst should review footnote disclosures to assess whether a company may be recognizing revenue prematurely or otherwise aggressively.

Example 24 illustrates another classic instance in which an analyst should look behind the accounting numbers.

EXAMPLE 24

Revenue Recognition Practices (2)

Sales on a **bill-and-hold basis** involve selling products but not delivering those products until a later date.[42] Sales on this basis have the effect of accelerating the recognition of those sales into an earlier reporting period. In its form 10-K filed 30 September 2008, Diebold (NYSE: DBD) provided the following note:

Revenues

Bill and Hold—The largest of the revenue recognition adjustments relates to the Company's previous long-standing method of accounting for bill and hold transactions under Staff Accounting Bulletin 104, Revenue Recognition in Financial Statements (SAB 104), in its North America and International businesses. On January 15, 2008, the Company announced that it had concluded its discussions with the OCA in regard to its practice of recognizing certain revenue on a bill and hold basis in its North America business segment. As a result of those discussions, the Company determined that its previous, long-standing method of accounting for bill and hold transactions was in error, representing a misapplication of GAAP. To correct for this error, the Company announced it would discontinue the use of bill and hold as a method of revenue recognition in its North America and International businesses and restate its financial statements for this change.

The Company completed an analysis of transactions and recorded adjusting journal entries related to revenue and costs recognized previously under a bill and hold basis that is now recognized upon customer acceptance of products at a customer location. Within the North America business segment, when the Company is contractually responsible for installation, customer acceptance will be upon completion of the installation of all of the items at a job site and the Company's demonstration that the items are in operable condition. Where items are contractually only delivered to a customer, revenue recognition of these items will continue upon shipment or delivery to a customer location depending on the terms in the contract. Within the International business segment, customer acceptance is upon either delivery or completion of the installation depending on the terms in the contract with the customer. The Company restated for transactions affecting both product revenue for hardware sales and service revenue for installation and other services that had been previously recognized on a bill and hold basis.

---

[42] For companies whose reports must conform to US SEC accounting regulations, revenue from bill-and-hold sales cannot be reported unless the risk of loss on the products transfers to the buyer and additional criteria are met. (SEC Staff Accounting Bulletin No. 101 specifies the criteria.)

Other Revenue Adjustments—The Company also adjusted for other specific revenue transactions in both its North America and International businesses related to transactions largely where the Company recognized revenue in incorrect periods. The majority of these adjustments were related to misapplication of GAAP related to revenue recognition requirements as defined within SAB 104. Generally, the Company recorded adjustments for transactions when the Company previously recognized revenue prior to title and/or risk of loss transferring to the customer.

In 2010, DBD agreed to pay $25 million to settle Securities and Exchange Commission charges that it manipulated its earnings from at least 2002 through 2007. During that period, the company misstated the company's reported pre-tax earnings by at least $127 million.

According to the SEC, DBD's financial management received reports, sometimes on a daily basis, comparing the company's actual earnings to analyst earnings forecasts. DBD's management would prepare "opportunity lists" of ways to close the gap between the company's actual financial results and analyst forecasts. Many of the methods were fraudulent accounting transactions designed to improperly recognize revenue or otherwise inflate DBD's financial performance. Among the fraudulent practices identified by the SEC were the following: improper use of bill and hold accounting; recognition of revenue on a lease agreement subject to a side buy-back agreement; manipulating reserves and accruals; improperly delaying and capitalizing expenses; and writing up the value of used inventory.

Example 25 briefly summarizes another example of aggressive revenue recognition practices.

EXAMPLE 25

Revenue Recognition Practices (3)

Groupon (NASDAQ GS: GRPN) is a deal-of-the-day website that features discounted gift certificates usable at local or national companies. Before going public in November 2011, GRPN amended its registration statement eight times. One SEC-mandated restatement forced it to change an auditor-sanctioned method of reporting revenue, reducing sales by more than 50 percent. Essentially, GRPN had initially counted the gross amount its members paid for coupons or certificates as revenue, without deducting the share (typically half or more) that it sends on to local merchants. The SEC also demanded GRPN remove from its offering document a non-GAAP metric it had invented called "adjusted consolidated segment operating income." This measure was considered misleading because it ignored marketing expenses which are one of the major risks of GRPN's business model.

Even when a company discloses its revenue recognition practices, the analyst cannot always determine precisely by how much sales may be overstated. If a company is engaging in questionable revenue recognition practices and the amount being manipulated is unknown, the analyst might do well to suggest avoiding investment in that company's securities. At the very least, the analyst should be skeptical and assign the company a higher risk premium than otherwise, which would result in a lower justified P/S.

3.3.2 *Valuation Based on Forecasted Fundamentals*

Like other multiples, P/S can be linked to DCF models. In terms of the Gordon growth model, we can state P/S as[43]

$$\frac{P_0}{S_0} = \frac{(E_0/S_0)\ (1-b)(1+g)}{r-g} \tag{6}$$

where E_0/S_0 is the business's profit margin. Although the profit margin is stated in terms of trailing sales and earnings, the analyst may use a long-term forecasted profit margin in Equation 6. Equation 6 states that the justified P/S is an increasing function of the profit margin and earnings growth rate, and the intuition behind Equation 6 generalizes to more-complex DCF models.

Profit margin is a determinant of the justified P/S not only directly but also through its effect on g. We can illustrate this concept by restating the equation for the sustainable growth rate [g = (Retention rate, b) × ROE], as follows:

$$g = b \times PM_0 \times \frac{Sales}{Total\ assets} \times \frac{Total\ assets}{Shareholders'\ equity}$$

where PM_0 is profit margin and the last three terms come from the DuPont analysis of ROE. An increase (decrease) in the profit margin produces a higher (lower) sustainable growth rate as long as sales do not decrease (increase) proportionately.[44] Example 26 illustrates the use of justified P/S and how to apply it in valuation.

EXAMPLE 26

Justified P/S Based on Forecasted Fundamentals

As a health care analyst, you are valuing the stocks of three medical equipment manufacturers, including the Swedish company Getinge AB (Stockholm: GETI) in March 2013. Based on an average of estimates obtained from capital asset pricing model (CAPM) and bond yield plus risk premium approaches, you estimate that GETI's required rate of return is 9 percent. You have gathered the following data from GETI's 2012 annual report (amounts in millions of Swedish krona, or SEK):

	2003	2004	2005	2006	2007	2008	2009	2010	2011	2012
Net sales	9,160	10,889	11,880	13,001	16,445	19,272	22,816	22,712	21,854	24,248
Growth rates (geometric)										
2003–2012	11.4%									
2008–2012	5.9%									
Year/Year		18.9%	9.1%	9.4%	26.5%	17.2%	18.4%	−0.5%	−3.8%	11.0%
Net profit	778	915	1,150	1,259	1,233	1,523	1,914	2,280	2,537	2,531
Growth rates										
2003–2012	14.0%									
2008–2012	13.5%									
Year/Year		17.6%	25.7%	9.5%	−2.1%	23.5%	25.7%	19.1%	11.3%	−0.2%

(continued)

---

[43] The Gordon growth model is $P_0 = D_0\ (1+g)/(r-g)$. Substituting $D_0 = E_0\ (1-b)$ into the previous equation produces $P_0 = E_0\ (1-b)(1+g)/(r-g)$. Dividing both sides by S_0 gives $P_0/S_0 = (E_0/S_0)(1-b)(1+g)/(r-g)$.
[44] That is, an increase (decrease) in the profit margin could be offset by a decrease (increase) in total asset turnover (sales/assets).

	2003	2004	2005	2006	2007	2008	2009	2010	2011	2012
Net profit margin	8.5%	8.4%	9.7%	9.7%	7.5%	7.9%	8.4%	10.0%	11.6%	10.4%
Averages										
2003–2012	9.2%									
2008–2012	9.7%									
Dividend payout ratio	35.1%	36.4%	35.4%	35.4%	39.3%	33.2%	34.3%	34.0%	35.3%	39.2%
Averages										
2003–2012	35.8%									
2008–2012	35.2%									

Although sales growth picked up in 2012, it has slowed considerably in recent years and you are concerned that trend will ultimately be reflected in profit margins. Given this consideration, you make the following long-term forecasts:

Profit margin = 9.0 percent

Dividend payout ratio = 35.0 percent

Earnings growth rate = 7.0 percent

1 Based on these data, calculate GETI's justified P/S.

2 Given a forecast of GETI's sales per share (in Swedish krona) for 2013 of SEK108.9, estimate the intrinsic value of GETI stock.

3 Given a market price for GETI of SEK196.2 on 31 March 2013 and your answer to Part 2, determine whether GETI stock appears to be fairly valued, overvalued, or undervalued.

Solution to 1:

From Equation 6, GETI's justified P/S is calculated as follows:

$$\frac{P_0}{S_0} = \frac{(E_0/S_0)(1-b)(1+g)}{r-g} = \frac{0.09 \times 0.35 \times (1+0.07)}{0.09-0.07} = 1.7$$

Solution to 2:

An estimate of the intrinsic value of GETI stock is 1.7 × SEK108.9 = SEK185.13.

Solution to 3:

GETI stock appears to be overvalued because its current market value of SEK196.20 is greater than its estimated intrinsic value of SEK185.13.

3.3.3 Valuation Based on Comparables

Using P/S in the method of comparables to value stocks follows the steps given in Section 3.1.5. As mentioned earlier, P/S ratios are usually reported on the basis of trailing sales. Analysts may also base relative valuations on P/S multiples calculated on forecasted sales. In doing so, analysts may make their own sales forecasts or may use forecasts supplied by data vendors.[45] In valuing stocks using the method of

---

[45] Although sales forecasts have historically been less readily available than earnings forecasts, several leading vendors of US market data currently provide forecasts of sales as well as such quantities as cash flow per share and dividends per share.

comparables, analysts should also gather information on profit margins, expected earnings growth, and risk. As always, the quality of accounting also merits investigation. Example 27 illustrates the use of P/S in the comparables approach.

EXAMPLE 27

P/S Comparables Approach

Continuing with the project to value Getinge AB, you have compiled the information on GETI and peer companies Smith & Nephew plc (London: SN) and CR Bard Inc. (NYSE: BCR) given in Exhibit 13.

Exhibit 13	P/S Comparables (as of 4 October 2013)		
Measure	GETI	SN	BCR
Price/Sales (ttm)	2.14	2.66	3.07
Profit Margin (ttm)	8.82%	13.21%	6.25%
Quarterly Revenue Growth (yoy)	7.20%	4.40%	2.30%
Total Debt/Equity (mrq)	115.86	9.83	94.97
Enterprise Value/Revenue (ttm)	2.79	2.73	3.28

Source: Yahoo Finance.

Use the data in Exhibit 13 to address the following:

1 Based on the P/S but referring to no other information, assess GETI's relative valuation.

2 State whether GETI is more closely comparable to SN or to BCR. Justify your answer.

Solution to 1:

Because the P/S for GETI, 2.14, is the lowest of the three P/S multiples, if no other information is referenced, GETI appears to be relatively undervalued.

Solution to 2:

On the basis of the information given, GETI appears to be more closely matched to SN than BCR. BCR's P/S is significantly higher than the P/S for GETI and SN. The profit margin and revenue growth are key fundamentals in the P/S approach, and despite BCR's higher P/S, its profit margin and revenue growth rate are both lower than those of GETI and SN. The big difference between GETI and SN is that GETI relies much more on debt as a funding source. Because of this, the enterprise value-to-revenue ratio arguably provides a more appropriate valuation measure than does P/S. We discuss enterprise value ratios later in this reading.

3.4 Price to Cash Flow

Price to cash flow is a widely reported valuation indicator. According to the *2012 BofA Merrill Lynch Institutional Factor Survey*, price to free cash flow trailed only P/E, beta, enterprise value/EBITDA, ROE, size, and P/B in popularity as a valuation factor and was used as a valuation metric by approximately half of the institutions surveyed.

In this section, we present price to cash flow based on alternative major cash flow concepts.[46] Because of the wide variety of cash flow concepts in use, the analyst should be especially careful to understand (and communicate) the exact definition of "cash flow" that is the basis for the analysis.

Analysts have offered the following rationales for the use of price to cash flow:

■ Cash flow is less subject to manipulation by management than earnings.

■ Because cash flow is generally more stable than earnings, price to cash flow is generally more stable than P/E.

■ Using price to cash flow rather than P/E addresses the issue of differences in accounting conservatism between companies (differences in the quality of earnings).

■ Differences in price to cash flow may be related to differences in long-run average returns, according to empirical research.[47]

Possible drawbacks to the use of price to cash flow include the following:

■ When cash flow from operations is defined as EPS plus noncash charges, items affecting actual cash flow from operations, such as noncash revenue and net changes in working capital, are ignored. So, for example, aggressive recognition of revenue (front-end loading) would not be accurately captured in the earnings-plus-noncash-charges definition because the measure would not reflect the divergence between revenues as reported and actual cash collections related to that revenue.

■ Theory views free cash flow to equity (FCFE) rather than cash flow as the appropriate variable for price-based valuation multiples. We can use P/FCFE but FCFE does have the possible drawback of being more volatile than cash flow for many businesses. FCFE is also more frequently negative than cash flow.

■ As analysts' use of cash flow has increased over time, some companies have increased their use of accounting methods that enhance cash flow measures. Operating cash flow, for example, can be enhanced by securitizing accounts receivable to speed up a company's operating cash inflow or by outsourcing the payment of accounts payable to slow down the company's operating cash outflow (while the outsource company continues to make timely payments and provides financing to cover any timing differences). Mulford and Comiskey (2005) describe a number of opportunistic accounting choices that companies can make to increase their reported operating cash flow.

■ Operating cash flow from the Statement of Cash Flows under IFRS may not be comparable to operating cash flow under US GAAP because IFRS allow more flexibility in classification of interest paid, interest received, and dividends received. Under US GAAP, all three of these items are classified in operating cash flow; but under IFRS, companies have the option to classify them as operating or investing (for interest and dividends received) and as operating or financing (for interest paid).

One approximation of cash flow in practical use is EPS plus per-share depreciation, amortization, and depletion. This simple approximation is used in Example 28 to highlight issues of interest to the analyst in valuation.

---

[46] "Price to cash flow" is used to refer to the ratio of share price to any one of these definitions of cash flow. P/CF is reserved for the ratio of price to the earnings plus noncash charges definition of cash flow, explained subsequently.

[47] For example, see O'Shaughnessy (2005).

Accounting Methods and Cash Flow

Consider two hypothetical companies, Company A and Company B, that have constant cash revenues and cash expenses (as well as a constant number of shares outstanding) in 2010, 2011, and 2012. In addition, both companies incur total depreciation of $15.00 per share during the three-year period and both use the same depreciation method for tax purposes. The two companies use different depreciation methods, however, for financial reporting. Company A spreads the depreciation expense evenly over the three years (straight-line depreciation, SLD). Because its revenues, expenses, and depreciation are constant over the period, Company A's EPS is also constant. In this example Company A's EPS is assumed to be $10 each year, as shown in Column 1 in Exhibit 14.

Company B is identical to Company A except that it uses accelerated depreciation. Company B's depreciation is 150 percent of SLD in 2007 and declines to 50 percent of SLD in 2009, as shown in Column 5.

Exhibit 14   Earnings Growth Rates and Cash Flow (All Amounts per Share)

Year	Company A			Company B		
	Earnings (1)	Depreciation (2)	Cash Flow (3)	Earnings (4)	Depreciation (5)	Cash Flow (6)
2010	$10.00	$5.00	$15.00	$7.50	$7.50	$15.00
2011	10.00	5.00	15.00	10.00	5.00	15.00
2012	10.00	5.00	15.00	12.50	2.50	15.00
Total		$15.00			$15.00	

Because of the different depreciation methods used by Company A and Company B for financial reporting purposes, Company A's EPS is flat at $10.00 (Column 1) whereas Company B's EPS (Column 4) shows 29 percent compound growth: $(\$12.50/\$7.50)^{1/2} - 1.00 = 0.29$. Thus, Company B appears to have positive earnings momentum. Analysts comparing Companies A and B might be misled by using the EPS numbers as reported instead of putting EPS on a comparable basis. For both companies, however, cash flow per share is level at $15.

Depreciation may be the simplest noncash charge to understand; write-offs and other noncash charges may offer more latitude for the management of earnings.

3.4.1 Determining Cash Flow

In practice, analysts and data vendors often use simple *approximations* of cash flow from operations in calculating cash flow for price to cash flow analysis. For many companies, depreciation and amortization are the major noncash charges regularly added to net income in the process of calculating cash flow from operations by the add-back method, so the approximation focuses on them. A representative approximation specifies cash flow per share as EPS plus per-share depreciation, amortization, and depletion.[48] We call this estimation the "earnings-plus-noncash-charges" definition and in this section, use the acronym CF for it. Keep in mind, however, that this definition is only one commonly used in calculating price to cash flow, not a technically accurate definition from an accounting perspective. We will also describe more technically accurate cash flow concepts: cash flow from operations, free cash flow to equity, and EBITDA (an estimate of pre-interest, pretax operating cash flow).[49]

Most frequently, trailing price to cash flows are reported. A trailing price to cash flow is calculated as the current market price divided by the sum of the most recent four quarters' cash flow per share. A fiscal-year definition is also possible, as in the case of EPS.

Example 29 illustrates the calculation of P/CF with cash flow defined as earnings plus noncash charges.

EXAMPLE 29

Calculating Price to Cash Flow with Cash Flow Defined as Earnings plus Noncash Charges

In 2012, Koninklijke Philips Electronics N.V. (Euronext: PHIA and NYSE: PHG) reported net income from continuing operations of €262 million, equal to EPS of €0.28. The company's depreciation and amortization was €1,433 million, or €1.53 per share. An AEX price for PHIA as of 31 July 2013 was €24.06. Calculate the P/CF for PHIA.

Solution:

CF (defined as EPS plus per-share depreciation, amortization, and depletion) is €0.28 + €1.53 = €1.81 per share. Thus, P/CF = €24.06/€1.81 = 13.3.

Rather than use an approximate EPS-plus-noncash charges concept of cash flow, analysts can use cash flow from operations (CFO) in a price multiple. CFO is found in the statement of cash flows. Similar to the adjustments to normalize earning, adjustments to CFO for components not expected to persist into future time periods may also be appropriate. In addition, adjustments to CFO may be required when comparing companies that use different accounting standards. For example, as noted above, under IFRS, companies have flexibility in classifying interest payments, interest receipts, and dividend receipts across operating, investing, and financing. US GAAP requires companies to classify interest payments, interest receipts, and dividend receipts as operating cash flows.

As an alternative to CF and CFO, the analyst can relate price to FCFE, the cash flow concept with the strongest link to valuation theory. Because the amounts of capital expenditures in proportion to CFO generally differ among companies being compared, the analyst may find that rankings by price to cash flow from operations (P/CFO) and by P/CF will differ from rankings by P/FCFE. Period-by-period FCFE may be more volatile than CFO (or CF), however, so a trailing P/FCFE is not necessarily

---

48 This representation is the definition of cash flow in Value Line, for example: "the total of net income plus non-cash charges (depreciation, amortization, and depletion) minus preferred dividends (if any)." (This definition appears in the Value Line online glossary—current as of July 2008.) To obtain cash flow per share, total cash flow is divided by the number of shares outstanding. Note that the term *depreciation* refers to fixed assets, *amortization* refers to intangible assets, and *depletion* refers to natural resources; all three accounting terms mean than an expenditure is systematically allocated over a period of time.

49 Grant and Parker (2001) point out that EBITDA as a cash flow approximation assumes that changes in working capital accounts are immaterial. The EPS-plus-noncash-charges definition makes the same assumption (it is, essentially, earnings before depreciation and amortization).

more informative in a valuation. For example, consider two similar businesses with the same CFO and capital expenditures over a two-year period. If the first company times its capital expenditures to fall toward the beginning of the period and the second times its capital expenditures to fall toward the end of the period, the P/FCFEs for the two stocks may differ sharply without representing a meaningful economic difference.[50] This concern can be addressed, at least in part, by using price to average free cash flow, as in Hackel, Livnat, and Rai (1994).

Another cash flow concept used in multiples is EBITDA (earnings before interest, taxes, depreciation, and amortization).[51] To forecast EBITDA, analysts usually start with their projections of EBIT and simply add depreciation and amortization to arrive at an estimate for EBITDA. In calculating EBITDA from historical numbers, one can start with earnings from continuing operations, excluding nonrecurring items. To that earnings number, interest, taxes, depreciation, and amortization are added.

In practice, both EV/EBITDA and P/EBITDA have been used by analysts as valuation metrics. EV/EBITDA has been the preferred metric, however, because its numerator includes the value of debt; therefore, it is the more appropriate method because EBITDA is pre-interest and is thus a flow to both debt and equity. EV/EBITDA is discussed in detail in a later section.

3.4.2 Valuation Based on Forecasted Fundamentals

The relationship between the justified price to cash flow and fundamentals follows from the familiar mathematics of the present value model. The justified price to cash flow, all else being equal, is inversely related to the stock's required rate of return and positively related to the growth rate(s) of expected future cash flows (however defined). We can find a justified price to cash flow based on fundamentals by finding the value of a stock using the most suitable DCF model and dividing that number by cash flow (based on our chosen definition of cash flow). Example 30 illustrates the process.

EXAMPLE 30

Justified Price to Cash Flow Based on Forecasted Fundamentals

As a technology analyst, you are working on the valuation of Western Digital (NYSE: WDC), a manufacturer of hard disk drives. As a first estimate of value, you are applying a FCFE model under the assumption of a stable long-term growth rate in FCFE:

$$V_0 = \frac{(1 + g)\text{FCFE}_0}{r - g}$$

where g is the expected growth rate of FCFE. You estimate trailing FCFE at $7.96 per share and trailing CF (based on the earnings plus noncash charges definition) at $12.00. Your other estimates are a 12.0 percent required rate of return and a 3.0 percent expected growth rate of FCFE.

1 What is the intrinsic value of WDC according to a constant-growth FCFE model?

---

50 The analyst could, however, appropriately use the FCFE discounted cash flow model value, which incorporates all expected future free cash flows to equity.

51 Another concept that has become popular is cash earnings, which has been defined in various ways, such as earnings plus amortization of intangibles or EBITDA minus net financial expenses.

2 What is the justified P/CF based on forecasted fundamentals?

3 What is the justified P/FCFE based on forecasted fundamentals?

Solution to 1:

Calculate intrinsic value as $(1.03 \times \$7.96)/(0.12 - 0.03) = \$91.10$.

Solution to 2:

Calculate a justified P/CF based on forecasted fundamentals as $\$91.10/\$12.00 = 7.6$.

Solution to 3:

The justified P/FCFE is $\$91.10/\$7.96 = 11.4$.

3.4.3 *Valuation Based on Comparables*

The method of comparables for valuing stocks based on price to cash flow follows the steps given previously and illustrated for P/E, P/B, and P/S. Example 31 is a simple exercise in the comparable method based on price to cash flow measures.

EXAMPLE 31

Price to Cash Flow and Comparables

Exhibit 15 provides information on P/CF, P/FCFE, and selected fundamentals as of 16 April 2012 for two hypothetical companies. Using the information in Exhibit 15, compare the valuations of the two companies.

Exhibit 15	Comparison of Two Companies (All Amounts per Share)						
Company	**Current Price (£)**	**Trailing CF per Share (£)**	**P/CF**	**Trailing FCFE per Share (£)**	**P/FCFE**	**Consensus Five-Year CF Growth Forecast (%)**	**Beta**
Company A	17.98	1.84	9.8	0.29	62	13.4	1.50
Company B	15.65	1.37	11.4	−.99	NM	10.6	1.50

Company A is selling at a P/CF (9.8) approximately 14 percent smaller than the P/CF of Company B (11.4). Based on that comparison, we expect that, all else equal, investors would anticipate a higher growth rate for Company B. Contrary to that expectation, however, the consensus five-year earnings growth forecast for Company A is 280 basis points higher than it is for Company B. As of the date of the comparison, Company A appears to be relatively undervalued compared with Company B, as judged by P/CF and expected growth. The information in Exhibit 15 on FCFE supports the proposition that Company A may be relatively undervalued. The positive FCFE for Company A indicates that operating cash flows and new debt borrowing are more than sufficient to cover capital expenditures. Negative FCFE for Company B suggests the need for external funding of growth.

3.5 Price to Dividends and Dividend Yield

The total return on an equity investment has a capital appreciation component and a dividend yield component. Dividend yield data are frequently reported to provide investors with an estimate of the dividend yield component in total return. Dividend yield is also used as a valuation indicator. Although the 2012 *BofA Merrill Lynch Institutional Factor Survey* did not survey this metric, in its surveys from 1989 to 2006 slightly more than one-quarter of respondents on average reported using dividend yield as a factor in the investment process.

Analysts have offered the following rationales for using dividend yields in valuation:

- Dividend yield is a component of total return.

- Dividends are a less risky component of total return than capital appreciation.

Possible drawbacks of using dividend yields include the following:

- Dividend yield is only one component of total return; not using all information related to expected return is suboptimal.

- Investors may trade off future earnings growth to receive higher current dividends. That is, holding return on equity constant, dividends paid now displace earnings in all future periods (a concept known as the **dividend displacement of earnings**).[52]

- The argument about the relative safety of dividends presupposes that market prices reflect in a biased way differences in the relative risk of the components of return.

3.5.1 *Calculation of Dividend Yield*

This reading so far has presented multiples with market price (or market capitalization) in the numerator. P/Ds have sometimes appeared in valuation, particularly with respect to indices. Many stocks, however, do not pay dividends, and the P/D ratio is undefined with zero in the denominator. For such non-dividend-paying stocks, dividend yield (D/P) *is* defined: It is equal to zero. For practical purposes, then, dividend yield is the preferred way to present this multiple.

Trailing dividend yield is generally calculated by using the dividend rate divided by the current market price per share. The annualized amount of the most recent dividend is known as the **dividend rate**. For companies paying quarterly dividends, the dividend rate is calculated as four times the most recent quarterly per-share dividend. (Some data sources use the dividends in the last four quarters as the dividend rate for purposes of a trailing dividend yield.) For companies that pay semiannual dividends comprising an interim dividend that typically differs in magnitude from the final dividend, the dividend rate is usually calculated as the most recent annual per-share dividend.

The dividend rate indicates the annual amount of dividends per share under the assumption of no increase or decrease over the year. The analyst's forecast of leading dividends could be higher or lower and is the basis of the leading dividend yield. The **leading dividend yield** is calculated as forecasted dividends per share over the next year divided by the current market price per share. Example 32 illustrates the calculation of dividend yield.

---

[52] Arnott and Asness (2003) and Zhou and Ruland (2006), however, show that caution must be exercised in assuming that dividends displace future earnings in practice, because dividend payout may be correlated with future profitability.

EXAMPLE 32

Calculating Dividend Yield

Exhibit 16 gives quarterly dividend data for Canadian telecommunications company BCE Inc. (NYSE: BCE) and semiannual dividend data for the ADRs of BT Group (NYSE: BT), formerly British Telecom.

Exhibit 16	Dividends Paid per Share for BCE Inc. and for BT Group ADRs	
Period	**BCE ($)**	**BT ADR ($)**
4Q:2011	0.508	
1Q:2012	0.518	0.390
2Q:2012	0.543	
3Q:2012	0.543	0.884
Total	2.112	1.274
4Q:2012	0.568	
1Q:2013	0.568	0.451
2Q:2013	0.583	
3Q:2013	0.583	0.994
Total	2.302	1.445

Source: Value Line.

1 Given a price per share for BCE of $42.70 during 4Q:2013, calculate this company's trailing dividend yield.

2 Given a price per ADR for BT of $55.30 during 4Q:2013, calculate the trailing dividend yield for the ADRs.

Solution to 1:

The dividend rate for BCE is $0.583 × 4 = $2.332. The dividend yield is $2.332/$42.70 = 0.0546 or 5.46 percent.

Solution to 2:

Because BT pays semiannual dividends that differ in magnitude between the interim and final dividends, the dividend rate for BT's ADR is the total dividend in the most recent year, $1.445. The dividend yield is $1.445/$55.30 = 0.0261 or 2.61 percent.

3.5.2 *Valuation Based on Forecasted Fundamentals*

The relationship of dividend yield to fundamentals can be illustrated in the context of the Gordon growth model. From that model, we obtain the expression

$$\frac{D_0}{P_0} = \frac{r-g}{1+g} \tag{7}$$

Equation 7 shows that dividend yield is negatively related to the expected rate of growth in dividends and positively related to the stock's required rate of return. The first point implies that the selection of stocks with relatively high dividend yields is consistent with an orientation to a value rather than growth investment style.

3.5.3 *Valuation Based on Comparables*

Using dividend yield with comparables is similar to the process that has been illustrated for other multiples. An analyst compares a company with its peers to determine whether it is attractively priced, considering its dividend yield and risk. The analyst should examine whether differences in expected growth explain the differences in dividend yield. Another consideration used by some investors is the security of the dividend (the probability that it will be reduced or eliminated). A useful metric in assessing the safety of the dividend is the payout ratio: A high payout relative to other companies operating in the same industry may indicate a less secure dividend because the dividend is less well covered by earnings. Balance sheet metrics are equally important in assessing the safety of the dividend, and relevant ratios to consider include the interest coverage ratio and the ratio of net debt to EBITDA. Example 33 illustrates use of the dividend yield in the method of comparables.

EXAMPLE 33

Dividend Yield Comparables

William Leiderman is a portfolio manager for a US pension fund's domestic equity portfolio. The portfolio is exempt from taxes, so any differences in the taxation of dividends and capital gains are not relevant. Leiderman's client requires high current income. Leiderman is considering the purchase of utility stocks for the fund in November 2013. In the course of his review he considers the four large-cap US electric utilities shown in Exhibit 17.

Exhibit 17	**Using Dividend Yield to Compare Stocks**			
Company	**Consensus Earnings Growth Forecast (%)**	**Beta**	**Dividend Yield (%)**	**Payout Ratio (%)**
Duke Energy (NYSE:DUK)	3.66	0.34	4.4	110
Pepco Holdings (NYSE: POM)	3.82	0.37	5.6	NMF
Portland General Electric Co. (NYSE:POR)	6.45	0.55	3.7	88
PPL Corp. (NYSE:PPL)	−2.40	0.26	4.8	58

Sources: www.finviz.com and Yahoo! Finance.

All of the securities exhibit similar low market risk; they each have a beta less than 1.00. Although POM has the highest dividend yield, its dividend payout ratio is not meaningful due to a negative EPS. DUK's dividend payout ratio of 110 percent, the highest of the group, also suggests that its dividend may be subject to greater risk. Leiderman notes that PPL's relatively low payout ratio means that the dividend is well supported; however, the expected negative earnings growth rate is a negative factor. Summing POR's dividend yield and expected earnings growth rate, Leiderman estimates POR's expected total return as about 10.2 percent; because the total return estimate is relatively attractive and because POR does not appear to have any strong negatives, Leiderman decides to focus his further analysis on POR.

4 ENTERPRISE VALUE MULTIPLES

Enterprise value multiples are multiples that relate the enterprise value of a company to some measure of value (typically, a pre-interest income measure). Perhaps the most frequently advanced argument for using enterprise value multiples rather than price multiples in valuation is that enterprise value multiples are relatively less sensitive to the effects of financial leverage than price multiples when one is comparing companies that use differing amounts of leverage. Enterprise value multiples, in defining the numerator as they do, take a control perspective (discussed in more detail later). Thus, even where leverage differences are not an issue, enterprise value multiples may complement the perspective of price multiples. Indeed, although some analysts strictly favor one type of multiple, other analysts report both price and enterprise value multiples.

4.1 Enterprise Value to EBITDA

Enterprise value to EBITDA is by far the most widely used enterprise value multiple.

Earlier, EBITDA was introduced as an estimate of pre-interest, pretax operating cash flow. Because EBITDA is a flow to both debt and equity, as noted, defining an EBITDA multiple by using a measure of total company value in the numerator, such as EV, is appropriate. Recall that **enterprise value** is total company value (the market value of debt, common equity, and preferred equity) minus the value of cash and short-term investments. Thus, EV/EBITDA is a valuation indicator for the overall company rather than solely its common stock. If, however, the analyst can assume that the business's debt and preferred stock (if any) are efficiently priced, the analyst can use EV/EBITDA to draw an inference about the valuation of common equity. Such an inference is often reasonable.

Analysts have offered the following rationales for using EV/EBITDA:

- EV/EBITDA is usually more appropriate than P/E alone for comparing companies with different financial leverage (debt), because EBITDA is a pre-interest earnings figure, in contrast to EPS, which is postinterest.

- By adding back depreciation and amortization, EBITDA controls for differences in depreciation and amortization among businesses, in contrast to net income, which is postdepreciation and postamortization. For this reason, EV/EBITDA is frequently used in the valuation of capital-intensive businesses (for example, cable companies and steel companies). Such businesses typically have substantial depreciation and amortization expenses.

- EBITDA is frequently positive when EPS is negative.

Possible drawbacks to using EV/EBITDA include the following:[53]

- EBITDA will overestimate cash flow from operations if working capital is growing. EBITDA also ignores the effects of differences in revenue recognition policy on cash flow from operations.
- Free cash flow to the firm (FCFF), which directly reflects the amount of the company's required capital expenditures, has a stronger link to valuation theory than does EBITDA. Only if depreciation expenses match capital expenditures do we expect EBITDA to reflect differences in businesses' capital programs. This qualification to EBITDA comparisons may be particularly meaningful for the capital-intensive businesses to which EV/EBITDA is often applied.

4.1.1 *Determining Enterprise Value*

We illustrated the calculation of EBITDA previously. As discussed, analysts commonly define enterprise value as follows:

> Market value of common equity (Number of shares outstanding × Price per share)
>
> **Plus:** Market value of preferred stock (if any)[54]
>
> **Plus:** Market value of debt
>
> **Less:** Cash and investments (specifically: cash, cash equivalents, and short-term investments)[55]
>
> **Equals:** Enterprise value

Cash and investments (sometimes termed **nonearning assets**) are subtracted because EV is designed to measure the net price an acquirer would pay for the company as a whole. The acquirer must buy out current equity and debt providers but then receives access to the cash and investments, which lower the net cost of the acquisition. (For example, cash and investments can be used to pay off debt or loans used to finance the purchase.) The same logic explains the use of market values: In repurchasing debt, an acquirer has to pay market prices. Some debt, however, may be private and it does not trade; some debt may be publicly traded but trade infrequently. When analysts do not have market values, they often use book values obtained from the balance sheet.[56] Example 34 illustrates the calculation of EV/EBITDA.

EXAMPLE 34

Calculating EV/EBITDA

Western Digital Corporation (NYSE: WDC) manufactures hard disk drives. Exhibit 18 presents the company's consolidated balance sheet as of 29 March 2013.

---

53 See Moody's (2000) and Grant and Parker (2001) for additional issues and concerns.
54 Minority interest, if any, usually should be added back unless it is already included elsewhere. **Minority interest** appears in the consolidated financial statements of a parent company that owns more than 50 percent but not 100 percent of a subsidiary; minority interest refers to that portion of equity in the subsidiary that is not owned by the parent.
55 Some analysts attempt to distinguish between cash and investments that are or are not needed in the operations of the company, subtracting only the nonoperating part in this calculation. However, making such a distinction is not always practical.
56 However, using so-called matrix price estimates of debt market values in such cases, where they are available, may be more accurate. Matrix price estimates are based on characteristics of the debt issue and information on how the marketplace prices those characteristics.

Exhibit 18	Western Digital Corporation Condensed Consolidated Balance Sheet (in Millions except Par Values; Unaudited)

Assets

Current assets:	
Cash and cash equivalents	$4,060
Accounts receivable, net	1,700
Inventories	1,197
Other current assets	383
Total current assets	7,340
Property and equipment, net	3,803
Goodwill and other intangible assets, net	2,610
Other noncurrent assets	174
Total assets	$13,927

Liabilities and Shareholders' Equity

Current liabilities:	
Accounts payable	$2,037
Accrued expenses	837
Accrued warranty	122
Current portion of long-term debt	230
Total current liabilities	3,226
Long-term debt	1,783
Other liabilities	495
Total liabilities	5,504
Commitments and contingencies (Notes 4 and 5)	
Shareholders' equity:	
Preferred stock, $0.01 par value; authorized—5 shares; outstanding—none	—
Common stock, $0.01 par value; authorized—450 shares; outstanding—238 shares	3
Additional paid-in capital	2,232
Accumulated comprehensive income (loss)	20
Retained earnings	7,073
Treasury stock—common shares at cost	(905)
Total shareholders' equity	8,423
Total liabilities and shareholders' equity	$13,927

Source: Company 10-Q

The balance sheet is labeled as unaudited because it is a quarterly balance sheet and US companies are required to have audits only for their annual financial statements.

From WDC's financial statements, the income statement and statement of cash flows for the year ended 29 June 2012 and for the nine months ended 29 March 2013 and 30 March 2012 provided the following items (in millions):

Item	Source	Year Ended 29 June 2012	Nine Months Ended 29 March 2013	Nine Months Ended 30 March 2012
Net income	Income statement	$1,612	$1,245	$867
Interest expense (net of interest income)	Income statement	14	35	8
Income tax provision	Income statement	145	207	88
Depreciation and amortization	Statement of cash flows	825	931	486

The company's share price as of 1 July 2013 was $63.06. Based on the above information, calculate EV/EBITDA.

Solution:

- For EV, we first calculate the total value of WDC's equity: 238 million shares outstanding times $63.06 price per share equals $15,008 million market capitalization.

  WDC has only one class of common stock, no preferred shares, and no minority interest. For companies that have multiple classes of common stock, market capitalization includes the total value of all classes of common stock. Similarly, for companies that have preferred stock and/or minority interest, the market value of preferred stock and the amount of minority interest are added to market capitalization.

  EV also includes the value of long-term debt. Per WDC's balance sheet, the amount of long-term debt is $2,013 million ($1,783 million plus the current portion of $230 million). Typically, the book value of long-term debt is used in EV. If, however, the market value of the debt is readily available and materially different from the book value, the market value should be used.

  EV excludes cash, cash equivalents, and short-term investments. Per WDC's balance sheet, the total of cash and cash equivalents is $4,060 million.

  So, WDC's EV is $15,008 million + 2,013 million – $4,060 million = $12,961 million.

- For EBITDA, we first calculate the trailing 12 month (TTM) information using the first nine months of the current fiscal year plus the last three months of the prior fiscal year. For example, the TTM net income equals $1,245 million from the first nine months ending 29 March 2013 plus $745 million from the last three months of the previous fiscal year ($1,612 million minus $867 million.) EBITDA is calculated as net income plus interest plus taxes plus depreciation and amortization. The TTM EBITDA totals $3,565 million. These calculations are summarized as follows:

EBITDA Component	Year Ended 29 June 2012	9 Months Ended 29 March 2013	9 Months Ended 30 March 2012	Total (TTM)
Net income	$1,612	$1,245	$867	$1,990
Interest	14	35	8	41
Taxes	145	207	88	264
Depreciation and amortization	825	931	486	1,270
EBITDA	$2,596	$2,418	$1,449	$3,565

WDC does not have preferred equity. Companies that do have preferred equity typically present in their financial statements net income available to common shareholders. In those cases, the EBITDA calculation uses net income available to *both* preferred and common equity holders.

We conclude that EV/EBITDA = ($12,961 million)/($3,565 million) = 3.6.

4.1.2 *Valuation Based on Forecasted Fundamentals*

As with other multiples, intuition about the fundamental drivers of enterprise value to EBITDA can help when applying the method of comparables. All else being equal, the justified EV/EBITDA based on fundamentals should be positively related to the expected growth rate in free cash flow to the firm, positively related to expected profitability as measured by return on invested capital, and negatively related to the business's weighted average cost of capital. **Return on invested capital** (ROIC) is calculated as operating profit after tax divided by total invested capital. In analyzing ratios such as EV/EBITDA, ROIC is the relevant measure of profitability because EBITDA flows to all providers of capital.

4.1.3 *Valuation Based on Comparables*

All else equal, a lower EV/EBITDA value relative to peers indicates that a company is relatively undervalued. An analyst's recommendations, however, are usually not completely determined by relative EV/EBITDA; from an analyst's perspective, EV/EBITDA is simply one piece of information to consider.

Example 35 presents a comparison of enterprise value multiples for four peer companies. The example includes a measure of total firm value, **total invested capital** (TIC), sometimes also known as the **market value of invested capital**, that is an alternative to enterprise value. Similar to EV, TIC includes the market value of equity and debt, but does not deduct cash and investments.

EXAMPLE 35

Comparable Enterprise Value Multiples

Exhibit 19 presents EV multiples for four companies in the data storage device industry: Western Digital Corporation (NYSE: WDC), Net App (NASDAQ GS: NTAP), EMC Corporation (NYSE: EMC), and Seagate Technology (NASDAQ GS: STX).

Exhibit 19	Enterprise Value Multiples for Industry Peers (amounts in $ million, except where indicated otherwise)			
Measure	WDC	NTAP	EMC	STX
Price	$70.72	$39.12	$23.64	$48.04
Times: shares outstanding (millions)	237	340	2,080	357
Equals: equity market cap	16,761	13,301	49,171	17,150
Plus: Debt (most recent quarter)	1,960	995	7,190	2,780
Plus: Preferred stock	—	—	—	—
Equals: Total Invested Capital (TIC)	18,721	14,296	56,361	19,930
Less: cash	4,310	5,080	11,150	2,190
Equals: Enterprise Value (EV)	$14,411	$9,216	$45,211	$17,740
EBITDA (TTM)	$3,320	$890	$5,330	$2,960
TIC/EBITDA	5.6	16.1	10.6	6.7
EV/EBITDA	4.3	10.4	8.5	6.0
Debt/Equity (book)	24.8%	24.8%	30.0%	79.2%
Profit margin (TTM)	6.38%	8.17%	12.45%	12.81%
Quarterly revenue growth (year over year)	−21.6%	27.9%	5.7%	−23.6%

Sources: Yahoo! Finance; calculations.

1 Exhibit 19 provides two alternative enterprise value multiples, TIC/EBITDA and EV/EBITDA. The ranking of the companies' multiples is identical by both multiples. In general, what could cause the rankings to vary?

2 Each EBITDA multiple incorporates a comparison with enterprise value. How do these multiples differ from price to cash flow multiples?

3 Based solely on the information in Exhibit 19, how does the valuation of WDC compare with that of the other three companies?

Solution to 1:

The difference between TIC and EV is that EV excludes cash, cash equivalents, and marketable securities. So, a material variation among companies in cash, cash equivalents, or marketable securities relative to EBITDA could cause the rankings to vary.

Solution to 2:

These multiples differ from price to cash flow multiples in that the numerator is a measure of firm value rather than share price, to match the denominator which is a pre-interest measure of earnings. These multiples thus provide a more appropriate comparison than price to cash flow when companies have significantly different capital structures.

Solution to 3:

Based on its lower TIC/EBITDA and EV/EBITDA multiples of 5.6 and 4.3, respectively, WDC appears undervalued relative to the other three companies. However, these lower valuation ratios may be warranted given WDC's low profit margin and declining revenue growth. Compared with STX, the enterprise value multiples of WDC are slightly lower which is consistent with it being less profitable than STX (profit margin of 6.38 percent versus 12.81 percent). The enterprise value multiples of NTAP are much higher than those of WDC, probably reflecting NTAP's recent relatively high revenue growth. Similarly, the enterprise value ratios for WDC are lower than those for EMC due also to differences in profitability and growth.

4.2 Other Enterprise Value Multiples

Although EV/EBITDA is the most widely known and used enterprise value multiple, other enterprise value multiples are used together with or in place of EV/EBITDA—either in a broad range of applications or for valuations in a specific industry. EV/FCFF is an example of a broadly used multiple; an example of a special-purpose multiple is EV/EBITDAR (where R stands for rent expense), which is favored by airline industry analysts. This section reviews the most common such multiples (except EV/sales, which is covered in the next section). In each case, a valuation metric could be formulated in terms of TIC rather than EV.

Major alternatives to using EBITDA in the denominator of enterprise value multiples include FCFF (free cash flow to the firm), EBITA (earnings before interest, taxes, and amortization), and EBIT (earnings before interest and taxes). Exhibit 20 summarizes the components of each of these measurements and how they relate to net income. Note that, in practice, analysts typically forecast EBITDA by forecasting EBIT and adding depreciation and amortization.

Exhibit 20	Alternative Denominators in Enterprise Value Multiples							
Free Cash Flow to the Firm =	Net Income	plus Interest Expense	minus Tax Savings on Interest	plus Depreciation	plus Amortization	less Investment in Working Capital	less Investment in Fixed Capital
EBITDA =	Net Income	plus Interest Expense	plus Taxes	plus Depreciation	plus Amortization		
EBITA =	Net Income	plus Interest Expense	plus Taxes		plus Amortization		
EBIT =	Net Income	plus Interest Expense	plus Taxes				

Note that the calculation of all the measures given in Exhibit 20 add interest back to net income, which reflects that these measures are flows relevant to all providers of both debt and equity capital. As one moves down the rows of Exhibit 20, the measures incorporate increasingly less precise information about a company's tax position and its capital investments, although each measure has a rationale. For example, EBITA may be chosen in cases in which amortization (associated with intangibles) but not depreciation (associated with tangibles) is a major expense for companies being compared. EBIT may be chosen where neither depreciation nor amortization is a major item.

In addition to enterprise value multiples based on financial measures, in some industries or sectors, the analyst may find it appropriate to examine enterprise value multiples based on a nonfinancial measurement that is specific to that industry or sector. For example, for satellite and cable TV broadcasters, an analyst might usefully examine EV to subscribers. For a resource-based company, a multiple based on reserves of the resource may be appropriate.

Regardless of the specific denominator used in an enterprise value multiple, the concept remains the same—namely, to relate the market value of the total company to some fundamental financial or nonfinancial measure of the company's value.

4.3 Enterprise Value to Sales

Enterprise value to sales is a major alternative to the price-to-sales ratio. The P/S multiple has the conceptual weakness that it fails to recognize that for a debt-financed company, not all sales belong to a company's equity investors. Some of the proceeds from the company's sales will be used to pay interest and principal to the providers of the company's debt capital. For example, a P/S for a company with little or no debt would not be comparable to a P/S for a company that is largely financed with debt. EV/S would be the basis for a valid comparison in such a case. In summary, EV/S is an alternative sales-based ratio that is particularly useful when comparing companies with diverse capital structures. Example 36 illustrates the calculation of EV/S multiples.

EXAMPLE 36

Calculating Enterprise Value to Sales

As described in Example 22, Stora Enso Oyj (Helsinki Stock Exchange: STERV) reported net sales of €10,814.8 million for 2012. Based on 788.6 million shares outstanding and a stock price of €6.72 on 16 September 2013, the total market value of the company's equity was €5,299.4 million. The company reported debt of €4,522.3 million, minority interest of €91.5 million, and cash of €1,849.9 million. Assume that the market value of the company's debt is equal to the amount reported. Calculate the company's EV/S.

Solution:

Enterprise value = €5,299.4 million + €4,522.3 million + €91.5 million − €1,849.9 million = €8,063.3 million. So, EV/S = €8,063.3 million/€10,814.8 million = 0.75.

4.4 Price and Enterprise Value Multiples in a Comparable Analysis: Some Illustrative Data

In previous sections, we explained the major price and enterprise value multiples. Analysts using multiples and a benchmark based on closely similar companies should be aware of the range of values for multiples for peer companies and should track the fundamentals that may explain differences. For the sake of illustration Exhibit 21 shows, for fiscal year 2007, the median value of various multiples by GICS economic sector, the median dividend payout ratio, and median values of selected fundamentals:

- ROE and its determinants (net profit margin, asset turnover, and financial leverage).
- The compound average growth rate in operating margin for the three years ending with FY 2007 (shown in the last column under "3-Year CAGR Op Margin").

Exhibit 21 is based on the Standard & Poor's Super 1500 Composite Index for US equities consisting of the S&P 500, the S&P Midcap 400 Index, and the S&P SmallCap 600 Index. GICS was previously described in Section 3.1.5.

At the level of aggregation shown in Exhibit 21, the data are, arguably, most relevant to relative sector valuation. For the purposes of valuing individual companies, analysts would most likely use more narrowly defined industry or sector classification.

Exhibit 21   Fundamental and Valuation Statistics by GICS Economic Sector: Median Values from S&P 1500, FY2007

GICS Sector (count)	Valuation Statistics							Fundamental Statistics					
	Trailing P/E	P/B	P/S	P/CF	Dividend Yield (%)	EV/ EBITDA	EV/S	Net Profit Margin (%)	Asset Turnover	Financial Leverage	ROE (%)	Dividend Payout Ratio (%)	3-Year CAGR Operating Margin (%)
Energy (85)	14.406	2.531	2.186	8.622	0.4	7.733	2.64	13.942	0.573	2.103	19.688	4.024	12.035
Materials (85)	15.343	2.254	0.888	9.588	1.4	7.686	1.095	5.568	0.995	2.465	15.728	17.874	4.157
Industrials (207)	17.275	2.578	1.045	11.642	1.0	8.979	1.209	6.089	1.139	2.143	15.262	16.066	5.337
Consumer Discretionary (279)	15.417	2.254	0.789	9.986	0.7	7.634	0.928	4.777	1.383	2.12	13.289	0	-2.682
Consumer Staples (80)	19.522	3.048	1.122	13.379	1.4	10.66	1.237	5.306	1.351	2.208	17.264	23.133	-0.88
Health Care (167)	23.027	3.088	2.061	15.762	0	11.623	2.274	6.637	0.83	1.854	12.399	0	-1.708
Financials (257)	14.648	1.559	1.888	11.186	3.1	9.482	4.017	13.113	0.113	5.848	10.348	41.691	-4.124
Information Technology (252)	20.205	2.444	2.162	45.073	0	11.594	1.811	7.929	0.743	1.587	10.444	0	1.524
Telecommunication Services (13)	19.585	2.485	1.527	5.266	0.8	6.681	2.345	7.109	0.471	2.367	5.43	6.862	-2.421
Utilities (75)	16.682	1.784	1.151	8.405	3.1	9.056	1.903	7.21	0.439	3.52	11.853	52.738	0.361
Overall (1,500)	17.148	2.246	1.398	11.328	0.8	9.108	1.626	7.318	0.839	2.227	12.701	8.051	0.181

Source: Standard & Poor's Research Insight.

INTERNATIONAL CONSIDERATIONS WHEN USING MULTIPLES

5

Clearly, to perform a relative-value analysis, an analyst must use comparable companies and underlying financial data prepared by applying comparable methods. Therefore, using relative-valuation methods in an international setting is difficult. Comparing companies across borders frequently involves differences in accounting methods, cultural differences, economic differences, and resulting differences in risk and growth opportunities. P/Es for individual companies in the same industry but in different countries have been found to vary widely.[57] Furthermore, P/Es of different national markets often vary substantially at any single point in time.

Although international accounting standards are converging, significant differences still exist across borders, sometimes making comparisons difficult. Even when harmonization of accounting principles is achieved, the need to adjust accounting data for comparability will remain. As we showed in earlier sections, even within a single country's accounting standards, differences between companies result from accounting choices (e.g., FIFO versus average cost for inventory valuation). Prior to 2008, the US SEC required non-US companies whose securities trade in US markets to provide a reconciliation between their earnings from home-country accounting principles to US GAAP. This requirement not only assisted the analyst in making necessary adjustments but also provided some insight into appropriate adjustments for other companies not required to provide this data. In December 2007, however, the SEC eliminated the reconciliation requirement for non-US companies that use IFRS. Research analyzing reconciliations by EU companies with US listings shows that most of those companies reported net income under IFRS that was higher than they would have reported under US GAAP and lower shareholders' equity than they would have under US GAAP, with a result that more of the sample companies reported higher ROE under IFRS than under US GAAP.[58]

Exhibit 22 presents a reconciliation of net earnings and shareholders' equity from IFRS to US GAAP for ASM International (Euronext: ASM; NASDAQ:ASMI). Headquartered in Almere, Netherlands, ASM is a leading supplier of semiconductor process equipment for wafer processing.

Exhibit 22	Principal Differences between IFRS and US GAAP for ASM (Years Ended 31 December; Euros in Thousands)		
Measure		**2012**	**2011**
Net earnings in accordance with IFRS		48,453	324,146
Allowance for inventory obsolescence		−335	1,639
Tax rate difference on eliminated intercompany profit		718	−768
Pensions		691	—
Debt issuance expenses credit facility		−446	55
Development expenses		−8,650	−8,908
Net earnings in accordance with US GAAP		40,431	316,164

(continued)

---

57 Copeland, Koller, and Murrin (1994, p. 375) provide an interesting example.
58 In Henry, Lin, and Yang (2009), 28% of the sample firms' ROE under IFRS is more than 5 percentage points higher than under US GAAP, whereas fewer than 10% of the sample report ROE more than 5 percentage points lower.

Exhibit 22 (Continued)		
Measure	**2012**	**2011**
Total equity in accordance with IFRS	1,095,366	991,841
Goodwill	10,481	10,647
Allowance for inventory obsolescence	−2,009	−1,626
Tax rate difference on eliminated intercompany profit	−49	−768
Debt issuance expenses credit facility	735	1,181
Development expenses	−51,386	−43,740
Pension plans	−3,329	179
Total equity in accordance with US GAAP	1,049,809	957,714

Source: ASM 2012 Annual Report.

In a study of companies filing such reconciliations to US GAAP, Harris and Muller (1999) classified common differences into seven categories, as shown in Exhibit 23.

Exhibit 23 Reconciliation of IFRS to US GAAP: Average Adjustment		
Category	**Earnings**	**Equity**
Differences in the treatment of goodwill	Minus	Plus
Deferred income taxes	Plus	Plus
Foreign exchange adjustments	Plus	Minus
Research and development costs	Minus	Minus
Pension expense	Minus	Plus
Tangible asset revaluations	Plus	Minus
Other	Minus	Minus

In a more recent study of reconciliation data, Henry, Lin, and Yang (2009) find that among 20 categories of reconciliations, the most frequently occurring adjustments are in the pension category (including post-retirement benefits) and the largest value of adjustments are in the goodwill category.

Although the SEC's decision to eliminate the requirement for reconciliation has eliminated an important resource for analysts, accounting research can provide some insight into areas where differences between IFRS and US GAAP have commonly arisen. Going forward, analysts must be aware of differences across standards and make adjustments when disclosures provide sufficient data to do so.

International accounting differences affect the comparability of all price multiples. Of the price multiples examined in this reading, P/CFO and P/FCFE will generally be least affected by accounting differences. P/B, P/E, and multiples based on such concepts as EBITDA, which start from accounting earnings, will generally be the most affected.

MOMENTUM VALUATION INDICATORS

6

The valuation indicators we call momentum indicators relate either price or a fundamental, such as earnings, to the time series of their own past values or, in some cases, to the fundamental's expected value. One style of growth investing uses positive momentum in various senses as a selection criterion, and practitioners sometimes refer to such strategies as "growth/momentum investment strategies." Momentum indicators based on price, such as the relative-strength indicator we will discuss here, have also been referred to as **technical indicators**. According to the *BofA Merrill Lynch Institutional Factor Survey*, various momentum indicators were used by many institutional investors. In this section, we review three representative momentum indicators: earnings surprise, standardized unexpected earnings, and relative strength.

To define standardized unexpected earnings, we define **unexpected earnings** (also called **earnings surprise**) as the difference between reported earnings and expected earnings:

$$UE_t = \text{EPS}_t - E(\text{EPS}_t)$$

where UE_t is the unexpected earnings for quarter t, EPS_t is the reported EPS for quarter t, and $E(\text{EPS}_t)$ is the expected EPS for the quarter.

For example, a stock with reported quarterly earnings of $1.05 and expected earnings of $1.00 would have a positive earnings surprise of $0.05. Often, the percent earnings surprise (i.e., earnings surprise divided by expected EPS) is reported by data providers; in this example, the percent earning surprise would be $0.05/$1.00 = 0.05 or 5 percent. When used directly as a valuation indicator, earnings surprise is generally scaled by a measure reflecting the variability or range in analysts' EPS estimates. The principle is that the less disagreement among analysts' forecasts, the more meaningful the EPS forecast error of a given size in relation to the mean. A way to accomplish such scaling is to divide unexpected earnings by the standard deviation of analysts' earnings forecasts, which we refer to as the **scaled earnings surprise**. Example 37 illustrates the calculation of such a scaled earnings surprise.

EXAMPLE 37

Calculating Scaled Earnings Surprise by Using Analysts' Forecasts

As of late 2012, the mean consensus earnings forecast for BP plc (LSE: BP.L; NYSE: BP) for the fiscal year ending December 2012 was $0.91. Of the 33 estimates, the low forecast was $0.87, the high forecast was $1.20, and the standard deviation was $0.0952. If actual reported earnings for 2012 come in equal to the high forecast, what would be the measure of the earnings surprise for BP scaled to reflect the dispersion in analysts' forecasts?

Solution:

In this case, scaled earnings surprise would be ($1.20 − $0.91)/$0.0952 = 3.05.

The rationale behind using earnings surprise is the thesis that positive surprises may be associated with persistent positive abnormal returns, or alpha. The same rationale lies behind a momentum indicator that is closely related to earnings surprise but more highly researched, namely, **standardized unexpected earnings** (SUE). The SUE measure is defined as

$$SUE_t = \frac{EPS_t - E(EPS_t)}{\sigma\left[EPS_t - E(EPS_t)\right]}$$

where

$$EPS_t = \text{actual EPS for time } t$$
$$E(EPS_t) = \text{expected EPS for time } t$$
$$\sigma[EPS_t - E(EPS_t)] = \text{standard deviation of } [EPS_t - E(EPS_t)] \text{ over some historical}$$
$$\text{time period}$$

In words, the numerator is the unexpected earnings at time t and the denominator is the standard deviation of past unexpected earnings over some period prior to time t—for example, the 20 quarters prior to t as in Latané and Jones (1979), the article that introduced the SUE concept.[59] In SUE, the magnitude of unexpected earnings is scaled by a measure of the size of historical forecast errors or surprises. The principle is that the smaller (larger) the historical size of forecast errors, the more (less) meaningful a given size of EPS forecast error.

Suppose that for a stock with a $0.05 earnings surprise, the standard deviation of past surprises is $0.20. The $0.05 surprise is relatively small compared with past forecast errors, which would be reflected in a SUE score of $0.05/$0.20 = 0.25. If the standard error of past surprises were smaller—say, $0.07—the SUE score would be $0.05/$0.07 = 0.71. Example 38 applies analysis of SUE to two electronics companies.

EXAMPLE 38

Unexpected Earnings

Exhibits 24 and 25 provide information about the earnings surprise history for two companies: Exxon Mobil Corporation (NYSE: XOM) and Volkswagon AG (Xetra: VOW).

Exhibit 24   Earnings Surprise History for Exxon Mobil Corporation

Quarter Ending	EPS Release Date	Mean Consensus EPS Forecast	Actual EPS	% Surprise	Std. Dev.	SUE Score
Sep 2013	31 Oct 2013	1.77	1.79	0.88	0.1250	0.16
Jun 2013	1 Aug 2013	1.90	1.55	−18.39	0.0997	−3.51
Mar 2013	25 Apr 2013	2.05	2.12	3.59	0.0745	0.94
Dec 2012	1 Feb 2013	2.00	2.20	10.20	0.0463	4.32

---

59 For a summary of the research on SUE, see Reilly and Brown (2006) or Brown (1997).

Exhibit 25	Earnings Surprise History for Volkswagen AG (in Euros)					
Quarter Ending	EPS Release Date	Mean Consensus EPS Forecast	Actual EPS	% Surprise	Std. Dev.	SUE Score
Sep 2013	30 Oct 2013	4.53	3.79	−16.37	0.2846	−2.60
Jun 2013	30 Jul 2013	5.10	5.86	14.99	0.3858	1.97
Mar 2013	24 Apr 2013	4.15	4.24	2.17	1.1250	0.08
Dec 2012	22 Feb 2013	5.56	3.54	−36.33	0.5658	−3.57

Source: Thomson Surprise Report.

1 Explain how XOM's SUE score of 0.16 for the quarter ending September 2013 is calculated.

2 Based on these exhibits, for which company were the consensus forecasts less accurate over the past four quarters?

3 Was the consensus forecast more accurate for XOM or VOW for the quarter ending March 2013?

Solution to 1:

The amount of XOM's unexpected earnings (i.e., its earnings surprise) for the quarter ending September 2013 was $1.79 − $1.77 = $0.02. Dividing by the standard deviation of $0.1250 gives a SUE score of 0.16.

Solution to 2:

The answer depends on whether accuracy is measured by the "% Surprise" or by the "SUE score." If accuracy is measured by the % Surprise, then VOW's consensus forecasts were less accurate: % Surprise varied from −36.33% to +14.99% for VOW versus −18.39% to +10.20% for XOM. Using SUE, XOM's consensus forecasts were less accurate: SUE varied from −3.51 to +4.32 for XOM versus −3.57 to +1.13 for VOW. The reason for these differing results is that the standard deviation of the earnings estimates is relatively smaller for XOM than it is for VOW.

Solution to 3:

For the quarter ending March 2013, the consensus forecast was more accurate for VOW than XOM. Both the % Surprise and SUE were lower for VOW in this quarter.

Another set of indicators, **relative-strength indicators**, compares a stock's performance during a particular period either with its own past performance or with the performance of some group of stocks. The simplest relative-strength indicator that compares a stock's performance during a period with its past performance is the stock's compound rate of return over some specified time horizon, such as six months or one year. This indicator has also been referred to as **price momentum** in the academic literature. Despite its simplicity, this measure has been used in numerous studies.[60]

---

60 See Salsman (1997) for an example.

The rationale behind its use is the thesis that patterns of persistence or reversal exist in stock returns that may be shown empirically to depend on the investor's time horizon (Lee and Swamina than 2000).

Other definitions of relative strength relate a stock's return over a recent period to its return over a longer period that includes the more recent period. For example, a classic study of technical momentum indicators (Brock, Lakonishok, and LeBaron 1992) examined trading strategies based on two technical rules—namely, a moving-average oscillator and a trading-range break (i.e., resistance and support levels)—in which buy and sell signals are determined by the relationship between a short period's moving average and a longer period's moving average (and bands around those averages). The reader should keep in mind that research on patterns of historical stock returns is notoriously vulnerable to data snooping and hindsight biases. Furthermore, investing strategies based purely on technical momentum indicators are viewed as inherently self-destructing, in that "once a useful technical rule (or price pattern) is discovered, it ought to be invalidated when the mass of traders attempts to exploit it" (Bodie, Kane, and Marcus 2008, p. 377). Yet, the possibility of discovering a profitable trading rule and exploiting it prior to mass use continues to motivate research.

A simple relative-strength indicator of the second type (i.e., the stock's performance relative to the performance of some group of stocks) is the stock's performance divided by the performance of an equity index. If the value of this ratio increases, the stock price increases relative to the index and displays positive relative strength. Often, the relative-strength indicator is scaled to 1.0 at the beginning of the study period. If the stock goes up at a higher (lower) rate than the index, then relative strength will be above (below) 1.0. Relative strength in this sense is often calculated for industries and individual stocks. Example 39 explores this indicator.

EXAMPLE 39

Relative Strength in Relation to an Equity Index

Exhibit 26 shows the values of the S&P 500 and three exchange-traded funds (ETFs) for the end of each of 18 months from April 2012 through September 2013. The ETFs are for long-term US Treasury securities, the STOXX Europe 50 Index, an emerging Europe SPDR. SPDR stands for Standard & Poor's Depositary Receipt.

Exhibit 26	A Relative Strength Comparison			
Date	S&P 500 Index	SPDR Barclays Long-Term Treasury (TLO)	SPDR Stoxx Europe 50 Index (FEU)	SPDR S&P Emerging Europe ETF (GUR)
2-Apr-2012	1397.91	65.77	29.46	39.55
1-May-2012	1310.33	70.86	26.32	32.42
1-Jun-2012	1362.16	69.98	28.45	35.96
2-Jul-2012	1379.32	72.29	28.71	36.06
1-Aug-2012	1406.58	71.38	29.75	37.89
4-Sep-2012	1440.67	69.93	30.52	39.46
1-Oct-2012	1412.16	69.76	30.92	39.05
1-Nov-2012	1416.18	70.49	31.51	39.25

Exhibit 26   (Continued)

Date	S&P 500 Index	SPDR Barclays Long-Term Treasury (TLO)	SPDR Stoxx Europe 50 Index (FEU)	SPDR S&P Emerging Europe ETF (GUR)
3-Dec-2012	1426.19	68.72	32.62	42.90
2-Jan-2013	1498.11	66.81	33.98	43.54
1-Feb-2013	1514.68	67.62	32.80	40.86
1-Mar-2013	1569.19	67.53	33.12	40.26
1-Apr-2013	1597.57	70.35	34.49	39.93
1-May-2013	1630.74	65.86	34.26	38.78
3-Jun-2013	1606.28	63.56	32.87	36.89
1-Jul-2013	1685.73	62.60	34.85	37.81
1-Aug-2013	1632.97	61.82	34.31	36.81
3-Sep-2013	1639.77	61.02	34.67	36.67

To produce the information for Exhibit 27, we divided each ETF value by the S&P 500 value for the same month and then scaled those results so that the value of the relative-strength indicator (RSTR) for April 2012 would equal 1.0. To illustrate, on 2 April 2012, the value of TLO divided by the S&P 500 was 65.77/1,397.91 = 0.0470. The RSTR for TLO on that date, by design, is then 0.0470/0.0470 = 1.0. In May, the value of TLO divided by the S&P 500 was 70.86/1,310.33 = 0.0541, which we scaled by the April number. The RSTR for 1 May 2012 for GLD is 0.0541/0.0470 = 1.1494, shown in Exhibit 27 as 1.149.

Exhibit 27   Relative-Strength Indicators

Date	RSTR SPDR Barclays Long-Term Treasury (TLO)	RSTR SPDR STOXX Europe 50 Index (FEU)	RSTR SPDR Emerging Europe (GUR)
2-Apr-2012	1.000	1.00	1.00
1-May-2012	1.149	0.953	0.875
1-Jun-2012	1.092	0.991	0.933
2-Jul-2012	1.114	0.988	0.924
1-Aug-2012	1.079	1.004	0.952
4-Sep-2012	1.032	1.005	0.968
1-Oct-2012	1.050	1.039	0.977
1-Nov-2012	1.058	1.056	0.980
3-Dec-2012	1.024	1.085	1.063
2-Jan-2013	0.948	1.076	1.027
1-Feb-2013	0.949	1.028	0.953
1-Mar-2013	0.915	1.002	0.907
1-Apr-2013	0.936	1.024	0.883
1-May-2013	0.858	0.997	0.841

(continued)

Date	RSTR SPDR Barclays Long-Term Treasury (TLO)	RSTR SPDR STOXX Europe 50 Index (FEU)	RSTR SPDR Emerging Europe (GUR)
Exhibit 27 (Continued)			
3-Jun-2013	0.841	0.971	0.812
1-Jul-2013	0.789	0.981	0.793
1-Aug-2013	0.805	0.997	0.797
3-Sep-2013	0.785	0.995	0.784

On the basis of Exhibits 26 and 27, address the following:

1 State the relative strength of long-term US Treasury securities, STOXX Europe 50 Index, and emerging Europe stocks over the entire time period April 2012 through September 2013. Interpret the relative strength for each sector over that period.

2 Discuss the relative performance of the STOXX Europe 50 Index ETF and the emerging Europe ETF in the period ending 3 December 2012.

Solution to 1:

The relative-strength indicator for long-term US Treasuries is 0.785. This number represents 0.785 − 1.000 = −0.215, or 21.5 percent under-performance relative to the S&P 500 over the time period. The relative-strength indicator for the STOXX Europe 50 Index is 0.995. This number represents 1.000 − 0.995 = −0.005, or 0.5 percent underperformance relative to the S&P 500 over the time period. The relative-strength indicator for the emerging Europe ETF is 0.784, indicating that it underperformed the S&P 500 by 21.6 percent over the time frame.

Solution to 2:

The December 2012 RSTR for the STOXX Europe 50 Index, at 1.085, is higher than in the prior month by 2.9 percent, whereas the emerging Europe RSTR, at 1.063, is higher than in the prior month by 8.3 percent. In December 2012, the emerging Europe ETF outperformed the STOXX Europe 50 Index ETF. The relative performance for that one month differs from the relative performance over the entire period, during which the STOXX Europe 50 Index significantly outperformed the emerging Europe ETF.

Overall, momentum indicators have a substantial following among professional investors. Some view momentum indicators as signals that should prompt an analyst to consider whether a stock price is moving successively *farther from* or successively *closer to* the fundamental valuations derived from models and multiples. In other words, an analyst might be correct about the intrinsic value of a firm and the momentum indicators might provide a clue about when the market price will converge with that intrinsic value. The use of such indicators continues to be a subject of active research in industry and in business schools.

VALUATION INDICATORS: ISSUES IN PRACTICE

All the valuation indicators discussed in this reading are quantitative aids but not necessarily solutions to the problem of security selection. In this section, we discuss some issues that arise in practice when averages are used to establish benchmark multiples and then illustrate the use of multiple valuation indicators.

7.1 Averaging Multiples: The Harmonic Mean

The harmonic mean and the weighted harmonic mean are often applied to average a group of price multiples.

Consider a hypothetical portfolio that contains two stocks. For simplicity, assume the portfolio owns 100 percent of the shares of each stock. One stock has a market capitalization of €715 million and earnings of €71.5 million, giving it a P/E of 10. The other stock has a market capitalization of €585 million and earnings of €29.25 million, for a P/E of 20. Note that the P/E for the portfolio is calculated directly by aggregating the companies' market capitalizations and earnings: (€715 + €585)/(€71.50 + €29.25) = €1,300/€100.75 = 12.90. The question that will be addressed is: What calculation of portfolio P/E, based on the individual stock P/Es, best reflects the value of 12.90?

If the ratio of an individual holding is represented by X_i, the expression for the simple **harmonic mean** of the ratio is

$$X_H = \frac{n}{\displaystyle\sum_{i=1}^{n}(1/X_i)} \qquad\qquad (8)$$

which is the reciprocal of the arithmetic mean of the reciprocals.

The expression for the **weighted harmonic mean** is

$$X_{WH} = \frac{1}{\displaystyle\sum_{i=1}^{n}(\omega_i/X_i)} \qquad\qquad (9)$$

where the w_i are portfolio value weights (summing to 1) and $X_i > 0$ for $i = 1, 2, ..., n$.

Exhibit 28 displays the calculation of the hypothetical portfolio's simple arithmetic mean P/E, weighted mean P/E, (simple) harmonic mean P/E, and weighted harmonic mean P/E.

Exhibit 28 Alternative Mean P/Es

Security	Market Cap (€ Millions)	Percent	Earnings (€ Millions)	Stock P/E	(1)	(2)	(3)	(4)
Stock 1	715	55	71.50	10	0.5 × 10	0.55 × 10	0.5 × 0.1	0.55 × 0.1
Stock 2	585	45	29.25	20	0.5 × 20	0.45 × 20	0.5 × 0.05	0.45 × 0.05
					15	14.5	0.075	0.0775
Arithmetic mean P/E (1)					**15**			
Weighted mean P/E (2)						**14.5**		

(continued)

Exhibit 28   (Continued)

| Security | Market Cap | | Earnings | Stock | | | | |
	(€ Millions)	Percent	(€ Millions)	P/E	(1)	(2)	(3)	(4)
Harmonic mean P/E (3)							1/0.075 = **13.33**	
Weighted harmonic mean P/E (4)								1/0.0775 = **12.90**

The weighted harmonic mean P/E precisely corresponds to the portfolio P/E value of 12.90. This example explains why index fund vendors frequently use the weighted harmonic mean to calculate the "average" P/E or average value of other price multiples for indices. In some applications, an analyst might not want or be able to incorporate the market value weight information needed to calculate the weighted harmonic mean. In such cases, the simple harmonic mean can still be calculated.

Note that the simple harmonic mean P/E is smaller than the arithmetic mean and closer to the directly calculated value of 12.90 in this example. The harmonic mean inherently gives less weight to higher P/Es and more weight to lower P/Es. In general, unless all the observations in a data set have the same value, the harmonic mean is less than the arithmetic mean.

As explained and illustrated earlier in this reading, using the median rather than the arithmetic mean to derive an average multiple mitigates the effect of outliers. The harmonic mean is sometimes also used to reduce the impact of large outliers—which are typically the major concern in using the arithmetic mean multiple—but not the impact of small outliers (i.e., those close to zero). The harmonic mean tends to mitigate the impact of large outliers. The harmonic mean may aggravate the impact of small outliers, but such outliers are bounded by zero on the downside.

We can use the group of telecommunications companies examined earlier in the reading (see Exhibit 5) to illustrate differences between the arithmetic mean and harmonic mean. This group includes two large outliers for P/E, Equinix at a P/E of 131.28 and Verizon at a P/E of 86.06. Exhibit 29 shows mean values including and excluding the outliers.

Exhibit 29   Arithmetic versus Harmonic Mean

Company	Trailing P/E (with Outliers)	Trailing P/E (No Outliers)
AT&T (NYSE: T)	25.73	25.73
BCE Inc. (NYSE: BCE; TSX: BCE)	14.49	14.49
Centurytel (NYSE: CTL)	18.86	18.86
Equinix (NASDAQ GS: EQIX)	131.28	
Frontier Communications Corp. (NASDAQ GS: FTR)	43.30	43.30
Verizon Communications (NYSE: VZ)	86.06	
Windstream Corp. (NYSE: WIN)	36.91	36.91
Arithmetic mean	50.95	27.86

Company	Trailing P/E (with Outliers)	Trailing P/E (No Outliers)
Median	36.91	25.73
Harmonic mean	30.39	23.69

Exhibit 29   (Continued)

Note that for the entire group, the mean (50.95) is far higher than the median (36.91) because of Equinix and Verizon. The harmonic mean (30.39) is much closer to the median and more plausible as representing central tendency. Once the outliers are eliminated, the values for the arithmetic mean (27.86), median (25.73), and harmonic mean (23.69) are more tightly grouped. The lower value for the harmonic mean reflects the fact that this approach mitigates the effect of the relatively high P/E for Frontier (43.30) and Windstream (36.91).

This example illustrates the importance for the analyst of understanding how an average has been calculated, particularly when the analyst is reviewing information prepared by another analyst, and the usefulness of examining several summary statistics.

7.2 Using Multiple Valuation Indicators

Because each carefully selected and calculated price multiple, momentum indicator, or fundamental may supply some piece of the puzzle of stock valuation, many investors and analysts use more than one valuation indicator (in addition to other criteria) in stock valuation and selection. Example 40 illustrates the use of multiple indicators.

EXAMPLE 40

Multiple Indicators in Stock Valuation

The following excerpts from past equity analyst reports illustrate the use of multiple ratios in communicating views about a stock's value. In the first excerpt, from a report on Colorpak Ltd. (Australian Stock Exchange: CKL), the analyst has used a discounted cash flow valuation as the preferred methodology but notes that the stock is also attractive when a price-to-earnings ratio (PER in the report) is used. In the second excerpt, from a report on AB InBev (Euronext Belgium: ABI), an analyst evaluates the stock price (then trading at 42.80) by using two multiples, price to earnings (P/E) and EV/EBITDA, in relation to revised forecasts.

Colorpak Ltd. (Australian Stock Exchange: CKL)

Our DCF for CKL is A$0.82ps, which represents a 44% prem. to the current price. Whilst the DCF valuation is our preferred methodology, we recognise that CKL also looks attractive on different metrics.

Applying a mid-cycle PER multiple of 10.5× (30% disc to mkt) to FY08 EPS of 7.6cps, we derive a valuation of A$0.80. Importantly, were the stock to reach our target of A$0.75ps in 12mths, CKL would be trading on a fwd PER of 9.1×, which we do not view as demanding. At current levels, the stock is also offering an attractive dividend yield of 5.7% (fully franked). [*Note*: "fully franked" is a concept specific to the Australian market and refers to tax treatment of the dividend.]

Mario Maia, CFA
Merrill Lynch (Australia)

AB InBev (Euronext Belgium: ABI)

Based on our slightly increased estimates, the shares are valued at a P/E and EV/EBITDA 2012 of 12.4x and 9x, slightly below the valuation of the large FMCG (fast-moving consumer goods) and spirits companies. Given its stronger profit growth, the brewer [ABI] could command a premium. We raise our target price from EUR52 to EUR53, implying a 24% upside. Buy.

Ton van Ooijen, CFA
Kepler Research

In selecting stocks, institutional investors surveyed in the *BofA Merrill Lynch Institutional Factor Surveys* from 1989 to 2012 used an average of 9.3 factors in selecting stocks (does not include 2008-2010 due to a lack of sufficient responses). The survey factors included not only price multiples, momentum indicators, and the DDM but also the fundamentals ROE, debt to equity, projected five-year EPS growth, EPS variability, EPS estimate dispersion, size, beta, foreign exposure, low price, and neglect. Exhibit 30 lists the factors classified by percentage of investors indicating that they use that factor in making investment decisions, out of 137 responders in 2012.

Exhibit 30	Frequency of Investor Usage of Factors in Making Investment Decisions

High (●) >50%; Med (♦) >30%<50%; Low (○) <30%

Factor	Frequency
P/E	●
Beta	●
EV/EBITDA	●
ROE	●
Size	●
P/B	●
P/FCF	♦
Share Repurchase	♦
Earnings Estimate Revision	♦
Margins	♦
Relative Strength	♦
EPS Momentum	♦
D/E	♦
EPS Variability	♦
DDM/DCF	♦
PEG	♦
Long-Term Price Trend	♦

Exhibit 30   (Continued)

High (●) >50%; Med (♦) >30%<50%; Low (○) <30%

Factor	Frequency
P/CF	♦
Analyst Neglect	♦
Dividend Growth	♦
Projected 5-Year EPS Growth	♦
Mean Reversion	♦
Normalized P/E	♦
P/S	♦
Net Debt/EBITDA	○
EPS Surprise	○
ROC	○
ROA	○
EPS Estimate Dispersion	○
Analyst Rating Revisions	○
Foreign Exposure	○
Long-term Price Trend w/ Short-Term Reversal	○
Trading Volume	○
Price Target	○
Ownership	○
Short-Term Price Trend	○
EV/Sales	○
Low Price	○
Altman Z-Score	○
Equity Duration	○

Source: BofA Merrill Lynch 2012 Institutional Factor Survey.

An issue concerning the use of ratios in an investing strategy is look-ahead bias. **Look-ahead bias** is the use of information that was not contemporaneously available in computing a quantity. Investment analysts often use historical data to back test an investment strategy that involves stock selection based on price multiples or other factors. When back testing, an analyst should be aware that time lags in the reporting of financial results create the potential for look-ahead bias in such research. For example, as of early January 2014, most companies had not reported EPS for the last quarter of 2013, so at that time, a company's trailing P/E would be based on EPS for the first, second, and third quarters of 2013 and the last quarter of 2012. Any investment strategy based on a trailing P/E that used actual EPS for the last quarter of 2013 could be implemented only after the data became available. Thus, if an analysis assumed that an investment was made in early January 2014 based on full-year 2013 data, the analysis would involve look-ahead bias. To avoid this bias an analyst would calculate the trailing P/E based on the most recent four quarters of EPS then being reported. The same principle applies to other multiples calculated on a trailing basis.

The application of a set of criteria to reduce an investment universe to a smaller set of investments is called **screening**. Stock screens often include not only criteria based on the valuation measures discussed in this reading but also on fundamental criteria that may explain differences in such measures. Computerized stock screening is an efficient way to narrow a search for investments and is a part of many stock selection disciplines. The limitations to many commercial databases and screening tools usually include lack of control by the user of the calculation of important inputs (such as EPS); the absence of qualitative factors in most databases is another important limitation. Example 41 illustrates the use of a screen in stock selection.

EXAMPLE 41

Using Screens to Find Stocks for a Portfolio

Janet Larsen manages an institutional portfolio and is currently looking for new stocks to add to the portfolio. Larsen has a commercial database with information on US stocks. She has designed several screens to select stocks with low P/Es and low P/B multiples. Because Larsen is aware that screening for low P/E and low P/B multiples may identify stocks with low expected growth, she also wants stocks that have a PEG less than 1.0. She decides to screen for stocks with a dividend yield of at least 3.0 percent and a total market capitalization over $10 billion. Exhibit 31 shows the number of stocks that successively met each of the five criteria as of January 2014 (so, the number of stocks that met all five criteria is 6).

Exhibit 31	Stock Screen
Criterion	**Stocks Meeting Each Criterion Successively**
P/E < 20.0	1,674
P/B < 2.0	1,135
PEG < 1.0	156
Dividend yield ≥ 3.0%	113
Market capitalization over $10 billion	6

Other information:

- The screening database indicates that the P/E was 19.4, P/B was 2.6, and the dividend yield was 2.1 percent for the S&P 500 as of the date of the screen.

- S&P's *US Style Indices Methodology* indicates that the style indices measure growth and value by the following six factors, which S&P standardizes and uses to compute growth and value scores for each company:

  Three Growth Factors

  Three-year change in EPS over price per share

  Three-year sales per share growth rate

  Momentum (12-month percentage price change)

  Three Value Factors

  Book value to price ratio

  Earnings to price ratio

  Sales to price ratio

- In July of 2013, the S&P Dow Jones US Index Committee raised the market cap guidelines used when selecting companies for the S&P 500, S&P Mid-Cap 400 and S&P Small-Cap 600. The new guidelines are:

    S&P 500: Over $4.6 billion

    S&P Mid-Cap 400: $1.2 to $5.1 billion

    S&P Small-Cap 600: $350 million to $1.6 billion

Using the information supplied, answer the following questions:

1 What type of valuation indicators does Larsen *not* include in her stock screen?

2 Characterize the overall orientation of Larsen as to investment style.

3 State two limitations of Larsen's stock screen.

Solution to 1:

Larsen has not included momentum indicators in the screen.

Solution to 2:

Larsen can be characterized as a large-cap value investor, based on the specified market capitalization. Although her screen does include a PEG, it excludes explicit growth rate criteria, such as those used by S&P, and it excludes momentum indicators usually associated with a growth orientation, such as positive earnings surprise. Larsen also uses a cutoff for P/B that is less than the average P/B for the S&P 500. Note that her criteria for multiples are all "less than" criteria.

Solution to 3:

Larsen does not include any profitability criteria or risk measurements. These omissions are a limitation because a stock's expected low profitability or high risk may explain its low P/E. Another limitation of her screen is that the computations of the value indicators in a commercial database may not reflect the appropriate adjustments to inputs. The absence of qualitative criteria is also a possible limitation.

Investors also apply all the metrics that we have illustrated in terms of individual stocks to industries and economic sectors. For example, average price multiples and momentum indicators can be used in sector rotation strategies to determine relatively under-or overvalued sectors.[61] (A sector rotation strategy is an investment strategy that overweights economic sectors that are anticipated to outperform or lead the overall market.)

SUMMARY

In this reading, we have defined and explained the most important valuation indicators in professional use and illustrated their application to a variety of valuation problems.

- Price multiples are ratios of a stock's price to some measure of value per share.

---

[61] Chan, Jegadeesh, and Lakonishok (1999) and Lee and Swaminathan (2000).

- Price multiples are most frequently applied to valuation in the method of comparables. This method involves using a price multiple to evaluate whether an asset is relatively undervalued, fairly valued, or overvalued in relation to a benchmark value of the multiple.

- The benchmark value of the multiple may be the multiple of a similar company or the median or average value of the multiple for a peer group of companies, an industry, an economic sector, an equity index, or the company's own median or average past values of the multiple.

- The economic rationale for the method of comparables is the law of one price.

- Price multiples may also be applied to valuation in the method based on forecasted fundamentals. Discounted cash flow (DCF) models provide the basis and rationale for this method. Fundamentals also interest analysts who use the method of comparables because differences between a price multiple and its benchmark value may be explained by differences in fundamentals.

- The key idea behind the use of price-to-earnings ratios (P/Es) is that earning power is a chief driver of investment value and earnings per share (EPS) is probably the primary focus of security analysts' attention. The EPS figure, however, is frequently subject to distortion, often volatile, and sometimes negative.

- The two alternative definitions of P/E are trailing P/E, based on the most recent four quarters of EPS, and forward P/E, based on next year's expected earnings.

- Analysts address the problem of cyclicality by normalizing EPS—that is, calculating the level of EPS that the business could achieve currently under midcyclical conditions (normalized EPS).

- Two methods to normalize EPS are the method of historical average EPS (calculated over the most recent full cycle) and the method of average return on equity (EPS = average ROE multiplied by current book value per share).

- Earnings yield (E/P) is the reciprocal of the P/E. When stocks have zero or negative EPS, a ranking by earnings yield is meaningful whereas a ranking by P/E is not.

- Historical trailing P/Es should be calculated with EPS lagged a sufficient amount of time to avoid look-ahead bias. The same principle applies to other multiples calculated on a trailing basis.

- The fundamental drivers of P/E are the expected earnings growth rate and the required rate of return. The justified P/E based on fundamentals bears a positive relationship to the first factor and an inverse relationship to the second factor.

- PEG (P/E to growth) is a tool to incorporate the impact of earnings growth on P/E. PEG is calculated as the ratio of the P/E to the consensus growth forecast. Stocks with low PEGs are, all else equal, more attractive than stocks with high PEGs.

- We can estimate terminal value in multistage DCF models by using price multiples based on comparables. The expression for terminal value, V_n, is (using P/E as the example)

$$V_n = \text{Benchmark value of trailing P/E} \times E_n$$

or

$$V_n = \text{Benchmark value of forward P/E} \times E_{n+1}$$

- Book value per share is intended to represent, on a per-share basis, the investment that common shareholders have in the company. Inflation, technological change, and accounting distortions, however, may impair the use of book value for this purpose.

- Book value is calculated as common shareholders' equity divided by the number of shares outstanding. Analysts adjust book value to accurately reflect the value of the shareholders' investment and to make P/B (the price-to-book ratio) more useful for comparing different stocks.

- The fundamental drivers of P/B are ROE and the required rate of return. The justified P/B based on fundamentals bears a positive relationship to the first factor and an inverse relationship to the second factor.

- An important rationale for using the price-to-sales ratio (P/S) is that sales, as the top line in an income statement, are generally less subject to distortion or manipulation than other fundamentals, such as EPS or book value. Sales are also more stable than earnings and are never negative.

- P/S fails to take into account differences in cost structure between businesses, may not properly reflect the situation of companies losing money, and may be subject to manipulation through revenue recognition practices.

- The fundamental drivers of P/S are profit margin, growth rate, and the required rate of return. The justified P/S based on fundamentals bears a positive relationship to the first two factors and an inverse relationship to the third factor.

- Enterprise value (EV) is total company value (the market value of debt, common equity, and preferred equity) minus the value of cash and investments.

- The ratio of EV to total sales is conceptually preferable to P/S because EV/S facilitates comparisons among companies with varying capital structures.

- A key idea behind the use of price to cash flow is that cash flow is less subject to manipulation than are earnings. Price to cash flow multiples are often more stable than P/E. Some common approximations to cash flow from operations have limitations, however, because they ignore items that may be subject to manipulation.

- The major cash flow (and related) concepts used in multiples are earnings plus noncash charges (CF), cash flow from operations (CFO), free cash flow to equity (FCFE), and earnings before interest, taxes, depreciation, and amortization (EBITDA).

- In calculating price to cash flow, the earnings-plus-noncash-charges concept is traditionally used, although FCFE has the strongest link to financial theory.

- CF and EBITDA are not strictly cash flow numbers because they do not account for noncash revenue and net changes in working capital.

- The fundamental drivers of price to cash flow, however defined, are the expected growth rate of future cash flow and the required rate of return. The justified price to cash flow based on fundamentals bears a positive relationship to the first factor and an inverse relationship to the second.

- EV/EBITDA is preferred to P/EBITDA because EBITDA, as a preinterest number, is a flow to all providers of capital.

- EV/EBITDA may be more appropriate than P/E for comparing companies with different amounts of financial leverage (debt).

- EV/EBITDA is frequently used in the valuation of capital-intensive businesses.

- The fundamental drivers of EV/EBITDA are the expected growth rate in free cash flow to the firm, profitability, and the weighted average cost of capital. The justified EV/EBITDA based on fundamentals bears a positive relationship to the first two factors and an inverse relationship to the third.

- Dividend yield has been used as a valuation indicator because it is a component of total return and is less risky than capital appreciation.

- Trailing dividend yield is calculated as four times the most recent quarterly per-share dividend divided by the current market price.

- The fundamental drivers of dividend yield are the expected growth rate in dividends and the required rate of return.

- Comparing companies across borders frequently involves dealing with differences in accounting standards, cultural differences, economic differences, and resulting differences in risk and growth opportunities.

- Momentum indicators relate either price or a fundamental to the time series of the price or fundamental's own past values (in some cases, to their expected values).

- Momentum valuation indicators include earnings surprise, standardized unexpected earnings (SUE), and relative strength.

- Unexpected earnings (or earnings surprise) equals the difference between reported earnings and expected earnings.

- SUE is unexpected earnings divided by the standard deviation in past unexpected earnings.

- Relative-strength indicators allow comparison of a stock's performance during a period either with its own past performance (first type) or with the performance of some group of stocks (second type). The rationale for using relative strength is the thesis that patterns of persistence or reversal in returns exist.

- Screening is the application of a set of criteria to reduce an investment universe to a smaller set of investments and is a part of many stock selection disciplines. In general, limitations of such screens include the lack of control in vendor-provided data of the calculation of important inputs and the absence of qualitative factors.

REFERENCES

Arnott, Robert D., and Clifford S. Asness. 2003. "Surprise! Higher Dividends = Higher Earnings Growth." *Financial Analysts Journal*, vol. 59, no. 1:70–87.

Aubert, Samuel, and Pierre Giot. 2007. "An international test of the Fed model." *Journal of Asset Management*, vol. 8, no. 2:86–100.

Bhojraj, Sanjeev, Charles M.C. Lee, and Derek K. Oler. 2003. "What's My Line? A Comparison of Industry Classification Schemes for Capital Market Research." *Journal of Accounting Research*, vol. 41, no. 5:745–774.

Bodie, Zvi, Alex Kane, and Alan J. Marcus. 2008. *Investments*, 7th edition. New York: McGraw-Hill.

Brock, William, Joseph Lakonishok, and Blake LeBaron. 1992. "Simple Technical Trading Rules and the Stochastic Properties of Stock Returns." *Journal of Finance*, vol. 47, no. 5:1731–1764.

Brown, Lawrence D. 1997. "Earnings Surprise Research: Synthesis and Perspectives." *Financial Analysts Journal*, vol. 53, no. 2:13–20.

Chan, L.K.C., and J. Lakonishok. 2004. "Value and Growth Investing: Review and Update." *Financial Analysts Journal*, vol. 60, no. 1:71–86.

Chan, Louis K.C., Narasimhan Jegadeesh, and Josef Lakonishok. 1999. "The Profitability of Momentum Strategies." *Financial Analysts Journal*, vol. 55, no. 6:80–90.

Chan, Louis K.C., Josef Lakonishok, and Bhaskaran Swaminathan. 2007. "Industry Classifications and Return Comovement." *Financial Analysts Journal*, vol. 63, no. 6:56–70.

Copeland, Tom, Tim Koller, and Jack Murrin. 1994. *Valuation: Measuring and Managing the Value of Companies*, 2nd edition. Hoboken, NJ: John Wiley & Sons.

Damodaran, Aswath. 2012. *Investment Valuation: Tools and Techniques for Determining the Value of Any Asset*, 3rd edition. Hoboken, NJ: John Wiley & Co.

Fairfield, Patricia M. 1994. "P/E, P/B and the Present Value of Future Dividends." *Financial Analysts Journal*, vol. 50, no. 4:23–31.

Fama, Eugene F., and Kenneth R. French. 1992. "The Cross-Section of Expected Stock Returns." *Journal of Finance*, vol. 47, no. 2:427–465.

Graham, Benjamin, and David L. Dodd. 1934. *Security Analysis*. McGraw-Hill Professional Publishing.

Grant, Julia, and Larry Parker. 2001. "EBITDA!" *Research in Accounting Regulation*, vol. 15:205–211.

Hackel, Kenneth S., Joshua Livnat, and Atul Rai. 1994. "The Free Cash Flow/Small-Cap Anomaly." *Financial Analysts Journal*, vol. 50, no. 5:33–42.

Harris, Robert S., and Felicia C. Marston. 1994. "Value versus Growth Stocks: Book-to-Market, Growth, and Beta." *Financial Analysts Journal*, vol. 50, no. 5:18–24.

Harris, Mary, and Karl A. Muller III. 1999. "The Market Valuation of IAS versus U.S. GAAP Accounting Measures using Form 20-F Reconciliations." *Journal of Accounting and Economics*, vol. 26, no. 1-3:285–312.

Henry, E., S. Lin, and Y. Yang. 2009. "The European–U.S. GAAP Gap: Amount, type, homogeneity, and value relevance of IFRS to U.S. GAAP Form 20-F reconciliations." *Accounting Horizons*, vol. 23, no. 2:121–150.

Kisor, Manown, Jr, and Volkert S. Whitbeck. 1963. "A New Tool in Investment Decision-Making." *Financial Analysts Journal*, vol. 19, no. 3:55–62.

Lakonishok, J., A. Shleifer, and R.W. Vishny. 1994. "Contrarian Investment, Extrapolation and Risk." *Journal of Finance*, vol. 49, no. 5:1541–1578.

Lander, Joel, Athanasios Orphanides, and Martha Douvogiannis. 1997. "Earnings, Forecasts and the Predictability of Stock Returns: Evidence from Trading the S&P." *Journal of Portfolio Management*, vol. 23, no. 4:24–35.

Latané, Henry A., and Charles P. Jones. 1979. "Standardized Unexpected Earnings—1971–77." *Journal of Finance*, vol. 34, no. 3:717–724.

Lee, Charles M.C., and Bhaskaran Swaminathan. 2000. "Price Momentum and Trading Volume." *Journal of Finance*, vol. 55, no. 5:2017–2069.

Lee, Charles M.C., James Myers, and Bhaskaran Swaminathan. 1999. "What is the Intrinsic Value of the Dow?" *Journal of Finance*, vol. 54, no. 5:1693–1741.

Liu, Jing, Doron Nissim, and Jacob Thomas. 2002. "Equity Valuation Using Multiples." *Journal of Accounting Research*, vol. 40, no. 1:136–172.

Liu, Jing, Doron Nissim, and Jacob Thomas. 2007. "Is Cash Flow King in Valuations?" *Financial Analysts Journal*, vol. 63, no. 2:56–68.

Malkiel, Burton, and John Cragg. 1970. "Expectations and the Structure of Share Prices." *American Economic Review*, vol. 60, no. 4:601–617.

Martin, Thomas A., Jr 1998. "Traditional Equity Valuation Methods." *Equity Research and Valuation Techniques*. Charlottesville, VA: AIMR.

Michaud, Richard. 1999. *Investment Styles, Market Anomalies, and Global Stock Selection*. Research Foundation of the ICFA: AIMR.

Moody's. 2000. *Putting EBITDA in Perspective*. Moody's Investors Service Global Credit Research.

Mulford, Charles W., and Eugene E. Comiskey. 2005. *Creative Cash Flow Reporting: Uncovering Sustainable Financial Performance*. Hoboken, NJ: John Wiley & Sons.

Nathan, Siva, Kumar Sivakumar, and Jayaraman Vijayakumar. 2001. "Returns to Trading Strategies Based on Price-to-Earnings and Price-to-Sales Ratios." *Journal of Investing*, vol. 10, no. 2:17–28.

O'Shaughnessy, James P. 2005. *What Works on Wall Street: A Guide to the Best-Performing Investment Strategies of All Time*, third edition. New York: McGraw-Hill Professional Publishing.

Pinto, Jerald, Howard Marmorstein, Thomas Robinson, John Stowe, and Dennis McLeavey. 2008. "A Survey of Equity Analysts' Valuation Practices." Working paper, 10 November.

Reilly, Frank K., and Keith C. Brown. 2006. *Investment Analysis and Portfolio Management*, 8th edition. Mason, OH: South-Western.

Richardson, Scott, and Irem Tuna. 2008. "Evaluating Financial Reporting Quality." *International Financial Statement Analysis*. Thomas Robinson, Hennie van Greuning, Elaine Henry, Michael Broihahn, eds. Hoboken, NJ: John Wiley & Sons.

Salsman, Richard M. 1997. "Using Market Prices to Guide Sector Rotation." *Economic Analysis for Investment Professionals*. Charlottesville, VA: AIMR. 48–55.

Senchack, A.J., Jr, and John D. Martin. 1987. "The Relative Performance of the PSR and PER Investment Strategies." *Financial Analysts Journal*, vol. 43, no. 2:46–56.

Siegel, Jeremy. 2002. *Stocks for the Long Run*, 3rd edition. New York: McGraw Hill.

Sloan, Richard G. 1996. "Do Stock Prices Fully Reflect Information in Accruals and Cash Flows About Future Earnings?" *Accounting Review*, vol. 71, no. 3:289–315.

Solnik, Bruno, and Dennis McLeavey. 2004. *International Investments*, 5th edition. Boston: Pearson Addison-Wesley.

Stimes, Peter C., and Stephen E. Wilcox. 2011. "Equity Market Valuation," Ch. 11. *Investments: Principles of Portfolio and Equity Analysis*, Hoboken, NJ: John Wiley & Sons, Inc.

Wild, John J., Leopold A. Bernstein, and K.R. Subramanyam. 2001. *Financial Statement Analysis*, 7th edition. New York: McGraw-Hill Irwin.

Yardeni, Edward. 2000. "How to Value Earnings Growth." *Topical Study #49*. Deutsche Banc Alex Brown.

Zhou, Ping, and William Ruland. 2006. "Dividend Payout and Future Earnings Growth." *Financial Analysts Journal*, vol. 62, no. 3:58–69.

PRACTICE PROBLEMS

1   As of February 2008, you are researching Jonash International, a hypothetical company subject to cyclical demand for its services. Jonash shares closed at $57.98 on 2 February 2007. You believe the 2003–2006 period reasonably captures average profitability:

Measure	2007	2006	2005	2004	2003
EPS	E$3.03	$1.45	$0.23	$2.13	$2.55
BV per share	E$19.20	$16.21	$14.52	$13.17	$11.84
ROE	E16.0%	8.9%	1.6%	16.3%	21.8%

   A   Define normalized EPS.

   B   Calculate a normalized EPS for Jonash based on the method of historical average EPS and then calculate the P/E based on normalized EPS.

   C   Calculate a normalized EPS for Jonash based on the method of average ROE and the P/E based on normalized EPS.

2   An analyst plans to use P/E and the method of comparables as a basis for recommending purchasing shares of one of two peer-group companies in the business of manufacturing personal digital assistants. Neither company has been profitable to date, and neither is expected to have positive EPS over the next year. Data on the companies' prices, trailing EPS, and expected growth rates in sales (five-year compounded rates) are given in the following table:

Company	Price	Trailing EPS	P/E	Expected Growth (Sales)
Hand	$22	−$2.20	NM	45%
Somersault	$10	−$1.25	NM	40%

   Unfortunately, because the earnings for both companies have been negative, their P/Es are not meaningful. On the basis of this information, address the following:

   A   Discuss how the analyst might make a relative valuation in this case.

   B   State which stock the analyst should recommend.

3   May Stewart, CFA, a retail analyst, is performing a P/E-based comparison of two hypothetical jewelry stores as of early 2009. She has the following data for Hallwhite Stores (HS) and Ruffany (RUF).

   ● HS is priced at $44. RUF is priced at $22.50.

   ● HS has a simple capital structure, earned $2.00 per share (basic and diluted) in 2008, and is expected to earn $2.20 (basic and diluted) in 2009.

   ● RUF has a complex capital structure as a result of its outstanding stock options. Moreover, it had several unusual items that reduced its basic EPS in 2008 to $0.50 (versus the $0.75 that it earned in 2007).

   ● For 2009, Stewart expects RUF to achieve net income of $30 million. RUF has 30 million shares outstanding and options outstanding for an additional 3,333,333 shares.

   A   Which P/E (trailing or forward) should Stewart use to compare the two companies' valuation?

Practice Problems and Solutions: *Equity Asset Valuation*, Second Edition, by Jerald E. Pinto, CFA, Elaine Henry, CFA, Thomas R. Robinson, CFA, and John D. Stowe, CFA. Copyright © 2009 by CFA Institute.

B Which of the two stocks is relatively more attractive when valued on the basis of P/Es (assuming that all other factors are approximately the same for both stocks)?

4 You are researching the valuation of the stock of a company in the food-processing industry. Suppose you intend to use the mean value of the forward P/Es for the food-processing industry stocks as the benchmark value of the multiple. This mean P/E is 18.0. The forward or expected EPS for the next year for the stock you are studying is $2.00. You calculate 18.0 × $2.00 = $36, which you take to be the intrinsic value of the stock based only on the information given here. Comparing $36 with the stock's current market price of $30, you conclude the stock is undervalued.

A Give two reasons why your conclusion that the stock is undervalued may be in error.

B What additional information about the stock and the peer group would support your original conclusion?

5 Suppose an analyst uses an equity index as a comparison asset in valuing a stock. In making a decision to recommend purchase of an individual stock, which price multiple(s) would cause concern about the impact of potential overvaluation of the equity index?

6 Christie Johnson, CFA, has been assigned to analyze Sundanci. Johnson assumes that Sundanci's earnings and dividends will grow at a constant rate of 13 percent. Exhibits 1 and 2 provide financial statements for the most recent two years (2007 and 2008) and other information for Sundanci.

Exhibit 1	Sundanci Actual 2007 and 2008 Financial Statements for Fiscal Years Ending 31 May (in Millions except Per-Share Data)	
Income Statement	**2007**	**2008**
Revenue	$474	$598
Depreciation	20	23
Other operating costs	368	460
Income before taxes	86	115
Taxes	26	35
Net income	60	80
Dividends	18	24
Earnings per share	$0.714	$0.952
Dividends per share	$0.214	$0.286
Common shares outstanding	84.0	84.0
Balance Sheet	**2007**	**2008**
Current assets	$201	$326
Net property, plant, and equipment	474	489
Total assets	675	815
Current liabilities	57	141

(continued)

Exhibit 1 (Continued)		
Balance Sheet	**2007**	**2008**
Long-term debt	0	0
Total liabilities	57	141
Shareholders' equity	618	674
Total liabilities and equity	675	815
Other Information		
Capital expenditures	34	38

Exhibit 2 Selected Financial Information	
Required rate of ROE	14%
Growth rate of industry	13%
Industry P/E	26

A Based on information in Exhibits 1 and 2 and on Johnson's assumptions for Sundanci, calculate justified trailing and forward P/Es for this company.

B Identify, within the context of the constant dividend growth model, how *each* of the following fundamental factors would affect the P/E:

i. The risk (beta) of Sundanci increases substantially.

ii. The estimated growth rate of Sundanci's earnings and dividends increases.

iii. The equity risk premium increases.

Note: A change in a fundamental factor is assumed to happen in isolation; interactive effects between factors are ignored. That is, every other item of the company is unchanged.

7 Tom Smithfield is valuing the stock of a food-processing business. He feels confident explicitly projecting earnings and dividends to three years (to $t = 3$). Other information and estimates are as follows:

- Required rate of return = 0.09.
- Average dividend payout rate for mature companies in the market = 0.45.
- Industry average ROE = 0.10.
- $E_3 = \$3.00$.
- Industry average P/E = 12.

On the basis of this information, answer the following questions:

A Compute terminal value (V_3) based on comparables.

B Contrast your answer in Part A to an estimate of terminal value based on the Gordon growth model.

8 Discuss three types of stocks or investment situations for which an analyst could appropriately use P/B in valuation.

9 Aratatech is a multinational distributor of semiconductor chips and related products to businesses. Its leading competitor around the world is Trymye Electronics. Aratatech has a current market price of $10.00, 20 million shares outstanding, annual sales of $1 billion, and a 5 percent profit margin. Trymye has a market price of $20.00, 30 million shares outstanding, annual sales of $1.6 billion, and a profit margin of 4.9 percent. Based on the information given, answer the following questions:

A Which of the two companies has a more attractive valuation based on P/S?

B Identify and explain one advantage of P/S over P/E as a valuation tool.

10 Wilhelm Müller, CFA, has organized the selected data on four food companies that appear below (TTM stands for trailing 12 months):

Measure	Hoppelli Foods	Telli Foods	Drisket Co.	Whiteline Foods
Stock price	$25.70	$11.77	$23.65	$24.61
Shares outstanding (thousands)	138,923	220,662	108,170	103,803
Market cap ($ millions)	3,570	2,597	2,558	2,555
Enterprise value ($ millions)	3,779	4,056	3,846	4,258
Sales ($ millions)	4,124	10,751	17,388	6,354
Operating income ($ millions)	285	135	186	396
Operating profit margin	6.91%	1.26%	1.07%	6.23%
Net income ($ millions)	182	88	122	252
TTM EPS	$1.30	$0.40	$1.14	$2.43
Return on equity	19.20%	4.10%	6.40%	23.00%
Net profit margin	4.41%	0.82%	0.70%	3.97%

On the basis of the data given, answer the following questions:

A Calculate the trailing P/E and EV/Sales for each company.

B Explain, on the basis of fundamentals, why these stocks have different EV/S multiples.

11 John Jones, CFA, is head of the research department at Peninsular Research. Peninsular has a client who has inquired about the valuation method best suited for comparing companies in an industry with the following characteristics:

● Principal competitors within the industry are located in the United States, France, Japan, and Brazil.

● The industry is currently operating at a cyclical low, with many companies reporting losses.

Jones recommends that the client consider the following valuation ratios:

1 P/E.

2 P/B.

3 EV/S.

Determine which *one* of the three valuation ratios is most appropriate for comparing companies in this industry. Support your answer with *one* reason that makes that ratio superior to either of the other two ratios in this case.

12 Giantin Growing AG (GG) is currently selling for €38.50, with TTM EPS and dividends per share of €1.36 and €0.91, respectively. The company's P/E is 28.3, P/B is 7.1, and P/S is 2.9. The ROE is 27.0 percent, and the profit margin on sales is 10.24 percent. The Treasury bond rate is 4.9 percent, the equity risk premium is 5.5 percent, and GG's beta is 1.2.

    A What is GG's required rate of return, based on the capital asset pricing model (CAPM)?

    B Assume that the dividend and earnings growth rates are 9 percent. What trailing P/E, P/B, and P/S multiples would be justified in light of the required rate of return in Part A and current values of the dividend payout ratio, ROE, and profit margin?

    C Given that the assumptions and constant growth model are appropriate, state and justify whether GG, based on fundamentals, appears to be fairly valued, overvalued, or undervalued.

13 Jorge Zaldys, CFA, is researching the relative valuation of two companies in the aerospace/defense industry, NCI Heavy Industries (NCI) and Relay Group International (RGI). He has gathered relevant information on the companies in the following table.

EBITDA Comparisons (in € Millions except Per-Share and Share-Count Data)		
Company	**RGI**	**NCI**
Price per share	150	100
Shares outstanding	5 million	2 million
Market value of debt	50	100
Book value of debt	52	112
Cash and investments	5	2
Net income	49.5	12
Net income from continuing operations	49.5	8
Interest expense	3	5
Depreciation and amortization	8	4
Taxes	2	3

Using the information in the table, answer the following questions:

    A Calculate P/EBITDA for NCI and RGI.

    B Calculate EV/EBITDA for NCI and RGI.

    C Which company should Zaldys recommend as relatively undervalued? Justify the selection.

14 Define the major alternative cash flow concepts, and state one limitation of each.

15 Data for two hypothetical companies in the pharmaceutical industry, DriveMed and MAT Technology, are given in the following table. For both companies, expenditures on fixed capital and working capital during the previous year reflect anticipated average expenditures over the foreseeable horizon.

Measure	DriveMed	MAT Technology
Current price	$46.00	$78.00
Trailing CF per share	$3.60	$6.00
P/CF	12.8	13.0
Trailing FCFE per share	$1.00	$5.00
P/FCFE	46.0	15.6
Consensus five-year growth forecast	15%	20%
Beta	1.25	1.25

On the basis of the information supplied, discuss the valuation of MAT Technology relative to DriveMed. Justify your conclusion.

16 Your value-oriented investment management firm recently hired a new analyst, Bob Westard, because of his expertise in the life sciences and biotechnology areas. At the firm's weekly meeting, during which each analyst proposes a stock idea for inclusion in the firm's approved list, Westard recommends Hitech Clothing International (HCI). He bases his recommendation on two considerations. First, HCI has pending patent applications but a P/E that he judges to be low in light of the potential earnings from the patented products. Second, HCI has had high relative strength versus the S&P 500 over the past month.

   A Explain the difference between Westard's two approaches—that is, the use of price multiples and the relative-strength approach.

   B State which, if any, of the bases for Westard's recommendation is consistent with the investment orientation of your firm.

17 Kirstin Kruse, a portfolio manager, has an important client who wants to alter the composition of her equity portfolio, which is currently a diversified portfolio of 60 global common stocks. Because of concerns about the economy and based on the thesis that the consumer staples sector will be less hurt than others in a recession, the client wants to add a group of stocks from the consumer staples sector. In addition, the client wants the stocks to meet the following criteria:

   - Stocks must be considered large cap (i.e., have a large market capitalization).
   - Stocks must have a dividend yield of at least 4.0 percent.
   - Stocks must have a forward P/E no greater than 15.

   The following table shows how many stocks satisfied each screen, which was run in July 2008.

Screen	Number Satisfying
Consumer staples sector	277
Large cap (> $9.7 billion in this database)	446
Dividend yield of at least 4.0%	1,609
P/E less than 15	2,994
All four screens	6

   The stocks meeting all four screens were Altria Group, Inc.; British American Tobacco (the company's ADR); Reynolds American, Inc.; Tesco PLC (the ADR); Unilever N.V. (the ADR); and Unilever PLC (the ADR).

   A Critique the construction of the screen.

   B Do these criteria identify appropriate additions to this client's portfolio?

Questions 18–24 relate to Mark Cannan

Mark Cannan is updating research reports on two well-established consumer companies before first quarter 2011 earnings reports are released. His supervisor, Sharolyn Ritter, has asked Cannan to use market-based valuations when updating the reports.

Delite Beverage is a manufacturer and distributor of soft drinks and recently acquired a major water bottling company in order to offer a broader product line. The acquisition will have a significant impact on Delite's future results.

You Fix It is a United States retail distributor of products for home improvement, primarily for those consumers who choose to do the work themselves. The home improvement industry is cyclical; the industry was adversely affected by the recent downturn in the economy, the level of foreclosures, and slow home sales. Although sales and earnings at You Fix It weakened, same store sales are beginning to improve as consumers undertake more home improvement projects. Poor performing stores were closed, resulting in significant restructuring charges in 2010.

Before approving Cannan's work, Ritter wants to discuss the calculations and choices of ratios used in the valuation of Delite and You Fix It. The data used by Cannan in his analysis is summarized in Exhibit 1.

Exhibit 1	Select Financial Data for Delite Beverage and You Fix It	
	Delite Beverage	**You Fix It**
2010 Earnings per share (EPS)	$3.44	$1.77
2011 estimated EPS	$3.50	$1.99
Book value per share end of year	$62.05	$11.64
Current share price	$65.50	$37.23
Sales (billions)	$32.13	$67.44
Free cash flow per share	$2.68	$0.21
Shares outstanding end of year	2,322,034,000	1,638,821,000

Cannan advises Ritter that he is considering three different approaches to value the shares of You Fix It:

Approach 1 Price-to-book (P/B) ratio

Approach 2 Price-to-earnings (P/E) ratio using trailing earnings

Approach 3 Price-to-earnings ratio using normalized earnings

Cannan tells Ritter that he calculated the price-to-sales ratio (P/S) for You Fix It, but chose not to use it in the valuation of the shares. Cannan states to Ritter that it is more appropriate to use the P/E ratio rather than the P/S ratio because:

Reason 1 Earnings are more stable than sales.

Reason 2 Earnings are less easily manipulated than sales.

Reason 3 The P/E ratio reflects financial leverage whereas the P/S ratio does not.

Cannan also informs Ritter that he did not use a price-to-cash flow multiple in valuing the shares of Delite or You Fix It. The reason is that he could not identify a cash flow measure that would both account for working capital and non-cash revenues, and also be after interest expense and thus not be mismatched with share price. Ritter advises Cannan that such a cash flow measure does exist.

Ritter provides Cannan with financial data on three close competitors as well as the overall beverage sector, which includes other competitors, in Exhibit 2. She asks Cannan to determine, based on the price-to-earnings growth (PEG) ratio, whether Delite shares are overvalued, fairly valued, or undervalued.

Exhibit 2	Beverage Sector Data	
	Forward P/E	**Earnings Growth**
Delite	—	12.41%
Fresh Iced Tea Company	16.59	9.52%
Nonutter Soda	15.64	11.94%
Tasty Root Beer	44.10	20%
Beverage sector average	16.40	10.80%

After providing Ritter his answer, Cannan is concerned about the inclusion of Tasty Root Beer in the comparables analysis. Specifically, Cannan asks Ritter:

> "I feel we should mitigate the effect of large outliers, but not the impact of small outliers (i.e., those close to zero), when calculating the beverage sector P/E. What measure of central tendency would you suggest we use to address this concern?"

Ritter requests that Cannan incorporate their discussion points before submitting the reports for final approval.

18 Based on the information in Exhibit 1, the *most appropriate* price-to-earnings ratio to use in the valuation of Delite is *closest* to:

A 18.71.

B 19.04.

C 24.44.

19 Based upon the information in Exhibit 1, the price-to-sales ratio for You Fix It is *closest* to:

A 0.28.

B 0.55.

C 0.90.

20 Which valuation approach would be *most* appropriate in valuing shares of You Fix It?

A Approach 1

B Approach 2

C Approach 3

21 Cannan's preference to use the P/E ratio over the P/S ratio is *best* supported by:

A Reason 1

B Reason 2

C Reason 3

22 The cash flow measure that Ritter would *most likely* recommend to address Cannan's concern is:

A free cash flow to equity.

    B earnings plus non-cash charges.

    C earnings before interest, tax, depreciation, and amortization.

23 Based upon the information in Exhibits 1 and 2, Cannan would most likely conclude that Delite's shares are:

    A overvalued.

    B undervalued.

    C fairly valued.

24 The measure of central tendency that Ritter will *most likely* recommend is the:

    A median.

    B harmonic mean.

    C arithmetic mean.

SOLUTIONS

1 **A** Normalized EPS is the level of earnings per share that the company could currently achieve under midcyclical conditions.

   B Averaging EPS over the 2003–2006 period, we find that ($2.55 + $2.13 + $0.23 + $1.45)/4 = $1.59. According to the method of historical average EPS, Jonash's normalized EPS is $1.59. The P/E based on this estimate is $57.98/1.59 = 36.5.

   C Averaging ROE over the 2003–2006 period, we find that (0.218 + 0.163 + 0.016 + 0.089)/4 = 0.1215. For current BV per share, you would use the estimated value of $19.20 for year-end 2007. According to the method of average ROE, 0.1215 × $19.20 = $2.33 is the normalized EPS. The P/E based on this estimate is $57.98/$2.33 = 24.9.

2 **A** The analyst can rank the two stocks by earnings yield (E/P). Whether EPS is positive or negative, a lower E/P reflects a richer (higher) valuation and a ranking from high to low E/P has a meaningful interpretation.

   In some cases, an analyst might handle negative EPS by using normalized EPS in its place. Neither business, however, has a history of profitability. When year-ahead EPS is expected to be positive, forward P/E is positive. Thus, the use of forward P/Es sometimes addresses the problem of trailing negative EPS. Forward P/E is not meaningful in this case, however, because next year's earnings are expected to be negative.

   B Hand has an E/P of −0.100, and Somersault has an E/P of −0.125. A higher earnings yield has an interpretation that is similar to that of a lower P/E, so Hand appears to be relatively undervalued. The difference in earnings yield cannot be explained by differences in sales growth forecasts. In fact, Hand has a higher expected sales growth rate than Somersault. Therefore, the analyst should recommend Hand.

3 **A** Because investing looks to the future, analysts often favor forward P/E when earnings forecasts are available, as they are here. A specific reason to use forward P/Es is the fact given that RUF had some unusual items affecting EPS for 2008. The data to make appropriate adjustments to RUF's 2008 EPS are not given. In summary, Stewart should use forward P/Es.

   B Because RUF has a complex capital structure, the P/Es of the two companies must be compared on the basis of diluted EPS.

   For HS, forward P/E = $44/2.20 = 20.

   For RUF, forward P/E per diluted share

   = $22.50/(30,000,000/33,333,333) = 25.

   Therefore, HS has the more attractive valuation at present.

   The problem illustrates some of the considerations that should be taken into account in using P/Es and the method of comparables.

4 **A** Your conclusion may be in error because of the following:

   ▪ The peer-group stocks themselves may be overvalued; that is, the mean P/E of 18 may be too high in terms of intrinsic value. If so, using 18 as a multiplier of the stock's expected EPS will lead to an estimate of stock value in excess of intrinsic value.

- The stock's fundamentals may differ from those of the mean food-processing industry stock. For example, if the stock's expected growth rate is lower than the mean industry growth rate and its risk is higher than the mean, the stock may deserve a lower P/E than the industry mean.

  In addition, mean P/E may be influenced by outliers.

  B The following additional evidence would support the original conclusion:

  - Evidence that stocks in the industry are, at least on average, fairly valued (that stock prices reflect fundamentals).

  - Evidence that no significant differences exist in the fundamental drivers of P/E for the stock being compared and the average industry stock.

5 In principle, the use of any price multiple for valuation is subject to the concern stated. If the stock market is overvalued, an asset that appears to be fairly or even undervalued in relation to an equity index may also be overvalued.

6 A The formula for calculating the justified forward P/E for a stable-growth company is the payout ratio divided by the difference between the required rate of return and the growth rate of dividends. If the P/E is being calculated on trailing earnings (Year 0), the payout ratio is increased by 1 plus the growth rate. According to the 2007 income statement, the payout ratio is 18/60 = 0.30; the 2008 income statement gives the same number (24/80 = 0.30). Thus,

P/E based on trailing earnings:

$$P/E = \left[\text{Payout ratio} \times (1 + g)\right]/(r - g)$$
$$= (0.30 \times 1.13)/(0.14 - 0.13) = 33.9$$

P/E based on next year's earnings:

$$P/E = \text{Payout ratio}/(r - g)$$
$$= 0.30/(0.14 - 0.13) = 30$$

B

Fundamental Factor	Effect on P/E	Explanation (Not Required in Question)
The risk (beta) of Sundanci increases substantially.	Decrease	P/E is a decreasing function of risk—that is, as risk increases, P/E decreases. Increases in the risk of Sundanci stock would be expected to lower its P/E.
The estimated growth rate of Sundanci's earnings and dividends increases.	Increase	P/E is an increasing function of the growth rate of the company—that is, the higher the expected growth, the higher the P/E. Sundanci would command a higher P/E if the market price were to incorporate expectations of a higher growth rate.
The equity risk premium increases.	Decrease	P/E is a decreasing function of the equity risk premium. An increased equity risk premium increases the required rate of return, which lowers the price of a stock relative to its earnings. A higher equity risk premium would be expected to lower Sundanci's P/E.

7 A V_n = Benchmark value of P/E $\times E_n$ = 12 $\times$ \$3.00 = \$36.0.

B   In the expression for sustainable growth rate $g = b \times ROE$, you can use $(1 - 0.45) = 0.55 = b$, and $ROE = 0.10$ (the industry average), obtaining $0.55 \times 0.10 = 0.055$. Given the required rate of return of 0.09, you obtain the estimate $\$3.00(0.45)(1.055)/(0.09 - 0.055) = \$40.69$. In this case, the estimate of terminal value obtained from the Gordon growth model is higher than the estimate based on multiples. The two estimates may differ for a number of reasons, including the sensitivity of the Gordon growth model to the values of the inputs.

8   Although the measurement of book value has a number of widely recognized shortcomings, P/B may still be applied fruitfully in several circumstances:

- The company is not expected to continue as a going concern. When a company is likely to be liquidated (so ongoing earnings and cash flow are not relevant), the value of its assets less its liabilities is of utmost importance. Naturally, the analyst must establish the fair value of these assets.

- The company is composed mainly of liquid assets, which is the case for finance, investment, insurance, and banking institutions.

- The company's EPS is highly variable or negative.

9 A   Aratatech: P/S = (\$10 price per share)/[(\$1 billion sales)/(20 million shares)] = $\$10/(\$1,000,000,000/20,000,000) = 0.2$

Trymye: P/S = (\$20 price per share)/[(\$1.6 billion sales)/(30 million shares)] = $\$20/(\$1,600,000,000/30,000,000) = 0.375$

Aratatech has a more attractive valuation than Trymye based on its lower P/S but comparable profit margin.

B   One advantage of P/S over P/E is that companies' accounting decisions typically have a much greater impact on reported earnings than they are likely to have on reported sales. Although companies are able to make a number of legitimate business and accounting decisions that affect earnings, their discretion over reported sales (revenue recognition) is limited. Another advantage is that sales are almost always positive, so using P/S eliminates issues that arise when EPS is zero or negative.

10 A   The P/Es are:

Hoppelli	25.70/1.30 = 19.8
Telli	11.77/0.40 = 29.4
Drisket	23.65/1.14 = 20.7
Whiteline	24.61/2.43 = 10.1

The EV/S multiples for each company are:

Hoppelli	3,779/4,124 = 0.916
Telli	4,056/10,751 = 0.377
Drisket	3,846/17,388 = 0.221
Whiteline	4,258/6,354 = 0.670

B   The data for the problem include measures of profitability, such as operating profit margin, ROE, and net profit margin. Because EV includes the market values of both debt and equity, logically the ranking based on EV/S should be compared with a pre-interest measure of profitability, namely, operating profit margin. The ranking of the stocks by EV/S from highest to lowest and the companies' operating margins are:

Company	EV/S	Operating Profit Margin (%)
Hoppelli	0.916	6.91
Whiteline	0.670	6.23
Telli	0.377	1.26
Drisket	0.221	1.07

The differences in EV/S appear to be explained, at least in part, by differences in cost structure as measured by operating profit margin.

11 For companies in the industry described, EV/S would be superior to either of the other two ratios. Among other considerations, EV/S is:

- more useful than P/E in valuing companies with negative earnings;

- better than either P/E or P/B for comparing companies in different countries that are likely to use different accounting standards (a consequence of the multinational nature of the industry);

- less subject to manipulation than earnings (i.e., through aggressive accounting decisions by management, who may be more motivated to manage earnings when a company is in a cyclical low, rather than in a high, and thus likely to report losses).

12 A Based on the CAPM, the required rate of return is 4.9% + 1.2 × 5.5% = 11.5%.

B The dividend payout ratio is €0.91/€1.36 = 0.669. The justified values for the three valuation ratios should be

$$\frac{P_0}{E_0} = \frac{(1-b) \times (1+g)}{r-g} = \frac{0.669 \times 1.09}{0.115 - 0.09} = \frac{0.7293}{0.025} = 29.2$$

$$\frac{P_0}{B_0} = \frac{ROE - g}{r-g} = \frac{0.27 - 0.09}{0.115 - 0.09} = \frac{0.18}{0.025} = 7.2$$

$$\frac{P_0}{S_0} = \frac{PM \times (1-b) \times (1+g)}{r-g} = \frac{0.1024 \times 0.669 \times 1.09}{0.115 - 0.09} = \frac{0.0747}{0.025} = 3.0$$

C The justified trailing P/E is higher than the trailing P/E (29.2 versus 28.3), the justified P/B is higher than the actual P/B (7.2 versus 7.1), and the justified P/S is higher than the actual P/S (3.0 versus 2.9). Therefore, based on these three measures, GG appears to be slightly undervalued.

13 A EBITDA = Net income (from continuing operations) + Interest expense + Taxes + Depreciation + Amortization

EBITDA for RGI = €49.5 million + €3 million + €2 million + €8 million = €62.5 million

Per-share EBITDA = (€62.5 million)/(5 million shares) = €12.5

P/EBITDA for RGI = €150/€12.5 = 12

EBITDA for NCI = €8 million + €5 million + €3 million + €4 million = €20 million

Per-share EBITDA = (€20 million)/(2 million shares) = €10

P/EBITDA for NCI = €100/€10 = 10

B For RGI:

Market value of equity = €150 × 5 million = €750 million

Market value of debt = €50

Total market value = €750 million + €50 = €800 million

EV = €800 million − €5 million (cash and investments) = €795 million

Now, Zaldys would divide EV by total (as opposed to per-share) EBITDA:

EV/EBITDA for RGI = (€795 million)/(€62.5 million) = 12.72

For NCI:

Market value of equity = €100 × 2 million = €200 million

Market value of debt = €100

Total market value = €200 million + €100 = €300 million

EV = €300 million − €2 million (cash and investments) = €298 million

Now, Zaldys would divide EV by total (as opposed to per-share) EBITDA:

EV/EBITDA for NCI = (€298 million)/(€20 million) = 14.9

C Zaldys should select RGI as relatively undervalued.

First, it is correct that NCI *appears* to be relatively undervalued based on P/EBITDA, because NCI has a lower P/EBITDA multiple:

- P/EBITDA = €150/€12.5 = 12 for RGI.
- P/EBITDA = €100/€10 = 10 for NCI.

RGI is relatively undervalued on the basis of EV/EBITDA, however, because RGI has the lower EV/EBITDA multiple:

- EV/EBITDA = (€795 million)/(€62.5 million) = 12.72 for RGI.
- EV/EBITDA = (€298 million)/(€20 million) = 14.9 for NCI.

EBITDA is a pre-interest flow; therefore, it is a flow to both debt and equity and the EV/EBITDA multiple is more appropriate than the P/EBITDA multiple. Zaldys would rely on EV/EBITDA to reach his decision if the two ratios conflicted. Note that P/EBITDA does not take into account differences in the use of financial leverage. Substantial differences in leverage exist in this case (NCI uses much more debt), so the preference for using EV/EBITDA rather than P/EBITDA is supported.

14 The major concepts are as follows:

- EPS plus per-share depreciation, amortization, and depletion (CF)

  Limitation: Ignores changes in working capital and noncash revenue; not a free cash flow concept.

- Cash flow from operations (CFO)

  Limitation: Not a free cash flow concept, so not directly linked to theory.

- Free cash flow to equity (FCFE)

  Limitation: Often more variable and more frequently negative than other cash flow concepts.

- Earnings before interest, taxes, depreciation, and amortization (EBITDA)

  Limitation: Ignores changes in working capital and noncash revenue; not a free cash flow concept. Relative to its use in P/EBITDA, EBITDA is mismatched with the numerator because it is a pre-interest concept.

15 MAT Technology is relatively undervalued compared with DriveMed on the basis of P/FCFE. MAT Tech's P/FCFE multiple is 34 percent the size of DriveMed's FCFE multiple (15.6/46 = 0.34, or 34 percent). The only comparison slightly in DriveMed's favor, or approximately equal for both companies,

is the comparison based on P/CF (i.e., 12.8 for DriveMed versus 13.0 for MAT Technology). However, FCFE is more strongly grounded in valuation theory than P/CF. Because DriveMed's and MAT Technology's expenditures for fixed capital and working capital during the previous year reflected anticipated average expenditures over the foreseeable horizon, you would have additional confidence in the P/FCFE comparison.

16 A   Relative strength is based strictly on price movement (a technical indicator). As used by Westard, the comparison is between the returns on HCI and the returns on the S&P 500. In contrast, the price multiple approaches are based on the relationship of current price, not to past prices, but to some measure of value such as EPS, book value, sales, or cash flow.

    B   Only the reference to the P/E in relationship to the pending patent applications in Westard's recommendation is consistent with the company's value orientation. High relative strength would be relevant for a portfolio managed with a growth/momentum investment style.

17 A   As a rule, a screen that includes a maximum P/E ratio should include criteria requiring positive earnings; otherwise, the screen could select companies with negative P/E ratios. The screen may be too narrowly focused on value measures. It did not include criteria related to expected growth, required rate of return, risk, or financial strength.

    B   The screen results in a very concentrated portfolio. The screen selected both of the parent companies of the Unilever Group: Unilever NV and Unilever PLC, which operate as a single business entity despite having separate legal identities and separate stock exchange listings. Thus, owning both stocks would provide no diversification benefits. In addition, the screen selected three tobacco companies, which typically pay high dividends. Again, owning all three stocks would provide little diversification.

18   A is correct. The forward P/E ratio should be used given the recent significant acquisition of the water bottling company. Since a major change such as an acquisition or divestiture can affect results, the forward P/E, also known as the leading P/E or prospective P/E, is the most appropriate P/E to use for Delite. Earnings estimates for 2011 should incorporate the performance of the water bottling company. The forward P/E is calculated as the current price divided by the projected earnings per share, or $65.50/$3.50 = 18.71.

19   C is correct. The price-to-sales ratio is calculated as price per share divided by annual net sales per share.

    Price per share = $37.23

    Annual net sales per share = $67.44 billion/1.638821 billion shares = $41.15

    Price-to-sales ratio (P/S) = $37.23/$41.15 = 0.90

20   C is correct. You Fix It is in the cyclical home improvement industry. The use of normalized earnings should address the problem of cyclicality in You Fix It earnings by estimating the level of earnings per share that the company could achieve currently under mid-cyclical conditions.

21   C is correct. The price to sales (P/S) ratio fails to consider differences in cost structures. Also, while share price reflects the effect of debt financing on profitability and risk, sales is a pre-financing income measure and does not incorporate the impact of debt in the firm's capital structure. Earnings reflect operating and financial leverage, and thus the price-to-earnings (P/E) ratio incorporates the impact of debt in the firm's capital structure.

22 A is correct. Free cash flow to equity (FCFE) is defined as cash flow available to shareholders after deducting all operating expenses, interest and debt payments as well as investments in working and fixed capital. Cannan's requirement that the cash flow include interest expense, working capital and noncash revenue is satisfied by FCFE.

23 C is correct. The P/E-to-growth (PEG) ratio is calculated by dividing a stock's P/E by the expected earnings growth rate, expressed as a percent. To calculate Delite's PEG ratio, first calculate the P/E ratio: $65.50/$3.50 = 18.71. In this case, the forward earnings should be used given the recent acquisition of the water bottling company. Next, calculate Delite's PEG ratio: 18.71/12.41 = 1.51.

Comparing Delite's PEG ratio of 1.51 to the PEG ratio of 1.74 (16.59/9.52) for Fresh Iced Tea, 1.31 (15.64/11.94) for Nonutter Soda, and to the beverage sector average of 1.52 (16.40/10.80), it appears that Delite's shares are fairly valued. This is determined by the fact that Delite's PEG ratio is in the middle of the range of PEG ratios and very close to the sector average. Therefore, the shares appear to be fairly valued.

24 B is correct. The harmonic mean is sometimes used to reduce the impact of large outliers—which are typically the major concern in using the arithmetic mean multiple—but not the impact of small outliers (i.e., those close to zero). The harmonic mean may aggravate the impact of small outliers, but such outliers are bounded by zero on the downside.

Residual Income Valuation

by Jerald E. Pinto, PhD, CFA, Elaine Henry, PhD, CFA,
Thomas R. Robinson, PhD, CFA, and John D. Stowe, PhD, CFA

Jerald E. Pinto, PhD, CFA, is at CFA Institute (USA). Elaine Henry, PhD, CFA, is at Fordham University (USA). Thomas R. Robinson, PhD, CFA, is at CFA Institute (USA). John D. Stowe, PhD, CFA, is at Ohio University (USA).

LEARNING OUTCOMES

Mastery	The candidate should be able to:
☐	a. calculate and interpret residual income, economic value added, and market value added;
☐	b. describe the uses of residual income models;
☐	c. calculate the intrinsic value of a common stock using the residual income model and compare value recognition in residual income and other present value models;
☐	d. explain fundamental determinants of residual income;
☐	e. explain the relation between residual income valuation and the justified price-to-book ratio based on forecasted fundamentals;
☐	f. calculate and interpret the intrinsic value of a common stock using single-stage (constant-growth) and multistage residual income models;
☐	g. calculate the implied growth rate in residual income, given the market price-to-book ratio and an estimate of the required rate of return on equity;
☐	h. explain continuing residual income and justify an estimate of continuing residual income at the forecast horizon, given company and industry prospects;
☐	i. compare residual income models to dividend discount and free cash flow models;
☐	j. explain strengths and weaknesses of residual income models and justify the selection of a residual income model to value a company's common stock;
☐	k. describe accounting issues in applying residual income models;
☐	l. evaluate whether a stock is overvalued, fairly valued, or undervalued based on a residual income model.

The data and examples for this reading were updated in 2014 by Professor Stephen Wilcox, CFA.

Equity Asset Valuation, Second Edition, by Jerald E. Pinto, CFA, Elaine Henry, CFA, Thomas R. Robinson, CFA, and John D. Stowe, CFA. Copyright © 2009 by CFA Institute.

1   INTRODUCTION

Residual income models of equity value have become widely recognized tools in both investment practice and research. Conceptually, residual income is net income less a charge (deduction) for common shareholders' opportunity cost in generating net income. It is the residual or remaining income after considering the costs of all of a company's capital. The appeal of residual income models stems from a shortcoming of traditional accounting. Specifically, although a company's income statement includes a charge for the cost of debt capital in the form of interest expense, it does not include a charge for the cost of equity capital. A company can have positive net income but may still not be adding value for shareholders if it does not earn more than its cost of equity capital. Residual income models explicitly recognize the costs of all the capital used in generating income.

As an economic concept, residual income has a long history, dating back to Alfred Marshall in the late 1800s.[1] As far back as the 1920s, General Motors used the concept in evaluating business segments.[2] More recently, residual income has received renewed attention and interest, sometimes under names such as economic profit, abnormal earnings, or economic value added. Although residual income concepts have been used in a variety of contexts, including the measurement of internal corporate performance, this reading will focus on the residual income model for estimating the intrinsic value of common stock. Among the questions we will study to help us apply residual income models are the following:

▪ How is residual income measured, and how can an analyst use residual income in valuation?

▪ How does residual income relate to fundamentals, such as return on equity and earnings growth rates?

▪ How is residual income linked to other valuation methods, such as a price-multiple approach?

▪ What accounting-based challenges arise in applying residual income valuation?

The reading is organized as follows: Section 2 develops the concept of residual income, introduces the use of residual income in valuation, and briefly presents alternative measures used in practice. Section 3 presents the residual income model and illustrates its use in valuing common stock. This section also shows practical applications, including the single-stage (constant-growth) residual income model and a multistage residual income model. Section 4 describes the relative strengths and weaknesses of residual income valuation compared to other valuation methods. Section 5 addresses accounting issues in the use of residual income valuation. The final section summarizes the reading and practice problems conclude.

2   RESIDUAL INCOME

Traditional financial statements, particularly the income statement, are prepared to reflect earnings available to owners. As a result, the income statement shows net income after deducting an expense for the cost of debt capital, that is, interest expense. The income statement does not, however, deduct dividends or other charges for equity

---

[1] Alfred Marshall, Book Two: Some Fundamental Notions, Chapter 4, "Income, Capital," in *Principles of Economics* (London; Macmillan and Co., Ltd., 1890).

[2] See, for example, Young (1999) and Lo and Lys (2000).

capital. Thus, traditional financial statements essentially let the owners decide whether earnings cover their opportunity costs. Conversely, the economic concept of residual income explicitly deducts the estimated cost of equity capital, the finance concept that measures shareholders' opportunity costs. The cost of equity is the marginal cost of equity, which is also referred to as the required rate of return on equity. The cost of equity is a marginal cost because it represents the cost of additional equity, whether generated internally or by selling more equity interests. Example 1 illustrates, in a stylized setting, the calculation and interpretation of residual income.[3]

EXAMPLE 1

Calculation of Residual Income

Axis Manufacturing Company, Inc. (AXCI), a very small company in terms of market capitalization, has total assets of €2 million financed 50 percent with debt and 50 percent with equity capital. The cost of debt is 7 percent before taxes; this example assumes that interest is tax deductible, so the after-tax cost of debt is 4.9 percent.[4] The cost of equity capital is 12 percent. The company has earnings before interest and taxes (EBIT) of €200,000 and a tax rate of 30 percent. Net income for AXCI can be determined as follows:

EBIT	€200,000
Less: Interest Expense	70,000
Pretax Income	€130,000
Less: Income Tax Expense	39,000
Net Income	€91,000

With earnings of €91,000, AXCI is clearly profitable in an accounting sense. But was the company's profitability adequate return for its owners? Unfortunately, it was not. To incorporate the cost of equity capital, compute residual income. One approach to calculating residual income is to deduct an **equity charge** (the estimated cost of equity capital in money terms) from net income. Compute the equity charge as follows:

$$\text{Equity charge} = \text{Equity capital} \times \text{Cost of equity capital}$$
$$= €1,000,000 \times 12\%$$
$$= €120,000.$$

As stated, residual income is equal to net income minus the equity charge:

Net Income	€91,000
Less: Equity Charge	120,000
Residual Income	€(29,000)

AXCI did not earn enough to cover the cost of equity capital. As a result, it has negative residual income. Although AXCI is profitable in an accounting sense, it is not profitable in an economic sense.

---

[3] To simplify this introduction, we assume that net income accurately reflects *clean surplus accounting*, which will be explained later in this reading. The discussions in this reading assume that companies' financing only consists of common equity and debt. In the case of a company that also has preferred stock financing, the calculation of residual income would reflect the deduction of preferred stock dividends from net income.
[4] In countries where corporate interest is not tax deductible, the after-tax cost of debt would equal the pretax cost of debt.

In Example 1, residual income is calculated based on net income and a charge for the cost of equity capital. Analysts will also encounter another approach to calculating residual income that yields the same results under certain assumptions. In this second approach, which takes the perspective of all providers of capital (both debt and equity), a **capital charge** (the company's total cost of capital in money terms) is subtracted from the company's after-tax operating profit. In the case of AXCI in Example 1, the capital charge is €169,000:

Equity charge	$0.12 \times €1,000,000 =$	€120,000
Debt charge	$0.07(1 - 0.30) \times €1,000,000 =$	49,000
Total capital charge		€169,000

The company's net operating profit after taxes (NOPAT) is €140,000 (€200,000 − 30% taxes). The capital charge of €169,000 is higher than the after-tax operating profit of €140,000 by €29,000, the same figure obtained in Example 1.

As illustrated in the following table, both approaches yield the same results in this case because of two assumptions. First, this example assumes that the marginal cost of debt equals the current cost of debt, that is, the cost used to determine net income. Specifically, in this instance, the after-tax interest expense incorporated in net income [€49,000 = €70,000 × (1 − 30%)] is equal to the after-tax cost of debt incorporated into the capital charge. Second, this example assumes that the weights used to calculate the capital charge are derived from the book value of debt and equity. Specifically, it uses the weights of 50 percent debt and 50 percent equity.

Approach 1		Reconciliation	Approach 2	
Net income	€91,000	Plus the after-tax interest expense of €49,000	Net operating profit after tax	€140,000
Less: Equity charge	120,000	Plus the after-tax capital charge for debt of €49,000	Less: Capital charge	169,000
Residual income	€(29,000)		Residual income	€(29,000)

That the company is not profitable in an economic sense can also be seen by comparing the company's cost of capital to its return on capital. Specifically, the company's capital charge is greater than its after-tax return on total assets or capital. The after-tax net operating return on total assets or capital is calculated as profits divided by total assets (or total capital). In this example, the after-tax net operating return on total assets is 7 percent (€140,000/€2,000,000), which is 1.45 percentage points less than the company's effective capital charge of 8.45 percent (€169,000/€2,000,000).[5]

2.1 The Use of Residual Income in Equity Valuation

A company that is generating more income than its cost of obtaining capital—that is, one with positive residual income—is creating value. Conversely, a company that is not generating enough income to cover its cost of capital—that is, a company with negative residual income—is destroying value. Thus, all else equal, higher (lower) residual income should be associated with higher (lower) valuations.

---

5 After-tax net operating profits as a percent of total assets or capital has been called **return on invested capital** (ROIC). Residual income can also be calculated as (ROIC − Effective capital charge) × Beginning capital.

To illustrate the effect of residual income on equity valuation using the case of AXCI presented in Example 1, assume the following:

- Initially, AXCI equity is selling for book value or €1 million with 100,000 shares outstanding. Thus, AXCI's book value per share and initial share price are both €10.

- Earnings per share (EPS) is €0.91 (€91,000/100,000 shares).

- Earnings will continue at the current level indefinitely.

- All net income is distributed as dividends.

Because AXCI is not earning its cost of equity, as shown in Example 1, the company's share price should fall. Given the information, AXCI is destroying €29,000 of value per year, which equals €0.29 per share (€29,000/100,000 shares). Discounted at 12 percent cost of equity, the present value of the perpetuity is €2.42 (€0.29/12%). The current share price minus the present value of the value being destroyed equals €7.58 (€10 − €2.42).

Another way to look at these data is to note that the earnings yield (E/P) for a no-growth company is an estimate of the expected rate of return. Therefore, when price reaches the point at which E/P equals the required rate of return on equity, an investment in the stock is expected to just cover the stock's required rate of return. With EPS of €0.91, the earnings yield is exactly 12 percent (AXCI's cost of equity) when its share price is €7.58333 (i.e., €0.91/€7.58333 = 12%). At a share price of €7.58333, the total market value of AXCI's equity is €758,333. When a company has negative residual income, shares are expected to sell at a discount to book value. In this example, AXCI's price-to-book ratio (P/B) at this level of discount from book value would be 0.7583. In contrast, if AXCI were earning positive residual income, then its shares should sell at a premium to book value. In summary, higher residual income is expected to be associated with higher market prices (and higher P/Bs), all else being equal.

Residual income (RI) models have been used to value both individual stocks[6] and the Dow Jones Industrial Average.[7] The models have also been proposed as a solution to measuring goodwill impairment by accounting standard setters (American Accounting Association Financial Accounting Standards Committee 2001). Recall that **impairment** in an accounting context means downward adjustment, and **goodwill** is an intangible asset that may appear on a company's balance sheet as a result of its purchase of another company.

Residual income and residual income models have been referred to by a variety of names. Residual income has sometimes been called **economic profit** because it is an estimate of the profit of the company after deducting the cost of all capital: debt and equity. In forecasting future residual income, the term **abnormal earnings** is also used. Under the assumption that in the long term the company is expected to earn its cost of capital (from all sources), any earnings in excess of the cost of capital can be termed abnormal earnings. The residual income model has also been called the **discounted abnormal earnings model** and the **Edwards–Bell–Ohlson model** after the names of researchers in the field. This reading focuses on a general residual income model that can be used by analysts using publicly available data and nonproprietary accounting adjustments. A number of commercial implementations of the approach, however, are also very well known. Before returning to the general residual income model in Section 3, we briefly discuss one such commercial implementation and the related concept of market value added.

---

6 See Fleck, Craig, Bodenstab, Harris, and Huh (2001).

7 See Lee and Swaminathan (1999) and Lee, Myers, and Swaminathan (1999).

2.2 Commercial Implementations

One example of several competing commercial implementations of the residual income concept is **economic value added** (EVA).[8] The previous section illustrated a calculation of residual income starting from net operating profit after taxes, and economic value added takes the same broad approach. Specifically, economic value added is computed as

$$\text{EVA} = \text{NOPAT} - (\text{C\%} \times \text{TC}) \tag{1}$$

where NOPAT is the company's net operating profit after taxes, C% is the cost of capital, and TC is total capital. In this model, both NOPAT and TC are determined under generally accepted accounting principles and adjusted for a number of items.[9] Some of the more common adjustments include the following:

- Research and development (R&D) expenses are capitalized and amortized rather than expensed (i.e., R&D expense, net of estimated amortization, is added back to earnings to compute NOPAT).

- In the case of strategic investments that are not expected to generate an immediate return, a charge for capital is suspended until a later date.

- Deferred taxes are eliminated such that only cash taxes are treated as an expense.

- Any inventory LIFO (last in, first out) reserve is added back to capital, and any increase in the LIFO reserve is added in when calculating NOPAT.

- Operating leases are treated as capital leases, and nonrecurring items are adjusted.

Because of the adjustments made in calculating EVA, a different numerical result will be obtained, in general, than that resulting from the use of the simple computation presented in Example 1. In practice, general (nonbranded) residual income valuation also considers the effect of accounting methods on reported results. Analysts' adjustments to reported accounting results in estimating residual income, however, will generally reflect some differences from the set specified for EVA. Section 5 of this reading will explore accounting considerations in more detail.

Over time, a company must generate economic profit for its market value to increase. A concept related to economic profit (and EVA) is market value added (MVA):

$$\text{MVA} = \text{Market value of the company}$$
$$- \text{Accounting book value of total capital} \tag{2}$$

A company that generates positive economic profit should have a market value in excess of the accounting book value of its capital.

Research on the ability of value-added concepts to explain equity value and stock returns has reached mixed conclusions. Peterson and Peterson (1996) found that value-added measures are slightly more highly correlated with stock returns than traditional measures, such as return on assets and return on equity. Bernstein and Pigler (1997) and Bernstein, Bayer, and Pigler (1998) found that value-added measures are no better at predicting stock performance than are such measures as earnings growth.

---

8 The acronym is trademarked by Stern Stewart & Company and is generally associated with a specific set of adjustments proposed by Stern Stewart & Co. The goal of these adjustments is to produce a value that is a good approximation of economic profit. For a complete discussion, see Stewart (1991) and Peterson and Peterson (1996).

9 See, for example, Ehrbar (1998).

A variety of commercial models related to the residual income concept have been marketed by other major accounting and consulting firms. Interestingly, the application focus of these models is not, in general, equity valuation. Rather, these implementations of the residual income concept are marketed primarily for measuring internal corporate performance and determining executive compensation.

THE RESIDUAL INCOME MODEL

3

In Section 2, we discussed the concept of residual income and briefly introduced the relationship of residual income to equity value. In the long term, companies that earn more than the cost of capital should sell for more than book value, and companies that earn less than the cost of capital should sell for less than book value. The **residual income model** of valuation analyzes the intrinsic value of equity as the sum of two components:

- the current book value of equity, and
- the present value of expected future residual income.

Note that when the change is made from valuing total shareholders' equity to directly valuing an individual common share, earnings per share rather than net income is used. According to the residual income model, the intrinsic value of common stock can be expressed as follows:

$$V_0 = B_0 + \sum_{t=1}^{\infty} \frac{\mathrm{RI}_t}{(1+r)^t} = B_0 + \sum_{t=1}^{\infty} \frac{E_t - rB_{t-1}}{(1+r)^t} \tag{3}$$

where

V_0 = value of a share of stock today (t = 0)

B_0 = current per-share book value of equity

B_t = expected per-share book value of equity at any time t

r = required rate of return on equity investment (cost of equity)

E_t = expected EPS for period t

RI_t = expected per-share residual income, equal to $E_t - rB_{t-1}$

The per-share residual income in period t, RI_t, is the EPS for the period, E_t, minus the per-share equity charge for the period, which is the required rate of return on equity times the book value per share at the beginning of the period, or rB_{t-1}. Whenever earnings per share exceed the per-share cost of equity, per-share residual income is positive; and whenever earnings are less, per-share residual income is negative. Example 2 illustrates the calculation of per-share residual income.

EXAMPLE 2

Per-Share Residual Income Forecasts

David Smith is evaluating the expected residual income as of the end of August 2013 of Silver Wheaton Corporation (NYSE: SLW). Established in 2004 in Vancouver, British Columbia, Silver Wheaton is the largest precious metal streaming company in the world. The company has a number of agreements whereby, in exchange for an upfront payment, it has the right to purchase all or a portion of the silver (and sometimes gold) production from mines located around the globe. Using an adjusted beta of 1.50 relative to the TSX 300 Index, a 10-year government bond yield of 2.8 percent, and an estimated equity risk premium of 4.2 percent, Smith uses the capital asset pricing model (CAPM) to estimate Silver Wheaton's required rate of return, r, at 9.1 percent [2.8 percent + 1.50(4.2 percent)]. Smith obtains the following as of the close on 23 August 2013:

Current market price	$27.70
Book value per share as of 31 December 2012	$8.77
Consensus annual earnings estimates	
FY 2013 (ending December)	$1.40
FY 2014	$1.60
Annualized dividend per share forecast	
FY 2013	$0.52
FY 2014	$0.60

What is the forecast residual income for fiscal years ended December 2013 and December 2014?

Solution:

Forecasted residual income and calculations are shown in Exhibit 1.

Exhibit 1	Silver Wheaton Corporation			
Year		**2013**		**2014**
Forecasting book value per share				
Beginning book value (B_{t-1})		$8.77		$9.65
Earnings per share forecast (E_t)	$1.40		$1.60	
Less dividend forecast (D_t)	0.52		0.60	
Add Change in retained earnings ($E_t - D_t$)		0.88		1.00
Forecast ending book value per share ($B_{t-1} + E_t - D_t$)		$9.65		$10.65
Calculating the equity charge				
Beginning book value per share	$8.77		$9.65	
Multiply cost of equity	× 0.091		× 0.091	
Per-share equity charge ($r \times B_{t-1}$)		$0.80		$0.88
Estimating per share residual income				
EPS forecast	$1.40		$1.60	
Less equity charge	0.80		0.88	
Per-share residual income		$0.60		$0.72

The use of Equation 3, the expression for the estimated intrinsic value of common stock, is illustrated in Example 3.

EXAMPLE 3

Using the Residual Income Model (1)

Bugg Properties' expected EPS is $2.00, $2.50, and $4.00 for the next three years. Analysts expect that Bugg will pay dividends of $1.00, $1.25, and $12.25 for the three years. The last dividend is anticipated to be a liquidating dividend; analysts expect Bugg will cease operations after Year 3. Bugg's current book value is $6.00 per share, and its required rate of return on equity is 10 percent.

1 Calculate per-share book value and residual income for the next three years.

2 Estimate the stock's value using the residual income model given in Equation

$$V_0 = B_0 + \sum_{t=1}^{\infty} \frac{E_t - rB_{t-1}}{(1 + r)^t}$$

3 Confirm your valuation estimate in Part 2 using the discounted dividend approach (i.e., estimating the value of a share as the present value of expected future dividends).

Solution to 1:

The book value and residual income for the next three years are shown in Exhibit 2.

Exhibit 2

Year	1	2	3
Beginning book value per share (B_{t-1})	$6.00	$7.00	$8.25
Net income per share (EPS)	2.00	2.50	4.00
Less dividends per share (D)	1.00	1.25	12.25
Change in retained earnings $(EPS - D)$	1.00	1.25	-8.25
Ending book value per share $(B_{t-1} + EPS - D)$	$7.00	$8.25	$0.00
Net income per share (EPS)	2.00	2.50	4.000
Less per-share equity charge (rB_{t-1})	0.60	0.70	0.825
Residual income (EPS − Equity charge)	$1.40	$1.80	$3.175

Solution to 2:

The value using the residual income model is

$$V_0 = 6.00 + \frac{1.40}{(1.10)} + \frac{1.80}{(1.10)^2} + \frac{3.175}{(1.10)^3}$$

$$= 6.00 + 1.2727 + 1.4876 + 2.3854$$

$$= \$11.15$$

Solution to 3:

The value using a discounted dividend approach is

$$V_0 = \frac{1.00}{(1.10)} + \frac{1.25}{(1.10)^2} + \frac{12.25}{(1.10)^3}$$

$$= 0.9091 + 1.0331 + 9.2036$$

$$= \$11.15$$

Example 3 illustrates two important points about residual income models. First, the RI model is fundamentally similar to other valuation models, such as the dividend discount model (DDM), and given consistent assumptions will yield equivalent results. Second, recognition of value typically occurs earlier in RI models than in DDM. In Example 3, the RI model attributes $6.00 of the $11.15 total value to the *first* time period. In contrast, the DDM model attributes $9.2036 of the $11.15 total value to the *final* time period. The rest of Section 3 develops the most familiar general expression for the RI model and illustrates the model's application.

3.1 The General Residual Income Model

The residual income model has a clear relationship to other valuation models, such as the dividend discount model. In fact, the residual income model given in Equation 3 can be derived from the DDM. The general expression for the DDM is

$$V_0 = \frac{D_1}{(1+r)^1} + \frac{D_2}{(1+r)^2} + \frac{D_3}{(1+r)^3} + \ldots$$

The **clean surplus relation** states the relationship among earnings, dividends, and book value as follows:

$$B_t = B_{t-1} + E_t - D_t$$

In other words, the ending book value of equity equals the beginning book value plus earnings minus dividends, apart from ownership transactions. The condition that income (earnings) reflects all changes in the book value of equity other than ownership transactions is known as clean surplus accounting. By rearranging the clean surplus relation, the dividend for each period can be viewed as the net income minus the earnings retained for the period, or net income minus the increase in book value:

$$D_t = E_t - (B_t - B_{t-1}) = E_t + B_{t-1} - B_t$$

Substituting $E_t + B_{t-1} - B_t$ for D_t in the expression for V_0 results in:

$$V_0 = \frac{E_1 + B_0 - B_1}{(1+r)^1} + \frac{E_2 + B_1 - B_2}{(1+r)^2} + \frac{E_3 + B_2 - B_3}{(1+r)^3} + \ldots$$

This equation can be rewritten as follows:

$$V_0 = B_0 + \frac{E_1 - rB_0}{(1+r)^1} + \frac{E_2 - rB_1}{(1+r)^2} + \frac{E_3 - rB_2}{(1+r)^3} + \ldots$$

Expressed with summation notation, the following equation restates the residual income model given in Equation 3:

$$V_0 = B_0 + \sum_{t=1}^{\infty} \frac{RI_t}{(1+r)^t} = B_0 + \sum_{t=1}^{\infty} \frac{E_t - rB_{t-1}}{(1+r)^t}$$

According to the expression, the value of a stock equals its book value per share plus the present value of expected future per-share residual income. Note that when the present value of expected future per-share residual income is positive (negative), intrinsic value, V_0, is greater (smaller) than book value per share, B_0.

The residual income model used in practice today has its origins largely in the academic work of Ohlson (1995) and Feltham and Ohlson (1995) along with the earlier work of Edwards and Bell (1961), although in the United States this method has been used to value small businesses in tax cases since the 1920s.[10] The general expression for the residual income model based on this work[11] can also be stated as:

$$V_0 = B_0 + \sum_{t=1}^{\infty} \frac{(ROE_t - r)B_{t-1}}{(1 + r)^t} \tag{4}$$

Equation 4 is equivalent to the expressions for V_0 given earlier because in any year, t, $RI_t = (ROE_t - r)B_{t-1}$. Other than the required rate of return on common stock, the inputs to the residual income model come from accounting data. Note that return on equity (ROE) in this context uses beginning book value of equity in the denominator, whereas in financial statement analysis ROE is frequently calculated using the average book value of equity in the denominator. Example 4 illustrates the estimation of value using Equation 4.

EXAMPLE 4

Using the Residual Income Model (2)

To recap the data from Example 3, Bugg Properties has expected earnings per share of $2.00, $2.50, and $4.00 and expected dividends per share of $1.00, $1.25, and $12.25 for the next three years. Analysts expect that the last dividend will be a liquidating dividend and that Bugg will cease operating after Year 3. Bugg's current book value per share is $6.00, and its estimated required rate of return on equity is 10 percent.

Using the above data, estimate the value of Bugg Properties' stock using a residual income model of the form:

$$V_0 = B_0 + \sum_{t=1}^{\infty} \frac{(ROE_t - r)B_{t-1}}{(1 + r)^t}$$

Solution:

To value the stock, forecast residual income. Exhibit 3 illustrates the calculation of residual income. (Note that Exhibit 3 arrives at the same estimates of residual income as Exhibit 2 in Example 3.)

Exhibit 3			
Year	**1**	**2**	**3**
Earnings per share	$2.00	$2.50	$4.00
Divided by beginning book value per share	÷ 6.00	÷ 7.00	÷ 8.25

(continued)

---

10 In tax valuation, the method is known as the **excess earnings method**. For example, see Hitchner (2006) and US IRS Revenue Ruling 68-609.

11 See, for example, Hirst and Hopkins (2000).

Exhibit 3   (Continued)

Year	1	2	3
ROE	0.3333	0.3571	0.4848
Less required rate of return on equity	– 0.1000	– 0.1000	– 0.1000
Abnormal rate of return (ROE – r)	0.2333	0.2571	0.3848
Multiply by beginning book value per share	× 6.00	× 7.00	× 8.25
Residual income (ROE – r) × Beginning BV	$1.400	$1.800	$3.175

Estimate the stock value as follows:

$$V_0 = 6.00 + \frac{1.40}{(1.10)} + \frac{1.80}{(1.10)^2} + \frac{3.175}{(1.10)^3}$$

$$= 6.00 + 1.2727 + 1.4876 + 2.3854$$

$$= \$11.15$$

Note that the value is identical to the estimate obtained using Equation 3, as illustrated in Example 3, because the assumptions are the same and Equations 3 and 4 are equivalent expressions:

$$V_0 = \frac{B_0 + \sum_{t=1}^{\infty} \frac{E_t - rB_{t-1}}{(1+r)^t}}{\text{Equation 3}} = \frac{B_0 + \sum_{t=1}^{\infty} \frac{(ROE_t - r)B_{t-1}}{(1+r)^t}}{\text{Equation 4}}$$

Example 4 showed that residual income value can be estimated using current book value, forecasts of earnings, forecasts of book value, and an estimate of the required rate of return on equity. The forecasts of earnings and book value translate into ROE forecasts.

EXAMPLE 5

Valuing a Company Using the General Residual Income Model

Robert Sumargo, an equity analyst, is considering the valuation of Google (NDQ:GOOG), in late 2013 when a recent closing price is $896.57. Sumargo notes that in general GOOG had a fairly high ROE during the past 10 years and that consensus analyst forecasts for EPS for the next two fiscal years reflect an expected ROE of around 19 percent. Sumargo expects that a high ROE may not be sustainable in the future. Sumargo usually takes a present value approach to valuation. As of the date of the valuation, GOOG does not pay dividends; although a discounted dividend valuation is possible, Sumargo does not feel confident about predicting the date of a dividend initiation. He decides to apply the residual income model to value GOOG, and uses the following data and assumptions:

▪ According to the CAPM, GOOG has a required rate of return of approximately 8.5 percent.

- GOOG's book value per share on 31 December 2012 was $217.54.

- ROE is expected to be 21 percent for 2013. Because of competitive pressures, Sumargo expects GOOG's ROE to decline in the following years and incorporates an assumed decline of 0.5 percent each year until it reaches the CAPM required rate of return.

- GOOG does not currently pay a dividend. Sumargo does not expect the company to pay a dividend in the foreseeable future, so all earnings will be reinvested. In addition, Sumargo expects that share repurchases will approximately offset new share issuances.

Compute the value of GOOG using the residual income model (Equation 4).

Solution:

Book value per share is initially $217.54. Based on a ROE forecast of 21 percent in the first year, the forecast EPS would be $45.68. Because no dividends are paid and the clean surplus relation is assumed to hold, book value at the end of the period is forecast to be $263.22 ($217.54 + $45.68). For 2013, residual income is measured as projected EPS of $45.68 minus an equity charge of $18.49, or $27.19. This is equivalent to the beginning book value per share of $217.54 times the difference between ROE of 21 percent and r of 8.5 percent [i.e., $217.54(0.21 − 0.085) = $27.19]. The present value of $27.19 at 8.5 percent for one year is $25.06. This process is continued year by year as presented in Exhibit 4. The value of GOOG using this residual income model would be the present value of each year's residual income plus the current book value per share. Because residual income is zero starting in 2038, no forecast is required beyond that period. The estimated value under this model is $920.24, as shown in Exhibit 4.

Exhibit 4	Valuation of GOOG Using the Residual Income Model							
Year	Projected Income EPS	Projected Dividend per Share	Book Value per Share	Forecast ROE (Based on Beginning Book Value)	Cost of Equity	Equity Charge	Residual Income (RI)	PV of BV and RI
	[Plus]	[Minus]	$217.54					217.54
2013	$45.68	$0.00	263.22	21.0%	8.5%	18.49	27.19	25.06
2014	53.96	0.00	317.18	20.5	8.5	22.37	31.59	26.83
2015	63.44	0.00	380.62	20.0	8.5	26.96	36.48	28.56
2016	74.22	0.00	454.84	19.5	8.5	32.35	41.87	30.21
2017	86.42	0.00	541.26	19.0	8.5	38.66	47.76	31.76
2018	100.13	0.00	641.40	18.5	8.5	46.01	54.13	33.18
2019	115.45	0.00	756.85	18.0	8.5	54.52	60.93	34.42
2020	132.45	0.00	889.30	17.5	8.5	64.33	68.12	35.47
2021	151.18	0.00	1,040.48	17.0	8.5	75.59	75.59	36.27
2022	171.68	0.00	1,212.15	16.5	8.5	88.44	83.24	36.81
2023	193.94	0.00	1,406.10	16.0	8.5	103.03	90.91	37.06
2024	217.95	0.00	1,624.04	15.5	8.5	119.52	98.43	36.98
2025	243.61	0.00	1,867.65	15.0	8.5	138.04	105.56	36.55
2026	270.81	0.00	2,138.46	14.5	8.5	158.75	112.06	35.76
2027	299.38	0.00	2,437.84	14.0	8.5	181.77	117.62	34.60
2028	329.11	0.00	2,766.95	13.5	8.5	207.22	121.89	33.04

(continued)

Exhibit 4	(Continued)							
Year	Projected Income EPS	Projected Dividend per Share	Book Value per Share	Forecast ROE (Based on Beginning Book Value)	Cost of Equity	Equity Charge	Residual Income (RI)	PV of BV and RI
2029	359.70	0.00	3,126.66	13.0	8.5	235.19	124.51	31.11
2030	390.83	0.00	3,517.49	12.5	8.5	265.77	125.07	28.80
2031	422.10	0.00	3,939.59	12.0	8.5	298.99	123.11	26.13
2032	453.05	0.00	4,392.64	11.5	8.5	334.86	118.19	23.12
2033	483.19	0.00	4,875.83	11.0	8.5	373.37	109.82	19.80
2034	511.96	0.00	5,387.79	10.5	8.5	414.45	97.52	16.20
2035	538.78	0.00	5,926.57	10.0	8.5	457.96	80.82	12.38
2036	563.02	0.00	6,489.60	9.5	8.5	503.76	59.27	8.37
2037	584.06	0.00	7,073.66	9.0	8.5	551.62	32.45	4.22
2038	601.26	0.00	7,674.92	8.5	8.5	601.26	0.00	0.00
Total							$920.24	

Note: PV is present value and BV is book value. This table was created in Excel, so numbers may differ from what will be obtained using a calculator, because of rounding.

Example 5 refers to the assumption of clean surplus accounting. The residual income model, as stated earlier, assumes clean surplus accounting. The clean surplus accounting assumption is illustrated in Exhibit 4, for example, in which ending book value per share is computed as beginning book value plus net income minus dividends. Under International Financial Reporting Standards (IFRS) and US generally accepted accounting principles (US GAAP), several items of income and expense occurring during a period, such as changes in the market value of certain securities, bypass the income statement and affect a company's book value of equity directly.[12] Strictly speaking, residual income models involve all items of income and expense (income under clean surplus accounting). If an analyst can reliably estimate material differences from clean surplus accounting expected in the future, an adjustment to net income may be appropriate. Section 5.1 explores violations of the clean surplus accounting assumption in more detail.

3.2 Fundamental Determinants of Residual Income

In general, the residual income model makes no assumptions about future earnings and dividend growth. If constant earnings and dividend growth are assumed, a version of the residual income model that usefully illustrates the fundamental drivers of residual

---

12 Items that bypass the income statement (dirty surplus items) are referred to as **other comprehensive income** (OCI). The relationship is Comprehensive income = Net income + Other comprehensive valuation.

income can be derived. The following expression is used for justified price-to-book ratio (P/B) based on forecasted fundamentals, assuming the Gordon (constant growth) DDM and the sustainable growth rate equation, $g = b \times ROE$:[13]

$$\frac{P_0}{B_0} = \frac{ROE - g}{r - g}$$

which is mathematically equivalent to:

$$\frac{P_0}{B_0} = 1 + \frac{ROE - r}{r - g}$$

The justified price is the stock's intrinsic value ($P_0 = V_0$). Therefore, using the previous equation and remembering that residual income is earnings less the cost of equity, or $(ROE \times B_0) - (r \times B_0)$, a stock's intrinsic value under the residual income model, assuming constant growth, can be expressed as:

$$V_0 = B_0 + \frac{ROE - r}{r - g} B_0 \tag{5}$$

Under this model, the estimated value of a share is the book value per share (B_0) plus the present value $[(ROE - r)B_0/(r - g)]$ of the expected stream of residual income. In the case of a company for which ROE exactly equals the cost of equity, the intrinsic value is equal to the book value per share. Equation 5 is considered a single-stage (or constant-growth) residual income model.

In an idealized world, where the book value of equity represents the fair value of net assets and clean surplus accounting prevails, the term B_0 reflects the value of assets owned by the company less its liabilities. The second term, $(ROE - r)B_0/(r - g)$, represents additional value expected because of the company's ability to generate returns in excess of its cost of equity; the second term is the present value of the company's expected economic profits. However, both IFRS and US GAAP allow companies to exclude some liabilities from their balance sheets, and neither set of rules reflects the fair value of many corporate assets. Internationally, however, a move toward fair value accounting is occurring, particularly for financial assets. Further, controversies, such as the failure of Enron Corporation in the United States, have highlighted the importance of identifying off-balance-sheet financing techniques.

The residual income model is most closely related to the P/B ratio. A stock's justified P/B ratio is directly related to expected future residual income. Another closely related concept is **Tobin's q**, the ratio of the market value of debt and equity to the replacement cost of total assets:[14]

$$\text{Tobin's } q = \frac{\text{Market value of debt and equity}}{\text{Replacement cost of total assets}}$$

Although similar to P/B, Tobin's q also has some obvious differences. The numerator includes the market value of total capital (debt as well as equity). The denominator uses total assets rather than equity. Further, assets are valued at replacement cost rather than at historical accounting cost; replacement costs take into account the effects of inflation. All else equal, Tobin's q is expected to be higher the greater the productivity of a company's assets.[15] One difficulty in computing Tobin's q is the lack of information on the replacement cost of assets. If available, market values of assets or replacement costs can be more useful in a valuation than historical costs.

---

13 Note that the sustainable growth rate formula itself can be derived from the clean surplus relation.
14 See Tobin (1969) or more recent work such as Landsman and Shapiro (1995).
15 Tobin theorized that q would average to 1 for all companies because the economic rents or profits earned by assets would average to zero.

3.3 Single-Stage Residual Income Valuation

The single-stage (constant-growth) residual income model assumes that a company has a constant return on equity and constant earnings growth rate through time. This model was given in Equation 5:

$$V_0 = B_0 + \frac{ROE - r}{r - g} B_0$$

EXAMPLE 6

Single-Stage Residual Income Model (1)

Joseph Yoh is evaluating a purchase of Canon, Inc. (NYSE: CAJ). Current book value per share is $26.24, and the current price per share is $34.68 (from Value Line, 26 July 2013). Yoh expects long-term ROE to be 11 percent and long-term growth to be 5.5 percent. Assuming a cost of equity of 9.5 percent, what is the intrinsic value of Canon stock calculated using a single-stage residual income model?

Solution:

$$V_0 = \$26.24 + \frac{0.11 - 0.095}{0.095 - 0.55} \$26.24$$

$$= \$36.08$$

Similar to the Gordon growth DDM, the single-stage RI model can be used to assess the market expectations of residual income growth—that is, an implied growth rate—by inputting the current price into the model and solving for g.

EXAMPLE 7

Single-Stage Residual Income Model (2)

Joseph Yoh is curious about the market-perceived growth rate, given that he is comfortable with his other inputs. By using the current price per share of $34.68 for Canon, Yoh solves the following equation for g:

$$\$34.68 = \$26.24 + \frac{0.11 - 0.095}{0.095 - g} \$26.24$$

He finds an implied growth rate of 4.84 percent.

In Examples 6 and 7, the company was valued at more than 1.3 times its book value because its ROE exceeded its cost of equity. If ROE was equal to the cost of equity, the company would be valued at book value. If ROE was lower than the cost of equity, the company would have negative residual income and be valued at less than book value. (When a company has no prospect of being able to cover its cost of capital, a liquidation of the company and redeployment of assets may be appropriate.)

In many applications, a drawback to the single-stage model is that it assumes the excess ROE above the cost of equity will persist indefinitely. More likely, a company's ROE will revert to a mean value of ROE over time, and at some point, the company's residual income will be zero. If a company or industry has an abnormally high ROE, other companies will enter the marketplace thus increasing competition and lowering returns for all companies. Similarly, if an industry has a low ROE, companies will exit the industry (through bankruptcy or otherwise) and ROE will tend to rise over time. As with the single-stage DDM, the single-stage residual income model also assumes a constant growth rate through time. In light of these considerations, the residual income model has been adapted in practice to handle declining residual income. For example, Lee and Swaminathan (1999) and Lee, Myers, and Swaminathan (1999) used a residual income model to value the Dow 30 by assuming that ROE fades (reverts) to the industry mean over time. Lee and Swaminathan found that the residual income model had more ability than traditional price multiples to predict future returns. Fortunately, other models are available that enable analysts to relax the assumption of indefinite persistence of excess returns. The following section describes a multistage residual income model.

3.4 Multistage Residual Income Valuation

As with other valuation approaches, such as DDM and free cash flow, a multistage residual income approach can be used to forecast residual income for a certain time horizon and then estimate a terminal value based on continuing residual income at the end of that time horizon. **Continuing residual income** is residual income after the forecast horizon. As with other valuation models, the forecast horizon for the initial stage should be based on the ability to explicitly forecast inputs in the model. Because ROE has been found to revert to mean levels over time and may decline to the cost of equity in a competitive environment, residual income approaches often model ROE fading toward the cost of equity. As ROE approaches the cost of equity, residual income approaches zero. An ROE equal to the cost of equity would result in residual income of zero.

In residual income valuation, the current book value often captures a large portion of total value and the terminal value may not be a large component of total value because book value is larger than the periodic residual income and because ROE may fade over time toward the cost of equity. This contrasts with other multistage approaches (DDM and DCF), in which the present value of the terminal value is frequently a significant portion of total value.

Analysts make a variety of assumptions concerning continuing residual income. Frequently, one of the following assumptions is made:

- residual income continues indefinitely at a positive level;
- residual income is zero from the terminal year forward;
- residual income declines to zero as ROE reverts to the cost of equity through time; or
- residual income reflects the reversion of ROE to some mean level.

The following examples illustrate several of these assumptions.

One finite-horizon model of residual income valuation assumes that at the end of time horizon T, a certain premium over book value ($P_T - B_T$) exists for the company, in which case, current value equals the following:[16]

$$V_0 = B_0 + \sum_{t=1}^{T} \frac{(E_t - rB_{t-1})}{(1+r)^t} + \frac{P_T - B_T}{(1+r)^T} \qquad (6)$$

---

16 See Bauman (1999).

Alternatively,

$$V_0 = B_0 + \sum_{t=1}^{T} \frac{(ROE_t - r)B_{t-1}}{(1 + r)^t} + \frac{P_T - B_T}{(1 + r)^T}$$

(7)

The last component in both specifications represents the premium over book value at the end of the forecast horizon. The longer the forecast period, the greater the chance that the company's residual income will converge to zero. For long forecast periods, this last term may be treated as zero. For shorter forecast periods, a forecast of the premium should be calculated.

EXAMPLE 8

Multistage Residual Income Model (1)

Diana Rosato, CFA, is considering an investment in Taiwan Semiconductor Manufacturing Ltd., a manufacturer and marketer of integrated circuits. Listed on the Taiwan Stock Exchange (Code: 2330), the company's stock is also traded on the New York Stock Exchange (NYSE: TSM). Rosato obtained the following facts and estimates as of August 2013:

- Current price equals TWD95.6.
- Cost of equity equals 12 percent.
- Taiwan Semiconductor's ROE has ranged from 18 percent to 22.9 percent during the period 2008–2012. The only time ROE was below 20 percent during that time period was in 2009.
- In 2012 the company paid a cash dividend of TWD2.9995.
- Book value per share was TWD28.8517 at the end of 2012.
- Rosato's forecasts of EPS are TWD7.162 for 2013 and TWD8.356 for 2014. She expects dividends of TWD2.9995 for 2013 and TWD3.2995 for 2014.
- Rosato expects Taiwan Semiconductor's ROE to be 25 percent from 2015 through 2019 and then decline to 20 percent through 2032.
- For the period after 2014, Rosato assumes an earnings retention ratio of 60 percent.
- Rosato assumes that after 2032, ROE will be 12 percent and residual income will be zero; therefore, the terminal value would be zero. Rosato's residual income model is shown in Exhibit 5.

Exhibit 5	Taiwan Semiconductor							
Year	Book Value (TWD)	Projected Income (TWD)	Dividend per Share (TWD)	Forecasted ROE (Beg. Equity, %)	COE (%)	COE (TWD)	Residual Income (TWD)	Present Value of Residual Income (TWD)
2012	28.8517							28.85
2013	33.0142	7.1620	2.9995	24.82	12.00	3.4622	3.6998	3.30
2014	38.0707	8.3560	3.2995	25.31	12.00	3.9617	4.3943	3.50
2015	43.7813	9.5177	3.8071	25.00	12.00	4.5685	4.9492	3.52
2016	50.3485	10.9453	4.3781	25.00	12.00	5.2538	5.6916	3.62
2017	57.9008	12.5871	5.0349	25.00	12.00	6.0418	6.5453	3.71
2018	66.5859	14.4752	5.7901	25.00	12.00	6.9481	7.5271	3.81

	Book Value (TWD)	Projected Income (TWD)	Dividend per Share (TWD)	Forecasted ROE (Beg. Equity, %)	COE (%)	COE (TWD)	Residual Income (TWD)	Present Value of Residual Income (TWD)
Exhibit 5	**(Continued)**							
Year								
2019	76.5738	16.6465	6.6586	25.00	12.00	7.9903	8.6562	3.92
2020	85.7626	15.3148	6.1259	20.00	12.00	9.1889	6.1259	2.47
2021	96.0541	17.1525	6.8610	20.00	12.00	10.2915	6.8610	2.47
2022	107.5806	19.2108	7.6843	20.00	12.00	11.5265	7.6843	2.47
2023	120.4903	21.5161	8.6065	20.00	12.00	12.9097	8.6065	2.47
2024	134.9492	24.0981	9.6392	20.00	12.00	14.4588	9.6392	2.47
2025	151.1431	26.9898	10.7959	20.00	12.00	16.1939	10.7959	2.47
2026	169.2802	30.2286	12.0914	20.00	12.00	18.1372	12.0914	2.47
2027	189.5938	33.8560	13.5424	20.00	12.00	20.3136	13.5424	2.47
2028	212.3451	37.9188	15.1675	20.00	12.00	22.7513	15.1675	2.47
2029	237.8265	42.4690	16.9876	20.00	12.00	25.4814	16.9876	2.47
2030	266.3657	47.5653	19.0261	20.00	12.00	28.5392	19.0261	2.47
2031	298.3296	53.2731	21.3093	20.00	12.00	31.9639	21.3093	2.47
2032	334.1291	59.6659	23.8664	20.00	12.00	35.7996	23.8664	2.47
						Present value TWD		86.41

Terminal Premium = 0.00

The market price of TWD95.6 exceeds the estimated value of TWD86.41. The market price reflects higher forecasts of residual income during the period to 2032, a higher terminal premium than Rosato forecasts, and/or a lower cost of equity. If Rosato is confident in her forecasts she may conclude that the company is overvalued in the current marketplace.

Lee and Swaminathan (1999) and Lee, Myers, and Swaminathan (1999) have presented a residual income model based on explicit forecasts of residual income for three years. Thereafter, ROE is forecast to fade to the industry mean value of ROE. The terminal value at the end of the forecast horizon (T) is estimated as the terminal-year residual income discounted in perpetuity. Lee and Swaminathan stated that this assumes any growth in earnings after T is value neutral. Exhibit 6 presents sector ROE data from Hemscott Americas, retrieved from Yahoo.com. (ROE data for specific industries can be retrieved from the same source.) In forecasting a fading ROE, the analyst should also consider any trends in industry ROE.

Exhibit 6	**US Sector ROEs**
Sectors	**ROE(%)**
Basic Materials	11.96
Conglomerates	22.60
Consumer Goods	14.54
Financial	9.78
Healthcare	18.60

(continued)

Exhibit 6	(Continued)
Sectors	**ROE(%)**
Industrial Goods	15.57
Services	17.69
Technology	16.47
Utilities	5.69

Source: Based on Hemscott Americas data retrieved from http://biz.yahoo.com on 28 August 2013.

EXAMPLE 9

Multistage Residual Income Model (2)

Rosato's supervisor questions her assumption that Taiwan Semiconductor will have no premium at the end of her forecast period. Rosato assesses the effect of a terminal value based on a perpetuity of Year 2032 residual income. She computes the following terminal value:

TV = TWD23.8664/0.12 = TWD198.8867

The present value of this terminal value is as follows:

PV = TWD198.8867/$(1.12)^{20}$ = TWD20.6179

Adding TWD20.6179 to the previous value of TWD86.41 (for which the terminal value was zero) yields a total value of TWD107.03. Because the current market price of TWD95.6 is less than TWD107.03, market participants expect a continuing residual income that is lower than her new assumptions and/or are forecasting a lower interim ROE. If Rosato agrees with her supervisor and is confident in her new forecasts, she may now conclude that the company is undervalued.

Another multistage model assumes that ROE fades over time to the cost of equity. In this approach, ROE can be explicitly forecast each period until reaching the cost of equity. The forecast would then end and the terminal value would be zero.

Dechow, Hutton, and Sloan (1999) presented an analysis of a residual income model in which residual income fades over time:[17]

$$V_0 = B_0 + \sum_{t=1}^{T-1} \frac{(E_t - rB_{t-1})}{(1+r)^t} + \frac{E_T - rB_{T-1}}{(1+r-\omega)(1+r)^{T-1}} \tag{8}$$

This model adds a persistence factor, ω, which is between zero and one. A persistence factor of one implies that residual income will not fade at all; rather it will continue at the same level indefinitely (i.e., in perpetuity). A persistence factor of zero implies that residual income will not continue after the initial forecast horizon. The higher the value of the persistence factor, the higher the stream of residual income in the final stage, and the higher the valuation, all else being equal. Dechow et al. found that in a large sample of company data from 1976 to 1995, the persistence factor equaled 0.62, which was interpreted by Bauman (1999) as equivalent to residual income

---

[17] See Dechow, Hutton, and Sloan (1999) and Bauman (1999).

decaying at an average rate of 38 percent a year. The persistence factor considers the long-run mean-reverting nature of ROE, assuming that in time ROE regresses toward r and that resulting residual income fades toward zero. Clearly, the persistence factor varies from company to company. For example, a company with a strong market leadership position would have a lower expected rate of decay (Bauman, 1999). Dechow et al. provided insight into some characteristics, listed in Exhibit 7, that can indicate a lower or higher level of persistence.

Exhibit 7 Final-Stage Residual Income Persistence

Lower Residual Income Persistence	Higher Residual Income Persistence
Extreme accounting rates of return (ROE)	Low dividend payout
Extreme levels of special items (e.g., non-recurring items)	High historical persistence in the industry
Extreme levels of accounting accruals	

Example 10 illustrates the assumption that continuing residual income will decline to zero as ROE approaches the required rate of return on equity.

EXAMPLE 10

Multistage Residual Income Model (3)

Rosato extends her analysis to consider the possibility that ROE will slowly decay toward r in 2033 and beyond, rather than using a perpetuity of Year 2032 residual income. Rosato estimates a persistence parameter of 0.60. The present value of the terminal value is determined as

$$\frac{E_T - rB_{T-1}}{(1 + r - \omega)(1 + r)^{T-1}}$$

with T equal to 21 and 2033 residual income equal to 26.7304 (23.8664 × 1.12), in which the 1.12 growth factor reflects a 12 percent growth rate calculated as the retention ratio times ROE, or (0.60)(20%) = 0.12.

$$\frac{26.73}{(1 + 0.12 - 0.60)(1.12)^{20}} = 5.33$$

Total value is TWD91.74 calculated by adding the present value of the terminal value, TWD5.33, to TWD86.41. Rosato concludes that if Taiwan Semiconductor's residual income does not persist at a stable level past 2032 and deteriorates through time, the shares are modestly overvalued at a price of TWD95.6.

RESIDUAL INCOME VALUATION IN RELATION TO OTHER APPROACHES

4

Before addressing accounting issues in using the residual income model, we briefly summarize the relationship of the residual income model to other valuation models.

Valuation models based on discounting dividends or on discounting free cash flows are as theoretically sound as the residual income model. Unlike the residual income model, however, the discounted dividend and free cash flow models forecast future cash flows and find the value of stock by discounting them back to the present by using the required return. Recall that the required return is the cost of equity for both the DDM and the free cash flows to equity (FCFE) model. For the free cash flow to the firm (FCFF) model, the required return is the overall weighted average cost of capital. The RI model approaches this process differently. It starts with a value based on the balance sheet, the book value of equity, and adjusts this value by adding the present values of expected future residual income. Thus, in theory, the recognition of value is different, but the total present value, whether using expected dividends, expected free cash flow, or book value plus expected residual income, should be consistent.[18]

Example 11 again illustrates the important point that the recognition of value in residual income models typically occurs earlier than in dividend discount models. In other words, residual income models tend to assign a relatively small portion of a security's total present value to the earnings that occur in later years. Note also that this example makes use of the fact that the present value of a perpetuity in the amount of X can be calculated as X/r.

EXAMPLE 11

Valuing a Perpetuity with the Residual Income Model

Assume the following data:

- A company will earn $1.00 per share forever.
- The company pays out all earnings as dividends.
- Book value per share is $6.00.
- The required rate of return on equity (or the percent cost of equity) is 10 percent.

1 Calculate the value of this stock using the DDM.
2 Calculate the level amount of per-share residual income that will be earned each year.
3 Calculate the value of the stock using a RI model.
4 Create a table summarizing the year-by-year valuation using the DDM and the RI model.

Solution to 1:

Because the dividend, D, is a perpetuity, the present value of D can be calculated as D/r.

$$V_0 = D/r = \$1.00/0.10 = \$10.00 \text{ per share}$$

Solution to 2:

Because each year all net income is paid out as dividends, book value per share will be constant at $6.00. Therefore, with a required rate of return on equity of 10 percent, for all future years, per-share residual income will be as follows:

$$\text{RI}_t = E_t - rB_{t-1} = \$1.00 - 0.10(\$6.00) = \$1.00 - \$0.60 = \$0.40$$

---

18 See, for example, Shrieves and Wachowicz (2001).

Solution to 3:

Using a residual income model, the estimated value equals the current book value per share plus the present value of future expected residual income (which in this example can be valued as a perpetuity):

V_0 = Book value + PV of expected future per-share residual income

= $6.00 + $0.40/0.10

= $6.00 + $4.00 = $10.00

Solution to 4:

Exhibit 8 summarizes the year-by-year valuation using the DDM and the RI models.

Exhibit 8	Value Recognition in the DDM and the RI Model			
	Dividend Discount Model		**Residual Income Model**	
Year	D_t	**PV of D_t**	B_0 **or RI_t**	**PV of B_0 or RI_t**
0			$6.00	$6.000
1	$1.00	$0.909	0.40	0.364
2	1.00	0.826	0.40	0.331
3	1.00	0.751	0.40	0.301
4	1.00	0.683	0.40	0.273
5	1.00	0.621	0.40	0.248
6	1.00	0.564	0.40	0.226
7	1.00	0.513	0.40	0.205
8	1.00	0.467	0.40	0.187
⋮	⋮	⋮	⋮	⋮
Total		$10.00		$10.00

In the RI model, most of the total value of the stock is attributed to the earlier periods. Specifically, the current book value of $6.00 represents 60 percent of the stock's total present value of $10.

In contrast, in the DDM, value is derived from the receipt of dividends, and typically, a smaller proportion of value is attributed to the earlier periods. Less than $1.00 of the total $10 derives from the first year's dividend, and collectively, the first five years' dividends ($0.909 + $0.826 + $0.751 + $0.683 + $0.621 = $3.79) contribute only about 38 percent of the total present value of $10.

As shown earlier and illustrated again in Example 11, the dividend discount and residual income models are in theory mutually consistent. Because of the real world uncertainty in forecasting distant cash flows, however, the earlier recognition of value in a residual income approach relative to other present value approaches is a practical advantage. In the dividend discount and free cash flow models, a stock's value is often modeled as the sum of the present value of individually forecasted dividends or free cash flows up to some terminal point plus the present value of the expected terminal value of the stock. In practice, a large fraction of a stock's total present value, in either the discounted dividend or free cash flow models, is represented by the present value of the expected terminal value. Substantial uncertainty, however, often surrounds the terminal value. In contrast, residual income valuations typically are less sensitive to terminal value estimates. (In some residual income valuation contexts the terminal value may actually be set equal to zero.) The derivation of value from the earlier portion of a forecast horizon is one reason residual income valuation can be a useful analytical tool.

4.1 Strengths and Weaknesses of the Residual Income Model

Now that the implementation of the residual income model has been illustrated with several examples, a summary of the strengths and weaknesses of the residual income approach follows:

The strengths of residual income models include the following:

- Terminal values do not make up a large portion of the total present value, relative to other models.
- RI models use readily available accounting data.
- The models can be readily applied to companies that do not pay dividends or to companies that do not have positive expected near-term free cash flows.
- The models can be used when cash flows are unpredictable.
- The models have an appealing focus on economic profitability.

The potential weaknesses of residual income models include the following:

- The models are based on accounting data that can be subject to manipulation by management.
- Accounting data used as inputs may require significant adjustments.
- The models require that the clean surplus relation holds, or that the analyst makes appropriate adjustments when the clean surplus relation does not hold. Section 5.1 discusses the clean surplus relation (or clean surplus accounting).
- The residual income model's use of accounting income assumes that the cost of debt capital is reflected appropriately by interest expense.

4.2 Broad Guidelines for Using a Residual Income Model

The above list of potential weaknesses helps explain the reading's focus in the following section on accounting considerations. In light of its strengths and weaknesses, the following are broad guidelines for using a residual income model in common stock valuation.

A residual income model is most appropriate when:

- a company does not pay dividends, or its dividends are not predictable;
- a company's expected free cash flows are negative within the analyst's comfortable forecast horizon; or
- great uncertainty exists in forecasting terminal values using an alternative present value approach.

Residual income models are least appropriate when:

- significant departures from clean surplus accounting exist, or
- significant determinants of residual income, such as book value and ROE, are not predictable.

Because various valuation models can be derived from the same underlying theoretical model, when fully consistent assumptions are used to forecast earnings, cash flow, dividends, book value, and residual income through a full set of pro forma (projected) financial statements, and the same required rate of return on equity is used as the discount rate, the same estimate of value should result when using each model. Practically speaking, however, it may not be possible to forecast each of these items with the same degree of certainty.[19] For example, if a company has near-term negative free cash flow and forecasts for the terminal value are uncertain, a residual income model may be more appropriate. But a company with positive, predictable cash flow that does not pay a dividend would be well suited for a discounted free cash flow valuation.

Residual income models, just like the discounted dividend and free cash flow models, can also be used to establish justified market multiples, such as price-to-earnings ratio (P/E) or P/B. For example, the value can be determined by using a residual income model and dividing by earnings to arrive at a justified P/E.

A residual income model can also be used in conjunction with other models to assess the consistency of results. If a wide variation of estimated value is found and each model appears appropriate, the inconsistency may lie with the assumptions used in the models. The analyst would need to perform additional work to determine whether the assumptions are mutually consistent and which model is most appropriate for the subject company.

ACCOUNTING AND INTERNATIONAL CONSIDERATIONS

5

To most accurately apply the residual income model in practice, the analyst may need to adjust book value of common equity for off-balance sheet items and adjust reported net income to obtain **comprehensive income** (all changes in equity other than contributions by, and distributions to, owners). In this section, we will discuss issues relating to these tasks.

Bauman (1999) has noted that the strength of the residual income model is that the two components (book value and future earnings) of the model have a balancing effect on each other, provided that the clean surplus relationship is followed:

> All other things held constant, companies making aggressive (conservative) accounting choices will report higher (lower) book values and lower (higher) future earnings. In the model, the present value of differences in future income is exactly offset by the initial differences in book value. (Bauman 1999, page 31)

Unfortunately, this argument has several problems in practice because the clean surplus relationship does not prevail, and analysts often use past earnings to predict future earnings. IFRS and US GAAP permit a variety of items to bypass the income statement and be reported directly in stockholders' equity. Further, off-balance sheet liabilities or nonoperating and nonrecurring items of income may obscure a company's financial performance. The analyst must thus be aware of such items when evaluating the book value of equity and return on equity to be used as inputs into a residual income model.

---

19 For a lively debate on this issue, see Penman and Sougiannis (1998), Penman (2001), Lundholm and O'Keefe (2001a), and Lundholm and O'Keefe (2001b).

With regard to the possibility that aggressive accounting choices will lead to lower reported future earnings, consider an example in which a company chooses to capitalize an expenditure in the current year rather than expense it. Doing so overstates current-year earnings as well as current book value. If an analyst uses current earnings (or ROE) naively in predicting future residual earnings, the RI model will overestimate the value of the company. Take, for example, a company with $1,000,000 of book value and $200,000 of earnings before taxes, after expensing an expenditure of $50,000. Ignoring taxes, this company has a ROE of 20 percent. If the company capitalized the expenditure rather than expensing it immediately, it would have a ROE of 23.81 percent ($250,000/$1,050,000). Although at some time in the future this capitalized item will likely be amortized or written off, thus reducing realized future earnings, analysts' expectations often rely on historical data. If capitalization of expenditures persists over time for a stable size company, ROE can decline because net income will normalize over the long term, but book value will be overstated. For a growing company, for which the expenditure in question is increasing, ROE can continue at high levels over time. In practice, because the RI model uses primarily accounting data as inputs, the model can be sensitive to accounting choices, and aggressive accounting methods (e.g., accelerating revenues or deferring expenses) can result in valuation errors. The analyst must, therefore, be particularly careful in analyzing a company's reported data for use in a residual income model.

Two principal drivers of residual earnings are ROE and book value. Analysts must understand how to use historical reported accounting data for these items to the extent they use historical data in forecasting future ROE and book value. Other readings have explained the DuPont analysis of ROE, which can be used as a tool in forecasting, and discussed the calculation of book value. We extend these discussions below with specific application to residual income valuation, particularly in addressing the following accounting considerations:

- violations of the clean surplus relationship;
- balance sheet adjustments for fair value;
- intangible assets;
- nonrecurring items;
- aggressive accounting practices; and
- international considerations.

In any valuation, close attention must be paid to the accounting practices of the company being valued. The following sections address the above issues as they particularly affect residual income valuation.

5.1 Violations of the Clean Surplus Relationship

One potential accounting issue in applying a residual income model is a violation of the clean surplus accounting assumption. Violations of this assumption occur when accounting standards permit charges directly to stockholders' equity, bypassing the income statement. An example is the case of changes in the market value of "available-for-sale" investments under US GAAP and "equity instruments measured at fair value through other comprehensive income" under IFRS. Under both IFRS (IFRS 9 Financial Instruments, paragraph 5.7.5) and US GAAP (ASC 320-10-35-1), these categories of investments are shown on the balance sheet at market value. Any unrealized change in their market value, however, is reflected in other comprehensive income rather than as income on the income statement.

As stated earlier, comprehensive income is defined as all changes in equity during a period other than contributions by, and distributions to, owners. Comprehensive income includes net income reported on the income statement and *other comprehensive income*, which is the result of other events and transactions that result in a change to equity but are not reported on the income statement. Items that commonly bypass the income statement include:[20]

- unrealized changes in the fair value of some financial instruments, as discussed above;
- foreign currency translation adjustments;
- certain pension adjustments;
- portion of gains and losses on certain hedging instruments;
- changes in revaluation surplus related to property, plant, and equipment or intangible assets (applicable under IFRS but not under US GAAP); and
- for certain categories of liabilities, change in fair value attributable to changes in the liability's credit risk (applicable under IFRS but not under US GAAP.

Under both international and US standards, such items as fair value changes for some financial instruments and foreign currency translation adjustments bypass the income statement. In addition, under IFRS, which unlike US GAAP permits revaluation of fixed assets (IAS 16, paragraph 39–42), some changes in the fair value of fixed assets also bypass the income statement and directly affect equity.

In all of these cases in which items bypass the income statement, the book value of equity is stated accurately because it includes "accumulated other comprehensive income," but net income is not stated properly from the perspective of residual income valuation. The analyst should be most concerned with the effect of these items on forecasts of net income and ROE (which has net income in the numerator), and hence residual income.[21] Because some items (including those listed above) bypass the income statement, they are excluded from historical ROE data. As noted by Frankel and Lee (1999), bias will be introduced into the valuation only if the present expected value of the clean surplus violations do not net to zero. In other words, reductions in income from some periods may be offset by increases from other periods. The analyst must examine the equity section of the balance sheet and the related statements of shareholders' equity and comprehensive income carefully for items that have bypassed the income statement. The analyst can then assess whether amounts are likely to be offsetting and can assess the effect on future ROE.

EXAMPLE 12

Evaluating Clean Surplus Violations

Excerpts from two companies' statements of changes in stockholders' equity are shown in Exhibits 9 and 10. The first statement, prepared under IFRS as of 31 December 2012, is for Nokia Corporation (NYSE: NOK), a leading manufacturer of mobile phones headquartered in Finland and with operations in four business segments: mobile phones, multimedia, enterprise solutions, and networks. The second statement, prepared under US GAAP as of 31 December 2012, is for SAP AG (NYSE: SAP), which is headquartered in Germany and is a worldwide provider of enterprise application software, including enterprise resource planning, customer relationship management, and supply chain management software.

---

20 See Frankel and Lee (1999).
21 The analyst should more precisely calculate historical ROE at the aggregate level (e.g., as net income divided by shareholders' equity) rather than as earnings per share divided by book value per share, because such actions as share issuance and share repurchases can distort ROE calculated on a per-share basis.

PART OF EXAMPLE 12

Exhibit 9   Nokia Corporation Statement of Changes in Shareholders' Equity (€ millions except number of shares)

	Number of shares (1,000's)	Share capital	Share issue premium	Treasury shares	Translation differences	Fair value and other reserves	Reserve for invested non-restrict. equity	Retained earnings	Before non-controlling interests	Non-controlling interests	Total
Balance as of December 31, 2011	3,710,189	246	362	-644	771	154	3,148	7,836	11,873	2,043	13,916
Translation differences					40				40	-2	38
Net investment hedges, net of tax					-67				-67		-67
Cash flow hedges, net of tax						-67			-67	47	-20
Available-for-sale investments, net of tax						36			36		36
Other increase, net								7	7	3	10
Loss								-3,106	-3,106	-683	-3,789
Total comprehensive income					-27	-31		-3,099	-3,157	-635	-3,792
Share-based compensation			1								
Excess tax benefit on share-based compensation			3								
Settlement of performance and restricted shares	796		-5	15			-12		-2		-2
Dividend								-742	-742	-22	-764
Convertible bond equity component			85						85		85
Total of other equity movements	796		84	15			-12	-742	-655	-22	-677
Balance at December 31, 2012	3,710,985	246	446	-629	744	123	3,136	3,995	8,061	1,386	9,447

Source: www.nokia.com.

Exhibit 10 SAP AG and Subsidiaries Statement of Changes in Shareholders' Equity (€ millions)

| | | | Equity attributable to owners of parent | | | | | | Non-controlling interests | Total equity |
| | | | | Other components of equity | | | | | | |
	Issued capital	Share premium	Retained earnings	Exchange differences	Available-for-sale financial assets	Cash flow hedges	Treasury sales	Total		
December 31, 2011	1,228	419	12,466	−19	9	−27	−1,377	12,699	8	12,707
Profit after tax			2,823					2,823	0	2,823
Other comprehensive income			−8	−217	13	47		−165		−165
Comprehensive income	0	0	2,815	−217	13	47	0	2,658	0	2,658
Share-based payments		41						41		41
Dividends			−1,310					−1,310		−1,310
Issuance of shares under share-based payments	1	14						15		15
Purchase of treasury shares							−53	−53		−53
Reissuance of treasury shares under share-based payments		18					93	111		111
Other			2					2	0	2
December 31, 2012	1,229	492	13,973	−236	22	20	−1,337	14,163	8	14,171

Source: www.sap.com.

For Nokia, items that have bypassed the income statement in 2012 are those in the columns labeled "Share issue premium," "Translation differences," "Fair value and other reserves," and "Reserve for invested non-restricted equity." For SAP, the amounts that bypassed the income statement in 2012 are "Share premium," "Exchange differences," "Available-for-sale financial assets," and "Cash flow hedges."

To illustrate the issues in interpreting these items, consider the columns "Translation differences" (Nokia) and "Exchange differences" (SAP). The amounts in these columns reflect currency translation adjustments to equity that have bypassed the income statement. For Nokia, the adjustment for the year 2012 was −€27 million. Because this is a negative adjustment to stockholders' equity, this item would have decreased income if it had been reported on the income statement. The balance is not increasing, however; it appears to be reversing to zero over time. For SAP, the translation adjustment for the year 2012 was −€217 million. Again, because this is a negative adjustment to stockholders' equity, this item would have decreased income if it had been reported on the income statement. In this case, the negative balance appears to be accumulating: It does not appear to be reversing (netting to zero) over time. If the analyst expects this trend to continue and has used historical data as the basis for initial estimates of ROE to be used in residual income valuation, a downward adjustment in that estimated future ROE might be warranted. It is possible, however, that future exchange rate movements will reverse this accumulation.

The examples in this reading have used the actual beginning equity and a forecasted level of ROE (return on beginning equity) to compute the forecasted net income. Because equity includes accumulated other comprehensive income (AOCI), the assumptions about future other comprehensive income (OCI) will affect forecasted net income and thus residual income. To illustrate, Exhibit 11 shows a hypothetical company's financials for a single previous year, labeled year $t-1$, followed by three different forecasts for the following two years. In year $t-1$, the company reports net income of $120, which is a 12 percent return on beginning equity of $1,000. The company paid no dividends, so ending retained earnings equal $120. In year $t-1$, the company also reports OCI of −$100, a loss, so the ending amount shown in AOCI is a −$100. (Companies typically label this line item "accumulated other comprehensive income (loss)," indicating that the amount is an accumulated loss when given in parentheses.)

All three forecasts in Exhibit 11 assume that ROE will be 12 percent and use this assumption to forecast net income for year t and $t+1$ by using the expression 0.12 × Beginning book value. Each forecast, however, incorporates different assumptions about future OCI. Forecast A assumes that the company will have no OCI in year t or year $t+1$, so the amount of AOCI does not change. Forecast B assumes that the company will continue to have the same amount of OCI in year t and year $t+1$ as it had in the prior year, so the amount of AOCI becomes more negative each year. Forecast C assumes that the company's OCI will reverse in year t, so at the end of year t, AOCI will be zero. As shown, because the forecasts use the assumed ROE to compute forecasted net income, the forecasts for net income and residual income in year $t+1$ vary significantly.

Because this example assumes all earnings are retained, a forecast of 12 percent ROE also implies that net income and residual income will grow at 12 percent. Only the year t to year $t+1$ under Forecast A, which assumes no future OCI, correctly reflects that relationship. Specifically, in Forecast A, both net income and residual income increase by 12 percent from year t to year $t+1$. Net income grows from $122.40 to $137.09, an increase of 12 percent [($137.09/$122.40) − 1]; and residual income grows from $20.40 to $22.85, an increase of 12 percent [($22.85/$20.40) − 1]. In contrast to

Exhibit 11   Hypothetical Company Alternative Forecasts with Different Assumptions about Comprehensive Income

	Actual	Forecast A		Forecast B		Forecast C	
Year	t−1	t	t+1	t	t+1	t	t+1
Beginning Balance Sheet							
Assets	$1,000.00	$1,020.00	$1,142.40	$1,020.00	$1,042.40	$1,020.00	$1,242.40
Liabilities	—	—	—	—	—	—	—
Common stock	1,000.00	1,000.00	1,000.00	1,000.00	1,000.00	1,000.00	1,000.00
Retained earnings	—	120.00	242.40	120.00	242.40	120.00	242.40
AOCI	—	(100.00)	(100.00)	(100.00)	(200.00)	(100.00)	—
Total equity	1,000.00	1,020.00	1,142.40	1,020.00	1,042.40	1,020.00	1,242.40
Total liabilities and total equity	$1,000.00	$1,020.00	$1,142.40	$1,020.00	$1,042.40	$1,020.00	$1,242.40
Net income	120.00	122.40	137.09	122.40	125.09	122.40	149.09
Dividends	—	—	—	—	—	—	—
Other comprehensive income	(100.00)	—	—	(100.00)	(100.00)	100.00	—
Ending Balance Sheet							
Assets	$1,020.00	$1,142.40	$1,279.49	$1,042.40	$1,067.49	$1,242.40	$1,391.49
Liabilities	—	—	—	—	—	—	—
Common stock	1,000.00	1,000.00	1,000.00	1,000.00	1,000.00	1,000.00	1,000.00
Retained earnings	120.00	242.40	379.49	242.40	367.49	242.40	391.49
AOCI	(100.00)	(100.00)	(100.00)	(200.00)	(300.00)	—	—
Total equity	$1,020.00	$1,142.40	$1,279.49	$1,042.40	$1,067.49	$1,242.40	$1,391.49
Total liabilities and total equity	$1,020.00	$1,142.40	$1,279.49	$1,042.40	$1,067.49	$1,242.40	$1,391.49
Residual income calculation based on beginning total equity							
Net income	120.00	122.40	137.09	122.40	125.09	122.40	149.09
Equity charge at 10 percent	100.00	102.00	114.24	102.00	104.24	102.00	124.24
Residual income	$20.00	$20.40	$22.85	$20.40	$20.85	$20.40	$24.85

Forecast A, neither Forecast B nor Forecast C correctly reflects the relationship between ROE and growth in income (net and residual). Growth in residual income from year *t* to year *t*+1 was 2.2 percent under Forecast B and 21.8 percent under Forecast C.

If, alternatively, the forecasts of future ROE and the residual income computation had incorporated total comprehensive income (net income plus OCI), the results of the residual income computation would have differed significantly. For example, suppose that in Forecast B, which assumes the company will continue to have the same amount of OCI, the estimated future ROE was 2.0 percent, using total comprehensive income [($120 – $100)/$1,000 = $20/$1,000]. If the residual income computation had then also used forecasted total comprehensive income at time *t*, the amount of residual income would be negative. Specifically, for time *t*, forecast comprehensive income would be $22.40 (net income plus other comprehensive income), the equity charge would be $102 (required return of 10 percent times beginning equity of $1,020), and residual income would be –$79.60 (comprehensive income of $22.40 minus equity charge of $102). Clearly, residual income on this basis significantly falls short of the positive $20.40 when the violation of clean surplus is ignored. As this example demonstrates, using an ROE forecast or a net income forecast that ignores violations of clean surplus accounting will distort estimates of residual income. Unless the present value of such distortions net to zero, using those forecasts will also distort valuations.

What are the implications for implementing a residual-income-based valuation? If future OCI is expected to be significant relative to net income and if the year-to-year amounts of OCI are not expected to net to zero, the analyst should attempt to incorporate these items so that residual income forecasts are closer to what they would be if the clean surplus relation held. Specifically, when possible, the analyst should incorporate explicit assumptions about future amounts of OCI.

Example 13 illustrates, by reference to the DDM value, the error that results when OCI is omitted from residual income calculations (assuming an analyst has a basis for forecasting future amounts of OCI).[22] The example also shows that the growth rate in residual income is generally not equal to the growth rate of net income or dividends.

EXAMPLE 13

Incorporating Adjustments in the Residual Income Model

Exhibit 12 gives per-share forecasts for Mannistore, Inc., a hypothetical company operating a chain of retail stores. The company's cost of capital is 10 percent.

Exhibit 12   Forecasts for Mannistore, Inc.

	Year				
Variable	**1**	**2**	**3**	**4**	**5**
Shareholders' equity					
t–1	$8.58	$10.32	$11.51	$14.68	$17.86
Plus net income	2.00	2.48	3.46	3.47	4.56
Less dividends	0.26	0.29	0.29	0.29	0.38

---

22 See Lundholm and O'Keefe (2001a and 2001b), who show how RI model and DDM valuations will differ when the analyst fails to include OCI in residual income calculations or makes inconsistent assumptions about the growth rates of net income, dividends, and residual income.

Exhibit 12	(Continued)				

	Year				
Variable	1	2	3	4	5
Less other comprehensive income	0.00	1.00	0.00	0.00	0.00
Equals shareholders' equity$_t$	$10.32	$11.51	$14.68	$17.86	$22.04

1 Assuming the forecasted terminal price of Mannistore's shares at the end of year 5 (time $t = 5$) is $68.40, estimate the value per share of Mannistore using the DDM.

2 Given that the forecast terminal price of Mannistore's shares at the end of year 5 (time $t = 5$) is $68.40, estimate the value of a share of Mannistore using the RI model and calculate residual income based on:

   A net income without adjustment, and

   B net income plus other comprehensive income.

3 Interpret your answers to Parts 2A and 2B.

4 Assume that a forecast of the terminal price of Mannistore's shares at the end of year 5 (time $t = 5$) is not available. Instead, an estimate of terminal price based on the Gordon growth model is appropriate. You estimate that the growth in net income and dividends from $t = 5$ to $t = 6$ will be 8 percent. Predict residual income for year 6, and based on that 8 percent growth estimate, determine the growth rate in forecasted residual income from $t = 5$ to $t = 6$.

Solution to 1:

The estimated value using the DDM is:

$$V_0 = \frac{\$0.26}{(1.10)^1} + \frac{\$0.29}{(1.10)^2} + \frac{\$0.29}{(1.10)^3} + \frac{\$0.29}{(1.10)^4} + \frac{\$0.38}{(1.10)^5}$$

$$+ \frac{\$68.40}{(1.10)^5} = \$43.59$$

Solution to 2:

A Calculating residual income as net income (NI) minus the equity charge, which is beginning shareholders' equity (SE) times the cost of equity capital (r), gives the following for years 1 through 5:

	Year				
	1	2	3	4	5
$RI = NI - (SE_{t-1} \times r)$	1.14	1.45	2.30	2.00	2.77

So, the estimated value using the RI model (using Equation 6), with residual income calculated based on net income, is:

$$V_0 = \$8.58 + \frac{\$1.14}{(1.10)^1} + \frac{\$1.45}{(1.10)^2} + \frac{\$2.30}{(1.10)^3} + \frac{\$2.00}{(1.10)^4} + \frac{\$2.77}{(1.10)^5}$$

$$+ \frac{\$68.40 - \$22.04}{(1.10)^5}$$

$$V_0 = \$8.58 + 35.84 = \$44.42$$

B Calculating residual income as net income adjusted for OCI (NI + OCI) minus the equity charge, which equals beginning shareholders' equity (SE) times the cost of equity capital (r), gives the following for years 1 through 5:

	Year				
	1	**2**	**3**	**4**	**5**
RI = (NI + OCI) − (SE$_{t-1}$ × r)	\$1.14	\$0.45	\$2.30	\$2.00	\$2.77

So, the estimated value using the RI model, with residual income based on net income adjusted for OCI, is:

$$V_0 = \$8.58 + \frac{\$1.14}{(1.10)^1} + \frac{\$.45}{(1.10)^2} + \frac{\$2.30}{(1.10)^3} + \frac{\$2.00}{(1.10)^4} + \frac{\$2.77}{(1.10)^5}$$

$$+ \frac{\$68.40 - \$22.04}{(1.10)^5}$$

$$V_0 = \$8.58 + 35.01 = \$43.59$$

Solution to 3:

The first calculation (2A) incorrectly omits an adjustment for a violation of the clean surplus relation. The second calculation (2B) includes an adjustment and yields the correct value estimate, which is consistent with the DDM estimate.

Solution to 4:

Given the estimated 8 percent growth in net income and dividends in year 6, the estimated year 6 net income is \$4.92 (\$4.56 × 1.08), and the estimated amount of year 6 dividends is \$0.42 (\$0.38 × 1.08).

Residual income will then equal \$2.72 (which is net income of \$4.92 minus the equity charge of beginning book value of \$22.04 times the cost of capital of 10 percent). So, the growth rate in residual income is negative at approximately −2 percent (\$2.72/\$2.77 − 1).

Lacking a basis for explicit assumptions about future amounts of OCI, the analyst should nonetheless be aware of the potential effect of OCI on residual income and adjust ROE accordingly. Finally, as noted above, the analyst may decide that an alternative valuation model is more appropriate.

5.2 Balance Sheet Adjustments for Fair Value

To have a reliable measure of book value of equity, an analyst should identify and scrutinize significant off-balance sheet assets and liabilities. Additionally, reported assets and liabilities should be adjusted to fair value when possible. Off-balance sheet assets and liabilities may become apparent through an examination of the financial statement footnotes. Probably the most common example is the use of operating leases. Operating leases do not affect the amount of equity (because leases involve both off-balance sheet assets that offset the off-balance sheet liabilities) but can affect an assessment of future earnings for the residual income component of value. Other assets and liabilities may be stated at values other than fair value. For example, inventory may be stated at LIFO and require adjustment to restate to current value. (LIFO is not permitted under IFRS.) The following are some common items to review for balance sheet adjustments. Note, however, that this list is not comprehensive:

- inventory;
- deferred tax assets and liabilities;
- operating leases;
- reserves and allowances (for example, bad debts); and
- intangible assets.

Additionally, the analyst should examine the financial statements and footnotes for items unique to the subject company.

5.3 Intangible Assets

Intangible assets can have a significant effect on book value. In the case of specifically identifiable intangibles that can be separated from the entity (e.g., sold), it is generally appropriate to include these in the determination of book value of equity. If these assets have a finite useful life, they will be amortized over time as an expense. Intangible assets, however, require special consideration because they are often not recognized as an asset unless they are obtained in an acquisition. For example, advertising expenditures can create a highly valuable brand, which is clearly an intangible asset. Advertising expenditures, however, are shown as an expense, and the value of a brand would not appear as an asset on the financial statements unless the company owning the brand was acquired.

To demonstrate this, consider a simplified example involving two companies, Alpha and Beta, with the following summary financial information (all amounts in thousands, except per-share data):

	Alpha	Beta
Cash	€1,600	€100
Property, plant, and equipment	3,400	900
Total assets	€5,000	€1,000
Equity	5,000	1,000
Net income	€600	€150

Each company pays out all net income as dividends (no growth), and the clean surplus relation holds. Alpha has a 12 percent ROE and Beta has a 15 percent ROE, both expected to continue indefinitely. Each has a 10 percent required rate of return. The fair market value of each company's property, plant, and equipment is the same as its book value. What is the value of each company in a residual income framework?

Using total book value rather than per-share data, the value of Alpha would be €6,000, determined as follows:[23]

$$V_0 = B_0 + \frac{ROE - r}{r - g}B_0 = 5{,}000 + \frac{0.12 - 0.10}{0.10 - 0.00}5{,}000 = 6{,}000$$

Similarly, the value of Beta would be €1,500:

$$V_0 = B_0 + \frac{ROE - r}{r - g}B_0 = 1{,}000 + \frac{0.15 - 0.10}{0.10 - 0.00}1{,}000 = 1{,}500$$

The value of the companies on a combined basis would be €7,500. Note that both companies are valued more highly than the book value of equity because they have ROE in excess of the required rate of return. Absent an acquisition transaction, the financial statements of Alpha and Beta do not reflect this value. If either is acquired, however, an acquirer would allocate the purchase price to the acquired assets, with any excess of the purchase price above the acquired assets shown as goodwill.

Suppose Alpha acquires Beta by paying Beta's former shareholders €1,500 in cash. Alpha has just paid €500 in excess of the value of Beta's total reported assets of €1,000. Assume that Beta's property, plant and equipment is already shown at its fair market value of €1,000, and that the €500 is considered to be the fair value of a license owned by Beta, say an exclusive right to provide a service. Assume further that the original cost of obtaining the license was an immaterial application fee, which does not appear on Beta's balance sheet, and that the license covers a period of 10 years. Because the entire purchase price of €1,500 is allocated to identifiable assets, no goodwill is recognized. The balance sheet of Alpha immediately after the acquisition would be:[24]

	Alpha
Cash	€200
Property, plant, and equipment	4,300
License	500
Total assets	€5,000
Equity	€5,000

Note that the total book value of Alpha's equity did not change, because the acquisition was made for cash and thus did not require Alpha to issue any new shares.

Making the assumption that the license is amortized over a 10-year period, the combined company's expected net income would be €700 (€600 + €150 − €50 amortization). If this net income number is used to derive expected ROE, the expected ROE would be 14 percent. Under a residual income model, with no adjustment for amortization, the value of the combined company would be:

$$V_0 = B_0 + \frac{ROE - r}{r - g}B_0 = 5{,}000 + \frac{0.14 - 0.10}{0.10 - 0.00}5{,}000 = 7{,}000$$

Why would the combined company be worth less than the two separate companies? If the assumption is made that a fair price was paid to Beta's former shareholders, the combined value should not be lower. The lower value using the residual income model results from a reduction in ROE as a result of the amortization of the intangible license

---

23 Results would be the same if calculated on a per-share basis.
24 For example, cash of €200 is calculated as €1,600 (cash of Alpha) + €100 (cash of Beta) − €1,500 (purchase price of Beta).

asset. If this asset were not amortized (or if the amortization expense was added back before computing ROE), net income would be €750 and ROE would be 15 percent. The value of the combined entity would be:

$$V_0 = B_0 + \frac{\text{ROE} - r}{r - g} B_0 = 5,000 + \frac{0.15 - 0.10}{0.10 - 0.00} 5,000 = 7,500$$

This amount, €7,500, is the same as the sum of the values of the companies on a separate basis.

Would the answer be different if the acquiring company used newly issued stock rather than cash in the acquisition? The form of currency used to pay for the transaction should not impact the total value. If Alpha used €1,500 of newly issued stock to acquire Beta, its balance sheet would be

	Alpha
Cash	€1,700
Property, plant, and equipment	4,300
License	500
Total assets	€6,500
Equity	€6,500

Projected earnings, excluding the amortization of the license, would be €750, and projected ROE would be 11.538 percent. Value under the residual income model would be:

$$V_0 = B_0 + \frac{\text{ROE} - r}{r - g} B_0 = 6,500 + \frac{0.11538 - 0.10}{0.10 - 0.00} 6,500 = 7,500$$

The overall value remains unchanged. The book value of equity is higher but offset by the effect on ROE. Once again, this example assumes that the buyer paid a fair value for the acquisition. If an acquirer overpays for an acquisition, the overpayment should become evident in a reduction in future residual income.

Research and development (R&D) costs provide another example of an intangible asset that must be given careful consideration. Under US GAAP, R&D is generally expensed to the income statement directly (except in certain cases such as ASC 985-20-25 which permits the capitalization of R&D expenses related to software development after product feasibility has been established). Also, under IFRS, some R&D costs can be capitalized and amortized over time. R&D expenditures are reflected in a company's ROE, and hence residual income, over the long term. If a company engages in unproductive R&D expenditures, these will lower residual income through the expenditures made. If a company engages in productive R&D expenditures, these should result in higher revenues to offset the expenditures over time. In summary, on a continuing basis for a mature company, ROE should reflect the productivity of R&D expenditures without requiring an adjustment.

As explained in Lundholm and Sloan (2007), including and subsequently amortizing an asset that was omitted from a company's reported assets has no effect on valuation under a residual income model. Such an adjustment would increase the estimated equity value by adding the asset to book value at time zero but decrease the estimated value by an equivalent amount, which would include a) the present value of the asset when amortized in the future and b) the present value of a periodic capital charge based on the amount of the asset times the cost of equity. Expensing R&D, however, results in an immediately lower ROE vis-à-vis capitalizing R&D. But expensing R&D will result in a slightly higher ROE relative to capitalizing R&D in future years because this capitalized R&D is amortized. Because ROE is used in a number of expressions derived from the residual income model and may also be used in forecasting net income, the analyst should carefully consider a company's R&D expenditures and their effect on long-term ROE.

5.4 Nonrecurring Items

In applying a residual income model, it is important to develop a forecast of future residual income based on recurring items. Companies often report nonrecurring charges as part of earnings, which can lead to overestimates and underestimates of future residual earnings if no adjustments are made. No adjustments to book value are necessary for these items, however, because nonrecurring gains and losses are reflected in the value of assets in place. Hirst and Hopkins (2000) noted that nonrecurring items sometimes result from accounting rules and at other times result from "strategic" management decisions. Regardless, they highlighted the importance of examining the financial statement notes and other sources for items that may warrant adjustment in determining recurring earnings, such as:

- unusual items;
- extraordinary items (applicable under US GAAP but not under IFRS);
- restructuring charges;
- discontinued operations; and
- accounting changes.

In some cases, management may record restructuring or unusual charges in every period. In these cases, the item may be considered an ordinary operating expense and may not require adjustment.

Companies sometimes inappropriately classify nonoperating gains as a reduction in operating expenses (such as selling, general, and administrative expenses). If material, this inappropriate classification can usually be uncovered by a careful reading of financial statement footnotes and press releases. Analysts should consider whether these items are likely to continue and contribute to residual income in time. More likely, they should be removed from operating earnings when forecasting residual income.

5.5 Other Aggressive Accounting Practices

Companies may engage in accounting practices that result in the overstatement of assets (book value) and/or overstatement of earnings. We discussed some of these practices in the preceding sections. Other activities that a company may engage in include accelerating revenues to the current period or deferring expenses to a later period.[25] Both activities simultaneously increase earnings and book value. For example, a company might ship unordered goods to customers at year-end, recording revenues and a receivable. As another example, a company could capitalize rather than expense a cash payment, resulting in lower expenses and an increase in assets.

Conversely, companies have also been criticized for the use of "cookie jar" reserves (reserves saved for future use), in which excess losses or expenses are recorded in an *earlier* period (for example, in conjunction with an acquisition or restructuring) and then used to reduce expenses and increase income in future periods. The analyst should carefully examine the use of reserves when assessing residual earnings. Overall, the analyst must evaluate a company's accounting policies carefully and consider the integrity of management when assessing the inputs in a residual income model.

---

25 See, for example, Schilit and Perler (2010).

5.6 International Considerations

Accounting standards differ internationally. These differences result in different measures of book value and earnings internationally and suggest that valuation models based on accrual accounting data might not perform as well as other present value models in international contexts. It is interesting to note, however, that Frankel and Lee (1999) found that the residual income model works well in valuing companies on an international basis. Using a simple residual income model without any of the adjustments discussed in this reading, they found that their residual income valuation model accounted for 70 percent of the cross-sectional variation of stock prices among 20 countries. Frankel and Lee concluded that there are three primary considerations in applying a residual income model internationally:

- the availability of reliable earnings forecasts;
- systematic violations of the clean surplus assumption; and
- "poor quality" accounting rules that result in delayed recognition of value changes.

Analysts should expect the model to work best in situations in which earnings forecasts are available, clean surplus violations are limited, and accounting rules do not result in delayed recognition. Because Frankel and Lee found good explanatory power for a residual income model using unadjusted accounting data, one expects that if adjustments are made to the reported data to correct for clean surplus and other violations, international comparisons should result in comparable valuations. For circumstances in which clean surplus violations exist, accounting choices result in delayed recognition, or accounting disclosures do not permit adjustment, the residual income model would not be appropriate and the analyst should consider a model less dependent on accounting data, such as a FCFE model.

It should be noted, however, that IFRS is increasingly becoming widely used. As of 2012, approximately 120 nations and reporting jurisdictions permit or require IFRS for domestic listed companies, although approximately 90 countries have fully conformed with IFRS as promulgated by the IASB and include a statement acknowledging such conformity in audit reports. Furthermore, standard setters in numerous countries continue to work toward convergence between IFRS and home-country GAAP. In time, concerns about the use of different accounting standards should become less severe. Nonetheless, even within a single set of accounting standards, companies make choices and estimates that can affect valuation.

SUMMARY

This reading has discussed the use of residual income models in valuation. Residual income is an appealing economic concept because it attempts to measure economic profit, which are profits after accounting for all opportunity costs of capital.

- Residual income is calculated as net income minus a deduction for the cost of equity capital. The deduction is called the equity charge and is equal to equity capital multiplied by the required rate of return on equity (the cost of equity capital in percent).
- Economic value added (EVA) is a commercial implementation of the residual income concept. EVA = NOPAT − (C% × TC), where NOPAT is net operating profit after taxes, C% is the percent cost of capital, and TC is total capital.

- Residual income models (including commercial implementations) are used not only for equity valuation but also to measure internal corporate performance and for determining executive compensation.

- We can forecast per-share residual income as forecasted earnings per share minus the required rate of return on equity multiplied by beginning book value per share. Alternatively, per-share residual income can be forecasted as beginning book value per share multiplied by the difference between forecasted ROE and the required rate of return on equity.

- In the residual income model, the intrinsic value of a share of common stock is the sum of book value per share and the present value of expected future per-share residual income. In the residual income model, the equivalent mathematical expressions for intrinsic value of a common stock are

$$V_0 = B_0 + \sum_{t=1}^{\infty} \frac{RI_t}{(1+r)^t} = B_0 + \sum_{t=1}^{\infty} \frac{E_t - rB_{t-1}}{(1+r)^t}$$

$$= B_0 + \sum_{t=1}^{\infty} \frac{(ROE_t - r)B_{t-1}}{(1+r)^t}$$

where

V_0 = value of a share of stock today ($t = 0$)
B_0 = current per-share book value of equity
B_t = expected per-share book value of equity at any time t
r = required rate of return on equity (cost of equity)
E_t = expected earnings per share for period t
RI_t = expected per-share residual income, equal to $E_t - rB_{t-1}$ or to (ROE $- r$) $\times$ B_{t-1}

- In most cases, value is recognized earlier in the residual income model compared with other present value models of stock value, such as the dividend discount model.

- Strengths of the residual income model include the following:
  - Terminal values do not make up a large portion of the value relative to other models.
  - The models use readily available accounting data.
  - The models can be used in the absence of dividends and near-term positive free cash flows.
  - The models can be used when cash flows are unpredictable.

- Weaknesses of the residual income model include the following:
  - The models are based on accounting data that can be subject to manipulation by management.
  - Accounting data used as inputs may require significant adjustments.
  - The models require that the clean surplus relation holds, or that the analyst makes appropriate adjustments when the clean surplus relation does not hold.

- The residual income model is most appropriate in the following cases:
  - A company is not paying dividends or if it exhibits an unpredictable dividend pattern.

- A company has negative free cash flow many years out but is expected to generate positive cash flow at some point in the future.
- A great deal of uncertainty exists in forecasting terminal values.

■ The fundamental determinants or drivers of residual income are book value of equity and return on equity.

■ Residual income valuation is most closely related to P/B. When the present value of expected future residual income is positive (negative), the justified P/B based on fundamentals is greater than (less than) one.

■ When fully consistent assumptions are used to forecast earnings, cash flow, dividends, book value, and residual income through a full set of pro forma (projected) financial statements, and the same required rate of return on equity is used as the discount rate, the same estimate of value should result from a residual income, dividend discount, or free cash flow valuation. In practice, however, analysts may find one model easier to apply and possibly arrive at different valuations using the different models.

■ Continuing residual income is residual income after the forecast horizon. Frequently, one of the following assumptions concerning continuing residual income is made:

- Residual income continues indefinitely at a positive level. (One variation of this assumption is that residual income continues indefinitely at the rate of inflation, meaning it is constant in real terms.)
- Residual income is zero from the terminal year forward.
- Residual income declines to zero as ROE reverts to the cost of equity over time.
- Residual income declines to some mean level.

■ The residual income model assumes the clean surplus relation of $B_t = B_{t-1} + E_t - D_t$. In other terms, the ending book value of equity equals the beginning book value plus earnings minus dividends, apart from ownership transactions.

■ In practice, to apply the residual income model most accurately, the analyst may need to:

- adjust book value of common equity for:
  - off-balance sheet items;
  - discrepancies from fair value; or
  - the amortization of certain intangible assets.
- adjust reported net income to reflect clean surplus accounting.
- adjust reported net income for nonrecurring items misclassified as recurring items.

REFERENCES

Bauman, Mark P. 1999. "Importance of Reported Book Value in Equity Valuation." *Journal of Financial Statement Analysis*, vol. 4, no. 2:31–40.

Bernstein, Richard, and Carmen Pigler. 1997. "An Analysis of EVA®." *Quantitative Viewpoint*. Merrill Lynch. 19 December.

Bernstein, Richard, Kari Bayer, and Carmen Pigler. 1998. "An Analysis of EVA® Part II." *Quantitative Viewpoint*. Merrill Lynch. 3 February.

Dechow, Patricia M., Amy P. Hutton, and Richard G. Sloan. 1999. "An Empirical Assessment of the Residual Income Valuation Model." *Journal of Accounting and Economics*, vol. 26, no. 1-3:1–34.

Edwards, Edgar O., and Philip W. Bell. 1961. *The Theory and Measurement of Business Income*. Berkeley, California: University of California Press.

Ehrbar, Al. 1998. *EVA: The Real Key to Creating Wealth*. John Wiley & Sons, Inc.

Feltham, Gerald A., and James A. Ohlson. 1995. "Valuation and Clean Surplus Accounting for Operating and Financial Activities." *Contemporary Accounting Research*, vol. 11, no. 4:689–731.

Fleck, Shelby A., Scott D. Craig, Michael Bodenstab, Trevor Harris, and Elmer Huh. 2001. *Technology: Electronics Manufacturing Services*. Industry Overview; Morgan Stanley Dean Witter. 28 March.

Frankel, Richard M., and Charles M.C. Lee. 1999. "Accounting Diversity and International Valuation." Working Paper, May.

Hirst, D. Eric, and Patrick E. Hopkins. 2000. *Earnings: Measurement, Disclosure, and the Impact on Equity Valuation*. Charlottesville, VA: Research Foundation of AIMR and Blackwell Series in Finance.

Hitchner, James R. 2006. *Financial Valuation: Applications and Models*, 2nd edition. Hoboken, NJ: John Wiley & Sons.

Landsman, Wayne, and Alan C. Shapiro. 1995. "Tobin's *q* and the Relation Between Accounting ROI and Economic Return." *Journal of Accounting, Auditing & Finance*, vol. 10:103–121.

Lee, Charles M.C., and Bhaskaran Swaminathan. 1999. "Valuing the Dow: A Bottom-Up Approach." *Financial Analysts Journal*, vol. 55, no. 5:4–23.

Lee, Charles M.C., James Myers, and Bhaskaran Swaminathan. 1999. "What is the Intrinsic Value of the Dow?" *Journal of Finance*, vol. 54, no. 5:1693–1741.

Lo, Kin, and Thomas Lys. 2000. "The Ohlson Model: Contributions to Valuation Theory, Limitations, and Empirical Applications." *Journal of Accounting, Auditing & Finance*, vol. 15, no. 3:337–367.

Lundholm, Russell J., and Terrence B. O'Keefe. 2001a. "Reconciling Value Estimates from the Discounted Cash Flow Model and the Residual Income Model." *Contemporary Accounting Research*, vol. 18, no. 2:311–335.

Lundholm, Russell J., and Terrence B. O'Keefe. 2001b. "On Comparing Residual Income and Discounted Cash Flow Models of Equity Valuation: A Response to Penman 2001." *Contemporary Accounting Research*, vol. 18, no. 4:693–696.

Lundholm, Russell J., and Richard G. Sloan. 2007. *Equity Valuation and Analysis with eVal*, 2nd edition. McGraw-Hill Irwin. New York.

Ohlson, James A. 1995. "Earnings, Book Values, and Dividends in Equity Valuation." *Contemporary Accounting Research*, vol. 11, no. 4:661–687.

Penman, Stephen H. 2001. "On Comparing Cash Flow and Accrual Accounting Models for Use in Equity Valuation: A Response to Lundholm and O'Keefe." *Contemporary Accounting Research*, vol. 18, no. 4:681–692.

Penman, Stephen H., and Theodore Sougiannis. 1998. "A Comparison of Dividend, Cash Flow and Earnings Approaches to Equity Valuation." *Contemporary Accounting Research*, vol. 15, no. 3:343–383.

Peterson, Pamela P., and David R. Peterson. 1996. *Company Performance and Measures of Value Added*. Charlottesville, VA: The Research Foundation of the ICFA.

Schilit, Howard, and Jeremy Perler. 2010. *Financial Shenanigans: How to Detect Accounting Gimmicks & Fraud in Financial Reports*, 3rd edition. New York: McGraw-Hill.

Shrieves, Ronald E., and John M. Wachowicz, Jr. 2001. "Free Cash Flow (FCF), Economic Value Added (EVA™), and Net Present Value (NPV): A Reconciliation of Variations of Discounted-Cash-Flow (DCF) Valuation." *Engineering Economist*, vol. 46, no. 1:33–52.

Stewart, G. Bennett III. 1991. *The Quest for Value*. New York: HarperCollins.

Tobin, James. 1969. "A General Equilibrium Approach to Monetary Theory." *Journal of Money, Credit and Banking*, vol. 1, no. 1:15–29.

Young, S. David. 1999. "Some Reflections on Accounting Adjustments and Economic Value Added." *Journal of Financial Statement Analysis*, vol. 4, no. 2:7–19.

PRACTICE PROBLEMS

1   Based on the following information, determine whether Vertically Integrated
    Manufacturing (VIM) earned any residual income for its shareholders:

    ● VIM had total assets of $3,000,000, financed with twice as much debt capital
      as equity capital.

    ● VIM's pretax cost of debt is 6 percent and cost of equity capital is
      10 percent.

    ● VIM had EBIT of $300,000 and was taxed at a rate of 40 percent.

    Calculate residual income by using the method based on deducting an equity
    charge.

2   Use the following information to estimate the intrinsic value of VIM's common
    stock using the residual income model:

    ● VIM had total assets of $3,000,000, financed with twice as much debt capital
      as equity capital.

    ● VIM's pretax cost of debt is 6 percent and cost of equity capital is
      10 percent.

    ● VIM had EBIT of $300,000 and was taxed at a rate of 40 percent. EBIT is
      expected to continue at $300,000 indefinitely.

    ● VIM's book value per share is $20.

    ● VIM has 50,000 shares of common stock outstanding.

3   Palmetto Steel, Inc. (PSI) maintains a dividend payout ratio of 80 percent
    because of its limited opportunities for expansion. Its return on equity is
    15 percent. The required rate of return on PSI equity is 12 percent, and its long-
    term growth rate is 3 percent. Compute the justified P/B based on forecasted
    fundamentals, consistent with the residual income model and a constant growth
    rate assumption.

4   Because New Market Products (NMP) markets consumer staples, it is able to
    make use of considerable debt in its capital structure; specifically, 90 percent
    of the company's total assets of $450,000,000 are financed with debt capital. Its
    cost of debt is 8 percent before taxes, and its cost of equity capital is 12 percent.
    NMP achieved a pretax income of $5.1 million in 2006 and had a tax rate of
    40 percent. What was NMP's residual income?

5   In 2007, Smithson–Williams Investments (SWI) achieved an operating profit
    after taxes of €10 million on total assets of €100 million. Half of its assets were
    financed with debt with a pretax cost of 9 percent. Its cost of equity capital is
    12 percent, and its tax rate is 40 percent. Did SWI achieve a positive residual
    income?

6   Calculate the economic value added (EVA) or residual income, as requested, for
    each of the following:

    A   NOPAT = $100

        Beginning book value of debt = $200

        Beginning book value of equity = $300

        WACC = 11 percent

        Calculate EVA.

Practice Problems and Solutions: *Equity Asset Valuation*, Second Edition, by Jerald E. Pinto, CFA, Elaine
Henry, CFA, Thomas R. Robinson, CFA, and John D. Stowe, CFA. Copyright © 2009 by CFA Institute.

B Net income = €5.00

Dividends = €1.00

Beginning book value of equity = €30.00

Required rate of return on equity = 11 percent

Calculate residual income.

C Return on equity = 18 percent

Required rate of return on equity = 12 percent

Beginning book value of equity = €30.00

Calculate residual income.

7 Jim Martin is using economic value added (EVA) and market value added (MVA) to measure the performance of Sundanci. Martin uses the fiscal year 2000 information below for his analysis.

● Adjusted net operating profit after tax (NOPAT) is $100 million.

● Total capital is $700 million (no debt).

● Closing stock price is $26.

● Total shares outstanding is 84 million.

● The cost of equity is 14 percent.

Calculate the following for Sundanci. Show your work.

A EVA for fiscal year 2000.

B MVA as of fiscal year-end 2000.

8 Protected Steel Corporation (PSC) has a book value of $6 per share. PSC is expected to earn $0.60 per share forever and pays out all of its earnings as dividends. The required rate of return on PSC's equity is 12 percent. Calculate the value of the stock using the following:

A Dividend discount model.

B Residual income model.

9 Notable Books (NB) is a family controlled company that dominates the retail book market. NB has book value of $10 per share, is expected to earn $2.00 forever, and pays out all of its earnings as dividends. Its required return on equity is 12.5 percent. Value the stock of NB using the following:

A Dividend discount model.

B Residual income model.

10 Simonson Investment Trust International (SITI) is expected to earn $4.00, $5.00, and $8.00 for the next three years. SITI will pay annual dividends of $2.00, $2.50, and $20.50 in each of these years. The last dividend includes a liquidating payment to shareholders at the end of Year 3 when the trust terminates. SITI's book value is $8 per share and its required return on equity is 10 percent.

A What is the current value per share of SITI according to the dividend discount model?

B Calculate per-share book value and residual income for SITI for each of the next 3 years and use those results to find the stock's value using the residual income model.

C Calculate return on equity and use it as an input to the residual income model to calculate SITI's value.

11 Foodsco Incorporated (FI), a leading distributor of food products and materials to restaurants and other institutions, has a remarkably steady track record in terms of both return on equity and growth. At year-end 2007, FI had a book value of $30 per share. For the foreseeable future, the company is expected to achieve a ROE of 15 percent (on trailing book value) and to pay out one-third of its earnings in dividends. The required return is 12 percent. Forecast FI's residual income for the year ending 31 December 2012.

12 Lendex Electronics (LE) had a great deal of turnover of top management for several years and was not followed by analysts during this period of turmoil. Because the company's performance has been improving steadily for the past three years, technology analyst Steve Kent recently reinitiated coverage of LE. A meeting with management confirmed Kent's positive impression of LE's operations and strategic plan. Kent decides LE merits further analysis.

Careful examination of LE's financial statements revealed that the company had negative other comprehensive income from changes in the value of available-for-sale securities in each of the past five years. How, if at all, should this observation about LE's other comprehensive income affect the figures that Kent uses for the company's ROE and book value for those years?

13 Retail fund manager Seymour Simms is considering the purchase of shares in upstart retailer Hot Topic Stores (HTS). The current book value of HTS is $20 per share, and its market price is $35. Simms expects long-term ROE to be 18 percent, long-term growth to be 10 percent, and cost of equity to be 14 percent. What conclusion would you expect Simms to arrive at if he uses a single-stage residual income model to value these shares?

14 Dayton Manufactured Homes (DMH) builds prefabricated homes and mobile homes. Favorable demographics and the likelihood of slow, steady increases in market share should enable DMH to maintain its ROE of 15 percent and growth rate of 10 percent through time. DMH has a book value of $30 per share and the required rate of return on its equity is 12 percent. Compute the value of its equity using the single-stage residual income model.

15 Use the following inputs and the finite horizon form of the residual income model to compute the value of Southern Trust Bank (STB) shares as of 31 December 2007:

- ROE will continue at 15 percent for the next five years (and 10 percent thereafter) with all earnings reinvested (no dividends paid).
- Cost of equity equals 10 percent.
- B_0 = $10 per share (at year-end 2007).
- Premium over book value at the end of five years will be 20 percent.

16 Shunichi Kobayashi is valuing United Parcel Service (NYSE: UPS). Kobayashi has made the following assumptions:

- Book value per share is estimated at $9.62 on 31 December 2007.
- EPS will be 22 percent of the beginning book value per share for the next eight years.
- Cash dividends paid will be 30 percent of EPS.
- At the end of the eight-year period, the market price per share will be three times the book value per share.
- The beta for UPS is 0.60, the risk-free rate is 5.00 percent, and the equity risk premium is 5.50 percent.

The current market price of UPS is $59.38, which indicates a current P/B of 6.2.

    A Prepare a table that shows the beginning and ending book values, net income, and cash dividends annually for the eight-year period.

    B Estimate the residual income and the present value of residual income for the eight years.

    C Estimate the value per share of UPS stock using the residual income model.

    D Estimate the value per share of UPS stock using the dividend discount model. How does this value compare with the estimate from the residual income model?

17 Boeing Company (NYSE: BA) has a current stock price of $49.86. It also has a P/B of 3.57 and book value per share of $13.97. Assume that the single-stage growth model is appropriate for valuing the company. Boeing's beta is 0.80, the risk-free rate is 5.00 percent, and the equity risk premium is 5.50 percent.

    A If the growth rate is 6 percent and the ROE is 20 percent, what is the justified P/B for Boeing?

    B If the growth rate is 6 percent, what ROE is required to yield Boeing's current P/B?

    C If the ROE is 20 percent, what growth rate is required for Boeing to have its current P/B?

Questions 18–25 relate to Mangoba Nkomo and Manga Mahlangu

Mangoba Nkomo, CFA, a senior equity analyst with Robertson-Butler Investments, South Africa, has been assigned a recent graduate, Manga Mahlangu, to assist in valuations. Mahlangu is interested in pursuing a career in equity analysis. In their first meeting, Nkomo and Mahlangu discuss the concept of residual income and its commercial applications. Nkomo asks Mahlangu to determine the market value added for a hypothetical South African firm using the data provided in Exhibit 1.

Exhibit 1	Hypothetical Firm Data (amounts in South African Rand)
Current share price	R25.43
Book value per share	R20.00
Total shares outstanding	30 million
Cost of equity	13%
Market value of debt	R55 million
Accounting book value of total capital	R650 million
Intrinsic share value of equity derived from residual income model	R22.00

Nkomo also shares his valuation report of the hypothetical firm with Mahlangu. Nkomo's report concludes that the intrinsic value of the hypothetical firm, based on the residual income model, is R22.00 per share. To assess Mahlangu's knowledge of residual income valuation, Nkomo asks Mahlangu two questions about the hypothetical firm:

    Question 1   What conclusion can we make about future residual earnings given the current book value per share and my estimate of intrinsic value per share?

Question 2 Suppose you estimated the intrinsic value of a firm's shares using a constant growth residual income model, and you found that your estimate of intrinsic value equaled the book value per share. What would that finding imply about that firm's return on equity?

Satisfied with Mahlangu's response, Nkomo requests that Mahlangu use the single-stage residual income (RI) model to determine the intrinsic value of the equity of Jackson Breweries, a brewery and bottling company, using data provided in Exhibit 2.

Exhibit 2 Jackson Breweries Data (amounts in South African Rand)

Constant long-term growth rate	9.5%
Constant long-term ROE	13%
Current market price per share	R150.70
Book value per share	R55.81
Cost of equity	11%

Nkomo also wants to update an earlier valuation of Amersheen, a food retailer. The valuation report, which was completed at the end of 2010, concluded an intrinsic value per share of R11.00 for Amersheen. The share price at that time was R8.25. Nkomo points out to Mahlangu that, in late 2010, Amersheen announced a significant restructuring charge, estimated at R2 million, that would be reported as part of operating earnings in Amersheen's 2010 annual income statement. Nkomo asks Mahlangu the following question about the restructuring charge:

Question 3 What was the correct way to treat the estimated R2 million restructuring charge in my 2010 valuation report?

Satisfied with Mahlangu's response, Nkomo mentions to Mahlangu that Amersheen recently (near the end of 2011) completed the acquisition of a chain of convenience stores. Nkomo requests that Mahlangu complete, as of the beginning of 2012, an updated valuation of Amersheen under two scenarios:

Scenario 1 Estimate the value of Amersheen shares using a multistage residual income (RI) model with the data provided in Exhibit 3. Under Scenario 1, expected ROE in 2015 is 26% but it is assumed that the firm's ROE will slowly decline towards the cost of equity thereafter.

Scenario 2 Estimate the value of Amersheen shares using a multistage residual income (RI) model with the data provided in Exhibit 3 but assume that, at the end of 2014, share price is expected to equal book value per share.

Exhibit 3 Amersheen Data (amounts in South African Rand)

Long-term growth rate starting in 2015	9.0%
Expected ROE in 2015	26%
Current market price per share	R16.55
Book value per share, beginning of 2012	R7.60
Cost of equity	10%
Persistence factor	0.70

(continued)

Exhibit 3	(Continued)		
	2012	**2013**	**2014**
Expected earnings per share	R3.28	R3.15	R2.90
Expected dividend per share	R2.46	R2.36	R2.06

18 Based upon the information in Exhibit 1, the market value added of the hypothetical firm is *closest* to:

A   R65 million.

B   R113 million.

C   R168 million.

19 The *most* appropriate response to Nkomo's Question 1 would be that the present value of future residual earnings is expected to be:

A   zero.

B   positive.

C   negative.

20 The *most* appropriate response to Nkomo's Question 2 would be that the firm's return on equity (ROE) is:

A   equal to the firm's cost of equity.

B   lower than the firm's cost of equity.

C   higher than the firm's cost of equity.

21 Based upon the information in Exhibit 2, the intrinsic value per share of the equity of Jackson Breweries is *closest* to:

A   R97.67.

B   R130.22.

C   R186.03.

22 If Nkomo's 2010 year-end estimate of Amersheen shares' intrinsic value was accurate, then Amersheen's shares were *most likely*:

A   overvalued.

B   undervalued.

C   fairly valued.

23 The *most* appropriate treatment of the estimated restructuring charge, in response to Nkomo's Question 3, would be:

A   an upward adjustment to book value.

B   an upward adjustment to the cost of equity.

C   to exclude it from the estimate of net income.

24 Under Scenario 1, the intrinsic value per share of the equity of Amersheen is *closest* to:

A   R13.29.

B   R15.57.

C   R16.31.

25 Under Scenario 2, the intrinsic value per share of the equity of Amersheen is *closest* to:

A   R13.29.

B R15.57.

C R16.31.

SOLUTIONS

1   Yes, VIM earned a positive residual income of $8,000.

EBIT	$300,000	
Interest	120,000	($2,000,000 × 6%)
Pretax income	$180,000	
Tax expense	72,000	
Net income	$108,000	

$$\text{Equity charge} = \text{Equity capital} \times \text{Required return on equity}$$
$$= (1/3)(\$3,000,000) \times 0.10$$
$$= \$1,000,000 \times 0.10 = \$100,000$$

$$\text{Residual income} = \text{Net income} - \text{Equity charge}$$
$$= \$108,000 - \$100,000 = \$8,000$$

2   According to the residual income model, the intrinsic value of a share of common stock equals book value per share plus the present value of expected future per-share residual income. Book value per share was given as $20. Noting that debt is $2,000,000 [(2/3)($3,000,000)] so that interest is $120,000 ($2,000,000 × 6%), VIM's residual income is $8,000, which is calculated (as in Problem 1) as follows:

$$\text{Residual income} = \text{Net income} - \text{Equity charge}$$
$$= \big[(\text{EBIT} - \text{Interest})(1 - \text{Tax rate})\big]$$
$$- \big[(\text{Equity capital})(\text{Required return on equity})\big]$$
$$= \big[(\$300,000 - \$120,000)(1 - 0.40)\big]$$
$$- \big[(\$1,000,000)(0.10)\big]$$
$$= \$108,000 - \$100,000$$
$$= \$8,000$$

Therefore, residual income per share is $0.16 per share ($8,000/50,000 shares). Because EBIT is expected to continue at the current level indefinitely, the expected per-share residual income of $0.16 is treated as a perpetuity. The present value of $0.16 is discounted at the required return on equity of 10 percent, so the present value of the residual income is $1.60 ($0.16/0.10).

$$\text{Intrinsic value} = \text{Book value per share} + \text{PV of expected future income}$$
$$\text{per-share residual income}$$
$$= \$20 + \$1.60 = \$21.60$$

3   With $g = b \times \text{ROE} = (1 - 0.80)(0.15) = (0.20)(0.15) = 0.03$,

$$P/B = (\text{ROE} - g)/(r - g)$$
$$= (0.15 - 0.03)/(0.12 - 0.03)$$
$$= 0.12/0.09 = 1.33$$

or

$$P/B = 1 + (\text{ROE} - r)/(r - g)$$
$$= 1 + (0.15 - 0.12)/(0.12 - 0.03)$$
$$= 1.33$$

4 In this problem (unlike Problems 1 and 2), interest expense has already been deducted in arriving at NMP's pretax income of $5.1 million.

Therefore,

Net income = Pretax income × (1 − Tax rate)
= $5.1 million × (1 − 0.4)
= $5.1 × 0.6 = $3.06 million

Equity charge = Total equity × Cost of equity capital
= (0.1 × $450 million) × 12%
= $45 million × 0.12 = $5,400,000

Residual income = Net income − Equity charge
= $3,0600,000 - $5,400,000 = −$2,340,000

NMP had negative residual income of −$2,340,000.

5 To achieve a positive residual income, a company's net operating profit after taxes as a percentage of its total assets can be compared with its weighted average cost of capital (WACC). For SWI,

NOPAT/Assets = €10 million / €100 million = 10%

WACC = Percent of debt × After-tax cost of debt
+ Percent of equity × Cost of equity
= (0.5)(0.09)(0.6) + (0.5)(0.12)
= (0.5)(0.054) + (0.5)(0.12) = 0.027 + 0.06 = 0.087
= 8.7%

Therefore, SWI's residual income was positive. Specifically, residual income equals €1.3 million [(0.10 − 0.087) × €100 million].

6 A EVA = NOPAT − WACC × Beginning book value of assets
= $100 − (11%) × ($200 + $300) = $100 − (11%)($500) = $45

B $RI_t = E_t - rB_{t-1}$
= €5.00 − (11%)(€30.00) = €5.00 − €3.30 = €1.70

C $RI_t = (\text{ROE}_t - r) \times B_{t-1}$
= (18% − 12%) × (€30) = €1.80

7 A Economic value added = Net operating profit after taxes − (Cost of capital × Total capital) = $100 million − (14% × $700 million) = $2 million. In the absence of information that would be required to calculate the weighted average cost of debt and equity, and given that Sundanci has no long-term debt, the only capital cost used is the required rate of return on equity of 14 percent.

B Market value added = Market value of capital − Total capital = $26 stock price × 84 million shares − $700 million = $1.48 billion

8 A Because the dividend is a perpetuity, the no-growth form of the DDM is applied as follows:

$$V_0 = D/r$$
$$= \$0.60/0.12 = \$5 \text{ per share}$$

B According to the residual income model, V_0 = Book value per share + Present value of expected future per-share residual income.

Residual income is calculated as:

$$\text{RI}_t = E - rB_{t-1}$$
$$= \$0.60 - (0.12)(\$6) = -\$0.12$$

Present value of perpetual stream of residual income is calculated as:

$$\text{RI}_t/r = -\$0.12/0.12 = -\$1.00$$

The value is calculated as:

$$V_0 = \$6.00 - \$1.00 = \$5.00 \text{ per share}$$

9 A According to the DDM, $V_0 = D/r$ for a no-growth company.

$$V_0 = \$2.00/0.125 = \$16 \text{ per share}$$

B Under the residual income model, $V_0 = B_0$ + Present value of expected future per-share residual income.

Residual income is calculated as:

$$\text{RI}_t = E - rB_{t-1}$$
$$= \$2 - (0.125)(\$10) = \$0.75$$

Present value of stream of residual income is calculated as:

$$\text{RI}_t/r = 0.75/0.125 = \$6$$

The value is calculated as:

$$V_0 = \$10 + \$6 = \$16 \text{ per share}$$

10 A V_0 = Present value of the future dividends

$$= \$2/1.10 + \$2.50/(1.1)^2 + \$20.50/(1.1)^3$$
$$= \$1.818 + \$2.066 + \$15.402 = \$19.286$$

B The book values and residual incomes for the next three years are as follows:

Year	1	2	3
Beginning book value	$ 8.00	$10.00	$12.50
Retained earnings (Net income – Dividends)	2.00	2.50	(12.50)
Ending book value	$10.00	$12.50	$ 0.00
Net income	$ 4.00	$ 5.00	$ 8.00
Less equity charge (r × Book value)	0.80	1.00	1.25
Residual income	$ 3.20	$ 4.00	$ 6.75

Under the residual income model,

$V_0 = B_0$ + Present value of expected future per-share residual income

$V_0 = \$8.00 + \$3.20/1.1 + \$4.00/(1.1)^2 + \$6.75/(1.1)^3$

$V_0 = 8.00 + \$2.909 + \$3.306 + \$5.071 = \$19.286$

C

Year	1	2	3
Net income (NI)	$4.00	$5.00	$8.00
Beginning book value (BV)	8.00	10.00	12.50
Return on equity (ROE) = NI/BV	50%	50%	64%
ROE – r	40%	40%	54%
Residual income (ROE – r) × BV	$3.20	$4.00	$6.75

Under the residual income model,

$V_0 = B_0 +$ Present value of expected future per-share residual income

$V_0 = \$8.00 + \$3.20/1.1 + \$4.00/(1.1)^2 + \$6.75/(1.1)^3$

$V_0 = 8.00 + \$2.909 + \$3.306 + \$5.071 = \$19.286$

Note: Because the residual incomes for each year are necessarily the same in Parts B and C, the results for stock valuation are identical.

11

Year	2008	2009	2012
Beginning book value	$30.00	$33.00	$43.92
Net income = ROE × Book value	4.50	4.95	6.59
Dividends = payout × Net income	1.50	1.65	2.20
Equity charge (r × Book value)	3.60	3.96	5.27
Residual income = Net income – Equity charge	0.90	0.99	1.32
Ending book value	$33.00	$36.30	$48.32

The table shows that residual income in Year 2008 is $0.90, which equals Beginning book value × (ROE – r) = $30 × (0.15 – 0.12). The Year 2009 column shows that residual income grew by 10 percent to $0.99, which follows from the fact that growth in residual income relates directly to the growth in net income as this example is configured. When both net income and dividends are a function of book value and return on equity is constant, then growth, g, can be predicted from (ROE)(1 – Dividend payout ratio). In this case, $g = 0.15 \times (1 - 0.333) = 0.10$ or 10 percent. Net income and residual income will grow by 10 percent annually.

Therefore, residual income in Year 2012 = (Residual income in Year 2008) × $(1.1)^4 = 0.90 \times 1.4641 = \$1.32$.

12 When such items as changes in the value of available-for-sale securities bypass the income statement, they are generally assumed to be nonoperating items that will fluctuate from year to year, although averaging to zero in a period of years. The evidence suggests, however, that changes in the value of available-for-sale securities are not averaging to zero but are persistently negative. Furthermore, these losses are bypassing the income statement. It appears that the company is either making an inaccurate assumption or misleading investors in one way or another. Accordingly, Kent might adjust LE's income downward by the amount of loss for other comprehensive income for each of those years. ROE would then decline commensurately. LE's book value would *not* be misstated because the decline in the value of these securities was already recognized and appears in the shareholders' equity account "Accumulated Other Comprehensive Income."

13 $V_0 = B_0 + (\text{ROE} - r)B_0/(r - g)$

$= \$20 + (0.18 - 0.14)(\$20)/(0.14 - 0.10)$

$= \$20 + \$20 = \$40$

Given the current market price is \$35 and the estimated value is \$40, Simms will probably conclude that the shares are somewhat undervalued.

14 $V_0 = B_0 + (\text{ROE} - r)B_0/(r - g)$

$= \$30 + (0.15 - 0.12)(\$30)/(0.12 - 0.10)$

$= \$30 + \$45 = \$75$ per share

15

Year	Net Income (Projected)	Ending Book Value	ROE (%)	Equity Charge (in Currency)	Residual Income	PV of RI
2007		\$10.00				
2008	\$1.50	11.50	15	\$1.00	\$0.50	\$0.45
2009	1.73	13.23	15	1.15	0.58	0.48
2010	1.99	15.22	15	1.32	0.67	0.50
2011	2.29	17.51	15	1.52	0.77	0.53
2012	2.63	20.14	15	1.75	0.88	0.55
						\$2.51

Using the finite horizon form of residual income valuation,

$V_0 = B_0 + $ Sum of discounted RIs + Premium (also discounted to present)

$= \$10 + \$2.51 + (0.20)(20.14)/(1.10)^5$

$= \$10 + \$2.51 + \$2.50 = \$15.01$

16 A Columns (a) through (d) in the table show calculations for beginning book value, net income, dividends, and ending book value.

	(a)	(b)	(c)	(d)	(e)	(f)
Year	Beginning Book Value	Net Income	Dividends	Ending Book Value	Residual Income	PV of RI
1	\$9.620	\$2.116	\$0.635	\$11.101	\$1.318	\$1.217
2	11.101	2.442	0.733	12.811	1.521	1.297
3	12.811	2.818	0.846	14.784	1.755	1.382
4	14.784	3.252	0.976	17.061	2.025	1.472
5	17.061	3.753	1.126	19.688	2.337	1.569
6	19.688	4.331	1.299	22.720	2.697	1.672
7	22.720	4.998	1.500	26.219	3.113	1.781
8	26.219	5.768	1.730	30.257	3.592	1.898
Total						\$12.288

For each year, net income is 22 percent of beginning book value. Dividends are 30 percent of net income. The ending book value equals the beginning book value plus net income minus dividends.

B Column (e) shows Residual income, which equals Net income − Cost of equity (%) × Beginning book value.

To find the cost of equity, use the CAPM:

$$r = R_F + \beta_i\left[E(R_M) - R_F\right] = 5\% + (0.60)(5.5\%) = 8.30\%$$

For Year 1 in the table above,

$$\text{Residual income} = RI_t = E - rB_{t-1}$$
$$= 2.116 - (8.30\%)(9.62)$$
$$= 2.116 - 0.798 = \$1.318$$

This same calculation is repeated for Years 2 through 8.

The final column of the table, (f), gives the present value of the calculated residual income, discounted at 8.30 percent.

C To find the stock value with the residual income method, use this equation:

$$V_0 = B_0 + \sum_{t=1}^{T}\frac{(E_t - rB_{t-1})}{(1+r)^t} + \frac{P_T - B_T}{(1+r)^T}$$

- In this equation, B_0 is the current book value per share of $9.62.
- The second term, the sum of the present values of the eight years' residual income is shown in the table, $12.288.
- To estimate the final term, the present value of the excess of the terminal stock price over the terminal book value, use the assumption that the terminal stock price is assumed to be 3.0 times the terminal book value. So, by assumption, the terminal stock price is $90.771 [$P_T = 3.0(30.257)$]. $P_T - B_T$ is $60.514 (90.771 - 30.257), and the present value of this amount discounted at 8.30 percent for eight years is $31.976.
- Summing the relevant terms gives a stock price of $53.884 ($V_0 = 9.62 + 12.288 + 31.976$).

D The appropriate DDM expression expresses the value of the stock as the sum of the present value of the dividends plus the present value of the terminal value:

$$V_0 = \sum_{t=1}^{T}\frac{D_t}{(1+r)^t} + \frac{P_T}{(1+r)^T}$$

Discounting the dividends from the table shown in the solution to Part A above at 8.30 percent gives:

Year	Dividend	PV of Dividend
1	$0.635	$0.586
2	0.733	0.625
3	0.846	0.666
4	0.976	0.709
5	1.126	0.756
6	1.299	0.805
7	1.500	0.858
8	1.730	0.914
All		$5.919

- The present value of the eight dividends is $5.92. The estimated terminal stock price, calculated in the solution to Part C above is $90.771, which equals $47.964 discounted at 8.30 percent for eight years.

- The value for the stock, the present value of the dividends plus the present value of the terminal stock price, is $V_0 = 5.92 + 47.964 = \$53.884$.

- The stock values estimated with the residual income model and the dividend discount model are identical. Because they are based on similar financial assumptions, this equivalency is expected. Even though the two models differ in their timing of the recognition of value, their final results are the same.

17 A The justified P/B can be found with the following formula:

$$\frac{P_0}{B_0} = 1 + \frac{ROE - r}{r - g}$$

ROE is 20 percent, g is 6 percent, and r is 9.4% $[R_F + \beta_i[E(R_M) - RF] = 5\% + (0.80)(5.5\%)]$. Substituting in the values gives a justified P/B of

$$\frac{P_0}{B_0} = 1 + \frac{0.20 - 0.094}{0.094 - 0.06} = 4.12$$

The assumed parameters give a justified P/B of 4.12, slightly above the current P/B of 3.57.

B To find the ROE that would result in a P/B of 3.57, we substitute 3.57, r, and g into the following equation:

$$\frac{P_0}{B_0} = 1 + \frac{ROE - r}{r - g}$$

This yields

$$3.57 = 1 + \frac{ROE - 0.094}{0.094 - 0.06}$$

Solving for ROE requires several steps to finally derive a ROE of 0.18138 or 18.1 percent. This value of ROE is consistent with a P/B of 3.57.

C To find the growth rate that would result with a P/B of 3.57, use the expression given in Part B, but solve for g instead of ROE:

$$\frac{P_0}{B_0} = 1 + \frac{ROE - r}{r - g}$$

Substituting in the values gives:

$$3.57 = 1 + \frac{0.20 - 0.094}{0.094 - g}$$

The growth rate g is 0.05275 or 5.3 percent. Assuming that the single-stage growth model is applicable to Boeing, the current P/B and current market price can be justified with values for ROE or g that are not much different from the starting values of 20 percent and 6 percent, respectively.

18 C is correct. Market value added equals the market value of firm minus total accounting book value of total capital.

Market value added = Market value of company – Accounting book value of total capital

Market value of firm = Market value of debt + Market value of equity

Market value of firm = R55 million + (30,000,000 × R25.43)

Market value of firm = R55 million + R762.9 million = R817.9 million

Market value added = R817.9 million – R650 million = R167.9 million, or approximately R168 million.

19 B is correct. The intrinsic value of R22.00 is greater than the current book value of R20.00. The residual income model states that the intrinsic value of a stock is its book value per share plus the present value of expected (future) per share residual income. The higher intrinsic value per share, relative to book value per share, indicates that the present value of expected per share residual income is positive.

20 A is correct because the intrinsic value is the book value per share, B_0, plus the expected residual income stream or $B_0 + [(ROE – r)B_0/(r-g)]$. If ROE equals the cost of equity (r), then $V_0 = B_0$. This implies that ROE is equal to the cost of the equity, and therefore there is no residual income contribution to the intrinsic value. As a result, intrinsic value would be equal to book value.

21 B is correct. With a single-stage residual income (RI) model, the intrinsic value, V_0, is calculated assuming a constant return on equity (ROE) and a constant earnings growth (g).

$$V_0 = B_0 + B_0 \frac{(ROE – r)}{(r – g)}$$

$$V_0 = R55.81 + R55.81 \frac{(0.13 – 0.11)}{(0.11 – 0.095)}$$

$$V_0 = R130.22$$

22 B is correct. The share price of R8.25 was lower than the intrinsic value of R11.00. Shares are considered undervalued when the current share price is less than intrinsic value per share.

23 C is correct. The restructuring charge is a nonrecurring item and not indicative of future earnings. In applying a residual income model, it is important to develop a forecast of future residual income based upon recurring items. Using the net income reported in Amersheen's 2010 net income statement to model subsequent future earnings, without adjustment for the restructuring charge, would understate the firm's future earnings. By upward adjusting the firm's net income, by adding back the R2 million restructuring charge to reflect the fact that the charge is nonrecurring, future earnings will be more accurately forecasted.

24 C is correct. As the multistage residual income model results in an intrinsic value of R16.31.

This variation of the multistage residual income model, in which residual income fades over time, is:

$$V_0 = B_0 + \sum_{t=1}^{T-1} \frac{(E_t – rB_{t-1})}{(1 + r)^t} + \frac{(E_T – rB_{T-1})}{(1 + r – \omega)(1 + r)^{T-1}}$$

where ω is the persistence factor.

The first step is to calculate residual income per share for years 2012–2015:

	2012	2013	2014	2015
Beginning book value per share	R7.60 (given)	R7.60 + R3.28 − R2.46 = R8.42	R8.42 + R3.15 − R2.36 = R9.21	R9.21 + 2.90 − R2.06 = R10.05
ROE	R3.28/R7.60 = 0.4316	R3.15/R8.42 = 0.3741	R2.90/R9.21 = 0.3149	26% (given)
Retention rate	1 − (R2.46/R3.28) = 0.25	1 − (R2.36/R3.15) = 0.2508	1 − (R2.06/R2.90) = 0.2897	N/A
Growth rate	0.4316 × 0.25 =0.1079	0.3741 × 0.2508 = 0.0938	0.3149 × 0.2897 = 0.0912	9% (given)
Equity charge per share	R7.60 × 0.10 = R0.76	R8.42 × 0.10 = R0.842	R9.21 × 0.10 = R0.921	R10.05 × 0.10 = R1.005
Residual income per share	R3.28 − R0.76 = R2.52	R3.15 − R0.842 = R2.31	R2.90 − 0.921 = R1.98	[0.26 × R10.05] − R1.005 = R1.608

ROE = earnings / book value

Growth rate = ROE × retention rate

Retention rate = 1 − (dividends/earnings)

Book value$_t$ = book value$_{t-1}$ + earnings$_{t-1}$ − dividends$_{t-1}$

Residual income per share = EPS − equity charge per share

Equity charge per share = book value per share$_t$ × cost of equity

Using the residual income per share for 2015 of R1.608, the second step is to calculate the present value of the terminal value:

$$PV \ of \ Terminal \ Value = \frac{R1.608}{(1 + 0.10 - 0.70)(1.10)^3} = R3.0203$$

Then, intrinsic value per share is:

$$V_0 = R7.60 + \frac{R2.52}{(1.10)} + \frac{R2.31}{(1.10)^2} + \frac{R1.98}{(1.10)^3} + R3.0203 = R16.31$$

25 A is correct. As the multistage residual income model results in an intrinsic value of R13.29. The multistage residual income model, is:

$$V_0 = B_0 + \sum_{t=1}^{T} \frac{(E_t - rB_{t-1})}{(1+r)^t} + \frac{(P_T - B_T)}{(1+r)^T}$$

The first step is to calculate residual income per share for years 2012–2014:

	2012	2013	2014
Beginning book value per share	R7.60 (given)	R7.60 + R3.28 − R2.46 = R8.42	R8.42 + R3.15 − R2.36 = R9.21
ROE	R3.28/R7.60 = 0.4316	R3.15/R8.42 = 0.3741	R2.90/R9.21 = 0.3149
Retention rate	1 − (R2.46/R3.28) = 0.25	1 − (R2.36/R3.15) = 0.2508	1 − (R2.06/R2.90) = 0.2897
Growth rate	0.4316 × 0.25=0.1079	0.3741 × 0.2508 = 0.0938	0.3149 × 0.2897= 0.0912
Equity charge per share	R7.60 × 0.10 = R0.76	R8.42 × 0.10 = R0.842	R9.21 × 0.10 = R0.921
Residual income per share	R3.28 − R0.76 = R2.52	R3.15 − R0.842 = R2.31	R2.90 − 0.921= R1.98

ROE = earnings / book value

Growth rate = ROE × retention rate

Retention rate = 1 − (dividends/earnings)

Book value$_t$ = book value$_{t-1}$ + earnings$_{t-1}$ – dividends$_{t-1}$

Residual income per share = EPS – equity charge per share

Equity charge per share = book value per share$_t$ × cost of equity

Under Scenario 2, at the end of 2014, it is assumed that share price will be equal to book value per share. This results in the second term in the equation above, the present value of the terminal value, being equal to zero.

Then, intrinsic value per share is:

$$V_0 = R\,7.60 + \frac{R\,2.52}{(1.10)} + \frac{R\,2.31}{(1.10)^2} + \frac{R\,1.98}{(1.10)^3} = R\,13.29$$

Private Company Valuation

by Raymond D. Rath, ASA, CFA

Raymond D. Rath, ASA, CFA, is at Globalview Advisors, LLC (USA).

LEARNING OUTCOMES

Mastery	The candidate should be able to:
☐	a. compare public and private company valuation;
☐	b. describe uses of private business valuation and explain applications of greatest concern to financial analysts;
☐	c. explain various definitions of value and demonstrate how different definitions can lead to different estimates of value;
☐	d. explain the income, market, and asset-based approaches to private company valuation and factors relevant to the selection of each approach;
☐	e. explain cash flow estimation issues related to private companies and adjustments required to estimate normalized earnings;
☐	f. calculate the value of a private company using free cash flow, capitalized cash flow, and/or excess earnings methods;
☐	g. explain factors that require adjustment when estimating the discount rate for private companies;
☐	h. compare models used to estimate the required rate of return to private company equity (for example, the CAPM, the expanded CAPM, and the build-up approach);
☐	i. calculate the value of a private company based on market approach methods and describe advantages and disadvantages of each method;
☐	j. describe the asset-based approach to private company valuation;
☐	k. explain and evaluate the effects on private company valuations of discounts and premiums based on control and marketability;
☐	l. describe the role of valuation standards in valuing private companies.

1 INTRODUCTION

The valuation of the equity of private companies is a major field of application for equity valuation.[1] Increasingly, generalist investment practitioners need to be familiar with issues associated with such valuations. Many public companies have start-up or other operations that can best be valued as if they were private companies. Companies may grow through the acquisition of competitors, including private companies, and analysts must be prepared to evaluate the price paid in such transactions. Furthermore, acquisitions often result in significant balances of intangible assets, including goodwill, that are reported on the balance sheets of acquiring companies. Goodwill balances require impairment assessment or formal testing on an annual basis (or more frequently if factors suggest impairment prior to an annual impairment test date) under International Financial Reporting Standards (IFRS) and US generally accepted accounting principles (GAAP). Impairment testing and other financial reporting initiatives increasingly result in the use of fair value estimates in financial statements. The concepts and methods discussed in this reading play important roles in this aspect of financial reporting. In addition, issues addressed in this reading arise in the types of investment held by venture capital and other types of private equity funds that constitute a significant allocation in many investors' portfolios. An expanded focus on the reported values of the investments held by private equity funds is leading to greater scrutiny of the valuation processes used and resulting value estimates.

This reading presents and illustrates key elements associated with the valuation of private companies and is organized as follows: Section 2 provides some background for understanding private company valuation, including typical contrasts between public and private companies and the major purposes for which private valuations are performed. Section 3 discusses the different definitions of value used in private company valuations and the idea that the valuation must address the definition of value relevant to the particular case. Section 4 discusses earnings normalization and cash flow estimation, introduces the three major approaches recognized in private company valuation, valuation discounts and premiums, and business valuation standards and practices. Section 5 summarizes the reading.

2 THE SCOPE OF PRIVATE COMPANY VALUATION

Private companies range from single-employee, unincorporated businesses to formerly public companies that have been taken private in management buyouts or other transactions. Numerous large, successful companies also exist that have remained private since inception, such as IKEA and Bosch in Europe and Cargill and Bechtel in the United States. The diverse characteristics of private companies and the absence of a universally recognized body providing guidance on valuation methods and assumptions have contributed to the development of diverse valuation practices.

---

[1] The term "appraisal" is often used in place of "valuation" in the contexts discussed in this reading. Appraisal and valuation are synonymous, as are appraiser and valuator.

2.1 Private and Public Company Valuation: Similarities and Contrasts

We can gain some insight into the challenges of private company valuation by examining company- and stock-specific factors that mark key differences between private and public companies.

2.1.1 Company-Specific Factors

Company-specific factors are those that characterize the company itself, including its lifecycle stage, size, markets, and the goals and characteristics of management.

- *Stage in lifecycle.* Private companies include companies at the earliest stages of development whereas public companies are typically further advanced in their lifecycle. Private companies may have minimal capital, assets, or employees. Private companies, however, also include large, stable, going concerns and failed companies in the process of liquidation. The stage of lifecycle influences the valuation process for a company.

- *Size.* Relative size—whether measured by income statement, balance sheet, or other measures—frequently distinguishes public and private companies; private companies in a given line of business tend to be smaller. Size has implications for the level of risk and, hence, relative valuation. Small size typically increases risk levels, and risk premiums for small size have often been applied in estimating required rates of return for private companies. For some private companies, small size may reduce growth prospects by reducing access to capital to fund growth of operations. The public equity markets are generally the best source for such funding. Conversely, for small companies, the costs of operating as a public company including compliance costs may outweigh any financing benefits.

- *Overlap of shareholders and management.* For many private companies, and in contrast to most public companies, top management has a controlling ownership interest. Therefore, they may not face the same pressure from external investors as public companies. Agency issues may also be mitigated in private companies.[2] For that reason, private company management may be able to take a longer term perspective in their decisions than public company management.

- *Quality/depth of management.* A small private company, especially if it has limited growth potential, would be expected to be less attractive to management candidates and have less management depth than a typical public company. The smaller scale of operation might also lead to less management depth compared with a public company. To the extent these considerations apply, they may increase risk and reduce growth prospects for the private company.

- *Quality of financial and other information.* Public companies are required to meet detailed requirements for the timely disclosure of financial and other information. Investment analysts may place significant demands on the management of a public company for high quality information. The more limited availability of financial and other information for private companies results in an increased burden for the prospective investor considering an equity investment or loan. This type of information difference presumably leads to greater uncertainty and, hence, risk. All else equal, the higher risk should lead to a relatively lower valuation. Although that may be the baseline case, note that in

---

2 **Agency issues** refer to such issues as monitoring costs arising from the sometimes conflicting interests of owners (principals) and managers (agents). See Aggarwal, Harrington, Kobor, and Drake (2008) for more information.

certain private company valuations, such as fairness opinions prepared in the context of an acquisition, the analyst usually has unlimited access to books, records, contracts, and other information that would not be available to the public stock analyst.

▪ *Pressure from short-term investors.* Earnings consistency and growth rates are often perceived as critical to the stock price performance of public companies. Continued management employment and levels of incentive compensation are often linked to stock price performance but many investors' interests may be of a trading or short-term nature. As a result, management may be motivated to try to support share price in the short term.[3] According to some observers, private companies typically do not experience similar stock price performance pressure and such companies can take a longer term investment focus.

▪ *Tax concerns.* Reduction of reported taxable income and corporate tax payments may be a more important goal for private companies compared with public companies because of greater benefit to the owners.

2.1.2 *Stock-Specific Factors*

In addition to company-specific factors, the characteristics of the stock of a private company frequently differ markedly from that of public companies.

▪ *Liquidity of equity interests in business.* Stock in private companies is generally much less liquid than otherwise similar interests in public companies. Private companies typically have fewer shareholders. Shares of a private company have not been registered for sale in the public stock markets. The limited number of existing and potential buyers reduces the value of the shares in private companies.

▪ *Concentration of control.*[4] Control of private companies is often concentrated in one or in very few investors. This concentration of control may lead to actions by a corporation that benefits some shareholders at the cost of other shareholders. Transactions with entities related to a control group at above-market prices would transfer value away from the noncontrolling shareholders of the corporation. Above-market compensation to a controlling shareholder is a typical perquisite.

▪ *Potential agreements restricting liquidity.* Private companies may have shareholder agreements in place that restrict the ability to sell shares. These agreements may reduce the marketability of equity interests.

Generally, stock-specific factors are a negative for private company valuation whereas company-specific factors are potentially positive or negative. The range of differences observed in private companies is such that the spectrum of risk and, therefore, the spectrum of return requirements are typically wider than for public companies. Another consequence is that the range of valuation methods and assumptions applied to private companies is typically more varied.

2.2 Reasons for Performing Valuations

Valuations of private businesses or equity interests therein fall into three groups: transaction-related, compliance-related, and litigation-related.

---

3 See *Breaking the Short-term Cycle*, CFA Institute Centre Publications (July 2006).
4 This factor could also be placed under company-specific factors.

Transactions encompass events affecting the ownership or financing of a business and represent a primary area of private company valuation. A variety of transaction types exist.

- *Private financing.* Raising capital is critical to development stage companies. To reduce risk and maintain influence, **venture capital investors** (as equity investors in such companies are known) typically invest through multiple rounds of financing tied to the achievement of key developments ("milestones"). A high level of uncertainty concerning expected future cash flows results in valuations that are often informal and based on negotiations between the company and investors.

- *Initial public offering (IPO).* An IPO is one liquidity option for a private company. Investment banking firms prepare valuations as part of the IPO process. A key element of an IPO-related valuation is frequently the identification of any public companies that are similar to the one going public.

- *Acquisition.* Acquisition can be an attractive liquidity option for development stage or mature companies. Acquisition related valuations may be performed (and negotiated) by management of the target and/or buyer. Smaller companies may be sold with the assistance of a business broker. The sale of many larger companies is handled by investment banking firms.

- *Bankruptcy.* For companies operating under bankruptcy protection, valuations of the business and its underlying assets may help assess whether a company is more valuable as a going concern or in liquidation. For viable going concerns operating in bankruptcy, insights from valuation may be critical to the restructuring of an overleveraged capital structure.

- *Share-based payment (compensation).* Share-based payments can be viewed as transactions between a company and its employees. These transactions often have accounting and tax implications to the issuer and the employee. Share-based payments can include stock option grants, restricted stock grants, and transactions involving an employee stock ownership plan (ESOP) in the United States and equivalent structures in other countries. Providing an incentive for improved employee performance is an important goal of such compensation mechanisms.

Compliance encompasses actions required by law or regulation. Compliance valuations are a second key area of valuation practice. Financial reporting and tax reporting are the two primary focuses of this type of valuation.

- *Financial reporting.* Financial reporting valuations are increasing in importance. Goodwill impairment is one of the most frequent financial reporting valuations that a securities analyst might observe.[5] Goodwill impairment tests require a business valuation for a cash-generating unit (IFRS)[6] of an entity or a reporting

---

5 Under IFRS, IAS 36, "Impairment of Assets," or IAS 38, "Intangible Assets," and under US GAAP, ASC 350 (formerly SFAS No. 142), "Goodwill and Other Intangible Assets," are the relevant accounting guidance. Under IFRS, IFRS 13, "Fair Value Measurements", and under US GAAP, ASC 820 (formerly SFAS No. 157), "Fair Value Measurements," provides additional guidance on measuring fair value.

6 IFRS 36, "Impairment of Assets," defines a **cash-generating unit** as the smallest identifiable group of assets that generates cash inflows that are largely independent of the cash inflows of other assets or groups of assets. ASC 350, "Goodwill and Other Intangible Assets," defines a **reporting unit** as an operating segment or one level below an operating segment (referred to as a component). A component of an operating segment is a reporting unit if the component constitutes a business for which discrete financial information is available and segment management regularly reviews the operating results of that component.

unit (US GAAP). Essentially, components of public companies are valued using private company valuation techniques. For private companies, stock option grants will frequently require valuations.[7]

■ *Tax reporting.* Tax reporting is a longstanding area that requires valuations of private companies. Tax-related reasons for valuations include corporate and individual tax reporting. A variety of corporate activities, such as corporate restructurings, transfer pricing, and property tax matters, may require valuations. An individual's tax requirements, such as those arising from estate and gift taxation in some jurisdictions, may generate a need for private company valuations.

Litigation—legal proceedings including those related to damages, lost profits, shareholder disputes, and divorce—often requires valuations. Litigation may affect public or private companies or may be between shareholders with no effect at the corporate level.

As the above descriptions make clear, each of the three major practice areas requires specialized knowledge and skills. This fact has led many valuation professionals to focus their efforts in one of these areas. Transactions, for example, often involve investment bankers. Compliance valuations are best performed by valuation professionals with knowledge of the relevant accounting or tax regulations. Litigation-related valuations require effective presentations in a legal setting.

Having provided an overview of the field of private company valuation, we can proceed to discussing how valuations are done. Logically, before developing an estimate of value, the valuator must understand the context of the valuation and its requirements. An important element in that process is knowledge of the definition(s) of value that the valuation must address (the subject of the next section).

3   DEFINITIONS (STANDARDS) OF VALUE

A **definition of value** (or **standard of value**) specifies how value is understood and, therefore, specifies a type of value. Identification of the correct definition of value to apply in a given valuation is a key step in developing an appropriate value estimate. The status of the company (in the sense of whether it is assumed to be a going concern or not)[8] and the use of the valuation are key elements in determining the definition of value to apply.

The major definitions of value may be summarized as follows.[9]

■ **Fair market value.** This term can be defined as the price, expressed in terms of cash equivalents, at which a property (asset) would change hands between a hypothetical willing and able buyer and a hypothetical willing and able seller, acting at "arm's length" in an open and unrestricted market, when neither is under compulsion to buy or sell and when both have reasonable knowledge of the relevant facts. Fair market value is most often used in a tax reporting context in the United States.

---

7 For IFRS, IFRS 2, "Share-Based Payment," and for US GAAP, ASC 718 (formerly SFAS No. 123R), "Share-Based Payment," are the relevant accounting guidance.

8 This assumption is sometimes referred to as the **premise of value**.

9 Definitions of fair market value, investment value, and intrinsic value are included in the International Glossary of Business Valuation Terms (IGBVT). The IGBVT was jointly developed by the American Institute of Certified Public Accountants, American Society of Appraisers, Canadian Institute of Chartered Business Valuators, National Association of Certified Valuation Analysts, and The Institute of Business Appraisers to improve appraisal practice through the use of consistent terminology.

- **Market value**. The International Valuation Standards Council (IVSC)[10] defines market value as "the estimated amount for which an asset or liability should exchange on the valuation date between a willing buyer and a willing seller in an arm's-length transaction, after proper marketing and where the parties had each acted knowledgeably, prudently, and without compulsion."[11] Market value is a definition of value often used in real estate and tangible asset appraisals when money is borrowed against the value of such assets.

- **Fair value** (financial reporting). Fair value is the definition of value used in financial reporting. Fair value shares many similarities with (fair) market value. The definition of fair value includes references to an arm's-length transaction (i.e., neither party is acting under duress) as well as the parties to a transaction being knowledgeable. Under IFRS (and US GAAP), fair value is defined as "the price that would be received to sell an asset or paid to transfer a liability in an orderly transaction between marketplace participant at the measurement date."[12] Note that this definition involves an **exit price**, the price that would be received to sell an asset (or be paid to transfer a liability).[13] An exit price should be less than or at most equal to the price paid to establish a position (an **entry price**).

- **Fair value** (litigation). In the United States, fair value is also a valuation definition as set forth by state statutes and legal precedents in certain litigation matters. Although definitions and interpretations may vary, the definition of fair value in a litigation context is generally similar to the previously given definitions for financial reporting.

- **Investment value**. Investment value can be defined as the value to a particular investor based on the investor's investment requirements and expectations. Investment value is important in the sale of a private company. The value of a company or asset may differ to different buyers as a result of differing perspectives on future earnings power and the level of risk of the company or asset, differing return requirements and financing costs of prospective buyers, and potential synergies of the acquisition with other assets owned by a prospective buyer. Investment value differs from the preceding value definitions in its greater focus on a specific buyer rather than value in a "market" context.

- **Intrinsic value**. Intrinsic value is often used in investment analysis. Intrinsic value can be defined as the value that an investor considers, on the basis of an evaluation or available facts, to be the "true" or "real" value that will become the

---

10 The IVSC is an international body that develops and maintains standards for the development, reporting, and disclosure of valuations, especially those that will be relied on by investors and other third-party stakeholders.

11 Some definitions of market value refer to value essentially on a cash equivalent basis. For example, real property is sometimes acquired with cash and seller financing (notes) in which the interest rate is different than the market rate. The cash equivalent value of the transaction would be its value if the note's value were adjusted to reflect a market interest rate. Another issue is contingent consideration, i.e., payments that are dependent on the occurrence of specified events (a more detailed definition is in Section 4.3.2), which may be an important component of certain acquisition payment structures. ASC 805 has expanded rules for the inclusion of contingent consideration in determining the total price paid in business acquisitions.

12 International Financial Reporting Standard No. 13, Fair Value Measurement and Accounting Standards Codification 820, Fair Value Measurement.

13 Market turmoil in 2008 and 2009 led to dramatically reduced liquidity in auction rate securities and large declines in quoted market prices. Some indicated that the exit price requirement of SFAS No. 157 (now ASC 820) resulted in significant asset markdowns and the reporting of unrealized losses as securities were marked to market. Public discussion of the implications of the exit price requirement under SFAS No. 157 and the impact of short-term market inefficiencies on asset pricing resulted from this turmoil.

market value when other investors reach the same conclusion. This definition attempts to capture the value of an asset absent any short-term pricing aberrations perceived as resulting in an asset value that is over or understated.

Different definitions of value can lead to different value estimates. To take a simple example, the investment value of an asset to a specific investor might be €100. This amount is not necessarily the same as the fair market value, market value, or fair value of the asset. Assume several other investors have investment values of €150 as a result of synergies or other factors and that it is believed that no other investors have investment values above €150. With sufficient investor interest at a value of €150, a fair market value estimate could be €150, recognizing the demand and supply schedules of buyers and sellers in the market.

An appraisal (valuation) should generally not be relied on for other than its intended purpose. Many private company valuations are performed for a specific purpose and reference a specific definition of value and valuation date that may not be relevant for another purpose. Prospective users must always consider whether a specific valuation and its definition of value are relevant for their situation.

To illustrate the point, consider an investor investigating the purchase of a controlling interest in a private company. The investor has access to a valuation prepared for tax reporting purposes of a small block of shares in the company. The value estimate in that report may not be relevant to this investor because it probably does not reflect the normalized earnings of the enterprise from the perspective of a majority shareholder who can influence corporate activities.[14] The valuation of the small block may include minority and/or marketability discounts that may not be appropriate in other contexts. A prospective buyer of the company relying on this valuation may miss an attractive acquisition candidate as expense adjustments and synergies may not have been considered. The valuation assumptions from the tax valuation would also require possible adjustments for use in a financial reporting context.

4   PRIVATE COMPANY VALUATION APPROACHES

Private company valuation experts distinguish three major approaches to valuation.

- The **income approach** values an asset as the present discounted value of the income expected from it. The income approach has several variations depending on the assumptions the valuator makes.

- The **market approach** values an asset based on pricing multiples from sales of assets viewed as similar to the subject asset. ("Pricing multiples" may refer to multiples based on share price or multiples based on a measure of total company value.)

- The **asset-based approach** values a private company based on the values of the underlying assets of the entity less the value of any related liabilities.

Valuation approaches for private companies are conceptually similar to those used for public companies although the labels used for them by experts in each field and the details of application may differ. The income approach corresponds to what are referred to as discounted cash flow models or present value models by public equities analysts. Along with asset-based models, discounted cash flow models are

---

14 Loosely, normalized earnings reflect adjustment for items that lessen the usefulness of the earnings number as a basis for comparison or forecasting. A more precise definition of normalized earnings is given in Section 4.1.1.

classified as absolute valuation models. By contrast, analysts use a relative valuation model when they apply a market-based approach in evaluating price and enterprise multiples relative to the value of a comparable.

Analysts select approach(es) depending on specific factors. The nature of operations and stage in lifecycle are important considerations. For a development stage company with the potential to operate as a successful large public company, the valuation methods may change over time. At the earliest stages of development, the company may best be valued using an asset-based approach because the going-concern premise of value may be uncertain and/or future cash flows may be extremely difficult to predict. With progress to a development stage company in a high growth mode, the company might be valued using a free cash flow method, which in private business appraisal is known as an income approach. A stable, mature company might be best valued on the basis of the market approach. Specific facts and circumstances may suggest different valuation methods.

Size is an important criterion in assessing valuation approaches and valuation methods. Multiples from public companies may not be appropriate for a small, relatively mature private company with very limited growth prospects. Comparisons to public companies are not a good basis of valuation for a private company if risk and growth prospects differ materially.

Public and private companies may consist of a variety of operating and nonoperating assets. Nonoperating assets are defined as assets not necessary to the ongoing operations of the business enterprise. Excess cash and investment balances are typical examples of nonoperating assets. In principle, the value of a company is the sum of the value of operating assets and the value of nonoperating assets. Thus, nonoperating assets should be included in the valuation of an enterprise regardless of the valuation approach or method being used.

Before we illustrate the application of the three approaches to valuation, we need to address certain typical issues relating to valuation model inputs that arise when valuing private companies.

4.1 Earnings Normalization and Cash Flow Estimation Issues

The next two sections cover earnings normalization and cash flow estimation in the context of private company valuation. Potential acquirers of private companies may find that current earnings reflect inefficiencies or redundancies that detract from their relevance as a baseline for forecasting future earnings under new ownership. In such cases, the earnings should be adjusted or "normalized" to a basis that is relevant for forecasting future results, given that the firm is acquired. Essentially, the valuator is seeking to understand accurately the earnings and cash flow capacity of the business enterprise if it is acquired and run efficiently.

4.1.1 Earnings Normalization Issues for Private Companies

Private company valuations may require significant adjustments to estimate the normalized earnings of the company. As defined in the International Glossary of Business Valuation Terms,[15] **normalized earnings** are "economic benefits adjusted for nonrecurring, non-economic, or other unusual items to eliminate anomalies and/or facilitate comparisons." As a result of the concentration of control in many private businesses, reported earnings may reflect discretionary expenses or expenses that are

---

15 The IGBVT is a glossary of frequently used business valuation terms that was developed through the joint efforts of the American Institute of Certified Public Accountants, the American Society of Appraisers, the Canadian Institute of Chartered Business Valuers, the National Association of Chartered Business Valuations, and the Institute of Business Appraisers.

not at arm's-length amounts. Tax and other motivations may also result in reporting earnings that may differ from the normalized earnings of a private company. The smaller size of many private companies potentially increases the relative impact on value of discretionary expenses.

When comparing the reported earnings of private companies with public companies, a key area of difference is the possible effect of transactions between the company and owners working in the business or with entities controlled by controlling shareholders. Many adjustments required to normalize earnings involve items that reduce the reported earnings of a profitable, private company. The controlling or sole shareholder is often active in the business and controls the Board of Directors and all policy and operating decisions. Above-market compensation or other expenses would reduce taxable income and income tax expense at the corporate level and subsequent taxes upon the payment of dividends to the controlling shareholder and other shareholders. Above-market expenses can also result in the controlling shareholder receiving a disproportionately high return in relation to other shareholders.

Compensation expense is a key area requiring possible adjustment. Profitable, private companies may report compensation expense to owner/employees above amounts that would be paid to a nonowner employee. Family members may also be included as employees and paid amounts above the market value of their services. For private companies with limited profits or reported losses, expenses may actually be understated with the reported income of the entity overstated. Owners active in the business may not take compensation commensurate with market levels required by an employee for similar activities.

A number of other areas exist for consideration for possible adjustments. Personal expenses may be included as expenses of the private company. Personal-use assets and excess entertainment expenses are areas for consideration. Personal residences, aircraft, and luxury or excessive use of corporate vehicles for personal use may require an adjustment. Life insurance and loans to shareholders merit review.

Real estate used by the private company is also an area for consideration. When a private company owns real estate, some analysts separate the real estate from the operating company. This separation consists of removing any revenues and expenses associated with the real estate from the income statement. If the company is using owned property in its business operations, adding a market rental charge for the use of the real estate to the expenses of the company would produce a more accurate estimate of the earnings of the business operations. Adjusting reported earnings to include a provision for the third party real estate costs would produce a value of the business operations excluding the owned real estate. Because the real estate is still owned by the entity, its value would represent a nonoperating asset of the entity. These adjustments for the financial impact of owned real estate can be appropriate because the business operations and real estate have different risk levels and growth expectations.

Without these adjustments to eliminate the effect of owned real estate on reported financial performance, the private company may be incorrectly valued. Rent charges for the use of real estate include return "of" and "on" investment components. Depreciation reflects return "of" investment. If real property is owned, depreciation expense would reflect the historical acquisition cost rather than current replacement cost. For owned real estate, the return "on" component of the rental charge would not be included at a market level charge. Application of a capitalization rate for the business operations to an earnings figure that includes some of the benefit from the owned real estate may misvalue the private company. The business operations and real estate may have different levels of risk and expected future growth that require separate valuation. If real estate is leased to the private company by a related entity, the level of expense may require an adjustment to a market rental rate. If real estate is leased from an unrelated party but the rental charge is not at a market level, an adjustment to normalize this expense may also be appropriate.

Example 1 illustrates a case in which a prospective buyer of a private business would need to make adjustments to reported financial results for a more accurate picture of the company's normalized earnings and value under new ownership.

Able Manufacturing: Normalized Earnings Adjustments

John Smith is the sole shareholder and CEO of Able Manufacturing, Inc. Smith has put Able up for sale in advance of his retirement. James Duvall, a manager in the corporate venturing unit of a public company, is evaluating the purchase of Able. Duvall notes the following facts affecting the most recent fiscal year's reported results:

- Smith's compensation for the year was $1.5 million. Duvall's executive compensation consultant believes a normalized compensation expense of $500,000 for a CEO of a company like Able is appropriate. Compensation is included in selling, general, and administrative expenses (SG&A).

- Certain corporate assets including ranch property and a condominium are in Duvall's judgment not required for the core operations of the company. Fiscal year expenses associated with the ranch and condominium were $400,000, including $300,000 of such operating expenses as property upkeep, property taxes, and insurance reflected in SG&A expenses, and depreciation expense of $100,000. All other asset balances (including cash) are believed to be at normal levels required to support current operations.

- Able's debt balance of $2,000,000 (interest rate of 7.5 percent) was lower than the optimal level of debt expected for the company. As reported interest expense did not reflect an optimal charge, Duvall believes the use of an earnings figure that excludes interest expense altogether, specifically operating income after taxes, will facilitate the assessment of Able.

Duvall uses the reported income statement to show the derivation of reported operating income after taxes, as given below.

Able Manufacturing, Inc.
Operating Income after Taxes

As of 31 December 2013	As Reported
Revenues	$50,000,000
Cost of goods sold	30,000,000
Gross profit	20,000,000
Selling, general, and admin. expenses	5,000,000
EBITDA	15,000,000
Depreciation and amortization	1,000,000
Earnings before interest and taxes	14,000,000
Pro forma taxes (at 40.0 percent)	5,600,000
Operating income after taxes	$8,400,000

Based only on the information given, address the following:

1   Identify the adjustments that Duvall would make to reported financials to estimate normalized operating income after taxes; that is, what the operating income after taxes would have been under ownership by Duvall's unit.

2   Based on your answer to Part 1, construct a pro forma statement of normalized operating income after taxes for Able.

Solution to 1:

First, SG&A should be reduced by $1,500,000 – $500,000 = $1,000,000 to reflect the expected level of salary expense under professional management at a market rate of compensation. Second, the ranch and condominium are nonoperating assets—they are not needed to generate revenues—so expense items should be adjusted to reflect their removal (e.g., through a sale). Two income statement lines are affected: SG&A expenses should be reduced by $300,000 and depreciation and amortization reduced by $100,000.

Solution to 2:

The pro forma statement of normalized operating income after taxes would be:

Able Manufacturing, Inc. Pro Forma Normalized Operating Income after Taxes	
As of 31 December 2013	**Pro Forma**
Revenues	$50,000,000
Cost of goods sold	30,000,000
Gross profit	20,000,000
Selling, general, and admin. expenses	3,700,000
EBITDA	16,300,000
Depreciation and amortization	900,000
Earnings before interest and taxes	15,400,000
Pro forma taxes (at 40.0 percent)	6,160,000
Operating income after taxes	$9,240,000

In addition to the various adjustments noted above, a variety of other areas exist for possible adjustment that are similar for the valuation of public and private companies (e.g., adjustments related to inventory accounting methods, depreciation assumptions, and capitalization versus expensing of various costs). Private companies may have their financial statements reviewed rather than audited. **Reviewed financial statements** provide an opinion letter with representations and assurances by the reviewing accountant that are less than those in audited financial statements. The preparation of reviewed rather than audited financial statements and other factors suggest a potentially greater need for analyst adjustments to the reported financials of some private companies. **Compiled financial statements** (that are not accompanied by an auditor's opinion letter) suggest an even greater need for analytical adjustments.

4.1.2 *Cash Flow Estimation Issues for Private Companies*

In addition to earnings normalization, cash flow estimation is an important element of the valuation process. Free cash flow (FCF) is the relevant concept of cash flow in this context. Free cash flow to the firm (FCFF) represents free cash flow at the business enterprise level and is used to value the firm or, indirectly, the firm's equity.[16] Alternatively, free cash flow to equity (FCFE) can be used to value equity directly.

Cash flow estimation for private companies raises some important challenges, including those related to the nature of the interest being valued, potentially acute uncertainties regarding future operations, and managerial involvement in forecasting.

The nature of assumptions in cash flow estimates depends on a variety of factors. The equity interest appraised and the intended use of the appraisal are key in determining the appropriate definition of value for a specific valuation. The assumptions included in cash flow estimates may differ if a small minority equity interest is appraised rather than the total equity of a business. For example, an investment value standard may lead to different cash flow estimates than a fair value standard related to a financial reporting valuation assignment.

In assessing future cash flow estimates, uncertainty regarding a potentially wide range of future cash flow possibilities also creates challenges for valuation using FCF. Many development stage companies and some mature companies are subject to significant uncertainties regarding future operations and cash flows. One possible solution involves projecting the different possible future scenarios. For a privately held development stage company, the possible scenarios could include initial public offering, acquisition, continued operation as a private company, or bankruptcy. For a larger, mature company, the scenarios might be chosen to cover the range of possible levels of growth and profitability.

In valuing an individual scenario, the discount rate chosen should reflect the risk of achieving the projected cash flows in that scenario. The probability of the occurrence of each scenario must also be estimated. The overall value estimate for a company is then a probability-weighted average of the company's estimated scenario values. Alternatively, the expected future cash flows based on the scenarios could be discounted using a conventional, single discount rate to obtain an overall value estimate. Although the trend is generally to more robust models, in current practice private company valuation more frequently reflects an average or most likely scenario than an explicit multiple scenario analysis.

Managers of private companies generally command much more information about their business than outside analysts. Management may develop cash flow forecasts to be used in a valuation with appraiser input, or appraisers may develop their own forecasts consulting management as needed. The appraiser should be aware of potential managerial biases, such as to possibly overstate values in the case of goodwill impairment testing or understate values in the case of incentive stock option grants. Appraisers should also pay attention to whether projections adequately capture capital needs.

The process for estimating FCFF and FCFE is similar for private and public companies. Revenues and expenses are generally adjusted to reflect the normalized earnings capacity of the private company. For FCFF, operating income after taxes is estimated by removing interest expense on debt and including a pro forma estimate of income taxes on operating income (i.e., EBIT minus estimated taxes, based on normalized earnings). Depreciation expense is added back because it is a noncash expense. A provision for capital expenditures required to replace the existing assets is subtracted to support the current level of operations. A provision for any additional capital expenditures required to fund future growth is also subtracted. A provision for

---

16 Some variation in terminology exists. Net cash flow and debt free net cash flow are variations of free cash flow to the firm.

incremental working capital required to fund revenue growth is also calculated and subtracted to arrive at FCFF. FCFE is found by subtracting after-tax interest expense from FCFF and adding net new borrowing.

Appraisers may choose between a FCFF and a FCFE approach based on the facts of the case. Some analysts believe that FCFF valuation is practically more robust than FCFE valuation when substantial capital structure changes are in view because the weighted average cost of capital (WACC), the discount rate used in a FCFF approach, is typically less sensitive than the cost of equity, the discount rate used in a FCFE approach, to changes in financial leverage. Apart from such considerations, there may be a tendency for appraisers at the largest firms and investment bankers to favor using FCFF and for appraisers at small firms to favor using FCFE.

EXAMPLE 2

Able Manufacturing: Pro Forma Free Cash Flow to the Firm

Duvall, the manager of the corporate venturing unit introduced in Example 1, has decided to make a bid for Able Manufacturing. Duvall has decided to use an income approach to value Able. As stated in Example 1, Able's debt is $2,000,000. Considering the nature of Able's business, its size, and the financial leverage used by competitors, Duvall has concluded that Able has a low level of debt relative to its capacity and that it will be optimal to increase its debt if Duvall's unit succeeds in purchasing Able. Because of that anticipated change in leverage, Duvall has decided to use a FCFF approach rather than FCFE to value Able.

Based on available information, Duvall makes the following assumptions:

- Long-term growth of revenues and after-tax operating income is 3 percent annually.
- The gross profit margin will remain at 40 percent.
- Depreciation will remain at 1.8 percent of sales.
- SG&A expenses can be maintained at the prior year's level of $3,700,000 at least for two years.
- Working capital equal to 10 percent of revenues is required (e.g., if the increase in revenues is $X from the prior year, additional working capital of 0.10 × $X would be needed).
- Capital expenditures are expected to equal projected depreciation expense (to support current operations) plus 5 percent of incremental revenues (to support future growth).

1   Should Duvall use reported earnings or normalized earnings in estimating FCFF for Able? Explain.

2   Forecast FCFF for Able for the upcoming year (from the perspective of a knowledgeable buyer).

Solution to 1:

For the valuation of Able in a purchase transaction, the normalized earnings of Able should be used to estimate FCFF. Normalized earnings would more accurately reflect the income expected by a willing buyer of Able than reported earnings.

Solution to 2:

Duvall assumed long-term growth of 3 percent into the foreseeable future. With the $50 million revenue base from the prior year and the 3 percent annual revenue growth, a $1.5 million increase in revenues is forecast when moving from the last historical year to the year ahead. Given depreciation of $927,000 and incremental sales of $1,500,000, forecast capital expenditure sum to $927,000 + 0.05($1,500,000) = $927,000 + $75,000 = $1,002,000. A requirement for incremental working capital of 10 percent of the increase in revenues equates to a $150,000 deduction in calculating free cash flow. Based on these assumptions, free cash flow to the firm of $9,358,800 was calculated as follows.

Able Manufacturing, Inc.
Calculation of Next Year's Projected Free Cash Flow to Firm

Revenues ($50,000,000 × 1.03 =)	$51,500,000
Cost of goods sold (0.60 × Revenues =)	30,900,000
Gross profit (Revenue − Cost of goods sold =)	20,600,000
SG&A expenses (maintained at 2013 level)	3,700,000
Pro forma EBITDA	16,900,000
Deprec. and amort. (0.018 × $51,500,000 =)	927,000
Pro forma earnings before interest and taxes	15,973,000
Pro forma taxes on EBIT (at 40.0 percent)	6,389,200
Operating income after tax	9,583,800
Plus: Depreciation and amortization	927,000
Less: Capital expenditures[a]	1,002,000
Less: Increase in working capital[b]	150,000
Free cash flow to firm	$9,358,800

[a] As explained in text, $927,000 + 0.05($1,500,000).
[b] 0.10($51,500,000 − $50,000,000).

4.2 Income Approach Methods of Private Company Valuation

The income approach obtains its conceptual support from the assumption that value is based on expectations of future income and cash flows. The income approach converts future economic benefits into a present value equivalent. For IFRS and US GAAP, assets are defined as probable future economic benefits. This definition provides strong support for the application of the income approach to valuation of an interest in a public or private company.

The three forms of income approach include the **free cash flow method** (often referred to as the **discounted cash flow method** in the appraisal community), the **capitalized cash flow method**, and **residual income method** (frequently referred to as the **excess earnings method** in the valuation community).[17]

- The free cash flow method values an asset based on estimates of future cash flows that are discounted to present value by using a discount rate reflective of the risks associated with the cash flows. For a going concern, this method

---

17 The residual income method is sometimes categorized under the asset approach because it involves marking the tangible assets to market and estimating the value of intangible assets including goodwill.

frequently includes a series of discrete cash flow projections followed by an estimate of the value of the business enterprise as a going concern at the end of the projection period.

■ The capitalized cash flow method (also referred to as the **capitalized income method** or **capitalization of earnings method**) values a private company by using a single representative estimate of economic benefits and dividing that by an appropriate capitalization rate to derive an indication of value.

■ For the valuation of a business enterprise, the excess earnings method consists of estimating the value of all of the intangible assets of the business by capitalizing future earnings in excess of the estimated return requirements associated with working capital and fixed assets. The value of the intangible assets is added to the values of working capital and fixed assets to arrive at the value of the business enterprise.

Whichever income approach method is used, an appropriate required rate of return estimate is needed for discounting expected future cash flows.

4.2.1 Required Rate of Return: Models and Estimation Issues

A variety of factors make estimating a required rate of return for a private company challenging.

■ *Application of size premiums.* In assessing private company valuations, size premiums are frequently used in developing equity return requirements by private company appraisers. This practice seems to be less prevalent in the valuation of public companies.[18] Furthermore, size premium estimates based on public company data for the smallest market cap segments can capture premiums for financial and/or operating distress that may not be relevant to the company being valued.

■ *Use of the CAPM.* Some parties have questioned whether the capital asset pricing model (CAPM) is appropriate for developing discount rate estimates for small private company valuations. In the United States, tax court cases involving private companies with little expectation of ever operating as public companies were one area where the CAPM was rejected. The perceived differences between the typically larger public companies and the smaller private company were key considerations. Small companies that have little prospect of going public or being acquired by a public company may be viewed as not comparable to the public companies for which market-data-based beta estimates are available.

■ *Expanded CAPM.* The **expanded CAPM**[19] is an adaptation of the CAPM that adds to the CAPM a premium for small size and company-specific risk.

■ *Elements of the build-up approach.* The build-up approach was introduced in the reading on return concepts. When **guideline public companies** (public-company comparables for the company being valued) are not available or of questionable comparability, appraisers may rely on a build-up method rather than the CAPM or other models. The build-up method is similar to the expanded CAPM but excludes the application of beta to the equity risk premium. Many view betas that are different from 1.0 as substantially reflecting industry risk factors and thus do not include an industry risk premium in the

---

18 Size premiums and other issues associated with the development of discount rates are discussed in depth in Pratt and Grabowski (2014), Chapter 14.
19 For more information see Pratt and Grabowski (2014), Chapter 10, where it is referred to as the modified CAPM.

expanded CAPM. In the build-up model, in which beta is implicitly assumed equal to 1.0, an argument exists to include an industry risk adjustment (premium or discount), although there are challenges in measuring industry risk adjustments. As the baseline implementation of the build-up model, we take the model with an industry risk adjustment.

- *Relative debt availability and cost of debt.* Correct estimation of the debt capacity of a private company is another valuation challenge. In calculating a WACC for a valuation based on FCFF, analysts should note that a private company may have less access to debt financing than a similar public company. This lesser access means the private company may need to rely more on equity financing, which would tend to increase its WACC. Furthermore, a private company's typically smaller size could lead to greater operating risk and a higher cost of debt.

- *Discount rates in an acquisition context.* In evaluating an acquisition, finance theory indicates that the cost of capital used should be based on the target company's capital structure and the riskiness of the target company's cash flows: The buyer's cost of capital is not relevant. In the context of acquisitions made by larger more mature companies of smaller riskier target companies, the buyer would be expected to have a lower cost of capital than the target. Both of these practices in general incorrectly transfer value from the buyer to the seller because the buyer would be paying the seller for possible value it brings to a transaction.[20]

- *Discount rate adjustment for projection risk.* Any lesser amount of information concerning a private company's operations or business model compared with a similar public company introduces greater uncertainty into projections that may lead to a higher required rate of return. As a second area of concern, management of a private company (on whom analysts may need to rely for forecasts) may have less experience forecasting future financial performance. Projections may reflect excessive optimism or pessimism. Any adjustments to a discount rate to account for projection risk or managerial inexperience in forecasting, however, would typically be highly judgmental.

EXAMPLE 3

Developing a Discount Rate for a Private Company

Duvall and his advisers have decided to use an income approach to value Able Manufacturing.

Because of its years of operating successfully and its owner's conservative nature, Able operated with little debt. Smith explored various sources of debt financing to operate Able with a lower overall cost of capital. Analysis of public companies in Able's industry indicated several guideline public companies for possible use in estimating a discount rate for Able. Duvall and his advisers agreed on the following estimates:

- Risk free rate: Estimated at 4.8 percent.

- Equity risk premium: The parties agreed that a 5 percent equity risk premium was appropriate.[21]

- Beta: A beta of 1.1 was estimated based on publicly traded companies in the same industry.

---

20 Damodaran (2002).
21 See the reading on return concepts and Chapter 8 in Pratt and Grabowski (2014) for further discussion of the equity risk premium.

- Small stock premium: The smaller size and less diversified operations suggest greater risk for Able relative to public companies. A small stock premium of 3 percent was included in the equity return calculation for these expected risks.[22]

- Company-specific risk premium: Assessment of Able indicated that beyond Smith's key role at the company, no other unusual elements created additional risk. A 1 percent company-specific risk adjustment was included.[23]

- Industry risk premium (build-up method only): The industry risk premium was 0 percent because no industry related factors were viewed as materially affecting the overall required return on equity estimate.

- Pretax cost of debt: Estimated at 7.5 percent.

- Ratio of debt to total capital for public companies in the same industry: Estimated at 20 percent.

- Optimal ratio of debt to total capital: The ratio was estimated at 10 percent based on discussions with various sources of financing. Able would not be able to achieve the industry capital structure based on its smaller size compared to public companies and the greater risk of its operations as a standalone company.

- Actual ratio of debt to total capital: For Able, the actual ratio was 2 percent.

- Combined corporate tax rate: Estimated at 40 percent.

Based only on the information given, address the following:

1 Calculate the required return on equity for Able using the CAPM.

2 Calculate the required return on equity for Able using the expanded CAPM.

3 Calculate the required return on equity for Able using the build-up method.

4 Discuss the selection of the capital structure weights to use in determining the weighted average cost of capital for Able.

5 Calculate the WACC for Able using the current capital structure and a 14 percent cost of equity.

6 Calculate the WACC for Able based on the optimal capital structure for Able and a 14 percent cost of equity.

Solution to 1:

According to the CAPM, Required return on share i = Current expected risk-free return + β_i (Equity risk premium) = 4.8% + 1.1(5%) = 10.30 percent.

Solution to 2:

The required rate of return is 14.3 percent, which is shown in the following tabular format.

---

22 If the CAPM were used to develop the equity required rate of return and similar risks were anticipated for the guideline public companies as for a smaller private company being valued, a small stock premium might not be warranted. As just described, the risk would likely be captured in the betas of the guideline public companies.

23 Estimation of company-specific risk has been a very subjective element of the valuation process. Several valuation professionals have presented methodologies to develop quantitative estimates of company-specific risk. These tools are being vetted in the valuation community.

Able Manufacturing, Inc.	
Expanded CAPM: Required Rate of Return on Equity	
Risk-free rate	4.8%
Plus: Equity risk premium adjusted for beta[a]	5.5
Plus: Small stock premium	3.0
Plus: Company-specific risk adjustment	1.0
Indicated required return on equity	14.3%

[a] 1.1 beta × 5 percent equity risk premium = 5.5 percent.

Solution to 3:

The required rate of return is 13.8 percent. Note the absence of a beta adjustment. Note too that the fact that beta (1.1) is close to 1.0 possibly suggests any industry risk adjustment that could be made would be small in magnitude.

Able Manufacturing, Inc.	
Build-Up Method: Required Rate of Return on Equity	
Risk-free rate	4.8%
Plus: Equity risk premium	5.0
Plus: Small stock premium	3.0
Plus: Industry risk premium	0.0
Plus: Company-specific risk adjustment	1.0
Indicated return on equity	13.8%

Solution to 4:

For valuation concerning the possible sale of Able, it is appropriate to assume the weights in the optimal capital structure in calculating WACC because an acquirer would be able and motivated to establish the optimum. The current capital structure of Able involves less debt than the optimal one; thus Able's WACC is currently higher than it needs to be. Note, however, that the weight on debt of similar large public companies may be higher than what is optimal for Able. Large public companies would be expected to have better access to public debt markets. Also, the small size of Able increases its risk relative to larger public companies. These two factors would tend to increase Able's cost of debt relative to a large public comparable and lead to a lower optimal weight of debt compared with such a public company.[24]

Solution to 5:

The cost of capital for Able based on the existing capital structure was calculated as follows:

---

[24] The AICPA practice aid, *Valuation of Privately-Held-Company Equity Securities Issued as Compensation*, (hereafter referred to as the "Stock Practice Aid") was released to provide technical guidance for the valuation of stock in the context of stock option grants and other share-based payments. Paragraph 119 notes that "one of the objectives and benefits of becoming a public enterprise is the ability to access the public capital markets, with the associated benefits of a lower cost of both equity and debt capital."

Able Manufacturing, Inc. Calculation of Weighted Average Cost of Capital Current Capital Structure		
Pre-tax cost of debt	7.5%	
Tax rate complement (1 − Tax rate)	0.60	
After-tax cost of debt	4.5%	
Weight	×0.02	
Weighted cost of debt		0.1%
Cost of equity	14.0%	
Weight	×0.98	
Weighted cost of equity		13.7%
Weighted average cost of capital		13.8%

Solution to 6:

The overall cost of capital using the optimal capital structure for Able reflected a higher level of debt financing. The WACC was calculated as follows:

Able Manufacturing, Inc. Calculation of Weighted Average Cost of Capital Optimal Capital Structure		
Pre-tax cost of debt	7.5%	
Tax rate complement (1 − Tax rate)	0.60	
After-tax cost of debt	4.5%	
Weight	0.10	
Weighted cost of debt		0.5%
Cost of equity	14.0%	
Weight	0.90	
Weighted cost of equity		12.6%
Weighted average cost of capital		13.1%

For early stage development companies, discount rate estimation concerns are magnified. Very high levels of company-specific risk, for example, may make use of the CAPM problematic. Several lifecycle stages exist with perceived broad ranges of absolute rate of return requirements for companies operating in each stage. Further, there can be uncertainty in classifying a company in a specific lifecycle stage.[25]

---

25 The AICPA practice aids *Assets Acquired in a Business Combination to Be Used in Research and Development Activities: A Focus on Software, Electronic Devices, and Pharmaceutical Industries* (hereafter referred to as the "IPRD Practice Aid") and the "Stock Practice Aid" provide descriptive information on various stages in the early lifecycle of development stage companies and estimated return requirements.

4.2.2 *Free Cash Flow Method*

Free cash flow valuation for private and public companies is substantially similar. For example, in the case of Able Manufacturing, a FCF valuation might involve projecting individually free cash flows for a number of years, finding the present value of those projected free cash flows, followed by finding the present value of a terminal value estimate that captures the business enterprise value at the end of the initial projection period. In principle, discrete free cash flow forecasts should be made until cash flows are expected to stabilize at a constant growth rate. Many practical implementations involve discrete cash flow projections for a period of five years.

To value the business enterprise at the end of the initial projection period, the capitalized cash flow method incorporating a sustainable long-term growth rate is a theoretically preferred method. Some appraisers, however, will calculate the terminal value using pricing multiples developed in the market approach. For a company in a high growth industry, market multiples would be expected to capture rapid growth in the near future and "normal" growth into the indefinite future. Using these multiples to estimate terminal value, the residual enterprise value may not be appropriate as rapid growth was incorporated twice: once in the cash flow projections over the projection period and also in the market multiple used in calculating the residual enterprise value.

4.2.3 *Capitalized Cash Flow Method*

The capitalized cash flow method (CCM) estimates value based on the expression for the value of a growing perpetuity and is essentially a stable growth (single stage) free cash flow model.[26] The CCM is only occasionally seen in the valuation of private companies—most often for the valuation of smaller private companies. The CCM is rarely used for the valuation of public companies, larger private companies, or in the context of acquisitions or financial reporting. The CCM may be appropriate, however, for valuing a private company in which no projections are available and an expectation of stable future operations exists. If market pricing evidence from public companies or transactions is limited, a CCM valuation may also be a feasible alternative.

For companies that are not expected to grow at a constant rate, FCF valuation using a series of discrete cash flow projections is theoretically preferable to the CCM. The CCM could provide assistance in assessing the discount rate or growth assumptions embedded in value indications from the market approach.

At the firm level, the formula for the capitalized cash flow to the firm is

$$V_f = FCFF_1/(WACC - g_f) \qquad (1)$$

where

$$V_f = \text{Value of the firm}$$
$$FCFF_1 = \text{Free cash flow to the firm for next twelve months}$$
$$WACC = \text{Weighted average cost of capital}$$
$$g_f = \text{Sustainable growth rate of free cash flow to the firm}$$

The value of equity is found as the value of the company less the market value of debt or $V_f -$ (Market value of debt). An implicit assumption in using WACC for discounting FCFF in Equation 1 is that a constant capital structure at market values in the future exists.

The capitalized cash flow method can also be used to value equity directly. In this instance, the inputs for free cash flow would reflect FCFE and the equity return requirement would be substituted for the WACC:

$$V = FCFE_1/(r - g) \qquad (2)$$

---

[26] See Pratt and Grabowski (2014), Chapter 4, for further discussion.

where r is the required return on equity and g is the sustainable growth rate of free cash flow to equity. In Equations 1 and 2 the denominator is known as the **capitalization rate**. Thus, the estimate of value in each is calculated as the forecasted Year 1 FCF divided by the capitalization rate. Example 4 illustrates the application of the CCM.

EXAMPLE 4

Valuation Using the Capitalized Cash Flow Method

Duvall and his team are comfortable with the normalized earnings, growth, and discount rate estimated for Able. Detailed projections for Able are not developed by management. Suppose that free cash flow to the firm is expected to grow at 3 percent per year going forward from the level of $9,358,800 forecast in Example 2.

1   Explain the rationale for the use of the capitalized cash flow method in this case.

2   Calculate the value of the equity of Able using the capitalized cash flow method and a WACC of 13.1 percent based on Able's optimal capital structure.

3   Calculate the value of the equity of Able using the WACC of 13.8 percent based on the existing capital structure.

4   Discuss factors leading to the difference in the computed values.

Solution to 1:

The capitalized cash flow method is appropriate given the assumption that free cash flow to the firm grows at a constant rate (here 3 percent) is accurate. Otherwise, at best it provides a rough value estimate.

Solution to 2:

With the estimated free cash flow to the firm, a capitalization rate of 10.1 percent (13.1 percent − 3 percent) was applied to derive a valuation indication for the business enterprise. Able's debt balance was subtracted to arrive at an equity value calculated as follows.

Able Manufacturing, Inc.		
Capitalized Cash Flow Method—Optimal Capital Structure		
Free cash flow to firm		$9,358,800
Weighted average cost of capital	13.1%	
Long-term growth rate	3.0%	
Capitalization rate		10.1%
Indicated value of invested capital		92,661,386
Less: Debt capital (actual, assumed to equal market value)		2,000,000
Indicated value of equity		$90,661,386

Solution to 3:

This calculation is similar to the one in the Solution to 2 except for the use of a capitalization rate of 10.8 percent (13.8 percent − 3 percent).

Able Manufacturing, Inc. Capitalized Cash Flow Method—Existing Capital Structure		
Free cash flow to firm		$9,358,800
Weighted average cost of capital	13.8%	
Long-term growth rate	3.0%	
Capitalization rate		10.8%
Indicated value of invested capital		86,655,556
Less: Debt capital		2,000,000
Indicated value of equity		$84,655,556

Solution to 4:

The low level of debt in the existing capital structure results in a higher WACC and a lower valuation conclusion for Able relative to the optimal capital structure.

4.2.4 Excess Earnings Method

In a business valuation context, the excess earnings method (EEM) involves estimating the earnings remaining after deducting amounts that reflect the required returns to working capital and fixed assets (i.e., the tangible assets). This residual amount of earnings (i.e., "excess earnings") is capitalized by using the growing perpetuity formula from the CCM to obtain an estimate of the value of intangible assets. Generally, the EEM has been used to value intangible assets and very small businesses when other such market approach methods are not feasible. For valuing the entire business, the values of working capital and fixed assets are added to the capitalized value of intangibles.

Applying the EEM to value a business enterprise would involve the following steps:

1 Estimate values of working capital and fixed assets (typically, fair value estimates are used). Suppose these are €200,000 and €800,000, respectively.

2 Determine the normalized earnings of the business enterprise. Suppose normalized earnings are €120,000 for the year just ended.

3 Develop discount rates for working capital and fixed assets. Working capital is viewed as the lowest risk and most liquid asset with the lowest required rate of return. Fixed assets require a somewhat greater rate of return. Intangible assets, given their limited liquidity and high risk, often require the highest return. Suppose the required returns on working capital and fixed assets are 5 percent and 11 percent, respectively.

4 Calculate required returns associated with working capital and fixed assets and subtract the required returns on working capital and fixed assets from the normalized earnings of the business enterprise to estimate the residual income; this residual income, if any, must reflect the value associated with intangible assets. In this case, residual income is €120,000 − 0.05(€200,000) − 0.11(€800,000) = €22,000. Assume that residual income grows at 3 percent per year.

5 Estimate discount rate and capitalization rate required for the valuation of the intangible assets.[27] This estimate typically represents all intangible assets.[28] The details of such a calculation are outside the scope of this reading; assume the discount rate is 12 percent.

6 Value intangible assets of the enterprise using the formula for a growing perpetuity. The total value of intangible assets is $(1.03)(€22,000)/(0.12 - 0.03) \approx$ 251,778. (Because €22,000 is associated with normalized income for the most recent year, it is increased by its assumed 3 percent growth rate to obtain a forecast of the year ahead residual income.)

7 Total of working capital, fixed assets, and intangibles equals the value of the business. The EEM estimate would be €200,000 + €800,000 + €251,778 = €1,251,778.

As mentioned, the EEM is only rarely used in pricing entire private businesses, and then only small ones. Some have viewed the specific return requirements for working capital, tangible assets, and the residual income associated with intangible assets as not readily measurable.[29]

For financial reporting, the concept of residual income is an important element of intangible asset valuations and has wide acceptance. Residual income is the subject of significant discussion among appraisers who perform purchase price allocation valuations of intangible assets pursuant to IFRS 3R or ASC 805 (formerly SFAS No. 141R).[30] An analyst considering intangible asset amortization and goodwill impairment issues would benefit from an understanding of residual income concepts. Interested readers are referred to two resources—"The Identification of Contributory Assets and the Calculation of Economic Rents" issued by The Appraisal Foundation and the "IPRD Practice Aid"—for further explanation of the concept and the valuation of intangible assets using residual income.

---

27 Significant judgment is associated with many of these estimates. If a weighted average cost of capital for the business enterprise has been calculated, a discount rate for intangible assets can be estimated. With values for working capital and fixed assets, discrete return requirements can be developed for these asset groups based on market return levels, borrowing costs, and other factors. With the WACC known and estimates for discount rates on working capital and fixed assets, the discount rate for intangible assets can be estimated as the amount that equates the WACC with the weighted values of working capital, fixed assets, and intangible assets. The best practice guide, The Identification of Contributory Assets and Calculation of Economic Rents, provides a detailed discussion of this process.

28 Valuations under ASC 805 and IAS 3R will typically consider separate intangible assets, such as customer relationships, technology, trade names, and the assembled work force, among others. Typically, only one or two intangible assets are valued based on residual income. Also, acquired intangible assets are valued based on their economic life rather than into perpetuity. Although overall customer relationships may grow over time, the customers acquired at the time of acquisition will decline over time.

29 Valuation professionals performing valuations of intangible assets for IAS 38 or ASC 805 often estimate return requirements for the various assets of a business enterprise. Individual discount rate estimates for each asset class can be compared to the WACC for an enterprise to confirm the reasonableness of the individual estimates. For further discussion, see the Appraisal Foundation's best practice guide, The Identification of Contributory Assets and Calculation of Economic Rents.

30 See 31 May 2010 guide, "The Identification of Contributory Assets and the Calculation of Economic Rents," issued by the Best Practices for Valuations for Financial Reporting: Intangible Asset Working Group organized by The Appraisal Foundation.

4.3 Market Approach Methods of Private Company Valuation

The market approach uses direct comparisons to public companies and acquired enterprises to estimate the fair value of an equity interest in a private company. Three major variations of the market approach exist:

- The **guideline public company method** (GPCM) establishes a value estimate based on the observed multiples from trading activity in the shares of public companies viewed as reasonably comparable to the subject private company. The multiples from the public companies are adjusted to reflect differences in the relative risk and growth prospects of the subject private company compared with the guideline public companies.

- The **guideline transactions method** (GTM) establishes a value estimate based on pricing multiples derived from the acquisition of control of entire public or private companies that were acquired. Whereas GPCM uses a multiple that could be associated with trades of any size, GTM uses a multiple that specifically relates to sales of entire companies.

- The **prior transaction method** (PTM) considers actual transactions in the stock of the subject private company. The actual price paid for shares or the pricing multiples implied by past transactions in the stock can be used for this method.

Because the market approach relies on data generated in actual market transactions, some consider it to be conceptually preferable to the income- and asset-based approaches for private company valuation. In the United States, tax courts assessing private company valuations have generally stated a preference for valuation based on market transactions although they often accept valuations based on the income approach. ASC 820 also presents a fair value hierarchy that gives the highest priority to market based evidence.[31] The primary assumption of the market approach is that transactions providing pricing evidence are reasonably comparable to the subject company.

A primary challenge in using the market approach is finding comparable companies and accurately assessing their pricing. All of the company-specific factors noted previously may lead to different levels of expected risk and growth for a private company relative to a public company. Market multiples reflect both expected risk and growth. Risk and growth assumptions should be extracted and multiples adjusted to reflect any differences of the subject company vis-à-vis the chosen comparable(s). The stock-specific factors associated with private companies may create additional uncertainties regarding levels of risk and growth.

The pricing of shares in public companies reflects stock price volatility as a result of, in part, their ready marketability. Rapid movements in the stock prices of public companies can lead to changes in pricing multiples that often serve as a basis for private company valuations. Interests in private companies have much more limited marketability and often require more extended time periods to completely sell. The

---

31 ASC 820 states that "To increase consistency and comparability in fair value measurements and related disclosures, the fair value hierarchy prioritizes the inputs to valuation techniques used to measure fair value into three broad levels. The fair value hierarchy gives the highest priority to quoted prices (unadjusted) in active markets for identical assets or liabilities (Level 1) and the lowest priority to unobservable inputs (Level 3)." ASC 820 notes that "The availability of inputs relative to the asset or liability and the relative reliability of the inputs might affect the selection of the valuation technique. However, the fair value hierarchy prioritizes the inputs to valuation techniques, not the valuation techniques." This last statement would suggest that the appropriate valuation approach would be dependent on the facts and circumstances unique to a particular valuation.

extended time period to sell such an interest in full and the likely movement of pricing multiples over the sale period create uncertainty in the determination of a pricing multiple and thus in the final value conclusion.

Factors for the identification of guideline companies are similar for public and private companies. Key factors include industry membership, form of operations, trends, and current operating status, among others. As previously noted, lifecycle and size differences may create significant challenges in applying the market approach.

Public and private company analysis may differ in the financial metrics used in the valuation process. Price-to-earnings methods are frequently cited in the valuation of public companies, with other multiples considered as well. For larger mature private companies, pricing multiples based on EBITDA and/or EBIT are frequently seen. EBITDA is best compared with the **market value of invested capital** (MVIC),[32] defined as the market value of debt and equity, in forming the valuation metric. With a calculation of MVIC for a private company, the value of debt can be subtracted to produce an estimate of equity value. As current transaction market values for debt are not available in many cases, some estimate of the market value of debt is needed. The use of the face value of debt as an estimate may be acceptable in many situations in which debt represents a small fraction of overall financing and operations are stable. For companies with highly leveraged financial conditions and/or significant volatility expected in future financial performance, the valuation of equity as the residual obtained by subtracting the face value of debt from the value of the business enterprise is frequently not appropriate.[33] Estimates of market value based on debt characteristics, known as matrix prices, are an alternative in such cases.

For many very small private companies with limited asset bases, net income based multiples may be more commonly used than EBITDA multiples. For extremely small companies, multiples of revenue may even be commonly applied. This convention considers the likely absence of meaningful financial data and the greater impact and subjectivity associated with such items as owner compensation.

Nonfinancial metrics may be an appropriate means of valuation for certain industries. These metrics would probably best be used in addition to financial metrics. Significant reliance on these metrics would be appropriate only if the nonfinancial measure is generally accepted within the industry. Examples of nonfinancial metrics include price per subscriber in cable and price per bed for hospital and skilled nursing and other healthcare facilities.

4.3.1 *Guideline Public Company Method*

In private company valuation as has been noted, valuation based on multiples of similar public companies is often referred to as the guideline public company method (GPCM). The valuation process is essentially similar for a public or a private company. A group of public companies is identified, the relevant pricing multiples for the guideline companies are derived, and adjustments to the multiples reflecting the relative risk and growth prospects of the subject company relative to the publicly traded companies are

---

32 In addition to MVIC, other similar terms include enterprise value (EV), business enterprise value (BEV), and firm value. Definitions for enterprise value vary but most frequently start with MVIC and subtract any cash and cash equivalents. BEV is typically synonymous with EV.

33 As noted in the "Stock Practice Aid" and observed in the capital markets, debt may not always be worth its face or par value because of repayment risk. Highly leveraged companies and/or companies with significant volatility of financial performance may have debt valued at significant discounts from face value. In these cases, option pricing theory can be used to value each debt and equity instrument as a separate call option on the business enterprise value of the company. Debt would be a senior call option with priority to payment of the business enterprise up to its face value and any unpaid interest. Preferred stock, common stock, and options would all represent different options with a call on the enterprise value. This concept is discussed in some depth in the "Stock Practice Aid."

made. For a private company, this method would lead to a conclusion of value. For a public company, application of this method helps assess over- or under-valuation of a company relative to similar companies at a specific point in time.

The primary advantage of this method is the potentially large pool of guideline companies and the significant descriptive, financial, and trading information available to the analyst/appraiser. Disadvantages include possible issues regarding comparability and subjectivity in the risk and growth adjustments to the pricing multiple.

Control premiums may be used in the valuation of a controlling interest in a company. Defined in the International Glossary of Business Valuation Terms (IGBVT), a **control premium** is an amount or a percentage by which the pro rata value of a controlling interest exceeds the pro rata value of a noncontrolling interest in a business enterprise, to reflect the power of control. For the valuation of a controlling interest, a control premium has often been added if the value is derived from the GPCM. The trading of interests in public companies typically reflects small blocks without control of the entity. Given this information, many but not all believe the resulting pricing multiples do not reflect control of the entity.[34]

A control premium adjustment may be appropriate depending on the specific facts. Historically, control premiums have been estimated based on transactions in which public companies were acquired. Several factors require careful consideration in estimating a control premium.

- *Type of transaction.* Some transaction databases classify acquisitions as either financial or strategic transactions. A **strategic transaction** involves a buyer that would benefit from certain synergies associated with owning the target firm. These synergies could include enhanced revenues, cost savings, or other possible benefits. A **financial transaction** involves a buyer having essentially no material synergies with the target. As examples, the purchase of a private company by a company in an unrelated industry or by a private equity firm would typically be a financial transaction. Compared with financial transactions, control premiums for an acquisition by a strategic buyer are typically larger because of the expected synergies.

- *Industry factors.* Industry sectors with acquisition activity are considered to be "in-play" at a valuation date; that is, pricing of public companies in the sector may reflect some part of a possible control premium in the share prices. Control premiums measured at a date significantly before a valuation date might reflect a different industry environment from that of the valuation date.

- *Form of consideration.* Transactions involving the exchange of significant amounts of stock (as opposed to all cash transactions) might be less relevant as a basis of measuring a control premium because of the possibility that acquiring companies time such transactions during periods when their management perceives that shares of their company are overvalued in the marketplace.

---

34 As of mid-2013, The Appraisal Foundation was preparing a document ("The Measurement and Application of Market Participant Acquisition Premiums") proposing major changes to make practice among appraisers more consistent in this area. In its draft form, the document was recommending that any control premium be justified based on an analysis of projected cash flows after an acquisition and, when justified, that control premiums be calculated at the MVIC rather than the equity level. New terminology in the area was also being discussed.

The multiple resulting from applying a control premium to pricing multiples from publicly-traded companies should be assessed for reasonableness.[35] Suppose that a public company, which is viewed as comparable to a private company being appraised, was acquired at an 8x pricing multiple. A control premium of 30 percent control is paid based on the stock's price prior to the acquisition. Pricing multiples for guideline public companies, however, are 10x at the valuation date. The application of a 30 percent control premium would suggest a 13x pricing multiple. The dramatically different value indications resulting from applying a 8x transaction multiple and a 13x multiple suggest the need for further investigation before accepting the 13x multiple. Comparability issues or dramatic pricing changes may be factors leading to this material difference.

EXAMPLE 5

Valuation Using Guideline Public Company Method

Duvall decides to use the GPCM to develop a value indication for Able that is independent of the FCF indication he is also pursuing. Duvall believes that many acquirors apply a multiple of market value of invested capital to EBITDA to value companies in Able's industry. A search for comparable public companies indicated several companies that might serve as guidelines or benchmarks for valuing Able; however, all of these were much larger than Able. Duvall's research on guideline public companies indicates the following:

■ The MVIC to EBITDA multiples of such public companies averages 7.0.

■ A combined downward adjustment of 15 percent for relative risk and growth characteristics of Able compared with the guideline public companies suggests an adjusted MVIC to EBITDA multiple of 5.95, rounded to 6, for Able.

■ A control premium of 20 percent was reported in a single strategic acquisition from several years ago. The transaction involved an exchange of stock with no cash consideration paid.

■ Duvall is not aware of any strategic buyers that might incorporate synergies into their valuation of Able.

■ Normalized EBITDA is $16,900,000.

■ Market value of debt capital is $2,000,000.

1 Explain the elements included in the calculation of a pricing multiple for Able.

2 Calculate the pricing multiple appropriate for Able including a control premium adjustment.

3 Calculate the value of Able using the guideline public company method.

---

[35] Appraisers performing private company valuations incorporate the control premium into the valuation calculation in a variety of different presentations. Many appraisers would not adjust the pricing multiple for a control premium. Rather, appraisers often use a multiple based on the guideline public companies and include a separate addition of the control premium in the calculation for the value estimate. The approach incorporating a control premium adjustment to the pricing multiple facilitates reconciliation of pricing multiples from public companies to those observed in transactions.

Solution to 1:

The value of Able in relation to a possible acquisition is desired. Pricing multiples from guideline public companies provide a starting point for the development of a pricing multiple. The pricing multiples for the guideline public companies must be adjusted to reflect any differences in risk and growth expectations for Able compared with the guideline public companies. As a final element, the pricing multiple should consider the inclusion of a control premium given the possible sale of Able.

Solution to 2:

Considering the absence of any strategic buyers, in the present instance a control premium of 0 percent is a reasonable baseline. There was a single strategic transaction for the acquisition of a public company several years prior to the acquisition. The age of the transaction, however, creates concern regarding the relevance of the indicated control premium.

Based on the information provided, the MVIC to EBITDA multiple for Able can be taken to approximately 6, reflecting no control premium adjustment.

Able Manufacturing, Inc.
Development of Pricing Multiple
for Guideline Public Company Method

Initial MVIC to EBITDA from public companies		7.0
Relative risk and growth adjustment for Able	−15%	(1.05)
Multiple before control adjustment		5.95
Control premium adjustment*	0%	0
Multiple after control adjustment		5.95
Rounded to		6.0

*Control premiums are measured based on the value of the equity or the MVIC of public companies before and after an acquisition. When an equity control premium has been estimated, a valuation on an MVIC basis (as is often the case in a transaction setting) would require an adjustment to the equity control premium. In the example, no control premium was concluded to be appropriate. Assuming an equity control premium of 30 percent was deemed appropriate based on different facts, a normalized capital structure of one-third debt and two-thirds equity would suggest a 20 percent control premium (two-thirds of 30 percent) if applied to an MVIC-multiple-based value from guideline public companies. Control premium data vary markedly and divergence in practice exists in this area of valuation.

Solution to 3:

Able Manufacturing, Inc.
Valuation Using Guideline Public Company Method

Normalized EBITDA	$16,900,000
Pricing multiple	6.0
Indicated value of invested capital	101,400,000
Less: Debt capital	2,000,000
Indicated value of equity	$99,400,000

4.3.2 *Guideline Transactions Method*

The guideline transactions method (GTM) is conceptually similar to the guideline public company method. Unlike the GPCM, the GTM uses pricing multiples derived from acquisitions of public or private companies. Transaction data available on publicly reported acquisitions is compiled from public filings by parties to the transaction with the regulatory bodies such as the Financial Conduct Authority in the United Kingdom or the Securities and Exchange Commission (SEC) in the United States. Data on transactions not subject to public disclosure may be available from certain transaction databases. As information may be limited and is generally not readily confirmed, many appraisers challenge the reliability of this data. All other things equal, transaction multiples would be the most relevant evidence for valuation of a controlling interest in a private company.

A number of factors need to be considered in assessing transaction-based pricing multiples.

- *Synergies.* The pricing of strategic acquisitions may include payment for anticipated synergies. The relevance of payments for synergies to the case at hand merits consideration.

- *Contingent consideration.* **Contingent consideration** represents potential future payments to the seller that are contingent on the achievement of certain agreed on occurrences. Obtaining some form of regulatory approval or achieving a targeted level of EBITDA are two types of contingencies. Contingent consideration may be included in the structure of acquisition. The inclusion of contingent consideration in the purchase price paid for an enterprise often reflects uncertainty regarding the future financial performance of the entity. ASC 805 changed the requirements for measuring and reporting contingent consideration in the context of a business combination.

- *Noncash consideration.* Acquisitions may include stock in the consideration. The cash equivalent value of a large block of stock may create uncertainty regarding the transaction price. For example, the 2001 merger of America Online (AOL) and Time Warner Corporation was a stock swap that occurred at a time when AOL stock was trading based on expectations of significant future growth. In 2002, the combined company reported two charges for goodwill impairment expense totaling $99 billion. The level of this impairment expense raises questions regarding whether the initial transaction price reflected temporary overvaluation of AOL stock relative to its intrinsic value.

- *Availability of transactions.* Meaningful transactions for a specific private company may be limited. The relevance of pricing indications from a transaction that occurred a significant period prior to a valuation date can be challenged—especially if evidence indicates changes in the subject company, industry, or economy between the transaction date and the valuation date.

- *Changes between transaction date and valuation date.* Unlike the guideline public company method, which develops pricing multiples based on stock prices at or very near the valuation date, the guideline transactions method relies on pricing evidence from acquisitions of control of firms at different points in the past. In many industries, transactions are limited and transactions several months or more from a valuation date may be the only transaction evidence available. Changes in the marketplace could result in differing risk and growth expectations requiring an adjustment to the pricing multiple.

Valuation Using Guideline Transactions Method

In addition to the income approach and the guideline public company method, the guideline transactions method was considered and applied. Duvall and his advisers noted:

- Pricing multiples from several recent acquisitions of private companies in the industry indicated a MVIC to EBITDA multiple of 6.0.

- Several of the acquisitions studied were viewed as similar to Able because of similar revenue bases and limited diversification. The overall risk and growth characteristics of the acquired companies and Able were viewed as similar.

1 Discuss differences between pricing multiples from the guideline transactions and guideline public company methods.

2 Explain the calculation of a pricing multiple using the guideline transactions method.

3 Calculate the pricing multiple appropriate for Able.

4 Calculate the value of Able using the guideline transactions method.

Solution to 1:

The guideline transactions method considers market transactions involving the acquisition of the total equity of companies. As such, the pricing multiple more accurately reflects the value of total companies. Pricing multiples from guideline public companies typically reflect public trading in small blocks of stock. The multiples may not reflect the value of the total equity of the public companies.

Solution to 2:

The pricing multiples from acquisitions are the basis for the pricing multiple. The risk and growth prospects of the acquired companies and the subject private company are assessed and an adjustment factor is applied. As the multiples reflect acquisitions of total equity, they reflect the value of total equity. No control premium adjustment is necessary.

Solution to 3:

Calculation of the initial pricing multiple follows:

Able Manufacturing, Inc. Development of Pricing Multiple for Guideline Transactions Method		
Initial MVIC to EBITDA from transactions		6.0
Relative risk and growth adjustment for Able	0%	0.0
Indicated multiple		6.0
Rounded to		6.0

Solution to 4:

Valuation using the guideline transactions method is similar to that from the guideline public company method except any control premium is already incorporated in the transaction multiple.

Able Manufacturing, Inc. Guideline Transactions Method	
EBITDA	$16,900,000
Pricing multiple	6.0
Indicated value of invested capital	101,400,000
Less: Debt capital	2,000,000
Indicated value of equity	$99,400,000

4.3.3 *Prior Transaction Method*

The prior transaction method (PTM) considers actual transactions in the stock of the subject company. Valuation can be based on either the actual price paid or the multiples implied from the transaction. The PTM is generally most relevant when considering the value of a minority equity interest in a company. For many private companies, there are no or very limited transactions in the stock.

If available, timely, and arm's length, the PTM would be expected to provide the most meaningful evidence of value. The PTM provides less reliable valuation evidence if transactions are infrequent. Also, uncertainly regarding the motivations of the parties, or special circumstances surrounding a prior transaction, can create uncertainty regarding the reliability of PTM data. Transactions at different points in time may require significant adjustment. As an example, an early state venture capital funded company experiences rapid value increases due to successful execution of their development plans. A transaction prior to the achievement of a significant value event might not provide meaningful value insights at a subsequent date.[36]

4.4 Asset-Based Approach to Private Company Valuation

The principle underlying the asset-based approach is that the value of ownership of an enterprise is equivalent to the fair value of its assets less the fair value of its liabilities. Of the three approaches to valuation, the asset-based approach (also referred to as the **cost approach** by many in the valuation profession) is generally considered to be the weakest from a conceptual standpoint for valuing an ongoing business enterprise.

The asset-based approach is rarely used for the valuation of going concerns. Reasons include the limited market data available to directly value intangible assets, difficulties in valuing certain tangible assets (such as special use plant and equipment), and the more readily available information to value operating companies as an integrated whole rather than on an asset-by-asset basis.

An operating company with nominal profits relative to the values of assets used and without prospects for doing better in the future might best be valued using an asset-based approach assuming the winding up of operations. In this case, its value as a going concern might be less than its value in liquidation (the value that could be realized through the liquidation of its assets) because the assets might be redeployed

---

36 The PTM can provide insights on the value of development stage entities when revenues and cash flows are highly speculative. Many development stage companies fund development activities through several rounds of equity financing. As such, there may be a series of prior transactions providing valuation evidence. The equity financing often involves the sale of preferred stock with liquidation preferences and rights to convert to common stock. As development stage entities often have complex capital structures with different classes of equity securities with differing rights, significant adjustments are required. This process is complex and requires significant judgment. The AICPA Toolkit *Valuation of Privately-Held Equity Securities Issued as Compensation* provides further insights.

by buyers to higher valued uses. Resource and financial companies might also be valued based on an asset-based approach. Banks and finance companies largely consist of loan and securities portfolios that can be priced based on market variables. In such cases a summation of individual asset value estimates may give a lower-bound-type estimate of the overall value of the company. The asset-based approach may be appropriate for the valuation of holding (investment) companies, such as real estate investment trusts (REITs) and closed end investment companies (CEICs). For these entities, the underlying assets typically consist of real estate or securities that were valued using the market and/or income approaches. An asset-based approach may also be appropriate for very small businesses with limited intangible value or early stage companies.

For the valuation of an interest in a pooled investment vehicle, certain factors may suggest a value different from the net asset value per share. Management fees and carried interest may lead to an expectation of proceeds available to an investor and a value estimate that is less than the net asset value per share.[37] The relative growth and profit as a result of management expertise may also merit an upward or downward adjustment to the net asset value. Other factors, such as the possible effect of tax attributes (tax basis in the assets held by the entity) and diversification, and professional management benefits may also affect value.

Example 7 illustrates four definitions of values that a private business appraiser used to value the financial services subsidiary of a public company.

EXAMPLE 7

Valuation of a Financial Services Company

In a valuation of a financial services company, a business appraiser estimated four values for the company using four different approaches, which he characterized as follows:

1 *Discounted cash flow approach.* The appraiser estimated value as the present value of projected FCFE for the next 10 years to which was added the present value of the capitalized value of the 11th-year cash flow.

2 *Market approach.* The appraiser used the GPCM with price-to-cash flow, price-to-book, and price-to-earnings multiples, and made adjustments to reflect differences in risk and growth, applying the resulting multiples to the company's cash flow, book value, and earnings, respectively.

3 *Adjusted book value approach, going-concern basis.* The appraiser adjusted the book values of assets and liabilities to better reflect market values and obtained the adjusted book value of equity, which was the estimate of value based on this approach. The definition of market value used was: "Market value is...the most probable price that an asset should bring in a

---

37 **Carried interest** or "carry" represents a share of any profits that is paid to the general partner (manager) of an investment partnership, such as a private equity or hedge fund, as a form of compensation designed to be an incentive to the manager to maximize performance of the investment fund. A manager's carried interest allocation is in addition to any investment that the manager may have in the investment partnership. To receive a carried interest, the manager typically must first return all capital contributed by the investors and in certain cases the fund must also return a previously agreed on rate of return (the *hurdle rate*) to investors.

competitive and open market under all conditions requisite to a fair sale, the buyer and seller each acting prudently and knowledgeably, and assuming the price is not affected by undue stimulus."

4 *Adjusted book value approach, orderly liquidation basis.* The appraiser adjusted the book values of assets and liabilities to better reflect orderly liquidation values and obtained the liquidation book value of equity, which was the estimate of value based on this approach. The definition of orderly liquidation value used was: "Orderly liquidation value [is] the price [the asset] would bring if exposed for sale on the open market, with a reasonable time allowed to find a purchaser, both buyer and seller having knowledge of the uses and purposes to which the asset is adapted and for which it is capable of being used, the seller being compelled to sell and the buyer being willing, but not compelled, to buy."

State and explain which of the above methods would be expected to produce the lowest value estimate.

Solution:

Methods 1, 2, and 3 recognize a going-concern value for the company; method 4 does not, so the value estimates under 4 should be the lowest. In general, using individual assets in a coordinated way in the operation of a business as implicitly assumed in 1 and 2 should increase value. Between 3 and 4, the element of the seller being compelled to sell should result in 4 being the lowest estimate.

4.5 Valuation Discounts and Premiums

Control and/or marketability adjustments are often included in valuations of interests in private companies. This area is one of the primary differences in the valuation of interests in private companies compared with public companies. The following chart is adapted from Hitchner[38] and presents the relationship of these concepts and other concepts discussed in this reading. As the chart indicates, the inclusion of discounts depends, in part, on the starting point of a valuation.

---

38 Hitchner (2006).

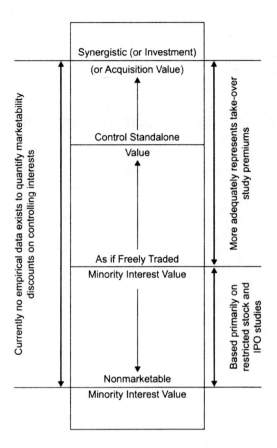

Starting at the top of the chart, the highest possible value indication for an entity would be its investment value to the optimal synergistic buyer. This value reflects a controlling interest assumption, which also increases value. Below the control value of the enterprise to a strategic buyer is the value of the enterprise to a standalone (financial) buyer. In this case, specific synergies to the buyer are not available. The "As If Freely Traded/Minority Interest Value" represents the value of a noncontrolling equity interest that is readily marketable. This value would be equivalent to the price at which most publicly traded companies trade in the market. The lowest level of value is the "Nonmarketable/Minority Interest Value." This value reflects the reduction to value associated with the lack of control and ready marketability associated with small equity interests in private companies.

The application of control premiums and lack of control and marketability discounts is fact-specific and estimates may vary dramatically. Variations in estimated discounts and premiums may relate to the challenging comparability of the data used to quantify discounts. Discounts may also vary based on interpretation of the importance of the size of shareholding and distribution of shares, the relationship of parties, state law affecting minority shareholder rights, and other factors.

The timing of a potential liquidity event is one key consideration. An interest in a private company that is pursuing either an IPO or a strategic sale might be valued with relatively modest valuation discounts. An equity interest in a private company that has not paid dividends and has no prospect for a liquidity event would likely require much higher valuation discounts.

4.5.1 *Lack of Control Discounts*

A **discount for lack of control** (DLOC) is an amount or percentage deducted from the pro rata share of 100 percent of the value of an equity interest in a business to reflect the absence of some or all of the powers of control.[39]

Lack of control discounts may be necessary for valuing noncontrolling equity interests in private companies if the value of total equity was developed on a controlling interests basis. The lack of control may be disadvantageous to an investor because of the inability to select directors, officers, and management that control the operations of an entity. Without control, an investor is unable to distribute cash or other property, to buy and sell assets, to obtain financing, and to bring about other actions, which could affect the value of the investment, the timing of distributions, and the ultimate return to the investor.

Although an interest may lack control, the effect on value of the lack of control is uncertain. The US SEC suggests that evidence of "disproportionate returns" is important in supporting the application of lack of control discounts. Disproportionate returns would result when control shareholders increase their returns through above-market compensation and other actions that reduce the returns available to minority shareholders. For private companies seeking a liquidity event through an IPO or strategic sale of the entity, the likelihood of actions by a control group that reduce the earnings of an entity is reduced.

Data available for estimating a lack of control discount are limited and interpretations can vary markedly. For interests in operating companies, control premium data from acquisitions of public companies had been used frequently in the past. The factors cited earlier in this reading on the calculation of a control premium should also be considered for estimating a lack of control discount. Noting the uncertainties in demonstrating the adverse financial impact of the lack of control of an interest and finding appropriate data to measure the lack of control, the equation used frequently in the calculation of a lack of control discount is:

$$\text{DLOC} = 1 - [1/(1 + \text{Control premium})].$$

For example, if a 20 percent control premium is assumed, the associated DLOC is $1 - (1/1.20) = 0.167$ or 16.7 percent.

The following sets forth the typical application of DLOC based on the different methods of valuation.

Method	Basis of Valuation	DLOC Expected?
GTM	Control	Yes
GPCM	Typically minority	No
CCM/FCF	Control or minority	Depends on cash flows

Valuation indications from the CCM and FCF methods of the income approach are generally agreed to be a controlling interest value if cash flows and the discount rate are estimated on a controlling interest basis. If control cash flows are not used and/or the discount rate does not reflect an optimal capital structure, the resulting value is generally believed to reflect a lack of control basis.

Some analysts believe trading in REITs and CEICs may provide a basis for the estimation of lack of control discounts as well. As individual REITs and CEICs may trade at premiums, discounts, or near their net asset value at different points in time, the use of this data to quantify the lack of control is challenging and outside the scope of this reading.

---

39 International Glossary of Business Valuation Terms.

4.5.2 Lack of Marketability Discounts

A **discount for lack of marketability** (DLOM) is an amount or percentage deducted from the value of an ownership interest to reflect the relative absence (compared with publicly traded companies) of a ready market for a company's shares.[40]

Lack of marketability discounts are frequently applied in the valuation of noncontrolling equity interests in private companies. Although a DLOM is different from a DLOC, the two discounts are often linked; that is, if a valuation is on a noncontrolling interest basis, a lack of marketability discount is typically appropriate. Key variables affecting a marketability discount include prospects for liquidity, contractual arrangements affecting marketability (such as lock-up agreements), restrictions on transferability, pool of potential buyers, risk or volatility, size and timing of distributions (duration of asset), uncertainty of value, and concentration of ownership.[41] At a minimum, an interest that lacks marketability involves a potential opportunity cost associated with the inability to redeploy investment funds.

Restricted stock transactions and IPOs are two types of data typically used to quantify lack of marketability discounts. Although generally agreed by valuation professionals as the best available data to support discounts, these sources are subject to significant differences in their interpretation.

In the United States, SEC Rule 144 provides certain restrictions on the resale of unregistered stock in public companies. Shares acquired prior to an IPO are an example of shares that might be subject to Rule 144 restrictions. These restrictions prevent resale of shares subject to the requirements of Rule 144 in an attempt to maintain an orderly trading market for the publicly traded shares. Restricted stock is essentially identical to freely traded stock of a public company except for the trading restrictions. Unlike interests in private companies, restricted stock transactions typically involve shares that will enjoy ready marketability in the near future.[42]

The relationship of stock sales prior to initial public offerings is another source of marketability discounts. In many companies (especially early stage or high growth companies) approaching an IPO, value may be increasing as levels of risk and uncertainty decline because the company is progressing in its development. Reduction in risk associated with realization of the predicted cash flows or a narrowing of the ranges of possible future cash flows would lead to a reduction in the discount rate.[43] Some studies have attempted to adjust for this factor.

A variety of models involving put options have also been used to quantify lack of marketability discounts. As the first step of this process, an at-the-money put option is priced. The value of the put option as a percentage of the value of the stock before any DLOM provides an estimate of the DLOM as a percentage. DLOM based on put options are used most often for equity interests in development stage companies. For these companies, liquidity in the short to intermediate term is frequently a key objective of investors.

The key assumptions are the expected term until a liquidity event and the level of volatility associated with the company. One advantage of the put option analysis is the ability to directly address perceived risk of the private company through the volatility

---

40 International Glossary of Business Valuation Terms.

41 As reported in paragraph 57 (page 24) of AICPA "Stock Practice Aid."

42 Some commentators have noted that the sale of blocks of restricted stock that significantly exceed public trading activity in the stock may be the most comparable data for quantifying a lack of marketability discount. If the block size significantly exceeds trading volumes, large blocks of restricted shares may still be illiquid when Rule 144 restrictions terminate. A private sale of this block may reflect a valuation discount related to the price risk associated with the holding.

43 The AICPA "Stock Practice Aid" comments on risk reductions in pre-IPO and IPO companies as follows: "The cost of equity capital for a private enterprise prior to its IPO generally ranges from 20 to 35 percent," in paragraph 117; and in paragraph 119, "By contrast, the cost of equity capital for a newly public enterprise generally ranges from 15 to 25 percent."

estimate. The volatility estimate may better capture the risks of the stock compared with restricted stock or IPO transactions in which volatility may be one of many variables influencing the level of discount. An estimate of volatility can be developed at the valuation date based on either historical volatilities of public companies or the volatility estimates embedded in the prices of publicly traded options. Put options only provide price protection (the protection lasts for the life of the option). The put option, however, does not provide liquidity for the asset holding, raising a concern on the use of this form of estimate of the DLOM. Put options also allow the holder of the underlying security to benefit from potential price increases in the value of the security and thus do not exactly model lack of marketability.

In addition to control and marketability discounts, a variety of other potential valuation discounts exist that may require consideration. These include key person discounts, portfolio discounts (discount for non-homogeneous assets), and possible discounts for nonvoting shares.

If both lack of control and lack of marketability discounts are appropriate, these discounts are applied in sequence and are essentially multiplicative rather than additive. The discounts are multiplicative as the valuation process involves discrete steps—first moving from a controlling to a noncontrolling basis and then moving from a marketable to a nonmarketable basis. For an equity interest in which a 10 percent lack of control discount and a 20 percent lack of marketability discount are believed to be appropriate, the total discount is 28 percent [1 − (1 − 10%)(1 − 20%)] rather than 30 percent (10% + 20%).

EXAMPLE 8

Application of Valuation Discounts

Suppose that Jane Doe owns 10 percent of the stock of Able, and that the remaining 90 percent is held by CEO John Smith. Smith is interested in selling Able to a third party. Smith advised Doe that if Able isn't sold he has no reason to purchase Doe's 10 percent interest. Assume the following:

- Valuation discounts assuming imminent transaction:
  - Lack of control discount = 0 percent.
  - Lack of marketability discount = 5 percent.
- Valuation discounts assuming continued operation as a private company:
  - Lack of control discount: incorporated through use of reported earnings rather than normalized earnings.
  - Lack of marketability discount = 25 percent.
- Indicated value of equity in operations:

- $96,000,000 in sale scenario.
- $80,000,000 in "stay private scenario."[44]

1 Discuss the relevance of valuation discounts assuming an imminent sale of Able.

2 Explain which estimate of equity value should be used and calculate the value of Doe's equity interest in Able assuming a sale is likely.

3 Discuss the relevance of valuation discounts assuming Able continues as a private company.

4 Explain which estimate of equity value should be used and calculate the value of Doe's equity interest assuming Able continues as a private company.

5 Contrast the valuation conclusions and discuss factors that contribute to the difference in the concluded values.

Solution to 1:

The sale of Able can only be completed with Smith's concurrence given his 90 percent equity interest. If a sale of Able seems imminent, valuation discounts associated with Doe's 10 percent equity interest would be modest. The controlling shareholder, Smith, would maximize the sales proceeds to himself and any other shareholder(s). Hence, the lack of control associated with a small minority equity interest would not be a factor.[45] The pending transaction being driven by the controlling shareholder reduces the adverse impact of the limited marketability of an interest in a private company.

Solution to 2:

If a sale is viewed as highly likely, the $96,000,000 equity value would be appropriate. This equity value uses normalized earnings and a discount rate based on an optimal capital structure in the calculation of the capitalization rate applied to earnings.

Able Manufacturing, Inc.
Valuation of Doe's 10 Percent Equity Interest
Sale of Company Viewed as Highly Likely

Indicated value of equity in operations	$96,000,000
Interest appraised	10%
Pro rata value of 10 percent equity interest	9,600,000
Less: Lack of control discount of 0 percent	0
Value assuming ready marketability	9,600,000
	(continued)

---

44 The treatment of nonoperating assets varies when a minority interest in the stock is appraised. Able holds nonoperating assets consisting of certain real estate. In the event of a sale, many buyers would not be interested in the nonoperating assets. The nonoperating assets could be distributed to the shareholders prior to the sale of the stock to a buyer. Alternatively, Able could sell the operating assets and liabilities to a buyer resulting in Able holding the real estate assets and cash from sale of the business operations. When liquidation of the entity is likely, inclusion of nonoperating assets values would seem appropriate. When continued operation as a private firm is expected, the benefit to minority shareholders from nonoperating assets is less certain. In this case, some appraisers would exclude these nonoperating assets from their equity valuation.

45 When the controlling stockholder sells, he is not always obligated to offer the minority shareholders the same price. The analyst should investigate this fact. Factors to consider include 1) intent of the controlling stockholder, 2) articles of incorporation, and 3) legal statutes on corporate governance and shareholder rights.

Able Manufacturing, Inc. **Valuation of Doe's 10 Percent Equity Interest** **Sale of Company Viewed as Highly Likely**	
Less: Lack of marketability discount of 5 percent	480,000
Indicated value of Doe's 10 percent equity interest	$9,120,000

Solution to 3:

If Smith has no intent to sell the company; the above-market expenses may continue. With the above-market expenses, the reported earnings would be lower than the normalized earnings. Use of reported earnings rather than normalized earnings is one possible means of capturing the adverse impact associated with the lack of control of a small minority equity interest.

Given the absence of any potential liquidity event and the above-market expenses, little market for the stock exists. A higher lack of marketability discount would be appropriate for the interest in this situation.

Solution to 4:

If continuing as a private company is viewed as highly likely, the $80,000,000 equity value would be appropriate. This equity value uses reported earnings and a discount rate based on the actual capital structure (not optimal) in the calculation of the capitalization rate applied to earnings.

Able Manufacturing, Inc. **Valuation of Doe's 10 Percent Equity Interest** **Continued Operation as a Private Company Likely**	
Indicated value of equity in operations	$80,000,000
Interest appraised	10%
Pro rata value of 10% equity interest	8,000,000
Less: Lack of control discount*	0
Value assuming ready marketability	8,000,000
Less: Lack of marketability discount of 25%	2,000,000
Indicated value of Doe's 10% equity interest	$6,000,000

*As noted in the example, the impact on the value of the 10 percent equity interest was assumed to be captured in the use of reported rather than normalized earnings. The actual capital structure was also used rather than the optimal capital structure. A wide range of practice exists in the treatment of the lack of control for a minority equity interest in a private firm.

Solution to 5:

The value of Doe's 10 percent minority equity interest differs markedly in the two scenarios. The imminent sale scenario results in a higher value indication for Doe's equity interest as a result of the higher value of the company and the lower valuation discounts. The value of the company would be higher because of the use of normalized earnings rather than reported earnings. A lower pricing multiple might also be warranted. The discount rate might be lower in the event an optimal capital structure is used rather than the existing structure. The lack of control is less important in the event of an imminent liquidity event such as a sale. The lack of marketability of a small equity interest is also less important in this instance.

We have seen that in private company valuation, as in most types of valuation beyond the simplest, a range of approaches and estimates can be argued even apart from differences resulting from different forecasts or business assumptions. A perception also exists that there is excessive divergence in valuation practices and estimates of value and that valuation standards could benefit the consumers of valuations. The next section briefly surveys the state of standardization initiatives.

4.6 Business Valuation Standards and Practices

Prior to recent increases in the use of fair value estimates in financial reporting, many business appraisers focused primarily on tax, divorce, and commercial litigation related valuations. The impact on third parties was limited and concern regarding the quality of appraisals was modest. Appraisers were perceived by some as advocates for their clients. The US savings and loan crisis of the late 1980s and early 1990s and the increasing role of fair value estimates in financial reporting under IFRS and US GAAP demonstrate the potential effect of valuation estimates on third parties. Increased third party reliance is contributing to a greater focus by a variety of parties on valuation estimates, practices, and standards.

The intent of valuation standards is to protect users of valuations and the community at large. Standards typically cover the development and reporting of the valuation. The Uniform Standards of Professional Appraisal Practice (USPAP) was instituted as a result of the failures of many savings and loan institutions in the United States (with a significant third party impact). Real estate appraisals that overvalued properties were perceived to have contributed to significant mortgage defaults that impaired the capital reserves and operating ability of many financial institutions.

USPAP was created by the Appraisal Foundation, a US quasi-governmental entity. The Appraisal Foundation is the congressionally authorized source of appraisal standards, practices, and appraiser qualifications. USPAP includes standards pertaining to fixed asset, real estate, and business valuations.[46]

Although USPAP includes business valuation related standards, business appraisers are typically not required by law to adhere to these standards.[47] Although many appraisals used in connection with mortgage lending require a USPAP compliant appraisal, business valuations—including valuations used for financial reporting by public companies—do not involve mandatory compliance with USPAP or other professional standards.

The 9th edition of International Valuation Standards (IVS) issued by the International Valuation Standards Council (IVSC) became effective on 1 January 2012. These standards have been adopted by many countries and valuation societies/institutes across the globe. Although previously primarily focused on real estate and tangible asset related issues, the 9th edition added sections for standards for Businesses and Business Interests and Intangible Assets, along with a separate Application Standard for valuations for financial reporting.

Valuation standards provide limited technical guidance as a result of the diverse and dynamic nature of valuations. Technical guidance has been released periodically, primarily for certain valuations used in a financial reporting context. In the late 1990s, the valuation of technology acquired in business combinations in the United States led to restatements of asset values in financial statements. Subsequently, the AICPA

---

46 USPAP standards 9 and 10 pertain to the valuation of interests in business enterprises or intangible assets. Standard 9 covers the development of a valuation estimate. Standard 10 covers the reporting of the results of an appraisal analysis.

47 Compliance with USPAP is required in the United States for "federally related transactions." Federally related transactions include loans made by a financial institution that include involvement of a federal financial regulatory agency.

released the IPRD Practice Aid providing guidance on the valuation of technology assets. In November 2011, a working draft of an updated Practice Aid was released for public review and comment. In June 2013, a second release of the Stock Practice Aid provided updated technical guidance for the valuation of stock in the context of stock option grants and other share-based payments. The Appraisal Foundation is also involved in efforts to provide technical guidance to appraisers. In May 2010, The Appraisal Foundation issued a document, *The Identification of Contributory Assets and the Calculation of Economic Rents*, providing guidance on the valuation of intangible assets. In June 2012, a working group released a draft of a "best practices" document, *The Valuation of Customer-Related Assets*, providing guidance in this area of intangible asset valuation. Other technical guidance documents are being prepared as well. The IVSC has also issued a Guidance Note, *Valuation of Intangible Assets*.

Future developments regarding valuation standards are possible. Users of valuation services are becoming increasingly aware of the importance of obtaining competent valuation services. Accounting and regulatory bodies and educators recognize the importance of fair value estimates and are increasing efforts in this area.

SUMMARY

This reading provides an overview of key elements of private company valuation and contrasts public and private company valuations.

- Company- and stock-specific factors may influence the selection of appropriate valuation methods and assumptions for private company valuations. Stock-specific factors may result in a lower value for an equity interest in a private company relative to a public company.

- Company-specific factors in which private companies differ from public companies include:
  - stage in lifecycle;
  - size;
  - overlap of shareholders and management;
  - quality/depth of management;
  - quality of financial and other information;
  - pressure from short-term investors;
  - tax concerns.

- Stock-specific factors that frequently affect the value of private companies include:
  - liquidity of equity interests in business;
  - concentration of control;
  - potential agreements restricting liquidity.

- Private company valuations are typically performed for three different reasons: transactions, compliance (financial or tax reporting), or litigation. Acquisition related valuation issues and financial reporting valuation issues are of greatest importance in assessing public companies.

- Different definitions (standards) of value exist. The use of a valuation and key elements pertaining to the appraised company will help determine the appropriate definition. Key definitions of value include:
  - fair market value;

- market value;
- fair value for financial reporting;
- fair value in a litigation context;
- investment value;
- intrinsic value.

■ Private company valuations may require adjustments to the income statements to develop estimates of the normalized earnings of the company. Adjustments may be required for nonrecurring, non-economic, or other unusual items to eliminate anomalies and/or facilitate comparisons.

■ Within the income approach, the free cash flow method is frequently used to value larger, mature private companies. For smaller companies or in special situations, the capitalized cash flow method and residual income method may also be used.

■ Within the market approach, three methods are regularly used: the guideline public company method, guideline transactions method, and prior transactions method.

■ An asset-based approach is infrequently used in the valuation of private companies. This approach may be appropriate for companies that are worth more in liquidation than as a going concern. This approach is also applied for asset holding companies, very small companies, or companies that were recently formed and have limited operating histories.

■ Control and marketability issues are important and challenging elements in the valuation of private companies and equity interests therein.

■ If publicly traded companies are used as the basis for pricing multiple(s), control premiums may be appropriate in measuring the value of the total equity of a private company. Control premiums have also been used to estimate lack of control discounts.

■ Discounts for lack of control are used to convert a controlling interest value into a noncontrolling equity interest value. Evidence of the adverse impact of the lack of control is an important consideration in assessing this discount.

■ Discounts for lack of marketability are often used in the valuation of noncontrolling equity interests in private companies. A DLOM may not be appropriate if there is a high likelihood of a liquidity event in the immediate future.

■ Quantification of DLOM can be challenging because of limited data, differences in the interpretation of available data, and different interpretations of the impact of the lack of marketability on a private company.

■ DLOM can be estimated based on 1) private sales of restricted stock in public companies relative to their freely traded share price, 2) private sales of stock in companies prior to a subsequent IPO, and 3) the pricing of put options.

■ The intent of valuation standards is to protect users of valuations and the community at large. Standards typically cover the development and reporting of a valuation.

■ A number of organizations have released valuation standards. No single set of valuation standards covers the valuation of private companies.

REFERENCES

Aggarwal, Raj, Cynthia Harrington, Adam Kobor, and Pamela P. Drake. 2008. "Capital Structure and Leverage." *Corporate Finance: A Practical Approach*. Michelle Clayman, Martin Fridson, and George Troughton, eds. Hoboken, NJ: John Wiley & Sons.

Damodaran, Aswath. 2002. *Investment Valuation Tools and Techniques for Determining the Value of Any Asset*. Hoboken, NJ: John Wiley & Sons.

Hitchner, James R. 2006. *Financial Valuation: Applications and Models*, second edition. Hoboken, NJ: John Wiley & Sons.

Pratt, Shannon P., and Roger J. Grabowski. 2014. *Cost of Capital: Applications and Examples*, fifth edition. Hoboken, NJ: John Wiley & Sons.

PRACTICE PROBLEMS

1   Two companies are considering the acquisition of Target Company. Buyer A is a strategic buyer and Buyer B is a financial buyer. The following information pertains to Target Company:

> Sales = £28,000,000
>
> Reported EBITDA = £4,500,000
>
> Reported executive compensation = £1,000,000
>
> Normalized executive compensation = £500,000
>
> Reduced SG&A from eliminating duplicate general and administrative functions = £600,000

Calculate the pro forma EBITDA estimates that the strategic and financial buyers would each develop in an acquisitions analysis of Target Company.

2   Using the build-up method and assuming that no adjustment for industry risk is required, calculate an equity discount rate for a small company, given the following information:

> Equity risk premium = 5.0 percent
>
> Mid-cap equity risk premium = 3.5 percent
>
> Small stock risk premium = 4.2 percent
>
> Income return on long-term bonds = 5.1 percent
>
> Total return on intermediate-term bonds = 5.3 percent
>
> Company-specific risk premium = 3.0 percent
>
> 20-year Treasury bond yield as of the valuation date = 4.5 percent

3   Using the capitalized cash flow method (CCM), calculate the fair market value of 100 percent of the equity of a hypothetical company, given the following information:

> Current year's reported free cash flow to equity = $1,400,000
>
> Current year's normalized free cash flow to equity = $1,800,000
>
> Long-term interest bearing debt = $2,000,000
>
> Weighted average cost of capital = 15 percent
>
> Equity discount rate = 18 percent
>
> Long-term growth rate of FCFE = 5.5 percent

4   You have been asked to value Pacific Corporation, Inc., using an excess earnings method, given the following information:

> Working capital balance = $2,000,000
>
> Fair value of fixed assets = $5,500,000
>
> Book value of fixed assets = $4,000,000
>
> Normalized earnings of firm = $1,000,000
>
> Required return on working capital = 5.0 percent
>
> Required return on fixed assets = 8.0 percent
>
> Required return on intangible assets = 15.0 percent
>
> Weighted average cost of capital = 10.0 percent
>
> Long-term growth rate of residual income = 5.0 percent

Based on this information:

A What is the value of Pacific's intangible assets?

B What is the market value of invested capital?

5 An appraiser has been asked to determine the combined level of valuation discounts for a small equity interest in a private company. The appraiser concluded that an appropriate control premium is 15 percent. A discount for lack of marketability was estimated at 25 percent. Given these factors, what is the combined discount?

The following information relates to Questions 6–11

Alan Chin, the chief executive officer of Thunder Corporation, has asked his chief financial officer, Constance Ebinosa, to prepare a valuation of Thunder for the purpose of selling the company to a private investment partnership. Thunder is a profitable $200 million annual sales US domiciled manufacturer of generic household products. Customers consist of several grocery store chains in the United States. Competitors include large companies such as Procter & Gamble, Clorox, and Unilever. Thunder has been in business for 15 years and is privately owned by the original shareholders, none of whom are employed by the company. The company's senior management has been in charge of the company's operations for most of the past 15 years and expects to remain in that capacity after any sale.

The partnership has expectations about Thunder similar to the current shareholders and management of Thunder. These investors expect to hold Thunder for an intermediate period of time and then bring the company public when market conditions are more favorable than currently.

Chin is concerned about what definition of value should be used when analyzing Thunder. He notes that the stock market has been very volatile recently. He also wonders whether fair market value can be realistically estimated when the most similar recent private market transactions may not have been at arm's length.

Chin asks Ebinosa whether there will be differences in the process of valuing a private company like Thunder compared with a public company. Ebinosa replies that differences do exist and mentions several factors an analyst must consider.

Ebinosa also explains that several approaches are available for valuing private companies. She mentions that one possibility is to use an asset-based approach because Thunder has a relatively large and efficient factory and warehouse for its products. A real estate appraiser can readily determine the value of these facilities. A second method would be the market approach and using an average of the price-to-earnings multiples for Procter & Gamble and Clorox. A third possibility is a discounted free cash flow approach. The latter would focus on a continuation of Thunder's trend of slow profitable growth during the past ten years.

The private investment partnership has mentioned that they are likely to use an income approach as one of their methods. Ebinosa decides to validate the estimates they make. She assumes for the next 12 months that Thunder's revenues increase by the long-term annual growth rate of 3 percent. She also makes the following assumptions to calculate the free cash flow to the firm for the next 12 months:

- Gross profit margin is 45 percent.
- Depreciation is 2 percent of revenues.
- Selling, general, and administrative expenses are 24 percent of revenues.

- Capital expenditures equal 125 percent of depreciation to support the current level of revenues.
- Additional capital expenditures of 15 percent of incremental revenues are needed to fund future growth.
- Working capital investment equals 8 percent of incremental revenues.
- Marginal tax rate on EBIT is 35 percent.

Chin knows that if an income approach is used then the choice of discount rate may have a large influence on the estimated value. He makes two statements regarding discount rate estimates:

1 If the CAPM method is used to estimate the discount rate with a beta estimate based on public companies with operations and revenues similar to Thunder, then a small stock premium should be added to the estimate.

2 The weighted average cost of capital of the private investment partnership should be used to value Thunder.

Ebinosa decides to calculate a value of Thunder's equity using the capitalized cash flow method (CCM) and decides to use the build-up method to estimate Thunder's required return on equity. She makes the following assumptions:

- Growth of FCFE is at a constant annual rate of 3 percent.
- Free cash flow to equity for the year ahead is $2.5 million.
- Risk free rate is 4.5 percent.
- Equity risk premium is 5.0 percent.
- Size premium is 2.0 percent.

6 Given Chin's concerns, the *most appropriate* definition of value for Thunder is:

A intrinsic value.

B investment value.

C fair market value.

7 The *least likely* factor that would be a source of differences in valuing Thunder compared with valuing a publicly traded company is:

A access to public debt markets.

B agency problems.

C the size of the company.

8 Ebinosa can *best* value Thunder using the:

A excess earnings approach.

B asset-based approach.

C discounted free cash flow approach.

9 The free cash flow to the firm is *closest* to:

A $23,031,000.

B $25,441,000.

C $36,091,000.

10 Regarding the two statements about discount rate estimates, Chin is:

A correct with respect to adding the small stock premium and correct with respect to the weighted average cost of capital.

B correct with respect to adding the small stock premium and incorrect with respect to the weighted average cost of capital.

    C incorrect with respect to adding the small stock premium and incorrect with respect to the weighted average cost of capital.

11 The indicated value of Thunder's equity using the build-up method and the capitalized cash flow method (CCM) based on free cash flow to equity is *closest* to:

    A $29.41 million.

    B $38.46 million.

    C $125.00 million.

The following information relates to Questions 12–17[1]

The Senior Vice President of Acquisitions for Northland Industries, Angela Lanton, and her head analyst, Michael Powell, are evaluating several potential investments. Northland is a diversified holding company for numerous businesses. One of Northland's divisions is a manufacturer of fine papers and that division has alerted Lanton about Oakstar Timber, a supplier that may be available for purchase. Oakstar's sole owner, Felix Tanteromo, has expressed interest in exchanging his ownership of Oakstar for a combination of cash and Northland Industries securities.

    Oakstar's main asset is 10,000 hectares of timberland in the western part of Canada. The land is a combination of new and old growth Douglas fir trees. The value of this timberland has been steadily increasing since Oakstar acquired it. Oakstar manages the land on a sustained yield basis (i.e., so it continues to produce timber indefinitely) and contracts with outside forestry companies to evaluate, harvest, and sell the timber. Oakstar's income is in the form of royalties (fees paid to Oakstar based on the number of cubic meters harvested). Oakstar's balance sheet as of 31 December 2008 is as follows.

Oakstar Timber Balance Sheet Year Ended 31 December 2008	
Assets	
Cash	$500,000
Inventory	25,000
Accounts receivable	50,000
Plant and equipment (cost less depreciation)	750,000
Land	10,000,000
Total assets	$11,325,000
Liabilities and Equity	
Accounts payables	$75,000
Long-term bank loan	1,500,000
Common stock	9,750,000
Total liabilities and equity	$11,325,000

---

1 Currency in Canadian dollars.

In addition to the balance sheet, Powell is gathering other data to assist in valuing Oakstar and has found information on recent sales of timberland in the western part of Canada. Douglas fir properties have averaged $6,178 per hectare for tracts that are not contiguous and do not have a developed road system for harvesting the timber. For tracts with these features, as possessed by Oakstar, the average price is $8,750 per hectare. Properties near urban areas and having potential for residential and recreational second home development command up to $20,000 per hectare. Oakstar's land lacks this potential. Lanton believes these values would form the basis of an asset-based valuation for Oakstar, with the additional assumption that other assets and liabilities on the balance sheet are assumed to be worth their stated values.

The second company under evaluation, FAMCO, Inc., is a family-owned electronic manufacturing company with annual sales of $120 million. The family wants to monetize the value of their ownership in FAMCO with a view to later investing part of the proceeds in a diversified stock portfolio. Lanton has asked Powell to obtain data for both an income-based and market-based valuation. Powell has obtained the recent annual income statement and additional data needed to calculate normalized earnings as follows.

FAMCO, Inc.
Income Statement
Year Ending 31 December 2008

Revenues		$120,000,000
Gross profit		85,000,000
Selling, general, and administrative expenses		23,000,000
Pro forma EBITDA		$62,000,000
Depreciation and amortization		3,500,000
Pro forma earnings before interest and taxes		$58,500,000
Less: Interest		1,000,000
Earnings before taxes (EBT)		$57,500,000
Pro forma taxes on EBT	40%	23,000,000
Operating income after tax		$34,500,000

Additional data for FAMCO is provided in the following table. Included are estimates by Powell of the compensation paid to family members and the smaller amount of salary expense for replacement employees if Northland acquires the company (reflecting perceived above-market compensation of the family group executives). He believes the current debt of FAMCO can be replaced with a more optimal level of debt at a lower interest rate. These will be reflected in a normalized income statement.

FAMCO, Inc.

Current debt level	$10,000,000
Current interest rate	10%
Salaries of employed family members	$7,000,000
Salaries of replacement employees	$5,400,000
New debt level	$25,000,000
New interest rate	8%

Powell also recognizes that a value needs to be assigned to FAMCO's intangibles consisting of patents and other intangible assets. Powell prepares an additional estimate of excess earnings and intangibles value using the capitalized cash flow method. He projects the following data for 2009:

FAMCO, Inc.—Intangibles Valuation Data	
Working capital balance	$10,000,000
Fair value of fixed assets	$45,000,000
Normalized income to the company	$35,000,000
Required return on working capital	8%
Required return on fixed assets	12%
Required return on intangible assets	20%
Weighted average cost of capital	14.5%
Future growth rate	6%

Lanton asks Powell to also use the market approach to valuation with a focus on the guideline transactions method. Powell prepares a table showing relevant information regarding three recent guideline transactions and market conditions at the time of the transactions. Powell's assumptions about FAMCO include its expected fast growth and moderate level of risk.

Target Firm	Target's Risk	Target's Growth	Consideration	Market Conditions
Firm 1	High	Slow	Cash	Normal, rising trend
Firm 2	Moderate	Fast	Stock	Prices near peak
Firm 3	Moderate	Fast	Cash	Normal, rising trend

Although Northland is interested in acquiring all of the stock of FAMCO, the acquisition of a 15 percent equity interest in FAMCO is also an option. Lanton asks Powell about the valuation of small equity interests in private entities and notes that control and marketability are important factors that lead to adjustments in value estimates for small equity interests. Powell mentions that the control premium paid for the most similar guideline firm used in the analysis suggests a discount for lack of control of 20 percent. The discount for lack of marketability was estimated at 15 percent.

12 Which of the following statements concerning asset-based valuation as applied to Oakstar is *most* accurate? The approach is applicable:

   A   only when a guideline public company for the valuation is not available.

   B   because natural resources with determinable market values constitute the majority of Oakstar's total value.

   C   because as a passive collector of royalties, Oakstar has no meaningful capital expenditures and free cash flow is irrelevant.

13 Using an asset-based approach, the value (net of debt) of Oakstar is *closest* to:

   A $62,250,000.

   B $87,250,000.

   C $199,750,000.

14 The normalized earnings after tax for FAMCO is *closest* to:

   A $32,940,000.

   B $34,260,000.

   C $34,860,000.

15 Using the excess earnings method, the value of the intangibles is *closest* to:

   A $144.0 million.

   B $205.7 million.

    C $338.8 million.

16 The guideline transaction that is *most likely* applicable to FAMCO is:

    A   Firm 1.

    B   Firm 2.

    C   Firm 3.

17 The total discount for both control and marketability is *closest* to:

    A   15 percent.

    B   32 percent.

    C   35 percent.

SOLUTIONS

1   A strategic buyer seeks to eliminate unnecessary expenses. The strategic buyer would adjust the reported EBITDA by the amount of the officers' excess compensation. A strategic buyer could also eliminate redundant manufacturing costs estimated at £600,000. The pro forma EBITDA a strategic buyer might use in its acquisition analysis is the reported EBITDA of £4,500,000 plus the nonmarket compensation expense of £500,000 plus the operating synergies (cost savings) of £600,000. The adjusted EBITDA for the strategic buyer is £4,500,000 + £500,000 + £600,000 = £5,600,000. The financial buyer would also make the adjustment to normalize officers' compensation but would not be able to eliminate redundant manufacturing expenses. Thus, adjusted EBITDA for the financial buyer would be £4,500,000 + £500,000 = £5,000,000.

2   The build-up method is substantially similar to the extended CAPM except that beta is excluded from the calculation. The equity return requirement is calculated as risk-free rate plus equity risk premium for large capitalization stocks plus small stock risk premium plus company-specific risk premium: 4.5 + 5.0 + 4.2 + 3.0 = 16.7 percent. Although practice may vary, in this case, there was no adjustment for industry risk.

3   There are FCFF and FCFE variations of the CCM. In this problem, the data permit the application of just the FCFE variation. According to that variation, the estimated value of equity equals the normalized free cash flow to equity estimate for next period divided by the capitalization rate for equity. The capitalization rate is the required rate of return for equity less the long-term growth rate in free cash flow to equity. Using the current $1.8 million of free cash flow to equity, the 18 percent equity discount rate, and the long-term growth rate of 5.5 percent yields a value indication of [($1.8 million)(1.055)]/(0.18 − 0.055) = $1.899 million/0.125 = $15.19 million.

4   The excess earnings consist of any remaining income after returns to working capital and fixed assets are considered. Fair value estimates and rate of return requirements for working capital and fixed assets are provided. The return required for working capital is $2,000,000 × 5.0 percent = $100,000 and the return required for fixed assets is $5,500,000 × 8.0 percent = $440,000, or $540,000 in total.

     A   The residual income for intangible assets is $460,000 (the normalized earnings of $1,000,000 less the $540,000 required return for working capital and fixed assets). The value of intangible assets can then be calculated using the capitalized cash flow method. The intangibles value is $4,830,000 based on $483,000 of year-ahead residual income available to the intangibles capitalized at 10.0 percent (15.0 percent discount rate for intangibles less 5.0 percent long-term growth rate of residual income).

     B   The market value of invested capital is the total of the values of working capital, fixed assets, and intangible assets. This value is $2,000,000 + $5,500,000 + $4,830,000 = $12,330,000.

5   The valuation of a small equity interest in a private company would typically be calculated on a basis that reflects the lack of control and lack of marketability of the interest. The control premium of 15 percent must first be used to provide an indication of a discount for lack of control (DLOC). A lack of control discount can be calculated using the formula Lack of control discount = 1 − [1/(1 + Control premium)]. In this case, a lack of control discount of approximately 13 percent is calculated as 1 − [1/(1 + 15%)]. The discount for lack of

marketability (DLOM) was specified. Valuation discounts are applied sequentially and are not added. The formula is (Pro rata control value) × (1 − DLOC) × (1 − DLOM). A combined discount of approximately 35 percent is calculated as 1 − (1 − 13%) × (1 − 25%) = 0.348 or 34.8 percent.

6 A is correct. Both the current shareholders and the future shareholders (the private investment group) share the same expectations. It is most reasonable to assume that both are concerned with Thunder's intrinsic value, which market prices should reflect when the company is brought public under less volatile market conditions.

7 B is correct. The size of Thunder and its probable lack of access to public debt markets are potential factors affecting the valuation of Thunder compared with a public company. Given that the separation of ownership and control at Thunder is similar to that at public companies, however, agency problems are not a distinguishing factor in its valuation.

8 C is correct. The excess earnings method would rarely be applied to value the equity of a company particularly when it is not needed to value intangibles. The asset-based approach is less appropriate because it is infrequently used to estimate the business enterprise value of operating companies. By contrast, the free cash flow method is broadly applicable and readily applied in this case.

9 A is correct. Using Ebinosa's assumptions:

Revenues ($200,000,000 × 1.03 =)		$206,000,000
Gross profit	45%[a]	92,700,000
Selling, general, and administrative expenses	24%[a]	49,440,000
Pro forma EBITDA		43,260,000
Depreciation	2%[a]	4,120,000
Pro forma EBIT		39,140,000
Pro forma taxes on EBIT	35%[b]	13,699,000
Operating income after tax		25,441,000
Plus: Depreciation		4,120,000
Less: Capital expenditures on current sales	125%[c]	5,150,000
Less: Capital expenditures to support future sales	15%[d]	900,000
Less: Working capital requirement	8%[d]	480,000
Free cash flow to the firm		$23,031,000

[a] Percent of revenues
[b] Percent of EBIT
[c] Percent of depreciation
[d] Percent of incremental revenues

10 C is correct. Both statements by Chin are incorrect. If the CAPM is used with public companies with similar operations and similar revenue size, as stated, then the calculation likely captures the small stock premium and should not be added to the estimate. Small stock premiums are associated with build-up models and the expanded CAPM, rather than the CAPM *per se*. The correct weighted average cost of capital should reflect the risk of Thunder's cash flows not the risk of the acquirer's cash flows.

11 A is correct. The return on equity is the sum of the risk free rate, equity risk premium, and the size premium for a total of 4.5 + 5.0 + 2.0 = 11.5 percent. The value of the firm using the CCM is $V = FCFE_1/(r − g) = 2.5/(0.115 − 0.03) = $29.41 million.

12 B is correct. Oakstar's primary asset is timberland whose market value can be determined from comparable land sales.

13 B is correct. In the absence of market value data for assets and liabilities, the analyst usually must use book value data (the reading explicitly makes the assumption that book values accurately reflect market values as well). Except for timberland, market values for assets are not available. Thus, all other assets are assumed to be valued by their book values, which sum to $500,000 + $25,000 + $50,000 + $750,000 = $1,325,000. The value of the land is determined by the value of $8,750 per hectare for properties comparable to Oakstar's. Thus, the value of Oakstar's land is $8,750 × 10,000 = $87,500,000. Liabilities are assumed to be worth the sum of their book value or $1,575,000. Thus, Estimated value = Total assets − Liabilities = $1,325,000 + $87,500,000 − $1,575,000 = $87,250,000.

14 C is correct. The new interest level is $2,000,000 instead of $1,000,000. SG&A expenses are reduced by $1,600,000 (= $5,400,000 − $7,000,000) to $21,400,000 by salary expense savings. Other than a calculation of a revised provision for taxes, no other changes to the income statement results in normalized earnings before tax of $58,100,000 and normalized earnings after tax of $34,860,000.

15 B is correct:

Return on working capital = 0.08 × $10,000,000 = $800,000

Return on fixed assets = 0.12 × $45,000,000 = $5,400,000

Return on intangibles = $35,000,000 − $800,000 − $5,400,000 = $28,800,000

Value of intangibles using CCM = $28,800,000/(0.20 − 0.06) = $205.71 million.

16 C is correct. Firm 3 matches FAMCO in both risk and growth. Firm 1 fails on these factors. In addition, Firm 3 is a better match to FAMCO than Firm 2 because the offer for Firm 3 was a cash offer in normal market conditions whereas Firm 2 was a stock offer in a boom market and the value does not reflect risk and growth in the immediate future.

17 B is correct. Both discounts apply and they are multiplicative rather than additive:

$1 - (1 - 0.20)(1 - 0.15) = 1 - 0.68 = 32$ percent

Glossary

Abandonment option   The ability to terminate a project at some future time if the financial results are disappointing.

Abnormal earnings   See *residual income.*

Abnormal return   The return on an asset in excess of the asset's required rate of return; the risk-adjusted return.

Absolute convergence   The idea that developing countries, regardless of their particular characteristics, will eventually catch up with the developed countries and match them in per capita output.

Absolute valuation model   A model that specifies an asset's intrinsic value.

Absolute version of PPP   The extension of the law of one price to the broad range of goods and services that are consumed in different countries.

Accounting estimates   Estimates used in calculating the value of assets or liabilities and in the amount of revenue and expense to allocate to a period. Examples of accounting estimates include, among others, the useful lives of depreciable assets, the salvage value of depreciable assets, product returns, warranty costs, and the amount of uncollectible receivables.

Acquirer   The company in a merger or acquisition that is acquiring the target.

Acquiring company   The company in a merger or acquisition that is acquiring the target.

Acquisition   The purchase of some portion of one company by another; the purchase may be for assets, a definable segment of another entity, or the purchase of an entire company.

Active factor risk   The contribution to active risk squared resulting from the portfolio's different-than-benchmark exposures relative to factors specified in the risk model.

Active return   The return on a portfolio minus the return on the portfolio's benchmark.

Active risk   The standard deviation of active returns.

Active risk squared   The variance of active returns; active risk raised to the second power.

Active specific risk   The contribution to active risk squared resulting from the portfolio's active weights on individual assets as those weights interact with assets' residual risk.

Add-on interest   A procedure for determining the interest on a bond or loan in which the interest is added onto the face value of a contract.

Adjusted funds from operations   Funds from operations (FFO) adjusted to remove any non-cash rent reported under straight-line rent accounting and to subtract maintenance-type capital expenditures and leasing costs, including leasing agents' commissions and tenants' improvement allowances.

Adjusted present value   (APV) As an approach to valuing a company, the sum of the value of the company, assuming no use of debt, and the net present value of any effects of debt on company value.

Adjusted R^2   A measure of goodness-of-fit of a regression that is adjusted for degrees of freedom and hence does not automatically increase when another independent variable is added to a regression.

Administrative regulations or administrative law   Rules issued by government agencies or other regulators.

Agency costs   Costs associated with the conflict of interest present when a company is managed by non-owners. Agency costs result from the inherent conflicts of interest between managers and equity owners.

Agency costs of equity   The smaller the stake that managers have in the company, the less is their share in bearing the cost of excessive perquisite consumption or not giving their best efforts in running the company.

Agency issues   Conflicts of interest that arise when the agent in an agency relationship has goals and incentives that differ from the principal to whom the agent owes a fiduciary duty. Also called *agency problems* or *principal–agent problems.*

Agency problem   A conflict of interest that arises when the agent in an agency relationship has goals and incentives that differ from the principal to whom the agent owes a fiduciary duty.

Alpha   The return on an asset in excess of the asset's required rate of return; the risk-adjusted return.

American Depositary Receipt   A negotiable certificate issued by a depositary bank that represents ownership in a non-US company's deposited equity (i.e., equity held in custody by the depositary bank in the company's home market).

American option   An option that can be exercised at any time until its expiration date.

Amortizing and accreting swaps   A swap in which the notional principal changes according to a formula related to changes in the underlying.

Analysis of variance (ANOVA)   The analysis of the total variability of a dataset (such as observations on the dependent variable in a regression) into components representing different sources of variation; with reference to regression, ANOVA provides the inputs for an F-test of the significance of the regression as a whole.

Arbitrage   1) The simultaneous purchase of an undervalued asset or portfolio and sale of an overvalued but equivalent asset or portfolio, in order to obtain a riskless profit on the price differential. Taking advantage of a market inefficiency in a risk-free manner. 2) The condition in a financial market in which equivalent assets or combinations of assets sell for two different prices, creating an opportunity to profit at no risk with no commitment of money. In a well-functioning financial market, few arbitrage opportunities are possible. 3) A risk-free operation that earns an expected positive net profit but requires no net investment of money.

Arbitrage-free models   Term structure models that project future interest rate paths that emanate from the existing term structure. Resulting prices are based on a no-arbitrage condition.

Arbitrage-free valuation   An approach to valuation that determines security values that are consistent with the absence of arbitrage opportunities.

Arbitrage opportunity   An opportunity to conduct an arbitrage; an opportunity to earn an expected positive net profit without risk and with no net investment of money.

Arbitrage portfolio   The portfolio that exploits an arbitrage opportunity.

Arrears swap   A type of interest rate swap in which the floating payment is set at the end of the period and the interest is paid at that same time.

Asset-backed securities   A type of bond issued by a legal entity called a *special purpose vehicle* (SPV), on a collection of assets that the SPV owns. Also, securities backed by receivables and loans other than mortgage loans.

Asset-based approach   Approach that values a private company based on the values of the underlying assets of the entity less the value of any related liabilities.

Asset-based valuation   An approach to valuing natural resource companies that estimates company value on the basis of the market value of the natural resources the company controls.

Asset beta   The unlevered beta; reflects the business risk of the assets; the asset's systematic risk.

Asset purchase   An acquisition in which the acquirer purchases the target company's assets and payment is made directly to the target company.

Asymmetric information   The differential of information between corporate insiders and outsiders regarding the company's performance and prospects. Managers typically have more information about the company's performance and prospects than owners and creditors.

At-the-money   An option in which the underlying value equals the exercise price.

Autocorrelation   The correlation of a time series with its own past values.

Autoregressive model (AR)   A time series regressed on its own past values, in which the independent variable is a lagged value of the dependent variable.

Available-for-sale investments   Debt and equity securities not classified as either held-to-maturity or fair value through profit or loss securities. The investor is willing to sell but not actively planning to sell. In general, available-for-sale securities are reported at fair value on the balance sheet.

Backward integration   A merger involving the purchase of a target ahead of the acquirer in the value or production chain; for example, to acquire a supplier.

Backwardation   A condition in the futures markets in which the benefits of holding an asset exceed the costs, leaving the futures price less than the spot price.

Bankruptcy   A declaration provided for by a country's laws that typically involves the establishment of a legal procedure that forces creditors to defer their claims.

Basic earnings per share   (EPS) Net earnings available to common shareholders (i.e., net income minus preferred dividends) divided by the weighted average number of common shares outstanding during the period.

Basis swap   1) An interest rate swap involving two floating rates. 2) A swap in which both parties pay a floating rate.

Basis trade   A trade based on the pricing of credit in the bond market versus the price of the same credit in the CDS market. To execute a basis trade, go long the "underpriced" credit and short the "overpriced" credit. A profit is realized when the price of credit between the short and long position converges.

Bear hug   A tactic used by acquirers to circumvent target management's objections to a proposed merger by submitting the proposal directly to the target company's board of directors.

Benchmark   A comparison portfolio; a point of reference or comparison.

Benchmark value of the multiple   In using the method of comparables, the value of a price multiple for the comparison asset; when we have comparison assets (a group), the mean or median value of the multiple for the group of assets.

Bill-and-hold basis   Sales on a bill-and-hold basis involve selling products but not delivering those products until a later date.

Binomial model   A model for pricing options in which the underlying price can move to only one of two possible new prices.

Binomial tree   The graphical representation of a model of asset price dynamics in which, at each period, the asset moves up with probability p or down with probability $(1 - p)$.

Blockage factor   An illiquidity discount that occurs when an investor sells a large amount of stock relative to its trading volume (assuming it is not large enough to constitute a controlling ownership).

Bond indenture   A legal contract specifying the terms of a bond issue.

Bond option   An option in which the underlying is a bond; primarily traded in over-the-counter markets.

Bond yield plus risk premium method   An estimate of the cost of common equity that is produced by summing the before-tax cost of debt and a risk premium that captures the additional yield on a company's stock relative to its bonds. The additional yield is often estimated using historical spreads between bond yields and stock yields.

Bonding costs   Costs borne by management to assure owners that they are working in the owners' best interest (e.g., implicit cost of non-compete agreements).

Book value   Shareholders' equity (total assets minus total liabilities) minus the value of preferred stock; common shareholders' equity.

Book value of equity   Shareholders' equity (total assets minus total liabilities) minus the value of preferred stock; common shareholders' equity.

Book value per share   The amount of book value (also called carrying value) of common equity per share of common stock, calculated by dividing the book value of shareholders' equity by the number of shares of common stock outstanding.

Bootstrapping   A statistical method for estimating a sample distribution based on the properties of an approximating distribution.

Bottom-up approach   With respect to forecasting, an approach that usually begins at the level of the individual company or a unit within the company.

Bottom-up investing   An approach to investing that focuses on the individual characteristics of securities rather than on macroeconomic or overall market forecasts.

Breakup value   The value derived using a sum-of-the-parts valuation.

Breusch–Pagan test   A test for conditional heteroskedasticity in the error term of a regression.

Broker   1) An agent who executes orders to buy or sell securities on behalf of a client in exchange for a commission. 2) *See* Futures commission merchants.

Brokerage   The business of acting as agents for buyers or sellers, usually in return for commissions.

Buy-side analysts   Analysts who work for investment management firms, trusts, and bank trust departments, and similar institutions.

Call   An option that gives the holder the right to buy an underlying asset from another party at a fixed price over a specific period of time.

Callable bond   Bond that includes an embedded call option that gives the issuer the right to redeem the bond issue prior to maturity, typically when interest rates have fallen or when the issuer's credit quality has improved.

Cannibalization   Cannibalization occurs when an investment takes customers and sales away from another part of the company.

Cap   1) A contract on an interest rate, whereby at periodic payment dates, the writer of the cap pays the difference between the market interest rate and a specified cap rate if, and only if, this difference is positive. This is equivalent to a stream of call options on the interest rate. 2) A combination of interest rate call options designed to hedge a borrower against rate increases on a floating-rate loan.

Cap rate   See *capitalization rate.*

Capital charge   The company's total cost of capital in money terms.

Capital deepening   An increase in the capital-to-labor ratio.

Capital rationing   A capital rationing environment assumes that the company has a fixed amount of funds to invest.

Capital structure   The mix of debt and equity that a company uses to finance its business; a company's specific mixture of long-term financing.

Capitalization of earnings method   In the context of private company valuation, valuation model based on an assumption of a constant growth rate of free cash flow to the firm or a constant growth rate of free cash flow to equity.

Capitalization rate   The divisor in the expression for the value of perpetuity. In the context of real estate, the divisor in the direct capitalization method of estimating value. The cap rate equals net operating income divided by value.

Capitalized cash flow method   In the context of private company valuation, valuation model based on an assumption of a constant growth rate of free cash flow to the firm or a constant growth rate of free cash flow to equity. Also called *capitalized cash flow model.*

Capitalized cash flow model   In the context of private company valuation, valuation model based on an assumption of a constant growth rate of free cash flow to the firm or a constant growth rate of free cash flow to equity. Also called *capitalized cash flow method.*

Capitalized income method   In the context of private company valuation, valuation model based on an assumption of a constant growth rate of free cash flow to the firm or a constant growth rate of free cash flow to equity.

Caplet   Each component call option in a cap.

Capped floater   Floating-rate bond with a cap provision that prevents the coupon rate from increasing above a specified maximum rate. It protects the issuer against rising interest rates.

Capped swap   A swap in which the floating payments have an upper limit.

Carried interest   A share of any profits that is paid to the general partner (manager) of an investment partnership, such as a private equity or hedge fund, as a form of compensation designed to be an incentive to the manager to maximize performance of the investment fund.

Carrying costs   The costs of holding an asset, generally a function of the physical characteristics of the underlying asset.

Cash available for distribution   Funds from operations (FFO) adjusted to remove any non-cash rent reported under straight-line rent accounting and to subtract maintenance-type capital expenditures and leasing costs, including leasing agents' commissions and tenants' improvement allowances.

Cash-generating unit   The smallest identifiable group of assets that generates cash inflows that are largely independent of the cash inflows of other assets or groups of assets.

Cash offering   A merger or acquisition that is to be paid for with cash; the cash for the merger might come from the acquiring company's existing assets or from a debt issue.

Cash settlement   A procedure used in certain derivative transactions that specifies that the long and short parties engage in the equivalent cash value of a delivery transaction.

Catalyst   An event or piece of information that causes the marketplace to re-evaluate the prospects of a company.

CDS spread   A periodic premium paid by the buyer to the seller that serves as a return over Libor required to protect against credit risk.

Chain rule of forecasting   A forecasting process in which the next period's value as predicted by the forecasting equation is substituted into the right-hand side of the equation to give a predicted value two periods ahead.

Cheapest-to-deliver   The debt instrument that can be purchased and delivered at the lowest cost yet has the same seniority as the reference obligation.

Clean surplus accounting   Accounting that satisfies the condition that all changes in the book value of equity other than transactions with owners are reflected in income. The bottom-line income reflects all changes in shareholders' equity arising from other than owner transactions. In the absence of owner transactions, the change in shareholders' equity should equal net income. No adjustments such as translation adjustments bypass the income statement and go directly to shareholders equity.

Clean surplus relation   The relationship between earnings, dividends, and book value in which ending book value is equal to the beginning book value plus earnings less dividends, apart from ownership transactions.

Clientele effect   The preference some investors have for shares that exhibit certain characteristics.

Club convergence   The idea that only rich and middle-income countries sharing a set of favorable attributes (i.e., are members of the "club") will converge to the income level of the richest countries.

Cobb–Douglas production function   A function of the form $Y = K^{\alpha} L^{1-\alpha}$ relating output (Y) to labor (L) and capital (K) inputs.

Cointegrated   Describes two time series that have a long-term financial or economic relationship such that they do not diverge from each other without bound in the long run.

Commercial real estate properties   Income-producing real estate properties, properties purchased with the intent to let, lease, or rent (in other words, produce income).

Common size statements   Financial statements in which all elements (accounts) are stated as a percentage of a key figure such as revenue for an income statement or total assets for a balance sheet.

Company fundamental factors   Factors related to the company's internal performance, such as factors relating to earnings growth, earnings variability, earnings momentum, and financial leverage.

Company share-related factors   Valuation measures and other factors related to share price or the trading characteristics of the shares, such as earnings yield, dividend yield, and book-to-market value.

Comparables   Assets used as benchmarks when applying the method of comparables to value an asset. Also called *comps*, *guideline assets*, or *guideline companies*.

Compiled financial statements   Financial statements that are not accompanied by an auditor's opinion letter.

Comprehensive income   All changes in equity other than contributions by, and distributions to, owners; income under clean surplus accounting; includes all changes in equity during a period except those resulting from investments by owners and distributions to owners; comprehensive income equals net income plus other comprehensive income.

Comps   Assets used as benchmarks when applying the method of comparables to value an asset.

Conditional convergence   The idea that convergence of per capita income is conditional on the countries having the same savings rate, population growth rate, and production function.

Conditional heteroskedasticity   Heteroskedasticity in the error variance that is correlated with the values of the independent variable(s) in the regression.

Conglomerate discount   The discount possibly applied by the market to the stock of a company operating in multiple, unrelated businesses.

Conglomerate merger   A merger involving companies that are in unrelated businesses.

Consolidation   The combining of the results of operations of subsidiaries with the parent company to present financial statements as if they were a single economic unit. The assets, liabilities, revenues and expenses of the subsidiaries are combined with those of the parent company, eliminating intercompany transactions.

Constant dividend payout ratio policy   A policy in which a constant percentage of net income is paid out in dividends.

Constant maturity swap   A swap in which the floating rate is the rate on a security known as a constant maturity treasury or CMT security.

Constant maturity treasury (CMT)   A hypothetical US Treasury note with a constant maturity. A CMT exists for various years in the range of 2 to 10.

Constant returns to scale   The condition that if all inputs into the production process are increased by a given percentage, then output rises by that same percentage.

Contango   A situation in a futures market where the current futures price is greater than the current spot price for the underlying asset.

Contingent consideration   Potential future payments to the seller that are contingent on the achievement of certain agreed on occurrences.

Continuing earnings   Earnings excluding nonrecurring components. Also referred to as *core earnings*, *persistent earnings*, or *underlying earnings*.

Continuing residual income   Residual income after the forecast horizon.

Continuing value   The analyst's estimate of a stock's value at a particular point in the future.

Continuous time   Time thought of as advancing in extremely small increments.

Control premium   An increment or premium to value associated with a controlling ownership interest in a company.

Convenience yield   The nonmonetary return offered by an asset when the asset is in short supply, often associated with assets with seasonal production processes.

Conventional cash flow   A conventional cash flow pattern is one with an initial outflow followed by a series of inflows.

Conversion factor   An adjustment used to facilitate delivery on bond futures contracts in which any of a number of bonds with different characteristics are eligible for delivery.

Conversion period   For a convertible bond, the period during which bondholders have the right to convert their bonds into shares.

Conversion price   For a convertible bond, the price per share at which the bond can be converted into shares.

Conversion ratio   For a convertible bond, the number of shares of common stock that a bondholder receives from converting the bond into shares.

Conversion value   For a convertible bond, the value of the bond if it is converted at the market price of the shares. Also called *parity value*.

Convertible bond   Bond with an embedded conversion option that gives the bondholder the right to convert their bonds into the issuer's common stock during a pre-determined period at a pre-determined price.

Core earnings   Earnings excluding nonrecurring components. Also referred to as *continuing earnings*, *persistent earnings*, or *underlying earnings*.

Corporate governance   The system of principles, policies, procedures, and clearly defined responsibilities and accountabilities used by stakeholders to overcome the conflicts of interest inherent in the corporate form.

Corporate raider   A person or organization seeking to profit by acquiring a company and reselling it, or seeking to profit from the takeover attempt itself (e.g., greenmail).

Corporation   A legal entity with rights similar to those of a person. The chief officers, executives, or top managers act as agents for the firm and are legally entitled to authorize corporate activities and to enter into contracts on behalf of the business.

Correlation analysis   The analysis of the strength of the linear relationship between two data series.

Cost approach   Approach that values a private company based on the values of the underlying assets of the entity less the value of any related liabilities. In the context of real estate, this approach estimates the value of a property based on what it would cost to buy the land and construct a new property on the site that has the same utility or functionality as the property being appraised.

Cost of carry   The cost associated with holding some asset, including financing, storage, and insurance costs. Any yield received on the asset is treated as a negative carrying cost.

Cost-of-carry model   A model for pricing futures contracts in which the futures price is determined by adding the cost of carry to the spot price.

Cost of debt   The cost of debt financing to a company, such as when it issues a bond or takes out a bank loan.

Cost of equity   The required rate of return on common stock.

Covariance stationary Describes a time series when its expected value and variance are constant and finite in all periods and when its covariance with itself for a fixed number of periods in the past or future is constant and finite in all periods.

Covered interest arbitrage A transaction executed in the foreign exchange market in which a currency is purchased (sold) and a forward contract is sold (purchased) to lock in the exchange rate for future delivery of the currency. This transaction should earn the risk-free rate of the investor's home country.

Covered interest rate parity Relationship among the spot exchange rate, forward exchange rate, and the interest rates in two currencies that ensures that the return on a hedged (i.e., covered) foreign risk-free investment is the same as the return on a domestic risk-free investment.

Cox–Ingersoll–Ross model A partial equilibrium term structure model that assumes interest rates are mean reverting and interest rate volatility is directly related to the level of interest rates.

Credit correlation The correlation of credits contained in an index CDS.

Credit curve The credit spreads for a range of maturities of a company's debt; applies to non-government borrowers and incorporates credit risk into each rate.

Credit default swap A derivative contract between two parties in which the buyer makes a series of cash payments to the seller and receives a promise of compensation for credit losses resulting from the default.

Credit derivative A derivative instrument in which the underlying is a measure of the credit quality of a borrower.

Credit event The outcome that triggers a payment from the credit protection seller to the credit protection buyer.

Credit protection buyer One party to a credit default swap; the buyer makes a series of cash payments to the seller and receives a promise of compensation for credit losses resulting from the default.

Credit protection seller One party to a credit default swap; the buyer makes a series of cash payments to the seller and receives a promise of compensation for credit losses resulting from the default.

Credit ratings Ordinal rankings of the credit risk of a company, government (sovereign), quasi-government, or asset-backed security.

Credit risk The risk that the borrower will not repay principal and interest. Also called *default risk*.

Credit scoring Ordinal rankings of a retail borrower's credit riskiness. It is called an *ordinal ranking* because it only orders borrowers' riskiness from highest to lowest.

Credit spreads The difference between the yields on default-free and credit risky zero-coupon bonds.

Currency option An option that allows the holder to buy (if a call) or sell (if a put) an underlying currency at a fixed exercise rate, expressed as an exchange rate.

Current credit risk The risk associated with the possibility that a payment currently due will not be made.

Current exchange rate For accounting purposes, the spot exchange rate on the balance sheet date.

Current rate method Approach to translating foreign currency financial statements for consolidation in which all assets and liabilities are translated at the current exchange rate. The current rate method is the prevalent method of translation.

Curvature One of the three factors (the other two are level and steepness) that empirically explain most of the changes in the shape of the yield curve. A shock to the curvature factor affects mid-maturity interest rates, resulting in the term structure becoming either more or less hump-shaped.

Curve trade Buying a CDS of one maturity and selling a CDS on the same reference entity with a different maturity.

Cyclical businesses Businesses with high sensitivity to business- or industry-cycle influences.

Daily settlement See *marking to market*.

Data mining The practice of determining a model by extensive searching through a dataset for statistically significant patterns.

Day trader A trader holding a position open somewhat longer than a scalper but closing all positions at the end of the day.

"Dead-hand" provision A poison pill provision that allows for the redemption or cancellation of a poison pill provision only by a vote of continuing directors (generally directors who were on the target company's board prior to the takeover attempt).

Debt ratings An objective measure of the quality and safety of a company's debt based upon an analysis of the company's ability to pay the promised cash flows, as well as an analysis of any indentures.

Decision rule With respect to hypothesis testing, the rule according to which the null hypothesis will be rejected or not rejected; involves the comparison of the test statistic to rejection point(s).

Deep-in-the-money Options that are far in-the-money.

Deep-out-of-the-money Options that are far out-of-the-money.

Default intensity Gives the probability of default over the next instant $[t, t + \Delta]$ when the economy is in state X_t.

Default probability See *probability of default*.

Default risk See *credit risk*.

Definition of value A specification of how "value" is to be understood in the context of a specific valuation.

Definitive merger agreement A contract signed by both parties to a merger that clarifies the details of the transaction, including the terms, warranties, conditions, termination details, and the rights of all parties.

Delivery A process used in a deliverable forward contract in which the long pays the agreed-upon price to the short, which in turn delivers the underlying asset to the long.

Delivery option The feature of a futures contract giving the short the right to make decisions about what, when, and where to deliver.

Delta The relationship between the option price and the underlying price, which reflects the sensitivity of the price of the option to changes in the price of the underlying.

Dependent variable The variable whose variation about its mean is to be explained by the regression; the left-hand-side variable in a regression equation.

Depository Trust and Clearinghouse Corporation A US-headquartered entity providing post-trade clearing, settlement, and information services.

Depreciated replacement cost In the context of real estate, the replacement cost of a building adjusted different types of depreciation.

Derivative A financial instrument whose value depends on the value of some underlying asset or factor (e.g., a stock price, an interest rate, or exchange rate).

Descriptive statistics The study of how data can be summarized effectively.

Diff swaps A swap in which the payments are based on the difference between interest rates in two countries but payments are made in only a single currency.

Diluted earnings per share (diluted EPS) Net income, minus preferred dividends, divided by the weighted average number of common shares outstanding considering all dilutive securities (e.g., convertible debt and options); the EPS that would result if all dilutive securities were converted into common shares.

Dilution A reduction in proportional ownership interest as a result of the issuance of new shares.

Diminishing marginal productivity When each additional unit of an input, keeping the other inputs unchanged, increases output by a smaller increment.

Direct capitalization method In the context of real estate, this method estimates the value of an income-producing property based on the level and quality of its net operating income.

Direct financing leases A type of finance lease, from a lessor perspective, where the present value of the lease payments (lease receivable) equals the carrying value of the leased asset. The revenues earned by the lessor are financing in nature.

Discount To reduce the value of a future payment in allowance for how far away it is in time; to calculate the present value of some future amount. Also, the amount by which an instrument is priced below its face value.

Discount factor The present value or price of a risk-free single-unit payment when discounted using the appropriate spot rate.

Discount for lack of control An amount or percentage deducted from the pro rata share of 100 percent of the value of an equity interest in a business to reflect the absence of some or all of the powers of control.

Discount for lack of marketability An amount of percentage deducted from the value of an ownership interest to reflect the relative absence of marketability.

Discount function Discount factors for the range of all possible maturities. The spot curve can be derived from the discount function and vice versa.

Discount interest A procedure for determining the interest on a loan or bond in which the interest is deducted from the face value in advance.

Discount rate Any rate used in finding the present value of a future cash flow.

Discounted abnormal earnings model A model of stock valuation that views intrinsic value of stock as the sum of book value per share plus the present value of the stock's expected future residual income per share.

Discounted cash flow (DCF) analysis In the context of merger analysis, it is an estimate of a target company's value found by discounting the company's expected future free cash flows to the present.

Discounted cash flow method Income approach that values an asset based on estimates of future cash flows discounted to present value by using a discount rate reflective of the risks associated with the cash flows. In the context of real estate, this method estimates the value of an income-producing property based by discounting future projected cash flows.

Discounted cash flow model A model of intrinsic value that views the value of an asset as the present value of the asset's expected future cash flows.

Discrete time Time thought of as advancing in distinct finite increments.

Discriminant analysis A multivariate classification technique used to discriminate between groups, such as companies that either will or will not become bankrupt during some time frame.

Diversified REITs REITs that own and operate in more than one type of property; they are more common in Europe and Asia than in the United States.

Divestiture The sale, liquidation, or spin-off of a division or subsidiary.

Dividend coverage ratio The ratio of net income to dividends.

Dividend discount model (DDM) A present value model of stock value that views the intrinsic value of a stock as present value of the stock's expected future dividends.

Dividend displacement of earnings The concept that dividends paid now displace earnings in all future periods.

Dividend imputation tax system A taxation system which effectively assures that corporate profits distributed as dividends are taxed just once, at the shareholder's tax rate.

Dividend payout ratio The ratio of cash dividends paid to earnings for a period.

Dividend policy The strategy a company follows with regard to the amount and timing of dividend payments.

Dividend rate the annualized amount of the most recent dividend.

Dominance An arbitrage opportunity when a financial asset with a risk-free payoff in the future must have a positive price today.

Double taxation system Corporate earnings are taxed twice when paid out as dividends. First, corporate earnings are taxed regardless of whether they will be distributed as dividends or retained at the G-13 corporate level, and second, dividends are taxed again at the individual shareholder level.

DOWNREIT A variation of the UPREIT structure under which the REIT owns more than one partnership and may own properties at both the REIT level and the partnership level.

Downstream A transaction between two related companies, an investor company (or a parent company) and an associate company (or a subsidiary) such that the investor company records a profit on its income statement. An example is a sale of inventory by the investor company to the associate or by a parent to a subsidiary company.

Due diligence Investigation and analysis in support of a recommendation; the failure to exercise due diligence may sometimes result in liability according to various securities laws.

Dummy variable A type of qualitative variable that takes on a value of 1 if a particular condition is true and 0 if that condition is false.

Duration A measure of an option-free bond's average maturity. Specifically, the weighted average maturity of all future cash flows paid by a security, in which the weights are the present value of these cash flows as a fraction of the bond's price. A measure of a bond's price sensitivity to interest rate movements.

Dutch disease A situation in which currency appreciation driven by strong export demand for resources makes other segments of the economy (particularly manufacturing) globally uncompetitive.

Dynamic hedging   A strategy in which a position is hedged by making frequent adjustments to the quantity of the instrument used for hedging in relation to the instrument being hedged.

Earnings surprise   The difference between reported EPS and expected EPS. Also referred to as *unexpected earnings*.

Earnings yield   EPS divided by price; the reciprocal of the P/E ratio.

Economic growth   The expansion of production possibilities that results from capital accumulation and technological change.

Economic obsolescence   In the context of real estate, a reduction in value due to current economic conditions.

Economic profit   See *residual income*.

Economic sectors   Large industry groupings.

Economic value added   (EVA°) A commercial implementation of the residual income concept; the computation of EVA° is the net operating profit after taxes minus the cost of capital, where these inputs are adjusted for a number of items.

Economies of scale   A situation in which average costs per unit of good or service produced fall as volume rises. In reference to mergers, the savings achieved through the consolidation of operations and elimination of duplicate resources.

Edwards–Bell–Ohlson model   A model of stock valuation that views intrinsic value of stock as the sum of book value per share plus the present value of the stock's expected future residual income per share.

Effective convexity   Sensitivity of duration to changes in interest rates.

Effective duration   Sensitivity of the bond's price to a 100 bps parallel shift of the benchmark yield curve, assuming no change in the bond's credit spread.

Embedded options   Contingency provisions found in a bond's indenture or offering circular representing rights that enable their holders to take advantage of interest rate movements. They can be exercised by the issuer, by the bondholder, or automatically depending on the course of interest rates.

Enterprise value   (EV) Total company value (the market value of debt, common equity, and preferred equity) minus the value of cash and investments.

Enterprise value multiple   A valuation multiple that relates the total market value of all sources of a company's capital (net of cash) to a measure of fundamental value for the entire company (such as a pre-interest earnings measure).

Entry price   The price paid to acquire an asset.

Equilibrium   The condition in which supply equals demand.

Equity carve-out   A form of restructuring that involves the creation of a new legal entity and the sale of equity in it to outsiders.

Equity charge   The estimated cost of equity capital in money terms.

Equity forward   A contract calling for the purchase of an individual stock, a stock portfolio, or a stock index at a later date at an agreed-upon price.

Equity options   Options on individual stocks; also known as stock options.

Equity REIT   A REIT that owns, operates, and/or selectively develops income-producing real estate.

Error autocorrelation   The autocorrelation of the error term.

Error term   The portion of the dependent variable that is not explained by the independent variable(s) in the regression.

Estimated parameters   With reference to a regression analysis, the estimated values of the population intercept and population slope coefficient(s) in a regression.

Eurodollar   A dollar deposited outside the United States.

European option   An option that can only be exercised on its expiration date.

Ex ante version of PPP   Hypothesis that expected changes in the spot exchange rate are equal to expected differences in national inflation rates. An extension of relative purchasing power parity to expected future changes in the exchange rate.

Ex-dividend   Trading ex-dividend refers to shares that no longer carry the right to the next dividend payment.

Ex-dividend date   The first date that a share trades without (i.e., "ex") the dividend.

Ex-dividend price   The price at which a share first trades without (i.e., "ex") the right to receive an upcoming dividend.

Excess earnings method   Income approach that estimates the value of all intangible assets of the business by capitalizing future earnings in excess of the estimated return requirements associated with working capital and fixed assets.

Exchange for physicals (EFP)   A permissible delivery procedure used by futures market participants, in which the long and short arrange a delivery procedure other than the normal procedures stipulated by the futures exchange.

Exchange ratio   The number of shares that target stockholders are to receive in exchange for each of their shares in the target company.

Exercise   The process of using an option to buy or sell the underlying. Also called *exercising the option*.

Exercise price   The fixed price at which an option holder can buy or sell the underlying. Also called *strike price, striking price*, or *strike*.

Exercise rate   The fixed rate at which the holder of an interest rate option can buy or sell the underlying. Also called *strike rate*.

Exercise value   The value of an asset given a hypothetically complete understanding of the asset's investment characteristics; the value obtained if an option is exercised based on current conditions. Also called *intrinsic value*.

Exercising the option   The process of using an option to buy or sell the underlying. Also called *exercise*.

Exit price   The price received to sell an asset or paid to transfer a liability.

Expanded CAPM   An adaptation of the CAPM that adds to the CAPM a premium for small size and company-specific risk.

Expected holding-period return   The expected total return on an asset over a stated holding period; for stocks, the sum of the expected dividend yield and the expected price appreciation over the holding period.

Expected loss   The probability of default multiplied by the loss given default; the full amount owed minus the expected recovery.

Expiration date   The date on which a derivative contract expires.

Exposure to foreign exchange risk   The risk of a change in value of an asset or liability denominated in a foreign currency due to a change in exchange rates.

Extendible bond   Bond with an embedded option that gives the bondholder the right to keep the bond for a number of years after maturity, possibly with a different coupon.

External growth   Company growth in output or sales that is achieved by buying the necessary resources externally (i.e., achieved through mergers and acquisitions).

External sustainability approach   An approach to assessing the equilibrium exchange rate that focuses on exchange rate adjustments required to ensure that a country's net foreign-asset/GDP ratio or net foreign-liability/GDP ratio stabilizes at a sustainable level.

Factor   A common or underlying element with which several variables are correlated.

Factor betas   An asset's sensitivity to a particular factor; a measure of the response of return to each unit of increase in a factor, holding all other factors constant.

Factor portfolio   See *pure factor portfolio.*

Factor price   The expected return in excess of the risk-free rate for a portfolio with a sensitivity of 1 to one factor and a sensitivity of 0 to all other factors.

Factor risk premium   The expected return in excess of the risk-free rate for a portfolio with a sensitivity of 1 to one factor and a sensitivity of 0 to all other factors. Also called *factor price.*

Factor sensitivity   See *factor betas.*

Failure to pay   When a borrower does not make a scheduled payment of principal or interest on any outstanding obligations after a grace period.

Fair market value   The market price of an asset or liability that trades regularly.

Fair value   The amount at which an asset (or liability) could be bought (or incurred) or sold (or settled) in a current transaction between willing parties, that is, other than in a forced or liquidation sale; as defined in IFRS and US GAAP, the price that would be received to sell an asset or paid to transfer a liability in an orderly transaction between market participants at the measurement date.

Fiduciary call   A combination of a European call and a risk-free bond that matures on the option expiration day and has a face value equal to the exercise price of the call.

Finance lease   Essentially, the purchase of some asset by the buyer (lessee) that is directly financed by the seller (lessor). Also called *capital lease.*

Financial contagion   A situation where financial shocks spread from their place of origin to other locales; in essence, a faltering economy infects other, healthier economies.

Financial distress   Heightened uncertainty regarding a company's ability to meet its various obligations because of lower or negative earnings.

Financial futures   Futures contracts in which the underlying is a stock, bond, or currency.

Financial risk   The risk that environmental, social, or governance risk factors will result in significant costs or other losses to a company and its shareholders; the risk arising from a company's obligation to meet required payments under its financing agreements.

Financial transaction   A purchase involving a buyer having essentially no material synergies with the target (e.g., the purchase of a private company by a company in an unrelated industry or by a private equity firm would typically be a financial transaction).

First-differencing   A transformation that subtracts the value of the time series in period $t - 1$ from its value in period t.

First-in, first-out (FIFO)   The first in, first out, method of accounting for inventory, which matches sales against the costs of items of inventory in the order in which they were placed in inventory.

First-order serial correlation   Correlation between adjacent observations in a time series.

Fitted parameters   With reference to a regression analysis, the estimated values of the population intercept and population slope coefficient(s) in a regression.

Fixed-rate perpetual preferred stock   Nonconvertible, noncallable preferred stock with a specified dividend rate that has a claim on earnings senior to the claim of common stock, and no maturity date.

Flip-in pill   A poison pill takeover defense that dilutes an acquirer's ownership in a target by giving other existing target company shareholders the right to buy additional target company shares at a discount.

Flip-over pill   A poison pill takeover defense that gives target company shareholders the right to purchase shares of the acquirer at a significant discount to the market price, which has the effect of causing dilution to all existing acquiring company shareholders.

Floor   A combination of interest rate put options designed to hedge a lender against lower rates on a floating-rate loan.

Floor traders   Market makers that buy and sell by quoting a bid and an ask price. They are the primary providers of liquidity to the market.

Floored floater   Floating-rate bond with a floor provision that prevents the coupon rate from decreasing below a specified minimum rate. It protects the investor against declining interest rates.

Floored swap   A swap in which the floating payments have a lower limit.

Floorlet   Each component put option in a floor.

Flotation cost   Fees charged to companies by investment bankers and other costs associated with raising new capital.

Forced conversion   For a convertible bond, when the issuer calls the bond and forces bondholders to convert their bonds into shares, which typically happens when the underlying share price increases above the conversion price.

Foreign currency transactions   Transactions that are denominated in a currency other than a company's functional currency.

Forward contract   An agreement between two parties in which one party, the buyer, agrees to buy from the other party, the seller, an underlying asset at a later date for a price established at the start of the contract.

Forward curve   The term structure of forward rates for loans made on a specific initiation date.

Forward dividend yield   A dividend yield based on the anticipated dividend during the next 12 months.

Forward integration   A merger involving the purchase of a target that is farther along the value or production chain; for example, to acquire a distributor.

Forward P/E   A P/E calculated on the basis of a forecast of EPS; a stock's current price divided by next year's expected earnings.

Forward price or forward rate   The fixed price or rate at which the transaction scheduled to occur at the expiration of a forward contract will take place. This price is agreed on at the initiation date of the contract.

Forward pricing model   The model that describes the valuation of forward contracts.

Forward rate   An interest rate that is determined today for a loan that will be initiated in a future time period.

Forward rate agreement (FRA)   A forward contract calling for one party to make a fixed interest payment and the other to make an interest payment at a rate to be determined at the contract expiration.

Forward rate model   The forward pricing model expressed in terms of spot and forward interest rates.

Forward swap   A forward contract to enter into a swap.

Franking credit   A tax credit received by shareholders for the taxes that a corporation paid on its distributed earnings.

Free cash flow   The actual cash that would be available to the company's investors after making all investments necessary to maintain the company as an ongoing enterprise (also referred to as free cash flow to the firm); the internally generated funds that can be distributed to the company's investors (e.g., shareholders and bondholders) without impairing the value of the company.

Free cash flow hypothesis   The hypothesis that higher debt levels discipline managers by forcing them to make fixed debt service payments and by reducing the company's free cash flow.

Free cash flow method   Income approach that values an asset based on estimates of future cash flows discounted to present value by using a discount rate reflective of the risks associated with the cash flows.

Free cash flow to equity   The cash flow available to a company's common shareholders after all operating expenses, interest, and principal payments have been made, and necessary investments in working and fixed capital have been made.

Free cash flow to equity model   A model of stock valuation that views a stock's intrinsic value as the present value of expected future free cash flows to equity.

Free cash flow to the firm   The cash flow available to the company's suppliers of capital after all operating expenses (including taxes) have been paid and necessary investments in working and fixed capital have been made.

Free cash flow to the firm model   A model of stock valuation that views the value of a firm as the present value of expected future free cash flows to the firm.

Friendly transaction   A potential business combination that is endorsed by the managers of both companies.

Functional currency   The currency of the primary economic environment in which an entity operates.

Functional obsolescence   In the context of real estate, a reduction in value due to a design that differs from that of a new building constructed for the intended use of the property.

Fundamental factor models   A multifactor model in which the factors are attributes of stocks or companies that are important in explaining cross-sectional differences in stock prices.

Fundamentals   Economic characteristics of a business such as profitability, financial strength, and risk.

Funds available for distribution   Funds from operations (FFO) adjusted to remove any non-cash rent reported under straight-line rent accounting and to subtract maintenance-type capital expenditures and leasing costs, including leasing agents' commissions and tenants' improvement allowances.

Funds from operations   Accounting net earnings excluding (1) depreciation charges on real estate, (2) deferred tax charges, and (3) gains or losses from sales of property and debt restructuring.

Futures commission merchants (FCMs)   Individuals or companies that execute futures transactions for other parties off the exchange.

Futures contract   A variation of a forward contract that has essentially the same basic definition but with some additional features, such as a clearinghouse guarantee against credit losses, a daily settlement of gains and losses, and an organized electronic or floor trading facility.

FX carry trade   An investment strategy that involves taking on long positions in high-yield currencies and short positions in low-yield currencies.

Gamma   A numerical measure of how sensitive an option's delta is to a change in the underlying.

Generalized least squares   A regression estimation technique that addresses heteroskedasticity of the error term.

Going-concern assumption   The assumption that the business will maintain its business activities into the foreseeable future.

Going-concern value   A business's value under a going-concern assumption.

Goodwill   An intangible asset that represents the excess of the purchase price of an acquired company over the value of the net identifiable assets acquired.

Gross domestic product   A money measure of the goods and services produced within a country's borders over a stated time period.

Gross lease   A lease under which the tenant pays a gross rent to the landlord who is responsible for all operating costs, utilities, maintenance expenses, and real estate taxes relating to the property.

Growth accounting equation   The production function written in the form of growth rates. For the basic Cobb–Douglas production function, it states that the growth rate of output equals the rate of technological change plus α times the growth rate of capital plus $(1 - \alpha)$ times the growth rate of labor.

Growth capital expenditures   Capital expenditures needed for expansion.

Growth option   The ability to make additional investments in a project at some future time if the financial results are strong. Also called *expansion option*.

Guideline assets   Assets used as benchmarks when applying the method of comparables to value an asset.

Guideline companies   Assets used as benchmarks when applying the method of comparables to value an asset.

Guideline public companies   Public-company comparables for the company being valued.

Guideline public company method   A variation of the market approach; establishes a value estimate based on the observed multiples from trading activity in the shares of public companies viewed as reasonably comparable to the subject private company.

Guideline transactions method   A variation of the market approach; establishes a value estimate based on pricing multiples derived from the acquisition of control of entire public or private companies that were acquired.

Harmonic mean   A type of weighted mean computed by averaging the reciprocals of the observations, then taking the reciprocal of that average.

Hazard rate   The probability that an event will occur, given that it has not already occurred.

Hazard rate estimation   A technique for estimating the probability of a binary event, such as default/no default, mortality/no mortality, and prepay/no prepay.

Health care REITs   REITs that invest in skilled nursing facilities (nursing homes), assisted living and independent residential facilities for retired persons, hospitals, medical office buildings, or rehabilitation centers.

Hedge ratio   The relationship of the quantity of an asset being hedged to the quantity of the derivative used for hedging.

Hedging   A general strategy usually thought of as reducing, if not eliminating, risk.

Held for trading investments   Debt or equity securities acquired with the intent to sell them in the near term.

Held-to-maturity investments   Debt (fixed-income) securities that a company intends to hold to maturity; these are presented at their original cost, updated for any amortization of discounts or premiums.

Herfindahl–Hirschman Index (HHI)   A measure of market concentration that is calculated by summing the squared market shares for competing companies in an industry; high HHI readings or mergers that would result in large HHI increases are more likely to result in regulatory challenges.

Heteroskedastic   With reference to the error term of regression, having a variance that differs across observations.

Heteroskedasticity   The property of having a nonconstant variance; refers to an error term with the property that its variance differs across observations.

Heteroskedasticity-consistent standard errors   Standard errors of the estimated parameters of a regression that correct for the presence of heteroskedasticity in the regression's error term.

Historical exchange rates   For accounting purposes, the exchange rates that existed when the assets and liabilities were initially recorded.

Ho–Lee model   The first arbitrage-free term structure model. The model is calibrated to market data and uses a binomial lattice approach to generate a distribution of possible future interest rates.

Holding period return   The return that an investor earns during a specified holding period; a synonym for total return.

Homoskedasticity   The property of having a constant variance; refers to an error term that is constant across observations.

Horizontal merger   A merger involving companies in the same line of business, usually as competitors.

Hostile transaction   An attempt to acquire a company against the wishes of the target's managers.

Hotel REITs   REITs that own hotel properties but, similar to health care REITs, in many countries they must refrain from operating their properties themselves to maintain their tax-advantaged REIT status.

Human capital   The accumulated knowledge and skill that workers acquire from education, training, or life experience.

Hybrid approach   With respect to forecasting, an approach that combines elements of both top-down and bottom-up analysis.

Hybrid REITs   REITs that own and operate income-producing real estate and invest in mortgages as well; REITs that have positions in both real estate assets and real estate debt.

I-spreads   Shortened form of "interpolated spreads" and a reference to a linearly interpolated yield.

Illiquidity discount   A reduction or discount to value that reflects the lack of depth of trading or liquidity in that asset's market.

Impairment   Diminishment in value as a result of carrying (book) value exceeding fair value and/or recoverable value.

Impairment of capital rule   A legal restriction that dividends cannot exceed retained earnings.

Implied repo rate   The rate of return from a cash-and-carry transaction implied by the futures price relative to the spot price.

Implied volatility   The volatility that option traders use to price an option, implied by the price of the option and a particular option-pricing model.

In-sample forecast errors   The residuals from a fitted time-series model within the sample period used to fit the model.

In-the-money   Options that, if exercised, would result in the value received being worth more than the payment required to exercise.

Income approach   Valuation approach that values an asset as the present discounted value of the income expected from it. In the context of real estate, this approach estimates the value of a property based on an expected rate of return; the estimated value is the present value of the expected future income from the property, including proceeds from resale at the end of a typical investment holding period.

Incremental cash flow   The cash flow that is realized because of a decision; the changes or increments to cash flows resulting from a decision or action.

Indenture   A written contract between a lender and borrower that specifies the terms of the loan, such as interest rate, interest payment schedule, maturity, etc.

Independent projects   Independent projects are projects whose cash flows are independent of each other.

Independent regulators   Regulators recognized and granted authority by a government body or agency. They are not government agencies per se and typically do not rely on government funding.

Independent variable   A variable used to explain the dependent variable in a regression; a right-hand-side variable in a regression equation.

Index amortizing swap   An interest rate swap in which the notional principal is indexed to the level of interest rates and declines with the level of interest rates according to a predefined schedule. This type of swap is frequently used to hedge securities that are prepaid as interest rates decline, such as mortgage-backed securities.

Index CDS   A type of credit default swap that involves a combination of borrowers.

Indexing   An investment strategy in which an investor constructs a portfolio to mirror the performance of a specified index.

Industrial REITs   REITs that hold portfolios of single-tenant or multi-tenant industrial properties that are used as warehouses, distribution centers, light manufacturing facilities, and small office or "flex" space.

Industry structure   An industry's underlying economic and technical characteristics.

Information ratio   (IR) Mean active return divided by active risk; or alpha divided by the standard deviation of diversifiable risk.

Informational frictions   Forces that restrict availability, quality, and/or flow of information and its use.

Initial margin requirement   The margin requirement on the first day of a transaction as well as on any day in which additional margin funds must be deposited.

Initial public offering   (IPO) The initial issuance of common stock registered for public trading by a formerly private corporation.

Inter-temporal rate of substitution the ratio of the marginal utility of consumption *s* periods in the future (the numerator) to the marginal utility of consumption today (the denominator).

Interest rate call An option in which the holder has the right to make a known interest payment and receive an unknown interest payment.

Interest rate cap A series of call options on an interest rate, with each option expiring at the date on which the floating loan rate will be reset, and with each option having the same exercise rate. A cap in general can have an underlying other than an interest rate.

Interest rate collar A combination of a long cap and a short floor, or a short cap and a long floor. A collar in general can have an underlying other than an interest rate.

Interest rate floor A series of put options on an interest rate, with each option expiring at the date on which the floating loan rate will be reset, and with each option having the same exercise rate. A floor in general can have an underlying other than the interest rate. Also called *floor*.

Interest rate option An option in which the underlying is an interest rate.

Interest rate parity A formula that expresses the equivalence or parity of spot and forward rates, after adjusting for differences in the interest rates.

Interest rate put An option in which the holder has the right to make an unknown interest payment and receive a known interest payment.

Interest rate risk Risk that interest rates will change such that the return earned is not commensurate with returns on comparable instruments in the marketplace.

Internal rate of return (IRR) Rate of return that discounts future cash flows from an investment to the exact amount of the investment; the discount rate that makes the present value of an investment's costs (outflows) equal to the present value of the investment's benefits (inflows).

Internal ratings Credit ratings developed internally and used by financial institutions or other entities to manage risk.

International Fisher effect Proposition that nominal interest rate differentials across currencies are determined by expected inflation differentials.

Intrinsic value The value of an asset given a hypothetically complete understanding of the asset's investment characteristics; the value obtained if an option is exercised based on current conditions. The difference between the spot exchange rate and the strike price of a currency.

Inverse price ratio The reciprocal of a price multiple, e.g., in the case of a P/E ratio, the "earnings yield" E/P (where P is share price and E is earnings per share).

Investment objectives Desired investment outcomes; includes risk objectives and return objectives.

Investment strategy An approach to investment analysis and security selection.

Investment value The value to a specific buyer, taking account of potential synergies based on the investor's requirements and expectations.

ISDA Master Agreement A standard or "master" agreement published by the International Swaps and Derivatives Association. The master agreement establishes the terms for each party involved in the transaction.

Judicial law Interpretations of courts.

Justified (fundamental) P/E The price-to-earnings ratio that is fair, warranted, or justified on the basis of forecasted fundamentals.

Justified price multiple The estimated fair value of the price multiple, usually based on forecasted fundamentals or comparables.

Key rate durations Sensitivity of a bond's price to changes in specific maturities on the benchmark yield curve. Also called *partial durations*.

kth order autocorrelation The correlation between observations in a time series separated by *k* periods.

Labor force Everyone of working age (ages 16 to 64) that either is employed or is available for work but not working.

Labor force participation rate The percentage of the working age population that is in the labor force.

Labor productivity The quantity of real GDP produced by an hour of labor. More generally, output per unit of labor input.

Labor productivity growth accounting equation States that potential GDP growth equals the growth rate of the labor input plus the growth rate of labor productivity.

Lack of marketability discount An extra return to investors to compensate for lack of a public market or lack of marketability.

Last-in, first-out (LIFO) The last in, first out, method of accounting for inventory, which matches sales against the costs of items of inventory in the reverse order the items were placed in inventory (i.e., inventory produced or acquired last are assumed to be sold first).

Law of one price Hypothesis that (1) identical goods should trade at the same price across countries when valued in terms of a common currency, or (2) two equivalent financial instruments or combinations of financial instruments can sell for only one price. The latter form is equivalent to the principle that no arbitrage opportunities are possible.

Leading dividend yield Forecasted dividends per share over the next year divided by current stock price.

Leading P/E A P/E calculated on the basis of a forecast of EPS; a stock's current price divided by next year's expected earnings.

Legal risk The risk that failures by company managers to effectively manage a company's environmental, social, and governance risk exposures will lead to lawsuits and other judicial remedies, resulting in potentially catastrophic losses for the company; the risk that the legal system will not enforce a contract in case of dispute or fraud.

Legislative and regulatory risk The risk that governmental laws and regulations directly or indirectly affecting a company's operations will change with potentially severe adverse effects on the company's continued profitability and even its long-term sustainability.

Lessee The party obtaining the use of an asset through a lease.

Lessor The owner of an asset that grants the right to use the asset to another party.

Level One of the three factors (the other two are steepness and curvature) that empirically explain most of the changes in the shape of the yield curve. A shock to the level factor changes the yield for all maturities by an almost identical amount.

Leveraged buyout (LBO) A transaction whereby the target company management team converts the target to a privately held company by using heavy borrowing to finance the purchase of the target company's outstanding shares.

Leveraged recapitalization A post-offer takeover defense mechanism that involves the assumption of a large amount of debt that is then used to finance share repurchases;

the effect is to dramatically change the company's capital structure while attempting to deliver a value to target shareholders in excess of a hostile bid.

Libor–OIS spread　The difference between Libor and the overnight indexed swap (OIS) rate.

Limit down　A limit move in the futures market in which the price at which a transaction would be made is at or below the lower limit.

Limit move　A condition in the futures markets in which the price at which a transaction would be made is at or beyond the price limits.

Limit up　A limit move in the futures market in which the price at which a transaction would be made is at or above the upper limit.

Linear association　A straight-line relationship, as opposed to a relationship that cannot be graphed as a straight line.

Linear regression　Regression that models the straight-line relationship between the dependent and independent variable(s).

Linear trend　A trend in which the dependent variable changes at a constant rate with time.

Liquidation　To sell the assets of a company, division, or subsidiary piecemeal, typically because of bankruptcy; the form of bankruptcy that allows for the orderly satisfaction of creditors' claims after which the company ceases to exist.

Liquidation value　The value of a company if the company were dissolved and its assets sold individually.

Liquidity preference theory　A term structure theory that asserts liquidity premiums exist to compensate investors for the added interest rate risk they face when lending long term.

Liquidity premium　The premium or incrementally higher yield that investors demand for lending long term.

Liquidity risk　The risk that a financial instrument cannot be purchased or sold without a significant concession in price due to the size of the market.

Local currency　The currency of the country where a company is located.

Local expectations theory　A term structure theory that contends the return for all bonds over short time periods is the risk-free rate.

Locals　Market makers that buy and sell by quoting a bid and an ask price. They are the primary providers of liquidity to the market.

Locational obsolescence　In the context of real estate, a reduction in value due to decreased desirability of the location of the building.

Locked limit　A condition in the futures markets in which a transaction cannot take place because the price would be beyond the limits.

Lockout period　Period during which a bond's issuer cannot call the bond.

Log-linear model　With reference to time-series models, a model in which the growth rate of the time series as a function of time is constant.

Log-log regression model　A regression that expresses the dependent and independent variables as natural logarithms.

Logit model　A qualitative-dependent-variable multiple regression model based on the logistic probability distribution.

London interbank offered rate　(Libor) Collective name for multiple rates at which a select set of banks believe they could borrow unsecured funds from other banks in the London interbank market for different currencies and different borrowing periods ranging from overnight to one year.

Long　The buyer of a derivative contract. Also refers to the position of owning a derivative.

Long/short trade　A long position in one CDS and a short position in another.

Long-term equity anticipatory securities　(LEAPS) Options originally created with expirations of several years.

Look-ahead bias　A bias caused by using information that was not available on the test date.

Loss given default　The amount that will be lost if a default occurs.

Lower bound　The lowest possible value of an option.

Macroeconomic balance approach　An approach to assessing the equilibrium exchange rate that focuses on exchange rate adjustments needed to close the gap between the medium-term expectation for a country's current account balance and that country's normal (or sustainable) current account balance.

Macroeconomic factor model　A multifactor model in which the factors are surprises in macroeconomic variables that significantly explain equity returns.

Macroeconomic factors　Factors related to the economy, such as the inflation rate, industrial production, or economic sector membership.

Maintenance capital expenditures　Capital expenditures needed to maintain operations at the current level.

Maintenance margin requirement　The margin requirement on any day other than the first day of a transaction.

Managerialism theories　Theories that posit that corporate executives are motivated to engage in mergers to maximize the size of their company rather than shareholder value.

Margin　The amount of money that a trader deposits in a margin account. The term is derived from the stock market practice in which an investor borrows a portion of the money required to purchase a certain amount of stock. In futures markets, there is no borrowing so the margin is more of a down payment or performance bond.

Marginal investor　An investor in a given share who is very likely to be part of the next trade in the share and who is therefore important in setting price.

Mark-to-market　The revaluation of a financial asset or liability to its current market value or fair value.

Market approach　Valuation approach that values an asset based on pricing multiples from sales of assets viewed as similar to the subject asset.

Market conversion premium per share　For a convertible bond, the difference between the market conversion price and the underlying share price, which allows investors to identify the premium or discount payable when buying a convertible bond rather than the underlying common stock.

Market conversion premium ratio　For a convertible bond, the market conversion premium per share expressed as a percentage of the current market price of the shares.

Market efficiency　A finance perspective on capital markets that deals with the relationship of price to intrinsic value. The **traditional efficient markets formulation** asserts that an asset's price is the best available estimate of its intrinsic value. The **rational efficient markets formulation** asserts that investors should expect to be rewarded for the costs of information gathering and analysis by higher gross returns.

Market timing   Asset allocation in which the investment in the market is increased if one forecasts that the market will outperform T-bills.

Market value   The estimated amount for which a property should exchange on the date of valuation between a willing buyer and a willing seller in an arm's-length transaction after proper marketing wherein the parties had each acted knowledgeably, prudently, and without compulsion.

Market value of invested capital   The market value of debt and equity.

Marking to market   A procedure used primarily in futures markets in which the parties to a contract settle the amount owed daily. Also known as the *daily settlement*.

Mature growth rate   The earnings growth rate in a company's mature phase; an earnings growth rate that can be sustained long term.

Mean reversion   The tendency of a time series to fall when its level is above its mean and rise when its level is below its mean; a mean-reverting time series tends to return to its long-term mean.

Merger   The absorption of one company by another; two companies become one entity and one or both of the pre-merger companies ceases to exist as a separate entity.

Method based on forecasted fundamentals   An approach to using price multiples that relates a price multiple to forecasts of fundamentals through a discounted cash flow model.

Method of comparables   An approach to valuation that involves using a price multiple to evaluate whether an asset is relatively fairly valued, relatively undervalued, or relatively overvalued when compared to a benchmark value of the multiple.

Minority Interest   The proportion of the ownership of a subsidiary not held by the parent (controlling) company.

Mispricing   Any departure of the market price of an asset from the asset's estimated intrinsic value.

Mixed offering   A merger or acquisition that is to be paid for with cash, securities, or some combination of the two.

Model specification   With reference to regression, the set of variables included in the regression and the regression equation's functional form.

Molodovsky effect   The observation that P/Es tend to be high on depressed EPS at the bottom of a business cycle, and tend to be low on unusually high EPS at the top of a business cycle.

Momentum indicators   Valuation indicators that relate either price or a fundamental (such as earnings) to the time series of their own past values (or in some cases to their expected value).

Monetary assets and liabilities   Assets and liabilities with value equal to the amount of currency contracted for, a fixed amount of currency. Examples are cash, accounts receivable, accounts payable, bonds payable, and mortgages payable. Inventory is not a monetary asset. Most liabilities are monetary.

Monetary/non-monetary method   Approach to translating foreign currency financial statements for consolidation in which monetary assets and liabilities are translated at the current exchange rate. Non-monetary assets and liabilities are translated at historical exchange rates (the exchange rates that existed when the assets and liabilities were acquired).

Monetizing   The conversion of the value of a financial transaction into currency.

Moneyness   The relationship between the price of the underlying and an option's exercise price.

Monitoring costs   Costs borne by owners to monitor the management of the company (e.g., board of director expenses).

Mortgage-backed securities   Asset-backed securitized debt obligations that represent rights to receive cash flows from portfolios of mortgage loans.

Mortgage REITs   REITs that invest the bulk of their assets in interest-bearing mortgages, mortgage securities, or short-term loans secured by real estate.

Mortgages   Loans with real estate serving as collateral for the loans.

Multi-family/residential REITs   REITs that invest in and manage rental apartments for lease to individual tenants, typically using one-year leases.

Multicollinearity   A regression assumption violation that occurs when two or more independent variables (or combinations of independent variables) are highly but not perfectly correlated with each other.

Multiple linear regression   Linear regression involving two or more independent variables.

Multiple linear regression model   A linear regression model with two or more independent variables.

Mutually exclusive projects   Mutually exclusive projects compete directly with each other. For example, if Projects A and B are mutually exclusive, you can choose A or B, but you cannot choose both.

***n*-Period moving average**   The average of the current and immediately prior $n - 1$ values of a time series.

Naked credit default swap   A position where the owner of the CDS does not have a position in the underlying credit.

Negative serial correlation   Serial correlation in which a positive error for one observation increases the chance of a negative error for another observation, and vice versa.

Net asset balance sheet exposure   When assets translated at the current exchange rate are greater in amount than liabilities translated at the current exchange rate. Assets exposed to translation gains or losses exceed the exposed liabilities.

Net asset value   The difference between assets and liabilities, all taken at current market values instead of accounting book values.

Net asset value per share   Net asset value divided by the number of shares outstanding.

Net lease   A lease under which the tenant pays a net rent to the landlord as well as an additional amount based on the tenant's pro rata share of the operating costs, utilities, maintenance expenses, and real estate taxes relating to the property.

Net liability balance sheet exposure   When liabilities translated at the current exchange rate are greater assets translated at the current exchange rate. Liabilities exposed to translation gains or losses exceed the exposed assets.

Net operating income   Gross rental revenue minus operating costs, but before deducting depreciation, corporate overhead, and interest expense. In the context of real estate, a measure of the income from the property after deducting operating expenses for such items as property taxes, insurance, maintenance, utilities, repairs, and insurance but before deducting any costs associated with financing and before deducting federal income taxes. It is similar to earnings before interest, taxes, depreciation, and amortization (EBITDA) in a financial reporting context.

Net operating profit less adjusted taxes (NOPLAT)   A company's operating profit with adjustments to normalize the effects of capital structure.

Net present value (NPV)   The present value of an investment's cash inflows (benefits) minus the present value of its cash outflows (costs).

Net realisable value   Estimated selling price in the ordinary course of business less the estimated costs necessary to make the sale.

Net regulatory burden   The private costs of regulation less the private benefits of regulation.

Net rent   A rent that consists of a stipulated rent to the landlord and a further amount based on their share of common area costs for utilities, maintenance, and property taxes.

Netting   When parties agree to exchange only the net amount owed from one party to the other.

Network externalities   The impact that users of a good, a service, or a technology have on other users of that product; it can be positive (e.g., a critical mass of users makes a product more useful) or negative (e.g., congestion makes the product less useful).

No-growth company   A company without positive expected net present value projects.

No-growth value per share   The value per share of a no-growth company, equal to the expected level amount of earnings divided by the stock's required rate of return.

Node   Each value on a binomial tree from which successive moves or outcomes branch.

Non-cash rent   An amount equal to the difference between the average contractual rent over a lease term (the straight-line rent) and the cash rent actually paid during a period. This figure is one of the deductions made from FFO to calculate AFFO.

Non-convergence trap   A situation in which a country remains relative poor, or even falls further behind, because it fails to t implement necessary institutional reforms and/or adopt leading technologies.

Non-monetary assets and liabilities   Assets and liabilities that are not monetary assets and liabilities. Non-monetary assets include inventory, fixed assets, and intangibles, and non-monetary liabilities include deferred revenue.

Non-renewable resources   Finite resources that are depleted once they are consumed; oil and coal are examples.

Nonconventional cash flow   In a nonconventional cash flow pattern, the initial outflow is not followed by inflows only, but the cash flows can flip from positive (inflows) to negative (outflows) again (or even change signs several times).

Nondeliverable forwards (NDFs)   Cash-settled forward contracts, used predominately with respect to foreign exchange forwards.

Nonearning assets   Cash and investments (specifically cash, cash equivalents, and short-term investments).

Nonlinear relation   An association or relationship between variables that cannot be graphed as a straight line.

Nonstationarity   With reference to a random variable, the property of having characteristics such as mean and variance that are not constant through time.

Normal backwardation   The condition in futures markets in which futures prices are lower than expected spot prices.

Normal contango   The condition in futures markets in which futures prices are higher than expected spot prices.

Normal EPS   The EPS that a business could achieve currently under mid-cyclical conditions. Also called *normalized EPS*.

Normalized earnings   The expected level of mid-cycle earnings for a company in the absence of any unusual or temporary factors that affect profitability (either positively or negatively).

Normalized EPS   The EPS that a business could achieve currently under mid-cyclical conditions. Also called *normal EPS*.

Normalized P/E   P/E based on normalized EPS data.

Notional amount   The amount of protection being purchased in a CDS.

NTM P/E   Next twelve months P/E: current market price divided by an estimated next twelve months EPS.

Off-market FRA   A contract in which the initial value is intentionally set at a value other than zero and therefore requires a cash payment at the start from one party to the other.

Off-the-run   A series of securities or indexes that were issued/created prior to the most recently issued/created series.

Office REITs   REITs that invest in and manage multi-tenanted office properties in central business districts of cities and suburban markets.

Offsetting   A transaction in exchange-listed derivative markets in which a party re-enters the market to close out a position.

On-the-run   The most recently issued/created series of securities or indexes.

One-sided durations   Effective durations when interest rates go up or down, which are better at capturing the interest rate sensitivity of bonds with embedded options that do not react symmetrically to positive and negative changes in interest rates of the same magnitude.

Operating lease   An agreement allowing the lessee to use some asset for a period of time; essentially a rental.

Operating risk   The risk attributed to the operating cost structure, in particular the use of fixed costs in operations; the risk arising from the mix of fixed and variable costs; the risk that a company's operations may be severely affected by environmental, social, and governance risk factors.

Operational risk   The risk of loss from failures in a company's systems and procedures, or from external events.

Opportunity cost   The value that investors forgo by choosing a particular course of action; the value of something in its best alternative use.

Optimal capital structure   The capital structure at which the value of the company is maximized.

Option   A financial instrument that gives one party the right, but not the obligation, to buy or sell an underlying asset from or to another party at a fixed price over a specific period of time. Also referred to as contingent claims.

Option-adjusted spread   (OAS) Constant spread that, when added to all the one-period forward rates on the interest rate tree, makes the arbitrage-free value of the bond equal to its market price.

Option premium   The amount of money a buyer pays and seller receives to engage in an option transaction.

Option price   The amount of money a buyer pays and seller receives to engage in an option transaction.

Orderly liquidation value   The estimated gross amount of money that could be realized from the liquidation sale of an asset or assets, given a reasonable amount of time to find a purchaser or purchasers.

Organic growth   Company growth in output or sales that is achieved by making investments internally (i.e., excludes growth achieved through mergers and acquisitions).

Other comprehensive income Changes to equity that bypass (are not reported in) the income statement; the difference between comprehensive income and net income.

Out-of-sample forecast errors The differences between actual and predicted value of time series outside the sample period used to fit the model.

Out-of-the-money Options that, if exercised, would require the payment of more money than the value received and therefore would not be currently exercised.

Overnight index swap (OIS) A swap in which the floating rate is the cumulative value of a single unit of currency invested at an overnight rate during the settlement period.

Pairs trading An approach to trading that uses pairs of closely related stocks, buying the relatively undervalued stock and selling short the relatively overvalued stock.

Par curve A hypothetical yield curve for coupon-paying Treasury securities that assumes all securities are priced at par.

Par swap A swap in which the fixed rate is set so that no money is exchanged at contract initiation.

Parameter instability The problem or issue of population regression parameters that have changed over time.

Partial equilibrium models Term structure models that make use of an assumed form of interest rate process. Underlying risk factors, such as the impact of changing interest rates on the economy, are not incorporated in the model.

Partial regression coefficients The slope coefficients in a multiple regression. Also called *partial slope coefficients*.

Partial slope coefficients The slope coefficients in a multiple regression. Also called *partial regression coefficients*.

Partnership A business owned and operated by more than one individual.

Payer swaption A swaption that allows the holder to enter into a swap as the fixed-rate payer and floating-rate receiver.

Payoff The value of an option at expiration.

Payout amount The payout ratio times the notional.

Payout policy The principles by which a company distributes cash to common shareholders by means of cash dividends and/or share repurchases.

Payout ratio An estimate of the expected credit loss.

Pecking order theory The theory that managers take into account how their actions might be interpreted by outsiders and thus order their preferences for various forms of corporate financing. Forms of financing that are least visible to outsiders (e.g., internally generated funds) are most preferable to managers and those that are most visible (e.g., equity) are least preferable.

PEG The P/E-to-growth ratio, calculated as the stock's P/E divided by the expected earnings growth rate.

Perfect capital markets Markets in which, by assumption, there are no taxes, transactions costs, or bankruptcy costs, and in which all investors have equal ("symmetric") information.

Performance appraisal The evaluation of risk-adjusted performance; the evaluation of investment skill.

Periodic inventory system An inventory accounting system in which inventory values and costs of sales are determined at the end of the accounting period.

Perpetual inventory system An inventory accounting system in which inventory values and costs of sales are continuously updated to reflect purchases and sales.

Perpetuity A perpetual annuity, or a set of never-ending level sequential cash flows, with the first cash flow occurring one period from now.

Persistent earnings Earnings excluding nonrecurring components. Also referred to as *core earnings, continuing earnings*, or *underlying earnings*.

Pet projects Projects in which influential managers want the corporation to invest. Often, unfortunately, pet projects are selected without undergoing normal capital budgeting analysis.

Physical deterioration In the context of real estate, a reduction in value due to wear and tear.

Physical settlement Involves actual delivery of the debt instrument in exchange for a payment by the credit protection seller of the notional amount of the contract.

Plain vanilla swap An interest rate swap in which one party pays a fixed rate and the other pays a floating rate, with both sets of payments in the same currency.

Poison pill A pre-offer takeover defense mechanism that makes it prohibitively costly for an acquirer to take control of a target without the prior approval of the target's board of directors.

Poison puts A pre-offer takeover defense mechanism that gives target company bondholders the right to sell their bonds back to the target at a pre-specified redemption price, typically at or above par value; this defense increases the need for cash and raises the cost of the acquisition.

Pooling of interests method A method of accounting in which combined companies were portrayed as if they had always operated as a single economic entity. Called pooling of interests under US GAAP and uniting of interests under IFRS. (No longer allowed under US GAAP or IFRS).

Portfolio balance approach A theory of exchange rate determination that emphasizes the portfolio investment decisions of global investors and the requirement that global investors willingly hold all outstanding securities denominated in each currency at prevailing prices and exchange rates.

Position trader A trader who typically holds positions open overnight.

Positive serial correlation Serial correlation in which a positive error for one observation increases the chance of a positive error for another observation, and a negative error for one observation increases the chance of a negative error for another observation.

Potential credit risk The risk associated with the possibility that a payment due at a later date will not be made.

Potential GDP The maximum amount of output an economy can sustainably produce without inducing an increase in the inflation rate. The output level that corresponds to full employment with consistent wage and price expectations.

Preferred habitat theory A term structure theory that contends that investors have maturity preferences and require yield incentives before they will buy bonds outside of their preferred maturities.

Premise of value The status of a company in the sense of whether it is assumed to be a going concern or not.

Premium The amount of money a buyer pays and seller receives to engage in an option transaction.

Premium leg The series of payments the credit protection buyer promises to make to the credit protection seller.

Present value model A model of intrinsic value that views the value of an asset as the present value of the asset's expected future cash flows.

Present value of growth opportunities The difference between the actual value per share and the no-growth value per share. Also called *value of growth*.

Present value of the expected loss Conceptually, the largest price one would be willing to pay on a bond to a third party (e.g., an insurer) to entirely remove the credit risk of purchasing and holding the bond.

Presentation currency The currency in which financial statement amounts are presented.

Price limits Limits imposed by a futures exchange on the price change that can occur from one day to the next.

Price momentum A valuation indicator based on past price movement.

Price multiples The ratio of a stock's market price to some measure of value per share.

Price-setting option The operational flexibility to adjust prices when demand varies from forecast. For example, when demand exceeds capacity, the company could benefit from the excess demand by increasing prices.

Priced risk Risk for which investors demand compensation for bearing (e.g., equity risk, company-specific factors, macroeconomic factors).

Principal–agent problem A conflict of interest that arises when the agent in an agency relationship has goals and incentives that differ from the principal to whom the agent owes a fiduciary duty.

Principal components analysis (PCA) A non-parametric method of extracting relevant information from high-dimensional data that uses the dependencies between variables to represent information in a more tractable, lower-dimensional form.

Principle of no arbitrage In well-functioning markets, prices will adjust until there are no arbitrage opportunities.

Prior transaction method A variation of the market approach; considers actual transactions in the stock of the subject private company.

Private market value The value derived using a sum-of-the-parts valuation.

Probability of default The probability that a bond issuer will not meet its contractual obligations on schedule.

Probability of survival The probability that a bond issuer will meet its contractual obligations on schedule.

Probit model A qualitative-dependent-variable multiple regression model based on the normal distribution.

Procedural law The body of law that focuses on the protection and enforcement of the substantive laws.

Production-flexibility The operational flexibility to alter production when demand varies from forecast. For example, if demand is strong, a company may profit from employees working overtime or from adding additional shifts.

Project sequencing To defer the decision to invest in a future project until the outcome of some or all of a current project is known. Projects are sequenced through time, so that investing in a project creates the option to invest in future projects.

Prospective P/E A P/E calculated on the basis of a forecast of EPS; a stock's current price divided by next year's expected earnings.

Protection leg The contingent payment that the credit protection seller may have to make to the credit protection buyer.

Protective put An option strategy in which a long position in an asset is combined with a long position in a put.

Proxy fight An attempt to take control of a company through a shareholder vote.

Proxy statement A public document that provides the material facts concerning matters on which shareholders will vote.

Prudential supervision Regulation and monitoring of the safety and soundness of financial institutions to promote financial stability, reduce system-wide risks, and protect customers of financial institutions.

Purchasing power gain A gain in value caused by changes in price levels. Monetary liabilities experience purchasing power gains during periods of inflation.

Purchasing power loss A loss in value caused by changes in price levels. Monetary assets experience purchasing power loss during periods of inflation.

Purchasing power parity (PPP) The idea that exchange rates move to equalize the purchasing power of different currencies.

Pure expectations theory A term structure theory that contends the forward rate is an unbiased predictor of the future spot rate. Also called the *unbiased expectations theory*.

Pure factor portfolio A portfolio with sensitivity of 1 to the factor in question and a sensitivity of 0 to all other factors.

Put An option that gives the holder the right to sell an underlying asset to another party at a fixed price over a specific period of time.

Put–call–forward parity The relationship among puts, calls, and forward contracts.

Put–call parity An equation expressing the equivalence (parity) of a portfolio of a call and a bond with a portfolio of a put and the underlying, which leads to the relationship between put and call prices.

Putable bond Bond that includes an embedded put option, which gives the bondholder the right to put back the bonds to the issuer prior to maturity, typically when interest rates have risen and higher-yielding bonds are available.

Qualitative dependent variables Dummy variables used as dependent variables rather than as independent variables.

Quality of earnings analysis The investigation of issues relating to the accuracy of reported accounting results as reflections of economic performance; quality of earnings analysis is broadly understood to include not only earnings management, but also balance sheet management.

Random walk A time series in which the value of the series in one period is the value of the series in the previous period plus an unpredictable random error.

Rational efficient markets formulation See *market efficiency*.

Real estate investment trusts (REITS) Tax-advantaged entities (companies or trusts) that typically own, operate, and—to a limited extent—develop income-producing real estate property.

Real estate operating companies Regular taxable real estate ownership companies that operate in the real estate industry in countries that do not have a tax-advantaged REIT regime in place or are engaged in real estate activities of a kind and to an extent that do not fit within their country's REIT framework.

Real exchange rate The relative purchasing power of two currencies, defined in terms of the *real* goods and services that each can buy at prevailing national price levels and nominal exchange rates. Measured as the ratio of national price levels expressed in a common currency.

Real interest rate parity The proposition that real interest rates will converge to the same level across different markets.

Real options Options that relate to investment decisions such as the option to time the start of a project, the option to adjust its scale, or the option to abandon a project that has begun.

Receiver swaption A swaption that allows the holder to enter into a swap as the fixed-rate receiver and floating-rate payer.

Reconstitution When dealers recombine appropriate individual zero-coupon securities and reproduce an underlying coupon Treasury.

Recovery rate The percentage of the loss recovered.

Reduced form models Models of credit analysis based on the outputs of a structural model but with different assumptions. The model's credit risk measures reflect changing economic conditions.

Reference entity The borrower on a single-name CDS.

Reference obligation A particular debt instrument issued by the borrower that is the designated instrument being covered.

Regime With reference to a time series, the underlying model generating the times series.

Regression coefficients The intercept and slope coefficient(s) of a regression.

Regulatory arbitrage Entities identify and use some aspect of regulations that allows them to exploit differences in economic substance and regulatory interpretation or in foreign and domestic regulatory regimes to their (the entities) advantage.

Regulatory burden The costs of regulation for the regulated entity.

Regulatory capture Theory that regulation often arises to enhance the interests of the regulated.

Regulatory competition Regulators may compete to provide a regulatory environment designed to attract certain entities.

Relative-strength indicators Valuation indicators that compare a stock's performance during a period either to its own past performance or to the performance of some group of stocks.

Relative valuation models A model that specifies an asset's value relative to the value of another asset.

Relative version of PPP Hypothesis that changes in (nominal) exchange rates over time are equal to national inflation rate differentials.

Renewable resources Resources that can be replenished, such as a forest.

Rental price of capital The cost per unit of time to rent a unit of capital.

Replacement cost In the context of real estate, the value of a building assuming it was built today using current construction costs and standards.

Replacement value The market value of a swap.

Reporting unit For financial reporting under US GAAP, an operating segment or one level below an operating segment (referred to as a component).

Reputational risk The risk that a company will suffer an extended diminution in market value relative to other companies in the same industry due to a demonstrated lack of concern for environmental, social, and governance risk factors.

Required rate of return The minimum rate of return required by an investor to invest in an asset, given the asset's riskiness.

Residential properties Properties that provide housing for individuals or families. Single-family properties may be owner-occupied or rental properties, whereas multi-family properties are rental properties even if the owner or manager occupies one of the units.

Residual autocorrelations The sample autocorrelations of the residuals.

Residual dividend policy A policy in which dividends are paid from any internally generated funds remaining after such funds are used to finance positive NPV projects.

Residual income Earnings for a given time period, minus a deduction for common shareholders' opportunity cost in generating the earnings. Also called *economic profit* or *abnormal earnings*.

Residual income method Income approach that estimates the value of all intangible assets of the business by capitalizing future earnings in excess of the estimated return requirements associated with working capital and fixed assets.

Residual income model (RIM) A model of stock valuation that views intrinsic value of stock as the sum of book value per share plus the present value of the stock's expected future residual income per share. Also called *discounted abnormal earnings model* or *Edwards–Bell–Ohlson model*.

Residual loss Agency costs that are incurred despite adequate monitoring and bonding of management.

Restructuring Reorganizing the financial structure of a firm.

Retail REITs REITs that invest in such retail properties as regional shopping malls or community/neighborhood shopping centers.

Return on capital employed Operating profit divided by capital employed (debt and equity capital).

Return on invested capital A measure of the after-tax profitability of the capital invested by the company's shareholders and debt holders.

Reviewed financial statements A type of non-audited financial statements; typically provide an opinion letter with representations and assurances by the reviewing accountant that are less than those in audited financial statements.

Rho The sensitivity of the option price to the risk-free rate.

Riding the yield curve A maturity trading strategy that involves buying bonds with a maturity longer than the intended investment horizon. Also called *rolling down the yield curve*.

Risk-neutral probabilities Weights that are used to compute a binomial option price. They are the probabilities that would apply if a risk-neutral investor valued an option.

Risk-neutral valuation The process by which options and other derivatives are priced by treating investors as though they were risk neutral.

Risk reversal An option position that consists of the purchase of an out-of-the-money call and the simultaneous sale of an out-of-the-money put with the same "delta," on the same underlying currency or security, and with the same expiration date.

Robust standard errors Standard errors of the estimated parameters of a regression that correct for the presence of heteroskedasticity in the regression's error term.

Roll When an investor moves from one series to a new one.

Rolling down the yield curve A maturity trading strategy that involves buying bonds with a maturity longer than the intended investment horizon. Also called *riding the yield curve*.

Root mean squared error (RMSE) The square root of the average squared forecast error; used to compare the out-of-sample forecasting performance of forecasting models.

Sales comparison approach In the context of real estate, this approach estimates value based on what similar or comparable properties (comparables) transacted for in the current market.

Sales-type leases A type of finance lease, from a lessor perspective, where the present value of the lease payments (lease receivable) exceeds the carrying value of the leased asset. The revenues earned by the lessor are operating (the profit on the sale) and financing (interest) in nature.

Scaled earnings surprise Unexpected earnings divided by the standard deviation of analysts' earnings forecasts.

Scalper A trader who offers to buy or sell futures contracts, holding the position for only a brief period of time. Scalpers attempt to profit by buying at the bid price and selling at the higher ask price.

Scatter plot A two-dimensional plot of pairs of observations on two data series.

Scenario analysis Analysis that involves changing multiple assumptions at the same time.

Screening The application of a set of criteria to reduce a set of potential investments to a smaller set having certain desired characteristics.

Seasonality A characteristic of a time series in which the data experiences regular and predictable periodic changes, e.g., fan sales are highest during the summer months.

Seats Memberships in a derivatives exchange.

Securities offering A merger or acquisition in which target shareholders are to receive shares of the acquirer's common stock as compensation.

Security selection risk See *active specific risk.*

Segmented markets theory A term structure theory that contends yields are solely a function of the supply and demand for funds of a particular maturity.

Self-regulating organizations Private, non-governmental organizations that both represent and regulate their members. Some self-regulating organizations are also independent regulators.

Sell-side analysts Analysts who work at brokerages.

Sensitivity analysis Analysis that shows the range of possible outcomes as specific assumptions are changed; involves changing one assumption at a time.

Serially correlated With reference to regression errors, errors that are correlated across observations.

Settlement In the case of a credit event, the process by which the two parties to a CDS contract satisfy their respective obligations.

Settlement date The date on which the parties to a swap make payments. Also called *payment date.*

Settlement period The time between settlement dates.

Settlement price The official price, designated by the clearinghouse, from which daily gains and losses will be determined and marked to market.

Shaping risk The sensitivity of a bond's price to the changing shape of the yield curve.

Shareholders' equity Total assets minus total liabilities.

Shark repellents A pre-offer takeover defense mechanism involving the corporate charter (e.g., staggered boards of directors and supermajority provisions).

Shopping center REITs that invest in such retail properties as regional shopping malls or community/neighborhood shopping centers.

Short The seller of a derivative contract. Also refers to the position of being short a derivative.

Single-name CDS Credit default swap on one specific borrower.

Sinking fund bond A bond which requires the issuer to set aside funds over time to retire the bond issue, thus reducing credit risk.

Sole proprietorship A business owned and operated by a single person.

Speculative value The difference between the market price of the option and its intrinsic value, determined by the uncertainty of the underlying over the remaining life of the option. Also called *time value.*

Spin-off A form of restructuring in which shareholders of a parent company receive a proportional number of shares in a new, separate entity; shareholders end up owning stock in two different companies where there used to be one.

Split-off A form of restructuring in which shareholders of the parent company are given shares in a newly created entity in exchange for their shares of the parent company.

Split-rate tax system In reference to corporate taxes, a split-rate system taxes earnings to be distributed as dividends at a different rate than earnings to be retained. Corporate profits distributed as dividends are taxed at a lower rate than those retained in the business.

Spot curve The term structure of spot rates for loans made today.

Spot rate The interest rate that is determined today for a risk-free, single-unit payment at a specified future date.

Spot yield curve The term structure of spot rates for loans made today.

Spurious correlation A correlation that misleadingly points toward associations between variables.

Stabilized NOI In the context of real estate, the expected NOI when a renovation is complete.

Stable dividend policy A policy in which regular dividends are paid that reflect long-run expected earnings. In contrast to a constant dividend payout ratio policy, a stable dividend policy does not reflect short-term volatility in earnings.

Standard deviation The positive square root of the variance; a measure of dispersion in the same units as the original data.

Standard of value A specification of how "value" is to be understood in the context of a specific valuation.

Standardized beta With reference to fundamental factor models, the value of the attribute for an asset minus the average value of the attribute across all stocks, divided by the standard deviation of the attribute across all stocks.

Standardized unexpected earnings (SUE) Unexpected earnings per share divided by the standard deviation of unexpected earnings per share over a specified prior time period.

Static trade-off theory of capital structure A theory pertaining to a company's optimal capital structure; the optimal level of debt is found at the point where additional debt would cause the costs of financial distress to increase by a greater amount than the benefit of the additional tax shield.

Statistical factor model A multifactor model in which statistical methods are applied to a set of historical returns to determine portfolios that best explain either historical return covariances or variances.

Statistically significant A result indicating that the null hypothesis can be rejected; with reference to an estimated regression coefficient, frequently understood to mean a result indicating that the corresponding population regression coefficient is different from 0.

Statutes Laws enacted by legislative bodies.

Statutory merger A merger in which one company ceases to exist as an identifiable entity and all its assets and liabilities become part of a purchasing company.

Steady state rate of growth The constant growth rate of output (or output per capita) which can or will be sustained indefinitely once it is reached. Key ratios, such as the capital–output ratio, are constant on the steady-state growth path.

Steepness One of the three factors (the other two are level and curvature) that empirically explain most of the changes in the shape of the yield curve. A shock to the steepness factor changes short-term yields more than long-term yields.

Sterilized intervention A policy measure in which a monetary authority buys or sells its own currency to mitigate undesired exchange rate movements and simultaneously offsets the impact on the money supply with transactions in other financial instruments (usually money market instruments).

Stock purchase An acquisition in which the acquirer gives the target company's shareholders some combination of cash and securities in exchange for shares of the target company's stock.

Storage costs The costs of holding an asset, generally a function of the physical characteristics of the underlying asset.

Storage REITs REITs that own and operate self-storage properties, sometimes referred to as mini-warehouse facilities.

Straight bond An underlying option-free bond with a specified issuer, issue date, maturity date, principal amount and repayment structure, coupon rate and payment structure, and currency denomination.

Straight-line rent The average annual rent under a multi-year lease agreement that contains contractual increases in rent during the life of the lease. For example if the rent is $100,000 in Year 1, $105,000 in Year 2, and $110,000 in Year 3, the average rent to be recognized each year as revenue under straight-line rent accounting is ($100,000 + $105,000 + $110,000)/3 = $105,000.

Straight-line rent adjustment See *non-cash rent*.

Strategic transaction A purchase involving a buyer that would benefit from certain synergies associated with owning the target firm.

Strike See *exercise price*.

Strike price See *exercise price*.

Strike rate The fixed rate at which the holder of an interest rate option can buy or sell the underlying. Also called *exercise rate*.

Striking price See *exercise price*.

Stripping A dealer's ability to separate a bond's individual cash flows and trade them as zero-coupon securities.

Structural models Structural models of credit analysis build on the insights of option pricing theory. They are based on the structure of a company's balance sheet.

Subsidiary merger A merger in which the company being purchased becomes a subsidiary of the purchaser.

Substantive law The body of law that focuses on the rights and responsibilities of entities and relationships among entities.

Succession event A change of corporate structure of the reference entity, such as through a merger, divestiture, spinoff, or any similar action, in which ultimate responsibility for the debt in question is unclear.

Sum-of-the-parts valuation A valuation that sums the estimated values of each of a company's businesses as if each business were an independent going concern.

Sunk cost A cost that has already been incurred.

Supernormal growth Above average or abnormally high growth rate in earnings per share.

Survivorship bias Bias that may result when failed or defunct companies are excluded from membership in a group.

Sustainable growth rate The rate of dividend (and earnings) growth that can be sustained over time for a given level of return on equity, keeping the capital structure constant and without issuing additional common stock.

Swap curve The term structure of swap rates.

Swap rate The interest rate for the fixed-rate leg of an interest rate swap.

Swap rate curve The term structure of swap rates.

Swap spread The difference between the fixed rate on an interest rate swap and the rate on a Treasury note with equivalent maturity; it reflects the general level of credit risk in the market.

Swaption An option to enter into a swap.

Synthetic call The combination of puts, the underlying, and risk-free bonds that replicates a call option.

Synthetic CDO Created by combining a portfolio of default-free securities with a combination of credit default swaps undertaken as protection sellers.

Synthetic forward contract The combination of the underlying, puts, calls, and risk-free bonds that replicates a forward contract.

Synthetic lease A lease that is structured to provide a company with the tax benefits of ownership while not requiring the asset to be reflected on the company's financial statements.

Synthetic put The combination of calls, the underlying, and risk-free bonds that replicates a put option.

Systematic risk Risk that affects the entire market or economy; it cannot be avoided and is inherent in the overall market. Systematic risk is also known as non-diversifiable or market risk.

Systemic risk The risk of failure of the financial system.

Takeover A merger; the term may be applied to any transaction, but is often used in reference to hostile transactions.

Takeover premium The amount by which the takeover price for each share of stock must exceed the current stock price in order to entice shareholders to relinquish control of the company to an acquirer.

Tangible book value per share Common shareholders' equity minus intangible assets reported on the balance sheet, divided by the number of shares outstanding.

Target The company in a merger or acquisition that is being acquired.

Target capital structure A company's chosen proportions of debt and equity.

Target company The company in a merger or acquisition that is being acquired.

Target payout ratio A strategic corporate goal representing the long-term proportion of earnings that the company intends to distribute to shareholders as dividends.

Technical indicators Momentum indicators based on price.

TED spread A measure of perceived credit risk determined as the difference between Libor and the T-bill yield of matching maturity.

Temporal method A variation of the monetary/non-monetary translation method that requires not only monetary assets and liabilities, but also non-monetary assets and liabilities that are measured at their current value on the balance sheet date to be translated at the current exchange rate. Assets and liabilities are translated at rates consistent with the timing of their measurement value. This method is typically used when the functional currency is other than the local currency.

Tender offer A public offer whereby the acquirer invites target shareholders to submit ("tender") their shares in return for the proposed payment.

Term premium The additional return required by lenders to invest in a bond to maturity net of the expected return from continually reinvesting at the short-term rate over that same time horizon.

Terminal price multiples The price multiple for a stock assumed to hold at a stated future time.

Terminal share price The share price at a particular point in the future.

Terminal value of the stock The analyst's estimate of a stock's value at a particular point in the future. Also called *continuing value of the stock*.

Termination date The date of the final payment on a swap; also, the swap's expiration date.

Theta The rate at which an option's time value decays.

Time series A set of observations on a variable's outcomes in different time periods.

Time to expiration The time remaining in the life of a derivative, typically expressed in years.

Time value The difference between the market price of the option and its intrinsic value, determined by the uncertainty of the underlying over the remaining life of the option. Also called *speculative value*.

Time value decay The loss in the value of an option resulting from movement of the option price towards its payoff value as the expiration day approaches.

Tobin's q The ratio of the market value of debt and equity to the replacement cost of total assets.

Top-down approach With respect to forecasting, an approach that usually begins at the level of the overall economy. Forecasts are then made at more narrowly defined levels, such as sector, industry, and market for a specific product.

Top-down investing An approach to investing that typically begins with macroeconomic forecasts.

Total factor productivity (TFP) A multiplicative scale factor that reflects the general level of productivity or technology in the economy. Changes in total factor productivity generate proportional changes in output for any input combination.

Total invested capital The sum of market value of common equity, book value of preferred equity, and face value of debt.

Total return swap A swap in which one party agrees to pay the total return on a security. Often used as a credit derivative, in which the underlying is a bond.

Tracking error The standard deviation of the differences between a portfolio's returns and its benchmark's returns; a synonym of active risk. Also called *tracking risk*.

Tracking risk The standard deviation of the differences between a portfolio's returns and its benchmark's returns; a synonym of active risk. Also called *tracking error*.

Trailing dividend yield Current market price divided by the most recent annualized dividend.

Trailing P/E A stock's current market price divided by the most recent four quarters of EPS (or the most recent two semi-annual periods for companies that report interim data semi-annually.) Also called *current P/E*.

Tranche CDS A type of credit default swap that covers a combination of borrowers but only up to pre-specified levels of losses.

Transaction exposure The risk of a change in value between the transaction date and the settlement date of an asset of liability denominated in a foreign currency.

Trend A long-term pattern of movement in a particular direction.

Triangular arbitrage An arbitrage transaction involving three currencies which attempts to exploit inconsistencies among pair wise exchange rates.

Unbiased expectations theory A term structure theory that contends the forward rate is an unbiased predictor of the future spot rate. Also called the *pure expectations theory*.

Unconditional heteroskedasticity Heteroskedasticity of the error term that is not correlated with the values of the independent variable(s) in the regression.

Uncovered interest rate parity The proposition that the expected return on an uncovered (i.e., unhedged) foreign currency (risk-free) investment should equal the return on a comparable domestic currency investment.

Underlying An asset that trades in a market in which buyers and sellers meet, decide on a price, and the seller then delivers the asset to the buyer and receives payment. The underlying is the asset or other derivative on which a particular derivative is based. The market for the underlying is also referred to as the spot market.

Underlying earnings Earnings excluding nonrecurring components. Also referred to as *continuing earnings*, *core earnings*, or *persistent earnings*.

Unexpected earnings The difference between reported EPS and expected EPS. Also referred to as an *earnings surprise*.

Unit root A time series that is not covariance stationary is said to have a unit root.

Uniting of interests method A method of accounting in which combined companies were portrayed as if they had always operated as a single economic entity. Called pooling of interests under US GAAP and uniting of interests under IFRS. (No longer allowed under US GAAP or IFRS).

Unlimited funds An unlimited funds environment assumes that the company can raise the funds it wants for all profitable projects simply by paying the required rate of return.

Unsterilized intervention A policy measure in which a monetary authority buys or sells its own currency to mitigate undesired exchange rate movements and does not offset the impact on the money supply with transactions in other financial instruments.

Upfront payment The difference between the credit spread and the standard rate paid by the protection if the standard rate is insufficient to compensate the protection seller. Also called *upfront premium*.

Upfront premium See *upfront payment*.

UPREITs An umbrella partnership REIT under which the REIT owns an operating partnership and serves as the general partner of the operating partnership. All or most of the properties are held in the operating partnership.

Upstream A transaction between two related companies, an investor company (or a parent company) and an associate company (or a subsidiary company) such that the associate company records a profit on its income statement. An example is a sale of inventory by the associate to the investor company or by a subsidiary to a parent company.

Valuation The process of determining the value of an asset or service on the basis of variables perceived to be related to future investment returns, or on the basis of comparisons with closely similar assets.

Value additivity   An arbitrage opportunity when the value of the whole equals the sum of the values of the parts.

Value at risk (VAR)   A money measure of the minimum value of losses expected during a specified time period at a given level of probability.

Value of growth   The difference between the actual value per share and the no-growth value per share.

Variance   The expected value (the probability-weighted average) of squared deviations from a random variable's expected value.

Variation margin   Additional margin that must be deposited in an amount sufficient to bring the balance up to the initial margin requirement.

Vasicek model   A partial equilibrium term structure model that assumes interest rates are mean reverting and interest rate volatility is a constant.

Vega   The relationship between option price and volatility.

Venture capital investors   Private equity investors in development-stage companies.

Vertical merger   A merger involving companies at different positions of the same production chain; for example, a supplier or a distributor.

Visibility   The extent to which a company's operations are predictable with substantial confidence.

Weighted average cost   An inventory accounting method that averages the total cost of available inventory items over the total units available for sale.

Weighted average cost of capital   (WACC) A weighted average of the after-tax required rates of return on a company's common stock, preferred stock, and long-term debt, where the weights are the fraction of each source of financing in the company's target capital structure.

Weighted harmonic mean   See *harmonic mean.*

White-corrected standard errors   A synonym for robust standard errors.

White knight   A third party that is sought out by the target company's board to purchase the target in lieu of a hostile bidder.

White squire   A third party that is sought out by the target company's board to purchase a substantial minority stake in the target—enough to block a hostile takeover without selling the entire company.

Winner's curse   The tendency for the winner in certain competitive bidding situations to overpay, whether because of overestimation of intrinsic value, emotion, or information asymmetries.

Write-down   A reduction in the value of an asset as stated in the balance sheet.

Yield curve factor model   A model or a description of yield curve movements that can be considered realistic when compared with historical data.

Z-spread   The constant basis point spread that needs to be added to the implied spot yield curve such that the discounted cash flows of a bond are equal to its current market price.

Zero   A bond that does not pay a coupon but is priced at a discount and pays its full face value at maturity.

Zero-cost collar   A transaction in which a position in the underlying is protected by buying a put and selling a call with the premium from the sale of the call offsetting the premium from the purchase of the put. It can also be used to protect a floating-rate borrower against interest rate increases with the premium on a long cap offsetting the premium on a short floor.

Zero-coupon bond   A bond that does not pay a coupon but is priced at a discount and pays its full face value at maturity.

Index

A

Abbott Laboratories, 200
AB InBev. *see* Anheuser-Busch InBev
abnormal earnings, 491
abnormal return, 7
absolute valuation models, 22–24
accounting estimates, 389n.12
accounting information, for equity
   valuation, 17–21
accounting methods
   for cash flow, 435
   and residual income model, 511–524
      accounting for intangible assets,
         521–524
      accounting for nonrecurring items,
         524
      aggressive accounting practices, 524
      balance sheet adjustments for fair
         value, 520–521
      clean surplus violations, 512–520
accounting standards, international
   differences, 451–452
Accounting Standards Codification
   (ASC) Topics
   "Business Combinations" (ASC 805),
      553n.11, 570, 576
   "Fair Value Measurement" (ASC 820),
      551n.5, 553n.12–13, 571
   "Goodwill and Other Intangible
      Assets" (ASC 350), 551n.5–6
   "Share-Based Payment" (ASC 718),
      552n.7
accumulated other comprehensive
   income (AOCI), 516
acquisitions, 9, 551
adaptive strategies
   characteristics of, 132
   defined, 131
   environment for, 133
   and life-cycle stages, 137
   prevalence of, 135
adjusted earnings, 388
adjusted historical estimates of equity
   risk premium, 61–64
adjusted present value (APV), 304n.2
ADR. *see* American Depositary Receipt
ADR ratio, 391–392
affiliates, income from, 164
after-tax interest, FCFF and, 308
AGA. *see* American Gas Association
agency issues, 549n.2
aggressive accounting practices, 524
aggressive estimates, 19
Ahold, 159–160, 178
AICPA. *see* American Institute of
   Certified Public Accountants
AIMR. *see* Association for Investment
   Management and Research
Air France-KLM, 200
airline industry, cost of goods sold in, 150
Albert Heijn, 150–151
Alleghany Corporation, 72–74

alpha, 7, 50
Altria Group, Inc., 475
Amazon, 200
AmBev, 169
American Depositary Receipt (ADR), 51,
   391–392
American Gas Association (AGA), 16n.
American Institute of Certified Public
   Accountants (AICPA), 17
   IGBVT, 552n.9
   IPRD Practice Aid, 566n.25, 570,
      587–588
   standards required by, 587–588
   Stock Practice Aid, 565n.24, 588
American Petroleum Institute (API), 16n.
   552n.9
American Society of Appraisers (ASA),
   552n.9
America Online, 576
amortization, 210
Amylin Pharmaceuticals, 145
analysts
   buy-side, 30
   CFO adjustments by, 332
   communication with, 10
   roles and responsibilities of, 30–32
   sell-side, 30–32
   trailing P/E adjustments by, 388–392
Anheuser-Busch Cos., 393
Anheuser-Busch InBev (AB InBev),
   169–172, 180, 462
Ansell Limited, 285
AOCI. *see* accumulated other
   comprehensive income
AOL Time Warner, 92, 97
API. *see* American Petroleum Institute
Apple
   long-term growth, 200
   and music industry, 105, 120
   price increases by, 177
   tablet computers, 185–186
   terminal value, 199
   threat of entry by, 108
appraisal, 548n.1
Appraisal Foundation, 570, 573n.34, 587,
   588
appraisers, cash flow forecasts by,
   559–560
APT. *see* arbitrage pricing theory
APV. *see* adjusted present value
Aqua America Inc., 248
arbitrage pricing theory (APT), 75
arithmetic mean, 56, 59–60, 460–461
ASA. *see* American Society of Appraisers
ASC Topics. *see* Accounting Standards
   Codification (ASC) Topics
ASM International, 451–452
asset-based valuation
   of equity, 23–24
   of private companies, 554, 578–580
assets
   guideline assets, 381
   intangible, 521–524, 548, 570

long-term, 165
nonearning, 443
nonfinancial, 424
nonoperating, 349, 555
non-traded, 72–75
personal-use, 556
return on, 275, 276, 405n.26
*Assets Acquired in a Business
   Combination to Be Used in Research
   and Development Activities* (IPRD
   Practice Aid), 566n.25, 570, 587–588
Association for Investment Management
   and Research (AIMR), 31–32
assumptions, long-term forecasting,
   200–201
AstraZeneca PLC, 388–389
AT&T, 404–407, 460
*The Auditor's Responsibility to Consider
   Fraud and Error in an Audit of
   Financial Statements* (International
   Federation of Accountants), 17
Australia
   FFM factors, 76n.45
   GDP growth rate, 243
   historical equity risk premium, 57, 59
Austria, 57, 59, 76n.45
availability, of transactions, 576
available-for-sale investments, 512
average return on equity, 390
Avon, 152, 153
Axis Manufacturing Company, Inc.,
   489–491

B

Baker Hughes Inc., 14–15
balance sheet modeling, 164–166
balance sheets
   adjustments for fair value on, 520–521
   and industry analysis, 110–111
   pro forma, 213–214
   quality of earnings indicators from, 18
   and statements of cash flows, 332
Baltika, 172–176
Bank of America, 385
Bank of Canada, 244
bankruptcy, 551
Barclays PLC, 421–424
bargaining power, 169–171, 202, 203
barriers to entry, 108–110
base case scenarios
   defined, 167
   for technological developments, 193, 194
basic earnings per share, 387
BCE Inc., 404–406, 440, 460
bear case scenario, 168, 193–195
Bechtel, 548
beer markets
   Brazilian, 169–170
   European, 177–178
   Russian, 172–176
   United Kingdom, 170–171
   United States, 177, 178

Beierdorf Consumer, 153
Belgium, 57, 59, 76n.45
benchmarking of operating costs, 152
benchmark value of the multiple, 401
benefits of scale, demand-side, 108
Berkshire Hathaway, 19
Best Buy, 117
beta
  factor, 75
  indexes and estimation of, 68
  for nonpublic companies, 73–75
  for public companies, 69–73
  unlevering, 73, 74
BEV. see business enterprise value
biases
  look-ahead, 463
  survivorship, 61
bill-and-hold basis, sales on, 429–430
blockage factors, 29
Bloomberg L.P., 69, 111, 268–270
Blume adjustment, 69
BNIC. see Bureau National
  Interprofessionnel du Cognac
Boeing Company, 92, 97, 532
BofA Merrill Lynch Institutional Factor
  Survey, 28, 239, 385, 433, 453, 462
bond indenture, 23
bond yield plus risk premium (BYPRP)
  method, 84–85
book-to-market ratio (B/P), 394
book value of equity (book value). see
  also price to book value (P/B)
  adjusting, 421–424
  defined, 380, 416
  determining, 419–424
  and residual income, 500–501
  in residual income model, 511–512
book value per share, 238, 416
  computing, 419–420
  and fair value accounting, 421–424
  tangible, 420–421
Bosch, 548
Boston Beer Co., 393
bottom-up approach
  forecasting, 22
  investing, 21n.7
  modeling operating costs, 146
  modeling revenue, 143, 144
  working capital projections, 164
Bowman, Thomas A., 32n.17
Boyd Gaming Corp., 396–397
B/P. see book-to-market ratio
BP p.l.c., 71–72, 398, 453
Brazilian beer market, 169–170
breakup value, 25
brewers, 150
Bridgestone, 402
British Airways, 283
British American Tobacco, 475
British Sky Broadcasting Group,
  283–284
brokerage, 30n.14
Brother Industries, Ltd., 285–286
BT Group, 440
Buffett, Warren, 19
build-up method
  for equity, 81–85
  for private company, 81–84, 562–563
bull case scenario, 168, 193–195

Bureau National Interprofessionnel du
  Cognac (BNIC), 202
"Business Combinations" (ASC 805),
  553n.11, 570, 576
"Business Combinations" (IFRS 3R), 570
"Business Combinations" (SFAS 141R),
  570
business context for equity valuation,
  11–21
  accounting information, 17–21
  financial reports, 14, 16
  industry and competitive analysis,
    12–14
  quality of earnings analysis, 17–21
  sources of information, 16–17
business-cycle influence, for trailing P/E,
  390–392
business cycle risk, 81
business enterprise value (BEV), 572n.32
business functions, strategic style for,
  136–137
business model, 13
business strategies, evaluating, 10. see
  also competitive strategy
business summary, research report, 35
buybacks (share repurchases), 233n.3,
  250–251
buyers. see customers
buy-side analysts, 30
BYPRP method. see bond yield plus risk
  premium method

C
CAGR. see compound annual growth rate
Cameron, 15
Canada
  dividend policy, 233
  FFM factors, 76n.45
  GDP growth rate, 243, 244
  historical equity risk premium, 57, 59
  regulatory requirements, 16
Canadian Institute of Chartered
  Business Valuators, 552n.9
cannibalization (technological)
  base case scenarios for, 193, 194
  bull and bear case scenarios for,
    193–195
  estimating impact of, 191–195
  quantifying potential for, 185–191
Canon, Inc., 502
capacity-based measures, modeling
  revenue with, 144
capex. see capital investment
capital
  cost of equity capital, 489
  fixed, 308
  human, 417
  invested
    market value of invested capital, 446,
      572
    return on invested capital, 106–107,
      446, 490n.5
    total invested capital, 446
  return on, 144
  weighted average cost of, 86–88,
    304–305, 563
  working
    and FCFF, 308–309
    and free cash flow, 317–318

on pro forma cash flow statements,
    210–211
  projections of, 164–165
capital asset pricing model (CAPM), 49
  and arithmetic mean, 59–60
  and equity risk premium, 55
  expanded, 562
  FFM vs., 79
  investors' expectations in, 50n.3
  for private company, 83–84
  and required rate of return for private
    company, 562
  required return on equity, 67–75
    beta for nonpublic companies,
      73–75
    beta for public companies, 69–73
    examples, 69–74
capital charge, 490
capital expenditures, 165, 308, 328–329
capital investment (capex), 210
capitalization of earnings method, 562
capitalization rate, 249, 568
capitalized cash flow method (CCM),
  305n.3, 561, 567–569
capitalized income method, 562
capital requirements, as barrier to entry,
  109
capital structure
  changing, 304
  and forecasting free cash flows,
    335–337
  and modeling financing expenses, 159
  projections of, 165
CAPM. see capital asset pricing model
Cargill, 548
Carlsberg, 170, 172, 183
Carl Zeiss Meditec AG, 259–260, 262
Carrefour SA
  dividend discount model, 240
  and European beer market, 178
  input and product prices at, 181–182
  justified P/E, 255–256
carried interest, 579n.37
cash flow from operations (CFO),
  236n.10
  adjusting, 320–324, 332
  FCFE from, 320–324
  FCFF from, 311–312, 320–324
  free cash flow vs., 303
  and price to cash flow, 434, 436
cash flows. see also free cash flow; price
  to cash flow (P/CF)
  and accounting methods, 435
  capitalized cash flow method of
    valuation, 305n.3, 561, 567–569
  DCF models
    as absolute valuation model, 22–23
    for equity valuation, 230
    forecasted fundamentals and
      multiples in, 383
    and free cash flows, 302
    residual income model vs., 508
    and valuation based on forecasted
      fundamentals, 397–399
  discounted cash flow method of
    valuation
    perpetuity calculations, 200
    private company valuation, 561–562,
      567

terminal value, 199
valuation inputs, 214–215
and discount rate selection, 88–89
earnings-plus-noncash-charges
definition, 436
estimation with private company
valuation, 559–561
for FCFE and FCFF approach to free
cash flow valuation, 303–304
future, for present value models,
231–233
operating, 18, 434
in present value models, 233–239
trailing price to cash flow, 436
cash flow statements. *see* statement of
cash flows
cash flow yield (CF/P), 394
cash-generating units, 551n.6
cash tax rate, 160–163
catalyst, valuation, 8
CCM. *see* capitalized cash flow
method
CEICs. *see* closed-end investment
companies
Centurytel, 404–406, 460
CFA Institute, 16
CFO. *see* cash flow from operations
CF/P. *see* cash flow yield
Charles Schwab Corporation, 426
Chase Bank, 118
Chemical Bank, 118
Chevron Corp., 286, 295
China
cognac industry, 202
revenue analysis, 141–143
strategic style, 136
Citigroup, Inc., 418
classical strategies
characteristics of, 131–132
defined, 131
environment for, 133
and life-cycle stages, 137
prevalence of, 134, 135
clean surplus accounting, 238n.12,
489n.3
and book value/future earnings,
511–512
and residual income model, 500
violations of, 512–520
clean surplus relation, 496
Clorox, 152n.2, 153
closed-end investment companies
(CEICs), 579, 582
Code of Ethics, 16, 32, 35–36
cognac industry, 202–203. *see also* Rémy
Cointreau Group
COGS. *see* cost of goods sold
Colgate-Palmolive Company (Colgate),
152, 153, 417–418
Colorpak Ltd., 461–462
common stock, required return for,
79–80
company
forecasting performance of, 11,
21–22
no-growth, 252–253
peer-company multiples for P/E,
403–407
positioning of, 104–105, 119

residual income model for valuation,
498–500
size of, 549, 555
company analysis. *see* financial
forecasting
company costs, 183
company culture, strategy style and,
136
company models, 202–215
company overview, 203–204
industry overview, 202–203
pro forma balance sheet, 213–214
pro forma cash flow statements,
209–214
capital investment forecast, 210
depreciation forecast, 210
and forecasted balance sheet,
213–214
working capital forecast, 210–211
pro forma income statements, 204–209
corporate income tax, 209
cost of goods sold, 205
non-operating expenses, 208–209
operating profit, 207–208
revenue forecasts, 204–205
selling, general, and administrative
costs, 205–207
valuation inputs, 214–215
company overview, 203–204
company sales, 179–181
company-specific factors
in forecast time horizon, 196
for private company valuation,
549–550
company strategy, sales and, 181
company units, strategic style for, 137
comparability, analyst adjustments for,
392
comparables (comps), 381
comparables-based valuation
enterprise value to EBITDA, 446–448
for markets, 381–383
P/E, 401–412
Fed Model, 409–411
historical P/E of company as
comparable, 411–412
industry and sector multiples, 407
overall market multiple, 407–411
peer-company multiples, 403–407
Yardeni model, 410
price to book value, 425–426
price to cash flow, 438
price to dividends, 441–442
price to sales, 432–433
in relative valuation models, 24, 25
with terminal price multiples, 415
compensation
and earnings normalization, 556
share-based employee, 10, 316–317,
551
competitive analysis, 12–16
competitive environment
and industry costs, 183
and strategic style, 129–130
competitive forces, 107–115, 168–177
for Anheuser-Busch InBev, 169–171
buyers (customers), 104, 112–113, 117
established rivals, 104, 114–115, 118
and financial forecasts, 168–177

and government regulation, 171
new entrants, 104, 108–111, 117
in Russian beer market, 172–176
substitutes, 104, 113–114, 118
suppliers, 104, 111, 117
competitive strategy, 103–127
and business context for valuation, 13
competitive forces, 107–115
defining industry in, 122–123
developing, 118–122
and drivers of profitability, 105–107
exploiting industry change in, 105,
119–120
and industry structure, 115–118,
120–122
positioning company in, 104–105, 119
practice problems, 125–126
solutions to problems, 127
suggestions for, 104–105
tactics, 105
value in, 122–124
compiled financial statements, 558
complements, 116–117
compliance valuations, of private
companies, 551–552
compound annual growth rate (CAGR),
189, 190
comprehensive income, 511, 516–520
Compustat, 69
conclusions
of equity valuation process, 12, 30–32
research report, 35
confidence, misplaced, 135
confidence risk, 80
conglomerate discounts, 27–28
*Consideration of Fraud in a Financial
Statement Audit* (American
Institute of Certified Public
Accountants), 17
consolidated affiliates, 164
consolidated income statement, 206–207
constant-growth FCFE model, 306–307
constant-growth FCFF model, 305–306
consumer goods market, 178–179
Continental AG, 402
contingent consideration, for
transaction-based price multiples,
576
continuing earnings, 388
continuing residual income, 503
continuing value, 260
contracts, 182–183
control
lack of control discounts, 582
and private company stock, 550
and required return for private
companies, 83
control premiums, 29, 573–574
cookie jar reserves, 524
Cooper Tire and Rubber, 402
core earnings, 388
corporate events, evaluating, 9
corporate income tax, 160–163, 209
cost approach, to private company
valuation, 578–580
cost of capital, weighted average. *see*
weighted average cost of capital
(WACC)
cost of debt, 50, 563

ost of equity, 50
ost of equity capital, 489
ost of goods sold (COGS), 149–151, 205
ost projections, 182–185
 company costs and inflation/deflation, 183–185
 industry costs and inflation/deflation, 182–183
 and input costs, 183–185
osts
 company, 183
 finance, 208–209
 fixed, 146–147
 industry, 182–183
 input, 177–185
  at Carrefour SA, 181–182
  and company costs, 183
  and company sales, 179–181
  and industry costs, 183
  and industry sales, 177–179
  at Nestlé and Lindt, 183–185
 operating, 146–158
 opportunity, 237
 overhead, 152
 switching, 109
 variable, 146, 188–189
ountry risk rating model, 86
ountry spread model, 86
CPI. see US Consumer Price Index (CPI)
raft Brew Alliance, Inc., 393
ross-sectional regression, for P/E, 399–400
ulture, strategy style and, 136
urrent P/E. see trailing P/E
ustomers (buyers)
 bargaining power of, 169–171, 203
 in beer markets, 170, 171
 and changes in industry structure, 117
 as competitive forces, 112–113
 in industry structure, 13
 and long-term profitability, 104
 neutralizing power of, 105
yclical businesses, 390
yclicality, 195–196

)
anone, 151
ays sales outstanding, 164
CF models. see discounted cash flow models
DM. see dividend discount model
ebt
 cost of, 50, 563
 government, 56–59
 market value of, 86–87, 305
ebt availability, 563
ebt ratio, 328
eclining growth phase, 137
eferred taxes, 316
efinition of value (term), 552–554
eflation, 177–185
 cost projection effects, 182–185
 sales projection effects, 177–182
  company sales, 179–181
  industry sales, 177–179
eimler, Mike, 132
emand, price elasticity of, 178, 179
emand-side benefits of scale, 108
emand-side estimates of equity risk premiums, 65n.28

DE Masterblenders, 183
Denmark
 FFM factors, 76n.45
 GDP growth rate, 244
 historical equity risk premium, 57, 59
depreciation, 210
developing markets, equity risk premium in, 62–63
Diebold, Inc., 429–430
diluted earnings per share, 387
dilution, 387n.10
Dime Savings Bank, 118
Dimson, Elroy, 85
discounted abnormal earnings model, 491
discounted cash flow method
 of developing terminal value, 199
 perpetuity calculations in, 200
 of private company valuation, 561–562, 567
 valuation inputs for, 214–215
discounted cash flow (DCF) models.
 see also specific types, e.g.: dividend discount model (DDM)
 as absolute valuation model, 22–23
 for equity valuation, 230
 forecasted fundamentals and multiples in, 383
 and free cash flows, 302
 residual income model vs., 508
 and valuation based on forecasted fundamentals, 397–399
discounted dividend valuation, 229–298
 about, 230–231
 dividend discount model, 239–242
  for multiple holding periods, 240–242
  for single holding period, 239–240
 Gordon growth model, 242–257
  dividend growth, earnings growth, and value appreciation in, 249–250
  equation, 242–249
  estimating required return, 256–257
  examples, 244–249
  implied dividend growth rate, 251–252
  with negative growth, 249
  for noncallable fixed-rate perpetual preferred stock, 248–249
  and present value of growth opportunities, 252–254
  and price-to-earnings ratio, 254–256
  and share repurchases, 250–251
 growth rates in, 273–279
  financial models and dividends, 278–279
  and retention rate/ROE analysis, 275–278
  sustainable, 273–274
 multistage models, 257–272
  H-model, 262–264
  for non-dividend-paying companies, 261–262
  spreadsheet modeling, 268–270
  three-stage model, 264–269
  two-stage dividend discount model, 258–261
 practice problems, 283–290
 present value models, 231–239

 for Coca-Cola Bottling Company and Hormel Foods, 234–236
 definitions of cash flows for, 233–239
 dividends in, 233–236
 free cash flows in, 236–237
 for future cash flows, 231–233
 residual income in, 237–238
 required return from, 271–272
 solutions to problems, 291–298
discount for lack of control (DLOC), 582
discount for lack of marketability (DLOM), 29, 583–584
discount rate, 231–232
 nominal, 88
 for private company, 559, 563–566
 real, 88, 337–338
 and required rate of return for private company, 563
 and returns, 53
 selection of, 88–89
discounts, 580–587
 application of, 584–586
 conglomerate, 27–28
 defined, 231
 illiquidity, 29
 for lack of control, 582
 for lack of marketability, 29, 583–584
 and premiums, 580–581
 in present value models, 60
disproportionate returns, 582
distribution channels, access to, 109
distribution expenses
 in modeling of operating costs, 151
 and pro forma income statements, 205–206
divestiture, equity valuation for, 9
dividend discount model (DDM), 239–242
 as absolute valuation model, 22–23
 for Coca-Cola Bottling Company and Hormel Foods, 234–236
 and dividends as returns, 233–236
 FCFF and FCFE vs., 302
 for multiple holding periods, 240–242
 multistage (see multistage dividend discount models)
 and residual income model, 496–497, 508–510
 and share repurchases, 250–251
 for single holding period, 239–240
dividend displacement of earnings, 274, 439
dividend policy, 164
dividend rate, 439
dividends. see also discounted dividend valuation; price to dividends (P/D)
 and FCFE, 319, 337
 and FCFF, 337
 financial policies and growth rate of, 276
 free cash flow vs., 332–334
 GAAP and IFRS on, 311
 in Gordon growth model, 249–250
 implied growth rate of, 251–252
 with negative growth, 249
 in present value models, 233–236
 spreadsheet model for, 278–279
dividends received, 434
dividend yield (D/P), 250, 394, 439–442

DLOC. *see* discount for lack of control
DLOM. *see* discount for lack of
    marketability
Dodd, David L., 384
dollar, US, 85
Donaldson Company, Inc., 26–27
Dow 30 Index, 503
Dow Jones, 402
Dow Jones Industrial Average, 391n.18
D/P. *see* dividend yield
due diligence, 31
Duke Energy, 441
DuPont. *see* E. I. DuPont de Nemours
    and Company
DuPont analysis of ROE, 270, 273,
    275–276, 431, 512
duration, 61n.21

E
E. I. DuPont de Nemours and Company
    (DuPont), 113, 260–261
earnings. *see also* price to earnings ratio
    (P/E)
  abnormal, 491
  adjusted, 388
  capitalization of earnings method, 562
  continuing, 388
  core, 388
  discounted abnormal earnings model,
    491
  dividend displacement of, 274, 439
  excess earnings method
    for private companies, 561, 562,
      569–570
    for residual income valuation,
      497n.10
  future, in residual income model,
    511–512
  in Gordon growth model, 249–250
  normalized, 196, 555–556
  persistent, 388
  press releases about, 16–17
  private company valuation and
    normalization of, 555–558
  quality of earnings analysis, 17–21
  scaled earnings surprise, 453
  standardized unexpected, 454–455
  trailing P/E with negative, zero, or low,
    392–394
  underlying, 388
  unexpected, 453–455
earnings before interest, taxes,
    depreciation, and amortization
    (EBITDA)
  adjusting, 325
  as cash flow approximation, 436n.49, 437
  enterprise value to (*see* enterprise value
    to EBITDA)
  and FCFE, 303, 324, 325
  and FCFF, 303, 324, 325, 333–334
  forecasting free cash flow with,
    333–334
  and market value of invested capital,
    572
earnings before interest, taxes and
    amortization (EBITA), 448
earnings before interest and taxes
    (EBIT)
  adjusting, 325

enterprise value to, 448
  FCFE from, 324, 325
  FCFF and FCFE vs., 303
  FCFF from, 324, 325
  forecasting, 328–329
earnings per share (EPS)
  basic, 387
  diluted, 387
  historical average, 390
  for nonrecurring items, 388–390
  normalized, 390–391
  and P/E multiples, 381, 385
  and technological cannibalization,
    189–191, 193–195
  trailing, 388–389
earnings-plus-noncash-charges
    definition of cash flow, 436
earnings surprise, 453–455
earnings yield, 393, 394
eBay, 108
EBIT. *see* earnings before interest and
    taxes
EBITA. *see* earnings before interest,
    taxes and amortization
EBITDA. *see* earnings before
    interest, taxes, depreciation, and
    amortization
economic disruption, 199
economic profit, 491
economic sectors, 401–403
  and control premiums, 573
  fundamental and valuation statistics,
    449–450
  price multiples for, 407
  ROE for, 505–506
economic value added (EVA), 492
economies of scale, 108, 147
Edison, Thomas, 134
Edwards–Bell–Ohlson model, 491
EEM. *see* excess earnings method
Efes, 172
effective tax rate, 160–163
efficiency, market, 7
efficiency ratios, 164
EIA. *see* Energy Information
    Administration
Electrolux, 117
Eli Lilly, 145
EMC Corporation, 446–448
emerging markets, country spread
    model for, 86
employee stock ownership plans
    (ESOPs), 551
Energen, 266–268
Energizer, 153
Energy Information Administration
    (EIA), 16n.
Enron Corporation, 31
enterprise value (EV), 442–448, 572n.32
enterprise value multiples, 442–450
  alternative denominators in, 448–449
  defined, 380, 442
  enterprise value to EBITDA, 442–448
    alternatives to, 448–449
    determining enterprise value,
      443–446
    valuation based on comparables,
      446–448
    valuation based on forecasted
      fundamentals, 446

enterprise value to sales, 449
  method of comparables for, 382
  price multiples vs., 449–450
enterprise value to earnings before
    interest, taxes and amortization
    (EV/EBITA), 448
enterprise value to earnings before
    interest and taxes (EV/EBIT), 448
enterprise value to EBITDA (EV/
    EBITDA), 442–448
  alternatives to, 448–449
  determining enterprise value, 443–446
  valuation based on comparables,
    446–448
  valuation based on forecasted
    fundamentals, 446
enterprise value to EBITDAR (EV/
    EBITDAR), 448
enterprise value to free cash flow to the
    firm (EV/FCFF), 448
enterprise value to sales (EV/S), 449
entry, industry, 119–120
entry price, 553
EPS. *see* earnings per share
equilibrium, 67
Equinix, 404–406, 460, 461
equity
  book value of equity
    adjusting, 421–424
    defined, 380, 416
    determining, 419–424
    and residual income, 500–501
    in residual income model, 511–512
  cost of, 50
  free cash flow to (*see* free cash flow to
    equity [FCFE])
  market value of, 86–87, 305
  required return on (*see* required return
    on equity)
  return on equity
    average, 390
    and clean surplus violations, 511–512
    and comprehensive income,
      516–518
    DuPont analysis, 270, 273, 275–276,
      431, 512
    and intangible assets, 521–524
    and residual income, 502–503
  shareholders', 416
  valuation of (*see* equity valuation)
equity capital, cost of, 489
equity charge, 489
equity premium puzzle, 60n.19
equity risk premium, 54–67
  and capital asset pricing model, 55
  demand-side estimates, 65n.28
  forward-looking estimates, 64–67
    Gordon growth model, 64–65
    macroeconomic model, 65–67
    surveys, 67
  historical estimates, 55–64
    adjusted, 61–64
    arithmetic/geometric mean, 59–60
    in developing markets, 62–63
    government bonds vs. bills, 60–61
    and returns of stocks vs. government
      debt, 56–59
  and required return on equity, 54–55
  supply-side estimates, 65–67

equity valuation, 5–46
  about, 5–6
  absolute valuation models, 22–24
  applications, 9–11
  for asset-based valuation, 23–24
  and market expectations, 10–11
  models for, 22–29
  practice problems, 40–43
  relative valuation models, 24–25
  research reports, 32–36
    contents, 32–34
    formats, 34–35
    responsibilities for reporting,
      35–36
  with residual income, 490–491
  solutions to problems, 44–46
  sum-of-the-parts valuation, 25–28
  types of value, 6–9
    fair market/investment value, 8
    going-concern/liquidation value, 8
    intrinsic value, 6–8
    summary, 9
  valuation process, 11–32
    applying valuation conclusions,
      30–32
    business context in, 11–21
    conversion of forecasts to valuations,
      29
    forecasting company performance,
      21–22
    selecting valuation models, 22–29
Erb, Claude, 86n.55
ESOPs. see employee stock ownership
    plans
established rivals
  in beer markets, 170, 171
  and changes in industry structure, 118
  in cognac industry, 202
  as competitive forces, 114–115
  competitive strategy for, 104
  and financial forecasts, 169–171
  limiting threats from, 105
Estée Lauder, 153
estimates
  accounting, 389n.12
  aggressive, 19
  of equity risk premium
    demand-side estimates, 65n.28
    forward-looking estimates, 64–67
    historical estimates, 55–64
    supply-side estimates, 65–67
  ex ante, 64–67
  of intrinsic value, 51–53
  of matrix price, 443n.56
  of required rate of return, 562–566
  of required return, 256–257
E*TRADE Financial Corp., 426
EU. see European Union
Europe, revenue analysis, 141, 142
European beer market, 177–178
European Petroleum Industry
    Association (EUROPIA), 16n.
European Union (EU), dividend policy,
    233, 234
Eurozone, Gordon growth model, 64
EV. see enterprise value
EVA. see economic value added
EV/EBIT. see enterprise value to
    earnings before interest and taxes

EV/EBITA. see enterprise value to
    earnings before interest, taxes and
    amortization
EV/EBITDA. see enterprise value to
    EBITDA
EV/EBITDAR. see enterprise value to
    EBITDAR
EV/FCFF. see enterprise value to free
    cash flow to the firm
EV/S. see enterprise value to sales
ex ante alpha, 50
ex ante estimates, 64–67
excess earnings method (EEM). see also
    residual income method
  for private companies, 561, 562,
    569–570
  for residual income valuation, 497n.10
exchange rates, required return on
    equity and, 85
excise duty, 173
executives, strategy selection mistakes
    of, 135–136
existing competitors. see established rivals
exit, industry, 119
exit barriers, 114
exit price, 553
expanded CAPM, 562
expected alpha, 50
expected holding-period return, 49
expected retaliation, in competitive
    strategy, 110, 111
expected return, 50–53
expenses
  distribution, 151, 205–206
  financing, 159–160
  interest, 159–160
  minority interest, 164
  non-operating, 159–163, 208–209
  as quality of earnings indicators, 18
  selling, general, and administrative,
    151–152, 205–207
ex post alpha, 50
Exxon Mobil Corporation, 71, 131, 132,
    454–455

F
Facebook, 129, 134
factor beta, 75
factor risk premium, 75
factor sensitivity, 75
fair market value, 8, 552
fairness opinions, rendering, 10
fair value
  balance sheet adjustments, 520–521
  defined, 8, 424n.34, 553
  standards for, 587–588
fair value accounting, book value per
    share and, 421–424
"Fair Value Measurement" (ASC 820),
    551n.5, 553n.12–13, 571
"Fair Value Measurement" (IFRS 13),
    553n.12
"Fair Value Measurement" (SFAS 157),
    29n.13, 551n.5, 553n.13
Fama, Eugene, 75
Fama–French model (FFM), 75–79, 400
FCFE. see free cash flow to equity
FCFF. see free cash flow to the firm
federally related transactions, 587n.47

FedEx, 134
Fed Model, 409–411
FFM. see Fama–French model
FIFO inventory accounting. see first-in,
    first-out inventory accounting
finance costs, 208–209
Financial Conduct Authority, 576
financial forecasting, 139–227
  about, 140
  company models, 202–215
    company overview, 203–204
    industry overview, 202–203
    pro forma balance sheet, 213–214
    pro forma cash flow statement,
      209–214
    pro forma income statement,
      204–209
    valuation inputs, 214–215
  competitive forces, 168–177
    for Anheuser-Busch InBev, 169–171
    five forces framework, 168–177
    and government regulation, 171
    in Russian beer market, 172–176
  financial modeling, 140–168
    balance sheet, 164–166
    cash flow statement, 164, 166
    income statement, 140–164
    scenario and sensitivity analyses,
      167–168
  inflation/deflation, 177–185
    cost projection effects, 182–185
    sales projection effects, 177–182
  long-term, 195–201
    assumptions in, 200–201
    historical valuation multiples in,
      198–199
    normalized revenue case study,
      196–201
  practice problems, 217–223
  solutions to problems, 224–227
  technological developments, 185–195
    base case scenarios for, 193, 194
    bull and bear case scenarios for,
      193–195
    estimating impact of cannibalization,
      191–195
    quantifying potential for
      cannibalization, 185–191
financial information, quality of,
    549–550
financial leverage, 405n.26, 412
financial modeling, 140–168
  balance sheet, 164–166
  of growth rates, 278–279
  income statement, 140–164
  scenario and sensitivity analyses,
    167–168
financial policies, ROA/dividend growth
    rate and, 276
financial ratios, in comparables-based
    valuation, 403
financial reports
  for equity valuation, 14, 16
  for private company valuation,
    551–552
financial statements, 558. see also
    specific statements
Financial Times Stock Exchange (FTSE),
    402

financial transactions, 573
financing activities, cash flow from, 311
financing expenses, 159–160
financing transactions, private company, 551
Finland, 57, 59, 76n.45
first-in, first-out (FIFO) inventory accounting, 392, 421
five-factor BIRR model, 80–81
five forces framework, 168–177, 202–203. *see also* competitive forces; competitive strategy
fixed capital, FCFF and, 308
fixed costs, 146–147
fixed-rate perpetual preferred stock, 248–249
flexibility, strategic, 137
food retailers, 179–180
forecasted fundamentals-based valuation
   enterprise value to EBITDA, 446
   forward P/E, 397–399
   justified P/E, 397–399
   of markets, 383–384
   price to book value, 424–425
   price to cash flow, 437–438
   price to dividends, 440–441
   price to earnings, 397–400
   price to sales, 431–432
forecasts. *see also* financial forecasting
   by appraisers and management, 559–560
   capital investment, 210
   of company performance, 11, 21–22
   corporate income tax, 209
   depreciation, 210
   dividend, 278–279
   equity valuations from, 12, 29
   FCFE, 327–329, 331
   FCFF, 327–331
   of free cash flow (*see* free cash flow, forecasts of)
   of growth, 276–278
   per-share residual income, 493–494
   revenue, 204–205
   sales, 331
   working capital, 210–211
Form 6-K, 16
Form 10-K, 16, 429–430
Form 10-Q, 16
Form 20-F, 16
forward dividend yield, 250
forward-looking estimates of equity risk premium, 64–67
   Gordon growth model, 64–65
   macroeconomic model, 65–67
   surveys, 67
forward P/E, 383, 386, 394–399
FPL Group, Inc., 256
franc, Swiss, 85
France
   FFM factors, 76n.45
   GDP growth rate, 244
   historical equity risk premium, 57, 59
free cash flow
   dividends vs., 332–334
   forecasts of, 307–337
      analyst adjustments to CFO, 332
      and capital structure, 335–337
      free cash flow vs. dividends, 332–334

mistakes with net income and EBITDA, 334
      noncash charges, 313–318
      working capital effects, 317–318
   in present value models, 236–237
   for private companies, 559–561
   and sales, 329–331
free cash flow method, of private company valuation, 561–562, 567
free cash flow to equity (FCFE)
   from CFO, 320–324
   defined, 303
   from EBIT, 324, 325
   from EBITDA, 324, 325
   from FCFF, 319–324
   forecasting, 327–329, 331
   and free cash flow as returns, 236–237
   free cash flow valuation approach, 303–307
      constant-growth FCFE model, 306–307
      defining cash flow, 303–304
      present value of FCFE, 305
      sensitivity analysis, 339–340
   negative, 304
   from net income, 320–324
   present value of, 305
   and price of cash flow, 434, 436–437
   for private companies, 559–560
   residual income model vs., 508
   from sales forecasts, 331
   single-stage model, 337–339
   three-stage growth model, 347
   two-stage free cash flow model, 340–347
   on uses-of-free-cash-flow-basis, 326–327
free cash flow to equity (FCFE) valuation model, 23
free cash flow to the firm (FCFF)
   defined, 303
   from EBIT, 324, 325
   from EBITDA, 324, 325
   FCFE from, 319–324
   forecasting, 327–331
   and free cash flow as returns, 236, 237
   free cash flow valuation approach, 303–306
      constant-growth FCFF model, 305–306
      defining cash flow, 303–304
      present value of FCFF, 304–305
      sensitivity analysis of, 339
   from net income, 307–310
   present value of, 304–305
   for private companies, 559–560
   residual income model vs., 508
   from statement of cash flows, 311–312
   three-stage growth model, 347–349
   two-stage free cash flow model, 340, 341
   on uses-of-free-cash-flow-basis, 326–327
free cash flow to the firm (FCFF) valuation model, 23
free cash flow valuation, 301–377
   about, 302
   FCFE approach, 303–307
      constant-growth FCFE model, 306–307

defining cash flow, 303–304
      present value of FCFE, 305
   FCFF approach, 303–306
      constant-growth FCFF model, 305–306
      defining cash flow, 303–304
      present value of FCFF, 304–305
   forecasting free cash flow, 307–337
      analyst adjustments to CFO, 332
      and capital structure, 335–337
      FCFE and FCFF from EBIT/EBITDA, 324–325
      FCFE and FCFF on uses-of-free-cash-flow basis, 326–327
      FCFE from FCFF, 319–324
      FCFF from net income, 307–310
      FCFF from statement of cash flows, 311–312
      forecasting FCFE and FCFF, 327–331
      free cash flow vs. dividends, 332–334
      mistakes with net income and EBITDA, 334
      noncash charges, 313–318
      working capital effects, 317–318
   model variations, 337–349
      for international stocks, 337–339
      and sensitivity analysis of FCFF and FCFE valuations, 339–340
      single-stage model, 337–339
      three-stage model, 347–349
      two-stage model, 340–347
   for nonoperating assets, 349
   practice problems, 353–365
   solutions to problems, 366–377
French, Kenneth, 75
front-end loading, 434
Frontier Communications Corp., 404–407, 460, 461
FTSE. *see* Financial Times Stock Exchange
FTSE Global Classification System, 402
Fuji, 107
fundamental P/E, 254–256
fundamentals. *see also* forecasted fundamentals-based valuation
   defined, 9
   forward P/E based on, 397–400
   market-based valuation with, 383–384
   in peer-group comparison, 405–407
   terminal price multiples based on, 414
future cash flows, for present value models, 231–233
future earnings, in residual income model, 511–512

G

GAAP. *see* generally accepted accounting principles
gains
   nonoperating, 524
   as quality of earnings indicators, 18
GATX Corporation, 402–403
GDP. *see* gross domestic product
General Electric, 117, 283, 291
generally accepted accounting principles (GAAP). *see also* US generally accepted accounting principles (US GAAP)
   adjusted earnings, 388
   and sales on bill-and-hold basis, 429, 430

General Motors, 283, 291, 488
general three-stage dividend discount
    model, 264–265
geographic analysis of revenue, 141
geographic scope, industries', 123
geometric mean, 56, 59–60
Germany
    FFM factors, 76n.45
    GDP growth rate, 244
    historical equity risk premium, 57, 59
Getinge AB, 431–433
GGM. *see* Gordon growth model
Global and Industry Classification
    System (GICS), 73, 402, 450
global financial crisis (2008), 199
going-concern assumption, 8
going-concern value, 8, 578
goodwill, 421, 491
"Goodwill and Other Intangible Assets"
    (ASC 350), 551n.5–6
"Goodwill and Other Intangible Assets"
    (SFAS 142), 551n.5
goodwill impairment, 491, 548, 551–552,
    576
Goodyear Tire & Rubber Company, 402
Google, Inc.
    and cannibalization of PC market, 186
    innovations by, 129
    long-term growth, 200
    present value of growth opportunities,
        253
    residual income model for valuation,
        498–500
Gordon growth model (GGM), 242–257
    dividend growth in, 249–250
    dividend yield from, 440–441
    earnings growth in, 249–250
    equation, 242–249
    equity risk premium from, 64–65
    examples, 244–249
    expected rate of return from, 256–257
    future dividend growth pattern, 241
    implied dividend growth rate, 251–252
    justified P/B from, 424
    justified P/E from, 254–256, 397–398
    with negative growth, 249
    for noncallable fixed-rate perpetual
        preferred stock, 248–249
    and present value of growth
        opportunities, 252–254
    and price-to-earnings ratio, 254–256
    P/S estimates from, 431
    required return from, 256–257
    and share repurchases, 250–251
    and terminal price multiples, 414–416
    in two-stage dividend discount model,
        258
    value appreciation in, 249–250
government bills, 57–58, 60–61
government bonds, 57, 59–61
government debt, returns for stock vs.,
    56–59
government policy, 109–110, 116
government regulations
    and competitive forces, 171
    and long-term forecasts, 199–200
GPCM. *see* guideline public company
    method
Graham, Benjamin, 19–20, 384

Great Plains Energy, 284
grocery segment, gross margins in,
    150–151
gross domestic product (GDP)
    in equity risk premium estimate, 65–67
    growth rate of, 243–244
    growth relative to GDP growth
        approach, 143
Grossman-Stiglitz paradox, 6
gross margin, 150–151
Groupon, 430
growth. *see also* Gordon growth model
    (GGM)
    constant-growth FCFE model, 306–307
    constant-growth FCFF model, 305–306
    dividend, 249–250
    and equity risk premium, 66
    forecasting, 276–278
    no-growth company, 252–253
    in perpetuity calculations, 200
    present value of growth opportunities,
        252–254
    sales, 330–331, 345–347
    supernormal, 257
    and survival strategies, 130
    value of, 252–254
growth capital expenditures, 165
growth phase, company, 137, 257,
    415–416
growth rates
    in dividend discount valuation,
        273–279
    implied dividend, 251–252
    as industry attribute, 116
    sustainable, 270, 273–274
    in three-stage dividend discount
        model, 266–268
    in two-stage model for free cash flow
        valuation, 341–347
growth relative to GDP growth
    approach, 143
Grupo Aeroportuario del Sureste, 201
Grupo Schincariol, 169
GTM. *see* guideline transactions method
guideline assets, 381
guideline companies, 381
guideline public company method
    (GPCM), 562, 571–575
guideline transactions method (GTM),
    571, 576–578

H
habits, unexamined, 135
Haier, 137
Halliburton Co., 14
Hammond, P. Brett, 67
harmonic mean, 459–461
Harvey, Campbell R., 86n.55
Hawawini, Gabriel, 165n.4, 165n.5
hedging strategies, 150, 182–183
Heineken, 169, 170, 172
Henkel, 152, 153
Hennessy, 207
Henry, E., 451n.58
historical analysis, business context for
    valuation and, 13–14
historical average earnings per share, 390
historical estimates of equity risk
    premium, 55–64

adjusted, 61–64
arithmetic/geometric mean, 59–60
in developing markets, 62–63
for long-term government bonds vs.
    short-term government bills,
    60–61
and returns of stocks vs. government
    debt, 56–59
historical P/E, 411–412
historical tables, research report, 35
historical valuation multiples,
    198–199
HML factor, 76
H-model, 258, 262–265
holding period returns, 48–49
holding periods
    DDM for multiple, 240–242
    DDM for single, 239–240
Home Depot, 117
Honda Motor Company, 411–412
Hong Kong, 76n.45
Hormel Foods, 234–236
human capital, 417
hybrid approach
    modeling operating costs, 146
    modeling revenue, 143, 144

I
IASB. *see* International Accounting
    Standards Board
IBM. *see* International Business
    Machines Corporation
ICB. *see* Industrial Classification
    Benchmark
IEA. *see* International Energy Agency
IFRS. *see* International Financial
    Reporting Standards
IGBVT. *see* International Glossary of
    Business Valuation Terms
IKEA, 548
illiquidity discounts, 29
impairment, 491
"Impairment of Assets" (IAS 36),
    551n.5–6
implied dividend growth rate,
    251–252
income
    accumulated other comprehensive,
        516
    comprehensive, 511, 516–520
    from consolidated affiliates, 164
    in equity risk premium estimate, 66
    interest, 158–159
    net
        adjusting, 320–324
        FCFE from, 320–324
        FCFF from, 307–310, 320–324
        and mistakes in forecasting free cash
            flows, 334
        and two-stage model for free cash
            flows, 343–345
    normalized operating, 161
    other comprehensive, 500n.12, 516–520
    per-share residual, 493–494
    persistence of, 506–507
    residual, 488–493 (*see also* residual
        income model; residual income
        valuation)
        calculation, 489–490

commercial implementations, 492–493
continuing residual income, 503
determinants of, 500–501
equity valuation with, 490–491
in present value models, 237–238
returns as, 237–238
income approach to private company valuation, 554, 561–570
capitalized cash flow method, 567–569
and discount rate for private company, 563–566
excess earnings method, 569–570
free cash flow method, 567
required rate of return from, 562–566
income models of valuation, 22n.8
income statement modeling, 140–164
non-operating costs, 159–163
operating costs, 146–158
revenue, 140–146
income statements
IFRS and US GAAP on, 140
in industry analysis, 110–111
pro forma, 204–209
corporate income tax, 209
cost of goods sold, 205
non-operating expenses, 208–209
operating profit, 207–208
revenue forecasts, 204–205
selling, general, and administrative costs, 205–207
income tax, corporate, 160–163, 209
incumbency advantages, 109
incumbent companies, rivalries with. see established rivals
indexes
and estimation of beta, 68
and relative strength indicators, 456–458
India, 62–63, 86
Industrial Classification Benchmark (ICB), 73, 402
industrial conglomerates, 402
industry(-ies)
classifications of, 401–403
defining, in competitive strategy, 122–123
exploiting, in competitive strategy, 119–120
industry structure vs. attributes of, 115–117
price multiples for, 407
profitability of, 106–107
selecting strategic style based on, 130–131, 133
industry analysis. see also financial forecasting
in competitive strategies, 110–111
for equity valuation, 12–14
mistakes with, 124
steps in, 123–124
industry costs, 182–183
industry factors, for control premiums, 573
industry leaders, reshaping of industry by, 121
industry overview, 202–203
industry sales, 177–179
industry structure, 115–118

attributes of industry vs., 115–117
changes in, 105, 117–118
as context for valuation, 12–13
shaping, with competitive strategy, 120–122
inflation, 177–185
cost projection effects, 182–185
company costs, 183–185
industry costs, 182–183
input costs at Lindt and Nestlé, 183–185
and equity risk premium, 66
and Fed Model, 410
and P/E, 412–414
sales projection effects, 177–182
company sales, 179–181
industry sales, 177–179
input costs at Carrefour SA, 181–182
and single-stage model of valuation, 337–338
inflation risk, 80
inflection points, long-term forecast, 199–200
information
for equity valuation, 16–21
quality of, 549–550
initial public offerings (IPOs), 10, 551, 583–584
input costs
at Carrefour SA, 181–182
and company costs, 183–185
and company sales, 179–181
and industry costs, 183
and industry sales, 177–179
at Nestlé and Lindt, 183–185
Institute of Business Appraisers, 552n.9
intangible assets
in excess earnings method, 570
and private company valuation, 548
in residual income valuations, 521–524
"Intangible Assets" (IAS 38), 551n.5, 570n.29
Intel Corporation, 10–11, 108, 121
interest
carried, 579n.37
FCFF and after-tax, 308
under GAAP and IFRS, 311
interest expense, 159–160
interest income, 158–159
interest paid, 434
interest rates, P/E of market and, 410–411
interest received, 434
internal rate of return (IRR), 53–54, 65
International Accounting Standards, 236n.10
"Impairment of Assets" (IAS 36), 551n.5–6
"Intangible Assets" (IAS 38), 551n.5, 570n.29
International Accounting Standards Board (IASB), 553n.12
International Business Machines Corporation (IBM)
competitive strategies, 108, 121
cost of equity, 84–85
forecasting growth for, 277–278
forward P/E, 395

sustainable growth rate calculation, 270
three-stage DDM, 265
weighted cost of capital, 87–88
international considerations
for market-based valuation, 451–452
with required return on equity, 85–86
for residual income model, 525
International Energy Agency (IEA), 16n.
International Federation of Accountants, 17
International Financial Reporting Standards (IFRS)
adjusted earnings, 388
available-for-sale investments, 512
book value of equity, 500, 511
business combinations, 570
fair value, 551n.5, 553, 587
goodwill impairment tests, 551
income statements, 140
intangible assets, 548
interest and dividends, 311
interest classifications, 436
LIFO inventory accounting, 521
nonfinancial assets, 424
operating cash flow, 434
prevalence of, 525
R&D expenditures, 417, 523
residual income, 501
share-based compensation, 316, 552n.7
US GAAP vs., 451–452
and US SEC reconciliation requirement, 451
International Glossary of Business Valuation Terms (IGBVT), 552n.9, 555
international stocks, free cash flow valuation for, 337–339
International Valuation Standards (IVS), 587
International Valuation Standards Council (IVSC), 553, 587, 588
internet software industry
shaping strategies for, 133, 134
strategy in oil industry vs., 129–130
intra-industry rivalry, 13
intrinsic value, 6–8
defined, 553–554
and discount rate, 53
estimates of, 51–53
and internal rate of return, 53–54
from residual income model, 493–496, 501
inventory, projecting future, 164
inventory accounting
and comparability, 392, 421
and fair value, 521
inventory turnover, 164
inverse price ratios, 393, 394
invested capital, 165n.4
market value of, 446, 572
return on, 106–107, 446, 490n.5
total, 446
investing activities, cash flow from, 311
investment decisions, market-based factors in, 462–463
investment strategy, forecast time horizon and, 195
investment value, 8, 553

investors
  short-term, 550
  venture capital, 551
iPad, 185–186
iPod, 120
IPOs. *see* initial public offerings
IPRD Practice Aid. *see Assets Acquired in a Business Combination to Be Used in Research and Development Activities*
Ireland
  FFM factors, 76n.45
  historical equity risk premium, 57, 59
IRR. *see* internal rate of return
Italy
  FFM factors, 76n.45
  GDP growth rate, 244
  historical equity risk premium, 57, 59
iTunes, 105, 117, 120
IVS. *see* International Valuation Standards
IVSC. *see* International Valuation Standards Council

J
Japan
  analysis of revenue for, 141, 142
  dividend policy, 233
  FFM factors, 76n.45
  GDP growth rate, 244
  historical equity risk premium, 57–59
Johnson & Johnson, 271–272
J.P. Morgan Chase & Company, 92, 97
justified P/B, 424–425, 501
justified P/CF, 437–438
justified P/E, 254–256, 397–399
justified price multiples, 384
justified P/S, 431–432
JVC, 117

K
Kansas City Southern Preferred, 249
Kimberly-Clark, 152n.2, 153
Kmart, 117
Kodak, 107, 199, 200
Koninklijke Philips Electronics N.V., 436
Korea, 141, 142

L
lack of control discounts, 582
lack of marketability discounts, 29, 583–584
Larsen & Toubro Ltd, 69–71, 93, 98
last-in, first-out (LIFO) inventory accounting, 392, 421, 521
law of one price, 382–383
leading dividend yield, 439
leading P/E, 254–255, 386
Leibowitz, Martin L., 67
leverage
  and FCFE/FCFF, 337
  financial, 405n.26, 412
  and ROE, 275
leveraged buyouts, 9
leverage ratios, 165
lifecycle, company's stage in, 137, 549
LIFO inventory accounting. *see* last-in, first-out inventory accounting
Lin, S., 451n.58
Lindt, 183–185
LinkedIn, 201

LIQ factor, 79
liquidation value, 8
liquidity
  illiquidity discounts, 29
  marketability vs., 80
  of private company stock, 550
litigation, 552, 553
Livent, Inc., 20–21
long-term assets, projections of, 165
long-term financial forecasting, 195–201
  assumptions in, 200–201
  historical valuation multiples in, 198–199
  normalized revenue case study, 196–201
long-term government bonds, 60–61
long-term growth, 200
look-ahead bias, 463
L'Oréal, 152–154
losses, as quality of earnings indicators, 18
low earnings, trailing P/E with, 393–394

M
McDonald's Corp, 253
macroeconomic model
  for equity risk premium, 65–67
  for required return on equity, 80–81
Macy's Inc., 253
maintenance capital expenditures, 165
Malaysia, 76n.45
malleability
  estimating level of, 136
  and strategic style, 130–131, 133
management, 549, 559
Manufacturers Hanover Corporation, 118
margin, gross, 150–151
marketability
  lack of marketability discounts, 29, 583–584
  liquidity vs., 80
  and required return for private companies, 82–83
market approach to private company valuation, 554, 571–578
  guideline public company method, 572–575
  guideline transactions method, 576–578
  prior transactions method, 578
market-based valuation, 379–485
  about, 380–381
  enterprise value multiples, 442–450
    alternative denominators in, 448–449
    enterprise value to EBITDA, 442–448
    enterprise value to sales, 449
    price multiples vs., 449–450
  harmonic mean, 459–461
  international considerations, 451–452
  issues with, 459–465
  method based on forecasted fundamentals, 383–384
  method of comparables, 381–383
  momentum indicators, 453–458
    relative strength indicators, 455–458
    scaled earnings surprise, 453
    and unexpected earnings, 453–455
  multiple indicators in, 461–465
  practice problems, 470–478
  price multiples, 384–442

price to book value, 416–426
price to cash flow, 433–438
price to dividends and dividend yield, 439–442
price to earnings ratio, 384–416
price to sales, 427–433
solutions to problems, 479–485
market bubble (1998-2000), 428
market capitalization, 408
market efficiency, 7
market expectations
  and equity valuation, 10–11
  inferring, 9–11
market growth and market share approach, 143–144
market multiple, for P/E, 407–411
market share, 143–144
market timing risk, 81
market value, 553
market value added (MVA), 492
market value of common equity (MVCE; MV[Equity]), 86–87, 305
market value of debt (MVD; MV[Debt]), 86–87, 305
market value of invested capital (MVIC), 446, 572
Marsh, Paul, 85
Marshall, Alfred, 488
matrix price estimates, 443n.56
mature growth phase, 137, 258, 415–416
mature growth rate, 258
mean
  arithmetic, 56, 59–60, 460–461
  geometric, 56, 59–60
  harmonic, 459–461
"The Measurement and Application of Market Participant Acquisition Premiums" (Appraisal Foundation), 573n.34
medical device manufacturing, 200
Mendocino Brewing Company, Inc., 393
Merck, 117
mergers, 9
Merrill Lynch Institutional Factor Survey. see BofA Merrill Lynch Institutional Factor Survey
method based on forecasted fundamentals, 383–384. *see also* forecasted fundamentals-based valuation
method of comparables. *see also* comparables-based valuation
  market-based valuation with, 381–383
  in relative valuation models, 24, 25
Michelin, 402
Microsoft Corporation
  cannibalization factor of tablet computers for, 185–195
  competitive strategy of, 108, 111, 116, 121
  in internet software industry, 129
  NTM P/E, 395
  required return on shares, 52–53, 77–79
Middlesex Water Company, 245–248
minority interest, 443n.54
minority interest expense, 164
mispricing, 7–8
Molodovsky, Nicholas, 390n.15

Molodovsky effect, 390
Molson-Coors Brewing Co., 170, 393
momentum indicators, 453–458
  defined, 381
  relative strength indicators, 455–458
  scaled earnings surprise, 453
  and unexpected earnings, 453–455
Mondelez International, 183
Moody's Investor Service, 410
Morgan Stanley Capital International
  (MSCI), 402
Morningstar, 69, 86
MSCI World index, 68
multicollinearity, 400
multifactor models for required return
  on equity, 75–81
  and arithmetic mean, 60
  Fama-French model, 75–79
  macroeconomic, 80–81
  Pastor–Stambaugh model, 79–80
  statistical, 80
multistage dividend discount models,
  257–272
  H-model, 262–264
  for non-dividend-paying companies,
    261–262
  spreadsheet modeling, 268–270
  three-stage model, 264–269
    with declining growth rates, 265–268
    with distinct stages, 264–265
  two-stage dividend discount model,
    258–261
    and P/E model, 260–261
    valuing stock with, 258–260
multistage residual income model,
  503–507
MV(Debt). *see* market value of debt
MV(Equity). *see* market value of
  common equity
MVA. *see* market value added
MVCE. *see* market value of common
  equity
MVD. *see* market value of debt
MVIC. *see* market value of invested
  capital
MySpace, 134

N
Nano, 134
NASDAQ Global Select Market
  (NASDAQ-GS), 10n.3, 52n.5
National Association of Certified
  Valuation Analysts, 552n.9
National Oilwell Varco Inc., 15
negative earnings, trailing P/E with, 393
negative growth, dividend with, 249
Nestlé, 183–185
Net App, 446–448
Netflix, 113
Netherlands
  FFM factors, 76n.45
  GDP growth rate, 244
  historical equity risk premium, 57, 59
net income
  adjusting, 320–324
  FCFE from, 320–324
  FCFF from, 307–310, 320–324
  mistakes in forecasting free cash flow
    with, 334

  and two-stage model for free cash
    flows, 343–345
net operating profit less adjusted taxes
  (NOPLAT), 165
network effects, 108
new entrants
  in beer markets, 170, 171
  and changes in industry structure, 117
  in cognac industry, 203
  as competitive forces, 108–111
  and financial forecasting, 169–171
  in industry structure, 13
  limiting threats from, 105
  and long-term profitability, 104
Newmont Mining, 92, 97
New York Times, 200
New Zealand, 57, 59, 76n.45
NextEra Energy, Inc., 256–257
next twelve month price-to-earnings
  ratio (NTM P/E), 395
no-growth company, 252–253
no-growth value per share, 253
Nokia Corporation
  clean surplus violations, 513,
    514, 516
  long-term forecasts for, 200
  statement of changes in stockholder
    equity, 514
nominal discount rate, 88
nominal GDP growth, 244
noncallable fixed-rate perpetual
  preferred stock, 248–249
noncash charges
  and FCFF, 307–308, 324
  and forecasting free cash flow, 313–318
noncash consideration, 576
non-dividend-paying companies, DDM
  for, 261–262
non-dividend paying stock, valuing,
  261–262
nonearning assets, 443
nonfinancial assets, 424
nonfinancial measurements, enterprise
  value for, 448–449
nonoperating assets, 349, 555
non-operating expenses
  modeling of, 159–163
  on pro forma income statements,
    208–209
nonoperating gains, 524
nonpublic companies, beta for, 73–75
nonrecurring items, 388–390, 524
nonstationarity, 56
non-traded assets, 72–75
NOPLAT. *see* net operating profit less
  adjusted taxes
normalized earnings, 196, 555–556
normalized earnings per share (normal
  EPS), 390–391
normalized operating income, 161
normalized P/Es, 387
normalized revenue, 196–201
North America
  analysis of revenue for, 141, 142
  Gordon growth model for, 64
Norway, 57, 59, 76n.45
Novo Nordisk, 141–146
NTM P/E. *see* next twelve month price-
  to-earnings ratio

O
Occidental Petroleum, 24
OCI. *see* other comprehensive income
off-balance sheet financing, 18
off-balance sheet liabilities, 421
oil industry, 129–132
one price, law of, 382–383
operating cash flow, 18, 434
operating costs, 146–158
operating income, normalized, 161
operating profit, 207–208
opportunity cost, 237
opportunity lists, 430
options
  put, 583
  real, 253–254
orderly liquidation value, 8
other comprehensive income (OCI),
  500n.12, 516–520
outliers, harmonic mean and, 460
overall market multiple, for P/E, 407–411
overhead costs, 152

P
Paccar, 104–105, 119
pairs trading, 24
Pastor–Stambaugh model (PSM), 79–80
payout ratio, 441
P/B. *see* price to book value
P/CF. *see* price to cash flow
P/D. *see* price to dividends
P/E. *see* price to earnings ratio
peer-company multiples, P/E, 403–407
PEG ratio, 405
P/E median, 411
Pepco Holdings, 441
Pepsi, 108
perpetual preferred stock, 248–249
perpetuities
  defined, 248
  residual income model for valuing,
    508–510
perpetuity calculations, long-term
  forecast, 200
per-share residual income forecasts,
  493–494
persistence, income, 506–507
persistent earnings, 388
personal computer industry, 185–195
personal-use assets, 556
Petroleo Brasileiro (Petrobras), 24,
  339–340
Petropolis, 169
planning cycles, 131–133
Playdom, 134
Playfish, 134
Porter, Michael E., 104, 108n.1, 116n.2, 168
Portland General Electric Co., 441, 442
PP&E. *see* property, plant, and
  equipment
PPL Corp., 441–442
PRAT model, 277–278
predictability
  estimating level of, 136
  and strategic style, 130–131, 133
predicted P/E, 399–400
preferred stock, 248–249, 335–337
premise of value (term), 552n.8
premiumization, 169

premiums. see also risk premiums
in build-up approaches, 81–83
control, 29, 573–574
defined, 54
and discounts in private company
valuation, 580–581
size, 562
present value
adjusted, 304n.2
of FCFE, 305
of FCFF, 304–305
present value models, 231–239
as absolute valuation models, 22–23
and build-up approaches, 81
for Coca-Cola Bottling Company and
Hormel Foods, 234–236
definitions of cash flows for, 233–239
dividends in, 233–236
free cash flows in, 236–237
for future cash flows, 231–233
and geometric mean, 60
residual income in, 237–238
present value of growth opportunities
(PVGO), 252–254
press releases, earnings, 16–17
price
entry, 553
exit, 553
growth rate implied by stock, 251–252
law of one, 382–383
terminal share, 242
value vs., 6–8
volume and price approach, 144
price competition, 114–115
price elasticity of demand, 178, 179
price momentum, 455–456
price multiples, 384–442
defined, 380
enterprise multiples vs., 449–450
for guideline transactions method, 576
justified, 384
method of comparables for, 381–382
price to book value, 416–426
price to cash flow, 433–438
price to earnings ratio, 384–416
price to sales, 427–433
from residual income model, 511
price to book value (P/B), 416–426
adjusting book value, 421–424
determining book value, 419–424
drawbacks to using, 417–418
and inverse ratio, 394
P/E vs., 416–417
rationale for, 416–417
and residual income, 501
valuation based on comparables,
425–426
valuation based on forecasted
fundamentals, 424–425
price to cash flow (P/CF), 433–438
accounting methods and cash flow, 435
determining cash flow, 435–437
drawbacks to using, 434
and inverse ratio, 394
price to dividends and dividend yield,
439–442
calculating dividend yield, 439–440
valuation based on comparables,
441–442

valuation based on forecasted
fundamentals, 440–441
rationale for, 434
valuation based on comparables, 438
valuation based on forecasted
fundamentals, 437–438
price to dividends (P/D), 439–442
calculating dividend yield, 439–440
and inverse ratio, 394
valuation based on comparables,
441–442
valuation based on forecasted
fundamentals, 440–441
price to earnings ratio (P/E), 384–416
alternative definitions, 386–387
based on cross-sectional regression,
399–400
in cross-country comparisons,
412–414
and dividend discount model, 260–261
forward P/E, 383, 394–399
and GGM equity risk premium
estimate, 65
and Gordon growth model, 254–256
harmonic mean, 459–461
and inflation, 412–414
and inverse, 394
and macroeconomic equity risk
premium estimate, 66
P/B vs., 416–417
and present value of opportunities, 254
in relative valuation model, 24
terminal price multiples, 414–416
based on comparables, 415
based on fundamentals, 414
in valuation of mature growth phase,
415–416
trailing P/E, 387–394
and business-cycle influence,
390–392
and comparability with other
companies, 392
with negative, zero, or low earnings,
392–394
and nonrecurring items, 388–390
and two-stage dividend discount
model, 260–261
valuation based on comparables,
400–412
historical P/E of company as
comparable, 411–412
industry and sector multiples, 407
overall market multiple, 407–411
peer-company multiples, 403–407
valuation based on forecasted
fundamentals, 397–400
justified P/E, 397–399
P/E based on cross-sectional
regression, 399–400
price to sales (P/S), 427–433
determining sales, 428–430
and inverse ratio, 394
and revenue recognition, 428–430
valuation based on comparables,
432–433
valuation based on forecasted
fundamentals, 431–432
prior transactions method (PTM), 571,
578

private company valuation, 547–600
about, 548
approaches, 554–588
asset-based approach, 578–580
build-up method for, 81–84
cash flow estimation issue, 559–561
discounts, 580–587
application of discounts, 584–586
lack of control discounts, 582
lack of marketability discounts,
583–584
and premiums, 580–581
earnings normalization issue, 555–558
equity valuation in, 10
income approach, 561–570
capitalized cash flow method,
567–569
and discount rate for private
company, 563–566
estimations of required rate of return,
562–566
excess earnings method, 569–570
free cash flow method, 567
market approach, 571–578
guideline public company method,
572–575
guideline transactions method,
576–578
prior transactions method, 578
practice problems, 591–597
public company valuation vs., 548–550
company-specific factors, 549–550
stock-specific factors in, 550
reasons for performing, 550–552
solutions to problems, 598–600
standards and practices for, 587–588
standards of value, 552–554
private market value, 25
Procter & Gamble, 152, 153
product line analysis of revenue, 141
Professional Conduct Statement, 32
profit
economic, 491
net operating profit less adjusted taxes,
165
operating, 207–208
profitability
drivers of, 105–107
in industry analysis, 110
and price competition, 114–115
redividing, 120–121
profit pool, expanding, 121–122
pro forma balance sheets, 213–214
pro forma cash flow statements,
209–214
capital investment forecast, 210
depreciation forecast, 210
and forecasted balance sheet, 213–214
forecasted cash flow statement,
211–213
working capital forecast, 210–211
pro forma income statements, 204–209
corporate income tax forecast, 209
cost of goods sold, 205
non-operating expenses, 208–209
operating profit, 207–208
revenue forecasts, 204–205
selling, general, and administrative
costs, 205–207

pro forma tables, research report, 35
projection risk, 563
property, plant, and equipment (PP&E), 165
prospective P/E, 386
P/S. *see* price to sales
PSM. *see* Pastor–Stambaugh model
PTM. *see* prior transactions method
public companies
   beta estimation for, 69–73
   valuation of private vs., 548–550
put options, 583
PVGO. *see* present value of growth opportunities

Q

quality of earnings analysis, 17–21

R

rational efficient markets formulation, 6–7
R&D expenditures. *see* research and development expenditures
real discount rate, 88, 337–338
real estate, 556
real estate investment trusts (REITs), 579, 582
realized alpha, 50
realized returns, 49
real options, 253–254
Reckitt Benckiser, 153
Reeves, Martin, 132
regression, cross-sectional, 399–400
Regulation FD (SEC), 16
regulations
   and competitive forces, 171
   and long-term forecasts, 199–200
regulatory information, in equity valuation, 16
REITs. *see* real estate investment trusts
relatively undervalued (term), 24
relative-strength indicators, 455–458
relative valuation models, 24–25
Rémy Cointreau Group, 202–215
   company overview, 203–204
   industry overview, 202–203
   pro forma balance sheet, 213–214
   pro forma cash flow statements, 209–214
   pro forma income statements, 204–209
   valuation inputs, 214–215
reporting units, 551n.6
reports
   financial, 14, 16, 551–552
   research, 32–36
required rate of return
   defined, 49–50
   expected return vs., 50
   from income approach to private company valuation, 562–566
   on Microsoft, 52–53
required return
   from dividend discount models, 271–272
   from Gordon growth model, 256–257
   and internal rate of return, 53–54
required return on equity, 67–86
   build-up method, 81–85
      bond yield plus risk premium, 84–85
      for private business valuation, 81–84
   CAPM model, 67–75

beta estimation for nonpublic companies, 73–75
beta estimation for public companies, 69–73
examples, 69–74
case studies, 52–53, 69–71, 77–79
and equity risk premium, 54–55
international issues, 85–86
multifactor models, 75–81
   Fama-French model, 75–79
   macroeconomic, 80–81
   Pastor–Stambaugh model, 79–80
   statistical, 80
research and development (R&D) expenditures, 152, 417, 523
research reporting, responsibilities for, 35–36
research reports, 32–36
   contents, 32–34
   example, 33–34
   format, 34–35
residual income, 488–493
   calculation, 489–490
   commercial implementations, 492–493
   continuing, 503
   determinants, 500–501
   equity valuation with, 490–491
   in present value models, 237–238
   returns as, 237–238
residual income method, for private company valuation, 561
residual income model, 383n.3, 493–507
   as absolute valuation model, 23
   accounting considerations, 511–524
      about, 511–512
      aggressive accounting practices, 524
      balance sheet adjustments for fair value, 520–521
      clean surplus violations, 512–520
      intangible assets, 521–524
      nonrecurring items, 524
   adjustments in, 518–520
   DDM vs., 496–497
   determinants of residual income, 500–501
   examples, 495–500
   general form, 496–500
   guidelines for use, 510–511
   international considerations, 525
   multistage model, 503–507
   other valuation models vs., 507–511
   per-share residual income forecasts, 493–494
   single-stage model, 502–503
   strengths and weaknesses of, 510
   for valuing a perpetuity, 508–510
residual income valuation, 487–545
   about, 488
   practice problems, 529–535
   and residual income, 488–493
      calculation, 489–490
      commercial implementations, 492–493
      determinants of residual income, 500–501
      equity valuation with residual income, 490–491
      residual income model, 493–507
      accounting considerations, 511–524

adjustments in, 518–520
determinants of residual income, 500–501
examples, 495–500
general form, 496–500
guidelines for use, 510–511
international considerations, 525
multistage model, 503–507
other valuation models vs., 507–511
per-share residual income forecasts, 493–494
single-stage model, 502–503
strengths and weaknesses of, 510
for valuing a perpetuity, 508–510
solutions to problems, 536–545
responsibilities, for research reporting, 35–36
restricted stock transactions, 583
restructuring charges, 313, 315, 316
retention rate, growth rate and, 275–278
Rethinking the Equity Risk Premium (Hammond, Leibowitz, and Siegel), 67
return(s), 47–100
   abnormal, 7
   and discount rate, 53, 88–89
   disproportionate, 582
   equity risk premium, 54–67
   expected, 50–53
   expected holding-period, 49
   holding period, 48–49
   importance of, 48
   internal rate of return, 53–54, 65
   from intrinsic value estimates, 51–53
   practice problems, 92–96
   realized, 49
   required, 49–50, 52–53
   required rate of return, 562–566
   required return on equity, 67–86
      build-up method, 81–85
      CAPM model, 67–75
      case studies, 52–53, 69–71, 77–79
      international issues, 85–86
      multifactor models, 75–81
      solutions to problems, 97–100
   and weighted average cost of capital, 86–88
return on assets (ROA), 405n.26
   and financial policies/dividend growth rate, 276
   and ROE, 275
return on capital approach, 144
return on capital employed (ROCE), 165
return on equity (ROE). *see also* required return on equity
   average, 390
   and clean surplus violations, 511–512
   and comprehensive income, 516–518
   DuPont analysis, 273, 275–276, 431, 512
   and growth rates, 275–278
   and intangible assets, 521–524
   mature-phase, 270
   and residual income, 502–503
return on invested capital (ROIC)
   and balance sheet modeling, 165
   defined, 446, 490n.5
   for US industries, 106–107
Reuters Company Research, 402–403

revenue(s)
 income statement modeling of, 140–146
 normalized, 196–201
 on pro forma income statements,
  204–205
 as quality of earnings indicators, 18
revenue recognition, price to sales and,
 428–430
reviewed financial statements, 558
Reynolds American, Inc., 475
risk(s)
 business cycle, 81
 confidence, 80
 country risk rating model, 86
 inflation, 80
 market timing, 81
 projection, 563
 in research reports, 35
 time horizon, 80
risk-free rate
 defined, 50
 for historical estimates of equity risk
  premium, 56, 60–61
risk premiums
 bond yield plus, 84–85
 equity, 54–67
  demand-side estimates, 65n.28
  forward-looking estimates, 64–67
  historical estimates, 55–64
  and required return on equity, 54–55
  supply-side estimates, 65–67
 factor, 75
Rite Aid, 147–150
rivals. see established rivals
RMRF factor, 75, 76
ROA. see return on assets
ROCE. see return on capital employed
ROE. see return on equity
ROIC. see return on invested capital
Rothblatt, Martine, 134
Rule 10b-18 (SEC), 234n.8
Rule 144 (SEC), 583
Russia, 172–176
Ryanair Holdings PLC, 317–318

S
SAB Miller, 172
sales. see also price to sales (P/S)
 cash flow valuation and growth in,
  330–331, 345–347
 company, 179–181
 and cost of goods sold, 150
 enterprise value to, 449
 and free cash flow, 329–331
 industry, 177–179
 for price to sales ratio, 428–430
sales forecasts, FCFE from, 331
sales projections, 177–182
 company sales, 179–181
 industry sales, 177–179
 and input cost increases, 181–182
sales-to-price ratio (S/P), 394
Samsung, 200
SAP AG, 109, 513, 515, 516
scaled earnings surprise, 453
scenario analysis, 167–168
Schlumberger Ltd., 14
scope of products/services, industries',
 123

Scotts Miracle-Gro, 108
screening, stock, 463–465
Seagate Technology, 446–448
SEC. see US Securities and Exchange
 Commission
sector rotation strategies, 465
sectors, economic. see economic sectors
Security Analysis (Graham and Dodd),
 384
segment analysis of revenue, 141
segmented markets, 68
selling, general, and administrative
 (SG&A) expenses
 in modeling of operating costs,
  151–152
 on pro forma income statements,
  205–207
selling expenses, 151
sell-side analysts, 30–32
semiconductor manufacturing, 200
Sensex. see S&P BSE Sensex Index
sensitivity analysis
 and absolute valuation models, 23
 converting forecasts to valuations with,
  29
 defined, 12
 of FCFE and FCFF approaches,
  339–340
 for financial forecasting, 167–168
SG&A expenses. see selling, general, and
 administrative expenses
shaping strategies
 characteristics of, 133–134
 defined, 131
 environment for, 133
 and life-cycle stages, 137
 prevalence of, 135
share-based employee compensation, 10,
 316–317, 551
"Share-Based Payment" (ASC 718),
 552n.7
"Share-Based Payment" (SFAS 123R),
 552n.7
share-based payments, 10
share count, 164
shareholder agreements, 550
shareholders
 communication with, 10
 in private company valuation, 549
shareholders' equity, 416
share repurchases, 233n.3, 250–251
Shell, 131
short-term government bills, 60–61
short-term investors, 550
Siegel, Laurence B., 67
Silver Wheaton Corporation, 493–494
Singapore, 76n.45
Singer–Terhaar method, 68n.34
single-stage model
 for free cash flow valuation, 337–339
 for residual income, 502–503
6-K, Form, 16
size, company, 549, 555
size premiums, 562
Skype, 113
SMB factor, 76
Sonoco Products Company, 244–245
Sony Corporation, 117
South Africa, 57, 59

S/P. see sales-to-price ratio
S&P. see Standard & Poor's Corporation
S&P 500 Composite Index, 408
S&P 500 Index, 449
 and Fed Model, 409
 GGM equity risk premium estimate,
  64–65
 macroeconomic equity risk premium
  estimate, 66–67
 market cap guidelines, 465
 relative strength indicators, 456–458
 survivorship bias in, 61n.23
Spain
 FFM factors, 76n.45
 historical equity risk premium, 57, 59
S&P BSE Sensex Index (Sensex), 62–63
S&P Dow Jones US Index Committee,
 464
SPDR. see Standard & Poor's Depositary
 Receipt
SPDR Barclays Long-Term Treasury,
 456–458
SPDR S&P Emerging Europe ETF,
 456–458
SPDR Stoxx Europe 50 Index, 456–458
special purpose entities, 161
specialty fashion retailing, 132
spin-offs, equity valuation for, 9
S&P Midcap 400 Index, 449, 465
spreadsheet modeling, 268–270
 for forecasting dividends, 278–279
 sustainable growth calculation, 270
 valuing stock with, 269–270
Sprint, 85
S&P SmallCap 600 Index, 449, 465
Staff Accounting Bulletin No. 101, SEC,
 428, 429n.42
Staff Accounting Bulletin No. 104, SEC,
 429
standardized unexpected earnings
 (SUE), 454–455
Standard & Poor's Corporation (S&P),
 402
Standard & Poor's Depositary Receipt
 (SPDR), 456–458
Standard & Poor's Super 1500
 Composite Index, 449, 450
Standards of Professional Conduct, 16,
 32, 35, 36
standards of value (term), 552–554
Standing Interpretations Committee
 Interpretation 31, 428–429
Starbucks, 108
statement of cash flows
 discrepancies of balance sheets and,
  332
 FCFF from, 311–312
 modeling, 166
 noncash charges on, 313–318
 pro forma, 209–214
  capital investment forecast, 210
  depreciation forecast, 210
  and forecasted balance sheet,
   213–214
  forecasted cash flow statement,
   211–213
  working capital forecast, 210–211
Statement of Financial Accounting
 Standards

"Business Combinations" (SFAS 141R), 570
"Fair Value Measurement" (SFAS 157), 551n.5, 553n.13
"Fair Value Measurements" (SFAS 157), 29n.13
"Goodwill and Other Intangible Assets" (SFAS 142), 551n.5
"Share-Based Payment" (SFAS 123R), 552n.7
statistical multifactor model, for required return on equity, 80
statutory tax rate, 160–161
Staunton, Mike, 85
Stern Stewart & Company, 492n.8
stock(s)
  common, 79–80
  and control premiums, 573–574
  international, 337–339
  noncallable fixed-rate perpetual preferred stock, 248–249
  non-dividend paying, 261–262
  perpetual preferred, 248–249
  preferred, 248–249, 335–337
  and private company valuation, 550
  restricted, 583
  returns on government debt vs., 56–59
  screening of, 463–465
  selection of, 9, 464–465
  terminal value of, 260
Stock Practice Aid. *see Valuation of Privately-Held Company Equity Securities Issued as Compensation*
stock price, growth rate implied by, 251–252
stock valuation
  with H-model, 263–264
  multiple valuation indicators in, 461–462
  for non-dividend paying stock, 261–262
  with spreadsheet modeling, 269–270
  with two-stage dividend discount model, 258–260
Stora Enso Oyj, 428, 449
STOXX Europe 50 Index, 456, 458
strategic style, 129–137
  adaptive, 131–133, 135, 137
  classical, 131–135, 137
  and competitive environment, 129–130
  finding your, 130–135
  and lifecycle stage, 137
  managing multiple, 136–137
  shaping, 131, 133–135, 137
  traps with selecting, 135–136
  visionary, 131, 133–135, 137
strategic transactions, 573
strategy planning, 130. *see also* strategic style
substitutes
  in beer markets, 170, 171
  and changes in industry structure, 118
  in cognac industry, 202
  as competitive forces, 113–114
  and financial forecasts, 169–171
  in industry structure, 13
  limiting threats from, 105
  and long-term profitability, 104
SUE. *see* standardized unexpected earnings

summary, research report, 35
sum-of-the-parts valuation, 25–28
supernormal growth, 257
suppliers
  bargaining power of, 169–171, 202
  in beer markets, 170, 171
  and changes in industry structure, 117
  as competitive forces, 111
  in industry structure, 13
  and long-term profitability, 104
  neutralizing power of, 105
supply-side economies of scale, 108
supply-side estimates of equity risk premiums, 65–67
surveys, equity risk premium from, 67
survival strategies, 130
survivorship bias, 61
sustainable growth rates, 270, 273–274
Sweden
  FFM factors, 76n.45
  GDP growth rate, 244
  historical equity risk premium, 57, 59
Swiss franc, 85
switching costs, 109
Switzerland
  FFM factors, 76n.45
  GDP growth rate, 244
  historical equity risk premium, 57–59
synergies, price multiples and, 576
Syngenta AG, 313–315
Sysco Company, 121, 181

T

table of contents, research report, 35
tablet computer industry, 185–195
Taiwan Semiconductor Manufacturing Company, 391–392, 504–507
Talisman Energy, Inc., 288–289
tangible book value per share, 420–421
Target, 109
target weights, WACC, 87
Tata, Ratan, 134
Tata Chemicals Ltd., 285
taxes
  deferred, 316
  modeling of, 159–163
  and private company valuation, 550, 552
  and weighted cost of capital, 86–88
tax rates
  cash, 160–163
  effective, 160–163
  statutory, 160–161
T-bonds. *see* US Treasury bonds
TD Ameritrade Holding Corp., 426
TD Bank Group, 419–420
technical indicators, 453
technological developments, 185–195
  base case scenarios, 193, 194
  bull and bear case scenarios, 193–195
  impact of cannibalization, 191–195
  potential for cannibalization, 185–191
technology
  as industry attribute, 116
  and long-term forecasts, 199–200
10-K, Form, 16, 429–430
10-Q, Form, 16
terminal price multiples, 414–416
  based on comparables, 415
  defined, 414

  multiple based on fundamentals, 414
  in valuation of mature growth phase, 415–416
terminal share price, 242
terminal value
  in long-term forecasts, 197–199
  of stock, 260
TerraNova Energy, 92, 97
Tesco PLC, 178, 475
Thomson First Call, 386, 395
3M, 196–198
three-stage models
  dividend discount, 264–269
    with declining growth rates, 265–268
    with distinct stages, 264–265
    future dividend growth pattern for, 241
  for free cash flow valuation, 347–349
TIC. *see* total invested capital
time frame, for comparable-based valuation, 409
time horizon
  for financial forecasting, 195
  in industry analysis, 110
time horizon risk, 80
time series approach, 144
Time Warner Corporation, 576
Tobin's q, 501
top-down approach
  forecasting, 21–22
  investing, 21n.7
  modeling operating costs, 146
  modeling revenue, 143–144
  working capital projections, 164–165
Toronto-Dominion Bank, 92, 419
total invested capital (TIC), 446
Total S.A., 71–72
Toyota Motor Corporation, 51, 399
Toys "R" Us, 117
trailing dividend yield, 439
trailing earnings per share, 388–389
trailing P/E, 387–394
  and business-cycle influence, 390–392
  calculating, 387–394
  and comparability with other companies, 392
  defined, 386
  justified, 254–256
  with negative, zero, or low earnings, 392–394
  and nonrecurring items, 388–390
trailing price to cash flow, 436
transaction date, 576
transition growth phase, 258
TREND formula, 196
20-F, Form, 16
two-stage models
  dividend discount, 258–261
    combining P/E model and, 260–261
    future dividend growth pattern for, 241
    valuing stock with, 258–260
  free cash flow, 340–347
    with declining growth rates, 343–347
    with declining net income, 343–345
    with declining sales growth, 345–347
    with fixed growth rates, 341–343

U

underlying earnings, 388
undervalued (term), 24, 85
unexpected earnings, 453–455
Uniform Standards of Professional
    Appraisal Practice (USPAP), 587
Unilever Group, 484
    company costs, 183
    input and product prices for, 178–179
    modeling of operating costs for,
        154–158
Unilever N.V., 475, 484
Unilever PLC, 475, 484
United Kingdom
    beer market, 170–171
    dividend policy, 233, 234
    FFM factors, 76n.45
    food inflation, 179–180
    GDP growth rate, 244
    Gordon growth model, 64
    historical equity risk premium, 57–59
United Parcel Service, 531–532
United States
    beer market, 177, 178
    book value, 417
    dividend policy, 233–234
    equity risk premium, 56
    FFM factors, 76n.45
    FFM model for equities market, 76
    GDP growth rate, 244
    GGM equity risk premium estimate,
        64–65
    historical equity risk premium, 57–59
    regulatory requirements, 16
    ROIC for industries in, 106–107
    savings and loan crisis (1980s-1990s),
        587
    sector ROEs, 505–506
    share repurchases, 250
    tax deductible interest, 308
US Consumer Price Index (CPI), 177
US dollar, 85
US generally accepted accounting
        principles (US GAAP)
    available-for-sale investments, 512
    book value of equity, 500, 511
    fair value, 553, 587
    goodwill impairment tests, 552
    IFRS vs., 451–452
    income statements, 140
    intangible assets, 548
    interest and dividends, 311
    interest classification, 436
    LIFO inventory accounting, 392
    nonfinancial assets, 424
    operating cash flow, 434
    R&D expenditures, 417, 523
    reconciliation requirement of,
        451–452
    residual income, 501
    share-based compensation, 316
US Securities and Exchange
        Commission (SEC)
    Diebold settlement with, 430

on discounts for lack of control, 582
    formalized revenue recognition
        practices, 428–429
    Groupon registration statement with,
        430
    and guideline transactions method,
        576
    reconciliation with GAAP as
        requirement, 451, 452
    Regulation FD, 16
    required filings with, 16
    Rule 10b-18, 234n.8
    Rule 144, 583
US Treasury bonds (T-bonds), 409
US Treasury securities (US Treasuries),
    86
unusual charges, 164
UPS, 134
US Bancorp, 418
uses-of-free-cash-flow-basis, 326–327
USPAP. see Uniform Standards of
    Professional Appraisal Practice
US Style Indices Methodology (S&P),
    464
utility providers, 199–200

V

valuation, 6, 35, 548n.1
valuation date, 576
valuation inputs, company model,
    214–215
*The Valuation of Customer-Related
    Assets* (Appraisal Foundation), 588
Valuation of Intangible Assets (IVSC
    Guidance Note), 588
*Valuation of Privately-Held Company
    Equity Securities Issued as
    Compensation* (Stock Practice Aid),
    565n.24, 588
value
    appreciation of, 249–250
    in competitive strategy, 122–124
    fair market, 8
    going-concern, 8
    intrinsic, 6–8
    investment, 8
    liquidation, 8
    and nonoperating assets, 349
    standards/definitions of, 552–554
    types of, 6–9
Value Line, 69, 407, 411, 436n.48
value of growth (term), 252–254
variable costs
    modeling, 146
    and technological cannibalization,
        188–189
venture capital investors, 551
Verizon Communications, Inc.,
    404–407, 460, 461
Viallet, Claude, 165n.4, 165n.5
Vinci SA, 263–264
visibility, 242
visionary strategies
    characteristics of, 134

defined, 131
    environment for, 133
    and life-cycle stages, 137
    prevalence of, 134, 135
Viskanta, Tadas, 86n.55
volatility, lack of marketability discounts
    and, 583–584
Volkswagen AG, 454–455
volume and price approach, 144
Vonage, 113

W

WACC. *see* weighted average cost of
    capital
Wachovia, 118
Walgreens, 147–149
Wal-Mart, 109, 117, 177
Washington Mutual, 118
Weatherford International Ltd., 15
weighted average cost of capital
    (WACC)
    and present value of FCFF, 304–305
    and required rate of return for private
        company, 563
    and returns, 86–88
weighted harmonic mean, 459–460
Wells Fargo & Company, 418
Western Digital Corporation, 437–438,
    443–448
Weyerhaeuser, 24
Whirlpool, 117
Williams, John Burr, 230, 241
Windstream Corp., 404–406, 460, 461
working capital
    and FCFF, 308–309
    and free cash flow, 317–318
    on pro forma cash flow statements,
        210–211
    projections of, 164–165
WPP Group PLC, 387
write-downs, 389n.12

X

XMI Corporation, 40–41, 45
XM satellite radio, 134

Y

Yahoo! Finance, 403
Yang, Y., 451n.58
Yardeni model, 410
yield
    in BYPRP method, 84–85
    cash flow, 394
    dividend, 250, 394, 439–442
    earnings, 393, 394
yield to maturity (YTM), 61, 84
YouTube, 113
YPF Sociedad Anonima, 338–339
YTM. *see* yield to maturity

Z

Zara, 132
zero earnings, trailing P/E with, 392
Zynga, 134